THE ARCHITECTURE OF JEFFERSON COUNTRY

Charlottesville and Albemarle County, Virginia

THE *Architecture of*

CHARLOTTESVILLE AND

Jefferson Country

ALBEMARLE COUNTY, VIRGINIA

K. EDWARD LAY

Color photographs by Bill Sublette

UNIVERSITY PRESS OF VIRGINIA

Charlottesville and London

THE UNIVERSITY PRESS OF VIRGINIA

© 2000 by K. Edward Lay

Printed in the United States of America on acid-free paper

First published in 2000

9 8 7 6 5 4 3 2

Design and composition by B. Williams & Associates
Printed and bound by Thomson-Shore, Inc.

Title page photograph: Birdwood, E19C. (Holsinger Studio, 1917, acc. no. 7862, neg. X-5449-B1, Special Collections, University of Virginia Library, Charlottesville)

Library of Congress Cataloging-in-Publication Data
Lay, K. Edward.
    The architecture of Jefferson country : Charlottesville and
Albemarle County, Virginia / K. Edward Lay ; color photographs by
Bill Sublette.
      p.   cm.
    Includes bibliographical references and index.
    ISBN 0-8139-1885-5 (cloth : alk. paper)
     1. Architecture — Virginia — Albemarle County.   2. Architecture —
Virginia — Charlottesville.   I. Title
NA730.V82A435   2000
720'.9755'48 — dc21   99-39178
                                        CIP

Dedicated to:

The memory of J. NORWOOD BOSSERMAN,
former Dean of the School of Architecture,
University of Virginia, who brought me to
the university in 1967 and for whom I was
Assistant/Associate Dean for six years. It was
he who brought together an august group of
people to serve as the Publication Committee
for this work, without whose tireless effort
and expertise it would not have been realized:
Sara Lee Barnes, Melinda Frierson, W. Douglas
Gilpin Jr., and Lloyd T. Smith Jr.

Contents

Illustrations

Preface

THIS BOOK IS A SURVEY OF ARCHITECTURE IN ALBE-marle County and Charlottesville intended for those who live, work, study, and shop in the more than 2,300 buildings identified. It also is an overview of the evolution of Virginia architecture and the characteristics of its different periods. Not only will it enhance local residents' knowledge of their surroundings, but it also will appeal to the building professions and others interested in Virginia architecture, history, and genealogy. Because of the extraordinary influence of Thomas Jefferson, the work of his master builders, and the effect of the School of Architecture at the University of Virginia, however, this study should be of interest well beyond the county and indeed appeal to a national and international audience. The county is unusually rich in historic buildings representing the vernacular tradition as well as a wide range of academic design (see appendix table 1). For architectural historians this survey will supply data for investigating numerous themes. For example, it can provide additional context for examining Jefferson as an architect, for following building technology, or for assessing the effect of various European building traditions. For historians it will contribute to the study of social and economic history. Practicing architects and builders may find inspiration for solutions to modern design problems.

This overview of the county and city's architectural history is arranged chronologically and traces the stylistic changes that have occurred here as well as throughout the United States. It includes information drawn from primary source material, such as court, tax, census, and insurance records and early maps, as well as from visual inspections. It also draws on the Virginia Department of Historic Resources county surveys, conducted primarily by the late Jeffrey M. O'Dell, and the Charlottesville city surveys, performed primarily by Eugenia Bibb, as well as the 1976 published survey by William C. Allen, Horner

Davis, Mary M. Shoemaker, and Dwight Young. It draws from a survey of more than 2,300 buildings on a computer database derived from my extensive files and recorded on CD-ROM. Far more data, photographic prints, and slides exist than could be included in the survey. Those interested in more information on a particular building might wish to review the CD-ROM database, my own voluminous files, the more than three hundred volumes of the work of my classes in the Fiske Kimball Fine Arts Library at the University of Virginia, the architectural survey files of the Virginia Department of Historic Resources in Richmond, the city of Charlottesville's historic building archives, and the files of the Albemarle County Historical Society.

The buildings represent the period from the first settlement of the county in the early eighteenth century until the beginning of World War II. Many buildings that no longer exist are represented, and in cases where early photographs prior to renovations are available, those images appear in preference to showing present-day altered states.

A single book cannot include every example of every architectural style. The object of this book is to present not only an overview of the county and city's most important buildings and styles but also as extensive a collection of local architecture in general as space will allow. Practically all of the extant structures built before the end of the antebellum era are included, as they represent the dominant national styles and types of the eighteenth and early nineteenth centuries: the Georgian, the Classical Revival, and the vernacular form. For the Victorian period that followed the Civil War, far fewer examples are included. Only a representative number of buildings constructed during the period between the turn of the twentieth century and World War II are part of this survey.

The architectural significance of Albemarle County

and Charlottesville rests on the continuing influence of Thomas Jefferson and his artistic achievements in his native county and elsewhere: the Richmond Capitol, his home Monticello, his Bedford County retreat Poplar Forest, and the University of Virginia. It is further supported by the many examples of Jeffersonian classicism later constructed by his master builders within the county's borders as well as beyond them. Still later, examples of other architectural idioms were built here—some were important works by nationally renowned architects—but none attained the popularity of the Classical Revival style. At the turn of the twentieth century, a period for the building arts known as the American Renaissance, the renewed interest of wealthy clients in eclectic architectural styles attracted some of the finest Beaux Arts architects in the country to Albemarle County and Charlottesville. Grand new buildings complemented and competed with the Jeffersonian models of a hundred years earlier. With the establishment of the School of Architecture at the University of Virginia in 1919 under Fiske Kimball, "the dean of American architectural history," the institution produced architects trained in historical styles, and many of them practiced locally as well as nationally. Consequently, Albemarle County and Charlottesville constitute an unusually rich microcosm of the major national architectural styles as well as the original models on which they were based.

Introduction

ALBEMARLE COUNTY, VIRGINIA, IS WELL KNOWN as the birthplace and home of Thomas Jefferson, one of the most important figures in American history. A man of many interests, not the least of them architecture, Jefferson designed in his native county two of the world's great examples of the building arts: a dwelling, Monticello, and an institution of higher learning, the University of Virginia. As a reflection of their importance, both of these structures appear on the United Nations Educational, Scientific, and Cultural Organization's World Heritage List, a roster of mankind's masterpieces of exceptional interest and universal value. There is no other county in the United States—which presently has a total of only twenty places on the list—with this distinction.

One can argue that no other American architect has surpassed Jefferson in his influence on the built environment of the United States. Just as every writer of fiction, according to Harold Bloom in *The Western Canon*, has since the time of Shakespeare written either in emulation of or in reaction to the bard, so has it been with the Classical Revival idiom that Jefferson introduced to his fellow countrymen more than two hundred years ago. Classical influences—either in imitation or in riposte—are seen throughout the United States in capitols, courthouses, post offices, churches, and houses by the hundreds of thousands. The story of American architecture is in large part the chronicle of the acceptance of the Classical Revival style and its subsequent manifestations (especially the Greek Revival and the Colonial Revival) by the vast majority of citizens and architects as the "official" architecture of the nation. Those styles that arose in reaction to the Classical Revival—Italianate, Egyptian Revival, Gothic Revival, International, Bauhaus, Modernist—

have never attained the same widespread levels of acceptance and esteem.

In many respects the architecture of Albemarle County and Charlottesville exemplifies the story of American architecture in microcosm. Virtually every style once or presently popular in the United States is represented locally, as well as the two principal works of Jefferson himself. Furthermore, the history of the county—its beginnings on the fringe of the western frontier, its settlement and growth, its roads and railroads and other improvements, its assemblage of towns and villages, its gradual shift from a farming to a broader-based economy—is typical in many ways of Virginia's, and indeed the nation's, history.

But in other ways the county's history is unique, as is its architectural genealogy. Two U.S. presidents have called Albemarle home while in office: Jefferson for his entire life aside from his absences in public service and James Monroe for much of the last third of his life, when he moved to the county to be near his friend Jefferson. Another president, Theodore Roosevelt, established a rustic retreat in Albemarle called Pine Knot. Acquired in 1905 and used by Roosevelt while in office, this simple dwelling foreshadowed Herbert Hoover's mountainside Camp Rapidan in Madison County, Virginia, and the camp in Maryland used by his successors.

Besides an abundance of presidents, Albemarle County and Charlottesville (which became an independent city in 1888) have harbored since 1819 one of the nation's premier public institutions of higher learning, Jefferson's University of Virginia. Its architect intended the "academical village"—the central composition of Rotunda, pavilions, and colonnades—to serve as a tangible example of Classical Revival architecture, to illustrate the proper use of architectural orders and proportions, and to function as library, home, and classroom for teachers and students. It is a tribute to Jefferson's genius that his masterpiece achieved all these goals.

The University of Virginia has grown far beyond Jefferson's village concept, both in size and influence. Today it is the dominant employer in Albemarle County, the principal reason for Charlottesville's expansion and multifaceted role as the seat of county and municipal government, a commercial center, and a "college town." The university as a center of learning attracts scholars, authors, and actors, among others; the amenities of school and city help spur economic growth; and the resulting prosperous mixture, combined with Albemarle County's historical and rural ambience, lures new residents and visitors alike.

The Albemarle County we behold today reflects some two and a half centuries of occupation and growth, of Virginian and American history. The tangible evidence of that history is the county's built environment. Houses, churches, schools, and commercial and public buildings; roads, canals, and railroads; farmlands, fields, and forests: whatever the hand of man has built or altered can tell us as well as any written record the story of Albemarle County and how it became the place it is today. That is the purpose of this book, to tell the story of Albemarle through its domestic, commercial, ecclesiastical, and institutional architecture from the early years of European settlement in the mid–eighteenth century until the beginning of World War II in 1939. This work includes examples of many of the architectural styles that have arisen and fallen in popularity over the years, from the Georgian to the Colonial Revival, that can be seen within the present boundaries of the county today.

It is important first to examine the context in which the built environment arose. The dwellings and other buildings constructed by the county's inhabitants reflect their taste, wealth, status, and values. They also are connected to the natural world in which they were built: the soil, terrain, watercourses, vegetation. Architecture makes little sense when separated from the history and natural conditions that influenced its creation. Without such a context, we cannot hope to understand why the houses in one part of the county look so different from those in another, why a simple frame dwelling stands on the same property as a grand mansion, why a village grew up and prospered at one road intersection while another village did not, why settlers from a particular ethnic group put down roots here but not there, and why the sizes, shapes, and styles of buildings changed over time.

A MATTER OF STYLE: NATIONAL AND LOCAL TRENDS

Stylistic changes in domestic architecture are influenced by many factors, including the inevitable rejection by one generation of the tastes and fashions of its predecessor, advances in the technologies used by the construction industry, the relative availability of building materials, external factors such as the aesthetic appeal of archaeological discoveries, and, of course, architects who lead public taste in new directions with the artistry of their creations. Most architectural change happens slowly and incompletely; one region may lag behind another in acceptance of a new building form or retain an older building form long after it has been supplanted elsewhere. Just as most social innovations today begin in California or Florida long before the rest of the country is aware of them, so most changes in architectural fashion still begin in urban areas and among the wealthy and spread slowly to the countryside and into the consciousness of middle-class citizens. Furthermore, new architectural styles seldom materialize full-blown and pure; instead, they evolve, thereby producing transitional buildings that contain elements of two or more styles.

Houses in virtually every style that achieved popularity in the United States have been built in Albemarle County, although here, as elsewhere, some styles were more popular than others (see appendix tables 2, 3). Over the years architectural historians have assigned various names to the dominant styles: Georgian, Federal, Roman Revival, Greek Revival, Victorian (including Gothic Revival, Italianate, Second Empire, and Queen Anne), and Eclectic (including Beaux Arts and Colonial Revival). In Albemarle and Charlottesville all of the styles but the Victorian gained widespread acceptance among architects and their clients, and there are some gems among the handful of Victorian examples here.

Insofar as eighteenth-century colonial houses were built in any particular style, that style was what architectural historians call Georgian, after the three kings of England who ruled successively during most of the period. Houses built in the Georgian style were symmetrical; that is, they had a central entrance door flanked on each side by one, two, or occasionally three rather narrow windows. A Georgian house might be three, five, or seven bays (openings on the first floor) wide. Usually, the house was two stories high and two rooms deep (this latter feature made the house a *double-pile*, a term used oddly enough to refer to its depth, not its height). In Virginia the chimneys generally were positioned on the gable ends of the house, either four in all (one for each first-floor room) or two altogether but centered on either end of the house so that the chimneys used a corner fireplace to heat each room.

Georgian-style houses are solid and dignified, and the larger brick ones especially were designed to impress the visitor with the owner's wealth and substance. To modern eyes such structures often appear a bit cold and austere on the outside (Frank Lloyd Wright supposedly called them "boxes with air holes"). Inside, however, their owners often lavished small fortunes on breathtaking woodwork, including intricately carved mantels and magnificent paneling. Such houses, always few in number and even rarer today, exemplify the best that the construction trades of their day had to offer in terms of craftsmanship and artistry.

Near the end of the eighteenth century, a new style gained in popularity. Today called the Federal style, it modified the Georgian style with Roman details and introduced the Classical Revival era that dominated American architecture for more than half a century. The basic Georgian plan and massing were altered by the introduction of nonrectangular spaces, and the finishing details — the woodwork and moldings and doorway surrounds — were lighter and more delicate than their predecessors and contained many references to ancient Roman architecture. A common design element of the Federal style, for instance, was a semicircular, lacy fanlight over the entrance door that reflected the Roman love of the arch.

The new style was profoundly influenced by two brothers, James and Robert Adam. British architects, the brothers Adam between 1773 and 1779 published *Works in Architecture*, an illustrated pattern book in which they set forth their principles. Their ideas took first Great Britain, then the United States, by storm. By 1800 the Adamesque Federal style began to supplant the Georgian, and it remained dominant until the 1830s.

Begun in the 1780s in Virginia, the Classical Revival style introduced during the Federal Revival period reached maturity about 1820 and remained popular for decades thereafter. Its high-style manifestation was the more literal and obvious inclusion of Roman temple elements by architects from Jefferson onward. Spurning the Georgian model (in part due to anti-British sentiment), its adherents reached further back in time for inspiration to the "original" and "pure" wellsprings of classical architecture, the Greek and Roman republics. Albemarle's own Thomas Jefferson was the first and principal advocate of the new style, which he introduced in his plan for the Virginia State Capitol in Richmond. He was soon joined by Benjamin Henry Latrobe, Charles Bulfinch, Robert Mills, and a host of other professional architects who spread the style far and wide in their designs for dwellings, churches, schools, and public buildings.

Jefferson's enthusiasm for ancient architecture arose in part from his conviction that the newly formed United States should develop an architecture to suit its politics: forthright, well balanced, moderate, and proportional, like Greek and Roman classical architecture. Contemporaneous archaeological discoveries in Greece, a nationwide desire to surpass the British in all things, and the natural tendency of the younger generation to reject the tastes of the older, all combined to ensure the success of the Classical Revival in America.

Although the Classical Revival era consisted of two stylistic phases, the Roman Revival (1800–1830) espoused by Jefferson and the Greek Revival (1830–60) that succeeded it, the two phases were not as neatly divided as the dates of their dominance in Albemarle County and Charlottesville suggest. Rather, the classical elements of the first overlapped and gradually melded with those of the second. The Classical Revival–style dwelling, like its predecessor the Georgian, was at least as frequently of wood-frame construction as of brick, but fewer of the frame houses have survived. Although the new style retained the symmetrical box form of its predecessors, rooflines were noticeably lower in pitch and sometimes (mainly during the Greek Revival phase) were concealed behind parapets. Below the roofline, the Greek Revival cornice was heavier and wider than its Roman or Federal counterpart. The hipped roof became popular, but occasionally the house was oriented so that a gable end faced the public way and functioned as the principal entrance. Porticoes in a variety of forms — single-story, two-tier, two-story or full-height, or full-facade — were common features of many Roman and some Greek Revival houses. Round or square columns, usually with Doric capitals but sometimes Ionic or Corinthian, supported the portico roofs, which were often pedimented during the Roman Revival and flat during the Greek. The Greek Revival portico sheltered an entrance door that typically was surrounded by sidelights and a rectangular transom instead of a semi-circular fanlight as in the Federal and Roman Revival styles. The facades of Greek Revival–style buildings commonly featured pilasters (projections from the wall surface that resemble flat columns). Inside, the elaborate carved mantels of the Georgian and Federal periods gave way to the simpler mantels of the Greek Revival, and door and window moldings likewise were simplified.

The Greek Revival reached its zenith in Virginia in the 1840s and 1850s. It was accompanied, or succeeded, by a variety of other "exotic" revivals, including the Gothic and the Italianate. Gothic Revival–style houses had steeply pitched roofs; paired front gables or single gables centered over the front door; decorative pierced woodwork (called bargeboards or vergeboards) under the eaves; the use of Gothic arches in windows, door surrounds, and porch-roof supports; and, frequently, an asymmetrical, irregular plan. Many Gothic Revival–style houses were small and intimate in scale compared with the dwellings built in the large and ponderous styles of the previous eras.

Italian villas and farmhouses inspired the Italianate style. Generally, Italianate houses were square or rectangular in shape, rather than irregular like the Gothic, but exhibited many features that gave them an air of verticality and countered their otherwise squatty appearance. Their windows were tall and narrow and frequently capped with arched hoods. Many Italianate houses sported towers, either off to one side or centered at the front. The roof eaves were deep and overhanging, but large decorative brackets under them gave an illusion of lift and height to the building. Sometimes a square observatory perched atop the roof, thereby adding vertical lines.

The appeal of the Gothic and Italianate styles lasted into the post–Civil War period. Gradually they were supplanted by what is commonly known as the Victorian style, named for the queen who reigned over Great Britain from 1837 to 1901. Although the styles most typically considered Victorian are the Second Empire and Queen Anne, the Italianate should be included as well.

Second Empire dwellings reached the height of their popularity in Virginia in the period from the 1860s to the 1880s. The style shared several features with the Italianate: window hoods, deep roof overhangs with decorative brackets, projecting towers, and cupolas. The principal difference was the adoption of the dual-pitched, hipped roof type called a mansard roof. Occasionally in Virginia dormers with rounded roofs projected from the steep lower slope of the mansard roof. Other decorative features of the style include iron cresting along the roofline, roof tiles or slates laid in contrasting patterns, and bay windows. Second Empire dwellings are more commonly found in towns or cities than in the countryside.

The somewhat inappropriately named Queen Anne style was introduced in England by architect Richard Norman Shaw in the mid–nineteenth century. Shaw and his followers looked not only to the architecture of Queen Anne's brief (1702–14) reign for inspiration but to earlier medieval and Elizabethan models. In the United States the style became wildly popular after 1880. Today, when most Americans think of a typical Victorian house, it is the Queen Anne style they are thinking of, with its irregular plans, nooks and crannies, wraparound porches supported by turned posts, corner towers, spindlework and gingerbread dripping from the eaves, bay windows, and scores of variations on these themes.

Just as the Queen Anne dwelling attained its apogee at the turn of the twentieth century, two other styles began gaining acceptance: the Craftsman and the Colonial Revival. The Craftsman style was largely the invention of two California brothers, Charles Sumner Greene and Henry Mather Greene, and may be the first example of an architectural style that swept the country from west to east rather than the other way around. The style is most often found in the one-story bungalow form: small, snug, inviting houses that present an impression of shelter and coziness through their low profiles, welcoming porches, and deep roof overhangs. Craftsman houses, as their name suggests, were renowned for their meticulous craftsmanship and careful wooden joinery. By publishing illustrations and floor plans in popular magazines, such as *Good Housekeeping* and *Ladies' Home Journal*, the brothers Greene capitalized on the growing interest in handmade arts and crafts. Craftsman-style bungalows are predominantly an urban and suburban house type.

The other turn-of-the-twentieth-century Eclectic styles, including the Colonial Revival and Beaux Arts, profited from the same interest in craftsmanship, but less directly and in a manner much more high-style than folksy. (The term *Colonial Revival*, according to Richard Guy Wilson in *The Making of Virginia Architecture*, is commonly interpreted to include the "entire period from Jamestown through the 1820s," or the truly colonial through the Roman and Greek Revivals.) Inspired by the celebration of the nation's centennial in 1876, architects and furniture designers rediscovered the country's Georgian and Federal roots. They did not copy the originals slavishly; rather, they embellished, combined, and reinterpreted old patterns to create new motifs undreamed of by colonial architects and cabinetmakers. Their efforts bore fruit immediately, although the Queen Anne style continued to dominate domestic architecture for another generation. In Albemarle County and Charlottesville, the new style's popularity increased after Stanford White redesigned the university's Rotunda following the fire of 1895 and enclosed the Lawn with classical-style buildings. With the additional boost given the idiom in the late 1920s by the restoration and reconstruction of Colonial Williamsburg, the Colonial Revival attained a level of acceptance with the American people that has never diminished.

The Common Architecture

Most authentic eighteenth-century Georgian houses were vernacular in design and fabrication. That is, their builders copied no particular style but instead adhered to the traditional floor plans and construction techniques of their time and place. They built what they knew. For this reason most unaltered vernacular dwellings can be dated only approximately by analyzing such diagnostic features as saw marks, nail types, brick patterns, and the like. Eventually, however, new architectural styles penetrated even the remotest corners of the countryside and influenced, if only subliminally, the tastes of builders and their clients. Some builders embellished vernacular houses—at the time of their construction or shortly thereafter by adding a few stylistic ornaments, such as rural renditions of sophisticated urban woodwork, that often provide clues to the age of a dwelling.

Floor plans offer additional clues. Often the simpler the plan and the fewer the rooms, the earlier the dwelling. The earliest houses in the county probably contained only one or two rooms—a hall, the more public space, and the more private parlor or chamber. Other early houses had a parlor and a small entry hall to one side (hence the term *side passage*). Later, another room might be added to the other side of the passage, thereby creating a two-room, center-passage house. Or that plan could be built all at once.

To house his family, the pioneer settler of Tidewater Virginia at first may have built a post-in-the-ground dwelling, an earthfast dwelling with a frame that consisted of poles stuck in the ground with smaller sticks and mud packed between them. Such houses, throwbacks to those constructed by the Jamestown colonists, went down almost as fast as they went up, since the wooden support-

ing members were in direct contact with the ground and quickly rotted or were attacked by termites. Many burned down, because their stick and mud chimneys frequently caught fire. None of these dwellings are known to have survived in either Tidewater or Piedmont Virginia, and it is uncertain whether any of this type ever were built in Albemarle County. Here no unmodified dwellings dating to the first half of the eighteenth century still stand, and only a relative handful from the second half; most can be confirmed only to the fourth quarter of the century. Fires and the other elements made the life spans of the pioneers' houses as brief as those of the pioneers themselves.

The one-room log cabin, introduced into America by Scandinavians and popularized by German immigrants early in the eighteenth century, soon became the pioneer dwelling of choice. Even easier to build than a post-in-the-ground house, it required only the skill to cut and notch logs. Stone piers raised the sills off the ground and postponed the inevitable collapse brought about by time and the weather. Contrary to "the log cabin myth" (the romantic modern conviction that every pioneer aspired to a little cabin in the woods), these structures were seen as necessary evils, drafty and leaky and bug-ridden, to be endured until something better could be built—and the sooner the better, most pioneer women agreed. None of these early dwellings have been identified in Albemarle County, although it is remotely possible that a handful could survive as farm outbuildings.

The log house was the next step up from the cabin and was intended as a permanent dwelling. It usually contained a loft or half story in addition to its one or more rooms, had stone chimneys or chimneys with stone bases and brick upper portions, and frequently was clad in weatherboards as soon as the family finances allowed it, in order to preserve the wooden walls. These dwellings were relatively well insulated and much more durable than log cabins. Well into the twentieth century, when wood of the necessary dimensions became rare and expensive, the popularity of the log house persisted. Most Piedmont and western Virginia counties boast at least a few log houses built between the late eighteenth and early twentieth centuries, and Albemarle is no exception.

Surviving vernacular frame houses outnumber log ones because they were built more recently and in greater numbers. Although frame houses were constructed in many configurations, the I-house was one of the most popular and persistent. The appearance of the I-house has remained constant over time: two stories high, one room deep, with a gable roof and either exterior end chimneys or interior ones. Typically of balloon-frame construction, a building innovation developed in the 1830s and widely adopted by the mid–nineteenth century, the I-house is straightforward and ubiquitous. A count of house types throughout the United States probably would reveal more I-houses than any other form. With various modifications and embellishments, I-houses continue to be built in housing developments everywhere, usually with such labels as "traditional" or "colonial."

THE TECHNOLOGY OF ARCHITECTURE

Frame dwellings became common once sawmills were built to ease the cutting of timber and sawing of weatherboards. Until the early 1800s frame buildings were of post-and-beam construction, and virtually every component was made by hand. The L-shaped posts rested on massive sill plates with beams laid atop the posts. The beams were secured to the posts with mortise-and-tenon joints held fast by hardwood pegs. Roof beams and rafters were similarly secured and then covered with planking and split wooden shingles (much thicker than the thin shakes so frequently used today and rounded on the exposed end instead of squared). The inside of the dwelling was finished with laths and plaster, while the outside was covered with weatherboards.

Before water-powered sawmills became available on the frontier, the wood used in the earliest frame houses was cut, split, and sawed by hand. The timber was cut and roughly squared off, then laid over a deep pit dug in the ground. Two men, one above ground and the other in the pit, employed a long saw to cut beams and planks from the log as they worked their way down its length. The man on top pulled up on the saw; the man in the pit pulled it down, sneezing and spitting sawdust. The pit-saw blade left identifying marks on beams and planks that help architectural historians assign dates to buildings. Sawmill blades left their own peculiar marks, particularly after 1800, when mills widely adopted the water-powered reciprocating saw.

Bricks were almost always made locally, usually next to the building site, unless the proper quality of clay was unavailable. Their size and shape give additional hints as to a building's age. Other clues to early construction are provided by the brick patterns used in foundations, walls, and chimneys. English bond, popular in the seventeenth century, alternated the long sides of bricks, called stretchers, and the short ends, or headers, from one row to the

next. In Flemish bond, which replaced English bond early in the eighteenth century, stretchers alternated with headers in the same row; the pattern was reversed in the next row. This pattern was attractive but relatively expensive to use because it required a large number of bricks; after 1780 it was often employed only on the front of brick buildings. Common or American bond (an entire row of headers followed by three rows of stretchers) was widely adopted after 1780 because of its cheapness. By 1820 the five-course American-bond pattern had succeeded the early three-course pattern in popularity, and there were other variations as well. Sometimes the three principal patterns are mentioned in documents as English brick, Flemish brick, or American brick; the phrases refer to the pattern in which the bricks were laid, not to their importation from England or Europe.

In the eighteenth century nails were handmade and costly, but in 1796 the first machine-cut nails became available. Still, they were relatively expensive by the standards of the day, and their use did not become common for several decades. Generally, the fewer the nails, the earlier the building.

By the early nineteenth century, the building trades had benefited from the Industrial Revolution and the principles of mass production. Soon after architectural pattern books and popular magazines broadcast the latest styles and floor plans, factories began turning out precast plaster moldings and machine-made woodwork. For the first time the prospective homeowner in the antebellum period could select a plan and order the appropriate parts and trim, which were then prefabricated and shipped to the construction site. By the early twentieth century, the prefabrication-to-order phenomenon reached its apogee when Sears, Roebuck and Company, among others, offered entire houses for sale by catalog.

The Sears houses were made possible by one of the most significant improvements in house construction, the balloon frame, which had been widely adopted by the mid–nineteenth century. Using lighter framing members, eventually standardized to two-by-four-inch boards nailed together, instead of the heavier and more expensive posts and beams of an earlier day, balloon-frame dwellings lent themselves to prefabrication as well as to a wide variety of floor plans. Today the balloon frame remains the most commonly employed nonmasonry construction method.

By the end of the nineteenth century, manufacturing technology had produced reinforced concrete, large sheets of plate glass, and structural steel. These components were combined to create new architectural wonders such as skyscrapers. They also made it possible for architects to design houses with corner windows and picture windows, cantilevered balconies, and poured-concrete slabs on which to place walls and partitions. The advent of indoor plumbing, gaslights, electricity, central heating, air-conditioning, and other innovations not only enabled but required architects to design new forms.

In the past, then, architectural styles were in large part dependent on the limited construction technologies and materials that were available. Today, however, this is far less the case. The vast array of technologies and materials used in house construction now makes it possible to build in any idiom. Homeowners may order up houses in favorite styles, or at least with any stylistic details they desire, and also construct dwellings with floor plans unrelated to particular historical styles. One may live in a newly built house that from all outward appearances is neo-Georgian, but was constructed of brick veneer over concrete block, has plastic rather than wooden sash, sports an attached garage, and lacks a front-to-rear central passage inside, much less a strict four-down and four-up room arrangement. As a result of the liberation of style from the constraints of building technology, America today is a happy patchwork quilt of architecture, with dozens of styles and idioms coexisting across the land. This is no less true in Albemarle County and Charlottesville.

Before one can build a house, of course, one must possess the land on which to build it. Throughout the history of Albemarle County, the search for the best and most affordable land on which to live and work has motivated the residents from the days of the first settlers. Let us begin where they began, with a look at the land.

The Land of Albemarle

Albemarle County was carved from Goochland County in 1744, and part of western Louisa County was added later. At its birth the new county included the future counties of Amherst, Appomattox, Buckingham, Fluvanna, Nelson, and part of Campbell.

Present-day Albemarle County is bounded on the northwest by the Blue Ridge from Afton Mountain to the northern end of Loft Mountain; on the north by the boundary with Greene and Orange Counties, which runs southeast from Loft Mountain almost to Gordonsville;

on the east by the boundary with Louisa and Fluvanna Counties, tending southwest to Scottsville on the James River; on the south by the James River upstream and west to the Rockfish River at Howardsville; and on the southwest by the Rockfish River upstream and north to a point near Schuyler in Nelson County, then northwest to Afton Mountain. The county's boundaries enclose some 750 square miles including Charlottesville, making Albemarle one of the half-dozen largest counties among Virginia's ninety-five in terms of landmass.

In *Gone with the Wind*, Gerald O'Hara tried to explain to his impatient young daughter Scarlett the importance of the land: "Land is the only thing in the world that amounts to anything, for 'tis the only thing in this world that lasts, and don't you be forgetting it!" O'Hara was referring to the land as the basis of agriculture and hence civilization. He would have agreed with Thomas Jefferson, who wrote in his *Notes on the State of Virginia* that "those who labour in the earth are the chosen people of God, if ever he had a chosen people." Jefferson went on to extol the virtues of husbandry (and the virtuousness of the husbandman) and proclaim, "While we have land to labour then, let us never wish to see our citizens occupied at a work-bench, or twirling a distaff."

It was for "land to labour" that the first European inhabitants of the county came searching in the 1730s and 1740s. Like the then-vanished Native Americans before them, these new settlers looked for fertile bottomland for planting their crops and elevated sites for building their houses. They found plenty of both, as well as countless streams and fine hardwood forests, in what is now present-day Albemarle. Since the western part of Albemarle County abuts the eastern wall of the Blue Ridge, most of its land drains to the south and east. None of the terrain is particularly flat, although the eastern part is more gently rolling than hilly. The elevation varies from more than 3,000 feet above sea level in the west to 400 in the east. Most of the hills (locally called mountains) are in the west near the Blue Ridge, and they bear such names as Appleberry Mountain, Long Arm Mountain, Turk's Mountain, and Buck's Elbow Mountain. Just southwest of Charlottesville stands a separate clump of hills called the Ragged Mountains; they provided the title for "A Tale of the Ragged Mountains" written by former university student Edgar Allan Poe. Otherwise, beginning roughly halfway between the Blue Ridge and Charlottesville, in the center of the county, the hills and "mountains" slowly give way to rolling farmland.

There is an exception, however, as one travels east. There is an abruptly rising range of hills and ridges that angle across the eastern half of the county. They extend southwest from near Gordonsville across the northeastern county boundary line to just west of Howardsville in the far southwest. Northeast of Charlottesville, they are known collectively as the Southwest Mountains, while southwest of the city they are called Carter's Mountain and Green Mountain. Although it is widely acknowledged that the Blue Ridge is one of the oldest mountain ranges in North America, the Southwest Mountains are even older. Furthermore, on their slopes and drainages are found the richest soils in the county and, formerly, the best hardwood forests.

Many streams water the land. From south to north Albemarle's principal rivers are the James, which forms the county's southern boundary and is the only easily navigable watercourse; the Rockfish, which enters the James in the county's southwest corner and constitutes its boundary here; the Hardware; and the Rivanna. The last-named is the longest and best-known river in Albemarle; it is formed from many creeks and two rivers—Moorman's and Mechum's—that arise in the eastern wrinkles of the Blue Ridge and ramble southeastwardly among the hills. The Rivanna River proper begins a half-dozen miles northwest of Charlottesville and snakes through the gap between the Southwest Mountains and Monticello Mountain, a small hill adjoining the north end of Carter's Mountain.

This, then, was the land as seen by its first European inhabitants: hilly in the western half and rolling in the eastern, except for the Southwest Mountains. Well-watered throughout, the soil is especially rich in the vicinity of the Southwest Mountains. It is not surprising, then, that the most prosperous settlers chose the eastern part of the county when they began immigrating to Albemarle in the 1730s.

SETTLEMENT AND GROWTH

By the time the first European pioneers arrived, the Native Americans had departed. The principal Saponi tribal village, Monasukapanough, which stood not far from Monticello and Charlottesville, was abandoned sometime before 1700. The Saponi and their allies, the Monacan, immigrated to southwestern Virginia and then into North Carolina.

Indians periodically passed through Albemarle after the first Europeans arrived, but the new settlers had nothing to fear from the passersby. Thomas Jefferson later recalled that when a youth, he encountered a traveling band of Indians who had left the highway to walk some miles out of their way to visit a Native American burial mound near Monticello and, he believed, to pay their respects. Then they quietly resumed their journey.

The Indians whom Jefferson saw may well have been treading a road that once was a path laid down by their ancestors. Since Albemarle lacked rivers that were easily navigable (except for the James), Jefferson's pioneer father and his contemporaries trekked into the wilderness along the Indians' trails, and settlers and wagons followed in their wake. Soon the county government ordered the improvement of these rutted paths, and work gangs of pioneers labored to widen and grade them until they might fairly be called roads. Periodically the government ordered the creation of new roads to connect the old, and within a few years the burgeoning county possessed a rudimentary transportation network.

Among the earliest and most important roads in Albemarle were the River Road, the Three Notch'd Road, and the Secretary's Road. The River Road, today's Route 6 and various county roads, ran along the bluffs to the north of the James River and linked the Piedmont with Tidewater by way of Richmond. The Three Notch'd Road began north of Richmond as the Mountain Road; it roughly followed present-day U.S. Route 250 through Charlottesville and for a few miles westward and then ran northwest through the Blue Ridge along a series of today's county roads. The Secretary's Road was named for John Carter, an early large landowner who served as secretary of the colony. Unlike the other two roads, this road trended southwest from the Three Notch'd Road just east of Charlottesville; it paralleled the Southwest Mountain range and eventually became the Lower Secretary's Road leading into present Nelson County. At that time (the 1730s and 1740s), nearby Scottsville lay close to the center of what was then a much larger Albemarle County. These roads, then, carried most of the weight of early migration into the area.

Some of the first European settlers of Albemarle County, such as John Carter, George Hoomes Jr., Nicholas Meriwether I, and Dr. George Nicholas, emigrated from the eastern Piedmont and Tidewater counties and secured patents of several thousands of acres in the Southwest Mountains during the late 1720s. Others, like Michael Woods, arrived in Albemarle from the Shenandoah Valley during the mid-1730s, among the first of many hundreds to cross the Blue Ridge from west to east.

Many of these early settlers acquired large tracts of land, but they soon were outnumbered by countless others who patented only 300 or 400 acres and then cleared as much as a man and his family could cultivate, leaving the remainder in woodlands.

The settlers found the land covered by extensive hardwood forests that contained little undergrowth. They cut down the smaller trees and girdled the larger ones; after the trees died, the pioneers chopped them down and planted corn among the stumps, which were left to rot. They used the wood for fuel and to build their cabins and houses.

Corn, wheat, and a few vegetables were planted to sustain the farmer, his family, and his beasts, but tobacco paid the bills and bought the goods that could not be made at home. A supremely labor-intensive crop, tobacco's profitability was linked directly to the amount of cheap labor that went into planting, caring for, and harvesting it. During the eighteenth and most of the nineteenth centuries in Albemarle, that labor was supplied by the farmer and his family, but most of all by slaves, who had arrived with the early white settlers. From the earliest days of settlement, then, the slave system took root and grew in the county beside the tobacco crop. By the end of the eighteenth century, however, the farmers of Albemarle had shifted from tobacco to grain production (particularly of wheat), due in part to the latter's profitability.

Most eighteenth- and nineteenth-century Virginia dwellings were built in a rural, not an urban, environment. Farms and plantations dotted the countryside, and towns and cities were few in number. Each farm was as self-sufficient as its owner could make it, for access to manufactured goods was limited by distance and the lack of a convenient transportation system. As soon as the farmer could build them, outbuildings sprang up around the principal dwelling. Usually these included at a minimum a "necessary house," a barn, and a separate kitchen to reduce the risk of fire. If the farmer became more affluent, he might add slave quarters, a smokehouse, corncrib, granary, stables, icehouse, laundry, office, overseer's house—a veritable village. Usually these structures were arranged near the main house, sometimes in a "plantation street" behind it. If the farm was large enough, the house servants' dwellings stood near the owner's house, while the quarters for the slaves who worked the fields were built some distance away. The slave quarters extant in Virginia today are of the former sort; the latter have almost all disappeared.

Most rural Virginians eagerly sought the development of towns and besieged the General Assembly with petitions for their creation. Farmers wanted nearby markets for their crops, access to goods at reasonable prices, and a center for social and political gatherings. The frontier was settled by families and groups of families, not by solitary woodsmen, despite the persistent legend of the lone pioneer that usually accompanies the log cabin myth.

Frontier communities or hamlets usually congealed around a river landing, a crossroads, or the county seat. Scottsville, the earliest village in present-day Albemarle County, had all three. Edward Scott owned a ferry here, and a branch of the Lower Secretary's Road intersected the River Road just to the west. When Albemarle was formed in 1744 from Goochland County, the first county court was held the next year at nearby Belle Grove, and Scottsville became the seat of government. The new county was named for William Anne Keppel, second earl of Albemarle and governor of Virginia from 1737 to 1754.

In 1761 Amherst and Buckingham Counties were formed from Albemarle while western Louisa County was added to its area. The county seat was soon moved from Scottsville north to the center of the reconfigured county, where a new town was laid out on fifty acres of high ground near the intersection of the Secretary's Road and Three Notch'd Road, just west of the Rivanna River and the Southwest Mountains. It was named Charlottesville for Queen Charlotte Sophia (1744–1818) of Mecklenberg-Strelitz, the wife of King George III. Nothing remains of the first courthouse in Scottsville.

Just as the county was the basic political unit within the colony, the parish was the basic ecclesiastical unit. Throughout Virginia's history until 1786, the Anglican Church was the established faith, and taxpayers supported the parish through special levies. By the third quarter of the eighteenth century, Albemarle comprised Fredericksville Parish north of the Three Notch'd Road and Saint Anne's Parish in the remainder of the county. In addition to the Anglicans, dissenting denominations (primarily Quakers, Presbyterians, Baptists, and Methodists) increased in numbers throughout the eighteenth century. All eventually built houses of worship—churches and chapels for the Anglicans, meetinghouses for the rest—although most of the dissenters worshiped in members' houses at first.

Most early farmhouses were simple utilitarian structures; so too were the first churches and meetinghouses. Only one eighteenth-century church building remains in the county: the frame Buck Mountain Church (Anglican), built in 1747 on Buck Mountain Road and moved in 1859 to Earlysville. It measured some 30 by 60 feet and survives today in a somewhat altered form.

The glebe house for Saint Anne's Parish also survives. Each colonial parish in Virginia contained a glebe, the dwelling and land owned by the parish that served to house and support the priest. After disestablishment in 1786, the General Assembly ordered that all glebes be sold and the money be used for the care of the poor. The Saint Anne's Parish glebe house, a frame dwelling, was built about 1765 in southern Albemarle and moved in 1946 to Clover Fields in the northern part.

Many gristmills existed in the county by the mid-eighteenth century—Peter Jefferson's, later inherited by his son Thomas, was probably the best known—but most have vanished. Colonel John Walker's 1764 Merrie Mill and Captain Thomas Walker Jr.'s 1783 mill still survive. A mill-related building that possibly dates to 1754, the miller's house for Cochran's mill, still stands as well.

In southern Albemarle, John Old mined iron ore; Jefferson mentioned the mines in *Notes on the State of Virginia*. Old, a Pennsylvanian by birth like so many other Virginia ironmasters, also built an iron furnace before the Revolutionary War on the Hardware River and a forge nearby on Ammonett Creek. Both have fallen into ruin.

The first tavern license in Albemarle County was issued in 1745 to Daniel Scott of Scottsville; his building has disappeared. Likewise, the 1773 Swan Tavern in Charlottesville is gone. Other eighteenth-century taverns, however, have survived in the countryside, including Nathaniel Burnley's, James Black's, the D. S. Tavern, Woodstock Hall, and Michie Tavern, which has been moved from Buck Mountain Road and much altered.

Often stores were built near taverns and other places, such as courthouses, where people congregated. No eighteenth-century store buildings are known to survive in Albemarle.

The Revolution in Albemarle County

On 19 April 1775 the long-simmering hostility between the American colonies and Great Britain erupted in a blaze of gunfire at Lexington in Massachusetts. A few days later, in Virginia, Governor John Murray, earl of Dunmore, seized the gunpowder stored in the public magazine in Williamsburg to prevent its falling into the hands of revolutionaries. In Albemarle County a group of developing revolutionaries, led by Lieutenant George Gilmer, marched toward Williamsburg to join like-minded citizens in demanding the return of the powder. On their way they encountered the firebrand Patrick Henry, who told them that Governor Dunmore had agreed to reimburse the colony for the gunpowder, and so they went home.

In May, Dunmore abandoned Williamsburg for the York River. There he took refuge on a British man-of-war, the *Fowey*, and issued various proclamations and ultimatums, including the promise of freedom for slaves who ran away and joined the British against the rebels. The next month Gilmer again led his militiamen on a march from the county to Williamsburg, which this time they reached. Once there, however, they found nothing to do and again marched home.

During the next several years, as the skirmishes with Great Britain evolved into full-scale warfare, many men from Albemarle enlisted in the Continental army or served in the local militia. The war itself did not affect the county until January 1779, however, and then it was in the form of some 4,000 British and Hessian prisoners captured in the battle of Saratoga in October 1777. They had been imprisoned in Massachusetts, but because the seat of war was in and around that state and food was scarce there, Congress voted to transfer them to Virginia. Colonel John Harvie, a member of Congress, offered his farm a few miles west of Charlottesville for the new prison camp. The prisoners marched several hundred miles overland in the dead of winter and arrived in Albemarle to find their camp unfinished. They had to complete it themselves.

The prisoners included not only soldiers but also camp women and children. Soon a veritable village of huts and other buildings, including a commissary store, a coffeehouse, and a theater—all known collectively as the Barracks (fig. 1)—arose on Harvie's farm off present-day Barracks Road. (None of the buildings remain today, and most of the site has been obliterated by the suburban growth around Charlottesville.) Given seed, equipment, and animals, the prisoners also raised the bulk of their own provisions. Many of the officers lived outside the Barracks: Major General William Phillips, the senior British officer, at Blenheim, the farm of Edward Carter, and Major General Baron von Riedesel, the ranking Hessian, at Colle, the former home of Dr. Philip Mazzei.

As the war dragged on, the numbers of Hessian soldiers seemed to dwindle, presumably as they escaped to their fellow countrymen in the Shenandoah Valley. By the end of 1780, only about 1,200 Hessians and 800 British re-

Fig. 1. Revolutionary War Barracks, 1779–80

mained of the original 4,000 prisoners. Life in Albemarle was good, the remaining prisoners seemed to agree. Riedesel and his family, for example, occasionally dined with Jefferson at Monticello.

Thomas Jefferson was Albemarle County's home-grown revolutionary. Unlike Patrick Henry, another great Virginia leader, Jefferson wielded his influence through the pen rather than the tongue. He wrote an authoritative pamphlet, *A Summary View of the Rights of British America*, that brought him to the attention of the other colonies. As a delegate to the Continental Congress in 1776, he wrote the Declaration of Independence, a core document of American democracy. From 2 June 1779 to 3 June 1781, Jefferson served as Virginia's second governor after independence, and he presided over the movement of the state capital from Williamsburg to Richmond in the spring of 1780.

The capital was relocated because of the perceived threat to Tidewater Virginia from the British army and navy. The threat soon became reality as waves of raids and battles swept the state. Early in June 1781 the war came directly to Albemarle County in a raid led by Lieutenant Colonel Banastre Tarleton, the noted British cavalry commander. Tarleton's mission, to destroy the much-needed supplies of the American army, was carried

out with alacrity as he and some 250 men rode toward Charlottesville.

Jefferson, near the end of his second term as Virginia's governor, and the General Assembly had abandoned Richmond on 10 May and made Charlottesville the temporary state capital. The Senate of Virginia probably met in the 1762 courthouse, while the House of Delegates convened in John Jouett's Swan Tavern, which stood just across the street. On the evening of 3 May, Jouett's son Jack happened to be stopping at the Cuckoo Tavern in Louisa County when Tarleton and his troopers arrived. Deducing their destination from their conversation, young Jouett left the tavern about 10:00 P.M., seconds ahead of Tarleton, and raced westward in the night to warn Jefferson and the legislators. Jouett, familiar with the shortest routes, galloped into Charlottesville about three hours later and sounded the alarm. Despite his early warning, however, the senators and delegates moved at a leisurely pace, and Tarleton very nearly bagged all of them. Tarleton stopped at Dr. Thomas Walker's house, Castle Hill, about 4:00 A.M. on 4 June as he approached Charlottesville. Here he frightened the family and captured several members of the General Assembly; then after half an hour he rode on to the town. Jefferson himself lingered over breakfast and did not leave Monticello with his family until he saw cavalrymen riding up the hill. He fled to Poplar Forest, and the government temporarily relocated to Staunton in the safe haven of the Shenandoah Valley.

Other than destroying some supplies and netting a handful of legislators, Tarleton's raid accomplished little besides embedding itself in local legend. Tarleton later reported that he also freed about twenty of the Saratoga prisoners. He left Albemarle County the next day, but not before — according to local tradition — resting under the shade of an oak tree (whose diseased remains were removed in 1997) at the eastern edge of Charlottesville. Thus ended the county's military role in the Revolutionary War.

The Early National Period

On 19 October 1781, at Yorktown, the war effectively ended with the surrender of the British forces under General Charles Cornwallis. Its independence precariously established, the fledgling United States contemplated its daunting political and financial problems and eventually replaced the Articles of Confederation with the Constitution "to form a more perfect Union."

In Albemarle County, with peace restored, the inhabitants traded their muskets for plowshares and returned to the everyday business of getting a living. The population grew as the process of westward migration, disrupted by the war, settled back into its usual patterns. By 1790, half a century after the first settlers had moved into the area, Albemarle's population stood at 12,585, including 6,835 whites, 5,579 black slaves, and 171 free blacks. Almost everyone lived on farms; the largest town, Charlottesville, probably had fewer than 200 inhabitants (its population was estimated at 300 in 1816). Even so, the General Assembly chartered Charlottesville as a town in 1801.

As the population increased and trade grew both to the east and the west, a few communities began to arise in the countryside. Scottsville continued to grow despite the removal of the government to Charlottesville, largely because of its position on the James, the county's most easily navigable watercourse. In 1789 the town of Milton was laid out on the land of Bennett Henderson on the south side of the Rivanna River, at the head of navigation in the northeastern quarter of the county. About 1793 the town of Warren was established at the head of Ballenger's Creek on the James River, on the land of Wilson Cary Nicholas a few miles upstream from Scottsville.

The feverish desire to create new towns to encourage commerce peaked early in the nineteenth century. In Albemarle, for example, North Milton was established about 1802 across the Rivanna River from the earlier Milton. Unlike its namesake, however, it did not prosper for long. Other would-be towns that fared similarly include Travellers' Grove (also called Pleasant Grove), laid out by Colonel John Everett near his house, Red Hill; New York, or Little York, a Pennsylvania German community built on the land of James Hays at the foot of the Blue Ridge near present-day U.S. Route 250; Morgantown, established near Ivy by Gideon Morgan; and Barterbrook near Eastham, northwest of Charlottesville.

It was during the years of growth between the end of the Revolution and the first decades of the nineteenth century that the Georgian style of architecture reached its zenith and began to be supplanted by the Federal style. Most builders, of course, continued to construct simple log dwellings or one-room frame vernacular houses. Few unaltered examples of these types remain in the county, for their owners expanded them as they prospered by adding rooms, passages, and second stories.

Few unaltered examples remain as well of the Georgian style, which was never as common in the county as other more recent styles. Perhaps the best frame Georgian specimen is Plain Dealing, a one-story house built about 1761 for John Biswell and later attached by an open hyphen to a 1789 frame I-house constructed for Samuel Dyer. Plain Dealing is noted for its elaborate interior paneling and mantels. Redlands, a stately two-story brick mansion built about 1798 for Robert Carter, is a transitional example. Its Georgian-style facade conceals a Federal-style interior that contains spectacular woodwork and an unusual segmental-shaped entry and drawing room.

Aside from dwellings, few substantial buildings were constructed during the last half of the eighteenth century and the first few years of the nineteenth century. Two exceptions are the second and third Albemarle County courthouses. The second, built in Charlottesville about 1762 after the county seat was moved from Scottsville, by 1800 had acquired a portico. The third, a handsomely detailed late Georgian brick building, was constructed by John Jordan, one of Thomas Jefferson's builders; it now forms the rear ell of the present courthouse.

Taverns, especially those associated with the courthouse, constituted the other major significant building type of the early national period. Benjamin Brown and David Ross built the Eagle Tavern about 1791 to the southeast of the courthouse and not far from the earlier Swan Tavern. Of frame construction and two stories high, the Eagle boasted a piazza or portico across the length of its facade.

Two stone taverns were built during the period, one in Charlottesville and the other in the country. George Nicholas constructed the Central Hotel on Market Street in Charlottesville about 1782; it burned in 1852. Nicholas's brother, Wilson Cary Nicholas, probably built the Warren Tavern in 1804; it was demolished about 1970.

The early national period in Albemarle County was but an introduction to the great era of architecture that would begin with the new century. It would start with the rebuilding of a private dwelling, continue through the construction of a university, and spread beyond the county's borders. Thomas Jefferson's architectural vision, broadcast by his designs and those of the workmen he employed, ultimately influenced other practitioners of the building arts throughout the United States.

Thomas Jefferson and His Master Builders (1800–1830s)

A man whose wide-ranging interests reflect his own complexities and self-contradictions, Thomas Jefferson exhibited throughout his life a need for order and control. Did this need arise from being uprooted from his home, Shadwell, while an infant to live at Tuckahoe through most of his boyhood, only to return to Shadwell at age nine? Was it caused by the early death of his vital, frontier-conquering father, which left young Thomas responsible for his sisters and younger brother and a mother with whom he had a distant relationship? Was it reinforced by the fire that destroyed Shadwell when Jefferson was twenty-six, thereby demolishing the structure that had sheltered him into manhood? Regardless of the cause or causes, Jefferson's awareness of the uncertainty of life and the swift passage of time compelled him to organize himself, impose order on his day, and control his environment. All of these needs and impulses found their outlet in the practice of architecture.

Architecture as a profession did not exist in the American colonies during Jefferson's youth. Most architects were either builders or gentlemen amateurs who imbibed basic principles from British and Italian pattern books. Eighteenth-century European architects looked to antiquity for appropriate models and thereby created the Classical Revival period of architecture. These architects published their ideas in pattern books or reissued older books that influenced their counterparts on the other side of the Atlantic, particularly Jefferson. Among the most important such works were Giacomo Leoni's edition of *The Architecture of A. Palladio; in Four Books* (1716–20), James Gibbs's *Book of Architecture* (1728), William Salmon's *Palladio Londinensis* (1734), and Robert Morris's *Select Architecture* (1755).

Jefferson was swept away by Palladianism—adherence to the architectural principles of the Italian Andrea Palladio—and the Roman models that inspired Palladio. In 1769, when the young Virginian began to clear the top of a little mountain and to build his house, Palladio became his mentor. As Jefferson designed the first version of Monticello, the three-bay central block rose two full stories, and a two-tier pedimented portico projected from the east front. Story-and-a-half wings with hipped roofs stood to either side, and a one-story octagonal bay was attached to each wing. Within the central block, both the first-floor parlor and the second-floor library had octagonal ends that were protected by another two-tier portico on the west front. In 1782 the marquis de Chastellux viewed the unfinished house and proclaimed that "Mr. Jefferson is the first American who has consulted the fine arts to know how he should shelter himself from the weather."

Jefferson never completed the house, which he began as a bachelor. Marriage and children followed by the death of his wife and five years in Paris during the 1780s prompted him to dismantle and reassemble Monticello in a new form. It was well that Jefferson professed to love "putting up and pulling down," for the second Monticello was not finished (if it ever truly was) until 1809. And it is ironic that a man who so desperately yearned for order and quiet spent some forty years living in the midst of a construction project.

The planning and construction of the second Monticello—the house we know today—solidified Jefferson's sophisticated architectural principles, which had been further refined in Paris. Even while abroad, he designed the first temple-form public building in America, the Virginia State Capitol, using a Roman temple, the Maison Carrée in Nîmes, France, as his model. The Capitol and the first Monticello were radical enough for their time, but the second Monticello was even more revolutionary. Besides sporting the first dome on a private residence in the United States, the remodeled dwelling may have been the first domestic structure designed to satisfy the particular and peculiar needs of its owner. When completed, the first floor contained three public rooms (entry hall–museum, parlor, and dining room), as well as an apartment or suite of private rooms for Jefferson (bedchamber, study or "cabinet," multiroom library, and greenhouse) and enough built-in gadgets to fill a patent office. Monticello thus broke the mold that subordinated a dwelling's function to the rigors of architectural style and within its highly idiosyncratic form wedded the two in a composition never before attempted in America.

Jefferson's concept for the University of Virginia was just as radical. The centerpiece was not a chapel, as on most church-affiliated campuses, but instead a temple of knowledge – a library. Modeled on the pagan Pantheon in Rome, Jefferson's Rotunda dominated the northern end of the Lawn and was flanked east and west by rows of two-story pavilions and one-story student rooms concealed behind Tuscan colonnades. Serpentine-walled gardens behind the Lawn buildings linked them with hotels (dining halls) and more student rooms in arcade-lined outer "ranges."

This "academical village" appears symmetrical and uniform at first glance, but as was usual with things Jeffersonian, appearances were deceiving. No two pavilions are identical. Indeed, Jefferson intended them all to be different, to serve as models of the orders of architecture. The result is a dynamic composition, at once alive and at peace.

Jefferson was assisted in refining his design not only by such eminent contemporary architects as B. Henry Latrobe and William Thornton but also by a talented corps of builders, some of whom had worked at Monticello. Preeminent among them were John Neilson and James Dinsmore, and others included John M. Perry, William B. Phillips, and Dabney Cosby. Several of these craftsmen designed and constructed dwellings, courthouses, and other buildings around the state and beyond, thereby spreading the doctrine of Jeffersonian classicism.

Jefferson's architectural vision was particularly avant-garde when compared with its predecessor, the Georgian style. The Federal or Roman Revival–style building differed radically from the Georgian, diverging especially in form, plan, and decorative details. Although exterior forms remained symmetrical, such new features as projecting fronts, centered gables, Palladian windows, and porticoes appeared. Inside, architects created nonrectangular spaces such as oval parlors and octagonal bays and frequently moved the stairs to lateral passages or tucked them away in narrow shafts as at Monticello. The mantels, moldings, and other decorative elements drew on classical models, particularly as interpreted by the brothers James and Robert Adam in their pattern book *Works in Architecture*. Jeffersonian classicism did not begin to dominate Virginia architecture until the 1820s, particularly after the university was completed and Jefferson's workmen went out into the world. Even then, it often manifested itself as a Federal-style structure incorporating Jeffersonian motifs.

Inside and outside Albemarle County, several buildings still stand that were designed by Jefferson's craftsmen. James Dinsmore, for example, built Estouteville (1827–30) on Green Mountain south of Charlottesville, and the tripartite Oak Lawn (1822), which lies within the city limits, is attributed to him. William B. Phillips designed Christ Episcopal Church, Glendower, near Keene; this Jeffersonian gem was constructed in 1831–32. But the influence of Jefferson's workmen may be even more evident outside the county's borders. John Neilson's best-known work, for instance, is Upper Bremo (1820) in Fluvanna County; it was designed for General John Hartwell Cocke with architectural details that were typically Jeffersonian. John M. Perry built several houses in Orange County, including Frascati (1821–23). Berry Hill (1824) in Orange is attributed to master builders William B. Phillips and Malcolm F. Crawford, who, together or separately, built houses and courthouses throughout the state. By 1830 Jeffersonian classicism permeated Virginia.

ALBEMARLE BEFORE THE WAR (1830s–1860)

The Classical Revival style promulgated by Jefferson and his disciples was based on Roman models as delineated by Italian, French, and English architects. Before long, American architects reached even deeper in time to resurrect the simpler, "purer" architecture of the Greeks and thus began the period known as the Greek Revival. Other, more exotic revivals followed, including the Gothic and the Egyptian, but only the Gothic and the Greek found favor in Albemarle. Another style, the Italianate, was based on Italian farmhouses and villas; it proved less popular nationally, and far less so in Albemarle, than the Greek Revival.

Two early nineteenth-century architectural pattern books helped to spread the Greek Revival gospel. The first, Asher Benjamin and Daniel Reynard's *The American Builder's Companion*, was originally published in 1806. In 1830 Benjamin revised it to instruct builders on the details of the new style and declared Roman Revivalism passé. (This was far from true in rural localities such as Albemarle County, which were slow to adopt new architectural trends.) Three years later Minard Lafever published *The Modern Builder's Guide*, which also proved popular with builders. The style reached its height of fashion in Virginia in the 1850s, when many older houses were "Greek Revivalized" with new porticoes and interior trim.

Albemarle County's collection of Greek Revival architecture includes transitional houses such as Cliffside, which overlooks Scottsville. Built in 1835, this brick three-bay, Federal-style house has handsome Greek Revival front and side porticoes. Pure examples of the style are abundant. Frame specimens include Mount Fair in Brown's Cove and Clover Fields, both of which were built about 1848, and the 1860 Jarman-Cree house near Crozet. Among brick examples, Hillcrest Farm, built in the late 1830s south of Charlottesville; Monticola, constructed in the early 1840s near Howardsville; and the 1853 Dr. John C. Hughes house in Charlottesville are all outstanding.

By the 1850s Albemarle and Charlottesville had developed a manifestation of the Greek Revival style that was common, if not particular, to the area. It took the form of a brick two-story dwelling over a high basement, was single- or double-pile in plan, and displayed four brick full-height pilasters on at least the front facade. The pilasters were topped with Tuscan or Doric capitals executed in either brick or wood and supported a typically prominent wide cornice that encircled the building. This form was repeated in numerous dwellings, including the Hughes house, the Abell-Gleason house, and Bonahora, all built in the 1850s in Charlottesville, and such rural examples as the 1840s Fairmount. It also appeared in public, commercial, and ecclesiastical buildings as well, including the 1851 Town Hall (later the Levy Opera House) and the 1854 Farish House hotel, both of which stand on or near Court Square, the midcentury Farmers' Bank, and the First Baptist Church of the same period.

During the period another structure was built that marked the first attempt by an architect of national repute to alter a Jefferson-designed edifice. Robert Mills, a former pupil of both Jefferson and Latrobe, in 1851 designed a Classical Revival addition known as the Annex or New Hall for the north front of the Rotunda. The new structure succeeded in its primary purpose—to provide much-needed classroom space and a public hall—but was far less successful as a work of architecture. Its failure (and near-universal unpopularity, especially after it served as the source of the infamous 1895 fire that de-

stroyed all but the walls of the Rotunda) is not so much due to its architectural details but to the overall effect of the structure. Mills faithfully replicated Jefferson's Rotunda cornice, window pediments, portico pediment, and colossal columns. He even had the Corinthian capitals cast in iron rather than carved from marble, a technological advance that Jefferson might have admired. But the Annex came to be regarded as a monstrous carbuncle on one of the most important buildings in the United States and a cautionary tale for any architect who would alter a Jefferson structure.

Simultaneously with the rise to dominance of the Greek Revival style, some architects initiated a reaction against strict adherence to the classical orders. The Gothic Revival style lent itself to irregular floor plans and to the cottage form, which Alexander J. Davis popularized in 1838 in *Rural Residences*. Blenheim, the seat of Andrew Stevenson, was built about 1846 in the Gothic Revival style. A story-and-a-half frame dwelling, Blenheim's most significant architectural features are its pointed Gothic windows and louvered shutters. Other examples of the style include the mid-nineteenth-century Perkins house on First Street, the Sunnyside remodeling of 1858 on Barracks Road, and the 1863 Fowler house on Ridge Street.

Italianate-style buildings, like their Gothic Revival counterparts, frequently broke away from the old rectangular forms to exhibit irregular plans. Andrew Jackson Downing, in *Cottage Residences* (1842) and *The Architecture of Country Houses* (1850), offered builders and owners many different facades and floor plans. Despite its popularity elsewhere, the style did not catch on in Albemarle. One of the few extant examples is the Tower House, constructed on Park Street in Charlottesville in the late 1850s for John Wood Jr.

Charlottesville grew rapidly during the antebellum period. By 1850 the county seat had almost 2,000 residents, while Scottsville had slightly fewer than 700 (the population of the entire county stood at about 26,000). Much of Charlottesville's growth, and the county's as well, may be traced to vast improvements in transportation. In 1816 the General Assembly created the Fund for Internal Improvement to invest money in turnpike, canal, navigation (river dredging), and—later—railroad companies. The companies were authorized to issue stock, and once private investors had subscribed to two-fifths of it, the state would purchase the remaining three-fifths. The companies expended most of these funds on construction and counted on tolls and freight fees to finance the costs of maintenance. Unfortunately for the investors, many of these companies eventually went bankrupt as maintenance expenses almost invariably exceeded revenues.

At first, however, money and enthusiasm seemed to guarantee success, and Albemarle's citizens joined early in the turnpike fever sweeping the state. The Rockfish Gap Turnpike, chartered by the General Assembly in 1818, ran from Scottsville to the gap. It followed approximately present-day Route 20 from Scottsville to Keene, then what are now Routes 712 and 692 to U.S. Route 250. In 1828 the legislature created the Rivanna and Rockfish Gap Turnpike (today's U.S. Route 250) to link the northeastern part of the county with the Shenandoah Valley by a road from Meriwether's Bridge on the Rivanna River to a junction with the Rockfish Gap Turnpike at Brooks's tavern. Other toll roads included the Staunton and James River Turnpike, established in 1827, and the Brown's Gap Turnpike (Routes 680, 810, and 629 from Mechum's River to that gap), a much-older road that was improved in the early 1850s. The Civil War ruined the turnpike companies because maintenance was neglected and tolls went uncollected; after the war most of the turnpikes were abandoned to the care of the counties.

Canal and river-improvement companies abounded during the antebellum period. By 1840 the James River and Kanawha Canal, which originated in Richmond, had reached Scottsville en route to its termination point near Covington. From there, the Kanawha Turnpike linked the end of the canal with the Ohio River, thus connecting the ports of Tidewater Virginia with the Midwest. On 2 March 1827 the General Assembly chartered the Rivanna Navigation Company to clear the county's only navigable internal river, an undertaking of more direct potential benefit to the county.

County residents, including Jefferson, had been attempting since the 1760s to open the Rivanna River to navigation and extend the improvement toward the mountains. The Rivanna Company was formed in 1806 to achieve that goal, but the work proceeded slowly; by 1820 the north and south forks had been improved for four or five miles upstream from their junction. The General Assembly chartered the Rivanna Navigation Company to take over the task from the old company and rebuild the system with additional locks and dams. The legislation authorized the new company to issue stock to raise the necessary capital and required it to begin work within two years after investors subscribed to half the stock and to complete the project within five years. Work proceeded at a glacial pace, however, and it took the threat of competition from the railroad in the 1850s to prompt the company managers to attempt to complete the project in a flurry of activity. It was too late, of course, and by 1860 the enterprise was all but dead.

By the 1830s railroads had begun to supplant canals even as the water systems enjoyed their heyday. Properly powered, a railroad train could carry more goods and passengers than several canalboats. And track could be laid almost anywhere a turnpike or other roadway could be constructed, thereby providing many more potential transportation routes than two navigable rivers. In the late 1840s the Virginia Central Railroad line was extended into Albemarle County and reached Charlottesville by 1850. Within four years trains ran over the line into the Shenandoah Valley.

The traffic on the turnpikes and railroads during the internal improvements boom resulted in the proliferation of stagecoach stops and taverns. The principal stagecoach routes linked Charlottesville to Lynchburg, Richmond, and Washington, D.C. On these and other roads, both old and new taverns catered to stage drivers and passengers, drovers, and other travelers. Some taverns stood at the intersections of major roads. For example, the Midway Hotel of 1818 was located at the junction of the Three Notch'd Road and the Lynchburg Road, while the 1788 La Fourche Tavern was at the intersection of the Three Notch'd Road and the Fredericksburg Road. Nathaniel Garland's tavern, built about 1802, still stands at the intersection of the Lynchburg Road and the turnpike to Staunton; it also served as a tollgate. At Mechum's River, near the Virginia Central Railroad depot, William Graves built Price's Hotel (named for its second owner, Charles H. Price) about 1850. Several of the antebellum taverns, long since converted to dwellings, still stand.

The prosperity of the antebellum years arose in part from improved farming practices and the shift to grain as the principal crop, as well as from the growth of commerce and industry. In the upper South the invention of the reaper helped keep the slave-based economy of the grain-producing regions profitable, as did the invention of the cotton gin in the lower South. The Agricultural Society of Albemarle, formed in 1817 with Thomas Jefferson as one of its founding members, encouraged good farming practices throughout a five-county region of Piedmont Virginia. Annual fairs and competitions, as well as a proliferation of farm-improvement magazines such as the *American Farmer*, intensified farmers' interest in selective stock breeding, crop rotation, and soil conservation.

Many new businesses and industries were established

during the period. The continuing shift from tobacco to grain as the primary crop resulted in the construction of many new mills, including Crozet Mill, Maupin's mill, and Patterson's mill. Eolus Gristmill, built in 1854, was one of the largest in the county. On the Rivanna River, William D. Meriwether's 1820s complex of mills evolved into the Charlottesville Woolen Mills. Tobacco remained an important cash crop, and tobacco warehouses continued to be built; the only one remaining is the Peter Field Jefferson warehouse, constructed in 1834 in Scottsville.

Dry goods stores sprouted around the county during the antebellum period. The Piedmont Store at White Hall was built about 1853 and still stands. In Charlottesville the Johnson W. Pitts house, located on West Main Street, was built in 1820 and later contained a dry goods store as well as a residence. The former Anderson Brothers' Bookstore on West Main Street opposite the University of Virginia housed a bookstore as early as 1852; the building itself, hidden beneath later cladding, dates from 1848.

Besides the establishment of the university, during the first half of the nineteenth century improvements were made in elementary education as well. Whereas earlier schools had been located on farms to serve a family or two or were supported by several families in a community, a growing awareness of the connection between education and the responsibilities of citizenship in the new republic prompted an eruption of schools and academies. In 1811 the General Assembly created the Literary Fund, from which loans were made to local governments for school construction. Occasionally the fund was augmented by donations from private citizens, as in the mid-1830s when the Reverend Martin Dawson financed the construction of two schools in Albemarle County and one in Nelson County through his will; the Literary Fund administered Dawson's bequest. By 1840 Albemarle County had eighteen academies or grammar schools and twenty-one primary schools, with about 400 students in each system. Despite these numbers, however, nothing approximating Jefferson's dream of universal public education existed until well after the Civil War. Education remained the domain of the few, not the right of the many. A handful of antebellum schools survive today.

By midcentury, Albemarle County had forty-five churches that were used by five denominations (Baptist, Episcopal, Methodist, Presbyterian, and Universalist). Several outstanding examples of contemporary architectural styles still stand. They include Mount Ed Baptist Church, a Greek Revival–style building constructed in

1856–57. The Howardsville Methodist Church, built in 1854, is a good example of the Greek Revival style. Grace Episcopal Church, built about 1847, designed by the nationally renowned architect William Strickland, is an exceedingly rare Gothic Revival–style gem.

In 1859, just before the outbreak of the Civil War, one of Jefferson's builders constructed a new facade for the Albemarle County Courthouse. Working from a design by William A. Pratt, the proctor of the university, George Wilson Spooner Jr. built a Gothic Revival addition to the old courthouse that became the new front entrance, complete with towers. As if embarrassed by this seeming betrayal of Jeffersonian classicism, which a later historian called an "architectural monstrosity," other hands began to remove the Gothic features almost immediately. By 1870 the towers were gone, and a portico supported by four Ionic columns sheltered the entrance. Eventually the Gothic doorway and window "eyebrows" were replaced, other changes were made as late as the 1930s, and the transformation of Pratt's Gothic courthouse into a proper Jeffersonian-style concoction was complete.

POSTWAR RECONSTRUCTION AND LATER VICTORIANISM (1865–1890s)

Fortunately for the citizens of Albemarle County, the battles of the Civil War largely took place elsewhere, thereby sparing the residents the destruction of crops and buildings suffered by other parts of the state. In June 1862 Major General Thomas J. "Stonewall" Jackson led his Valley Army down the Brown's Gap Turnpike en route to Richmond to join in the defense of the Confederate capital; no fighting occurred in the county then. The only military engagement here came late in the war, on 29 February 1864, when Brigadier General George Armstrong Custer led some 1,500 cavalrymen on a diversionary raid. Custer's mission was to draw attention from a simultaneous Union cavalry raid on Richmond led by Brigadier General H. Judson Kilpatrick and Colonel Ulric Dahlgren. At Rio Hill, just north of Charlottesville, Custer attacked the winter camp of four batteries of the Stuart Horse Artillery under Captain Marcellus N. Moorman. Custer destroyed most of the huts but withdrew when Moorman shelled his men.

Barely a year later, on 3 March 1865, Custer returned to Albemarle and this time occupied Charlottesville, which Mayor Christopher Fowler surrendered without a fight. The Union army under Major General Philip H. Sheridan had just defeated Lieutenant General Jubal A.

Early's Confederate army at the battle of Waynesboro and was on the march to Richmond. Custer's men occupied Charlottesville for two days, tore up the Virginia Central Railroad tracks, and burned the depot. They also guarded the university, major public buildings, and many private homes; there was little looting or destruction of private property.

The major effect of the war on the county lay in its aftermath, particularly in the liberation of the slaves. Hundreds of them fled in Custer's wake, while the remainder were freed at war's end. The shock of sudden freedom affected both races, and the federal government created the Freedmen's Bureau to assist the former slaves in making the transition. By 1870 Albemarle's African Americans comprised a majority of the population of 27,544: 14,994 blacks and 12,550 whites.

The Virginia Constitution of 1869, adopted as required under federal Reconstruction legislation, established Virginia's first statewide system of public schools. Most localities already possessed several private schools and academies for whites, and Albemarle was no exception. But these schools catered to the children of those in the white upper social and economic strata, while the less prosperous did not fare as well. Under the new constitution the public schools would be available to all, white and black alike. Although the new system at first met with widespread opposition from Conservatives, soon an influx of money from the Literary Fund and from private sources such as the Janes and Rosenwald foundations, as well as the contributions of the citizens themselves, launched waves of racially segregated school construction throughout the state. Several of the early public schools still stand.

For the most part, late nineteenth- and early twentieth-century rural schools were utilitarian in design. The Miller School of Albemarle is a rare exception. Established by a bequest from philanthropist Samuel Miller in 1869, the school was organized in 1874. The Main Building, begun that year, is a spectacular example of High Victorian Gothic architecture. It was designed by Richmond architects D. Wiley Anderson and Albert M. Lybrock, the latter being one of the country's most eminent practitioners of the style.

The Gothic Revival style was adapted more successfully for certain types of buildings than for others. To the public its use for a courthouse seemed inappropriate, and it was never used as commonly for dwellings as the Greek Revival style. Yet when executed in stone and castellated, the style became enormously popular in a mode now sometimes called "collegiate Gothic," with Virginia Military Institute in Lexington being a premier example. Its appeal was even more widespread when applied to ecclesiastical architecture, and Gothic Revival–style churches continue to be constructed, often in a less formal style called "carpenter Gothic." Saint John's Episcopal Church in Scottsville, built in 1875, is a good example, with board-and-batten walls, pointed Gothic windows, and a scrollwork vergeboard.

An explosion of church construction followed the Civil War as African Americans left white-dominated churches to form their own congregations and build their own houses of worship. One of the grander black churches, Mount Zion Baptist Church in Charlottesville, was designed by George Wilson Spooner Jr. and constructed of brick in the Gothic Revival style in 1884. In the countryside black congregations usually built simpler frame churches, such as another Mount Zion Baptist Church located in the northern part of the county.

Most dwellings built during the late nineteenth century were vernacular I-houses, but a few excellent samples of the Second Empire and Queen Anne styles also exist. The Price-Poore house in Charlottesville, which was modified several times after its initial construction about 1839, is an evolved example of the former style. Among the finest Queen Anne–style dwellings are the 1894 brick Marshall-Rucker house on Park Street in Charlottesville and the frame Kirklea near Ivy, constructed about 1896.

During the postwar period a near frenzy of railroad acquisition and construction began as economic activity resumed in a rush. The Virginia Central Railroad eventually was absorbed by the Chesapeake and Ohio Railroad, and the Orange and Alexandria (whose line had been extended to Charlottesville in 1881) by the Southern Railway. Two brick depots still stand in Charlottesville, the 1885 Southern Railway depot and the 1905 C&O depot. None of the antebellum rural depots survive, except for a portion of the one at Keswick.

Downtown Charlottesville underwent a spate of commercial construction late in the nineteenth century and early in the twentieth century, and today these buildings form the core of the downtown financial and shopping district. Most are of brick and stand two or more stories tall; many have elaborate cornices. They vary enough to interest the eye and yet still create an architecturally cohesive district.

On 2 March 1888 the General Assembly amended Charlottesville's town charter and established it as an incorporated city. Under Virginia's system of independent cities, this meant that Charlottesville gained its own tax base, court system, police force, and separate political identity. Typical of the era, the new city's boosters promoted its amenities (both actual and hoped-for) to attract new investors and encourage growth. The movement of rural residents into the city because of improved employment opportunities created a demand for inexpensive housing close to but not in the commercial center. Land developers and architects heard the call and hastened to respond.

THE ECLECTIC ERA (1890s–1930s)

The demand for new and affordable housing in Albemarle County and Charlottesville that arose in the late nineteenth century invited incursions of nontraditional architectural styles, many of which included references to older types. Among the new styles were the Bungalow, Dutch Colonial, Craftsman, American Foursquare, Tudor Revival, and Modern. They were attractive in part because most were small in size (so that a housewife might clean them with little or no assistance from servants) and irregular in floor plan (reflecting a redefinition of public and private spaces); they also contained indoor plumbing and other modern conveniences and instead of nearby stalls for horses frequently possessed adjoining garages for automobiles. Once again, changes in technology and lifestyle resulted in corresponding changes in architectural design.

Many of these new houses were constructed apart from Charlottesville's old downtown in what were termed suburbs. Suburban developments encouraged a certain uniformity of house size and style that could charm or bore, depending on the skill of the project architect. This new way of life — not entirely rural, not quite urban — was possible only because of improvements in roads, automobiles, and streetcar systems. Now one no longer needed to live above the store or within walking distance of one's employer.

Some architects catered to the taste of the well-to-do for large but modern dwellings located in such developments as Farmington, which rose up around the old plantation (converted to a country club) in the 1920s, or on miniature estates sited on well-traveled roads into Charlottesville. Often such houses were built in distinctive styles, such as Villa Crawford (recently the Keswick Hall), a Georgian Revival–Italian Villa confection erected about 1912. Royal Orchard, patterned in 1913 after a Newport, Rhode Island, mansion, has a medieval interior designed

four years later by John Russell Pope. Casa Maria was built between 1919 and 1922 in a Spanish-Mediterranean style, while Recoleta, constructed about 1939–40, was called Spanish Colonial Revival.

The Jeffersonian legacy, meanwhile, continued to hold sway at the University of Virginia after a flirtation with Victorianism exemplified by the Brooks Museum of 1876 and the Gothic chapel of 1890. The classical resurgence was born of disaster — the 1895 Rotunda fire — although the 1893 Fayerweather Hall gymnasium, designed by John Kevan Peebles and J. Edwin R. Carpenter, had reintroduced the theme. Stanford White, a principal in the renowned firm of McKim, Mead and White, was retained to draw plans for a reconstructed Rotunda. White gave the building a north portico and altered the interior space to create one enormous dome room. Just as significantly, he enclosed the south end of the Lawn (something that had been proposed before but not executed until the fire destroyed the Annex classrooms) with three new Classical Revival buildings: Rouss Hall on the east, Cocke Hall on the west, and Cabell Hall on the south. During the next decade a host of such structures arose on the grounds, including Randall Hall (1899) and University Hospital (1901), both designed by Paul J. Pelz, the architect of the Library of Congress. Similar buildings included Madison Hall (1905), designed by Parish and Schroeder; Garrett Hall (1908), by McKim, Mead and White; Minor Hall (1911), by John Kevan Peebles and Warren H. Manning; and Peabody Hall (1912), by Carlow, Ferguson and Taylor.

In 1904, in the midst of its building campaign, the university eliminated its ancient system of government by the faculty and inaugurated its first president, the nationally renowned educator Edwin Anderson Alderman. During the ensuing years until his death in 1931, Alderman campaigned tirelessly and successfully to expand the institution's schools and construct new buildings — almost invariably designed in the new classical style — to house them. Statues of Homer, Jefferson, and Washington were erected on the central grounds, and the Schools of Education, Law, and Medicine grew rapidly as well. Under Fiske Kimball, who came to the university in 1919 to direct the newly created architectural curriculum, the School of Architecture gained considerable stature.

The classical influence extended well beyond the university's boundaries into the community and found a receptive audience, as many Virginians were attracted to Colonial Revival architecture after it figured so prominently in the Jamestown Tercentennial Celebration in Norfolk in 1907. Architect-designed buildings, some by university faculty and graduates, proliferated throughout Charlottesville and Albemarle County and beyond, spreading the style widely. Near the university, for example, Stanislaw Makielski designed the Phi Kappa Psi and Beta Theta Pi fraternity houses of 1928 and 1929. In 1910 Eugene Bradbury's Four Acres was completed farther away on Rugby Road, and Makielski designed the 1929 Dulaney house, also on Rugby Road. Bradbury had designed Lewis Mountain in 1909; it was constructed just west of the university.

Twentieth-century classical or Beaux Arts public buildings in Charlottesville include the present-day Jefferson-Madison Regional Library, designed by Percy Ash as a post office and built in 1904, and Walter Dabney Blair's Beaux Arts masterpiece, the McIntire Public Library, which was completed in 1922 and presently houses the Albemarle County Historical Society. The conversion of the Albemarle County Courthouse from Gothic Revival to the new classical style was completed in the 1930s. Several Charlottesville schools, the 1916 McGuffey Elementary School by Ferguson, Calrow and Wrenn among them, were built in the style. Classical-style churches include the First Methodist Church, designed by Joseph Hudnut and completed in 1924, and Saint Paul's Memorial Church (Episcopal), designed by Eugene Bradbury and built in 1925. Charlottesville's two early skyscrapers, the National Bank and Trust Company building of 1920 by William Johnston Marsh and the Monticello Hotel, designed by Stanhope S. Johnson and completed in 1926, are in the Beaux Arts tradition.

In Albemarle County the classical style found expression in Ednam, designed by D. Wiley Anderson and built in 1901 just south of Farmington. Other rural examples include Westover, completed in 1916 and designed by Claude K. Howell; Kenridge, designed by William Johnston Marsh and completed about 1922; and Tiverton, a house that dated to the 1920s but was rebuilt in 1937 by architect Carl Linder after a fire destroyed its interior. In addition, dozens of similar dwellings, large and small, are scattered throughout the county.

The Triumph of Tradition (1910s–1930s and Beyond)

Although many architectural styles have come and gone, Virginians in general and Albemarle Countians in particular have never lost their love of the Georgian and Classical Revival styles. Collectively termed Colonial (by real estate agents in particular), these styles have persisted throughout the United States in the genre known as Colonial Revival.

It is especially fitting, therefore, that one of the earliest expressions of Colonial Revival architecture in America stands in Albemarle County. Cobham Park, built about 1856 as a summerhouse for William Cabell Rives Jr., is essentially a Georgian Revival mansion with the form and architectural details of that style. It preceded by a generation the accepted date for the beginning of the style, the 1880s.

It is also fitting that Sidney Fiske Kimball built Shack Mountain, his retirement home, near Charlottesville. Kimball is known as the dean of architectural history in America, the father of the University of Virginia School of Architecture, and the man who almost singlehandedly restored the reputation of "Thomas Jefferson, Architect," through his respected book of that title. Shack Mountain, built in 1935–36, is a Jeffersonian-style pavilion that is considered Kimball's masterwork.

Among Fiske Kimball's many projects was the restoration of Colonial Williamsburg, for which he was one of the advising architects. The widespread publicity given the undertaking and its subsequent success as a tourist attraction gave the Colonial Revival style a boost in popularity that has continued to this day and shows no signs of abating. So widespread is its appeal that sometimes earlier dwellings built in other architectural styles have been "Colonial Revivalized" or "Williamsburged," frequently to their detriment. Properly executed by such masterful architects as Kimball, William Lawrence Bottomley, Stanhope Johnson, and others, however, such handsome works as Shack Mountain, Rose Hill, and Gallison Hall have been the happy result.

The style has also found widespread acceptance for modern middle-class houses, as hundreds of developments attest. The popularity of the Colonial Revival dwelling is credited to its combination of tradition and modernity: within the standard rectangular footprint and behind the conservative facade, countless floor plans and spatial relationships are possible because of modern construction materials. One therefore may own a house that offers a link to the past (however ersatz) with all of the modern conveniences and none of the old inconveniences.

For example, with the arrival of radio, television, and air-conditioning, porches lost their former function as summer living rooms and became merely decorative, while the life of the house turned inward as never before. The extension of electrical service to rural areas provided, ultimately, for the construction of housing developments (or bedroom suburbs) that were not suburban at all but separated from the city by miles of farmland. Their existence was also made possible, of course, by the ribbons of concrete that enabled their inhabitants to drive to work, return home, reenter the air-conditioned and centrally heated dwelling, and thereby avoid virtually all contact with other residents. This physical and emotional distancing would not have been possible in an earlier time, when one walked to work with one's fellow employees or jostled for a seat on a crowded streetcar.

Modern Times

Although Albemarle County and Charlottesville have changed dramatically during the last half century, much of their historical flavor still abides. Monticello and the "academical village" at the University of Virginia continue to epitomize the county's architectural achievements. They also continue to attract and challenge architects of national and international repute who come to the county to design houses and other buildings. The shadow of Jefferson lingers, and invariably invites comparisons and provokes professional competition, to Albemarle's benefit.

As a result, the county is blessed with vernacular buildings and stylistic masterpieces by the hundreds that enrich the environment and please the eye. Most of them have been built to harmonize with the countryside, not to clash with it. Visitor and resident alike still find it easy to look past the blacktop and other modern features and see the houses and farms and patterns of land use that our forebears evolved over some two and a half centuries. The Albemarle of old, as John Adams said of Jefferson, "still lives."

The county is no longer primarily agricultural, however, nor has it been for many years. The number of farmers—the chosen people of God, as Jefferson called them—has plunged, as has the number of farms in the county: during the five-year period between 1964 and 1969, for example, the number of farms declined from 964 to 706, a decrease of 27 percent. Meanwhile, the population of the county has increased hugely, from about 38,000 in 1970 to around 68,000 in 1990.

Outside Charlottesville and away from the commercial sprawl on U.S. Route 29 North, most of the county remains overwhelmingly rural. The character of that rural ambience has changed, however, from that of fifty or more years ago. Rather than a bucolic countryside containing thousands of small farms that support an agricultural economy, rural Albemarle has come to resemble a community of estates and country gentlemen's seats. Instead of a farm-based county, Albemarle now is thought of primarily as home to the wealthy and famous, including writers, actors, and sports figures. It is also heavily promoted as a retirement community and tourism destination. Modern inhabitants of Albemarle tend to live on the land but make their livings not from the land itself as of old but from the image of the land instead —an image of ancient houses and great natural beauty. Fortunately, for the time being at least, the image is also reality.

Charlottesville has become a regional capital as well as the county seat, while experiencing significantly less population growth than the surrounding county. In 1970 about 39,000 people lived in the city; twenty years later that number had increased by only a thousand, due no doubt to the relative lack of available space within the city's boundaries. In the intervening years Charlottesville countered the competition from suburban shopping malls by creating a downtown mall, anchoring one end of it with a large new hotel, and promoting its unique ambience of restaurants, boutiques, and bookstores. Unlike many other urban downtowns, Charlottesville's remains lively, with many fine commercial buildings restored and preserved.

Much of the development in the city and the county has been inspired by the growth of the University of Virginia. The school not only has grown in terms of its faculty, student population, and infrastructure but has also attracted new residents because of its expanded role in the cultural and economic life of the region. From intercollegiate sports to the performing arts, from executive institutes to government-funded research projects, the university offers scores of incentives to attract new residents. Its success, however, has been accompanied by the seeds of potential destruction.

Historian John Hammond Moore, in *Albemarle: Jefferson's County, 1727-1976*, observed that the county's "greatest problem is how to regulate growth so as to retain the flavor of years gone by." A quarter century later, it remains among the county's stiffest challenges, as its citizens and elected officials juggle the frequently conflicting demands of economic development and historic preservation. The very factors that attract investors and tourists and invite new residents—lovely scenery, old houses, the rural atmosphere—often are threatened or obliterated by the shopping centers, residential developments, and highway construction projects that are necessary to support the growth of the local population and economy. Uncontrolled, urban sprawl may destroy in decades the historic fabric that has existed for centuries.

Yet one must have faith in the ability of the citizens of Albemarle and Charlottesville, new and old, to make wise decisions about growth. Time and again over the years they have proved themselves to be faithful stewards of their historic and scenic heritage. They have supported surveys of the county's historic buildings and sites. They have formed groups to educate their fellow citizens about the unique heritage of their community. They have preserved Albemarle County and Charlottesville's collection of some of the nation's best architecture, not as a petrified and prettified outdoor museum but rather as a living community that changes to meet their needs without severing vital links to the past.

May they continue to do so.

John S. Salmon

ALBEMARLE COUNTY

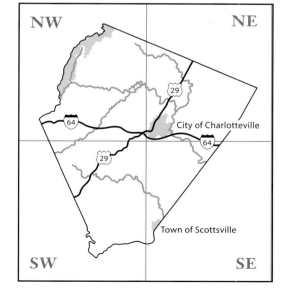

NW NE

City of Charlottesville

Town of Scottsville

SW SE

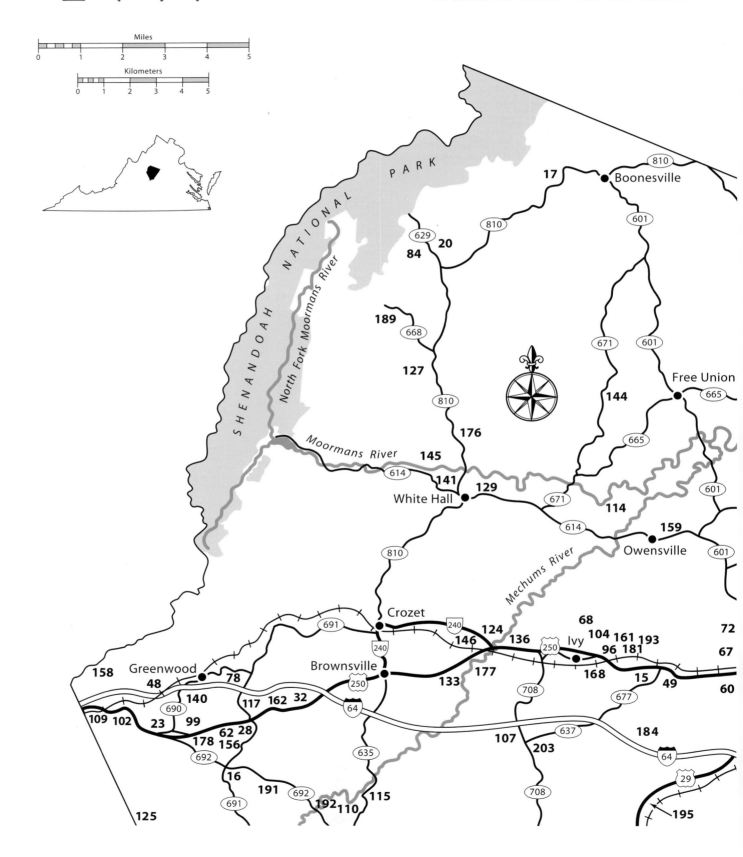

NW

ALBEMARLE

COUNTY

NE

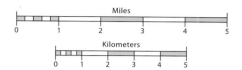

Miles
0 1 2 3 4 5

Kilometers
0 1 2 3 4 5

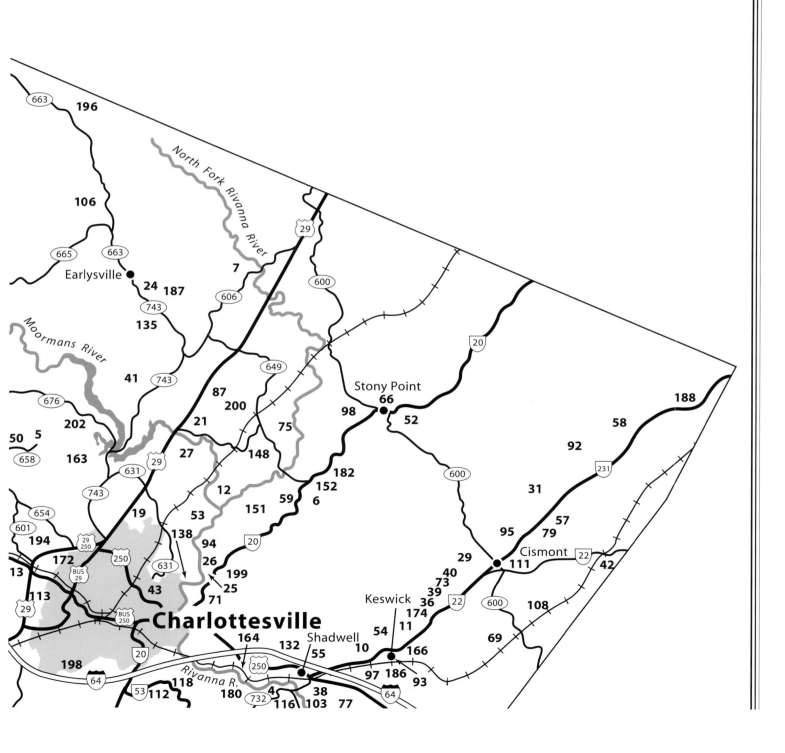

663 **196**

North Fork Rivanna River

29

106

665 663

Earlysville

Moormans River

663
24 187
743
135

606

600

7

41 743

649

676

202
50 5
658 **163**
631
29

743

654
601
194

13

113
29

29
250

250
BUS
29

172

BUS
250

Charlottesville

20

198

64

53 **112**
118

87
200

21

27

148

12

53

138

94
26

43

71

180 732
116 **103**

75

59

151

20

199
25

164

250

132
55

4

38

77

Stony Point
66

98
52

182
152
6

600

600

31

95

29
40
73
39
36
174
11

Keswick
54
10

22

22

600

Cismont
111 22
42

57
79

108

69

Shadwell
93
97 186

64

188

58

92

231

231

188

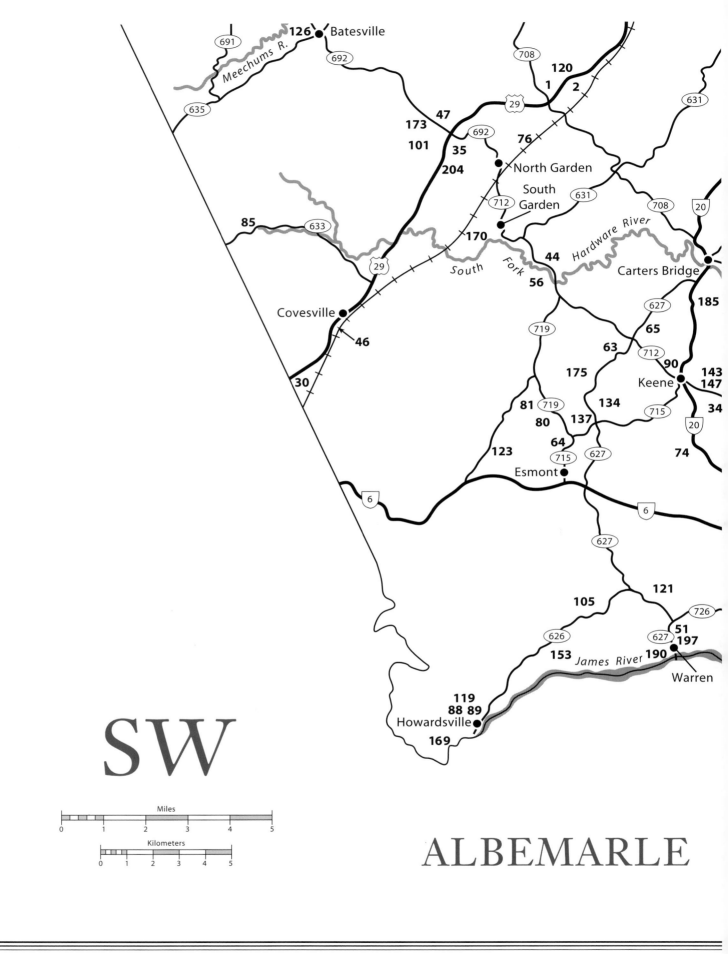

126 Batesville
691
Meechums R.
692
635
708
120
1 29 **2**
631
47
173
101 692
35 **76**
204 North Garden
South
Garden 631
712
708 20
85
633 **170** Hardware River
29 **44** Carters Bridge
South Fork **56** **185**
627
Covesville 65
719 **63**
46 712
175 **90** **143**
Keene **147**
30 **81** 719 **134** 715 **34**
80 **137**
123 **64** 627 **74**
715
Esmont
6
627
121
105 726
626 **51**
627 **197**
153 James River **190**
Warren
119
88 **89**
Howardsville
169

SW

Miles
0 1 2 3 4 5

Kilometers
0 1 2 3 4 5

ALBEMARLE

179
631
70

183
20

91
171
160
45
732
53

729

100
Boyd Tavern ●
250
64

150

22

3
734

18
616

201
20

122

165
155
20

61
795

167
729

157
627

14

149

620

53

8
708
795

618

729
618

130
618

620

142
712

128
139
795

20

86

6

33
37
726
9

Scottsville
154
131

625

83 **82**

James River

Hatton Ferry ●

Hardware River

Rivanna River

SE

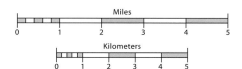

COUNTY

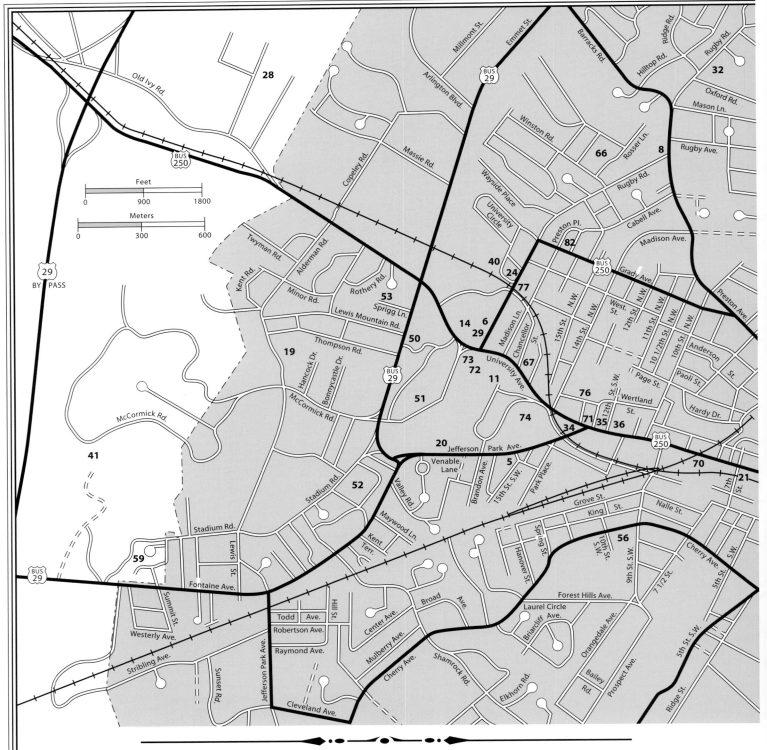

1. Abell-Gleason house
2. Albemarle County Courthouse (including Confederate statue)
3. Albemarle County Jail
4. Armstrong Knitting Factory
5. Barringer mansion
6. Bayly Art Museum
7. Belmont
8. Belvoir
9. Beth Israel Synagogue
10. Bonahora
11. Brooks Museum

12. Butler-Norris town houses
13. C&O Depot
14. Carr's Hill
15. Carter-Gilmer town houses
16. Christ Episcopal Church
17. Clermont
18. Cochran's millhouse
19. Confederate statue (in university cemetery)
20. Dawson's Row
21. Delevan Baptist Church
22. Duke house

23. Enderly
24. Faculty Apartments
25. Farish House Tavern (including Eagle Tavern)
26. The Farm (18th. century house)
27. The Farm (19th. century house)
28. Faulkner House
29. Fayerweather Hall
30. First Methodist Church
31. First Presbyterian Church
32. Four Acres
33. Fowler house

34. George Rogers Clark statue
35. Heiskell-Livers town houses
36. John Vowles town houses
37. Hodges-Gleason house
38. Holy Comforter Catholic Church
39. Jones-Williams house
40. Lambeth Field Colonnades
41. Leander-McCormick Observatory
42. Levy Opera House (including Town Hall)

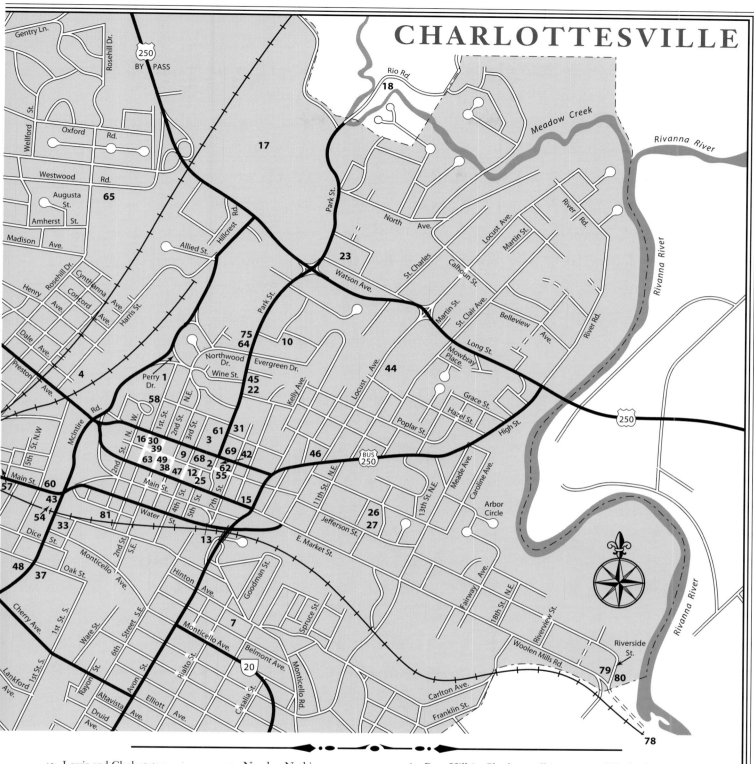

CHARLOTTESVILLE

43. Lewis and Clark statue
44. Locust Grove
45. Marshall-Rucker house
46. Martha Jefferson Hospital
47. Massie-Wills town houses
48. McAllister-Andrews house
49. McIntire Library
50. Memorial Gym
51. Monroe Hill
52. Montebello
53. Morea
54. Mount Zion Baptist Church

55. Number Nothing
56. Oak Lawn
57. Paxton Place
58. Perkins house
59. Piedmont (at University of Virginia)
60. Pitts-Inge house
61. Price-Poore house
62. Redland Club (including Swan Tavern)
63. Robert E. Lee statue
64. Robertson house

65. Rose Hill (at Charlottesville)
66. Rugby
67. Saint Paul's Episcopal Church
68. Stonewall Jackson statue
69. Tower House
70. Union Depot
71. University Baptist Church
72. University of Virginia
73. University of Virginia Chapel
74. University of Virginia Hospital
75. Watson house

76. Wertland
77. Westminster Presbyterian Church
78. Woolen Mills
79. Woolen Mills Chapel
80. Woolen Mills Tavern
81. Word-Wertenbaker house
82. Wyndhurst

Far more historic buildings exist in the city than can be shown here.

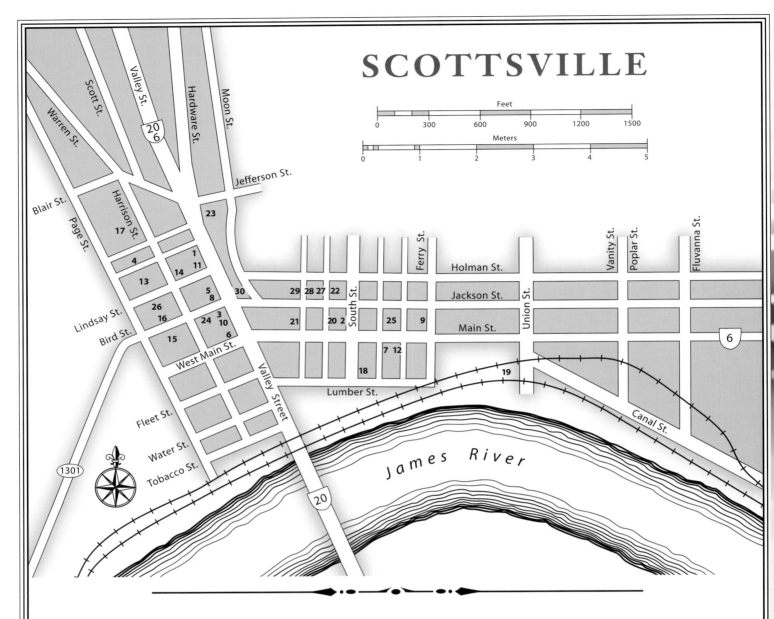

SCOTTSVILLE

Adapted from 1818 plat—many streets no longer extant

1. Apothecary Shop
2. Barclay house
3. Beal building
4. Blair house
5. Butler Funeral Home
6. Carlton House hotel
7. Colonial House
8. Columbia Hotel
9. Doll House
10. Grifflin building
11. Harris building
12. Herndon house
13. Jeffries-Bruce house
14. Lindsay house
15. Old Hall
16. Saint John's Episcopal Church
17. Scottsville Baptist Church
18. Scottsville Canal tobacco warehouse
19. Scottsville Depot
20. Scottsville Disciples of Christ Church
21. Scottsville Methodist Church
22. Scottsville Methodist Parsonage
23. Scottsville Factory
24. Scottsville Presbyterian Church
25. Scottsville Tavern
26. The Shadows
27. Staples house
28. The Terrace
29. Thompkins house
30. Victory Hall

I

The Georgian Period

BACKGROUND

The first Englishmen in Virginia built houses and other structures that resembled the familiar forms that they had left behind. Thus buildings constructed during the pre-Georgian architectural period in Virginia (1607–1700) exhibited the characteristics of Jacobean styles, either frame buildings, often single-cell or hall-parlor in plan, with heavy mortise-and-tenon joinery and summer beams or structures employing English-bond brickwork overall and massive pyramidal or ramped buttress-type T-plan chimneys, with casement windows and steep roofs. No buildings from this period exist in Albemarle County, because English settlers from Tidewater did not reach the area until the early eighteenth century, and by then what is called the Georgian style had taken hold.

The dominance of the style of architecture we call Georgian began in Virginia with the construction of the Wren Building for the College of William and Mary in Williamsburg about 1699; Jefferson's State Capitol in Richmond ended it in the 1780s. In its high-style buildings, the Georgian drew its examples from the Renaissance Revival and was influenced by the sixteenth-century work of Andrea Palladio as illustrated in English pattern books. In Albemarle County, which was on the western edge of Virginia civilization for much of the Georgian period, architecture most often manifested itself in familiar, vernacular forms: one-story frame dwellings, ubiquitous I-houses and log houses, and pyramidal-roofed outbuildings.

Albemarle County was formed from Goochland County in 1744 and encompassed the present-day counties of Amherst, Buckingham, Fluvanna, and Nelson, as well as the northern portions of Appomattox, Bedford, and Campbell. In 1761 the county's size was reduced to exclude all but present-day Fluvanna; it simultaneously acquired the western part of what is now Louisa County.[1]

Although a road from what is now Orange County traversed the area of Albemarle about 1726, the first official order for the construction of a road (present-day Route 6, or the River Road, along the James River) was issued by the Goochland County Court on 21 December 1731. Martin King's Road entered the present county limits on 19 September 1732, and about 1733 the Old Mountain Road (Route 22) from Louisa County was extended into the area. All male tithables (white males age nineteen and older and black males age fifteen and older) were responsible for the upkeep and construction of the roads through the property on which they resided. The first court order for a bridge in present-day Albemarle, over Mechunk Creek, was issued on 15 May 1739; it was not built until more than a year later.[2]

In the 1730s, before Albemarle was created, the Three Notch'd Road (present-day U.S. Route 250, also called the Mountain Road and later known as Three Chopt Road) followed an ancient Indian buffalo-hunting path through the region. The route ran from Richmond to Woods's Gap (Jarman's Gap) in the Blue Ridge Mountains west of Crozet. The first mountains encountered along its path from Richmond were the Chestnut or Southwest Mountains just east of modern Charlottesville. The first settlers in the area obtained patents for land located to the east of these barrier mountains. As the road emerged from a water gap formed by the Rivanna River between Southwest Mountain and Carter's Mountain, it crossed the Rivanna River at Secretary's Ford, just north of Monticello Mountain, and continued into the area now known as the Woolen Mills. From here, it traveled up the ridge that

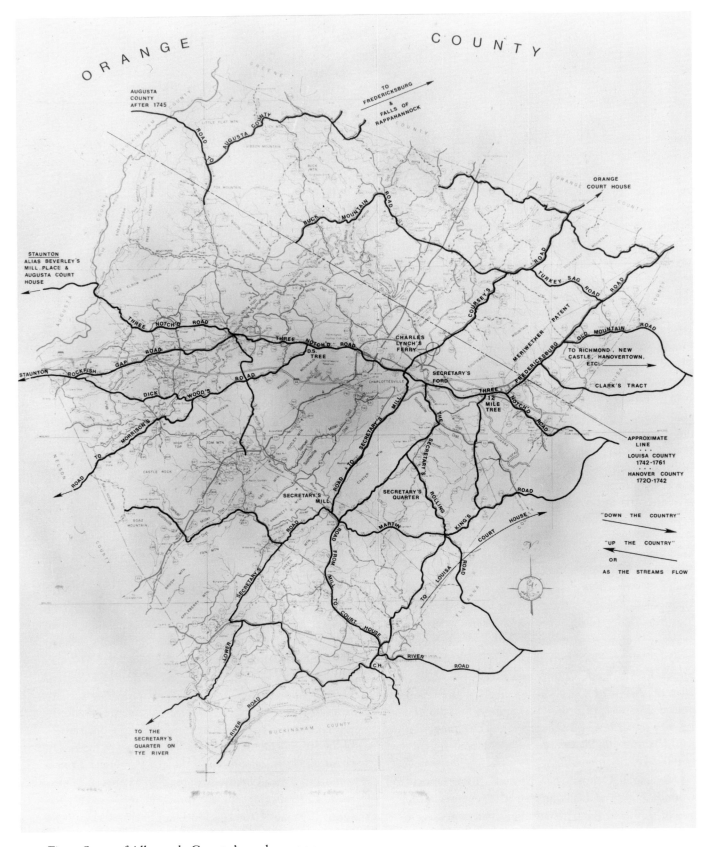

Fig. 2. Some of Albemarle County's roads, c. 1745

later became Belmont, back again to the present downtown mall, along West Main Street and south of the University of Virginia by Midmont to what would become U.S. Route 250 West. The road did not take its alternate path along University Avenue until about 1790 when the swamp there, now the intersection of University Avenue and Emmet Street, was partly drained. The remnants of that swamp still existed into the mid–twentieth century when it was completely drained for the county's first shopping center at Barracks Road (fig. 2). It was not until 1920 that state funds were provided for county roads.[3]

The settlers who traveled west on the Three Notch'd Road in the early eighteenth century were predominantly Englishmen from Tidewater Virginia who were searching for new land to complete the trinity of Virginia wealth: land, slaves, and tobacco. Often overseers and slaves were sent ahead to clear and cultivate the land some years before the owners' arrival; without the labor of slaves, many landowners would not have been able to sustain their farms. One planter wrote a creditor in 1765 that "I had rather sell anything [but] the negroes . . . as it would hurt the estate."[4]

An estimated one-tenth of the county population was composed of Germans and Scotch-Irish who migrated down the fertile Shenandoah Valley from the port at Philadelphia.[5] Coming into the region from the west through Woods's Gap beginning in 1734, they introduced the Lutheran and Presbyterian dissenting denominations to an essentially Anglican area.

Virginia's colonial government issued the first patent for land in the county to Nicholas Meriwether I in 1719. By 1730 he had patented about 18,000 acres (fig. 3) on the eastern slope of the Chestnut or Southwest Mountains, where both Clover Fields and Castle Hill became the seats of the Meriwether and Walker families, respectively. Three years earlier George Hoomes Jr. had obtained a patent for 3,100 acres in the area. Other patents soon were issued for tracts on which many architecturally important dwellings later were constructed. Dr. George Nicholas of Williamsburg patented 2,600 acres on the north bank of the James River, where Mount Warren became the seat. Allen Howard patented land on which Westcote was built as well as the later town of Howardsville. By 1735 Charles Hudson of Hanover County had acquired more than 5,500 acres where he constructed Mount Air. Francis Eppes patented 6,500 acres around Green Mountain, and later Enniscorthy, Woodville, Tallwood, and Estouteville were built here. Major Thomas Carr of King William County patented almost 10,000 acres north of present-day Charlottesville before his death in 1738; here Bentivar, Carrsbrook, and Dunlora were later constructed. Secretary of the Colony John Carter owned more than 9,000 acres to the south, on which Blenheim and Redlands were constructed. By 1745, 191 patents had been granted conveying approximately 160,000 acres of land in Albemarle County, approximately a third of its present area. Six patents exceeded 5,000 acres, and forty-six were for more than 1,000 acres; the average tract was 831 acres in size.[6]

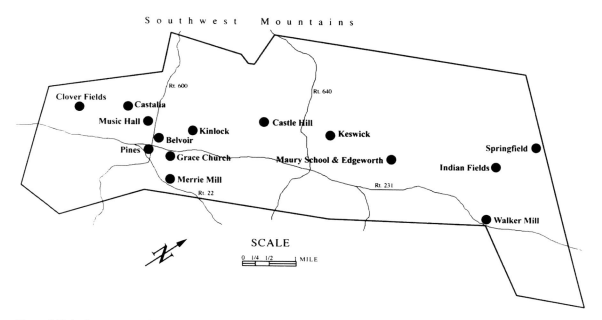

Fig. 3. Nicholas Meriwether land grants, 1727–30

Primogeniture, the English system under which the eldest male heir inherited the title, the seat, and frequently the entire estate, had been practiced in the Virginia colony from its earliest days. The purpose of the system was to protect and perpetuate the family estate rather than to endow the many children of the early planters. While some of these planters acquired such extensive holdings that they were able to provide lavishly for many children and even grandchildren in Tidewater Virginia, by the mid–eighteenth century a number of the disinherited younger sons had begun the migration westward, and some came to Albemarle. By midcentury the size of the average grant in the county had decreased to 470 acres.[7]

Tobacco had been the leading crop in Virginia since John Rolfe of Surry County first planted it in 1612, and by the early eighteenth century, Virginia's central Piedmont offered new tobacco land to replace the depleted farms in the east. In the eighteenth century tobacco became the staple crop for export to England in Albemarle County as elsewhere; hemp and ginseng also found foreign markets. Beef and pork were sold locally, and rye, wheat, barley, and Indian corn were grown for local consumption. Early in the eighteenth century, hogsheads of tobacco were packed into barrels in prizing houses on plantations and rolled by oxen to the James River where they were placed in dugout canoes lashed together for their trip downriver to the fall line at Westham, just west of present-day Richmond. But after a devastating flood in 1771, Anthony Benjamin Rucker, a tobacco planter from what is now Amherst County, designed a flat-bottomed bateau with pointed ends that was less apt to overturn and could carry larger loads. The 50-foot-long barge held as many as sixteen hogsheads, the measure of a quantity of tobacco. By the advent of the James River and Kanawha Canal in the 1820s, it has been estimated that there were 500 bateaux employing 1,500 men on the James River.[8]

Founded in 1817, the Agricultural Society of Albemarle became a nationally influential organization through its advocacy of such reforms as crop rotation, contour plowing, selective breeding, and use of animal manure as fertilizer. Its membership included such prominent Virginians as Thomas Jefferson, Wilson Cary Nicholas, Thomas Mann Randolph Jr., Peter Minor, and Dabney Minor, all of Albemarle County. Notable nonresident members included Joseph C. Cabell of Edgewood in Amherst County; General John Hartwell Cocke of Bremo in Fluvanna County; and James Barbour of Barboursville and James Madison of Montpelier, both in Or-

ange County. Although large tobacco crops continued into the mid–nineteenth century, by the close of the eighteenth century wheat had become the principal crop.[9]

Near the end of the eighteenth century and well into the nineteenth, some local buildings were insured against fire by the "Mutual Assurance Society against Fire on Buildings of the State of Virginia," incorporated on 22 December 1794. The policies provide the value of each building insured, its replacement cost, and a perimeter building plan indicating the wall and roof cladding, the number of stories, and the material used for the underpinning or foundation. Outbuildings were often shown. Sometimes elevations or axonometric drawings were included that indicated chimneys, window and door openings, and the roof type. Although local agents probably drew the plans, elevations, and axonometric sketches for these records, it is not inconceivable that Jefferson himself rendered those for Monticello. The majority of insured properties were large country dwellings or town houses, but taverns, mills, and stores were also included. On 10 August 1798 the company issued the first insurance policy in Albemarle County, to Craven Peyton for his frame house on East Main Street in Milton. In 1820 the Mutual Assurance Society ceased insuring frame structures, and after 1822 it only insured urban buildings, eventually restricting its operations to Richmond. The last-known policies for Charlottesville properties were issued on 20 December 1860 for a two-story brick dwelling built by George Wilson Spooner Jr. for James P. Holcombe on the southeast corner of Third and High Streets and for a similar building in the southeastern part of the town that was owned by Charles Carter.

Other insurance companies provided coverage during the early nineteenth century, but their records no longer exist. For example, in 1831 the *Virginia Advocate* carried an advertisement by John O. Lay, agent for the Aetna and Protection Company of Richmond, offering protection insurance "policies on Dwelling Houses, Furniture, Libraries, Goods & Merchandize, Machinery, and on Mills and Stock contained therein."[10]

In 1886 the Sanborn-Perris Map Company began producing maps for insurance companies that showed buildings located in cities and towns throughout the United States, including Albemarle County. The maps are color-coded, accurately drawn plats that indicate each building's plan, form, function, materials, number of stories, windows, and cornice material. The maps are extremely useful in identifying the locations of buildings no longer extant and dating the additions to existing ones.[11]

In 1744, the year after Thomas Jefferson's birth at Shadwell, Albemarle County was formed. The first county court convened in February of the following year, when nine magistrates were sworn in at Scott's Landing on the James River: Captain Thomas Ballou, Dr. William Cabell, Captain James Daniel, Lieutenant Joshua Fry, Edwin Hickman, Major Allen Howard, Peter Jefferson, Charles Lynch, and Captain Joseph Thompson. Colonel William Randolph, who owned the Edgehill property in Albemarle County but resided at Tuckahoe in Goochland County, was appointed clerk, and Edmund Gray became the county attorney. The members of the House of Burgesses from Albemarle County from 1745 until the Revolution were Colonel William Cabell, William Cabell Jr., Edward Carter, Henry Fry, John Fry, Joshua Fry, Major Allen Howard, Peter Jefferson, Thomas Jefferson, Charles Lewis, Charles Lynch, John Nicholas, Colonel John Walker, and Dr. Thomas Walker. Also in 1745 the first courthouse was established at Belle Grove near what became Scott's Landing, named for the ferry here. By 1842 Scottsville (fig. 4) contained twenty-one stores, one tobacco factory, three taverns, and four churches. By the start of the Civil War, the town had a population of 1,500 and boasted of having twenty-four "mechanics."[12]

The county's boundaries were reduced in 1761, and in December of the following year, Charlottesville was established one mile west of the Rivanna River water gap on a gently sloping knoll. Charlottesville was named for Queen Charlotte Sophia, spouse of England's King George III. Colonel Richard Randolph acquired the site and conveyed it to Dr. Thomas Walker to be sold for the benefit of the county, and the county seat was then relocated here from its previous location near Scottsville. The town was laid out (fig. 5) on fifty acres that were situated, according to a 1737 patent issued to William Taylor, between the properties of Nicholas Lewis's The Farm on the east, John Carter's land on the south,

Fig. 4. Plat of Scottsville, 1818–73

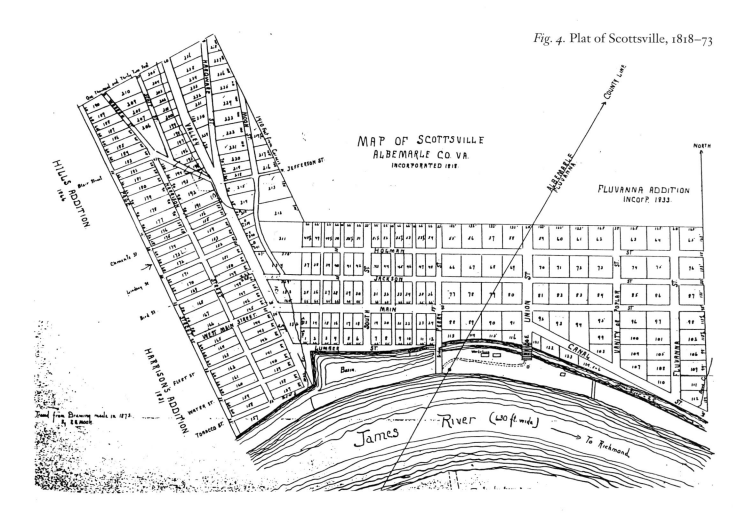

Fig. 5. Plat of downtown Charlottesville, 1762–1830

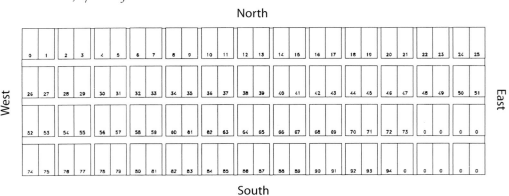

Fig. 6. Plat of Milton, 1790

28

Hanover Countian Abraham Lewis's property on the west, and Charles Lynch's Pen Park to the north. Divided into fifty-six half-acre plots in a rectangular pattern, with the courthouse just beyond the northeastern boundary on the highest ground, the town lay on the land bounded by present-day South, McIntire, Jefferson, and Sixth Streets for two blocks on either side of the Three Notch'd Road.[13]

Within three years of Charlottesville's creation, forty-seven lots had been sold. Nevertheless, British major Thomas Anburey observed in 1779 that all that existed in the town were "a courthouse, one tavern [The Swan], and a dozen little houses." Obviously, although all but nine lots had been sold, few had been developed into more than vegetable gardens. Eighteen years later, however, Jedediah Morse claimed that the town had grown to forty-five houses together with its courthouse and jail. In 1773 John Jouett built the Swan Tavern just to the east of Court Square; another, the Eagle Tavern, was erected south of the courthouse in 1791. Neither of these buildings remains today. In the 1790s Charlottesville annexed additions to the north, thereby increasing the number of its lots to eighty-two.[14]

The town of Milton (fig. 6) was laid out in 1789 at the head of navigation on the Rivanna (River Anna) River in four rows of twenty-six one-half-acre lots, two to a block, on 100 acres of the land of Bennett Henderson on the south side of the river at a spot called the Shallows. Trustees for the sale of the lots were Edward Carter of Blenheim, deputy sheriff and magistrate William Clark, Charles Lilburn Lewis of Mount Eagle, Howell Lewis of Lewis Level, Edward Moore of Crutchfield, Wilson Cary Nicholas of Mount Warren, and Francis Walker of Keswick. Within ten years twenty lots had been sold, and by 1810 the census taker recorded twenty-nine white heads of household and a large community of free blacks. Until the War of 1812, Milton remained the commercial center of the county and a major port through which goods from as far away as the Shenandoah Valley were shipped eastward. It was here that Chastain Cocke built, at the cost of $500, a low, 16-foot-wide bridge on submerged cribs filled with rock. By 1815 the town consisted of a public tobacco warehouse and a large merchant mill, both erected by the Hendersons, and about twenty-five houses. Although once approaching the size of Charlottesville, with which it was linked by several roads (fig. 7), Milton declined during the 1820s after the university was established near the county seat and Charlottesville grew in response. The Locust Grove Tavern and Jail still

exists, as does Milton Farm. An older tavern dating to 1747 in Milton was razed in 1887.[15]

Dr. George Nicholas had received a patent for land on the James River in 1729. At the mouth of Ballenger's Creek about 1793, the town of Warren grew up around the facilities for shipping wheat used by his grandson Wilson Cary Nicholas, who lived here at Mount Warren. The younger Nicholas was born in 1761 in Williamsburg and attended the College of William and Mary, where he studied law under George Wythe as Jefferson had done. During the Revolutionary War he married Margaret Smith of Baltimore. The town included the 1759 gristmill owned by his father, Robert Carter Nicholas, as well as two other mills, Nicholas's tobacco inspection warehouse, Samuel Shelton's 1796 distillery, Jacob Kinney's Stone Tavern, a blacksmith shop, a few houses, and a ferry over the James River. Only about twelve half-acre lots were purchased. In 1803 Nicholas sold most of his land and buildings to William Walker, John Staples, and Samuel Shelton. In 1812 John Patterson of Baltimore, who had married Nicholas's daughter in 1795, resided just outside the town at Oakland. Although Nicholas had built the house for his daughter and son-in-law, Patterson was obviously a talented draftsman, for he later presented design suggestions for General John Hartwell Cocke's Bremo. In 1819 the Pattersons returned to the Baltimore area. Remaining in the county was Nicholas's fourth daughter, Jane Hollins Nicholas Randolph, who had married Thomas Jefferson Randolph, the president's grandson, although the Randolph family disapproved of the marriage. The William Walker house, Donegal (Oakland), and the remnants of Nicholas's Mount Warren still remain at Warren; the stone tavern was razed in the 1970s and the country store and depot even more recently.[16]

At the turn of the nineteenth century, five other planned towns were proposed but met with little success. The largest, North Milton, was laid out in 1802 on the land of Thomas Mann Randolph Jr. on the north side of the Rivanna. The trustees for the sale of the lots included Dr. William Bache of Franklin; Governor James Barbour of Orange County; George Divers of Farmington; Edward Garland of Head of Creek Plantation; David Higginbotham of Morven; William D. Meriwether of Clover Fields; Edward Moore of Crutchfield; Hore Browse Trist of Birdwood; and Francis Walker of Keswick. By 1816 at least nine lots had been purchased by Obadiah Britt, George Bruce, Julius Clarkson, John Fogg, William D. Meriwether, Hannah Proctor, and John Watson. North Milton too contained a tobacco

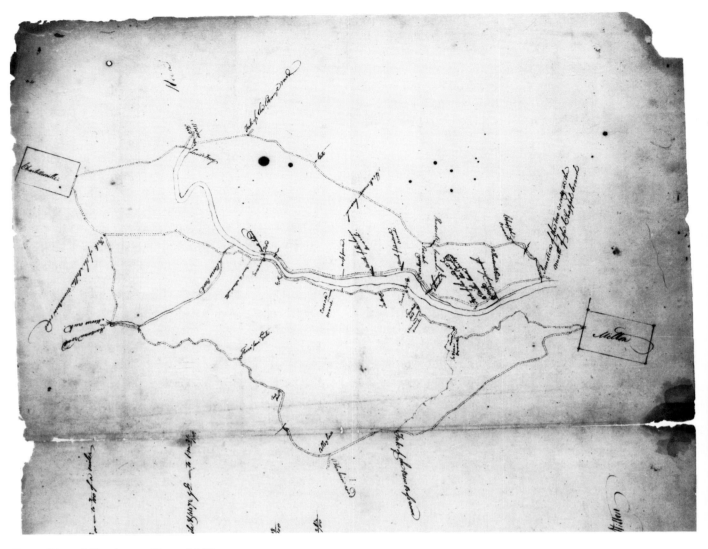

Fig. 7. Plat of Charlottesville and Milton

warehouse, but the community was overshadowed by the earlier Milton across the river. All of the town that remains today is Clifton.[17]

The other four towns in Albemarle County grew even less than North Milton. Travellers' Grove (Pleasant Grove) near Red Hill was planned by Colonel John Everett. New York (Little York) along U.S. Route 250 at the foot of the Blue Ridge was planned by James Hays and inhabited by Pennsylvania Germans. In its heyday it contained a tavern, church, blacksmith shop, and tanyard (only the Brooksville Tavern still survives). Morgantown, laid out near Ivy by Gideon Morgan, included Benjamin Harden's tavern (Albemarle Hotel). Barterbrook, near Eastham, contained the Pinch'em-slyly Tavern.[18]

The community of Shadwell developed around Thomas Jefferson's birthplace and his mills along the north bank of the Rivanna River. By 1835, almost a decade after Jefferson's death, it included a large carding factory that employed about a hundred workers, a large merchant mill, and a sawmill, as well as stores and dwellings. Alberene evolved from the soapstone quarries; Hatton and Howardsville, at the confluence of the James and Rockfish Rivers, around river transportation. Other towns developed around railroad depots during the nineteenth century: Keswick, Greenwood, Lindsay, Cobham, Campbell's, Ivy (Woodville), Hickory Hill, Proffit, and Crozet (Wayland's). Nonetheless, except for Crozet, other communities that probably were not developed as planned towns prospered better over the years than those that were. Such unplanned communities include Batesville (around Oliver's store), Brownsville, Covesville, Earlysville, Esmont, and White Hall (at Glenn's store).[19]

EIGHTEENTH-CENTURY ARCHITECTURAL DETAILS

The characteristic construction details that date buildings to the Georgian period include wrought-iron roseheaded nails, pit-sawed framing members inscribed with Roman numerals, mortise-and-tenon joints, and L-shaped corner posts. Brick buildings (fig. 8) commonly featured Flemish-bond brickwork on all walls above the water table, while frame structures were sheathed with weatherboards that were beaded to prevent splintering. Casement windows disappeared in favor of vertically sliding window sash with one-and-a-half-inch-wide muntins and six-over-nine-, nine-over-six-, nine-over-nine-, and six-over-six-light double-hung sash configurations. Roofs were covered with thick wooden shingles with rounded ends. Most rooflines were unbroken or were pierced by shed-roofed dormers with beaded flush siding laid parallel to the roof slope. Later dormers had pedimented or hipped roofs. Chimneys, usually located on the gable ends of buildings, often were double-ramped; that is, they had two sloping shoulders with smooth, flat tile washes or stepped-brick weatherings.

Inside, doors were hung with wrought-iron H and HL hinges, fireplace openings were simple and often lacked mantel shelves, and the central stair passage extended from the front to the rear of the house. Pents or closets sometimes were built between the chimneys and served as china presses, bookcases, powder rooms, or butteries for the servants' pantry. Often, too, beaded joists were left exposed in high-ceilinged rooms. Sometimes elongated single-story porches included a porch room that served many functions. Wall studs occasionally were infilled with brick nogging to help fireproof, ratproof, sound-proof, and insulate the building.

LOG DWELLINGS

By the time Albemarle County was formed in 1744, the frontier had moved westward to the Allegheny Mountains, but the ubiquitous housing type of the frontier era, the log cabin, still survived. As early as 1803, however, a distinction was made between a log cabin—a round-log, temporary dwelling—and a log house—a hewed-log, permanent dwelling. It is doubtful that any log cabins exist here today, whereas a multitude of log houses, often imbedded in later structures, dot the countryside.[20]

The typical log house (fig. 9) measured 16 by 16 feet or 16 by 20 feet laid out in a proportional system related to the diagonal of the square (1:1.414) or to the golden mean related to the diagonal of half the square (1:1.732 or 5:8) (fig. 10). Logs more than 20 feet in length not only were unwieldy, but their significant taper also caused a marked increase in the width of the chinking from one end to the other. Although the unique water-shedding V-notch was the common corner joint, full- and half-dovetail notching or diamond-and-square notching was used on occasion, usually for outbuildings. Chinking was made of split wood inserted diagonally between the logs, or stones or small branches inserted horizontally, and then covered with mud mixed with animal hair and straw. The hewed logs of the walls rose to the roof eaves, where horizontal weatherboards were nailed to upright studs in the gable

Brick Bonds

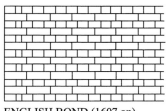

ENGLISH BOND (1607 on)

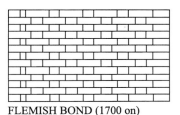

FLEMISH BOND (1700 on)

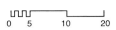

THREE-COURSE
AMERICAN BOND (1780 on)

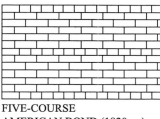

FIVE-COURSE
AMERICAN BOND (1820 on)

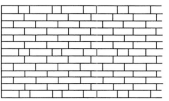

FIVE-COURSE AMERICAN BOND
WITH FLEMISH VARIANT (1780 on)

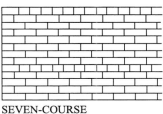

SEVEN-COURSE
AMERICAN BOND (1860 on)

RUNNING BOND

Fig. 8. Brick bonds

Fig. 9. Typical log house, 18c/19c

ends. Two or three logs extended the roof eaves above the loft floor to create greater headroom in the upper space.

Often, too, as in frame houses, one or two exterior stone chimneys (depending on the number of rooms within) were located at either end of the dwelling and frequently included above the fireplace openings a brick shaft that did not touch the wood. The use of brick atop stone addressed two problems: moisture and chimney fires. In masonry structures moisture is sometimes drawn by osmosis from the ground (hence the term *rising damp*) to damage the mortar at the lower levels, while water often penetrates and erodes the mortar at the upper levels. Rising damp can be corrected by improving the drainage around the building, but erosion from the top often requires disassembly, and it is easier to install and replace brick than stone at the upper level. The separation of the brick shaft from the gable end and roof (sometimes executed with a noticeable tilt away from the structure) served two purposes. First, it avoided the necessity of installing flashing around the chimney if it penetrated the roof. Second, because the lime mortar was forever be-

ing eroded and allowing sparks to escape between bricks, the separation further served as a fire prevention measure. In case of a chimney fire in the upper brick portion, it could be pulled away from the dwelling easily; often, too, a wooden ladder was left on the roof slope to provide access to the chimney in case of a flue fire. Because the fireplace served not only for heating but also for cooking, a shed-roofed room to serve as the kitchen was attached, initially or later, to a gable end or to the rear of the house. To reduce the dangers of fire further, settlers often built separate kitchens.

The doors of a log house were usually batten (vertical beaded boards secured with clinched nails to horizontal beaded rails). The clinching of the nail was called deadening; hence the expression "dead as a doornail." Often there were no sash windows because glass was expensive and difficult to transport to the frontier; in addition, window glass was sometimes subject to taxation, as in the case of the tax on "glass windows" passed by the General Assembly in 1780 or the direct tax levied by Congress in 1798. Therefore, to enhance the light inside, the interior

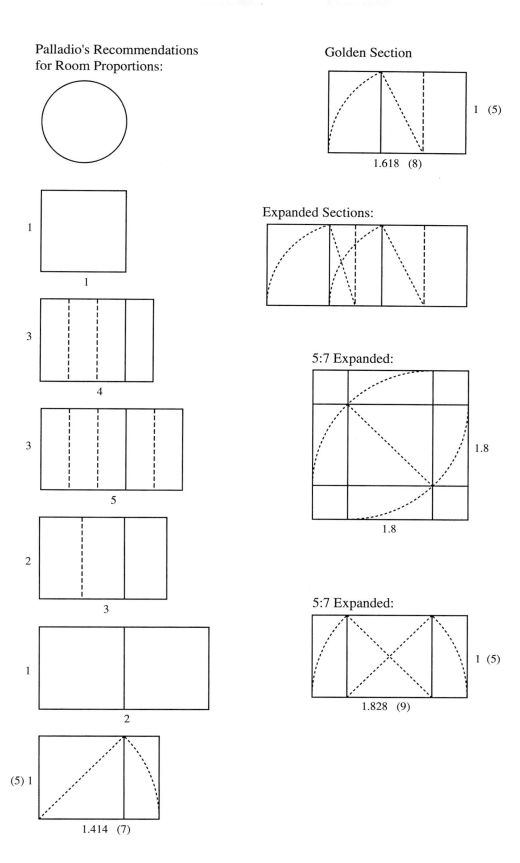

Palladio's Recommendations
for Room Proportions:

Golden Section

1 (5)

1.618 (8)

Expanded Sections:

5:7 Expanded:

1.8

1.8

5:7 Expanded:

1 (5)

1.828 (9)

1

1

3

4

3

5

2

3

1

2

(5) 1

1.414 (7)

Fig. 10. Proportional systems

walls were whitewashed and the doors left open as much as possible during daylight hours. Sometimes the exterior was whitewashed in the belief that it would keep water out. Other times, nothing was applied to the exterior, in keeping with the proverb "too poor to paint, too proud to whitewash." Frequently the entire dwelling was sheathed with horizontal weatherboards (fig. 11) either from the outset or soon after, for the sake of appearance or to protect pine logs that never were meant to be exposed to the weather. Because of the summer humidity, brick or stone piers supported the dwelling at its corners to permit air circulation under the flooring. Often, too, an open porch at the front sheltered the entrance door and cooled the air entering the building.[21]

Dogtrot Log Houses

When the settler desired a larger building, he erected two log rooms or pens a few feet apart and enclosed the space

Fig. 11. Shifflett log house with siding, Brown's Cove

Fig. 12. Fan Mountain dogtrot log house

between them both front and rear with horizontal weatherboards nailed over upright studs. This resulted in a floor plan called a dogtrot or possum trot. One example may still survive on Fan Mountain (fig. 12). Another, the late eighteenth-century James Harris house, formerly was on Route 614 at White Hall.[22]

Saddlebag Log Houses

In another version of the log house called the saddlebag plan, the two pens were built abutting each other, and a chimney stood at the juncture to provide each with a fireplace opening. The only unaltered example in the county is at Nydrie. Others were located until recent years at Wakefield (fig. 13) and Old Poorhouse Farm.[23]

FRAME HOUSES

A variety of house plans and elevation types (figs. 14, 15) prevailed during the Georgian period and continued to be popular through succeeding architectural periods. The dwellings of each era exhibited the various wall claddings and decorative details peculiar to that era.

Claim Houses

Beginning early in the eighteenth century, the House of Burgesses passed acts designed to discourage frontier land speculation because often land stood empty while speculators tried to sell tracts or waited for values to rise. The

Fig. 13. Wakefield saddlebag log house

GERMANIC THREE-ROOM PLAN

KAMMER

KÜCHE

STUBE

GERMANIC TWO-DOOR HOUSE

HALL-PARLOR

HALL   PARLOR

I-HOUSE

Fig. 14. House forms

GEORGIAN

2/3 GEORGIAN TOWN HOUSE

1/3 GEORGIAN TOWN HOUSE

Fig. 15. Georgian house forms

colonial government wanted actual settlers on the frontier, both to help defend the colony and to pay taxes. To encourage settlement the acts required anyone obtaining a patent for unoccupied land to "seat" it within three years by clearing and cultivating at least three acres of every fifty and by constructing "one good dwelling house, after the manner of Virginia building, to contain at least twenty foot in length, and sixteen foot in breadth." A few dwellings in the county are said to be claim houses, but it is doubtful that any actually still exist.[24]

One-Story Frame Dwellings

Thomas Jefferson in his *Notes on the State of Virginia* (1787) cited a popular belief that brick walls admitted rain and resulted in damp buildings (frequently true but due to poor drainage and rising damp rather than rainstorms). He predicted that buildings of "scantling and plank" would last only a half century, "whereas when buildings are of durable materials [meaning brick], every new edifice is an actual and permanent acquisition to the state, adding to its value as well as to its ornament."[25] Although brick struc-

tures predominate today among surviving early buildings, as Jefferson foresaw, the majority of eighteenth-century houses were of frame construction, for wood was more easily obtained and less expensive than brick. They usually were one or one and a half stories in height, of the single-cell plan, and with an exterior gable-end chimney. An open winder or enclosed box stair allowed access to an attic chamber (usually a bedchamber) in the half story.

Besides Dr. Thomas Walker's Castle Hill, Robert Lewis's Belvoir, Thomas Mann Randolph's Edgehill, Joshua Fry's Viewmont, and Peter Jefferson's Shadwell, Fry and Jefferson noted Clover Fields (fig. 16), the seat of the Meriwethers, on their 1751 map of Virginia.[26] The first house at Clover Fields, built for Nicholas Meriwether I about 1747, probably was located at present-day Castalia. It and the other dwellings began as one-story houses but have been either destroyed or enlarged by subsequent construction.

The one-story frame Joel Terrell house that was located on the site of the present parking garage at Main and Fifth Streets in Charlottesville allegedly was built

Fig. 16. Clover Fields old house, 18c

about 1762. If this date is correct, it was one of the oldest houses in the county and the first house built in Charlottesville. The Farmers' Bank replaced it in 1850.[27]

Dr. Philip Mazzei, the Italian friend of Jefferson, completed his one-story frame house at Colle (fig. 17) near Monticello about 1774. Here he experimented with grape vineyards and silkworm culture. Upon returning to Europe in 1779 during the Revolutionary War, he rented Colle to a German prisoner of war, Major General Baron von Riedesel; Mazzei returned to America in 1785 to find his vineyards destroyed by the general's horses. The house was replaced in 1933 by one designed by William Adams Delano. Architect Milton Grigg reused paneling, chair rails, and mantels from the old house in Michie Tavern.[28]

Dr. George Gilmer, father-in-law of William Wirt, the biographer of Patrick Henry who served as attorney general of the United States under both Presidents John Quincy Adams and James Monroe, gave Wirt part of his Pen Park property. Here Wirt built Rose Hill (fig. 18), a one-story frame house with double-ramped chimneys

and a steep roof. In 1815 it was purchased by Richard Sampson of Goochland County, who in 1819 sold it to John H. Craven. The house was located on Westwood Road near Rose Hill Drive within the present limits of Charlottesville but was razed about 1933.[29]

James Monroe—fifth president of the United States, minister to France, and twice governor of Virginia—settled in Albemarle County in 1789 to be near his friend Thomas Jefferson after selling his family's holding in Westmoreland County. He first bought 950 acres that later included the University of Virginia; then in 1793 he purchased 3,500 acres nearer Monticello. The following year, when he was appointed minister to France, he had to leave Highland (Ash Lawn) (fig. 19), his "cabin castle," unfinished until December 1799. Monroe was forced to sell the property in 1825 to satisfy debts, at which time he made his principal residence Oak Hill in Loudoun County. The one-story frame Highland was drastically altered in subsequent years. The Reverend John E. Massey owned it from 1867 to 1930; he attached a frame I-house to it in 1882. In 1930 philanthropist Jay Winston

Fig. 17. Colle, c. 1774

Fig. 18. (top) Rose Hill, 18c

Fig. 19. (bottom) Highland (Ash Lawn), 1799

Johns bought it and opened it to the public. It is now operated as a museum by the College of William and Mary.[30]

One-Story Frame Single-Cell Dwellings

The single-cell house was the most common early house type in the county. One of the oldest, built about 1770, served as a hunting lodge near Key West for the Key family and was expanded over the years to become Windie Knowe. About 1840 the Key family sold it to Richard Terrell of Louisa County, who traded it with his son-in-law, William W. Minor, for Minor's property Glen Echo. Minor made additions to the house at midcentury and operated a successful vineyard here in the late nineteenth century.[31]

Oaklawn, near Earlysville, was built for George Twyman sometime in the eighteenth century. It contains such period earmarks as hewed beams, pit-sawed timbers, wrought-iron nails, wide-paneled wainscoting, a mantel with an arched opening, a wooden box lock, a winder stair, a high ceiling with beaded joists, nine-over-nine sash windows, and brick cellar walls of Flemish bond on the exterior and English bond on the interior.[32]

A one-story, single-cell frame house was built in 1789 on lot 24 in Warren. In 1839, as the mercantile establishment of Robinson and McLaurain, it was sold to John S. Nicholas. By 1850 it was the property of Dr. Charles L. Wingfield, a medical doctor. Additions and alterations to the house over the years greatly expanded its form to two stories with wings and a two-tier portico. Behind the house is a summer kitchen with pit-sawed joists and rafters fastened using mortise-and-tenon construction and pegged at the roof peak. It remained in the Wingfield family until 1938.[33]

Another house that began as a single-cell dwelling and later was expanded into a hall-parlor configuration is Plainview Farm. Built for the Ballard family near Free Union, it contains beaded ceiling joists and L-shaped corner posts and has recently been restored. Yet another example is Solitude, built either for Christopher Wingfield or his son Charles and nestled into Carter's Mountain on Route 20 between Charlottesville and Carter's Bridge. The one-story frame house contains beaded joists and original beaded exterior boards that were feathered by splitting to overlap and were fastened by rosehead nails. One weatherboard contains the date 1807 inscribed in Roman numerals, the year the house was expanded. This later section contains brick nogging in its walls between its mortise-and-tenon framing.[34]

In 1730 John Carter, a son of Robert "King" Carter, patented 9,350 acres around what is now called Carter's Mountain. In 1796 William Champe Carter sold a portion of this property, then called Indian Camp, to William Short of Philadelphia, who during the Revolutionary War had been a member of General George Washington's staff. Short later served as minister to The Hague in the Netherlands, diplomatic representative to Spain, minister to France, and Jefferson's secretary. Shortly after the transaction, he built a one-story frame dwelling (fig. 20) that contains an unusual means of access to the loft—a ship's ladder. Short lived here until 1813, when he sold the tract to David Higginbotham, a Milton merchant, who built a brick house and renamed the property Morven.[35]

Hugh Morris patented 400 acres on the branches of Totier Creek near Warren in 1747 and built his house here. The eastern single-cell portion of Morrisena (figs. 21, 22) appears to be older than the western part, which contains a center passage and another room that probably date to the early nineteenth century. An ell to the north was added even later.

Fig. 20. Indian Camp (Morven), 1796

Fig. 21. Morrisena, 18c

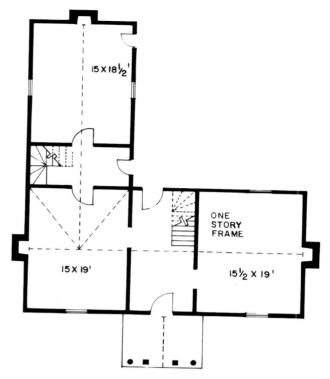

Fig. 22. Morrisena, 18c, plan

Red stone chimneys, L-shaped corner posts, split laths, pit-sawed mortise-and-tenon members, and beaded weatherboards occur throughout the structure. Surviving outbuildings include a kitchen and smokehouse. Today John Lacy Morris Jr. is the seventh generation of the Morris family to reside on the property.[36]

Glentivar, on Route 691 near Greenwood, probably evolved from an eighteenth-century single-cell frame building into a rambling mid-nineteenth-century two-story dwelling. Its older portion exhibits beaded joists, pit-sawed structural members, nonpedestal chair rails (they lack a shelf), and older door trim with double cyma reversa moldings (each one convex at the top and concave at the bottom) with large pegs.[37]

The stack house, a larger and rarer version of the single-cell house, is two stories in height with one room over another. Such two-story one-room-plan dwellings were rare in Tidewater Virginia but more common in the Valley and Piedmont of Virginia in the late eighteenth century. None from this early period are known to exist in Albemarle County, probably because they have been modified into larger house forms.

One-Story Frame Hall-Parlor Dwellings

A larger version of the one-story building type had two rooms: an entrance hall and a parlor or chamber. This type and plan—the story and one-half structure with hall-passage-parlor plan and end chimneys—persisted from the seventeenth century well into the nineteenth century. The second room, usually the "best" room, served as the master bedchamber and sometimes as the more formal room or parlor. The chamber also served as the dining room; it was not until the mid–eighteenth cen-

tury that the dining room came into its own. Later, after a central entrance passage evolved, this hallway often functioned as a summer living room; although an unheated, single-pile space, it offered cross ventilation when the front and back doors stood open.[38]

One of the earliest extant hall-parlor-plan houses in the county is Findowrie (figs. 23, 24) at Campbell's, allegedly built for Thomas Darsie before the mid–eighteenth century. More likely it was built for either John Clark or Joseph Brand about 1778. Regardless of the date, it is one of the oldest virtually unaltered houses in the area; the original section of Castle Hill, its near contemporary, was erected in the 1760s. Joseph W. Campbell, Findowrie's mid-nineteenth-century owner, operated the first steam sawmill in the county and supplied timber to the nearby Virginia Central Railroad, which reached that part of Albemarle County in 1848. That same year he began to supply stone from the Rougemont quarries to build Grace Episcopal Church at Cismont. Six generations of Campbell descendants owned Findowrie until it was sold out of the family in 1991.

The house features one-and-one-quarter-inch window muntins, a paneled overmantel, beaded weatherboards, beaded flush horizontal wallboards on the porch,

Fig. 23. Findowrie, c. 1778

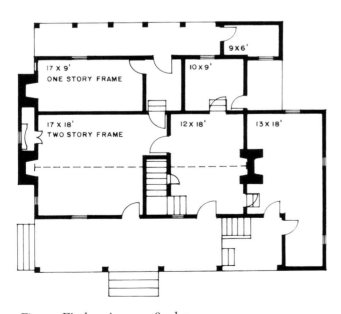

Fig. 24. Findowrie, c. 1778, plan

a winter kitchen with an oven, a chimney pent or closet with shelves between the chimneys, and a double-ramp (containing two sloping, corbeled-brick washes or shoulders on each side) Flemish-bond chimney. A hook is still attached to the dining-room ceiling, from which a punkah probably was suspended. The concept for these early ceiling fans to cool the air and keep flies from the dining-room table originated in India; a few American punkahs still survive, mostly in the Deep South. A chair rail and picture molding, obviously to accommodate a painting, occur on the parlor wall and resemble those found in the glebe house of Saint Anne's Parish. Upstairs in the attic the sills beneath the dormer windows slide to reveal storage spaces underneath as at Maxfield, a house built about 1764 near Keswick. The outbuildings at Findowrie included an ash house, well house, lumber house, smokehouse, corncrib, barn, and summer kitchen.

Fig. 25. Belle Grove, 18c, sketch

press that contains a viewing hole to the outside parterres, or ornamental garden. The house has been drastically altered several times over the years.[42]

Believed to have been built about 1780 for James Minor, Land's End is west of Stony Point in the western watershed of the Southwest Mountains. The house exhibits a double-ramped chimney in Flemish bond and a chimney pent that served as a buttery. It also has beaded weatherboards, flush horizontal beaded boards under the portico, nine-over-six window sash, and a winder stair.[43]

The property also contained Campbell's lime kilns; he burned and sold lime in the community.[39]

Edward Scott received a land patent for 550 acres along Totier Creek just north of the James River in 1732. According to local tradition, the house Belle Grove (fig. 25) built here by his son, Daniel, served as a temporary courthouse until the new courthouse was completed in 1745 on the property. The visible architectural evidence, however, cannot confirm this early date. A single-cell outbuilding dating to about 1800 was connected with a hyphen to the house in the twentieth century.[40]

Mount Walla (fig. 26), built around 1770 by John Scott, commands the bluff overlooking Scottsville and its horseshoe bend on the James River. It was acquired in 1836 by Peter Field Jefferson, grandnephew of the president, and includes a summer kitchen and smokehouse.[41]

After a house fire about 1839, Dr. Thomas Walker Meriwether built what is now the east wing of Kinloch near Cismont. It may have been added to a 1764 hall-parlor frame house constructed for the overseer of Belvoir. A curious feature of the house is a china

Old Mooreland, west of Red Hill in southwestern Albemarle, originally had exterior gable-end chimneys, beaded weatherboards, wooden shingles, six-panel doors with HL hinges, and a stone-walled cellar. It is reputed to be the first house in the county to have glazed windows and is said to have been built for Stephen Moore, a Revolutionary War veteran.[44]

Perhaps built about 1780 for Samuel Tompkins in Scottsville, the hall-parlor-plan Colonial House features a double-ramped chimney, beaded weatherboards, nine-

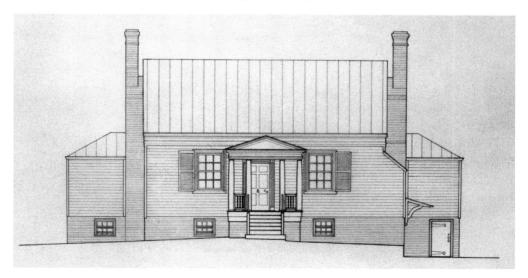

Fig. 26. Mount Walla, c. 1770, elevation

over-nine window sash, wooden wainscots, six-panel doors with wooden box locks and HL hinges, and a winder stair. A one-story frame addition, originally a detached outbuilding, has a chimney pent or closet.[45]

Old Linden probably was erected for Nicholas Beary near Crossroads, west of North Garden, in the late eighteenth century. The house is framed with pit-sawed timbers with incised Roman numerals to facilitate construction, beaded joists, and rosehead nails; the doors feature vertical beaded boards and HL hinges.[46]

Built for Richard Durrett in 1781 on land patented by his father in 1738, Wakefield was later the birthplace of state senator Nathaniel B. Early on 30 July 1866; Earlysville was named for his family. The house contains a Flemish-bond chimney facade with tiled washes (bricks laid wide-side-up on the sloping parts of the chimney sides) and English bond on the sides. The original windows were nine-over-six sash. The porch shelters a facade of flush horizontal boards and terminates in a room within the porch similar to those at Temple Hill, Findowrie, High Meadows, and Ash Lawn. Outbuildings included a kitchen and saddlebag log slave quarters.[47]

John Brown probably built the Brown-Parrott house in the 1780s on Beaver Creek on present-day Route 680 near Mechum's River. Its exterior gable-end chimneys were constructed of Flemish-bond brick and featured stepped weatherings (bricks set in steps rather than laid to form a smooth surface, as with tiled washes); glazed headers formed a diamond diapering pattern. The house's six-panel doors had HL hinges, and its interior had a raised-panel wainscot. Other features included beaded weatherboards attached with rosehead nails, L-shaped corner posts, and a winter kitchen in the cellar. It was razed in 1977.[48]

James Kinsolving began purchasing land along Mechum's River in 1788 and had acquired more than 1,400 acres by the time of his death in 1829. He made his home at Temple Hill, which includes an exterior bulkhead for access to the cellar. Outbuildings included a smokehouse and an icehouse.[49]

The grandson of Benjamin Franklin, Dr. William Bache, built Franklin about

1795 just northeast of Charlottesville on the western slope of the Southwest Mountains. It began as a one-story frame hall-parlor house. In 1800 a two-room, one-story addition was attached to its southern gable end; this addition incorporated a diagonally set chimney to serve the two rooms from the existing house chimney. Jefferson sent Bache three nine-over-nine sash windows with twelve-inch square panes for this addition.[50]

Bell Mount, another one-story frame hall-parlor-plan house, was built for Pleasant Dawson on Route 795 along the Hardware River. It not only possessed typical eighteenth-century features—beaded weatherboards, rosehead wrought-iron nails, pit-sawed sill plates, pegged mortise-and-tenon joinery, and three-course American-bond brick chimney and cellar walls—but its eastern addition featured a six-over-six sash window at attic floor level above a nine-over-six window on the first floor. Bell Mount was demolished in 1969. In 1996–97 Mount Ida, a late eighteenth-century Buckingham County dwelling that contains exquisite interior woodwork, was relocated to the foundation of Bell Mount.[51]

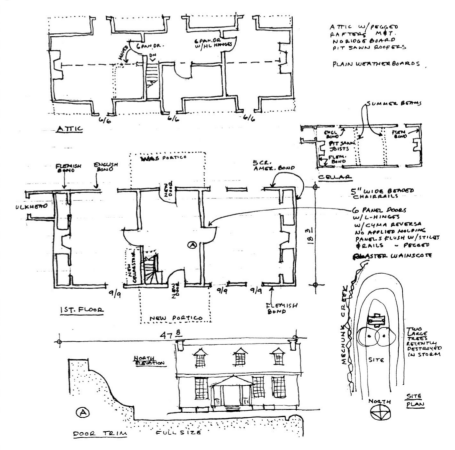

Fig. 27. Michie house, c. 1785, field notes

One-Story Frame Two-Room, Center-Passage Dwellings

The Michie house (fig. 27), believed to have been built around 1785, commands Mechunk Creek from atop a ridge near Cobham. A one-story frame dwelling with single-pile rooms on either side of an off-center passage, it is underpinned with a Flemish-bond foundation and contains pit-sawed mortise-and-tenon construction and nine-over-nine sash.[52]

The late eighteenth-century Locust Hill, an unusual one-story frame house on Route 626 north of Howardsville, was built for the Jourden family. It is the only house of its period in the county with a mansard roof.[53]

One-Story Frame Double-Pile Dwellings

The original house near Keswick at Belvoir (fig. 28), now called Maxfield, was built about 1764 by Dr. Thomas Walker's oldest son, Colonel John Walker, later an aide to George Washington and a U.S. senator. In 1781 some of Lieutenant Colonel Banastre Tarleton's British troopers raided Belvoir, where they hoped to capture Colonel Walker, an active revolutionary, but were disappointed. About 1790, when a larger house was built, the first one was moved to Milton by Francis Walker. It was relocated again in the mid–nineteenth century by Thomas Walker Lewis to its present site near Cismont, where William E. Money operated a boys school in the early twentieth century. Although Maxfield is a one-story frame dwelling, it has a center passage and is double-pile (two rooms deep).[54]

Two-Story Frame Dwellings

By 1799 Randolph Lewis, the son of Thomas Jefferson's sister Lucy, owned Buck Island on the north side of the Rivanna River. The house, whose floor plan is unknown, was a 20-by-42-foot frame structure with a semicircular portico and a brick springhouse. David Michie purchased the property from Lewis in 1805.[55]

TWO-STORY FRAME HALL-PARLOR DWELLINGS Few two-story frame hall-parlor-plan houses existed in this period. In addition to the 1757 portion of Woodstock Hall, another late eighteenth-century example is Upper

Fig. 28. Belvoir (Maxfield), c. 1764

Plantation (fig. 29), near Simeon just east of Carter's Mountain. It has beaded weatherboards, three-course American-bond chimneys, pit-sawed timbers, and nine-over-six sash. A one-story frame ell also contains a three-course American-bond chimney but with double-ramped stepped washes rather than single ones. This building probably was added to the two-story portion but could have been an older one relocated and attached to the house. In 1934 the owners engaged architect Milton Grigg to remodel the house.[56]

THE FRAME I-HOUSE In 1936 the cultural geographer Fred B. Kniffen identified a recurring house form in Illinois, Indiana, and Iowa that he dubbed the "I-house" in reference to his findings in these three states. He did not fully understand then that this house type had proliferated throughout America with little reference to any one time period or architectural style. This popular house form was passed on from generation to generation through the collective memory of individuals rather than pattern-book examples, in a truly vernacular fashion. It is often regarded as the poor man's Georgian dwelling, since it is half the size of a typical Georgian house. Except for being single-pile (one room deep) rather than double-pile, it possesses all the other Georgian charac-

Fig. 29. Upper Plantation, L18c

teristics: two stories high, with a center passage and a high basement. The earlier versions had gable-end chimneys, either exterior or flush with the outside wall; in the late nineteenth century, however, after coal replaced wood as the dominant heating fuel, the chimney stacks became smaller and were situated on the interior along the center-passage walls. Also, the roofline often was broken during this period by a central gable above the entrance to the house.

Longwood, near Earlysville in northwestern Albemarle, was built as a frame I-house about 1765 for James Michie. Afterward, an addition was constructed that served as a store operated until about the end of the eighteenth century by a descendant also named James Michie. The Michies had emigrated from Scotland to Pennsylvania and then Virginia, where John Michie purchased land in Albemarle from Major John Henry, the father of Patrick Henry. In his late eighteenth-century will, John Michie of The Horseshoe near Free Union mentioned that three of his sons, James, Patrick, and William, "have made considerable improvements in the land they now occupy, which lands are my property, and make a part of the residium before divided." These properties appear to have been William's tavern, Patrick's Chestnut Avenue, and James's Longwood. A side ell was added about 1820, and a frame school for black students was built about 1900. The property remained in the Michie family until 1904; General Philip Peyton bought it in 1940.[57]

River Lawn, between Warren and Howardsville in the southeastern part of the county, is on a tract that was part of the John Lewis land patent of 1741. It may have been built for Joseph Joplin about 1765 and altered about 1800 by the Argyle family. Its uneven three-bay window spacing is testimony to its evolution over time and suggests that the house was added onto later. It once had a two-tier portico featuring a Chinese railing that faced the James River. Much of its present detail is Greek Revival in style and probably was added in the mid–nineteenth century.[58]

Once owned by the Yancey family, the frame I-house Castlewood at Yancey Mills may have been built in 1790. Another two-story building was once attached to the main house but has since been detached, moved a short distance away, and then reconnected to the main structure with a hyphen.[59]

Bellair (fig. 30), southeast of Carter's Bridge near Carter's Mountain, was built for a Presbyterian minister, the Reverend Charles Wingfield Jr., perhaps as early as 1794 when he was appointed a county magistrate. Martin Dawson, a successful merchant from Milton who willed

Fig. 30. Bellair, c. 1794

much of his estate to the University of Virginia and the State Literary Fund, acquired it in 1822. Martin Thacker added the wings for him. The Methodist minister Walker Timberlake purchased the property in 1843. In the 1930s it was renovated by architect Marshall Wells.[60]

TWO-STORY FRAME DOUBLE-PILE DWELLINGS WITH CENTER PASSAGE (GEORGIAN PLAN) The prototypical Georgian house form consisted of a symmetrical and orthogonal (rectangular) plan and a two-story, double-pile dwelling with a high basement. The Georgian house had three-, five-, or seven-bay facades with its front door centered and a center passage extending from the front of the house all the way to the rear wall; the back part of the passage contained the stair to the private bedchambers on the second floor. Often an arch located midway down the passage separated the public area from the private and distinguished between the space for the reception of guests in the front and the private stair in the rear. Chimneys sometimes were located inside the house between the front and rear rooms. More often, however, two separate exterior chimneys were built on each gable end, or

single gable-end chimneys served corner fireplace openings in each room.

Colonel Joshua Fry was born in England and educated at Oxford. About 1720 he became a professor of mathematics at the College of William and Mary. As a surveyor he produced a definitive map of Virginia with Peter Jefferson in 1751 while living at Viewmont at Carter's Bridge near the south end of Carter's Mountain. In 1754, on an expedition during the French and Indian War, Fry was killed by his own horse near Cumberland, Maryland. In his memory his second in command, George Washington, allegedly had carved on a tree there: "Under this oak tree, lies the body of the good, the just and the noble Fry." Perhaps because of their association, Washington's birthday seems to have been a special occasion in the county. In 1825 the newspaper announced a "Birth-Night Ball" in the Central Hotel. Three years later John L. Keller announced that he would exhibit a "Washington Birthday Cake" at the home of Samuel Leitch Jr. The "very large and rich plumb cake elegantly ornamented with a fine candy pyramid" was "to be from 8 to 10 feet in circumference."[61]

Viewmont may have been constructed by 1737, the year Fry's eldest son, John, was born. In 1786 Governor Edmund Randolph purchased it. The original house burned before 1800 and was rebuilt on the foundation; the new dwelling (fig. 31, 32) retained the old, massive chimneys. Randolph sold the property in 1798 to William Champe Carter, who in turn sold it in 1803 to Captain John Harris, who at the time of his death in 1832 owned eight large estates and was the wealthiest man in the county. One of his Moon family nephews, who inherited the estate, fathered Charlotte "Lottie" Digges Moon, who became famous as a Baptist missionary to China from 1873 until her death in 1912. The 140-year-old Viewmont, again destroyed by fire in 1939, was a two-story frame double-pile house with a center passage and massive brick multiple-ramp, gable-end chimneys. The interior featured interesting mantels and overmantels and a built-in china press. A third house was built on the site in 1941 by architect Charles Baker and incorporated the original chimney brick in its walls.[62]

Old Woodville (fig. 33), on Green Mountain in the southern part of the county, was built in 1796 for Walter Coles Sr., the eldest son of John Coles II, as a typical three-bay Georgian-plan house. The date is said to have been inscribed on a chimney brick that also contained the initials of the builder, William Bates. Coles added the dining-room (west) wing in 1832, eliminating in the process a pent closet situated between the chimneys. One of Jefferson's builders, Hugh Chisholm, executed the plasterwork. A Mutual Assurance Society policy issued in 1799 described a 36-by-34-foot two-story frame house underpinned with a stone foundation. Small porticoes or porches sheltered the north and south fronts, with two chimneys located at each gable end.[63]

BRICK DWELLINGS

One-Story Brick Dwellings

ONE-STORY BRICK SINGLE-CELL DWELLINGS Patrick Michie's brick Chestnut Avenue plantation, on present-

Fig. 31. Viewmont, 18c, 1800

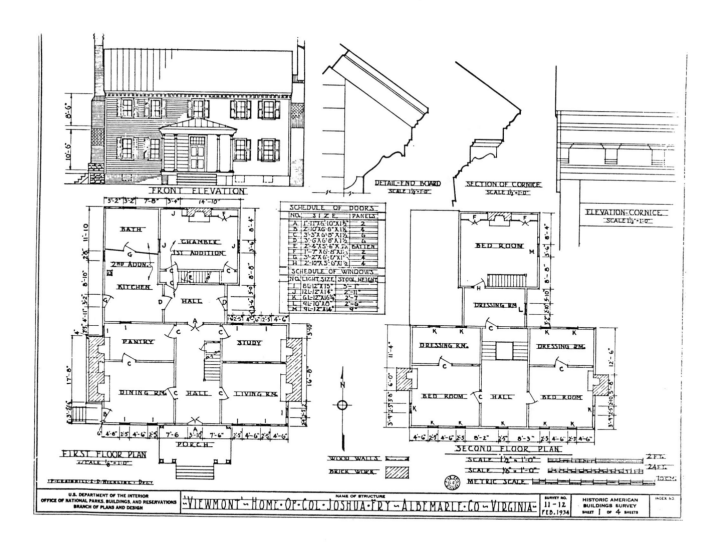

Fig. 32. (above) Viewmont, 18c,
1800, plan

Fig. 33. (left) Old Woodville,
1796, elevation

Fig. 34. Chestnut Avenue plantation office, 18c

day Route 622 near Earlysville, burned in the early twentieth century, but its plantation office (fig. 34) survived until 1985, when it was razed. The office was a one-story, single-cell brick building with a cellar containing a fireplace. Two exterior walls were of Flemish bond with glazed headers while the other two contained three-course American bond. Two rows of glazed raking-course headers adorned the entrance gable.[64] At least two other county properties, Monroe Hill and Limestone Farm, possessed one-story, single-cell brick outbuildings that served as law offices.

ONE-STORY BRICK HALL-PARLOR DWELLINGS
One-story, hall-parlor brick houses often have much earlier dates than are evident from the examination of visual details. Captain Thomas Carr, for example, built Glen Echo northeast of Charlottesville near present-day Proffit in the eighteenth century. He later built Carrsbrook, where he resided from the 1780s until 1794 when he relocated to the North Garden area, where he died in 1807. When

James D. Allen, who had purchased Glen Echo in the 1820s, sold the house to William W. Minor of nearby Gale Hill in 1836, it was considered an old place. Minor exchanged it for Windie Knowe in 1844, so that the latter's owner, Richmond Terrell, could live closer to his daughter, who then resided at Gale Hill. Another one-story, hall-parlor brick house for which tradition claims a mid-eighteenth-century date is the older house at Glendower, south of Keene. Its exterior walls are of Flemish bond.[65]

The old brick house at The Farm (fig. 35) on Twelfth Street at East Jefferson Street claims a 1770 date, according to local tradition, as the home of Nicholas Lewis. Its double-ramp chimney contains an oven, and the wooden timbers are pit-sawed with mortise-and-tenon joinery. A 1735 house on the property burned before the Revolution. During that war the British officer Lieutenant Colonel Tarleton stayed overnight here on 4 June 1781 and incarcerated one of his prisoners, Assemblyman Daniel Boone, in the property's "coal house." It seems more likely, however, that the present brick house was a summer kitchen for a 22-by-48-foot two-story frame house that was on the property in the latter part of the eighteenth century. During the first half of the 1820s, Samuel O. Minor conducted a boarding school for boys on the property. In the first half of the nineteenth century, the brick house served as a carriage house for the newer farmhouse, built about 1825. Because of Tarleton's visit to The Farm, a large oak tree here is believed by some to be the genuine Tarleton's Oak rather than the traditional one that survived at the corner of High and Ninth Streets until cut down in 1997.[66]

Fig. 35. The Farm, 1770

Two-Story Brick Hall-Parlor Dwellings

Robert Bolling sold Glen Esk (fig. 36) at North Garden to Marshall Durrett in 1803. Bolling probably built the two-story, hall-parlor house shortly before then, as Flemish-bond brick was used in the walls, with three-course American bond in the cellar. The property was originally part of the Robert Lewis patent of 5,200 acres. The two-door facade contained nine-over-nine sash on the first floor and six-over-six on the second. Wooden wainscots and iron strap and H-hinge door hardware adorned the interior. The house was razed in 1997, and the flooring and two double-leaf doors with iron strap hinges were removed and installed in Annandale in Orange County.[67]

SINGLE-CELL STONE DWELLINGS

Very few stone dwellings were constructed east of the Blue Ridge in Albemarle County. In 1747 David Rees patented 400 acres on which the stone single-cell house at Carrsgrove is located (now within the city limits of Charlottesville on Stribling Avenue). The dwelling, which has two-foot-thick walls, measures about 16 by 18 feet on the interior. Another single-cell stone house, Tuckedaway, is on U.S. Route 250 west of Charlottesville and may date to the late eighteenth century. It measures about 14 by 19 feet on the interior with walls more than two feet thick. In the second quarter of the nineteenth century, a two-story, hall-parlor log addition was made to the south. Thomas Jefferson Randolph, Jefferson's grandson, built a similar stone house (fig. 37) at Tufton near Simeon, probably early in the nineteenth century.[68]

REASSEMBLED HOUSES

A few eighteenth-century houses have been disassembled from elsewhere in the state and then brought to the county and reassembled. Sometimes the elements of older buildings are recombined to form new structures, and occasionally groups of buildings are gathered together. The Michie Tavern complex forms the largest reassembled grouping in the county.

Normandale, off U.S. Route 250 west of Charlottesville, combines two eighteenth-century frame houses: the 1797 Harris house from Nelson County and the 1738 Carr

Fig. 36. Glen Esk, 18c

Fig. 37. Tufton stone house, E19C

house from Smithfield. They were relocated and reassembled near Mechum's River in 1975–76 by architect Don Swofford and builders William G. Hodges and Paul Grady.[69]

The nineteenth-century Halifax House was removed from Halifax County and reassembled at the D. S. Tavern, also located west of Charlottesville. It is a one-story frame hall-parlor, three-bay house with nine-over-nine windows.

TRANSITION DWELLINGS

Buildings do not usually fall neatly into stylistic categories, nor are they always easy to date by their saw marks, brick bonds, nail types, and molding shapes because often these details vary within the same building. It is extremely rare to find a building that exhibits any one pure architectural style or that contains technical features from a single time period. Occasionally other sources such as construction contracts, land tax records, letters, and newspaper advertisements can provide hints as to a building's date of construction, but such records are rare and often inconclusive.

Architectural historians, therefore, must resort to dating buildings through their stylistic and technical features—an inexact science at best. Little is written on the subject; certainly there is no single, authoritative source of information. Much of what is written about molding profiles, door and window patterns, brick bonds, saw marks, and nail chronology is based on individual observations rather than on any substantial and systematic recording of buildings that exhibit these features and that have been dated through other means. Furthermore, advances in technology, such as the replacement of hand pit-sawing by water-powered reciprocating sawmills, occurred at different times in different localities. Likewise, stylistic changes took place slowly as aesthetic tastes changed, and such changes occurred more rapidly in cities than in the conservative countryside.

Vernacular building forms and plans have outlasted every architectural style. The ubiquitous I-house is a form in point. It is found throughout the county (indeed, throughout the country) in almost every stylistic period, changing only its decorative dress as each period of fashion changed.

Perhaps a combination of the architectural historians'

concern for dates and style and the cultural geographers' and the folklorists' concern for form provides the most profitable avenue for definitive architectural investigations. Prototypical buildings — the earliest surviving examples of each type and style — and their features should be correlated with the historical periods in which they were constructed rather than simply listed in surveys of county architecture, in order to understand the reasons for their evolution.

The ways in which dwellings were enlarged to adapt to their owners' changing needs, for example, can also provide further insights into the popularity of certain features in different time periods. In addition to the ubiquitous T-plan and L-plan configurations, historically there have been three typical patterns of enlargement: telescopic, ends built first, and H-plan. These late eighteenth- and early nineteenth-century patterns can assist present-day owners in building appropriate additions to historic houses that will preserve their integrity.

Telescopic Enlargement

Perhaps the most common method of constructing additions was by telescoping the dwelling, or adding new parts to expand it in a linear fashion. One-story, late eighteenth-century frame houses — and their variant, two-story stack houses — often were expanded in the early nineteenth century gable end to gable end by adding a two-story brick addition.

Benjamin Brown Sr. came from Hanover County by way of Louisa County to northwest Albemarle in the mid–eighteenth century. Here, in what became known as Brown's Cove, he had accumulated more than 6,000 acres on Doyle's River by the time of his death in 1762. His eleven children inherited the property. His daughter Lucretia, who married Robert Harris Jr., probably built the one-story frame hall-parlor portion of Headquarters (figs. 38, 39) before they moved to Surry County, North Carolina, in 1785. The features of the house include Flemish-bond chimneys with penciled mortar joints (painted with white lime to make the brick stand out and appear more regular from a distance), three-course American bond in the cellar, beaded weatherboards attached by cut nails with hammered heads, joists and floorboards sawed with a reciprocating saw, and sawdust insulation in the walls. Some of these features reflect construction that occurred after 1800, for Brightberry Brown extended the

Fig. 38. Headquarters, 1769, 1818

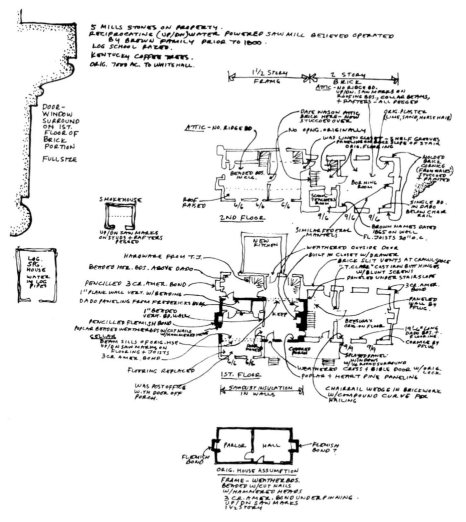

Fig. 39. Headquarters, 1769, 1818, field notes

frame house west toward the mountains in 1812. In addition, the house burned and was rebuilt in 1818, when Thomas H. Brown bought nails and hinges from Jefferson's foundry for use in the new work. The 1818 two-story, hall-parlor brick portion that completed the telescopic form contains an exterior molded-brick cornice, Flemish-bond facade, and three-course American-bond sides. Underground threaded wooden water pipes supplied water to the house.[70]

The Home Tract (fig. 40) in Ivy is a telescopic house in which the brick portion was assumed to predate the frame portion. However, the discovery of beaded weatherboards, a typical eighteenth-century feature, on the frame wall that abuts the brick house wall suggests that the frame house was built first. Here again the frame

house features a hall-parlor plan and possibly was originally one story high, while the two-story brick portion contains one room above another (as a stack house) and exhibits a Flemish-bond facade, four-course American-bond sides (an early nineteenth-century feature), and a double-row brick mousetooth cornice.[71]

Spring Hill Farm (fig. 41), also in Ivy, has a two-story frame section with a two-thirds Georgian plan (a double-pile house with a side passage) attached to a brick stack house; as at Home Tract, the brick section was believed to be the earlier of the two. Apparently, however, the frame section dates to the late eighteenth century and the brick part to about 1814.[72]

Mountain View near Crozet apparently was completed about 1800 as a two-story, hall-parlor-plan frame house with brick nogging in its walls. Perhaps, however, the second story was added much later, since its roof contains a ridgeboard —a construction feature not much in use until about 1860. A single-cell, two-story brick unit was added about 1820, together with an interior stair between the two parts. The brick portion has a Flemish-bond facade and three-course American bond with Flemish variant on the sides.[73]

Brightberry, another Brown family house in Brown's Cove, was built for Captain Brightberry Brown about 1818 as a two-story, hall-parlor frame dwelling. It features a chimney with three-course American bond, beaded weatherboards with cut nails, and mortise-and-tenon structural members that bear the marks of a reciprocating saw. About 1848 a two-story, hip-roofed frame addition completed its telescopic form. An investigation of the addition's cellar revealed that Brightberry began its existence earlier as a single-cell house. Around 1805 Brightberry Brown and Captain William Jarman built the Brown's Gap Turnpike, which extended from the Three Notch'd Road at Mechum's River through Brown's Cove to the Shenandoah Valley—a route later used by Stonewall Jackson in 1862. Brown also patented a water-powered loom in 1814.[74]

Fig. 40. (top) Home Tract, 1803, 1812

Fig. 41. (bottom) Spring Hill Farm, L18c, c. 1814, sketch

Ends Built First

Another method of enlarging a dwelling consisted of building the wings first. Two one-story frame houses were built, and the center portion was added later, frequently in response to a new style coming into vogue.

Although the Shenandoah Valley was rich in limestone and much favored as fertile agricultural land by Germanic farmers, only a few pockets of limestone exist in Albemarle County. Here limestone was likely to be burned in a kiln and then mixed with sand and water to make mortar for bricklaying. Limestone Farm (fig. 42), east of Charlottesville, contains a pocket of limestone; here Jefferson obtained lime for the mortar used at Monticello and the University of Virginia. A law office on the Limestone Farm property contains a beam bearing the date 1794 and the initials R. S., probably for Robert Sharp, the property's owner after 1773. James Monroe bought Limestone Farm in 1800, and it became the home of his brother Andrew. After 1827 Dr. George C. Blaetterman, first professor of modern languages at the University of Virginia, resided here periodically and added a Classical Revival–style central section between the two one-story, eighteenth-century frame units. The addition's square columns later were replaced with round ones, perhaps in 1928.

Although Blaetterman was highly recommended for his position in 1821 and Richard Rush, the American am-bassador to England, interviewed him, evidence of Blaetterman's low character emerged when he beat his wife in public; he was asked to resign his chair in 1840. In 1850 he was found lying dead in the snow at Limestone Farm, the victim of a "fit of apoplexy."[75]

H-Plan

The third method of enlargement produces the H-plan. The earliest-known pattern-book examples of this plan appear in Stephan Primatt's *City and Country Purchaser and Builder* of 1667 and Sebastiano Serlio's *Architettura*, republished in London in 1611.[76] In addition to the quintessential early eighteenth-century Virginia example, the Lee family seat Stratford Hall, perhaps the earliest extant example in Virginia is Tuckahoe in Goochland County; it dates from about 1720, and its addition was built about 1740. This plantation became Jefferson's boyhood home from 1745 to 1752 when his father moved the family there while he cared for his orphaned godson, Thomas Mann Randolph.

The H-plan dwelling usually evolved after a one-story house was built and then, when more space was needed, another house was constructed parallel to the first one but facing in the opposite direction. The two houses were then connected by a hyphen that often served as a summer living room; it typically had a single-pile plan for cross ventilation and contained no fireplaces, contrary to the Primatt plan that contained fireplaces. The hyphen

Fig. 42. Limestone Farm, L18c, 1828

touched the old and the new as little as possible, thereby avoiding roofing and flashing problems while retaining the integrity of both the old and the new houses.

The H-plan house typically was not constructed in a single building campaign; rather, its growth occurred over a span of years. Some of the earliest examples in Albemarle County, however, were built entirely in the eighteenth century as was Tuckahoe. John Carter, secretary of the colony and eldest son of Robert "King" Carter, obtained a patent in 1730 for 9,350 acres northeast of present-day Carter's Bridge. He maintained a mill here, and his son Edward built the first house at Blenheim, where a captive British commander, Major General William Phillips, resided while a prisoner during the Revolutionary War. The house consisted of a one-story frame house connected by a 15-by-29-foot hyphen to a 19-by-59-foot two-story frame house. The property was offered for sale at public auction in 1840; it burned by the mid–nineteenth century.[77]

Plain Dealing (fig. 43) consists of a one-story frame house (originally hall-parlor) built about 1761 for John

Biswell that was attached by an open hyphen to a 1789 frame I-house constructed for Samuel Dyer. The interior contains some of the finest paneling in the county, including arched closets, stop-fluted pilasters, and pedimented mantelpieces. Dyer was born in Bristol, England, in 1756 and eventually opened a store proclaiming a "plain deal" on the property, near present-day Keene on what was then John Coles's rolling road. In the mid–nineteenth century Plain Dealing became the home of the Reverend Joseph P. B. Wilmer, later the Episcopal bishop of New Orleans. From 1944 to 1952 it was the home of Princess Djordjadze (born Audrey Emery), who had been married to one of the assassins of the monk Rasputin in Russia.[78]

Many more of these H-plan dwellings were comprised of eighteenth-century houses that outgrew their owners' needs in the early nineteenth century and were expanded by adding a Federal house to the original Georgian house, then connecting them with a hyphen. Often the addition was log or frame rather than brick.

Several examples of the plan exist in the county. Keswick (fig. 44), on Turkey Sag Road east of Charlottesville,

Fig. 43. Plain Dealing, 1761, 1789

Fig. 44. Keswick, c. 1764, 1818, 1832

Fig. 45. (below) Mount Warren, c. 1780
Fig. 46. (right) Mount Warren, c. 1780, plan

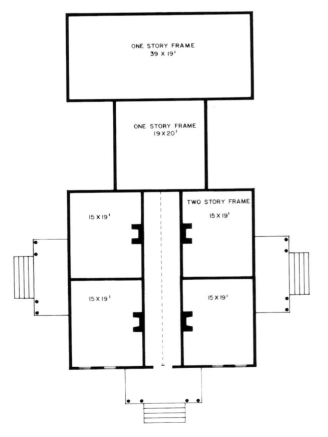

ONE STORY FRAME
39 X 19'

ONE STORY FRAME
19 X 20'

TWO STORY FRAME

15 X 19'

15 X 19'

15 X 19'

15 X 19'

was built about 1764 as a hunting lodge for Dr. Thomas Walker of Castle Hill and was developed into a two-story log house in 1818 for Dr. Mann Page, who married Walker's daughter that year. Its one-story frame H-addition was added in 1832. Governor Wilson Cary Nicholas built Mount Warren (figs. 45, 46) at Warren about 1780. Its H-plan consisted of a 20-by-40-foot one-story frame house connected by a 20-by-20-foot hyphen to a 40-by-40-foot two-story frame dwelling with three classical porticoes. The house burned about 1926. John R. Campbell's Buck Island and Captain Edward Moore's Crutchfield in the county and the Maupin-Bibb house in Charlottesville are other examples of one-story frame houses connected by hyphens to two-story dwellings.[79]

Often, however, the Federal addition was of brick construction. The one-story frame portion of Edgmont (near Stony Point) was built by a member of the Key family about 1780. Dr. John Gilmer, who made one of the first attempts to treat smallpox by inoculation, commissioned the construction of a Federal I-house addition in 1827 by

carpenter Thomas R. Blackburn. The five-bay brick addition contains doorways with fanlights and sidelights on both levels. About 1899 Henry Magruder gave its one-story paired-column portico to Hugh Minor for use at The Riggory and replaced it with a Victorian veranda.[80]

Castle Hill (fig. 47), which is listed on the National Register of Historic Places, is one of the oldest extant plantations in Albemarle County and has an unusually rich history. In 1781, during the Revolutionary War, Lieutenant Colonel Tarleton and his British cavalry were delayed in their raid on Charlottesville by a leisurely breakfast at the house, according to tradition. Castle Hill's H-plan form is especially interesting, as are its landscape and eighteenth- and early nineteenth-century outbuildings, all of which contribute to its magnificent setting.[81]

Between 1727 and 1730 Nicholas Meriwether II (1667–1744) obtained in three separate land patents about 18,000 acres on the eastern slope of the Southwest Mountains, in the center of which stands Castle Hill. After Meriwether's son Nicholas III (1699–1739) died, his

Fig. 47. Castle Hill, 1764, engraving

widow, Mildred Thornton Meriwether (1721–1778), still occupied the property when she married Dr. Thomas Walker (1715–1794) in 1741. Walker became an eminent physician and explorer, a surveyor of the Virginia–North Carolina border, a member of the House of Burgesses, quartermaster general during the French and Indian War, and guardian to Thomas Jefferson. In 1770 he formed a partnership with John Wilkinson, Edward Carter, William Cabell, and Alexander Trent in the Albemarle Iron Works. By 1782 Walker was the fourth-wealthiest person in the county, just after Thomas Jefferson. His estate included eighty-six slaves, ninety-three head of cattle, twenty-two horses, and a two-wheel riding carriage. In 1787, although the Castle Hill tract had been significantly reduced in size, he still owned the fourth-highest number of acres in the county with a total of 6,150. That same year he and John Coles II of Enniscorthy recorded the second-largest number of slaves at seventy-five each, Jefferson having the largest number at eighty.[82]

The first house in which the Walkers resided at Castle Hill burned. The site of this house might very well be indicated by the saddlebag-plan log house foundation on the nearby property called Castalia. Walker built the present one-story frame portion (fig. 48) of the dwelling at Castle Hill as either a single-cell structure or a hall-parlor design that was later expanded with a gable-end addition. Today a frame wing of the main house, it contains eighteenth-century details such as pit-sawed timbers, beaded weatherboards attached to the studs by hand-wrought rosehead nails, wide one-and-a-half-inch muntins in its nine-over-nine-light double-hung sash, paneled wainscoting, fan-louvered lunettes over powder-room doors, floor-to-ceiling wood-paneled walls in the parlor, and a dogleg stair with molded handrail, turned banisters, and scrolled end brackets.

Thomas Walker's youngest son, Francis Walker (1764–1806), married Jane Byrd Nelson, the daughter of Governor Thomas Nelson of Yorktown, and inherited Castle Hill. In 1800 Francis Walker was the third-wealthiest person in the county with seventy-seven slaves, twenty-seven horses, a four-wheel coach, and 6,522 acres. In 1815 his estate owned 105 cattle, the second-highest number in the county. The house, valued at $1,200, contained four sideboards, a bureau, two dressers, two mirrors, a clock, five pictures larger than twelve inches, and one of the only two organs in the county.[83]

After Walker's death in 1806, his daughter Judith Page Walker (1802–1882) — who married U.S. senator William Cabell Rives (1793–1868), twice minister to France and

member of the Confederate Congress — inherited Castle Hill in 1819 and resided here until her death. Both Riveses were authors. William Rives wrote biographies of John Hampden and James Madison, while Judith Rives, a novelist, described life at Castle Hill in one of her works, *Home and the World*. In it she stated that "the house . . . like the grounds showed the work of successive generations. The original structure had received many additions, some of the latest claiming a title to architectural taste. . . . The more ancient portion of the building . . . always seemed to possess a special attraction for the family." The parlor windows in the newer portion "commanded a view of the extensive lawn in front of the house. One side of it gave entrance to a conservatory filled with tropical fruit trees and flowering plants." During the Riveses' tenure they expanded the house to the east to complete the H-shaped plan and thereby increased the dwelling's assessed value to $5,000 in 1820, when the total value of the property stood at $47,868. By 1821 the number of acres had declined to 3,700, but Rives owned thirty-nine slaves, the fourth-highest number in the county.[84]

Captain John M. Perry, who was one of Jefferson's master brickmasons, built the two-story, five-bay, Flemish-bond brick addition. It contains several Federal features, including a graceful elliptical stair in the summer living-room hyphen, attenuated mantels with patera and colonnettes, and an entrance doorway with an elliptical fanlight, sidelights, and a one-story tetrastyle Tuscan portico with a Chinese railing.

Perry's construction contract with Rives, dated 10 August 1823, refers to the use of similar Federal features in other Perry work.[85] For example, the exterior of the addition was to be faced with "rubbed stretchers in the manner of the Rotunda at the University"; the windows, interior doors, and general woodwork to be "after the style" of the work done on his recent Pavilion V at the university in conjunction with James Dinsmore; and the front door and the interior and exterior cornices to be similar to that of Perry's Frascati, built about 1821–23 in Orange County for Colonel Philip Pendleton Barbour. The agreement further stipulated that the new structure would have a portico with a "handsome Chinese railing" and be "supported on four columns with stone caps and bases." In 1844 columned conservatories with triple-hung windows were added to each end of Perry's brick addition by another Jefferson brickmason, William B. Phillips.

During her long tenure at Castle Hill, Judith Walker Rives served as hostess to presidents, crowned heads of

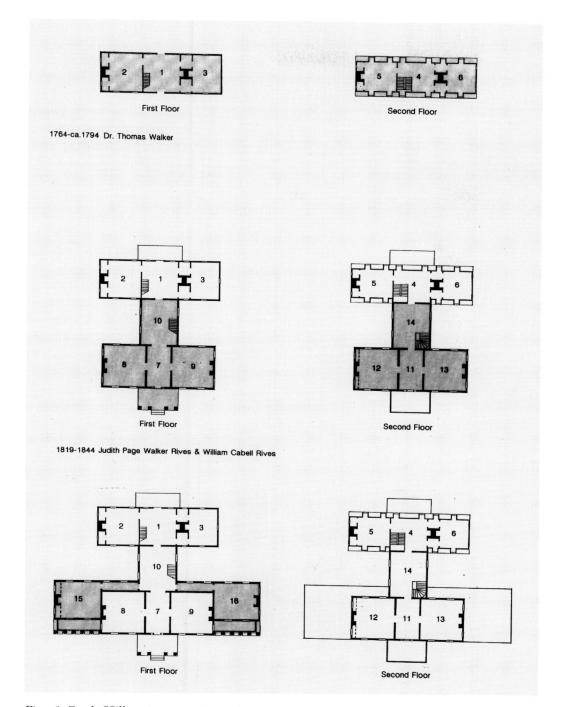

First Floor

Second Floor

1764-ca.1794 Dr. Thomas Walker

First Floor

Second Floor

1819-1844 Judith Page Walker Rives & William Cabell Rives

First Floor

Second Floor

Fig. 48. Castle Hill, 1764, 1824, 1844, plan

Europe, the Rothschilds, Henry Clay, Daniel Webster, and numerous other prominent figures. By 1870 she was listed as the sixth-wealthiest county resident, although her property had been reduced to 1,762 acres. Colonel Alfred Landon Rives, son of William and Judith Rives, inherited Castle Hill. Born here in 1830, Rives served as chief of engineers to General Robert E. Lee during the Civil War and later as president of the Mobile and Ohio Railroad. After Rives died in 1903 and his widow, Sarah Catherine MacMurdo Rives, died in 1909, their novelist daughter, Amélie (1863–1945), who had married a famous Russian portrait painter, Prince Pierre Troubetzkoy (1864–1936), inherited the property. After her death Castle Hill was sold out of the family to Colonel Clark J. Lawrence and his wife Eleanor, who renovated it in 1948 with the aid of local architect Marshall Wells. Additional renovations have been made by subsequent owners Don Michael and

Audrey Bird, Russell and Margaret Pace, Gary and Anne Lieberthal, and Gardner and Jennie Larned.[86]

Owners of other eighteenth-century houses completed their H-plans in the mid–nineteenth century during the Greek Revival period. One example, Pen Park (fig. 49), was located on the Rivanna River at Lynch's ferry. It probably was built after 1777 as a one-story frame house, possibly by Dr. George Gilmer, who purchased the property then from John Harvie. In the mid–eighteenth century, the Quaker Charles Lynch had resided here in a log house. By the mid–nineteenth century, a frame I-house was connected to the older dwelling with a hyphen, possibly by John H. Craven, who resided here from 1819 to 1845. The house burned in the 1920s. In 1866 a German owner, William Hotopp, began to operate a vineyard here; the remnant of a wine cellar still exists on the property.[87]

The Riggory (fig. 50), near Stony Point, was another frame I-house that was added in 1849 to a one-story frame house with a hyphen. The original 1796 portion was built for Hugh Minor, and Franklin Minor conducted a classical school for boys here during the first half of the nineteenth century. According to local tradition, the house contained the first running water in the county; it oper-

Fig. 49. (above) Pen Park, c. 1777, M19C

Fig. 50. (right) Paired square-column portico at The Riggory, 1796, 1849

ated using a well siphon, but during the Civil War the well was disassembled, and its lead water pipes were melted for bullets.[88]

Other H-plan dwellings received brick Greek Revival additions instead of frame. The Reverend Ebenezer Boyden, rector of Grace Episcopal Church, built an 1849 brick I-house addition connected with a hyphen to a late eighteenth-century one-story frame house at Holly Fork near Cismont. Another example of a Greek Revival brick I-house addition built onto a late eighteenth-century one-story frame house is Valmontis (fig. 51) near Bartersbrook. The property contains its original frame smokehouse and slave quarters, and the cellar walls of the frame portion exhibit an English-bond cellar foundation and a double-ramped chimney with Flemish-bond facade and three-course American-bond sides. The I-house constructed about 1829 for David Carr features Flemish bond with penciled mortar joints on two sides and five-course American bond on the other two. It also features a stuccoed, paired-column portico built of pie-shaped bricks that shelters an entrance doorway surrounded by sidelights and a flat transom. The doors in the brick addition contain eight panels in a double-cross pattern.[89]

Other H-plan complexes received Victorian additions. Mount Air (fig. 52), a one-story frame house at Proffit, was connected to a later frame Victorian I-house that features bay windows and a center gable. In 1883 Scottsville merchant Charles B. Harris added a Victorian brick I-house to the 1831–32 one-story brick house at Scottsville called High Meadows; the earlier portion, built for Peter White, contains a porch room. The mid-nineteenth-century one-story frame dwelling called Walnut Grove was connected about 1872 to a frame Victorian I-house built for the Rodes family.[90]

Farm Outbuildings

About 1780 British major Thomas Anburey reflected on Albemarle County's plantations:

> The plantations are scattered here and there . . . over the land which is thickly covered with timber. On these there is a dwelling house, with kitchen, smokehouse, and other outhouses detached, and from the various buildings each plantation has the appearance of a small village. At some distance from the houses are peach and apple orchards, and scattered over the plantations are the negroe's huts, and tobacco barns, which are large and built of wood for the cure of that article. . . . Most of

the planters consign the care of their plantations and negroes to an overseer; even the man whose house we rent has an overseer, though he could with ease superintend it himself.[91]

Architectural historian Camille Wells examined a thousand newspaper advertisements published in the *Virginia Gazette* between 1736 and 1781. She discovered that the farm outbuildings most frequently mentioned were kitchens, followed by dairies, smokehouses, and slave quarters, then barns and tobacco houses. The advertisements revealed that 90 percent of the houses were of

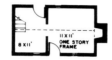

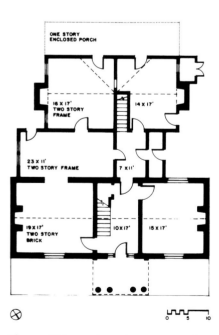

Fig. 51. Valmontis, L18c, c. 1829, plan

Fig. 52. Mount Air, 18c, c. 1865

wood-frame construction with outbuildings and 70 percent had but one- or two-room plans and were one story in height. Seventy-five percent were estimated to have had cat and clay chimneys (with wood poles laid horizontally to form a rectangular shaft and covered with mud), the last one being recorded in the county earlier in the twentieth century.[92]

Twelve of the advertisements published between 1765 and 1775 pertained to Albemarle County tracts that varied in size from 200 to 3,000 acres. The crops most frequently cited were tobacco, peach orchards, apple orchards, wheat, and corn. Fenced open land was mentioned twice, and cattle and hogs were among the most common livestock. Nine tracts contained dwellings or overseers' houses. Although farm buildings often were lumped together as "all convenient outhouses," many advertisements separately listed tobacco "houses," three listed gristmills (one with two wheels), and some mentioned barns, slave quarters, and counting or "compting" houses. One contained a loom shop as well as a fulling mill. Since

summer kitchens, dairies, smokehouses, stables, and corncribs were rarely mentioned, they obviously were embraced by the all-inclusive term *outhouse*, together with necessary houses (privies), which were never mentioned. Neill Campbell also advertised a "pretty large copper still, well fixed, which will be sold with the land." And although some residents were selling their slaves as well as their real estate, Samuel Stockton wished to acquire more slaves, stating that "I will take one half the value of it money in negroes."[93]

Two types of barns predominated in Albemarle County: English ground barns used to store grain (primarily wheat) and Germanic bank barns—so named because they were built against the bank or side of a hill—used for grain storage and threshing on the upper level and the stabling of cattle below. A ramp led to the upper level of a bank barn, and the stable opened into a fenced yard where hay was tossed from the forebay above. Few early examples of either barn type survive. The 1810 Sutherland barn (fig. 53), an excellent example of a brick

Fig. 53. Sutherland English ground barn, 1810

ground barn, still stands near Crossroads, while an early frame ground barn at Clover Fields is now a part of the Clover Hill property. The latter contains mortise-and-tenon pegged joinery, pit-sawed members, and columns with lamb's-tongues—a cyma curve between each of the square column's four beveled corners that makes it octagonal. A rare example of an eighteenth-century bank barn was located at Enniscorthy; the barn also served as an animal-operated gristmill. Although this barn and the Stockton Creek barn near Mirador have been razed, another early bank barn is located on the Ezekiel Wilhoit Jr. property (fig. 54) near Nortonsville. Horse-powered threshing machines were housed in barns at Sherwood and at Redlands near Carter's Bridge.[94]

A few examples of other barn types remain in the county. For instance, the double-crib log barn at Ben-Coolyn (fig. 55) near Keswick is a unique survivor from the mid–nineteenth century.[95] And an exquisite stone barn designed by architect Eimerto Cappelino in 1929 exists at Castalia near Cismont.

Vertical frame tobacco barns originally dotted the county. Few remain today—those at Underhill Farm (fig. 56) near Edgehill and Dovedale near Stony Point are rare examples. Each plantation also had a prizing house where tobacco was packed into the huge barrels or hogsheads

Fig. 54. Ezekiel Wilhoit Jr. bank barn, 19c

Fig. 55. Ben-Coolyn double-crib barn, M19C

Fig. 56. Underhill Farm tobacco barn, 19C

Fig. 57. Ingleridge horse barn, E20C

that were a standard measure of quantity. No prizing houses are known to exist today.

Large horse stables once were common in the county, and many were described by their owners in Mutual Assurance Society policies. For example, a very large one-story brick stable, 18 feet wide by 90 feet long, was insured in 1812 at Donegal near Warren. Elegant brick stables designed by Richmond architect D. Wiley Anderson for Harry Douglas Forsyth and built about 1898 still stand at Nydrie on Green Mountain. They were expanded by Ray Alan Van Clief in 1932. Under his son Daniel G. Van Clief, this stud farm consigned many yearlings to Saratoga and produced a long line of derby winners here. Impressive frame horse barns built in the twentieth century are located on Garth Road at Ingleridge (fig. 57) and Ingleside. The latter farm has produced three Kentucky Derby winners and is an acclaimed training center.[96]

Chicken coops (fig. 58) and hog pens housed other farm animals. Examples of corncribs, which usually were ventilated with wooden slats and elevated on masonry piers with flanges for ratproofing, remain at Hatton Grange (fig. 59) at Hatton and at Westbury at Batesville.

Slave quarters (fig. 60) usually were located in two places on each plantation. Those close to the main house served as dwellings for the slaves involved in chores within the main house itself, while those situated far from the house served as quarters for the farmhands.[97]

Virtually every southern plantation had a detached summer kitchen (fig. 61) that frequently contained a central chimney which also served a laundry opposite its kitchen side. Sometimes the loft space above functioned as slave quarters. Winter kitchens usually were located in

Fig. 58. Auburn Hill chicken coop, 19c

Fig. 59. Hatton Grange corncrib, 19c

Fig. 60. Valmontis slave
quarters, 19C

Fig. 61. (above) Fosteria summer kitchen, 19C

Fig. 62. (above right) Enniscorthy smokehouse, 19C

the cellars of the main house and were entered through an exterior bulkhead.

Almost every farm had its lumber house, in which not only lumber but also farm supplies and equipment were stored. Smokehouses (fig. 62), where meat was cured by drying and smoking, and dairies (fig. 63), where milk and butter were kept cool, usually were housed in square dependencies that commonly had pyramidal roofs topped with wooden finials. Dairy floors were recessed into the ground to give better insulation to the dairy products, and some were built over natural springs to help cool them; wooden grills provided ventilation. Inside smoke-

Fig. 63. Castle Hill dairy, 19C

houses, meat was hung from wooden or iron hooks embedded in the roof joists. Smokehouse framing studs were placed close together to defeat thieves even if they pried weatherboards off the walls. Icehouses (fig. 64), which held ice cut from a nearby pond or river, usually were round pits dug deep into the earth and lined with stone or logs tilted upright. The top enclosure was either square

or circular and had a pulley attached to its roof interior to hoist the ice. Orangeries (fig. 65), built to shelter citrus trees, and greenhouses, for the growing of flowering plants and vegetables, sometimes stood as separate buildings and other times were attached to the main house. Privies (also called necessary houses) often had multiple seats as in early Roman times. Other service buildings constructed for the well-being of the family included schools (fig. 66), chapels (fig. 67), and libraries (fig. 68). The plantation office or counting house, from which the owner or overseer administered the farm operations, usually was located close to the main dwelling, as was the carriage house (fig. 69). Wells (figs. 70, 71) for underground water and cisterns for the storage of rainwater usually were roofed. Often in the latter part of the nineteenth century, iron tanks to hold water were built into the attic space of dwellings. In the early twentieth century, some property owners constructed water towers (fig. 72) to store water that then flowed by gravity to the house, while

Fig. 64. (left) Hampstead icehouse, 19c

Fig. 65. (below) Castle Hill orangery, 1844

Fig. 66. (left) Dawson's mill plantation school, 19c

Fig. 67. (above) Blenheim chapel, 19c

Fig. 68. Blenheim library, 19c

Fig. 69. Carr's Hill carriage house, 1907

Fig. 70. (left) Giddings's well house, 19c

Fig. 71. (below) Findowrie well house, 19c

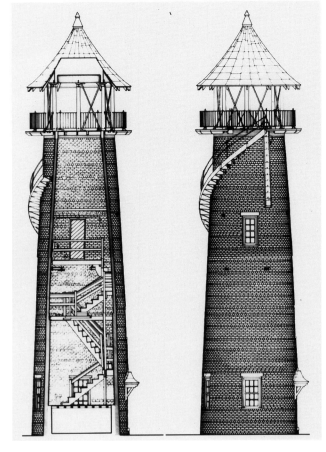

Fig. 72. Birdwood water tower, E20C, section and elevation

others used windmills to pump water from wells. Water towers and windmills became vertical elements in the farm landscape, as did silos for the storage of grain. At about the same time, when electricity replaced gaslight, the Delco house, which housed the storage battery, became a common farm fixture.

It has been said that the country house was the greatest contribution made by England to the visual arts. Virginia's eighteenth- and nineteenth-century rural Georgian houses made a similar contribution. In Virginia, however, such dwellings were not merely weekend or summer residences but year-round communities based on land, slaves, and tobacco—the trinity of eighteenth-century Virginia wealth. On the Virginia plantation the main house was the heart of a small village formed by its outbuildings. Two examples out of many in Albemarle County may serve to represent an entirely vanished culture.

Clover Fields has remained the seat of the Meriwethers

since the family first patented land in the county in 1730. Occupants of the houses here today are the tenth- and eleventh-generation descendants of Nicholas Meriwether II, the recipient of that patent, and seventh- and eighth-generation direct descendants of Thomas Jefferson.

The plantation included such dependencies as a summer kitchen-laundry, bake oven, smokehouse, icehouse, springhouse, privies, overseer's house, slave quarters, weaver's house, tobacco barn, crop barn, stable, corncrib, granary, gristmill, sawmill, carpenter's shop, and doctor's office—all contributing to the household economy. Here too is a unique combination smokehouse and dairy.

The rectangular garden plan persisted in America long after the informal "English" gardens were adopted in England, possibly because of a felt need to impose order on this country's wilderness. At Clover Fields a nine-square garden was aligned on center with the main house and also with a mountain peak in the distance in the sixteenth-century Palladian manner. Here in the garden the family not only grew vegetables and flowers but also buried their ancestors, as at Westover on the James River, where several generations of the Byrd family are buried in the formal garden just yards from the mansion.

English boxwood more than two hundred years old survive at Clover Fields, as well as 75- and 140-year-old peonies and pear trees planted in the 1840s. Such crops as clover, tobacco, corn, wheat, timothy, oats, buckwheat, cherries, chestnuts, crab apples, and grapes are recorded in the farm journals. The Meriwethers practiced crop rotation, fertilized with manure, and used a three-horse McCormick threshing machine.

The keen interest in scientific agriculture evinced by Thomas Jefferson and James Madison, among other farmers in the region, inspired the founding in 1817 of the Agricultural Society of Albemarle, an organization of national influence. Its first president, Thomas Mann Randolph Jr., invented a hillside plow. In 1828 the society held a competition to select the best farms in the area; it awarded John Rodgers's Keswick first prize, John H. Craven's Pen Park second prize, and William Douglas Meriwether's Clover Fields third place and made Peter Minor's Ridgway runner-up. Minor, together with Cyrus McCormick, had further improved the moldboard plow. Jefferson had earlier invented the moldboard plow of "least resistence."

In 1782 the Meriwethers paid taxes on fifty slaves who labored on 2,100 acres at Clover Fields. The family also owned thirty-nine head of cattle and fifteen horses. By 1817 the farm animal population included four saddle horses, five workhorses, six oxen, thirty-three horned cattle, sixty hogs, and forty-five sheep.[98]

The beautiful grounds and plantings at Castle Hill (fig. 73), the other outstanding eighteenth-century Albemarle County plantation, are largely the result of Judith Rives's interest in landscaping. Eighteenth- and early nineteenth-century outbuildings line either side of a flat rectangular bowling green somewhat centered on Walnut Mountain to the northwest in the manner of Palladian villas. A frame office and a carpenter shop stand on the southwestern edge of the green, while a wooden wool-carding house as well as frame and brick smokehouses line the other side. A well house, slave quarters, dairy, and summer kitchen are located northeast of the house, and on the southwest there were once a stable, a carriage house, and terraced gardens. In front of the brick section is an hourglass-shaped lawn in the English landscape tradition; it is about 800 feet long and is bordered on three sides by impressive boxwood and magnificent trees. The lane from the public road to the house is lined with cedar trees.[99]

PUBLIC ARCHITECTURE

Courthouses

In 1745, the year after the establishment of Albemarle County, the county court ordered Thomas Bellew, William Cabell, Major Allen Howard, Peter Jefferson, and Charles Lynch to find a site for the new courthouse and appointed John Anthony surveyor for a road from the courthouse to Martin King's Road. According to a 1936 Works Progress Administration survey, this first courthouse, built about 1749, was a frame building on an English-bond foundation that measured 20 by 36 feet. Samuel Scott allegedly erected it at his own expense, patterning it after the Goochland County Courthouse. Its exact location is believed to be a flat area just to the south of the old house at Belle Grove near Daniel Scott's ferry. The courthouse remained standing through the Revolution, when it was used as an arsenal. Stone capitals and bases said to be from the courthouse are presently located outside the Scottsville Museum, and bricks from the foundations were buried near the dairy silos on the site.[100]

Late in November 1762 Colonel William Cabell gave his bond for the construction of the second courthouse, to be located on Court Square in Charlottesville, but he turned over the task to John Moore in April 1763 when the building was partially completed. The courthouse was to be patterned after the Henrico County Courthouse,

with a floor of eight-inch flagstones, and was to cost £375.10. In 1792 the courthouse square was enclosed within a rail fence, and by 1800 the courthouse facade included a tetrastyle portico.[101]

Jails

In 1745 the Albemarle County Court ordered Benjamin Woodson and John Henderson to mark off boundaries for the first county jail at Belle Grove. Then, about 1749 before the Scottsville courthouse was built, Samuel Scott had William Terrell erect an 18-by-42-foot frame gaol on an English-bond foundation as well as a stock and pillory. The second jail was built about 1766 on Court Square in Charlottesville, also by William Terrell, and the third jail, a two-story stone building 16 by 16 feet in plan, was erected by Henry Gambrell in 1785. In 1798 Thomas Whitlow erected the fourth jail for £1,000. The pillory, stocks, and whipping post were repaired in 1807 and restored again in 1820 — obviously they were well used. In 1846 the jail was improved at a cost of $3,000, and in 1857 James Lobban and Andrew Brown erected a new whipping post. In 1875 the jail was repointed and whitewashed, and rainspouts were installed to delay deterioration until a new jail could be completed across the street.[102]

ECCLESIASTICAL BUILDINGS

Churches

THE ANGLICAN (EPISCOPAL) CHURCH The Church of England was the official or established church in Virginia until it was disestablished after the Revolutionary War. As early as the 1720s, the Anglican Mountain Chapel, a log building, was located on the Edgehill property owned by Colonel William Randolph in the Shadwell area on the Three Notch'd Road (Old Mountain Road). Albemarle County contained two Anglican parishes during the eighteenth century. In 1742 Saint Anne's Parish was formed from Saint James's Parish in Goochland County, and Fredericksville Parish was established in 1761. Its border with Saint Anne's Parish followed the Rivanna River and the Three Notch'd Road. (In 1839, Walker's Parish was carved from Fredericksville Parish.)[103]

On 16 April 1745 the Saint Anne's Parish vestry decided to build three Anglican churches "below the mountains." Within a year Francis Smith, who had been involved in other Anglican construction projects in Virginia, built the "Middle" church (Belvoir or Walker's). It was to be completed by Christmas Day 1746 and

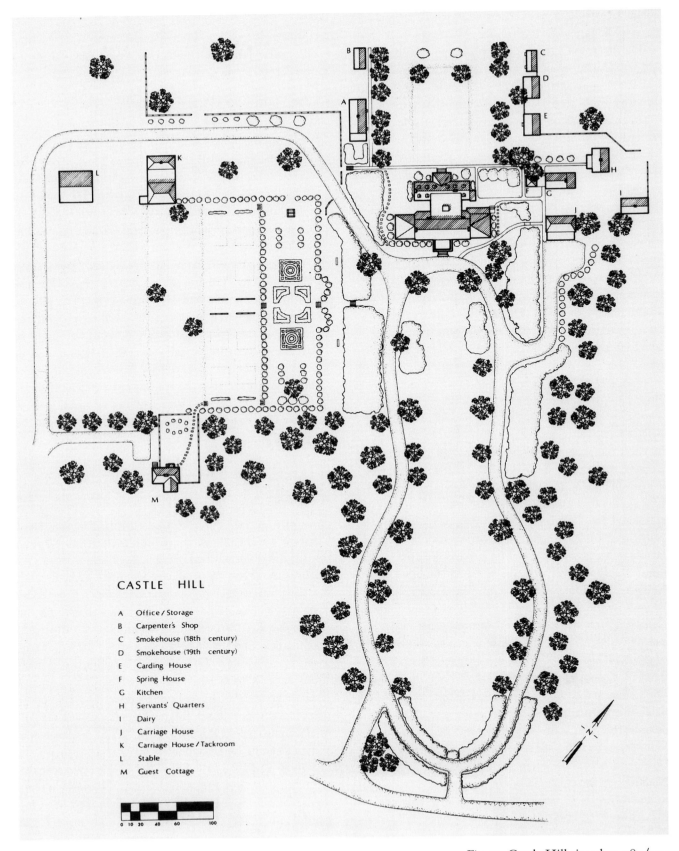

CASTLE HILL

A   Office / Storage
B   Carpenter's Shop
C   Smokehouse (18th century)
D   Smokehouse (19th century)
E   Carding House
F   Spring House
G   Kitchen
H   Servants' Quarters
I   Dairy
J   Carriage House
K   Carriage House / Tackroom
L   Stable
M   Guest Cottage

0 10 20   40   60   100

Fig. 73. Castle Hill site plan, 18c/19c

located at the old Mountain Chapel, but was designed to be eight feet shorter and with two fewer windows. Today a boulder in front of Grace Church near Cismont marks its site.[104]

The second early Anglican church, located "above the Little Mountains," is Buck Mountain Church (fig. 74), built in 1747 on Buck Mountain Road on the property of David Mills. Of frame construction and about 30 by 60 feet, it contained a gallery for slaves in the west end. By 1801 the Baptist Church occupied it, but by 1833 it returned to Episcopalian hands. In 1859 the church was moved to Earlysville from its original location. It retains the approximate dimensions specified in the parish records as well as much of its original fabric.[105]

The third church, the "lowest church," was built in the eighteenth century at Church Hill, just south of Crossroads on the North Garden tract of Hugh Morris. The vestry ordered that it be of frame construction and 20 by 40 feet in dimension. It was to contain three windows with nine-over-nine sash on each side and two four-over-four windows on the west end, as well as a "double window" over the communion table. In the 1770s a brick church was planned nearby, but its construction was in-terrupted by the Revolution. The five-course American-bond brick Trinity (Garden) Episcopal Church was finally completed in 1835 close by at Crossroads. It has four windows with nine-over-nine sash and a double-leaf door. In 1892 it was converted into a public school, and then to a residence in 1922.[106]

Two other eighteenth-century Anglican churches were built in Saint Anne's Parish. Ballenger's Creek Church still stood near Boiling Spring at the turn of the twentieth century but was converted into a residence and eventually razed.[107] Forge Church, constructed shortly before the Revolution, was just north of the Hardware River near Eolus Mills. It was still standing in the nineteenth century but had been converted into a barn and eventually was burned.

The Saint Anne's Parish glebe land was sold to Joseph Cabell in 1779. Some years later the General Assembly ordered the glebe lands of the disestablished church across the state sold and the funds to be used to support the poor and for other endeavors. The University of Virginia, for example, later was constructed in part with funds derived from the sale of the Saint Anne's Parish glebe land.[108]

Fig. 74. Buck Mountain Anglican Church, 1747

THE QUAKERS Christopher Clark, a Louisa County Quaker, and Nicholas Meriwether I purchased land on Sugarloaf Mountain among the Southwest Mountains in Albemarle County in 1742. Here they established the first Friends' meetinghouse, Sugarloaf Mountain Friends, on the site of present-day Bridle Spur Farm. Clark's stay in the county was short-lived; after twelve years he moved to what became Lynchburg in Bedford County. His daughter Sarah married Charles Lynch, whose family founded that town.[109]

THE PRESBYTERIAN CHURCH In the eighteenth century Germans and Scotch-Irish traveled the Great Wagon Road down the fertile Shenandoah Valley from the port at Philadelphia. Coming into Albemarle County from the west through Woods's Gap in 1734, they brought the Lutheran and Presbyterian denominations to an essentially Anglican region. The Scotch-Irish, led by Michael Woods and William Wallace, settled close to the Blue Ridge Mountains and erected the Rockfish Presbyterian Church and a school in what is now Nelson County in 1746. It has been estimated that Germans and Scotch-Irish made up 10 percent of Albemarle County's population in the eighteenth century.[110]

Other eighteenth-century Presbyterian churches included the 1740s Mountain Plains Church, named after Michael Woods's plantation at Mechum's River, the 1741 D. S. Church at the intersection of Dick Woods's Road and the Three Notch'd Road, the 1756 North Garden Presbyterian Church, and the 1769 log Cove Church, replaced in 1809 by the present building. The D. S. Church (the initials are believed to stand for Dissenters) was dissolved in 1811. Both the current Cove Church, in 1880, and Mountain Plains, in 1959, were damaged by tornadoes.[111]

THE BAPTIST CHURCH William "Baptist Billy" Woods was numbered among the influential early Baptist ministers in Albemarle County; he succeeded Wilson Cary Nicholas, who had been elected to the U.S. Senate, as a member of the Virginia House of Delegates during the session of 1799–1800. Another, the Reverend Martin Dawson, served as president of the Rivanna Navigation Company, and his bequest to the University of Virginia funded the construction of Dawson's Row in the 1850s. The first Baptist congregation in the county was organized in 1773 at Lewis's meetinghouse on the David Lewis property just west of Charlottesville. The congregation was called Albemarle Baptist, then Buck Mountain Baptist in 1801 when it took over that former Anglican

church. In 1775 the Totier Baptist and Ballenger's Creek Baptist congregations were formed. Nine years later the log Preddy's Creek Baptist Church was built on land acquired from Colonel Nimrod Bramham. The present frame church on the same site allegedly dates from the early nineteenth century.[112]

THE METHODIST CHURCH In 1795 Henry Austin conveyed land near the Greene County line near Nortonsville for Austin's meetinghouse, now known as Bingham's Methodist Church.[113]

The Anglican Glebe

The residence (usually a house and farm) furnished the clergy of the Anglican Church was called a glebe; it provided living quarters and financial support for priests until the late eighteenth century. The frame glebe house of Saint Anne's Parish (figs. 75, 76) was built about 1765 in the southern part of the county and was relocated in 1946 to Clover Fields in the north. The log or frame glebe house of Fredericksville Parish at Edgeworth became the Reverend James Maury's classical school, then in 1825 the home of General William Fitzhugh Gordon. It burned in February 1835.[114]

MANUFACTURING BUILDINGS

Mills and Millhouses

Merchant mills, which produced flour or meal from grain brought in by local farmers, formed the center of activity in rural communities and thereby made the miller a prominent person. Often, in fact, communities grew up around mills, which were constructed in the floodplains of rivers and streams. The mill's first floor was usually of stone, with two or three frame floors above and two in the attic to handle the process of sifting grain. Sometimes these upper floors were constructed of stone or brick.[115]

Most mills were built to the standards found in Oliver Evans's *The Young Millwright and Miller's Guide* of 1795. Even the inventive Thomas Jefferson agreed to pay Evans for using his patents in rebuilding the family mill at Shadwell.[116] Originally, waterwheels were made of wood, and it was not until 1852 that John Fitz Wheel Company of Hanover, Pennsylvania, began manufacturing metal wheels that quickly became the vogue. These metal wheels in turn often were sacrificed as scrap iron during various wars.

Barns too sometimes sheltered animal-operated gristmills, in which a mule or other work animal was hitched

Fig. 75. Glebe of Saint Anne's Parish, c. 1765

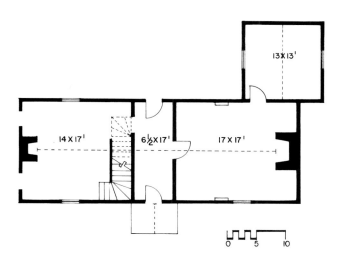

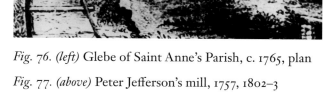

Fig. 76. (left) Glebe of Saint Anne's Parish, c. 1765, plan

Fig. 77. (above) Peter Jefferson's mill, 1757, 1802–3

to a beam that turned grindstones when the animal walked in a circle around them. One such mill was in the barn at Enniscorthy on Green Mountain that was demolished in 1993.

The early records of Albemarle County mention several mills. The first, a water-powered gristmill on Preddy's Creek, appeared in 1742. Three more mills were noted in 1745: John Key's, Davis Stockton's, and Moses Higginbottom's. And the following year the records

mentioned Secretary Carter's mill on the Hardware River at Carter's Bridge.[117]

Peter Jefferson's mill on the Rivanna River at Shadwell was built about 1757. It was damaged in the "Great Freshet" of 1771 and rebuilt (figs. 77, 78) in 1802–3 for his son Thomas as a 40-by-60-foot three-story building with two attic floors and two waterwheels. John M. Perry was the carpenter and James Walker the millwright. In 1829 Thomas Jefferson's heirs sold the mill complex for

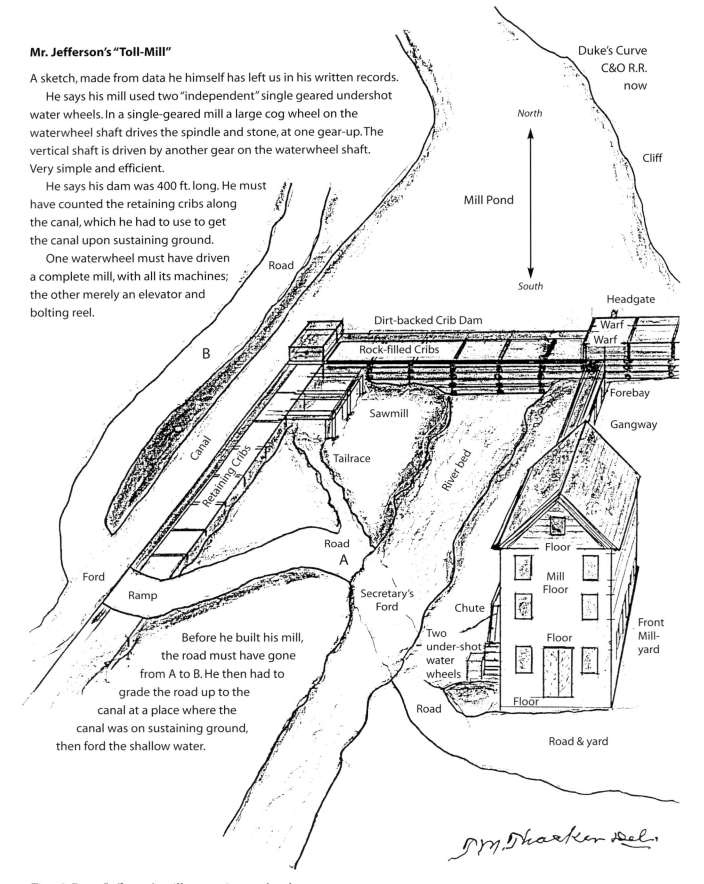

Mr. Jefferson's "Toll-Mill"

A sketch, made from data he himself has left us in his written records.

He says his mill used two "independent" single geared undershot water wheels. In a single-geared mill a large cog wheel on the waterwheel shaft drives the spindle and stone, at one gear-up. The vertical shaft is driven by another gear on the waterwheel shaft. Very simple and efficient.

He says his dam was 400 ft. long. He must have counted the retaining cribs along the canal, which he had to use to get the canal upon sustaining ground.

One waterwheel must have driven a complete mill, with all its machines; the other merely an elevator and bolting reel.

Before he built his mill, the road must have gone from A to B. He then had to grade the road up to the canal at a place where the canal was on sustaining ground, then ford the shallow water.

Fig. 78. Peter Jefferson's mill, 1757, 1802–3, sketch

$10,000 to John Bowie Magruder, his son Colonel James R. Magruder, and his son-in-law John Timberlake; Timberlake became the sole owner in 1843. In 1851 a devastating fire ravaged the mills, entirely destroying the cotton factory here. By 1860 the mill had been rebuilt and was advertised for sale as the "most valuable site for manufacturing and milling purposes." The tract consisted of 370 acres and contained a 50-by-140-foot five-story brick cotton factory, a flour mill, a gristmill, a sawmill, and a millhouse, as well as housing for 150 employees. The war intervened, however, and no sale was made. In 1898 Charlottesville Woolen Mills acquired the tract.[118]

Parts of other gristmill complexes that date to the mid–eighteenth century still stand in Albemarle County. The stone John Cochran's millhouse (figs. 79, 80), on Meadow Creek just north of Charlottesville, dates perhaps to 1754. The property contained a 36-by-50-foot three-story stone mill. It was part of the Pen Park property that John Harvie Jr. owned from 1750 to 1786. Harvie's father served as one of the guardians of Thomas Jefferson after Peter Jefferson's death. In 1786 Dr. George Gilmer, one of Jefferson's physicians, purchased the mill;

in 1852 John Cochran acquired it. In the Germanic fashion the millhouse was built over a spring that issues from the cellar floor. The mill itself no longer survives. Merrie Mill (fig. 81), built about 1764 at Cismont for Colonel John Walker of Belvoir, is two stories high, constructed of stone with one frame story above, and contains double attics. It is abandoned and in a ruinous condition.[119]

Several extant mills and millhouses date from the latter part of the eighteenth century. Walker's mill (fig. 82), constructed by Thomas Walker Jr. near the Orange County line on present-day Route 231, contained a date stone above the entrance inscribed "T. W. 1783." Its wooden waterwheel was replaced by a metal wheel made by the Fitz Wheel Company of Hanover, Pennsylvania, which began making metal wheels in 1852. It burned in 1983 and has since been converted into a dwelling. Its earlier one-story frame millhouse (fig. 83) was on a hill across Happy or Howard Creek and dated to about 1756. It was relocated in 1973 to the Buena Vista property. Samuel Dyer's mill (fig. 84) and millhouse on Totier Creek at Glendower dated to about 1790. The 38-by-40-foot mill had two stories of stone with a frame story above and served as a merchant

Fig. 79. John Cochran's millhouse, c. 1754

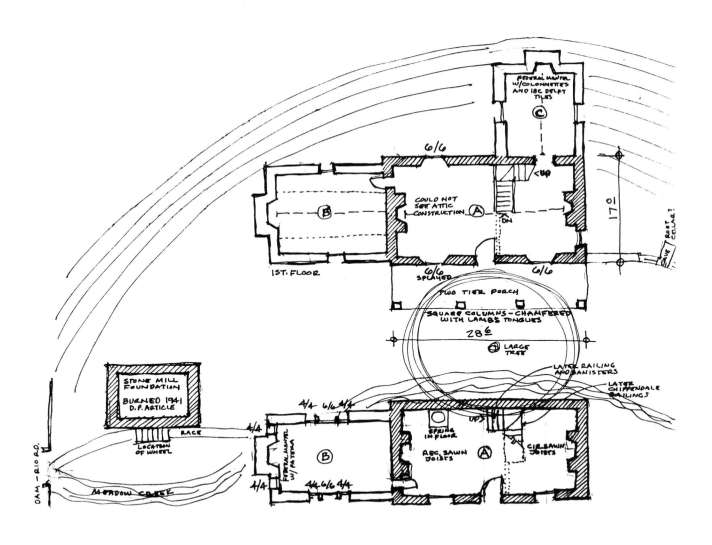

STONE MILL
FOUNDATION
BURNED 1941
D. P. ARTICLE

Fig. 80. (above) John Cochran's millhouse, c. 1754, plan

Fig. 81. (right) Merrie Mill, c. 1764

Fig. 82. Thomas Walker Jr.'s mill, 1783

Fig. 83. Thomas Walker Jr.'s millhouse, c. 1756

Fig. 84. Samuel Dyer's mill, c. 1790

mill for Samuel Dyer. Tsuquatantia (fig. 85), the 1792 mill-house built for James Powell Cocke's gristmill on the Hardware River at Edgemont, is only one of two hall-parlor, two-story stone millhouses extant in the county, the other being Cochran's. After Cocke's death in 1829, the mill was operated successively by the Coles and Johnson families and remained a commercial operation until the 1930s. It burned in the 1940s, and parts of its machinery were reinstalled in an outbuilding at Morrisena. The 1795 Jarman-Harris mill on Mechum's River, built by Captain William Jarman, burned in 1860 and was rebuilt in 1869 by R. F. Harris, but it burned again in 1951, and today only the two-story log millhouse survives. Hartman's mill was on Moore's Creek south of Charlottesville; a mill had stood on that site since the eighteenth century. Later, the Farish family operated Hartman's mill.[120]

At Warren was located Robert Carter Nicholas's 1759 gristmill as well as two later mills near the James River at the mouth of Ballenger's Creek. One was a merchant mill, a 40-by-60-foot brick structure with three waterwheels that was built about 1793. It was operated by the partnership of Samuel Shelton, William Walker, and John Staples.[121] Another

large merchant mill, erected by the Henderson family, was at Milton.

Warehouses

Tobacco warehouses once were located at every river port in the county. John Henderson's warehouses were constructed in Milton as early as 1789. All its buildings were one-story frame structures: three warehouses, including one 112 feet long, one scale house, and a transfer house. Across the Rivanna River in North Milton was the one-story, 42-by-200-foot-long stone warehouse owned by Thomas Mann Randolph Jr. of Edgehill and the one-story, 40-by-200-foot-long stone and frame warehouse of John H. Craven, John P. Sampson, and Stapleton C. Sneed. By 1803 William Robertson and Jacob Kinney's warehouses were built near Warren. One-story frame structures, they included three warehouses and a counting house or scale house.[122]

Furnaces and Forges

In the second half of the eighteenth century, John Old of Berks County, Pennsylvania, established an iron furnace on the Hardware River and a forge on Ammonett Branch near Garland's tavern. These enterprises evolved into the Albemarle Iron Works, in which John Wilkinson and Thomas Walker of Castle Hill were partners. Ruins of both structures still can be seen. Another eighteenth-century forge was located near Carter's Bridge. In the nineteenth century the Bateman Foundry at Howardsville produced plow castings.[123]

Fig. 85. Tsuquatantia millhouse, 1792

COMMERCIAL BUILDINGS

Taverns

Eighteenth- and nineteenth-century travelers noted that they could "scarcely pass ten or twenty miles without seeing an ordinary. They all resemble each other, having a porch in front, the length of the house, almost covered with handbills. They have no sign. These Virginia taverns take their name from the person who keeps the house, who is often a man of consequence." The typical ordinary consisted of "a little house placed in a solitary situation in the middle of the woods" that also served as the dwelling of its owner, and it frequently accommodated many lodgers in cramped quarters.[124]

Several terms were used in reference to these accommodations, all of which offered food, drink, lodging, and stabling but no doubt differed widely in the quality of service. An ordinary (apparently derived from the ordinary or set meals it offered), also called a public house or house of public entertainment, was used as a hotel by travelers. A house of private entertainment was a short-term boardinghouse where lodgers typically stayed a few days at most. Taverns offered more elaborate amenities, and they also served as community social centers where people gathered for gaming and to conduct business. Sometimes they functioned as stagecoach stops, as stores, and, if located on a turnpike, as tollhouses.[125]

Primarily to control the sale of liquor, county courts licensed public accommodations and also set the rates they could charge. The licenses were renewable annually, and state license fees were charged after the Revolutionary War. The first tavern license issued in Albemarle County after its creation was given to Daniel Scott on 25 July 1745. His tavern probably was located at Belle Grove; until recently, a 26-by-40-foot Flemish-bond foundation was visible here. The first county court order book (1744–48) reported licenses issued to five innkeepers, including Peter Jefferson.[126]

Nathaniel Burnley's tavern (fig. 86), on Corsey's Road at Stony Point, includes a one-story log portion that allegedly dates from 1740, making it perhaps the earliest such structure in Albemarle County. The one-story

Fig. 86. Nathaniel Burnley's tavern, 1740, 1776

Fig. 87. (right)
James Black's tavern, 1746

Fig. 88. (below)
D. S. Tavern, 1741

frame section of the building contains a board inscribed with the date 1776. The county records confirm that in the eighteenth century Thomas Burch kept a tavern at Stony Point, and as early as 1805 William Smith and Nathan Breedlove operated one here. By 1829 Nathaniel Burnley ran it. In 1938–39 Audrey Emery relocated the tavern to Key West in Albemarle County with the aid of architect Milton Grigg.[127]

Another extant inn, allegedly dating to 1746, James Black's tavern (fig. 87), for which Black obtained licenses in the 1780s and 1790s, is a one-story log structure on the former Rockfish Gap Turnpike. Here, in the fall of 1777, General George Rogers Clark was a lodger. In 1819 Alexander Garrett, the proctor of the university, bought the tavern.[128]

The D. S. Tavern (fig. 88), owned by U.S. Supreme Court justice John Marshall from 1809 to 1813, is at the zero milepost on the Three Notch'd Road. The letters

D. S. probably refer either to Davis (or David) Stockton, who blazed a trail from Williamsburg to "the wilds of Goochland" in the mid–eighteenth century, or to the dissenters at the Presbyterian church nearby. One of the most interesting features of this two-story log and frame building is its tap-bar "cage," into which are inscribed the date 1786 and the initials C. B., presumably for Claudius Buster who kept a tavern here from about 1785 to 1807. The older log section of the tavern is said to have been a 1741 claim house. In 1977 Clarence J. and Mary Ann Elder meticulously restored the building.[129]

A second tavern lovingly restored by the Elders and Munsey and Jean Wheby in 1985 is the frame Woodstock Hall (fig. 89) on Dick Woods's Road, which joined the Three Notch'd Road at the D. S. Tavern. Woodstock Hall's two-story, hall-parlor wing probably was built by David Lewis as a dwelling in 1757. Richard Woods acquired the place about 1771, and it was here that the duc de La Rochefoucauld-Liancourt lodged in 1796. He wrote that "Mr. Woods inn is so good and cleanly . . . that I cannot forbear mentioning those circumstances with

pleasure." The two-story frame Roman Revival–style wing added in 1808 has a date board on which is inscribed "Hell and Damnation—Captain Woods" and "January 14, 1808." The inscriptions may have been written by Richard's son, surveyor William Woods Sr., a captain in the Albemarle County Light Infantry. Both Woodses, father and son, owned racehorses, some of which were acquired from the stables of John Randolph of Roanoke. Of the twelve persons licensed to operate ordinaries in 1805, the personal property tax lists for that year showed that William Woods Sr. was assessed the highest amount. This 1808 section was built as though it were the center pavilion of a tripartite house. A five-course American-bond brick kitchen and slave quarters with a mousetooth brick cornice is also on the property.[130]

The Michie Tavern (fig. 90) is perhaps the best-known ordinary in Albemarle County. William Michie opened it in 1784 in his dwelling built some twelve years earlier on the Buck Mountain Road in the northern part of the county (Major John Henry, the father of Patrick Henry, first acquired the land in 1746). The tavern was disman-

Fig. 89. Woodstock Hall, 1757, 1808

tled and reassembled near Monticello in 1927–28 to exhibit the extensive antique furniture collection owned by Mrs. Mark Henderson. On the road to Monticello, the tavern attracted tourists in an era of improved roads, the ease of travel that the automobile offered, and increased leisure time. Part of the tavern served as Milton Grigg's architectural office after he purchased the building in 1932. Michie Tavern features an exterior porch taproom

and interior woodwork and mantels that were removed from Colle. Today the tavern is part of a museum complex of relocated historic buildings. One of the outbuildings, the necessary house, was listed in records as containing a rope suspended over the privy hole by a frustrated innkeeper so that drunken guests who got stuck could pull themselves out.[131]

The marquis de Lafayette visited Boyd's tavern (fig. 91) on the Three Notch'd Road during the Revolution as well as on his return to America in 1824 and enjoyed its arrack punch. Built about 1780, the tavern was purchased in 1803 by Thomas Duckett Boyd, later allegedly a builder at the university. Boyd's tavern burned twice, in 1790 and in 1868, and was restored once again in 1978.[132]

The two-story frame La Fourche Tavern, also on the Three Notch'd Road but at the intersection with the Fredericksburg road, was built by John Everett in 1788. Originally called Travellers' Grove, its original portion forms the nucleus of extensive additions.[133]

Fig. 90. (left) William Michie's tavern, c. 1772

Fig. 91. (below) Thomas Duckett Boyd's tavern, c. 1780, 1868

In Charlottesville two taverns were built adjacent to Court Square in the eighteenth century, and by 1835 three hotels and one tavern operated in the town. The first, the Swan Tavern, was constructed by John Jouett Sr. in 1773 just east of the square. In 1781 Jouett's son Jack made his famous ride from Cuckoo Tavern in Louisa County to warn Jefferson of the approach of the British raiding party commanded by Lieutenant Colonel Banastre Tarleton. Since the Swan Tavern was near the courthouse, it apparently drew rowdy crowds; eventually proprietor Jesse Davenport closed the public barroom and sold liquor only to lodgers in their rooms to maintain "a calm and quiet house." The brick Redland Club constructed in 1832 now occupies the Swan Tavern site.[134]

The second early Charlottesville ordinary, the Eagle Tavern, was built on town lot number 1 southeast of the courthouse about 1791 for Benjamin Brown and David Ross. It was a two-story, 33-by-66-foot frame building with a piazza that sheltered the length of its street facade, and a one-story, 23-by-57-foot brick dining-room addition in back. At the turn of the nineteenth century, it was operated first by John M. Sheppard, then by Thomas Wells, in 1829 by Opie Norris and William D. Fitch, and in 1833 by John Vowles.[135] Fitch also ran a tavern in the Dyer house on the corner of Seventh and East Jefferson Streets.

EDUCATIONAL BUILDINGS

A farm or plantation sometimes included a school among its outbuildings, where family children could be instructed by tutors. Several still stand in the county, such as those at Arrowhead, Cliffside, and Dawson's mill. The stone foundation of the original house at Arrowhead, built about 1828 by Dr. Charles E. and Frances E. Meriwether, is still evident in the cellar of the present house, built for Henry Carter Moore. At the turn of the twentieth century, wings were added for Samuel Baker Woods, Charlottesville's first twentieth-century mayor and the son of the Reverend Edgar Woods, the author in 1901 of the first definitive Albemarle County history.[136]

In the eighteenth century the Reverend James Maury's Anglican classical school at Edgeworth numbered as alumni five signers of the Declaration of Independence and U.S. presidents Jefferson and Madison. The property had been the Fredericksville Parish glebe. In 1825 William Fitzhugh Gordon purchased it as a residence; it burned in February 1835, and Gordon then built the present Edgeworth. In the late eighteenth century,

the Reverend Samuel Black's classical school was conducted for Presbyterians in his home near Mechum's River.[137]

TRANSPORTATION STRUCTURES

Ferries

The first mention of ferries in the county court order books appeared in the mid-1740s with Daniel Scott's ferry on the James River at Scottsville and Captain Charles Lynch's ferry on the Rivanna River at Pen Park. About the mid–twentieth century, two ferries remained in the county on the James River at Hatton and Warren. Today only the Hatton Ferry survives.[138]

Road Bridges

The first bridge in the county was built in 1740 over Mechunk Creek. The county court order books from 1749 through 1782 were destroyed by the British during the Revolution, but a 1783 order mentioned that John Prince had built a bridge over the Hardware River the previous year. Many of the bridges were weatherboarded and covered to protect the structure from the elements, such as the Free Bridge (fig. 92) over the Rivanna River at the eastern entrance to Charlottesville.[139]

Canals

The Rivanna River was opened for navigation about 1789. Founded in 1827, the Rivanna Navigation Company invested more than $350,000 through 1860 in a canal system from Moore's Creek at Charlottesville along the Rivanna to Point of Fork at Columbia in Fluvanna County.[140]

The James River and Kanawha Company was formed in 1785 and acquired by the state in 1820. Its canal paralleled the north side of the James River and finally opened all of its 147½ miles between Richmond and Lynchburg in 1840.

Remnants of canal locks still exist as well as a 30-foot-wide stone aqueduct (fig. 93) at Warren on the James River; the Pireus dam built by William D. Meriwether in 1829 can still be seen at the Charlottesville Woolen Mills site on the Rivanna River. Other dams, locks, and culverts exist at Milton, Shadwell, Stump Island, Hatton, and Warren. Neither canal system reached its full potential before the advent of railroads, the beginning of the Civil War, and the floods of 1870 and 1877 brought about their demise. Canal traffic finally ceased in the early 1880s, and new railroad tracks were laid on the old James River and Kanawha Canal towpaths.[141]

Fig. 92. (above)
Free Bridge over
Rivanna River,
19C, engraving

Fig. 93. (right)
James River and
Kanawha Canal
stone aqueduct at
Warren, M19C

II

Thomas Jefferson and His Builders

THE JEFFERSON INFLUENCE

At Thomas Jefferson's 250th Birthday Celebration at the University of Virginia on 13 April 1993, Mikhail Gorbachev stated that "having once begun a dialogue with Jefferson, one continues the conversation forever." Jefferson, as a new member of Congress, was referred to as "a gentleman of thirty-two who could calculate an eclipse, survey an estate, tie an artery, plan an edifice, try a cause, break a horse, dance a minuet, and play the violin." The man who would become the nation's third president was born on 13 April 1743 at Shadwell and died on the Fourth of July 1826, within a few hours of the death of John Adams and fifty years to the day after the publication of the Declaration of Independence, which Jefferson wrote. He has been described as "the man of this millennium." During his lifetime he played many other roles — lawyer, colonial legislator, revolutionary leader, governor, diplomat, secretary of state, vice president, architect, and landscape architect. He spoke five languages, read in seven languages, and accumulated three libraries, the largest containing about 7,000 volumes. Our understanding of Jefferson is enriched by the fact that he left some 65,000 documents behind, including 19,000 of his personal letters and more than 500 drawings. From these voluminous records, and from the buildings Jefferson designed, it may be argued that his political influence was equaled by his architectural significance.[1]

In 1780 the state capital was moved from Williamsburg to Richmond, and Jefferson was appointed to head a committee for the public buildings to be constructed there. In 1784 he replaced Benjamin Franklin as minister to France, and during a visit to Nîmes, he saw the first-century B.C. Maison Carrée, considered by Jefferson "the best morsel of ancient architecture now remaining." It became his model for the new Virginia Capitol and as such

ushered in the Classical Revival period, being the first building patterned after an ancient Roman temple. It antedated by twenty years the 1807 Madeleine in Paris, one of the first European temple reproductions. Peter Harrison's Redwood Library in Newport, Rhode Island, had preceded it in 1750, but that structure's form was not from an extant ancient temple but from Palladian influences in eighteenth-century publications; in addition, as a state capitol Jefferson's temple had much greater influence. At Jefferson's request a plaster model of the Maison Carrée was constructed, "only changing the order from the Corinthian to Ionic, on account of the difficulty of the Corinthian capitals," and shipped to Richmond to be used together with Jefferson's drawings in the construction of the capitol.[2]

Monticello

At a presidential reception for Nobel Prize winners in 1962, President John F. Kennedy told his guests that they represented the most extraordinary assemblage of talent and knowledge ever gathered at the White House with the possible exception of occasions when Thomas Jefferson dined alone. Jefferson began to put his talent and knowledge to the service of architecture almost twenty years before he designed the Virginia State Capitol when, at the age of twenty-six, he leveled a hilltop and began to build his house Monticello (Little Mountain) in 1768. The first house was a tripartite form similar to the William Finnie (formerly James Semple) house in Williamsburg, but Monticello had a two-tier portico and demioctagonal rooms, one of the first such figural spaces in America. Its facade resembled Palladio's Villa Pisani at Montagnana in Italy.[3]

While in France, Jefferson observed a contemporary

building under construction across from the Louvre. He later wrote that Monticello "is not without precedent in my own history. While at Paris, I was violently smitten with the 'Hotel de Salm,' and used to go to the Tuileries almost daily to look at it." That private home's dome affected the evolution of Jefferson's thinking about the use of one at Monticello, and its U-shaped colonnade later influenced the design of the University of Virginia. Seven years after Jefferson's return to America in 1789, he began to alter his main house (fig. 94), enlarging it to thirty-three rooms with thirteen skylights, replacing the two-tier portico with a tetrastyle templelike one, and introducing a dome—the first visible on the exterior of an American house—and the half floor, which he had seen at the Hôtel de Salm. As he exclaimed, "Architecture is my delight, and putting up and pulling down one of my favorite amusements." In 1809, when Jefferson retired from the presidency at the age of sixty-five, Monticello was virtually complete, the culmination of forty years of pulling down and putting up. This remarkable house by one of the nation's most revered founding fathers is an amalgam of Roman, Palladian, and French architectural ideals. The Thomas Jefferson Memorial Foundation has maintained the estate since 1923.[4]

Octagonal Houses

Jefferson designed a house for his friend James Powell Cocke in 1793 at Edgemont in southern Albemarle County. The house exhibited a demioctagonal salon projection patterned after Palladio's Villa Capra in Vicenza. In 1802 Jefferson designed an octagonal addition to an earlier farmhouse in the county, Farmington, owned by another friend, George Divers.

In 1804 Jefferson envisioned an octagonal house in combination with rectangular spaces for his daughter Maria, wife of John W. Eppes, and leveled the site east of Charlottesville at Pantops to accommodate it. The house was never built because Maria died that year, but two years later he began a similar dwelling on land inherited by his late wife from her family. It was ninety miles away from Monticello in Bedford County and was designed to be a country retreat.[5] Jefferson patterned Poplar Forest,

Fig. 94. Monticello, 1768–1809, engraving

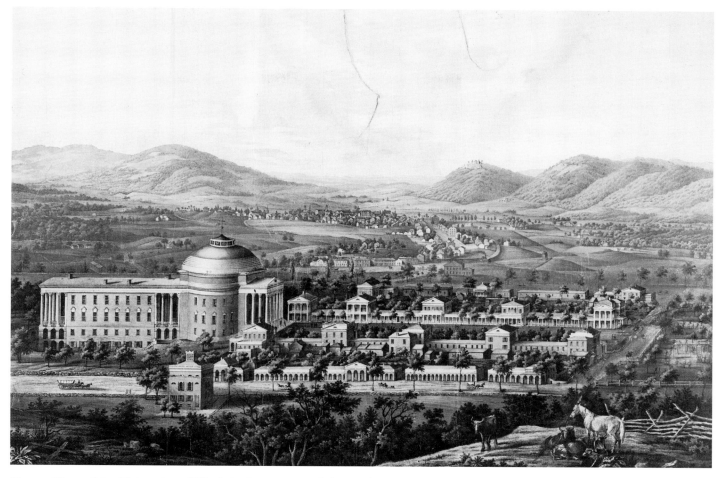

Fig. 95. View of the University of Virginia, from an 1856 lithograph

the first octagonal house built in America, after a plate in William Kent's *Designs of Inigo Jones* of 1727. It is a perfect cube in which the chimneys form diagonals to create octagonal rooms; he also laid out its grounds with geometric precision. Poplar Forest features a rear facade that demonstrates the first use of a portico over an arcade; the second was Jefferson's later use of the same portico design on Pavilion VII at the University of Virginia.[6]

The University of Virginia

Jefferson wished his gravestone epitaph to read "Author of the Declaration of Independence, of the Statute of Virginia for Religious Freedom, and the Father of the University of Virginia" because, as he stated, it was "by these as testimonials that I have lived I wish most to be remembered." Jefferson's crowning architectural achievement, the University of Virginia (figs. 95, 96), was designated by the American Institute of Architects in 1976 as the "proudest achievement of American architecture in the past 200

years." It was begun in 1817, when he was seventy-four years old, and completed at his death at age eighty-three in 1826. The Lawn, as he wrote, was the "hobby of my old age." He referred to the University of Virginia as the "last of my mortal cares, and the last service that I can render my country." He also referred to it as his "academical village," "based on the illimitable freedom of the human mind." As early as 1805 Jefferson stated that his "university would be a village, not a big building," and when he envisioned his Central College, he thought of it as the "germ from which a great tree may spread itself."[7]

In 1818 the Virginia General Assembly granted $15,000 to establish a state university and the next year chartered the University of Virginia at the site of Central College. The university opened for classes in 1825 and since then has matriculated many significant people, including poet Edgar Allan Poe, typhoid and yellow fever conqueror Walter Reed, U.S. president Woodrow Wilson, polar explorer Richard E. Byrd, U.S. vice president Alben

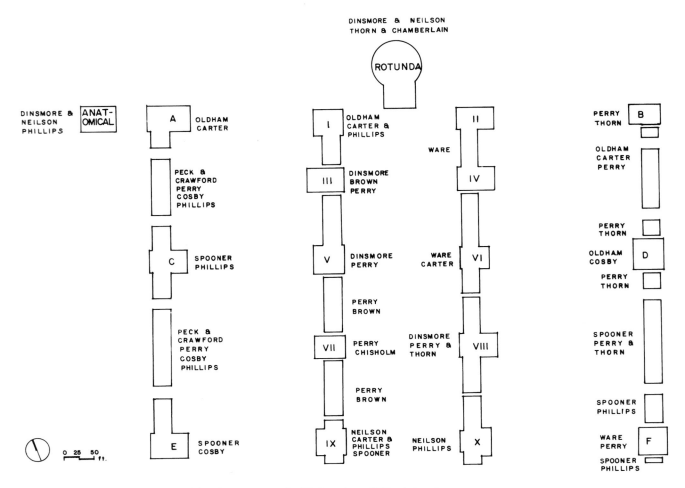

Fig. 96. Principal carpenters and brickmasons at the University of Virginia, 1817–25

Barkley, Attorney General Robert F. Kennedy, Senator Edward M. Kennedy, and at least seven governors.[8]

Jefferson revered the work of the sixteenth-century Italian architect Andrea Palladio. In fact, he owned five editions of Palladio's *Quattro Libri*; one was a pocket version. Isaac Coles, one of Jefferson's friends, paraphrased his attitude toward Palladio and his architectural philosophy for a mutual friend, General John Hartwell Cocke, in 1816: "Palladio he said 'was the Bible.' You should get it and stick close to it. . . . The height of a room should be equal to its width. . . . The Tuscan order was too plain—it would do for your barns, etc., but was not fit for a dwelling House—the Doric would not cost much more & would be vastly handsomer. . . . Dinsmore he recommends . . . as a good and faithful workman [who] would build you a house without any false architecture, so much the rage at present."[9]

Jefferson based his designs for the university on both Palladio's examples and his own knowledge of ancient ar-

chitecture. The Roman Pantheon of 126 A.D., with which Jefferson was familiar through the books of Palladio and others, served as model for the Lawn's Rotunda. This domed building to house the library became a half-scale version of the Pantheon; its central position in Jefferson's composition was suggested by architect B. Henry Latrobe. The Hôtel de Salm already had influenced Jefferson's remodeling of Monticello; with its colonnaded courtyard, it also might have inspired the Lawn itself. Certainly, the Château de Marly near Versailles and the Certosa di Pavia, which he also visited, have similarities to the layout of the buildings that form the Lawn. In 1810 Jefferson had recommended such a plan for the University of Tennessee, and his plan in turn resembled Union College in Schenectady, New York, designed by Jean Jacques Ramée and built two years earlier, although there is no evidence Jefferson knew of its plan.[10]

For the site of the university, Jefferson preferred a tract owned by John Kelly north of the Three Notch'd Road half a mile west of Charlottesville, but Kelly would not sell it. Advertisements for sites resulted in offers from John H. Craven to part with his land north of town; Nicholas Lewis, his land that lay east of town; and John M. Perry, his tract one mile west (fig. 97). Perry's offer was the least expensive, and the cornerstone of Pavilion VII was laid on 6 October 1817 with Perry and three U.S. presidents, Jefferson, Madison, and Monroe, present.[11]

Jefferson, his master joiner James Dinsmore, and Captain Edmund Bacon, his overseer for twenty years at Monticello, earlier had laid out the foundation of the university. As Bacon recalled about 1861:

My instruction was to get 10 able-bodied hands to commence the work. I soon got them, and Mr. Jefferson started . . . to lay off the foundation. . . . An Irishman named Dinsmore and I went along with him. . . . I went to Davy Isaacs's store and got a ball of twine, and Dinsmore found some shingles and made some pegs. . . . Mr. Jefferson looked over the ground some time and then stuck down a peg . . . and then directed me to where to carry the line, and I stuck the second. He carried one end of the line, and I the other, in laying of the foundation. He had a little rule in his pocket . . . a small 12 inch rule . . .

3 inches long when folded . . . that he always carried with him, and with this he measured off the ground and laid off the entire foundation, and then set the men at work.

Bacon later stated that "Dinsmore . . . was the most ingenious hand to work with wood I ever knew. He could make anything. He made a great deal of nice mahogany furniture [and] helped make the carriage" together with the slave John Hemings.[12]

At 3:00 P.M. on 5 November 1824, to celebrate the return of the marquis de Lafayette to America, a dinner was held in the partially completed Rotunda. Some 400 guests sat at tables arranged in three concentric circles. A feeble Jefferson came down the mountain from Monticello for the affair, and James Dinsmore was one of many to give a toast to "Mr. Jefferson," in his case to "Thomas Jefferson, founder of the University of Virginia."[13]

Anatomical Hall, a dissection theater, was one of the last buildings of Jefferson's design and was completed after his death. It was square in plan with stepped seating on all four sides and surrounded by wall lunettes and a lantern at its roof peak. It was razed in 1938 when Alderman Library was built, the only Jefferson-designed building at the university to be razed, other than a student room.[14]

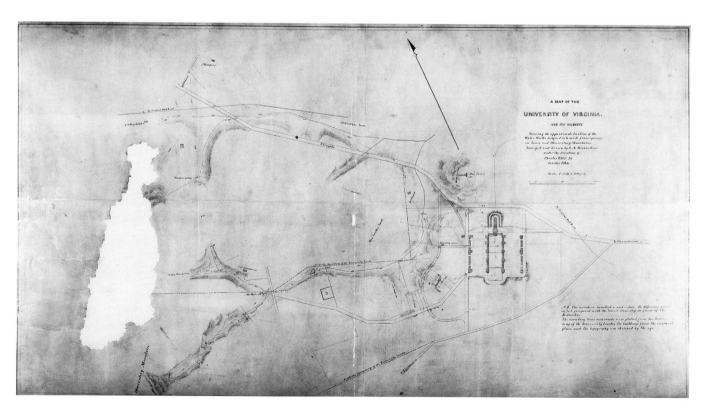

Fig. 97. Plat of the University of Virginia and its vicinity, 1850s

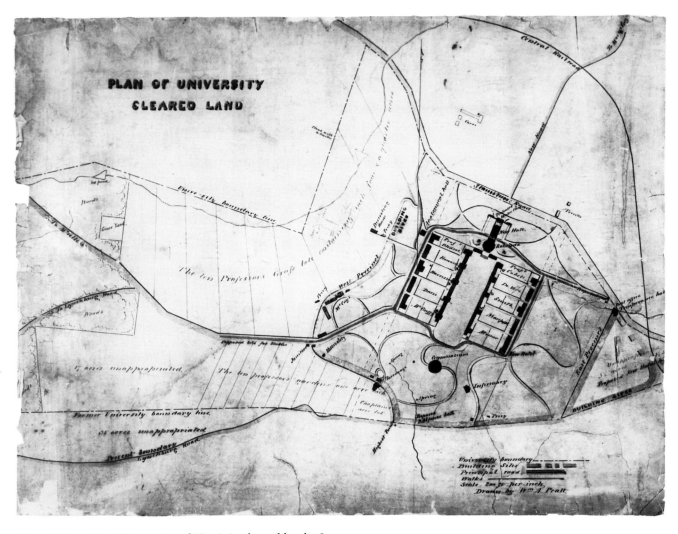

Fig. 98. Plat of the University of Virginia cleared land, 1850s

As with Monticello, Jefferson's university and Lawn are studies in the contradictions and inconsistencies that so enrich architecture. Although the academical village appears to be symmetrical, it is a subtle study in asymmetry. No two of its ten Pavilion plans are alike. Pavilion doors do not align across the Lawn, and each pavilion exhibits a different architectural facade composition, in keeping with Jefferson's intention that they serve the students as models of the different orders of ancient architecture.

The Lawn itself has receding terraces that slope from north to south as do the west gardens, while just to the west of the West Range, the land slopes from south to north. The east gardens are twenty feet wider than those on the west and slope steeply from west to east. And the brick serpentine wall–enclosed pavilion gardens on both sides expand from north to south to accommodate the increasing

number of student rooms between pavilions. All of this can only be comprehended by moving about the exterior spaces.

Beyond the gardens on each side are the Ranges, which include three hotels, where students dined. Behind each hotel a serpentine wall subdivided the gardens, which probably were intended to provide plots for growing vegetables for hotel use. Between each garden was a macadamized alley that permitted access to the Lawn from the Ranges, in perhaps one of the first uses of such paving in America.[15] Archaeological research is being conducted to determine if this was the original paving, as it was on the road at the edge of the West Range. The increasing number of student rooms and the sloping parterres gave the illusion of greater perspective from the south where the Lawn was entered from the old Three Notch'd Road. At this point was constructed an element that functioned as a ha-ha, in this case a lower parterre with a retaining wall that prevented cattle from entering the Lawn and, because the feature was devoid of a fence, allowed an unobstructed view. Jefferson intended the Lawn itself to be expanded by extending its student rooms, pavilions, and colonnades to the south as needed.

Aside from grass, the Lawn at first had little landscaping, but by 1830 it contained double rows of locust trees along each side.[16] By midcentury, grass fields to the west and garden plots to the southwest of the Lawn were designated for use by the ten faculty members (fig. 98).

In most colleges of the day, especially those laid out in a similar manner, the central building was the chapel. At the University of Virginia, however, the central Rotunda, patterned after Rome's Pantheon, became the school's center of learning, the library. In its dome room, which utilized a wooden Philibert de l'Orme truss as at Monticello to support the roof, Jefferson envisioned the ceiling painted blue with gilt stars to depict the constellations. Had the project been completed, it would have produced the first planetarium in America. The Rotunda's double-curved spaces on the two lower levels were the first such cyma spaces seen in the United States.

The East and West Ranges, with student rooms between their hotels, each have an all-weather passage composed of brick arcades; one-story, Tuscan-columned colonnades on each side of the Lawn serve the same purpose. It has been recently observed that the colonnade originally had its columns of pie-shaped bricks covered probably with unpainted brownish stucco to resemble stone and its bases and capitals cut from stone, as Jefferson himself suggested: "Would it not be best to make the internal columns of well-burnt brick, moulded in portions of circles adapted to the diminution of the columns? Burlington, in his notes on Palladio, tells us that he found most of the buildings erected under Palladio's direction, and described in his architecture, to have their columns made of brick in this way and covered with stucco. I know an instance of a range of six or eight columns in Virginia, twenty feet high, well proportioned and properly diminished, executed by a common bricklayer. The bases and capitals would of course be of hewn stone."[17] The colonnade passages on each side of the Lawn were connected at the Rotunda by two below-ground-level all-weather wings lighted by lunettes. These spaces formed the gymnasia, where Jefferson expected students to exercise.

The roofs of the Lawn colonnades, edged with wooden Chinese railings, were used by professors as private exterior passages linking the second floors of the pavilions, where the professors lived. These roofs were constructed in a manner similar to those on the Monticello terraces to form V-shaped conductors of rainwater to gutters and eventually to cisterns. Several of the pavilions had balconies hung with wrought-iron rods so they would not engage the columns. This is believed to be the first use of such suspended balconies in America.[18]

The lower Lawn level of each pavilion contained classrooms and sometimes an office. The land then sloped off enough to the rear of the pavilions to allow direct entrance to a ground-floor kitchen and sometimes a dining room. The pavilions originally had parapet walls that obscured their gables and gave the impression of flat roofs. Intricately folded Welsh tin covered the roofs themselves, similar to the roofing installed at Monticello after Jefferson had one of his master builders inspect an example in the Shenandoah Valley in 1818.

A JEFFERSON LEGACY: HIS MASTER BUILDERS

Thomas Jefferson employed more than 200 able craftsmen and builders during the late eighteenth and early nineteenth centuries to build his home, Monticello; his Bedford County retreat, Poplar Forest; and the University of Virginia. This number did not include the builders' slaves who also labored on the buildings or other workmen employed by the builders.[19]

The construction of the university on the former John M. Perry tract a mile west of Charlottesville in the foothills of the Ragged Mountains began in 1817, and that undertaking spurred similar activity throughout the community. Speculative development soon began along the Three Notch'd Road running through the open fields between the university and downtown. Such was the impact of Jefferson's construction project that the local labor pool was soon exhausted. Years earlier, in 1796, the duc de La Rochefoucauld-Liancourt had noted in his *Travels through the United States* that "there are not four stone masons in the whole county of Albemarle," and as late as 1819 one of Jefferson's master carpenters complained of "the difficulties we labor under here in procuring good workmen." Even before the university became a reality, Jefferson showed his concern by proposing a county technical school to offer instruction in architecture for builders and those interested in the fine arts. The school never materialized.[20]

The lack of sufficiently skilled local builders for the

university was quickly apparent, and advertisements in Staunton, Richmond, and Philadelphia newspapers in 1819 brought many to the university, including twenty from Philadelphia alone. Others came from as far away as Northern Ireland (then called Ulster), England, and Italy.[21] These carpenters, brickmasons, stonemasons, plasterers, painters, glaziers, and other craftsmen not only lived in the community but also undertook other projects in the region. Some of them were well-read and obviously educated. After Jefferson's death in 1826, many continued to practice their crafts in the area and produced some very fine buildings. A few deserve special mention because of their numerous contributions to the architecture of the community.

Two Ulster Builders

Referring on his seventy-fourth birthday to the construction of the university, Jefferson wrote: "I suppose the superintendence of the buildings will rest chiefly on myself as most convenient. So far as it does I should wish to commit it to yourself and Mr. Nelson . . . it will open a great field of future employment for you."[22] He was writing to forty-six-year-old James Dinsmore and referring to John Neilson, a two-man team of builders who had lived and worked at Monticello from 1798 and 1804, respectively, until 1808. They had been in President James Madison's employ at Montpelier until 1810 and then worked on Upper Bremo between 1817 and 1820. These two accomplished Ulstermen became Jefferson's most prominent master builders at the university and the overseers of his work. True to Jefferson's prediction, they remained in the forefront of American building activity until their deaths.

James Dinsmore, born about 1771, became a naturalized American citizen in Philadelphia on 5 June 1798. His tools, purchased there at Jefferson's expense, were sent to Monticello eight days later, and that October, Jefferson paid his travel expenses to Charlottesville. Until 1808 Dinsmore worked as a master carpenter at Monticello and also made window sash for Poplar Forest. On 14 April 1809 both he and Neilson left Monticello to work at Montpelier, where they added many classical details including a delightful Doric garden temple, probably from the design of Dr. William Thornton. In 1811 Dinsmore acquired a saw- and merchant mill at Pen Park north of Charlottesville in partnership with John H. Craven, who purchased Dinsmore's share in the enterprise four years later.[23]

Meanwhile, British troops had burned the nation's Capitol in 1814, and Jefferson recommended both Dins-

more and Neilson to B. Henry Latrobe for restoration work there:

[I] offer you two house joiners of the very first order both in their knolege in architecture, and their practical abilities. James Dinsmore . . . a more faithful, sober, honest and respectable man I have never known. . . . John Nielson, the other one . . . I have found him also an honest, sober, and excellent man. They have done the whole [work] of the joiner; work of my house, to which I can affirm I have never seen any superior in US. After they had finished with me they worked 2 or 3 years for the President [Madison], to whom, therefore they are well known. Mr. [Robert] Mills also knows them personally and their works.

It remains uncertain whether Dinsmore and Neilson ever actually worked on the Capitol. Latrobe mentioned in a 12 July 1815 letter to Jefferson that "Mr. Nelson arrived here, (as I understand for the 2d time) a few days ago, and is now in the city. Mr. Dinsmore I have not seen. But the Commissioners have not appointed either of them to any situation." By 1817 Dinsmore was in Petersburg, where he prepared some drawings for James Monroe for a house near Monroe's Highland.[24]

In subsequent years Dinsmore resided in Charlottesville in a tripartite house on West Main Street and speculated in property along that thoroughfare. Between 1818 and 1825, when the university began classes, he subdivided thirteen contiguous lots between what are now Tenth and Fourteenth Streets (fig. 99). Two purchasers of these lots were also Jefferson builders: Malcolm F. Crawford, a university carpenter, and Irishman John Gorman, a stonemason. Lyman Peck, also a carpenter, rented a dwelling here. Structures dating to the period include the razed Peter Heiskell house and the surviving Alexander St. Clair Heiskell and John Vowles town houses. Others built town houses along this street; the Johnson W. Pitts house (1820) and Paxton Place (1824) still stand. The Pitts house was purchased by an African American after the Civil War and thereby became one of Charlottesville's oldest black-owned stores. In 1819 Dinsmore purchased town lot number 22, and in 1827 he deeded a portion of that plot to the Presbyterian Church. He also owned more than 500 acres just south of town that he called Orange Dale.[25]

The tripartite house Oak Lawn, built for Colonel Nimrod Bramham in 1822 and perhaps the finest extant house within the Charlottesville city limits, is attributed to Dinsmore. During his tenure at the University of Virginia,

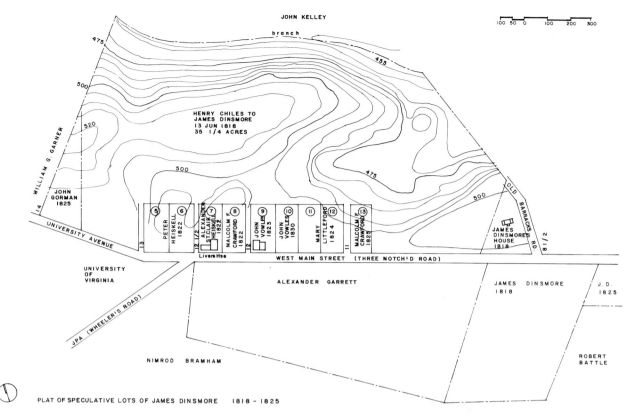

Fig. 99. Plat of the speculative lots of James Dinsmore, 1818–25

Dinsmore was the principal master carpenter for Pavilions III, V, and VIII, fourteen dormitories, and — in collaboration with John Neilson — the Rotunda and Anatomical Hall. Estouteville, on Green Mountain south of Charlottesville, is another of Dinsmore's crowning achievements. Constructed between 1827 and 1830, Estouteville is noted for its grand Tuscan exterior porticoes and great interior hall with an elaborate Doric frieze. Dinsmore may also have designed the exquisite Greek Revival–style Fluvanna County Courthouse. His brother John allegedly supervised this building's construction, as well as that of Estouteville, in 1830–31 after Dinsmore's death.[26]

On 13 May 1830, at the age of fifty-nine, Dinsmore drowned in the Rivanna River at Ridgway, northeast of Charlottesville. A week later his carpenter nephew Andrew committed suicide. Dinsmore's father had been twice married and sired sixteen children, several of whom came to America, but Dinsmore himself was probably unmarried. The Dinsmore family lineage can be traced to Achenmead, Scotland, in the early seventeenth century, but the family relocated to Northern Ireland about 1667, as did many lowland Protestant Scots. At the time of his death, his kinfolk resided in Ballymoney, County Antrim, in Northern Ireland.[27]

Dinsmore's will named his oldest brother, John, as his principal heir. Two other surviving brothers received bequests of $500: Robert, in Ireland, and William, who lived at Rock Hill in Charlottesville and later at Orange Dale. Another brother, Samuel, of Havre de Grace, Maryland, received $300 and Dinsmore's chest of tools, except for a set of bench tools and three saws "to my boy, John Boles," a free black cabinetmaker from Milton. Dinsmore's will also reflects his compassionate and sentimental nature. He wished that his slave Stella and her children should live with his brother John, "but in case she should object to going with him she is at liberty to chuse her master." The sum of $500 went to Charles Stewart "in consideration of his fidelity and helpless situation," and James Dinsmore Pickands, the oldest son of his deceased Philadelphia friend Thomas Pickands, was named "in consideration of . . . the affection I have for him."[28]

The auction of his personal property on 15 October 1830

included "twelve or fifteen negroes . . . all his household and kitchen furniture; his library of well selected books, among which are Low's *Encyclopedia*, and many other valuable works; his stock, among which are three horses, and one very valuable cow; his farming utensils, ploughs, harrows, etc., wagon and gear; an excellent horse cart; entire crop of wheat, rye, corn, oats, fodder, hay, etc. together with many other articles of personal property, remaining on the premises, too tedious to enumerate."[29]

While at Monticello, Dinsmore worked with Jefferson's talented slave John Hemings, a carpenter and house joiner. As early as 1793 Hemings was making window frames at Monticello and later the Chinese railings and venetian blinds for the porticoes here. In 1810 he made sash for Poplar Forest and in 1819 made venetian blinds there as well.[30]

Jefferson's other principal builder, Ulsterman John Neilson, was born before 1775 in Northern Ireland, where he was apprenticed to an architect-builder, a Mr. Hunter, in Belfast. Neilson and two of his brothers were accused of participating in the June 1798 insurrection there after guns were found in the house of their widowed mother, a schoolmistress, in Ballycarry, County Antrim. William Neilson, the youngest of the three, was hanged, and Samuel and John Neilson were exiled (Samuel for life and John for seven years) without trial under the Banishment Act. The brothers sailed from Belfast in May 1799; the French captured their ship, but it was retaken by the British and sailed to the West Indies. Samuel Neilson died on the voyage. John Neilson, fearing that he would be recruited into the British army, escaped to America, where he was naturalized in Philadelphia on 28 September 1804. From then until 1808 he lived and worked at Monticello. The following year he moved to Montpelier, where he worked until 1810. Neilson's most important work is Upper Bremo (commonly referred to simply as Bremo), which has been called "one of the finest Jeffersonian buildings not designed by Jefferson." The house is atop a bluff on the north side of the James River in Fluvanna County. It was built between 1817 and 1820 for General John Hartwell Cocke, who was a brigadier general in the War of 1812, a founder of the University of Virginia and a member of its Board of Visitors for thirty-three years, a president of the National Temperance Union, a senior vice president of the American Colonization Society, and the commissioner of roads for Virginia.[31]

Although Bremo is one story high on the northern facade, the land drops off enough toward the James River to the south for the structure to become two stories on its river front. But whereas Monticello was built into its hill in a U-shape, Bremo was erected in linear form atop a bluff, a site similar to Palladio's Villa Barbaro at Maser in Italy. The house contains many Jeffersonian features: 20-foot cubic spaces, dependencies recessed into the hillside, upper windows at floor level to reduce apparent scale, bed alcoves, a rotating food-serving door, and small stairs tucked away. It also has the first jalousies in America in its distyle-in-muris (two columns between square pillars or pilasters) river facade, the lower level of which was an orangery. On the north or land front is a ha-ha, a ditch that allows an unobstructed view from the house while preventing cattle from entering the front yard. The central block of the dwelling contains blind or false windows, and in the wings are plastered Palladian motifs that Cocke referred to as his "sham venetians." On the upper level, there are early built-in closets in the bedchamber as well as a transverse passage. The grounds contain diamond-notched log structures, pisé (rammed earth) buildings, and stone outbuildings with brick in the gables, in cornices, and above openings where stone would have been more difficult to place. The stone barn, perhaps the only classical example in America, was built in 1816.[32]

During Neilson's subsequent tenure at the university, he was the master carpenter for Pavilions IX and X and seven dormitories, as well for the Rotunda and the Anatomical Hall that he built with Dinsmore. Neilson constructed his own brick house on the south side of West Main Street in Random Row, in the Vinegar Hill vicinity. He built another house nearby on the north side of the street that his partner's nephew Andrew Dinsmore purchased in 1827. Neilson also owned a brick house at the intersection of West Main Street and Wheeler's Road, across from the present-day University Baptist Church.[33]

During Christmas 1826, while staying at his country house near Keene called Refuge, Neilson developed a "violent cold." This malady, combined with the sad news of his daughter's death, brought on an extended illness from which he died the following 24 June. Neilson was buried in an unmarked grave in Charlottesville's "public burying ground" (Maplewood Cemetery or its predecessor, now the site of the First Presbyterian Church on Park Street). Accounts for settlement of his estate indicate several buildings that are probably by his hand, including the now-altered Lewis Level near North Garden and the Southall-Venable house in Charlottesville, which later was razed for Lee Park.[34]

Neilson's will divided his estate among his wife, Mary, his brother Jackson, the children of his sisters Isabella and

Sarah, and a family friend, Mary Ann McCracken, all of Northern Ireland. The twelve-page inventory of his estate gives a vivid insight into the education and interests of this extraordinary man. His library, composed of 248 titles, contained encyclopedias, histories, literature, novels, travel accounts, orations, lectures, and books about botany, mathematics, and architecture. He owned drawing and artist's instruments, carpentry and gardening tools, and a camera obscura. The inventory also listed eleven slaves, numerous livestock, and various crops. Neilson obviously was a learned man of some financial means with desirable property. His library and household furniture were sold within two months of his death.[35]

Among Neilson's numerous prints and drawings were Latrobe's "View of the Capitol of the United States," "Jefferson's House in Bedford," the "Portico of Diocletian," and "Napoleon's Entry in Paris." He also owned medallions of Napoleon, Benjamin Franklin, and George Washington. While corresponding with Neilson's nephew in Ireland, the attorney for his estate mentioned that he had "discovered an excellent profile of your uncle among his prints, the correctness of the likeness will be admitted by all. . . . I reserved it for . . . one of his family." This profile, undoubtedly made with his camera obscura, was sent to his widow, who was then living in Belfast.[36]

Neilson's own drawings and paintings included a "book of drawings of the U.Va. by Jno. Neilson," a "book of drawings of the Ionic, Doric & Corinthian Orders," a "book of observations of the orders of architecture and intended to accompany this book of drawings of the orders," "3 books of drawings with drawings on oil paper," "a book of drawings and designs," renderings of the "Rotunda and two pavilions," and his "plan for University of Virginia with two ground plans." This list of his drawings and artist's implements suggests the possibility that some of the renderings attributed to Jefferson's granddaughter Cornelia Jefferson Randolph are actually those of John Neilson. Likewise, grid-paper drawings of the final Bremo, also attributed to Cornelia Randolph, are probably the original Neilson drawings that had long been missing.[37]

Apparently Neilson made other drawings, too. The original study for the Maverick engraving (fig. 100) of the University of Virginia is attributed to him. In 1823 he was selected to execute drawings for the Nelson County Jail with Phillips and Crawford as builders, and in that same year he sent Jefferson his rendering of "the north front of the Rotunda." That drawing is probably the one referred to in a letter from Neilson to General John Hartwell Cocke that depicted the Rotunda and the two end pavil-

ions. Another sketch, adapted from Palladio's *Quattro Libri*, book 4, plate 60, that depicts a scroll modillion for the University of Virginia Rotunda "Museum," is identified in the university proctor's papers as being by Neilson.[38]

Another of Jefferson's craftsmen, John Gorman, was born in Ireland in 1786. He immigrated to Lynchburg, where he worked both in a quarry and at Poplar Forest, where he laid and polished the hearths. He came to the university in 1819, after Jefferson noted in recommending him for a position there, "I find him well informed, industrious, very skillful, sober & good humored, and think he will be a valuable acquisition. He understands the business from the quarrying to conducting the work to the outlines for the sculptor." While at the university Gorman executed all the stone caps, bases, sills, wall copings, and newel blocks for the Rotunda, all of the ten pavilions, and Hotels A, C, D, E, and F. His fee amounted to about $250 for each pavilion.[39]

In 1821 Gorman declared his intention to become a U.S. citizen. Four years later he purchased one of Dinsmore's lots (probably lot number 1) on West Main Street, and here he built his house. Gorman died here an "insolvent debtor" on 23 August 1827, leaving a wife and their infant child, Mary Ann, and is buried in Maplewood Cemetery. The property, which had been in trusteeship to satisfy debts to Dinsmore's and Neilson's estates, was sold in 1842 to Alexander St. Clair Heiskell.[40]

Builders Associated with the Perry Family

Captain John M. Perry, born late in the 1770s, was first associated with construction at Monticello in 1800 together with his brothers Jesse and Reuben. In 1804 John Perry performed carpentry work on Jefferson's mill. In 1806 and 1807 he was a carpenter at Poplar Forest and also covered the terraces at Monticello with sheet iron. He worked at Monticello until 1809. Reuben Perry was subsequently engaged as a carpenter at Poplar Forest in 1812, where he made the molds for the iron firebacks, and he may also have worked at Point of Honor in Lynchburg. In the 1830s he employed his skills in Prince Edward County and later in Raleigh and Charlotte, North Carolina. Interestingly, Reuben Perry's inventory of books listed "one Biddle and two Pains," probably pattern books by Owen Biddle and William Pain.[41]

John M. Perry owned various properties in Albemarle County. In 1804 he purchased more than 200 acres in the Buck Island (Buckeye Land) area. Ten years later he bought the John Nicholas property, which had formerly belonged to James Monroe; Perry sold this tract in 1817 as

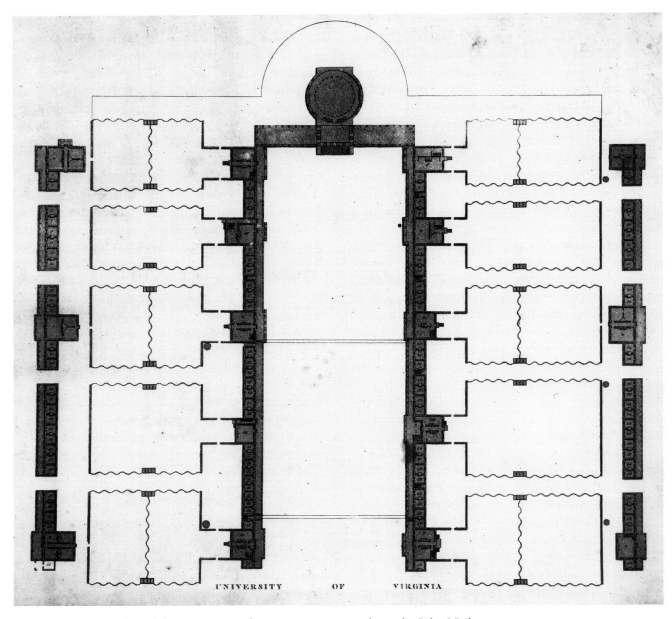

Fig. 100. Maverick Plan of the University of Virginia, 1822, 1825, drawn by John Neilson

the construction site for the University of Virginia. A year earlier Perry, now a local magistrate, had bought town lot 34. From 1819 until 1834 he owned Hydraulic Mills, which produced a hundred thousand feet of lumber annually. In 1820, the same year he advertised in the *Central Gazette* for the capture and return of one of his thirty-seven slaves, he built for himself the Federal-style house Montebello near the university. His business accounts reveal that he collected books on history, grammar, and mathematics; he also bought whiskey and the "best madera wine."[42]

A master carpenter and brickmason, Perry sold the Nicholas tract, including the house and outbuildings now known as Monroe Hill, with the provision that he be hired as a builder for the university. As a result, he received more remuneration during his tenure at the university than any other craftsman — more than $30,000. He worked on the Rotunda, all ten pavilions and six hotels, most of the student rooms, the serpentine brick garden walls, and the privies. He was the principal carpenter for the first building constructed at the university, Pavilion VII, with Hugh Chisholm as brickmason. Perry was also the principal brick-mason on Pavilions III, V, and VIII, along with Hotels B and F, with Richard Ware as carpenter. In 1817 Perry participated in the Pavilion VII cornerstone-laying ceremony with one current and two former presidents of the United States: Monroe, Jefferson, and Madison.[43]

It was during Perry's tenure with the university that he built Frascati in Orange County for U.S. Supreme Court justice Colonel Philip Pendleton Barbour, brother of Governor James Barbour of Barboursville; the Castle Hill addition for U.S. senator William Cabell Rives; and the original Charlottesville Presbyterian Church with George Wilson Spooner Jr. In 1826, as a justice of the peace, Perry appraised Jefferson's estate. Three years later he began selling off his own real estate, and in 1835 he placed his personal property in trust and moved to Missouri. Perry died in the late 1830s in Mississippi.[44]

During Perry's years at the university he worked in association with three other brickmasons, Matthew Brown, Curtis Carter, and Abiah B. Thorn, and with carpenters Hugh Chisholm, Richard Ware, and James Dinsmore. Matthew Brown, Perry's associate on Pavilion III who also built sixteen of the student rooms, was from Lynchburg. Curtis Carter was principal brickmason for Pavilion VI and Hotel A, and he was a partner with William B. Phillips on Pavilions I and IX as well as some of the student rooms. Between 1816 and 1818 Carter, a Virginia native, had executed the fine brickwork of architect Robert Mills's Brockenbrough house (which some years later served as the White House of the Confederacy) in Richmond.[45]

Irishman Hugh Chisholm, born in the 1770s, began working at Monticello in 1796, occasionally with his brother, and also was employed as a brickmason, carpenter, and plasterer at Poplar Forest and Montpelier as well as at the university. At Monticello he built twenty brick pillars under the terrace wings and installed the cast-iron lunettes in the all-weather passage. Abiah B. Thorn, from Philadelphia, was a brickmason in partnership with Perry on Pavilion VIII, Hotel B, and several student rooms; he was a partner with Nathaniel Chamberlain on the Rotunda.[46]

Another Philadelphian, Richard Ware, had moved to Delaware to escape debtors' prison. He arrived in Charlottesville by way of Richmond in 1819 with the recommendation of architect Robert Mills, with whom he had worked on Philadelphia projects. Ware was the principal carpenter and brickmason for thirteen student rooms and for Pavilions II, IV, and VI, as well as master

carpenter on Hotel F. For his work he received more than $27,000, second only to Perry in remuneration for services rendered to the university during this booming period of construction.[47]

Another of the original builders at the university, George Wilson Spooner Jr., was born to George W. B. and Sally Drake Spooner of Fredericksburg in 1798. From 1817 to 1819 he worked under Neilson at Upper Bremo. By 1819 Spooner was employed at the university. In that year he wrote to the proctor that he was boarding with Perry because it was more convenient to his university work. Within two years he married Perry's eldest daughter, Elizabeth, and when Perry left for Missouri, the Spooners occupied Montebello. Spooner was the principal carpenter for Hotels C and E and for several student rooms. He also worked for Dinsmore on the Rotunda and for Neilson on Pavilion IX. Spooner's association with the university was long-lived. In 1832 he was placed in charge of collecting money for a monument to Jefferson which was never built. During the 1845–46 academic year, he became acting proctor of the university. He supervised the construction of Robert Mills's Rotunda Annex in 1853, and two years later he built the now razed Temperance Hall just east of the university along Main Street.[48]

Also an active builder and property owner in Charlottesville, Spooner added a distyle-in-muris portico to the facade of Christ Church in 1853. Six years later he added to the Albemarle County Courthouse a Gothic Revival facade with gables and towers from a design by William A. Pratt (1818–1879), superintendent of buildings at the university from 1858 to 1865. Also in 1859, Pratt submitted drawings for a new steeple for Christ Church. He had formerly lived in Pratt's Castle in Richmond, where he had been involved in the planning of Richmond's Hollywood Cemetery. In 1856 Spooner was instrumental in acquiring Paul Balze's copy of the painting of Raphael's *School of Athens* for the Rotunda Annex. Spooner also rented out buildings on town lots he owned, numbers 73 and 74. By 1860 the value of his real estate rose to $9,000, and his personal property was assessed at $3,200.[49]

William B. Phillips and His Associates

Another master builder, William B. Phillips, born about 1790 in Virginia, moved to Charlottesville in 1818 to work at the university. He was the principal brickmason for the Rotunda, the Anatomical Hall, Pavilion X, Hotel C, the serpentine garden walls and the cisterns, several student rooms, and, in partnership with Curtis Carter, Pavilions I and IX. He also was the principal builder for two other university buildings, the Proctor's House and the Overseer's House, and Jefferson viewed his work at the university as "the best work done there."[50]

Phillips is credited with other projects in Charlottesville and Albemarle County as well as in other parts of the state: Berry Hill south of the town of Orange in 1824; The Farm for John A. G. Davis near Charlottesville just south of the older Nicholas Lewis one in 1825–27; Edgehill for Thomas Jefferson Randolph near Shadwell in 1828; Christ Church Glendower near Keene in southwestern Albemarle (with James W. Widderfield and James Walker) in 1832; the Orange County Jail in 1837 (Richard S. Boulware executed the ironwork); Greenfield, with its paired-column Ionic portico, on the eastern edge of Orange in 1838; and the brick garden wall of Christ Church in downtown Charlottesville that same year. About 1839 Phillips also executed the brickwork for Sweet Springs resort in what later became West Virginia, and in 1844 he added the classical orangeries to Perry's Castle Hill. Albemarle resident John Kelley recommended him in 1830 to build Randolph-Macon College in Boydton, writing that "Mr. Wm. B. Phillips . . . is a man of the strictest veracity, and sobriety, and not inferior to any man in the State of Virginia as a workman in his line of business, as to stile and neatness . . . you may be acquainted with Col. John Coles of this county who has put up a splendid building just now completed, the brickwork was done by Mr. Phillips." The Coles building in Albemarle County was Estouteville, which Dinsmore had designed.[51]

Phillips owned twelve town lots, some with buildings. In 1830 he advertised for sale 440 acres on Adams's Creek in Fluvanna County, together with "his house and lots in the town of Charlottesville." The notice further stated that "if not shortly sold, that on the main street will be for rent" as a "private residence or a place of business." In 1833 Phillips purchased part of the Colle estate south of Charlottesville, where he built his own home, Sunnyfields, valued in 1840 at $4,000. He also owned a three-acre brickyard one-half mile southwest of the courthouse, as well as 175 acres on Buck Island Creek. By 1850 his real estate holdings were valued at $25,000. Phillips married Barbara O. Pendleton, the sister-in-law of university painter and glazer John Vowles, who had been born in Bristol, England, in 1797. All are buried in Maplewood Cemetery; Phillips died on 24 April 1861, a few years after his wife.[52]

Phillips's master carpenter for Christ Church Glendower, James W. Widderfield, also a Virginian, was born in 1789. He had been a journeyman carpenter for Dins-

more and Neilson from 1819 to 1821 while working at the university. In 1833 he married Eliza J. Branham; by 1850 they were living next to George Wilson Spooner Jr. His oil portrait (fig. 101) by the local painter John Toole shows him with his carpenter's tools.[53]

Phillips also associated with two other builders, Crawford and Boulware, to complete some of the finest courthouses and dwellings in Virginia. Malcolm F. Crawford, born in Maine in 1794, was the principal carpenter in partnership with Lyman Peck for twenty-seven of the university student rooms. The partners also built a summerhouse for St. George Tucker at Edgewood in Nelson County in 1822. Crawford also owned the land where Christ Church in Charlottesville was constructed. In 1828 Crawford and Phillips built the new Edgehill to replace the house Jefferson had designed for his daughter here. They also built courthouses in Greene (1838), Page (1833), and possibly Caroline (c. 1830) Counties, and with Virginian Richard S. Boulware, born in 1800, they built the 1830 Madison County Courthouse and several dwellings there. Later,

Fig. 101. Portrait of James W. Widderfield, b. 1789

Crawford built two more courthouses, for Spotsylvania and Rappahannock Counties. About 1840 he built West End in Louisa County with Colonel James R. Magruder, who purchased Perry's Frascati after the Civil War. Magruder's father, John Bowie Magruder, was a lumber supplier for the university.[54]

In 1825 Crawford, then living in New Kent County, married Amanda M. F. Craven, the daughter of John H. Craven. Craven had been in partnership with Dinsmore from 1811 to 1815 in the Pen Park Mill; he owned two Dinsmore lots on the north side of West Main Street and Charlottesville town lot number 66. In 1850 his Albemarle County real estate was valued at $12,000. Ten years later he seems to have been living in Camden County, Georgia.[55]

Captain James Oldham, born in the 1770s, was a carpenter at Monticello from 1801 to 1808. Jefferson described Oldham as "an able workman in house joinery, skilled in the orders of architecture," and he lent Oldham his portable copy of Palladio's *Quattro Libri* when Oldham was unable to secure his own copy. By 1809 Oldham had submitted plans for a powder magazine for the penitentiary in Richmond. Between 1812 and 1813 he worked on alterations to Jefferson's Capitol in Richmond and on the Executive Mansion there as well. In 1818 Oldham planned to move to St. Louis from his home in Richmond, but he soon returned to Charlottesville as the principal carpenter for Pavilion I, for Hotel A with Curtis Carter, for Hotel D with Dabney Cosby, and on thirteen student rooms.[56]

Oldham was an irascible man with the distinction of being the only workman to sue the university, first writing an anonymous letter in 1823 accusing the proctor of fraud. Of Oldham, Jefferson noted: "[He] worked on my house for some years, is as faithful a workman as I have ever known, and I have believed him to be an honest man. But his temper is unhappy. Disagreements with his brother-workmen occasioned his leaving my service, without any displeasure between him and myself; and knowing his skill and fidelity as a workman I got him employed at the University. He soon got into a misunderstanding there with the Proctor. . . . I did suppose however that his self respect would [prevent his attacking] an adversary from behind the mask of an anonymous information." The lawsuit was not settled until 1832. In 1812 Oldham had married Mary Gambell, the daughter of Henry and Charlotte Gambell, in Richmond. They lived on the Three Notch'd Road near Ivy and operated a tavern there. Among Oldham's estate when he died in 1843 were drawing instruments, books, and carpenter's tools.[57]

The Irish Cosbys had been in Virginia since 1626. One

Fig. 102. Portrait of Dabney Cosby, 1779–1862

of that talented lineage, Dabney Cosby (fig. 102), was born in Louisa County on 11 August 1779. Cosby was the principal brickmason for Hotels D and E and for eight student rooms. Of the several recommendations in 1819 supporting his application to work at the university, one was from the noted Virginia legislator and judge Archibald Stuart of Staunton. Stuart, who had built for himself in 1791 one of the earliest examples of a tetrastyle porticoed house in Virginia, stated that "Dabney Cosby . . . is a man of Industry, Energy and I believe Capacity and may be relyed on to execute whatever he undertakes. Mr. C. has for years been more extensively employed in his line than any man in the county."[58]

In 1821 Cosby specifically requested that Oldham be his carpenter for the West Range at the university. That same year he wrote the proctor that "should it be deemed advisable to proceed to the erection of the pantheon [Rotunda] this season, and I be consider'd trustworthy, it would be a source of much pride and gratification to me, to see it executed in a stile, which for neatness and strength, should equal it in importance, and granduer of design." The Rotunda job did not materialize for him. By this time he had moved from Louisa County to Staunton, along with his wife, Frances Davenport Tapp Cosby, who was of Welsh descent, their fourteen children, and twenty-three slaves. Two sons became architects: Dabney Minor Cosby (1813–1898) in Halifax County and John Wayt Cosby (b. 1815) in Raleigh, North Carolina.[59]

In 1824 Dabney Cosby moved to Buckingham County and by 1830 to Prince Edward County. He continued his distinguished career, constructing college buildings, churches, and courthouses throughout Southside Virginia. Among the Virginia buildings attributed to him are Randolph-Macon College (1830) then located in Mecklenburg County, Venable Hall at Hampden-Sydney College (1830) in Prince Edward County, Tabb Street Presbyterian Church (1844) in Petersburg (for architect Thomas U. Walter), and county courthouses in Buckingham (1822), Goochland (1826; in collaboration with Valentine Parrish), Lunenburg (1827), Sussex (1828), and Halifax (1838). In 1839 he moved to Raleigh, North Carolina, where he built about thirty more buildings. He also worked with architect A. J. Davis on university buildings at Chapel Hill. Cosby died in Raleigh on 8 July 1862.[60]

Other Builders Associated with Jefferson

Only a few of the many workmen at the university actually did the majority of the work in their given field. Joseph Antrim, an Irishman who owned 246 acres in the county and had plastered the dining room at Poplar Forest in 1819, executed all the plasterwork for the Rotunda and all of the pavilions, hotels, and student rooms. He received about $580 for each pavilion and more than $2,100 for the Rotunda.[61]

William John Coffee (1773–c. 1846), who arrived in New York from England in 1816, executed the interior plaster ornaments at Poplar Forest and may have done work at Monticello. He sculpted terra-cotta busts of Jefferson and his granddaughters as well as those of many other county residents. Coffee also made all the composition and leaden ornaments on the Rotunda and in all the pavilions at about $36 per pavilion. Even at this seemingly low price the university felt overcharged, and an exchange of correspondence between the proctor and Coffee ensued. One of Coffee's last letters began: "I am surprized you have lost temper at a man merely because he wished to be paid."[62]

Edward Lowber painted all the pavilions, hotels, and student rooms and supplied all the glass, glazing, and two coats of sash paint. His fee for each pavilion amounted to about $400.[63]

Although there is no evidence that John Jordan (fig. 103)

Fig. 103. Portrait of John Jordan, 1777–1854

worked at the university, he flourished as a brickmason in the area during the same period as these other craftsmen. Of Irish descent, he was born in 1777 in Goochland County and died in 1854. He worked at Monticello from about 1803 to 1806 and in 1803 built the north part of the present Albemarle County Courthouse, which was used as a "common temple" for religious services; three presidents, Jefferson, Madison, and Monroe, all worshiped there. Earlier, Jordan had lived in Hanover County, but by 1801 he was in Lexington, Rockbridge County, from which he operated several mills and an iron-smelting business in five counties. In 1802 Jordan married Lucy Winn, the sister of John Winn, a Charlottesville merchant and postmaster who sold building supplies to the university. The Jordans had twelve sons and two daughters.[64]

Jordan later built several buildings in Rockbridge County, including Little Stono (1816); his own house, Stono (1818); and Centre Hall (c. 1824) at Washington and Lee. Of interest in Jordan's work are the great similarities between Stono, Little Stono, and Belmont, John Winn's

Fig. 104. Portrait of William Dunkum, 1777–1846

house in Charlottesville. All of these dwellings exhibit the three-bay pedimented center pavilion with lower side wings like the William Finnie house in Williamsburg, Jefferson's first version of Monticello, and Oak Lawn in Charlottesville.[65]

Although little evidence exists to confirm it, according to local tradition two sons of John and Mary Phoebe Bradley Dunkum (Duncomt) of Stafford County worked for Jefferson. The elder son, John Dunkum, was born in 1775 in Cumberland County, arrived in Albemarle County in 1807, and built his own brick I-house, Woodland, about 1810 on the road from Charlottesville to Carter's Bridge (present-day Route 20). When John Dunkum died in December 1855, he owned personal property valued at almost $17,000, including carpenter's tools and twenty-two slaves.[66]

His brother, William Dunkum, was born on 23 March 1777 in Cumberland County. The younger Dunkum also built his own brick I-house, Brookhill, on Route 20. A third house on the same road long believed to be associated with the Dunkum family—the brick two-story, hall-parlor Rolling Acres—actually was built in the 1820s by Martin Thacker for his son Wilson Harvey Thacker (b. 1800) who

Fig. 105. Daniel F. Carr house, c. 1830

married Mary B. Wingfield. About the time of William Dunkum's arrival in the county in 1803, he erected the first brick house in Charlottesville, for Joseph Bishop in Random Row on Vinegar Hill. Adjacent to Court Square in Charlottesville, he built a two-story brick house for Twyman Wayt in the McKee block and a house in the 400 block of East Jefferson Street for Lewellyn Wood. He also may have built houses for his sons: the brick I-house Tudor Grove for William Lewis Dunkum, who married Elizabeth Bradley in 1832, and a frame house for Elijah Dunkum in 1843 on Ridge Street in Charlottesville as well as a two-story brick dwelling here the following year. Frances Gentry became William Dunkum's second wife on 18 December 1823. At Dunkum's death on 21 May 1846, he owned personal property assessed at more than $14,000, including fifty-four books, many carpenter's tools, twenty-six slaves, and an oil portrait (fig. 104) of himself by John Toole.[67]

Rarely in the history of American architecture have craftsmen and master builders of major monuments had such a profound long-term impact on the built environment. Many buildings besides those named here, both in Charlottesville and in the surrounding region, were built by these men. Most still survive, but unfortunately one of the best examples in the city has been lost. Judging from its stylistic features, undoubtedly the fine distyle-in-muris brick house (fig. 105) built for Daniel F. Carr about 1830 on West Main Street was designed and constructed by one of Jefferson's master builders. It was razed in 1975 and sold for the price of its bricks.[68]

D. S. Tavern, 1741, 1786

Plain Dealing, 1761, 1789

Edgemont, c. 1796

Red Hills, 1797, c. 1805

Sunny Bank, 1797

Monticello, 1768–1809

Redlands, 1798

Farmington, 1803

University of Virginia Lawn, 1817–26

Esmont, c. 1819

Malvern, E19C

Birdwood, 1819

Oak Lawn, 1822

Estouteville, 1827–30

Heiskell-Livers town house, 1827, 1842

Vowles town house, 1823, c. 1830

Old Hall, 1830

Mount View School at Cliffside

Cliffside, 1835

Abell-Gleason house, 1859

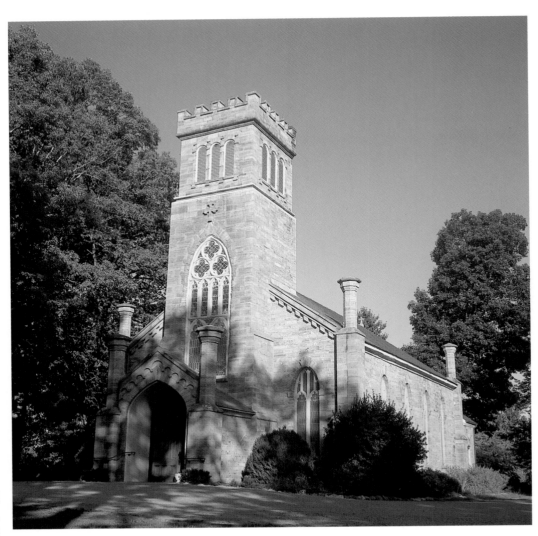

Grace Episcopal
Church, 1847,
1896

Marshall-Rucker house, 1894

Carr's Hill, 1909

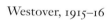
Westover, 1915–16

Shack Mountain, 1935–36

The Roman Revival (1800–1830)

BACKGROUND

In the closing years of the eighteenth century, the popularity of the Georgian style waned as architects turned for inspiration to classical architectural models and thereby inaugurated the Classical Revival style. The new style took two forms in Virginia, the Roman Revival, of which Thomas Jefferson was one of the earliest proponents, and the Greek Revival, which overlapped and then succeeded it in popular acceptance.

The Federal period, which introduced the Roman Revival, is generally bounded by the years 1780 and 1820. The beginning and ending of the popularity of the style in such rural counties as Albemarle, however, were delayed by a decade or more. The Federal style was based on classical models imaginatively interpreted with lightness and delicacy by the British architects James and Robert Adam (hence the Adamesque Federal style) and reinterpreted in the United States by New England architects such as Charles Bulfinch and Samuel McIntire. During the period Jefferson was further influenced by contemporary French examples as well as ancient Roman models. Because of Jefferson's and his master builders' importance to Albemarle's and Virginia's early nineteenth-century architectural design, moreover, the style persisted longer in the county and state than in the rest of the country.

American pattern books came into vogue during the early years of the new republic and promoted the Federal style. The first publication in America of a British pattern book was Abraham Swan's *The British Architect* in 1775 in Philadelphia. The American Asher Benjamin published *The Country Builder's Assistant* twenty-four years later; it was the first original American book on architecture. In 1806, in collaboration with Daniel Reynard, Benjamin published his popular *American Builder's Companion*, and

soon other American architects followed his example. Although architectural historians long have regarded Benjamin's books as the most influential of their era, the recent rediscovery of details in the less-expensive pattern books by the lesser-known William Pain (1730–1790) that appear in many Virginia buildings suggests that Pain may have been more influential in the state.[1] Together with the pattern books, professionally trained architects entered the scene about this time as well. B. Henry Latrobe (1764–1820), trained in Europe, was the first; Robert Mills (1781–1855) was the first native-trained architect.

The characteristic details of the Adamesque Federal style included Flemish-bond brick facades with three-course American bond below the water table and on the side and rear walls. The brickwork often featured penciled mortar joints,[2] cornices of molded brick that formed cyma curves, mousetooth or houndstooth cornices of diagonally set bricks, and chimney curtains—brick parapet walls that connect two gable-end chimneys and mask the gable roofs. Federal-style windows, like the woodwork generally, were more delicate than Georgian ones, with narrower three-quarter-inch-wide muntins and plaster lintels designed to resemble stonework. The Federal style introduced new types of windows, including triple-hung, lunette (thermal), blind (false), tripartite, and Palladian windows, as well as fanlights over doorways. Likewise, the appearance of doors changed with the increasing popularity of double-leaf front doors, six-panel "cross and Bible" doors, and blind or false doors. Four-column, paired-column, and two-tiered porticoes sheltered entrances. Roofs of blue-black Buckingham County slate first came into use in the late eighteenth century and metal roofs in the first quarter of the nineteenth century. Inside, attenuated fireplace mantel shelves appeared, often supported by slender colonnettes. Rectangular banisters replaced the carved and turned ones of the preceding period. Interior doors were hung from cast-iron butt hinges and self-closing hinges, improvements over the old wrought-iron hinges.

Throughout the Classical Revival period, which ended in Albemarle County at about the time the Civil War began, certain architectural features were commonly found on both Roman Revival and Greek Revival buildings. Perhaps the most popular innovation, particularly in hot and humid Virginia, was the piazza. The portrait painter John Singleton Copley, when building his own house in Boston, stated that piazzas, or open verandas that span the height and length of a house, "are so cool that I think I should not be able to like a house without."[3] Although the piazza was not introduced in America until the eighteenth century, as at Mount Vernon, it persisted well into

the nineteenth century, especially during the Classical Revival period. Often builders constructed piazzas on the north side of houses as a welcome place to escape the Virginia heat and humidity (fig. 106).

Double-ramped chimneys, which came into vogue in the eighteenth century, persisted into the nineteenth century, especially on one-story frame houses (fig. 107). The Flemish-bond brick pattern (a header centered above and below each stretcher) remained popular for facades during the Classical Revival period. The header was the same size brick as the stretcher, but it was simply laid perpendicular to the stretcher to bond the wall together. The Flemish-bond pattern required specially made brick closers at the end of each row, at the corners and openings of buildings; they were either queen's closers (about two-thirds the length of a header) (fig. 108) or king's closers (about two-thirds the length of a stretcher). Many other special-

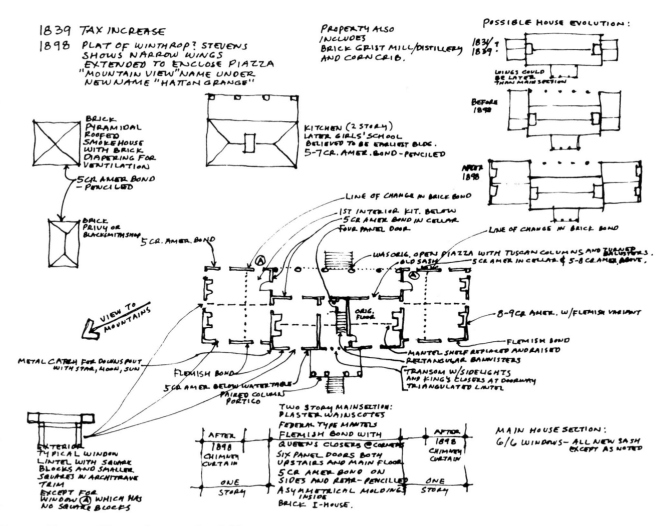

Fig. 106. Piazza at Hatton Grange, 1831, field notes

Fig. 107. Double-ramped chimney at Jarman house, E19C

Fig. 108. Mousetooth and molded cornices and queen's closers, Butler-Norris town house, c. 1808

purpose bricks were made, including molded bricks for cornices or water tables and for Tuscan or Doric capitals, as well as rounded and pie-shaped bricks to construct the column shafts themselves (fig. 109).

Inside the buildings, the Federal mantel (fig. 110), unlike the Georgian, had an attenuated, cutout shelf with patera, garlands, or swags in its frieze. After 1800 paired colonnettes often supported the frieze. Although carpenters referred to the popular pattern books to learn the features of the new styles, they often modified them to suit their own preferences. Stair-end scroll brackets, for example, were highly individualized and perhaps were used as signature pieces by carpenters from one project to another (fig. 111).

Some architectural features were closely associated with the Roman Revival period, including several varieties of brickwork. Brick chimney curtains and parapets often

were used in double-pile houses to join the gable-end chimney stacks (fig. 112). At least ten country dwellings survive in Albemarle County that feature exterior corbeled (projecting) cornices made of molded bricks to form a cyma curve.[4] Usually these cornices are stuccoed and whitewashed (fig. 113). Among the popular exterior brick corbeled cornices were those that featured a row or two of diagonally set brick; they were known as mousetooth or houndstooth cornices (fig. 114). On the other hand, many Federal features were executed in wood. Some exterior wooden cornices, for example, had elaborate moldings, such as the rope (fig. 115) or the bead-and-reel.

The Roman Revival period introduced new window treatments. Semicircular lunettes (fig. 116) derived from the thermal windows of ancient Roman baths appeared in the gables and tympanums of pediments. The lunettes had different muntin configurations; the Gothic motif

Fig. 109. *(right)* Pie-shaped column bricks
at Bentivar, L18c, c. 1830

Fig. 110. *(below)* Federal mantel at Cliffside, E19c

Fig. 112. Brick chimney curtains at Southall-Venable house, E19C

Fig. 113. (left) Molded-brick cornice at Mount Armour, c. 1790

Fig. 114. (below) Brick mousetooth cornice at Home Tract, 1803

Fig. 111. Stair scroll brackets at Edgmont, 1827

Fig. 115. Exterior wood cornice at Summer Hill, 1820s

Fig. 116. Lunette in tympanum at Pavilion X, 1822, elevation

Fig. 117. Fanlight doorway at Cliffside, E19C

was a popular one that Jefferson used. Semicircular and elliptical fanlights with radiating muntins often were constructed above doorways to admit light into entrance halls (fig. 117). Tall windows with triple-hung sash and sills set at floor level were a favorite feature employed by the architect Charles Bulfinch after 1788 and by Jefferson in the construction of his revised version of Monticello. These windows improved air circulation when the top and bottom sashes were centered over the middle sash. They also enabled the window to function as a doorway when the center and bottom sash were raised and portable wooden steps were placed outside (fig. 118). Blind or false windows were used when necessary to make a building appear more symmetrical, especially when the placement of a chimney or the appearance of a stairway behind a real window would have threatened the aesthetic effect. Usually the false

window consisted of closed blinds (shutters with louvers) over a recessed brick wall (fig. 119).

Besides all these stylistic changes, technological advances that were introduced by the beginning of the nineteenth century benefited the local building trades. Although the first water-powered gristmill in the county appeared on Preddy's Creek in 1742,[5] it was not until 1801 that George West built Albemarle's first recorded sawmill on the "old Woods's Gap road," thereby adding the reciprocating or up-and-down saw to the older hand method of pit-sawing lumber. Cut nails were introduced about the turn of the century, but the heads were still hand hammered into a rosette shape. Jefferson had purchased a nail machine in 1796, producing cut nails for sale at Monticello. Mass-produced, elaborate cast-plaster ceiling medallions and moldings exhibiting circular and oval patera, garlands and

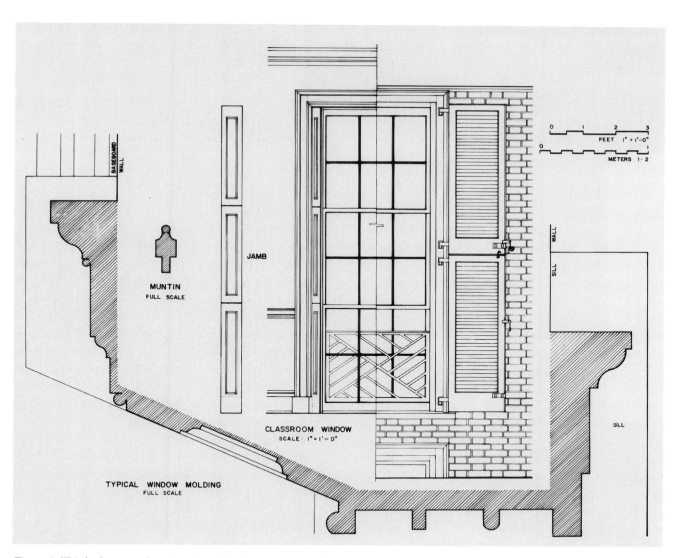

Fig. 118. Triple-hung sash at Pavilion IV, 1819, measured drawing

Fig. 119. False windows in gable end at Jones-Williams house, 1814

swags, reeds, flutes, interlaces, and floral and wave motifs came into vogue. Itinerant painters employed their graining and marbleizing techniques to make pine wood resemble the more elegant mahogany or marble.

New floor plans and room arrangements emerged to suit the new architectural styles. Stairs were repositioned from the center passage into side passages, thereby permitting the clearer separation of the public and private realms within dwellings. Jefferson noted admiringly that in Parisian houses "great staircases are avoided, which are expensive and occupy a space which would make a good room in every story."[6] The central passage no longer continued through the house but was separated into an entrance space with a salon beyond. Major interior spaces were no longer restricted in shape to the square or rectangular but became figural or irregular: octagonal, circular, oval, segmental.

The former frontier grew sophisticated and prosperous. By 1782 three of the one hundred wealthiest and most influential Virginians owned land in Albemarle County: Edward Carter of Blenheim, son of Secretary John Car-

ter; Robert Carter Nicholas, son of Dr. George Nicholas and absentee owner of present-day Warren; and Thomas Jefferson of Monticello. The county's tax lists show that its fourth- through thirteenth-wealthiest landowners were Dr. Thomas Walker of Castle Hill; John Coles II of Enniscorthy; Charles B. J. Lewis; Robert Nelson, absentee owner of land in the North and South Garden area and son of Council president William Nelson of Yorktown; Martin Key of the Key West area, son of John Key; John Scott of Belle Grove; Colonel John Walker of Belvoir; Margaret Douglas Meriwether of Clover Fields, widow of Nicholas Meriwether I; Thomas Mann Randolph Sr. of Tuckahoe, absentee owner of Edgehill; and the Viewmont estate of Colonel John Fry, son of Colonel Joshua Fry.[7]

According to the 1787 real estate and personal property tax lists, Edward Carter of Blenheim remained the county's wealthiest person with 9,700 acres, 227 taxable slaves, 60 horses and mules, 116 head of cattle, and a carriage. In 1789, the year that Robert Carter began to build Redlands in Albemarle County, Virginia became the tenth state in the Union, and the following year Virginian George Washington became the first president. The wealthiest person in Albemarle County in 1800 was future governor Wilson Cary Nicholas of Mount Warren, who had the highest-valued personal property and real estate with more than 7,700 acres of land. Robert Carter of Redlands owned the second-highest number of acres. Nicholas paid taxes on more slaves, 97, and more horses, 58, than any other person. He also claimed a studhorse as well as a coach and a chariot. His nearest competitor was John Coles II of Enniscorthy, who had but half that wealth. Coles also claimed a chariot and a phaeton. But between the end of the Revolutionary War and 1800, real estate had dropped to one-tenth of its value due to the war and the availability of cheap land in the Midwest.[8]

In 1801 Albemarle's Thomas Jefferson became the nation's third president. The following year he designed an addition with demioctagonal ends for Farmington, a 1779 Albemarle County farmhouse. John Jordan, the Rockbridge County brickmason, completed his work on the Albemarle County Courthouse in 1803. He also worked at Monticello and was still living in the county in 1805. James Madison of nearby Orange County succeeded his friend Jefferson as president (1809–17), and Jefferson returned home to Albemarle to finish the construction of Monticello and also to build his retreat, Poplar Forest, in Bedford County. Years of turmoil with Great Britain erupted in the War of 1812 during Madison's tenure, and although the young United States emerged the victor, it cost the nation's treasury dearly. Several states, including Virginia, incurred enormous expenses by repeatedly calling out the militia to defend against British attacks. In 1815, to pay for the just-ended war, the state increased the number of items of personal property subject to taxation. Besides the usual slaves and horses, the commonwealth taxed clocks, watches, musical instruments, paintings, carriages, billiard tables, and many other articles. Of almost 250 households on the tax lists, eighteen persons took out ordinary licenses; the tax rolls noted forty gristmills, five sawmills, sixty-three farm icehouses, and carriages sported by forty-one households. Although the enlarged list of taxable items increased the amount of revenue collected in 1815, the broad levy was never repeated because of the time and expense involved.[9]

These tax rolls provide a glimpse of the cultural life of early nineteenth-century Albemarle County. Some residents were musically inclined; Thomas Jefferson, for example, was taxed on a harpsichord (he is known to have played the violin and his late wife the pianoforte). Hugh Nelson of Belvoir and Francis Walker of Castle Hill owned organs. Na-

thaniel Anderson of Saint Anne's Parish Glebe, John R. Campbell of Buck Island, Mary Eliza Coles Carter of Redlands, John Estes, David Higginbotham of Morven, Christopher Hudson of Mount Air, and Reuben Lindsay of Springfield, all owned pianofortes. In addition to Monticello's sixteen oil portraits and one crayon portrait, eight more oils and two more crayons were owned by other households. The crayon portraits may very well have been made by Charles-Balthazar-Julien Févret de Saint-Mémin, an exiled French aristocrat who drew many profile portraits in preparation for his miniatures and engravings. According to the 1815 tax books, only one person other than Jefferson—James Powell Cocke of Edgemont—adorned his windows with the fashionable venetian blinds. Other stylish items in county homes included mahogany furniture, carpets, calico and worsted curtains, silver pitchers and teapots, and cut-glass decanters as well as 93 looking glasses, 93 bookcases, and 120 clocks.[10]

James Monroe, a sometime resident of Albemarle County, became the nation's fifth president in 1817 and remained in office until 1825, during which time the University of Virginia was constructed. Two years after Monroe's first inauguration, the nationwide financial panic of 1819 occurred. In Virginia the next year, buildings were valued separately from land for the first time in the land tax books. George Divers's Farmington dwelling had the highest value in the county at $22,500, with Monticello valued at $12,000 and Elijah May's Cedars Tavern at Yancey's mills at $11,000.[11] The county court issued twenty-one ordinary licenses, of which seven were to proprietors of "Houses of Private Entertainment" (essentially restaurants located in private homes). Thirty merchants also purchased licenses. Among the industries operating in the county in 1820 were ten tanneries, seven tobacco factories, seventeen sawmills, twelve flour mills, four wool-carding machines, and two distilleries.

LOG DWELLINGS

Log construction remained popular throughout the nineteenth century. John Carr built Green Mountain near Boonesville in 1802 for his daughter, Eliza, who married her cousin Thomas Salmon. Later Dr. Thomas Martin Dunn was born here. This one-story log house, with its nine-over-six sash windows and shed dormers, probably evolved from a single-cell dwelling into two rooms, each with its own front door. The one-story, single-cell, V-notched chestnut log Bishop house near Woodridge contained stone chimneys with brick necks to heat both the main part of the house and its shed addition. A one-story frame kitchen and slave quarters with central chimney and two front doors served as a dependency to the property. Another log house with the same characteristics is located at the Goodwin farm just southwest of Charlottesville.[12]

Two Scotch-Irish brothers surnamed Wallace emigrated from Pennsylvania with Michael Woods and settled in Albemarle County. One, William Wallace, married his cousin Hannah Woods and patented 800 acres in the western part of the county between 1737 and 1741. In 1765 he purchased 200 more acres on a branch of Stockton's Creek, where he built a house that was destroyed before 1790. His son, William Wallace II, built his log house named Meadowbrook nearby in the late eighteenth century. It began as a one-story log house with full dovetail notching and a penciled three-course American-bond chimney. Later it was expanded to two stories with V-notch log construction.[13]

The earliest part of The Shadows on Route 676 is a single-cell log house from the first half of the nineteenth century. After 1870 it was expanded into a two-story, center-passage dwelling, and during the 1940s it was heavily remodeled, acquiring wings, stucco cladding, a two-story tetrastyle portico with a Chinese railing, and a classical aedicule doorway—framed by pilasters and crowned with a pediment—from another building. Zachariah Shackelford built Dovedale, a log house with an unusual floor plan, east of Stony Point about 1806. The original one-story log house appears to have been a double-pile, one-third Georgian plan, with a diagonally set stone chimney. The property had a row of slave quarters, an icehouse, a log smokehouse, a log stable, a log tobacco barn, and a bank barn. The original house was expanded several times throughout the Victorian period.[14]

Log Hall-Parlor Dwellings

In 1734 Thomas Sowell obtained a patent for 550 acres near Carter's Bridge, where either his son John or his grandson Benjamin built the extant one-story log hall-parlor Oak Crest. Jonathan Leathers, who married Benjamin Sowell's daughter, acquired it in 1853. The double-pen log Dunn house near Nortonsville was later raised to two floors but retains its original penciled five-course American-bond chimney with a stepped-brick wash. The house dates to about 1825. Ragged Mountain Farm (fig. 120), another hall-parlor log dwelling, is on Route 681 in southwestern

Fig. 120. Ragged Mountain Farm, E19c

Fig. 121. Piedmont, c. 1807

Albemarle. The house contains pit-sawed joists, mortise-and-tenon construction, and a six-panel door with panels raised beyond the stiles and rails.[15]

Log-plank construction was relatively common in the Shenandoah Valley, but few examples are known in Albemarle County. This method of construction required rectangular sawed logs, on whose ends were cut tongues that fitted into grooves in a square vertical member at each corner. The edges of the logs were smooth and even, causing each plank to fit snugly against the one below, thus eliminating any space between the logs that would have to be chinked. The one-story, hall-parlor Fielding near Ivy is such a plank building. Inherited by Thomas Fielding Lewis in 1838, the property had been owned by his wife's grandmother Lucy Meriwether Lewis Marks, the mother of the explorer Meriwether Lewis. The property includes a twentieth-century frame water tower built into the house.[16]

Two-Story Log Dwellings

William Wallace II died in 1809 at Piedmont (figs. 121, 122) near Meadowbrook. Probably he or his son, William Wallace III, built this later two-story, one-over-one log house between 1805 and 1809. Michael Wallace, the son of

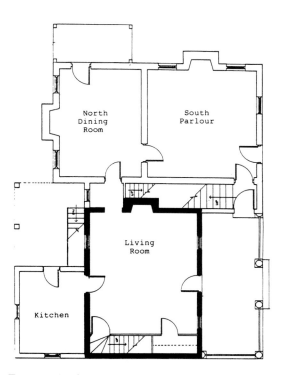

Fig. 122. Piedmont, c. 1807, plan

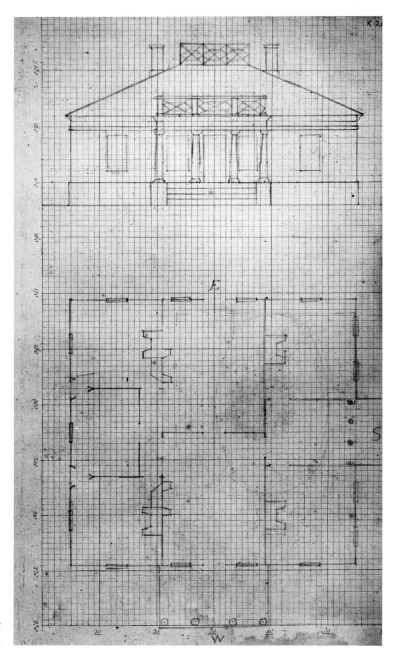

Fig. 123. Edgehill, c. 1798, drawing by Thomas Jefferson

William Wallace III, built a two-story brick Greek Revival addition with a penciled Flemish-bond facade, five-course American-bond sides, and exterior molded-brick cornice. A log smokehouse and log slave quarters still stand on the property, along with the ruins of a kitchen. Colonel James O. Carr's house, which he built on Meadow Creek on land owned by his father, Garland Carr, was another two-story log house but with a center chimney. It probably evolved from a one-over-one-room dwelling. The property also contained a larger frame house, The Meadows, and a kitchen. All of these buildings were razed for the expansion of Seminole Square Shopping Center in the 1980s and 1990s.[17]

One-Story Frame Dwellings

In 1735 Colonel William Randolph of Tuckahoe in Goochland County patented 2,400 acres on the eastern slope of the Southwest Mountains. This property, as well as Tuckahoe, passed to his son, Thomas Mann Randolph Sr. Later the Southwest Mountains property was acquired by his son Thomas Mann Randolph Jr., who married Jefferson's daughter Martha in 1790. They received the house Varina south of Richmond as a wedding gift from his father, but Jefferson encouraged them to relocate on the Albemarle County property, Edgehill. He even designed a house for them here, a one-story frame house with a hipped roof, a paired-column portico, and a distyle-in-muris side portico (fig. 123). The plan was double-pile with an entrance hall and, beyond it, a salon. After living at nearby Belmont for a few years, the couple moved to Edgehill in 1799. Thomas Mann Randolph was elected governor in 1819, which caused his frequent absence from the county; at such times his family resided at Monticello. Because of Randolph's large debts, it fell to his eldest son, Thomas Jefferson Randolph, the president's favorite grandson, to purchase Edgehill in 1826 and build a large brick house for the family here in 1828 after his grandfather died and Monticello was sold.

The one-story frame Doll House in Scottsville has a center-passage plan with a room on either side. Dating to the early nineteenth century, it might have begun with a hall-parlor plan. The one-story frame Millburne, northwest of Mirador, was the home of William Ramsay as early as 1802. By 1816 an 8-foot-wide piazza had been built to shelter its 38-foot-long facade. The property included a 60-foot-long barn and a combination mill and distillery.[18]

One-Story Frame Single-Cell Dwellings

The ubiquitous single-cell, one-story frame house persisted well into the nineteenth century. The Herndon house, a one-story dwelling in Scottsville, began as a single-cell frame house. Its features include double-ramped brick chimneys, beaded siding, and nine-over-six sash windows. Built by the Minor family, Barrsden at Eastham contains several early nineteenth-century one-story, single-cell houses; some adjoin one another while others stand separately. One house is log with beaded joists, and another is frame

with a stone chimney. After 1883 Albert Holladay purchased the property and operated a vineyard here until Prohibition was enacted in 1919. His burgundy wine won first place at the 1893 Columbian Exposition in Chicago.[19]

The early nineteenth-century house at Quiet Entry near Keene is another example of a single-cell dwelling. Its features include a stone chimney as well as beaded weatherboards attached by cut nails with hammered heads. A hall-parlor addition expanded the house in the 1820s. Merry Oaks (fig. 124), built about 1830 near Burnley's Sta-

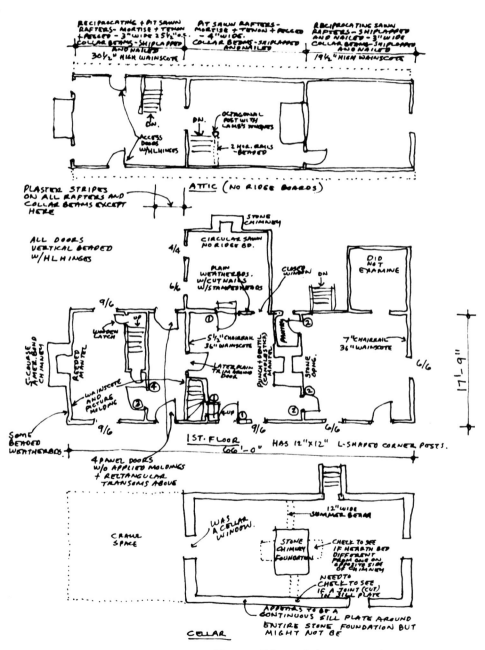

Fig. 124. Merry Oaks, c. 1830, field notes

Fig. 125. Maple Hill Cottage, c. 1820

tion, probably began as a one-story, single-cell frame house or perhaps as a hall-parlor-plan dwelling with a center chimney. Edwin Temple Douglass (1812–1893) resided here in the nineteenth century. The Douglass family had been in this area as early as 1761.[20]

One-Story Frame Hall-Parlor Dwellings

The one-story frame hall-parlor-plan house also remained popular until well into the nineteenth century. Pleasant Hill, for example, is on Ballenger's Creek near Tapscott. It was probably built about 1801 or 1804 (according to a dated cellar beam, the last numeral of which is illegible) for Benjamin and Dorothy Childress Dawson. One of their daughters married Peter Turner and inherited the house, which features two double-ramped chimneys in three-course American bond.[21]

Hampstead, a one-story frame house built for William S. Dabney on present-day Route 719 near Esmont, retains a hall-parlor plan, two front doors, and a center chimney. An inscribed timber in the house dates its construction to 1804, and a circular brick icehouse remains on the property. Mechum's River Farm near Batesville was built as a hall-parlor house about 1810 for the Burch family, which had immigrated to Albemarle from Caroline County in 1763. In the 1840s the dwelling was expanded

and modernized with Greek Revival details. A single-cell, one-story building on the property may predate the hall-parlor house.[22]

Solitude, near Crossroads, probably was constructed for William Alcock about 1810. Its two double-ramped chimneys exhibit three-course and five-course American bond, and its surviving dependencies include a smokehouse and a kitchen. Henry Gantt of Prince George's County, Maryland, bought this one-story frame hall-parlor house in 1813. After winning $40,000 in the Maryland lottery in 1821, Gantt returned home, and his son Dr. John W. Gantt succeeded to ownership of the farm. In 1837 Dr. Gantt sold it to Joseph L. Sutherland, and it remains in the Sutherland family to this day.[23]

The frame hall-parlor Maple Hill Cottage (fig. 125) was built about 1820 on the east side of present-day Route 20 across from Totier Creek Farm. The Giles family owned it at the end of the Civil War. The house was relocated in 1976 to another site a few miles south and on the opposite side of Route 20. The Pleasant Sowell house, also on the east side of Route 20 but north of Carter's Bridge, was relocated in 1993 to the Michie Tavern complex. Sowell operated a furniture and coffin-making factory near Sowell's Creek and probably built the hall-parlor house about the time of his marriage to Sarah Garland in 1824.[24]

One-Story Frame Double-Pile Dwellings

The one-story frame Edwards house near Burnley Station may date to 1800. It has a massive 12-foot-wide stone chimney that serves double-pile rooms in a one-third Georgian plan. Dragon beams parallel the diagonally set chimney in the cellar and are notched at an angle into a summer beam. Another one-story frame house, but with a two-thirds Georgian plan (double-pile with a side passage) is the early nineteenth-century Darby's Folly (figs. 126, 127), built off Barracks Road for the Garth family.[25]

TWO-STORY FRAME DWELLINGS

Two-Story Frame Hall-Parlor Dwellings

The two-story frame house called Forest Hill (fig. 128) began with a hall-parlor plan. That it might have served as a tavern is suggested by its exterior room doors and exterior stairs to its two-tier veranda that is supported by square chamfered columns. Situated on the Rivanna River south of Milton, Forest Hill was built for Robert Rives about 1802, sold to John Watson in 1813, and bought by Tandy Wilhoit in 1889. The two-tier tetrastyle portico on its north facade was added during the twentieth century.[26]

The Frame I-House

The I-house, one of the most popular vernacular house forms in the United States, persisted as well in Albemarle County throughout all of the eighteenth- and nineteenth-century architectural stylistic periods. Many examples of this common form still stand in the county. Among them is Clifton, which Thomas Mann Randolph Jr. built near North Milton at about the same time that Thomas Jefferson designed the house at Edgehill for the Randolphs so that they could be close to him at Monticello. The house probably served as a warehouse as well as Randolph's business office. In 1826 he became estranged from his family over a disagreement about Jefferson's will and moved into the office at Clifton, where he lived in seclusion. In 1828, due to ill health, he moved into the North Pavilion at Monticello and died there four months later. The house at Clifton has been expanded considerably and now serves as a bed-and-breakfast inn.[27]

Fig. 126. Darby's Folly, E19C

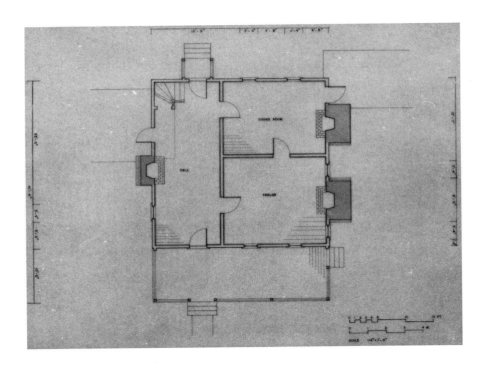

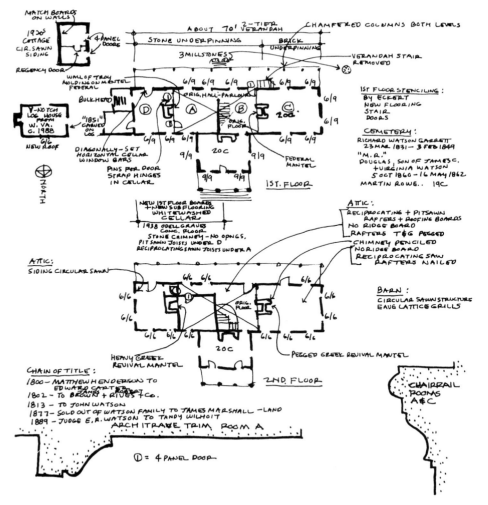

Fig. 127. (above) Darby's Folly, E19C, plan

Fig. 128. (left) Forest Hill, c. 1802, field notes

The German Ezekiel Wilhoit Sr. purchased land near Nortonsville from William Johnson in 1823. Milton Wilhoit, one of his sons, acquired the tract while another son, Ezekiel Wilhoit Jr., who married Louisa Frances Eddins, lived nearby in a frame I-house built in the 1820s. The brothers jointly owned the saw- and gristmills where their properties joined and around which the small community of Wilhoit developed. The Ezekiel Wilhoit Jr. property contains many outbuildings, including slave quarters, kitchen, dairy, icehouse, well house, smokehouse, carriage house, blacksmith's shop, corncrib, springhouse, chicken houses, tobacco barns, and ground and bank barns.[28]

ONE-STORY BRICK DWELLINGS

One-Story Brick Hall-Parlor Dwellings

The red clay soil of Albemarle continued to serve as a ready source of on-site material for bricks. Many brick houses were small one-story dwellings with a hall-parlor plan. The eccentric Pennsylvania German John Yeargain resided in a one-story frame house constructed about 1800 at 220 Court Square, where he maintained a liquor store, having been issued a tavern license in 1796. The 18-by-36-foot footprint of that house is identical to that of the present mid-

nineteenth-century dwelling: a one-story, hall-parlor brick house with stepped-gable parapet walls and two front doors. Later the property served as law offices for Virginia Supreme Court of Appeals justice William J. Robertson, and then for U.S. senator Thomas Staples Martin.[29]

Midmont, at the western edge of Charlottesville, evolved from a one-story, hall-parlor brick house with a penciled Flemish-bond facade and mousetooth cornice. Its next addition exhibited three-course American bond, another five-course, and yet another six- and seven-course, making it an interesting example of building accretions. In 1833 Jesse Pitman Lewis sold the property to Thomas Walker Maury, who conducted a private school here. Local attorney and historian Bernard Peyton Chamberlain bought the house in 1929.[30]

Bachelor's Quarters (fig. 129), northwest of Crossroads, probably was built for the White family about 1800. Later a minister operated a school here. The house has a penciled Flemish-bond facade with three- and four-course American bond on the other walls. The attic rafters, inscribed with Roman numerals, are shiplapped and pegged, and their purlins are pit-sawed. It once had wooden shingles and a batten door with beaded boards.[31]

Jesse Garth built Cherry Valley on Route 601 on land

Fig. 129. Bachelor's Quarters, c. 1800

his father, Thomas Garth Sr., had purchased in 1777 from Christopher Harris. Originally built as a one-story dwelling with a penciled Flemish-bond facade and three-course American-bond sides, the house was constructed with a hall-parlor plan and a date brick incised "JG 1805." In the 1820s the house underwent extensive modifications. It was raised to two stories, a center passage and a two-story brick gable-end wing were constructed, a gable roof with a center gable reusing the original rafters was placed over the entire building, and a molded cyma recta four-brick cornice was added. Abandoned since 1949, the vandalized house was razed in 1997.[32]

Littleberry Moon, who moved to Albemarle from Buckingham County, became a wealthy Scottsville merchant. After marrying Sallie Price Perkins in 1812, he built the brick I-house portion of Riverview overlooking the James River. Its two-tier portico with octagonal columns utilizes lamb's-tongues to make the transition from a square shape at the base of each column to the octagon above. About 1865 Benjamin Darneille added a dining room and kitchen to the east; they later were connected to the existing brick summer kitchen. An early brick wing of the old house probably served as Moon's office.[33]

Joshua Wheeler built such a house (fig. 130) in 1820 on U.S. Route 29 south of Charlottesville. With five-course American bond below the first floor and American bond with Flemish variant bond above, the three-bay brick house with brick gable parapets was painted red with penciled mortar joints. Joshua Wheeler had purchased the property, then known as Little Egypt, in 1819 from Clairborne Gooch, and it remained in the Wheeler family until 1856 when it was sold to William Kirby.[34]

One-Story Brick Double-Pile Piano Nobile Dwellings (Exposed Full Cellar)

Some one-story brick buildings were double-pile with a cellar fully exposed above ground. Thus the exterior stair rose a full flight to the front door that entered the piano nobile or living space, with servant quarters below in the Palladian manner. The William Walker house (fig. 131) at Warren was built in 1803–5 by Walker's brother, James, who worked for Jefferson as a carpenter and millwright. The entire house is constructed of three-course American bond with a cyma reversa brick water table over a high basement, plastered jack arches above nine-over-nine sash windows, and a hipped roof.[35]

Major Thomas Carr (1678–1738) of King William County accumulated more than 10,000 acres between 1730 and 1737 along the north fork of the Rivanna on the west side of the Southwest Mountains. He gave most of this land to his son, John (1706–1778), of Bear Castle in Louisa County. John Carr's descendants built elegant Jeffersonian-type houses in Albemarle County: one son built Bentivar, another built Dunlora, and a third built Glen Echo and Carrsbrook. Carr's youngest son, Garland (1754–1837), built the single-story, double-pile Bentivar in the fork of the north and south branches of the Rivanna River. His youngest child, Mary Winston Carr, is believed to have been born here in 1796. The house burned on 27 April 1830, and a new one (fig. 132) was erected shortly thereafter as a one-story, double-pile brick house with a fully exposed cellar. Originally the house stair arrived at a small portico with

Fig. 130. Joshua Wheeler house, 1820

Fig. 131. William Walker house, 1803–5

Fig. 132. Bentivar, c. 1790, c. 1830

columns made of pie-shaped bricks. Other features include a Flemish-bond facade with the other three walls of five-course American bond with Flemish variant, a stuccoed molded-brick cornice on all four sides, a hipped roof culminating in a belvedere, and nine-over-nine sash above nine-over-three cellar windows.[36]

Samuel Carr (1745–1777) probably built the first house at Dunlora just south of the fork of the Rivanna and across the river from Bentivar. His nephew and namesake, Colonel Samuel Carr (1771–1855), had a brick house (fig. 133) built here in 1828 by Thomas R. Blackburn and William B. Phillips that was similar to Bentivar. This newer house also had an exposed cellar, an exterior stair to a piano nobile portico, and a hipped roof with belvedere. In 1846 the property passed to a descendant, William S. Dabney, who willed the western part of the Dunlora property to his former slaves at the end of the Civil War; the tract became known as the Free State. The house was burned by an arsonist in 1916, then renovated by architect Eugene Bradbury, who altered the entrance and lowered it to the first-floor ground level.[37]

TWO-STORY BRICK DWELLINGS

The Brick Stack House

Built in the late 1820s on present-day Route 692, the old Staunton–James River Turnpike, Rosneath began as a brick one-over-one stack house with a Flemish-bond facade. The Carr family may have built it as a hunting

lodge. The house was enlarged in 1845, and in 1910 a living room was added on the northwest. A summer kitchen and chicken house remain on the property.[38]

Two-Story Brick Hall-Parlor Dwellings

John Rodes Sr. of Louisa County built the two-story log Midway in 1765, halfway between Brown's Gap and Charlottesville. In 1807 a two-story, hall-parlor house (fig. 134) with a penciled Flemish-bond facade and four-course American-bond sides was built here for Captain John Rodes III. It contains stepped gables and a double-row brick mousetooth cornice. About 1820 another two-story, hall-parlor house was built on line with the older one, but about fifteen feet to the west. It is constructed of three-course American bond below five-course. Both brick units, which have been joined by a hyphen, have wooden wainscots on the first floor. A brick summer kitchen of three-course American bond stands outside the formal gardens designed in 1936 by Charles Gillette.[39]

Another two-story, hall-parlor house also named Midway was built about 1810 on present-day Route 791 near Crozet. This three-bay, three-course American-bond house features posts and beams bearing reciprocating-saw marks, as well as mortise-and-tenon-pegged joinery. In addition, the Flemish-bond brick house Rose Valley near White Hall was constructed on the hall-parlor plan in 1820. It received an ell addition in 1850. Samuel Barksdale probably constructed Pleasant Hill, a one-story frame house on the old Lynchburg Road (Route 706). About 1840, on the marriage of his son John H. Barksdale to Martha Catherine Dunkum, daughter of brickmason William Dunkum, a two-story, two-bay hall-parlor brick house was built on the site. It features a Flemish-bond facade, dual windows, and parapeted gable-end walls.[40]

Charles Munday built the brick hall-parlor Woodburne (figs. 135, 136) near Proffit, probably in the 1820s. It has a penciled Flemish-bond facade and five-course American bond on the other three sides. Pomegranate, another hall-parlor-plan house, is near the Miller School, built most likely for

Fig. 133. Dunlora, 1828

Fig. 134. Midway, 1807, c. 1820

Fig. 135. Woodburne, 1820s

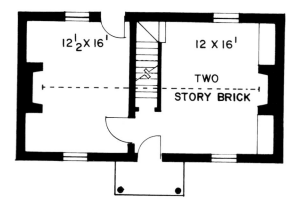

Fig. 136. Woodburne, 1820s, plan

Joseph Grayson about 1823. It displays a molded-brick cornice, a penciled Flemish-bond facade, and six-over-nine sash on the first floor. Dr. Reuben Lewis, brother of the explorer Meriwether Lewis, built Valley Point Farm at Ivy about 1825. Among its features are a side-passage plan

with a gable lunette, a molded-brick cornice, nine-over-nine sash on the first floor with nine-over-six on the second, and a Flemish-bond facade with remaining walls in five-course American bond.[41]

A member of the White family probably built The Anchorage on what is today's U.S. Route 29 near Red Hill before 1826. It was constructed with the hall-parlor plan and displays penciled three-course American-bond brickwork. Later an ell of five-course American bond was added, and the entire house was Victorianized. Samuel Overton Moon built his hall-parlor house, Westbury, in Batesville in the late 1820s. The house was expanded before midcentury to include another two-story brick unit, and the entire house was Victorianized after the Civil War. At his death in 1870, Moon was one of the richest persons in the county. The Walters-Page house, another two-story brick dwelling with a hall-parlor plan, is also in Batesville. It was built about 1830 for Mrs. Polly Walters. A casing for a foot-operated punkah remains in the house.[42]

Fig. 137. Red Hills, c. 1797, c. 1821

The Brick I-House

The I-house with its different wall construction and its various stylistic decorations continued throughout the nineteenth century as one of the most popular house forms in America as well as in Albemarle County, where examples abound. Red Hills, for instance, with its penciled Flemish-bond brick, was built around 1821 for Dr. Francis Carr, later the secretary of the University of Virginia's first faculty. Interestingly, the two one-story brick wings (fig. 137) to the back of the house extend into the I-house wall, indicating that they were built first, allegedly about 1797. In 1880 the German-born Adolph C. H. F. Russow, who had rented the property, purchased it and took a prize in Paris for his wine from the vineyards here. This unique house has been restored in recent years by James and Ann Eddins.[43]

Bezaleel Garland Brown built the brick I-house called Walnut Level in Brown's Cove about 1810, when he married Elizabeth Early Michie. Two sides are constructed of Flemish bond while the other two are of three-course American bond. Mount Pleasant, an early nineteenth-century brick I-house, is on the Hardware River northeast of Scottsville. Flemish bond was used on all four walls, but with three-course American bond below the water table. One gable end contains a two-story, three-columned portico with a balcony suspended by wrought-iron rods. A two-story frame ell addition is underpinned with five-course American-bond brickwork. Mount Armour, an early nineteenth-century brick I-house situated near the Nelson County line in the southwestern part of Albemarle, has a Flemish-bond facade with five-course American bond on the other walls and a molded five-brick cornice. The first floor contains semicircular relieving arches of gauged bricks above six-over-six sash.[44]

Jefferson builder John Dunkum constructed his two-story, three-bay brick I-house, Woodland (fig. 138), near Carter's Bridge about 1820. He used penciled Flemish bond on three sides and five-course American bond on the

Fig. 138. Woodland, c. 1820

rear elevation, as well as mousetooth cornices. An early L-wing addition with the same Flemish bond and cornice contains a winter kitchen in its cellar. Two early outbuildings, a summer kitchen with pit-sawed beaded siding attached with rosehead nails and a log granary, still stand on the property. The remnants of the circular stone walls of the icehouse can be seen across U.S. Route 20 to the west. In 1929 architect Lloyd C. Mayers made additions and alterations to the main house.[45]

As early as 1825 John Patton resided on West Main Street in a three-bay brick I-house with a hipped roof, paired-square-column portico, and tripartite window that survived until the mid-1950s. Christian Wertenbaker, a native of Germany, moved from Columbia in Fluvanna County to the newly established town of Milton in Albemarle about 1789. His son, William Wertenbaker, a former sheriff and lawyer, was appointed by Jefferson as the second university librarian in 1826. The library at that time contained 8,000 volumes, one of the largest collections in the country. Wertenbaker's house, Wertland (fig. 139), was built soon after his appointment. After Wertenbaker's death in 1882, a Victorian porch was added to the house in 1886. An I-house exhibiting American bond but with Flemish vari-

ant is Clover Hill near Keswick. It was built in 1830 for Dr. Thomas Walker Meriwether, whose daughter Mildred and her husband, George W. Macon, resided here for many years. Still standing here is a double-pen log granary and a barn with pit-sawed mortise-and-tenon joinery and octagonal columns with lamb's-tongues. These structures date from the earlier Clover Fields property adjacent to the south.[46]

Two-Story Brick Double-Pile Dwellings

In 1788 James Monroe purchased a town house one block from the courthouse and an 800-acre farm west of town that he called his "lower plantation." In 1790 he built Monroe Hill along with a law office on the farm. From 1794 until 1797 his brother Joseph resided here temporarily while Monroe served as minister to France. In 1799, after becoming governor of Virginia, James Monroe moved to Highland near Monticello. In 1814 the builder John M. Perry acquired the Monroe Hill property and probably expanded the main house into its present double-pile, five-bay form with a brick dentil cornice. He sold it three years later for the use of the University of Virginia, and Proctor Arthur P. Brockenbrough resided here. In 1848 arcaded

Fig. 139. Wertland, L1820s

student rooms were added to the house, and after the Civil War, George Sidney Ford remodeled the main dwelling.[47]

The grand brick Georgian plan survived well into the nineteenth century beneath Federal and Greek Revival garb. The 48-by-42-foot house called The Farm (figs. 140, 141), now within the eastern city limits of Charlottesville, is a three-bay version. It has triple-hung sash windows on three elevations. Other features include a one-story paired-column portico of pie-shaped bricks with Chinese railings, double-leaf entrance doors surrounded by a fanlight and sidelights, recessed arched openings around the dining-room mantel, and clay floor insulation. The house was begun about 1825 and first occupied in 1827 as the residence of John A. G. Davis, who became professor of law and chairman of the faculty at the

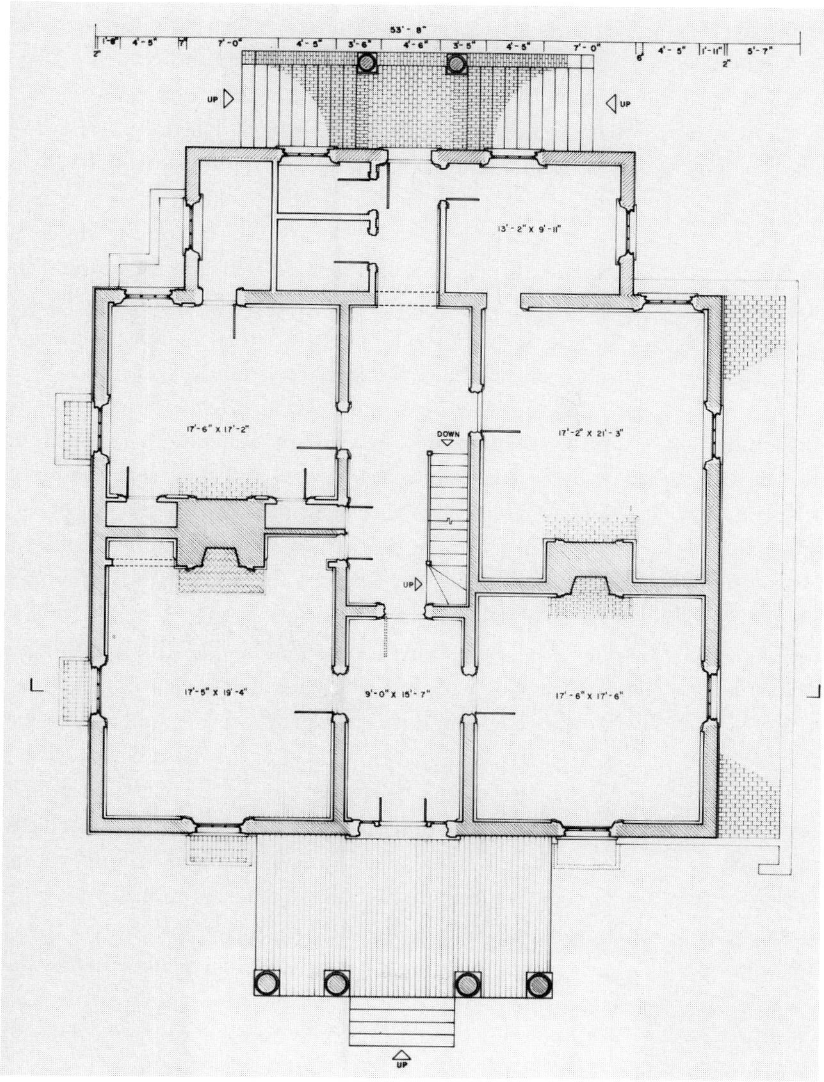

Fig. 140. (above) The Farm, 1825–27

Fig. 141. (left) The Farm, 1825–27, plan

University of Virginia. Professor Davis's death in 1840 outside his Lawn pavilion at the hands of a rowdy student prompted the establishment of the honor system at the university two years later. George R. B. Michie, founder of what became a well-known law-publishing company, purchased the house in 1909. After being in disrepair for a number of years, the house was restored in 1993 by owner-architects Jo Lawson and Michael Bednar.[48]

William B. Phillips and Malcolm F. Crawford built a similar house in 1828 to replace the original dwelling near Shadwell at Edgehill, for which Thomas Jefferson Randolph had obtained title in 1826. According to a letter written in 1827, only the parlor and dining room remained of the first house; "the rest has fallen down." This original remnant, by then only a two-room, one-story frame house, was moved to make way for the new 38-by-46-foot, three-bay brick dwelling constructed in 1828. In 1829, in order to pay the inherited debts of Thomas Mann Randolph Jr. and Thomas Jefferson, Edgehill became The Edgehill School for Young Ladies. Although the interior of the 1828 house burned in 1916, the dwelling as it stands today closely resembles the drawings attributed to Phillips and Crawford for the 1828 structure. Discovered in recent excavations, an unusual feature, a brick-walled and -floored fossé, surrounded the building. This early nineteenth-century waterproofing measure relied on a retaining wall several feet outside the cellar wall to keep ground moisture away from the cellar. As at The Farm, the second Edgehill had a hipped roof and a one-story paired-column portico with Chinese railings.[49]

Five-bay facades were more common with the Georgian plan than the three-bay versions. Glendower, built about 1810 on present-day Route 20 south of Keene, is a good example of the former, with its two-story penciled Flemish-bond walls, nine-over-nine sash windows on the first floor with six-over-nine on the second, and a hipped roof that culminated in a cupola. Its two two-tier porticoes were designed by a New Jersey architect early in the twentieth century. An early brick kitchen-laundry remains on the property as well as a school that was built for black children.[50]

The 1814 John Russell Jones house on East Jefferson Street in Charlottesville began as a two-story brick L-plan but became double-pile with the completion of its northwest corner. Its doorway has a fanlight with sidelights, and its four-bay gable-end facade has four false windows where the blinds were permanently closed over brick recesses. Jones was a mercantile partner with his brother-in-law Colonel Nimrod Bramham and became the first pres-

ident of the local branch of the Farmers' Bank of Virginia. The dwelling housed the law office of George Allen, governor of Virginia from 1994 to 1998.[51]

The Barracks, located off Barracks Road, was built in 1819 for Garland Garth on the site of the Revolutionary War British and Hessian prisoner-of-war barracks, which occupied a tract owned during the war by Colonel John Harvie of Belmont. The house has lunettes in both gables and a penciled Flemish-bond facade with five-course American bond on the other three sides. In 1930 W. Duncan Lee, a Richmond architect, made changes to the house while Richmond landscape architect Charles Gillette added the formal gardens. Bezaleel Brown Jr. built the five-bay, two-story brick house called Licking in Brown's Cove about 1822. It featured nine-over-nine sash windows on the first floor and six-over-nine above. It burned about 1940 and was razed in 1984.[52]

The Scotch-Irishman John Kelly of Lancaster County became a successful merchant in partnership with his nephew and son-in-law, Opie Norris, and owned a large amount of land between the town and the university. Kelly was a founder of the South Plains Presbyterian Church and was also instrumental in building the Charlottesville Presbyterian Church. In 1828 Kelly constructed a five-bay, two-story brick house (fig. 142) on Park Street at Maple; it was noted for a chimney curtain between its double-pile chimneys. It was razed in the twentieth century and is now the site of the present First Presbyterian Church, the successor of the one Kelly helped to found.[53]

Many other two-story, double-pile brick Federal houses did not have center passages extending from front to rear and containing the stair. Instead, they had an entrance hall and a salon to the rear for greater privacy. For example, James "Cutfinger" Minor built his home Brookhill (figs. 143, 144) on the Rivanna River north of town about 1815. According to local tradition, Minor earned his sobriquet as a young court clerk when he cut off the forefinger of his writing hand to end his clerking days after he had become disenchanted with the prospect of spending the rest of his life working indoors. In 1857 the dentist Dr. Charles Minor, James Minor's cousin, conducted a school for boys at the house. The double-pile dwelling has an unheated entrance hall, beyond which are a parlor and a dining room. The latter contains a built-in cherry china press with drawers below, one of which unfolds to become a writing surface. On the outside of the house, the penciled Flemish-bond facade and other walls of three-course American bond contain a raised-brick belt course between the first and second floors and a molded-brick cornice above.

Fig. 142. John Kelly house, 1828

Similarities exist between James Minor's Brookhill and Ridgway, the home of his first cousin, Peter Minor, at Eastham, where master joiner James Dinsmore died in 1830. Both dwellings have similar double-pile floor plans, two-story Flemish-bond facades, five-bay fronts and four-bay backs, tucked-away stairs, center passages leading to two rear rooms, and special built-in closets beside the fireplaces. Ridgway's facade, however, was converted into the Gothic Revival style about the mid–nineteenth century.[54]

In 1821 David Higginbotham built a five-bay, double-pile, two-story brick house at Morven (fig. 145) that was similar in floor plan to Brookhill, although the previous year Jefferson had designed for him a more complex house with three octagonal bays. Morven's unheated entrance hall contains an enclosed stair to one side. One of the two first-floor rear rooms has an arched alcove and the other a marble caryatid mantel relocated from elsewhere in the house. Martin Thacker, the craftsman who built Redlands, also built this house. The turn-of-the-century renovation of Morven

Fig. 143. Brookhill, c. 1815

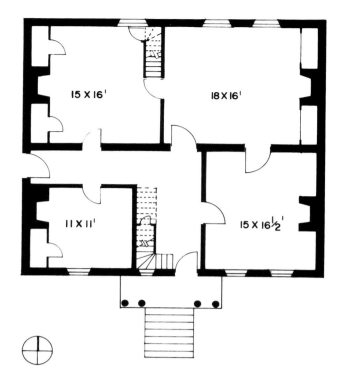

Fig. 144. (right) Brookhill, c. 1815, plan

Fig. 145. (below) Morven, 1821

has been attributed to Baltimore architect Howard Sill, who was working at Redlands about the same time. In 1926 Charles A. Stone purchased Morven and established a noted thoroughbred stud farm here. Four years later Annette Hoyt Flanders directed the restoration of the formal gardens. In the 1980s the property sold for $8.5 million, the highest price to that time in county history. Under the ownership of John Werner Kluge, the grounds have been embellished with the outdoor sculpture of Aristide Maillol, Auguste Rodin, Marino Marini, Magdalena Abakanowicz, Robert Graham, Giacomo Manzu, Arturo Martini, Alberto Giacometti, Henry Moore, and Robert Arneson.[55]

Esmont (fig. 146), at the intersection of Routes 715 and 719 in the southern part of the county, is a three-bay version of Morven that contains an entrance hall with private rooms beyond. The house was built about 1816 for Dr. Charles L. Cocke, a nephew of James Powell Cocke of Edgemont and a cousin of John Hartwell Cocke of Bremo. In 1848 Bedford Brown purchased Esmont. The house is exquisitely composed with fine Flemish-bond brickwork believed to have been laid by William B. Phillips. Esmont exhibits many refined details including a 48-by-45-foot plan with full exterior Doric entablature, plaster belt courses, Chinese Chippendale railings, King of Prussia marble mantels, plaster ceiling ornaments, silver-plated locks, and cut-glass door knobs. Its entrance hall features a wooden parquet floor with a herringbone pattern equaled only by that at Monticello. The triple-sash tripartite windows so favored by Latrobe are found on all four first-floor walls and extend to floor level. The brackets of

Fig. 147. Bel Aire, c. 1825

the stairs, which are located to the side of the entrance hall, are similar to those at Carrsbrook, Plain Dealing, and Dunkum's Brookhill. The cellar contains clay floor insulation and tapered leveling wedges above the posts that support the summer beams.[56]

James Michie, a county sheriff and magistrate, built Bel Aire (fig. 147) on the north fork of the Rivanna River near Piney Mountain about 1825. The two-story brick house includes chimney curtains in the gables with a lunette in the west gable and a brick recess in the first floor below probably for a blind window. Its four-bay facade had two front doors sheltered by a one-story paired-brick-column portico; one door has been replaced with a window. The double-pile floor plan consists of four rooms with no center passage.[57]

The Brick Town House

Just as the full Georgian plan continued to be built well into the nineteenth century, so did its smaller town-house variations. In urban areas such dwellings were constructed with narrower facades to accommodate the smaller town lots. A two-thirds version, usually three-bay, was double-pile with a side entrance passage, while the one-third version, usually two-bay, was simply a double-pile house without the side entrance passage. These basic Georgian town-house plans were embellished with the decorative motifs of the Federal, Greek Revival, and Victorian periods. The one-third versions with no side passage were the rarer of the two. Opie Norris, for example, received lot number 4 on East Jefferson Street in Charlottesville as John Kelly's son-in-law. It is believed that the Scotch-Irish

Fig. 146. Esmont, c. 1819

cabinetmaker Edward Butler and his son James, alias Nolly, built the two-story Flemish-bond brick Butler-Norris town house (fig. 148) on the lot about 1808. The house is probably the oldest extant house in downtown and is the only house in the city with a molded-brick cornice. It has nine-over-six sash windows, and its mantels incorporate candlestick moldings.[58]

In the 1820s the brick Norris-McCue town house was built adjacent to the Butler-Norris house to the east, but with a brick mousetooth cornice, five-course American bond, and six-over-nine sash windows. A five-foot-wide passage separates the two houses — a common feature that allowed access to the rear door for service and private entry from the street. The Barclay town house in Scottsville also exhibits the one-third plan. Possibly built by John B. Hart after his purchase of a lot in 1830, the house gives evidence of earlier construction, because the west sidewall contains three-course American bond that changes to five-course by the second floor. In 1850 Dr. James Turner Barclay, who had owned Monticello, purchased the house next door to the Disciples of Christ Church he had built four years earlier. He spent several years as a missionary in Jerusalem.[59]

Most town houses were of the two-thirds Georgian type. Alexander St. Clair Heiskell built one example, the Heiskell-Livers town house (fig. 149), at 1211 West Main Street in 1827. James Dinsmore, who had owned speculative lots here, may have designed it. John Breckenridge purchased the property in 1831 and sold it to Clement P. McKennie seven years later; the deed described it as the lot "on which Alexander St. Clair Heiskell erected a valuable brick dwelling house and other improvements." McKennie, whose family resided here for seventy-five years, was the publisher of the *Central Gazette* newspaper and later established a bookstore at The Corner that evolved into the University Bookstore. The town house has a chimney curtain in its gable. A sun parlor, two sleeping porches, and portico were added by John L. Livers after he acquired the property in 1915. Adjacent to it on the west is a second house constructed by Heiskell in 1842.[60]

John Vowles built another town-house pair on the Dinsmore lots on West Main Street: 1111 (figs. 150, 151) built in 1823 and 1113 about 1830. Both have two-third Georgian plans, Flemish-bond fa-

cades, and flat transoms over their entrance doors. Number 1111 has a chimney curtain, a circular plaster medallion with dogwood blossoms in the entrance ceiling, and a mantel with candlestick moldings, while 1113 has a triple-hung sash window and diagonally set fireplaces. In 1839 Michael Johnson bought the properties; he in turn sold them to Mary E. Dunkum in 1850. Another West Main Street town house, Paxton Place, was built for J. D. Paxton about 1824. It has a mousetooth cornice and a lunette below its brick chimney curtain. Dr. Charles Carter built the Carter-Gilmer town house on a corner of East Jefferson Street, as well as his detached one-story brick office, after acquiring the land in 1825. The first two stories of the sides of the house that face the two streets at the intersection are of

Fig. 148. Butler-Norris town house, c. 1808

Fig. 149. Heiskell-Livers town house, 1827, 1842

Fig. 150. (above) John Vowles town house, 1823, c. 1830, elevation

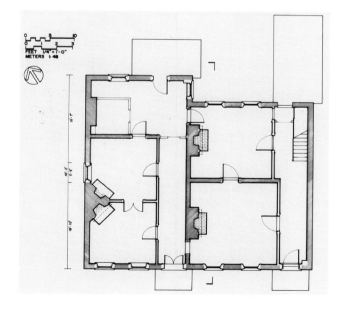

Fig. 151. (right) John Vowles town house, 1823, c. 1830, plan

Flemish bond, while the sides that face the garden are of five-course American bond. The third floor obviously was added later because its bond changes to five-course American with Flemish variant. The Massie-Wills town houses in the 200 block of Fourth Street were built for Dr. Hardin Massie. In 1830 he built number 215 with nine-over-six sash windows on the first floor and six-over-six above, a chimney curtain, brick dentil cornice, and a Flemish-bond facade with five-course American bond below the water table. Another side-passage house was built to the south in 1840 with a carriage passage between the two houses. Frederick Wills connected them in the 1870s.[61]

FIGURAL SPACES

Spaces that were nonorthogonal (irregular) became popular during the Federal period, and their plans employed segmental, circular, oval, cyma, and octagonal forms. Louis LeVau utilized the elliptical salon as early as the mid–seventeenth century at Vaux-le-Vicomte in France, and projecting segmental salons were shown in Sir John Soane's *Plans, Elevations, and Sections of Buildings*, published in 1788 in London.

One-Story Frame Dwellings with Figural Spaces

James Powell Cocke was born at Malvern Hill in Henrico County in 1748 and served Henrico as a justice. Seeking a healthier, malaria-free climate, he moved first to Augusta County and then to Albemarle, where he built Edgemont (fig. 152) near Alberene about 1796. The building date is taken from a reference to the house in a letter from Jefferson to Wilson Cary Nicholas that year. "Discovered" in ruins in 1936 by architect Milton Grigg and the pioneer woman architectural photographer Frances Benjamin Johnston, Edgemont was attributed to Jefferson because of its similarity to his design for Edgehill and to Woodberry Forest in Orange County, which he designed for William Madison, brother of President James Madison. Dinsmore and Neilson, Jefferson's builder-architects, could not have been involved in the construction of Edgemont as they had not yet arrived in the county. Cocke had considered a William Bates as the builder of his house in 1793, but whether he actually executed the final building is unknown.

Edgemont, based on Andrea Palladio's Villa Capra (Rotunda) in Vicenza, is a bank house: one story at its entrance, which is centered on a hill to the south, but drop-

Fig. 152. Edgemont, c. 1796

ping off to two stories to the north, which faces its parterres. According to Grigg, Edgemont's rusticated frame walls were originally "sanded" and the joints painted in a contrasting color to make the walls look like stone. Its upper octagonal salon is directly over the dining room at the rear garden level. Grigg restored and altered the house in 1938 for Dr. Graham Clark and in 1946 for William Snead. The south and west porticoes are original, but Grigg added the other two. The octagonal space projection on the north side of the house had a portico base but no portico; Grigg supplied one, patterning it after Jefferson's colonnade-over-arcade facades at Poplar Forest and Pavilion VII. The Chinese Chippendale railings are conjectural, as are the wooden corner quoins. An uncoursed rubblestone outbuilding in the northeast garden corner was replicated by Grigg in the northwest corner as a dovecote. Grigg designed underground passages with lunettes, patterned after the university's gymnasia and Monticello's underground passage, to connect his two new outbuildings to the main house. He replaced the missing staircase with one from a Charlottesville house, reinstated a Palladian screen motif in the entrance hall, and added a plaster ceiling medallion and pediment over the salon doorway.

Today we consider that the best way to restore an old building is to retain as much of the original fabric as possible and to make as few changes as needed. Earlier in the twentieth century, old houses frequently were embellished — often in grander ways than originally intended — as they were renovated to make them more elegant as well as more livable. The renovation of Edgemont is of just that sort, and although not the preferred way to restore a building today, it is in its own right a masterpiece from the hand of Milton L. Grigg.[62]

Two-Story Brick Dwellings with Figural Spaces

Thomas Jefferson's first Monticello, begun in the early 1770s, constituted the first figural space in the English colonies with its demioctagonal forms. His decision to build on top of a mountain and to connect recessed dependencies with the main house was unique in America.[63] After returning from France in 1789, Jefferson began transforming Monticello to reduce the apparent height of the front facade and to introduce the first dome exposed on the exterior of an American house, but his duties as secretary of state from 1790 to 1793 slowed his progress. In 1796 he had the two-tier east portico dismantled; the present east portico was erected in 1804, using the original stone Doric columns. In 1800 he began construction of the Philibert de l'Orme, or Delorme, dome, and about

1823 the brick-shaft columns were finally installed to replace the tulip poplar tree trunks holding up the entablature of the west portico. By 1809, forty years after its beginning, Monticello's interior was completed, thereby doubling the size of the original house. True to Jefferson's use of dynamic spaces, with no two rooms alike on the interior of what appears symmetrical on the exterior, Monticello's intricate composition is grasped experientially as one moves about the complex. As at the university, the inconsistencies and contradictions of Monticello's design produce a visually exciting and dynamic dwelling.

To these dynamic qualities may be added illusion, especially on Monticello's exterior. Under the portico, its wooden cladding is rusticated and sanded to resemble stone, mahogany wooden muntins are used here to make the sash less noticeable, two-dimensional roof balusters at the dome wall appear to be round, and the lowering of the second-floor windows to floor level reduces the perceived height of the north facade. Jefferson designed several exterior features to work with the natural environment, not against it, for the convenience of Monticello's residents. A board-covered terrace over the lower servant passage, for example, contains troughs beneath it to divert rainwater into cisterns. Similar troughs were used to support brick insulation in the passage under the main house. Two roofs covered the earth-insulated ice pit, thereby preserving the ice for a longer time. Freshly caught fish were kept in a garden pond near the house. Jefferson also brought the outdoors inside with a green-painted entrance floor and grass planted in the west portico floor, operable skylights throughout the house, and storm windows and doors that soften the effects of weather on the northwest. Furthermore, his generous use of tall, triple-hung windows and glass doors made Monticello one of the lightest and airiest houses of its time.

One of Jefferson's most modern traits was his love of gadgets and conveniences, which he incorporated into Monticello's design wherever he saw an opportunity. He either invented or adapted such innovative features as self-opening double-leaf doors, bedchambers with entry alcoves and two doors for sound-deadening and privacy, Rumford stoves, recessed bed alcoves (one of which positioned his own bed between his dressing room and study), three indoor privies, portable bookcases, wine-bottle dumbwaiters, and a lazy Susan dining-room door. A weathervane atop the eastern portico can be read from indoors because it is connected by a rod to a pointer and dial under the portico. The entrance hall contains an indoor-outdoor seven-day clock with cannonball weights that designate the days of the week as they sink past labels on the wall (Saturday is in the basement, via a hole in the floor), and a folding ladder used to wind the clock still stands in a corner. Other unusual features include an intricately formed Welsh tin roof and a parquet salon floor, to name but a few among dozens.[64]

After Jefferson's death in 1826, the house and grounds began to deteriorate, yet their sad condition did not keep trespassers and souvenir hunters away. In 1828 his grandson and executor Thomas Jefferson Randolph advertised in the local newspaper that "in consequence of the ruinous trespasses committed . . . on the estate of Thomas Jefferson, he must prohibit all persons whatsoever from hunting or ranging over the same, with the assurance that the most rigorous steps will be taken to enforce this prohibition." A few months later Randolph advertised the sale of the property "divided to suit purchasers. . . . The sale is being made for the payment of the testator's debts."[65]

Monticello, though the first house with figural space in the county, was not the last. Redlands (figs. 153, 154) was another. John Carter, a son of Robert "King" Carter, received a grant for 9,350 acres around what is now Carter's Mountain. By 1789 John Carter's son Edward, of Blenheim, had sent a foreman with twenty-five slaves to dig the foundation for a house in a hillside grove of large trees, then called West Oak, six miles west of Blenheim. This was the site of Redlands. Martin Thacker built Redlands for Edward Carter's son Robert, who had married Mary Eliza Coles in 1798. About 1812 a Mr. Heston from Lynchburg and his workman, Thomas Billups, worked on the interior of the present house, completing the first floor by 1813 except for one mantel. While the house was being built in 1798, the Carters lived just east of it in a frame hall-parlor-plan dwelling that burned about 1915. Early in the twentieth century, Baltimore architect Howard Sill renovated the brick house and completed the interior of the sec-

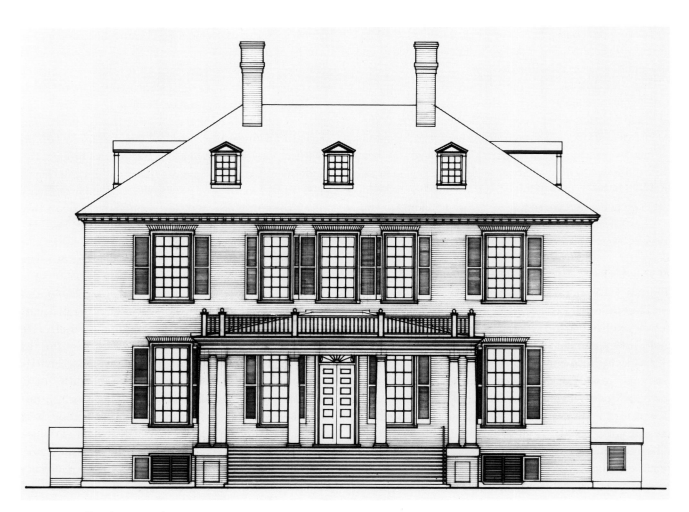

Fig. 153. Redlands, 1798, elevation

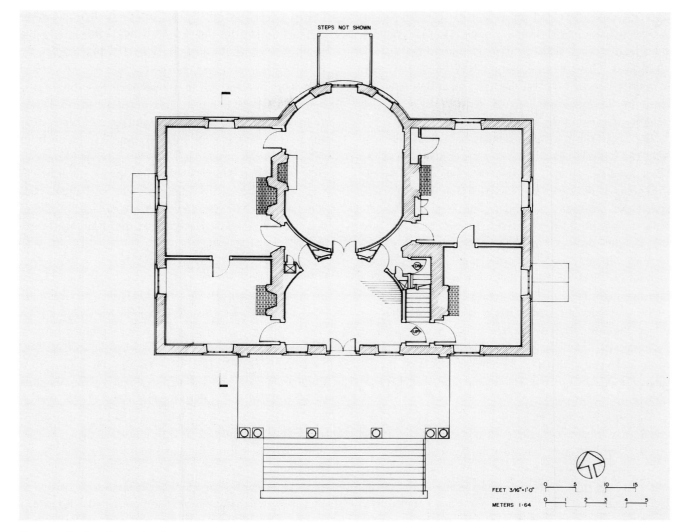

STEPS NOT SHOWN

FEET 3/16"=1'0"
METERS 1:64

Fig. 154. Redlands, 1798, plan

ond floor; he also renovated nearby Morven. At the time of Sill's death in 1927, he was an associate in the well-known architectural firm led by John Russell Pope.

The house presents a five-bay Georgian facade on the south front, but the north elevation reveals its projecting Federal segmental salon. (Alexander Parrish executed similar segmental spaces in the Wickham-Valentine house in Richmond in 1812.) Redlands contains seventeen rooms with twelve fireplaces that open from just two chimney stacks. The attic construction consists of three massive king-post trusses, and its first floor utilizes corn shucks for insulation. The interior contains a bed alcove, a dumbwaiter to transport food from the cellar kitchen to the first-floor dining room, and a shaft paralleling the stairwell from the second floor that may have been used to convey chamber pots to the cellar.

Its name derived from the red clay soil, the house was built on the southeastern side of Carter's Mountain, commanding the crest of a knoll amid large trees and with splendid views of the mountains to the southwest. To the east were boxwood-lined flower and vegetable gardens consisting of twelve squares; some were laid out in the form of a Maltese cross, a reflection of Robert Carter's Masonic affiliation. Redlands remains in the Carter family to this day, and a remarkable assemblage of portraits, furniture, and other family possessions reflects their long tenure. Recently the Thomas Jefferson Chapter of the Association for the Preservation of Virginia Antiquities recognized the Carters for their generations of stewardship at Redlands.[66]

In 1758 Francis Jerdone I, who would become a Loyalist during the Revolutionary War, acquired Farmington just west of town on Ivy Creek on present-day U.S. Route 250. In 1785 his son sold the property to Dr. Thomas Walker's son-in-law George Divers, the first owner of the tract to reside here. Divers probably built the two-thirds Georgian plan brick house in 1792, perhaps as an addition to an existing log house to the west. A detached brick service wing was located to the south.

In 1802 Divers commissioned his friend Thomas Jefferson to design an addition for the eastern end of the brick dwelling. Jefferson planned (figs. 155, 156) an octagonal wing with a tetrastyle portico and probably also added the one-story passage to the service wing. As Jefferson was president at the time, he was not available to oversee the construction. The result was not to his satisfaction: columns were out of proportion, and the demioctagonal ends lacked a full entablature around them. The interior was built as an asymmetrical space with an offset partition. Ordered for Monticello in 1792, the bull's-eye upper windows arrived too late and thus were used at Farmington. The cellar included a vaulted wine storage room and a ceiling with bricks between the joists for insulation. Log slave quarters and a circular icehouse also were located on the property.

Subsequent owners made significant alterations. General Bernard Peyton remodeled the house in 1852–54 in the Greek Revival manner, adding a small portico with cast-iron capitals on the north side of the original brick house and a passage over the lower service wing on the south. He also removed the Jeffersonian interior entablatures, which portrayed griffins, and added a second floor and center passages on each level within the octagonal space. In 1898 Warner Wood removed the log building to the west and replaced it with a two-story brick addition of four rooms. In 1929 Farmington was again remodeled, this time by architect Edmund Campbell, to serve as one of the most prestigious country clubs in Virginia. Campbell removed the interior floors and partitions in the octagon above the first-floor level to create a single two-story symmetrical space. Architects Marshall Wells and Floyd Johnson later made alterations and additions.[67]

TRIPARTITE DWELLINGS

The first version of Monticello and James Dinsmore's own home were both tripartite forms similar to the so-called James Semple house of about 1780 in Williamsburg, which actually was built for William Finnie and often has been attributed to Jefferson. In 1809 St. George Tucker referred to the dwelling as the "handsomest house in town."

The tripartite house form consisted of a two-story center pavilion, usually three bays wide, with a pedimented gable facing the front and lower side wings; it often exhibited a one-story paired-column portico at the entrance. It was built on the T-plan, with an unheated central entrance passage that contained a stair and permitted access to the three rooms that projected to each side and the rear. Some early sources for the tripartite form are found in plates from William Halfpenny's *Useful Architecture*, published in 1752, and Robert Morris's *Select Architecture*, published in 1755. Disseminated by Jefferson's master builders and popularized in Minard Lefever's *Modern Builder's Guide* of 1833, which espoused square columns, the form spread south through the Carolinas.[68]

Frame Tripartite Dwellings

An 1836 fire destroyed the second Belvoir, a frame tripartite house built near Keswick in 1790 for Colonel John Walker. After Walker's death in 1809, the house became the property of his only grandchild, Eliza Kinloch Nelson, the wife of Hugh Nelson, who was the son of Governor Thomas Nelson and the first Speaker of the Virginia House of Delegates, a federal court judge, U.S. congressman, and minister to Spain. The house had a two-story center pavilion, 48 by 30 feet, with lower side wings, a fanlight over the front door, and a bull's-eye window in its tympanum.[69]

Springfield, another frame tripartite house, burned in 1897. It was north of Edgeworth off present-day Route 641 near the Orange County line. Springfield was built about 1800 for the Revolutionary War hero Reuben Lindsay, who had emigrated from Westmoreland County in 1776. He married a daughter of Dr. Thomas Walker. Springfield's two-story center pavilion measured 50 by 20 feet and had lower side wings. The farm contained a kitchen, smokehouse, dairy, and a later six-sided stone tower of unknown use that had a pyramidal roof. Several frame tripartite houses with single-pile projections to the rear are still extant. Andrew Hart (1754–1832) came from Scotland about 1780 and established himself as a successful store owner at Jumping Hill near North Garden. In 1797 he built Sunny Bank (fig. 157) at South Garden as a frame tripartite house with two-tier portico columns, each fashioned from a single poplar trunk. Its lower side wings were expanded to two stories in the early nineteenth century. The house remains in the Hart family to this day.[70]

Jefferson's master joiner, James Dinsmore, built his own frame tripartite house (fig. 158) among his other West Main Street dwellings in Charlottesville in the early

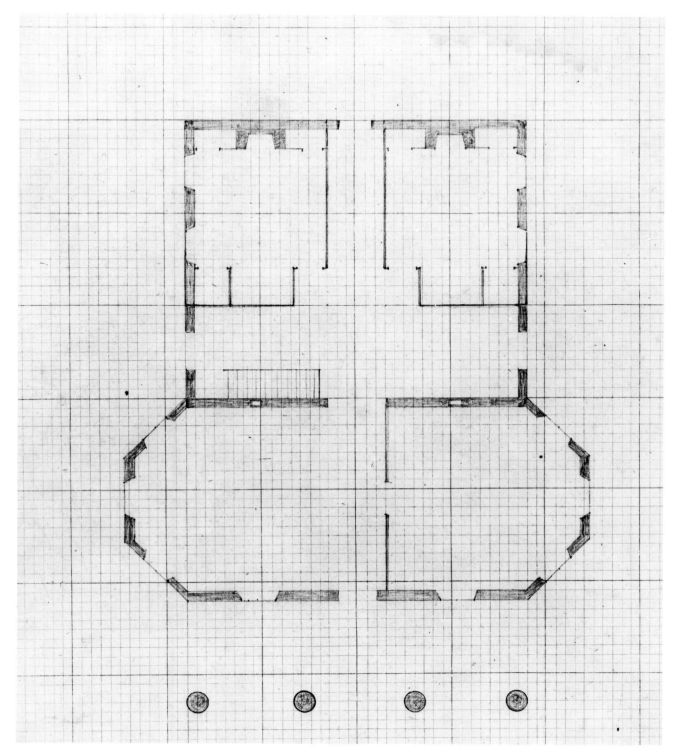

Fig. 155. Farmington, 1802, plan by Thomas Jefferson

Fig. 156. (above) Farmington, 1802, elevation by Thomas Jefferson

Fig. 157. (right) Sunny Bank, 1797

144

Fig. 158. James Dinsmore's house, E19C

nineteenth century. It had a two-story, three-bay center pavilion with a one-story paired-column portico and lower side wings. At the time of his death in 1830, the property was described as having a garden, kitchen, smokehouse, large workshop, corncrib, and stable. The house was razed in 1960. The frame tripartite house at Howardsville, in its ruinous state, has but one wing now. Its two-story, three-bay center pavilion has a one-story paired-square-column portico with Chinese railings.[71]

Jefferson's brother-in-law and friend Dabney Carr died in 1773, leaving a wife and six children. Jefferson's sister Martha moved the family into Monticello where the oldest son, Peter, aged three, was reared and educated under the influence of his famous uncle. While Jefferson was minister to France, he arranged for James Madison to serve as Peter's guardian and enrolled the boy at Walker Maury's classical grammar school in Williamsburg. Afterward, Peter studied under George Wythe at the College of William and Mary. In 1793 he began a law practice in Albemarle County, and from 1798 until his death in 1815, he resided at Carrsbrook (fig. 159) north of Charlottesville on the south fork of the Rivanna River. The house had been

built in the 1780s by his uncle Thomas Carr (c. 1735–1807), son of John Carr of Bear Castle, and was sold to Wilson Cary Nicholas in 1794. Peter Carr married Nicholas's wife's sister three years later and acquired the house. He served in the Virginia General Assembly, was Jefferson's personal secretary, and ran a private school at his home beginning in 1811 until his death in 1815. Carrsbrook's three-bay, two-story central pavilion has a rear passage to its pavilion wings, thus creating a five-part composition. There is no evidence that Jefferson designed the house.[72]

Brick Tripartite Dwellings

The earliest brick tripartite house in Albemarle County was the first Monticello, while the earliest unaltered extant example is Mountain Grove (figs. 160, 161) near Damon, built for Revolutionary War captain Benjamin Harris in 1803–4. A man of wealth and prominence, Harris signed the county's "Declaration of Independence" in 1779; he became a magistrate in 1791 and sheriff in 1815. The proportions among Mountain Grove's facade, plan, and landscape are all based on the golden section (a proportional system based on the diagonal of half of a square) with 248-foot-

Fig. 159. Carrsbrook, 1780s

Fig. 160. Mountain Grove, 1803–4

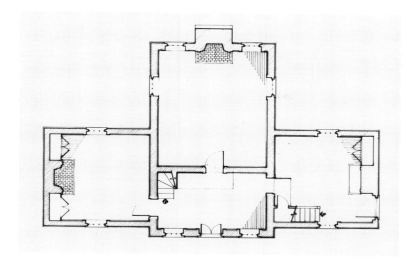

Fig. 161. Mountain Grove, 1803–4, plan

transom above. A bull's-eye window pierces the tympanum, and wooden scrolled modillions surround the roof eaves. Its interior has grained and paneled wainscots. The mantelpieces include carved mantels and overmantels with candlestick moldings, reeding, and consoles. The mantel in the main salon boasts herringbone latticework, garlands, stippling, marbleizing, and graining based on William Pain's *Builders' Pocket Treasury* of 1763. Many of the interior doors at Mountain Grove are grained with pen-lined panel fields to simulate mahogany.[73]

based on the diagonal of half of a square) with 248-foot-square plantation quadrangles. The front elevation has stuccoed jack arches to resemble stone over the doors and windows, molded-brick water tables, penciled three-course American bond, nine-over-nine sash windows with nine-over-six above, and a double-leaf front door with a flat

The brick tripartite house on Park Street built for Governor Thomas Walker Gilmer about 1820 had a four-bay center pavilion with a lunette in the gable and triangular lintels over the windows. Gilmer, who later served as U.S. secretary of the navy, was killed in an explosion while aboard the gunboat *Princeton* in 1844. In 1849 Drury Wood purchased the dwelling, which was replaced in 1901 by another brick house that in turn gave way for the present First Presbyterian Church on Park Street. James Dinsmore built a tripartite brick house (fig. 162) with two-story brick wings

Fig. 162. Francis B. Dyer house, c. 1820

and stepped gables about 1820 for Francis B. Dyer at Seventh and East Jefferson Streets in Charlottesville. William D. Fitch, the proprietor of the Eagle Tavern, operated a public house here. General Alexander Archer Vandegrift was born in the house in 1888, and from 1889 to 1903 it served as a boardinghouse for Major Horace W. Jones's School for Boys. It was razed in 1955.[74]

One of the finest houses in Charlottesville is the brick tripartite Oak Lawn (figs. 163, 164), built in 1822 for Colonel Nimrod Bramham, who served in the Virginia House of Delegates. Bramham had operated a store in 1797 where the Turkey Sag Road met Coursey's Road (present-day Route 20 North) and in 1806 was operating another store on the west side of Court Square. In 1847, two years after his death, the property was sold to the Reverend James Fife, a native of Scotland. Fife became city engineer for Richmond, lived for a while in Goochland County, was ordained a Baptist minister, and purchased Rock Hill just north of Charlottesville in 1839. Oak Lawn remains in the Fife family to this day.[75]

In 1813 John Manoah Carr, a nephew of Dabney Carr, sold John Winn a property that contained a 1790s one-story frame house. Winn served as Charlottesville postmaster for many years and built the Jefferson Hotel on Court Square in 1828. His brother-in-law was the master brickmason John Jordan, who is believed to have built Winn's brick tripartite house Belmont (fig. 165) on the property from which the southeast portion of Charlottesville, the Belmont subdivision of the 1890s, derives its name. The second-floor wings were added about 1840, probably

Fig. 163. (above) Oak Lawn, 1822, sketch

Fig. 164. (right) Oak Lawn, 1822, plan

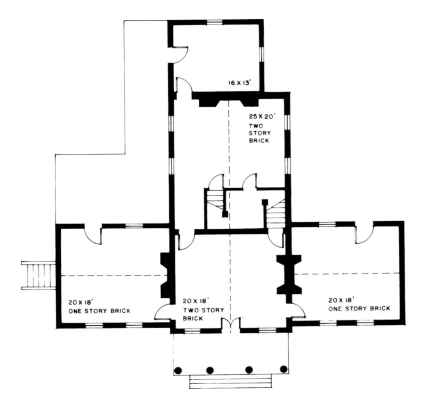

Fig. 165. Belmont, E19C, c. 1840

by Winn's son. The square-columned tetrastyle portico shelters a balcony with Chinese railings suspended by wrought-iron rods. A lunette adorns the portico's tympanum. A 16-foot-wide wooden entry-hall arch with a keystone is stored in the cellar. In 1857 Slaughter W. Ficklin purchased Belmont, made the property into one of the leading stock farms in America, and imported the first Percheron-Norman heavy-duty workhorses to Virginia. His famous stallion, Black Hawk, a mare, Daisy, and another stallion, Raspin, are buried on the property. Ficklin's brother, Major Benjamin Franklin Ficklin, the general superintendent of the Pony Express, briefly became the owner of Monticello in 1864, after it had been seized by the Confederate government. In 1865 he was jailed as an accomplice in President Abraham Lincoln's assassination but was cleared of any wrongdoing.[76]

In 1824 William Huntington's estate was advertised as a house "with wings on each side." It was listed as "a very handsome brick building" on "two-and-a-half acres immediately on the road [Main Street] . . . calculated for almost any business." Already this part of Main Street between the university and downtown Charlottesville was undergoing the conversion of houses to businesses with the development of the University of Virginia.[77]

Center Two-Story Pavilion without Wings

Another variation of the tripartite plan consisted of the center pavilion without the lower side wings. The Woodstock Hall frame addition of 1808 is an example of the plan, as is the nearby brick Malvern (figs. 166, 167) on Route 708 at Route 637. Malvern, originally called Oakland, may have been built by Menan Mills and his wife Frances, daughter of John Jouett, the owner of the Swan Tavern, in the early nineteenth century. The entrance of this two-story, three-bay house was intended for the center of the gable end, which has a lunette in the tympanum, but later was located on the west side. The entrance hall contains an elaborate freestanding stair, and the parlor beyond it has a fine Federal mantel. From 1902 to 1910 Malvern was the home of Benjamin E. Wheeler, who served as the mayor of Charlottesville from 1920 to 1922. In 1969–70 the house was restored under the guidance of architectural historian Clay Lancaster.[78]

Fig. 166. Malvern, E19C

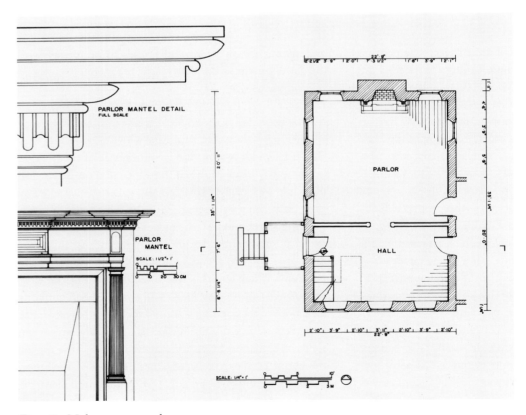

Fig. 167. Malvern, E19C, plan

I-Houses with Wings

In another variation of the tripartite house, the center pavilion is turned sideways to create an I-house with lower side wings. Begun in 1784 by John Coles II, the second Enniscorthy on Green Mountain had been transformed by 1810 into a 200-foot-long frame I-house containing one-story frame wings with a 12-by-60-foot-long piazza in back. The workmen included carpenters Francis Wethered and John Hall, brickmason John Harris, and Henry Martin, who supplied hardware and furnishings. When the house burned in December 1839, the family took up residence nearby in the mid-eighteenth-century one-story log house called the Cabin-in-the-Grove until they completed a third dwelling a decade later. This log house had been built for John Coles I. In 1984 it was torn down, and its logs were incorporated into another house in the county.[79]

Captain John M. Perry, the university brickmason, built his brick I-house with wings, Montebello (figs. 168, 169), just southwest of the university in 1819–20. From 1836 to 1865 his son-in-law George Wilson Spooner Jr. occupied the house. After the Civil War it was rented by William Mynn Thornton, later the first dean of the Engineering School. In 1917 Isaac Kimber Moran, the university bursar, bought it; his family lived here until they sold it to the university in 1961.[80]

PORTICOED DWELLINGS

In the Classical Revival period, the five basic column orders were built with varying heights and proportions calculated on the diameter of the column's base relative to its height. For Roman Revival architects, this meant that the

Fig. 168. Montebello, 1819–20. Rear view showing piazza addition.

Tuscan column rose approximately seven column diameters in height, the Doric eight diameters, the Ionic nine, the Corinthian ten, and the Composite eleven.

Two-Story Brick Double-Pile Dwellings with Tetrastyle Porticoes

Talbot Hamlin noted that Jefferson's "influence found its most characteristic expression in the pedimented two-story classical entrance porch."[81] The four-column, usually two-story, portico with a pediment, a lunette in the tympanum, and a fanlight above the doorway, became the symbol of the Roman Revival temple. Tuscan or Doric porticoes were common, and often a second-floor balcony was suspended by wrought-iron rods so as not to engage the

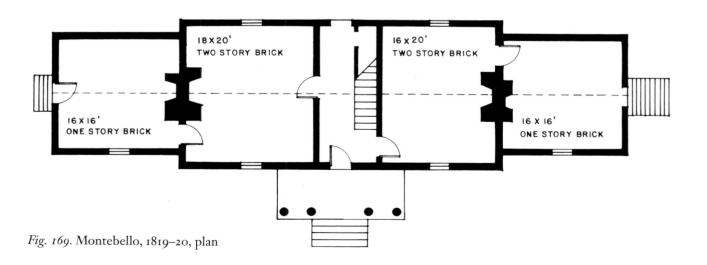

Fig. 169. Montebello, 1819–20, plan

columns. Such porticoes evoked the memory of Palladio's Villa Pisani at Montagnana in Italy.

In 1817 William Garth purchased property just west of Charlottesville and the university. As early as 1810 the tract had been called Birdwood (fig. 170), and in 1828 the Birdwood Jockey Club, among whose members was Jefferson workman Lyman Peck, advertised horse races here. Allegedly using workmen from the university, Garth built a mansion on the tract. The double-pile, two-story brick house contains a two-story Roman Doric tetrastyle portico with an elliptical fanlight doorway, tympanum lunette, and Chinese balcony suspended by wrought-iron rods. Recessed brick panels are found between floors, as well as flat stone lintels over windows. In 1909 civil engineer Hollis Rinehart Sr. altered the house and added a magnifi-

cent brick water tower (see fig. 72). In 1921 Henry L. Fonda purchased the property, where he raised Hereford cattle and horses that won ribbons at Madison Square Garden in New York. Birdwood is now owned by the University of Virginia.[82]

Master joiner John Neilson probably built the tetrastyle house called Lewis Level between Porters and Warren in the 1820s for Howell Lewis, a great-grandson of Robert Lewis of Belvoir (Howell Lewis was indebted to Neilson's estate after the joiner's death). In 1824 Lewis sold the property to William Morris, a son of Hugh Rice Morris, and moved to The Anchorage two years later. Lewis Level was the home of Lady Blanca Rosenstiel during the twentieth century.[83]

The frame Calycanthus Hill was built in 1799 on Green

Fig. 170. Birdwood, E19C

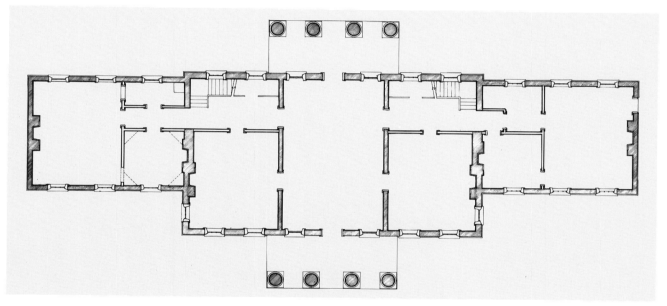

Fig. 171. (top) Estouteville, 1827–30, elevation

Fig. 172. (bottom) Estouteville, 1827–30, plan

Mountain for John Coles III, who married Selina Skipwith of Prestwould in Mecklenburg County. Master joiner James Dinsmore, assisted by brickmason William B. Phillips, built Estouteville (figs. 171, 172) immediately to the south of it between 1827 and 1830. The older house, after being converted to an orangery, burned in 1856. The newer two-story brick house with wings features two magnificent two-story Tuscan tetrastyle porticoes. Its seven-bay Flemish-bond facade is 152 feet long and contains doorways with fanlights, lunettes in the tympanums, and stone sills, lintels, and steps.

The entrance to Estouteville opens into a single-pile summer living room with a Doric entablature adorned with bucrania (composition ornaments in the form of ox skulls, the symbol of fertility in early Roman times) adapted from a plate in Palladio's *Quattro Libri*, as well as an ornate plaster ceiling medallion from Asher Benjamin's *American Builder's Companion*. Throughout the upper floor classical Ionic-columned mahogany closets from 1832 retain the labels of the cabinetmaker John Needles of Baltimore. As in all the other Coles properties, the house is set atop a ridge, faces south, has mountain views to the west, and contains elaborate formal gardens to the east. Interestingly, the house features a rear passage that connects its wings; it is similar to a passage in James Madison's Montpelier, which Dinsmore had remodeled.[84]

The structure's great interior stairs are recessed into this rear transverse passage. Using Dinsmore's original drawings, Milton Grigg produced an *analytique* rendering while attending the University of Virginia School of Architecture.

Single-Tier Portico with Paired Columns

Jefferson utilized the one-story portico with grouped or coupled columns on the one-story frame houses he designed. This portico became perhaps the most common entry form on houses constructed thereafter and was widely disseminated by Jefferson's master builders. Examples include Woodberry Forest in Orange County, built in 1793 for William Madison, brother of President James Madison; Edgemont, built in 1796 for James Powell Cocke; and Edgehill, the house Jefferson designed in 1798 for his daughter Martha. The Farm, a later example, was built just east of the Albemarle County courthouse for the Davis family in the 1820s. Frequently porticoes of this type had two wooden benches perpendicular to the facade that served as railings.

Two-Tier Porticoes

The two-tier portico, sometimes constructed with paired columns and often with a pedimented roof, became quite popular in the early nineteenth century. About 1800 Garrett White built on the Nicholas Beary property near Crossroads the two-story brick Linden Farm; it has a two-tier portico with chamfered columns, Flemish-bond facade, and molded-brick cornice. The four-bay facade originally contained two doors. Colonel Joseph Joplin erected a house on the James River between Tapscott and Howardsville about 1765. About 1800 the Argyle family acquired the property and built the present house River Lawn in the form of a frame I-house with wings. Its two-tier portico facing the river has since been removed.[85]

Fig. 173. Tallwood, c. 1803, c. 1826

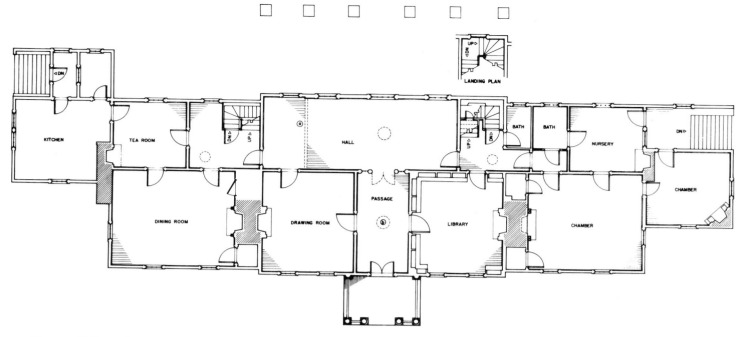

Fig. 174. Tallwood, c. 1803, c. 1826, plan

Tallwood (figs. 173, 174) on Green Mountain was one of the finest examples of a frame Federal house in Albemarle County. It contained more than twenty-five rooms. The original central section, five bays wide and one story high on a raised stone foundation, was built for Tucker Coles about 1803. He married Helen Skipwith of Prestwould in Mecklenburg County in 1810 and was a close friend of Jefferson and Monroe. A second floor was added by 1820, and two frame wings were telescoped onto either side of the central portion about 1826, producing an overall length of 134 feet. The house was sheathed with beaded weatherboards. A two-tier pedimented portico supported by Tuscan columns, featuring Chinese railings and a semicircular fanlight over the doorway, sheltered the south entrance, and a Tuscan-columned piazza with balustrade was attached to the north facade. The house was centered on an allée of trees with formal gardens to the east. In 1903 a wrought-iron entrance gate on the Green Mountain Road was designed by Olinto Ceccarelli of San Cimenano, Tuscany, Italy. Tallwood's dining room featured a classical punkah brought back from India in 1857 by a member of the Skipwith family. The many outbuildings on the property included stables, a carriage house, barns, a corncrib, a circular stone icehouse, smokehouses, a dairy, a laundry, a two-story brick summer kitchen with a cellar, and log slave quarters. Today the house is in ruins.[86]

East Belmont near Keswick was the western portion of

Fig. 175. East Belmont, 1811

Colonel John Harvie's Belmont and was purchased by John Rogers Sr.; here he built a frame house in 1811. Rogers, the first cousin of explorer General George Rogers Clark, served as overseer at Monticello while Jefferson was in France. In 1825 his son John Rogers Jr. added a brick I-house (fig. 175). It was built by the black brickmason Lewis Level with a fanlight doorway. A scar on the brick facade indicates a one-story portico was replaced by a two-tier one featuring square columns and Chinese railings.[87]

Fig. 176. Monroe Hill law office, c. 1789

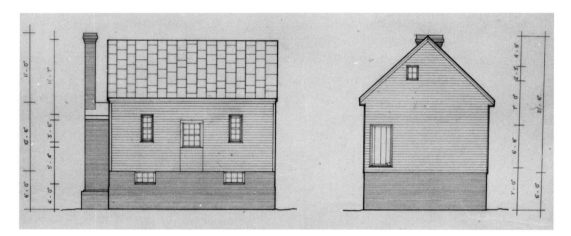

Fig. 177. Limestone Farm law office, 1794, elevation

LAW OFFICES

Many town attorneys maintained offices near the courthouse, but if a lawyer was also a farm or plantation owner, he usually built a law office as an outbuilding on his grounds. Two of James Monroe's properties included law offices: one at Monroe Hill (fig. 176) built about 1789 and the other built in 1794 at Limestone Farm (fig. 177), which he acquired in 1800. William Wirt's law office (fig. 178), on the other hand, was at 611 East Main Street in Charlottesville. This early nineteenth-century one-story brick building, containing a mousetooth cornice and six-over-nine sash, was razed in 1968 to build the present city hall.[88]

Fig. 178. William Wirt's law office, E19C

Courthouse and Court Square

The third Albemarle County Courthouse (fig. 179) was built in 1803 to the east of the second one from plans drawn by George Divers, William D. Meriwether, and Isaac Miller. Its cost was "not to exceed $5,000." It was constructed of brick by Jefferson builder John Jordan, who was subsequently hired in 1811 to enclose Court Square with a brick and stone wall. Because the first church was not erected in Charlottesville until 1824, the third courthouse was used for all gatherings including religious services.

Within a few years of its construction, alterations to the courthouse began. In 1815 its cupola was repaired, and a bell bearing the inscription "Geo. Hadderty Founder Philadelphia 1809" probably was installed at that time. In 1818 Jacob Wimer installed "Franklins" (lightning rods) purchased from James Leitch. Tin replaced the wood-shingled roof in 1825. In 1859 another Jefferson builder, George Wilson Spooner Jr., added to the courthouse a $9,400 Gothic Revival-style facade with towers de-signed by William A. Pratt, university proctor. About 1870 Spooner's son George Wallace Spooner removed these towers and added a tetrastyle portico with Ionic columns. Other alterations occurred in 1897. In 1926 the bench and jury box were moved from the west wall to the north end. Twelve years later architects Milton Grigg and Floyd Johnson removed the stucco on the 1859 facade to expose the brickwork and laid a new brick facade over it, with a new Ionic tetrastyle portico as well. The brickwork of the 1803 courthouse, which had been painted, later was sandblasted to reveal the Flemish-bond pattern. At this time too the Victorian interior was removed. One of the last major changes to the courthouse was made in 1963 with the addition of a small judge's chamber designed by Floyd Johnson. The iron balcony railing was removed then and installed at Mount Moriah Methodist Church in rural Albemarle.[89]

Changes were proposed for or made to Court Square as well as to the courthouse itself. In 1824 offices were suggested for each corner of the square for the use of Valentine W. Southall, Francis B. Dyer, William Hunter Meri-

Fig. 179. Albemarle County Courthouse, Charlottesville, 1803

wether, and the county clerk's assistant. Seven years went by, however, before a small office building was constructed in the northeastern corner of the square. In 1847 Malcolm F. Crawford, another Jefferson builder, and Thomas Wood were appointed to investigate whether to construct more office buildings on the square, but it was not until 1855 that Drury Wood and W. T. Early were permitted to do so on the eastern side. In 1856 the court ordered that the square be enclosed and paved according to a plan by William S. Dabney. A stone wall with an iron railing was then built for $1,500.

Jails

In addition to the official jail on Court Square in Charlottesville, smaller communities sometimes created their own facilities to hold miscreants temporarily. About 1812 the Milton town jail was in the cellar of Locust Grove Tavern. In the late nineteenth century, a building in Batesville served as a jail there.

Poorhouses

Until the disestablishment of the Anglican Church following the Revolutionary War, the care of the poor, elderly, and disabled who were without family support was the responsibility of each parish in Virginia. Usually the parish levied a special tax each year, then distributed the money to individuals or families to cover the expenses of housing and feeding those unable to fend for themselves. After disestablishment, the General Assembly ordered the parish lands or glebes to be sold and the revenue applied to caring for the needy. Each county and city in Virginia appointed overseers of the poor to fulfill this obligation. Eventually, as the number of those willing to serve as custodians declined, local governments erected almshouses or poorhouses and hired paid staff to tend to the inmates. Most poorhouses were built in rural areas on farms bought or donated for the purpose (hence the term *poor farm*).[90]

Although an almshouse is believed to have existed in Albemarle in the eighteenth century, the county purchased the land for its first known almshouse (fig. 180), just west of the present-day Barracks Road Shopping Center, from John Alphin in 1806. The poor farm consisted of overseer Anderson's house centered at the end of two rows of buildings comprising a kitchen and five log saddlebag houses for the occupants. This, in turn, was centered to the east on a garden and a field containing a cemetery. A stable and spring were located to the south. In 1870

Richard Thomas Walker Duke Sr. of adjoining Sunnyside acquired the property. That same year the land and building near Keswick for the second poorhouse, known as Old Poorhouse Farm (fig. 181), was conveyed to the county by Quintus L. Williams. Here too were a two-story log saddlebag house, a privy for multiple use, and a large cemetery with unmarked graves. The third poorhouse was on U.S. Route 29 south of Charlottesville. An Elderly Ladies' Home was located in Charlottesville in the early twentieth century.[91]

ECCLESIASTICAL BUILDINGS

In Charlottesville the courthouse served as a place of worship for several denominations until churches were constructed in the town in the early nineteenth century. Jefferson wrote in 1822:

> In our village of Charlottesville, there is a good degree of religion, with a small [amount] only of fanaticism. We have four sects, but without either church or meetinghouse. The courthouse is the common temple, one Sunday in the month to each. Here, Episcopalian and Presbyterian, Methodist and Baptist, meet together. . . . The diffusion of instruction . . . will be the remote remedy to this fever of fanaticism; while the more proximate one will be the progress of Unitarianism. That this will, ere long, be the religion of the majority from north to south, I have no doubt. In our university you know there is no Professorship of Divinity.[92]

By the mid–nineteenth century forty-five churches had been built in Charlottesville and Albemarle County to serve five denominations. In the order of their appearance in the county, the denominations were the Episcopal, Presbyterian, Baptist, Methodist, and Universalist.[93]

The Unitarian-Universalist Church

In religion Jefferson was considered a deist or freethinker by others and referred to himself as a materialist. For much of his life he was interested in Unitarian beliefs. His interest caused him political problems, especially when he attempted to employ a Unitarian as a member of the university faculty, for many traditional Christians regarded Unitarians as atheists. Although a Universalist church was recorded in the county in 1850, it was not until one hundred years later that Stanislaw Makielski designed the brick Unitarian Church on Rugby Road.[94]

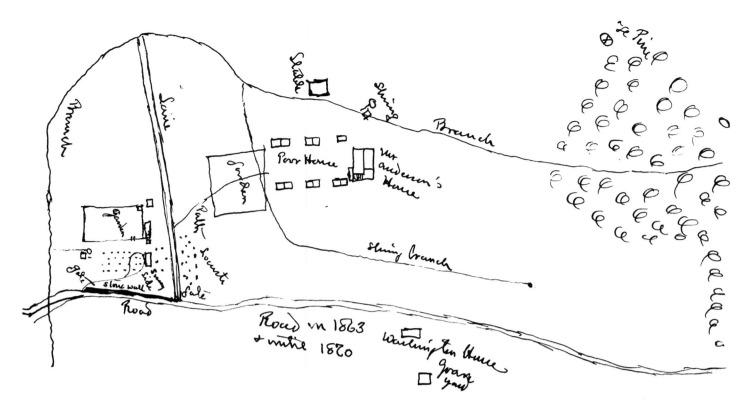

Fig. 180. Plat of county's first almshouse, 1806

Fig. 181. Old Poorhouse Farm, 19c

The Episcopal Church

The first church in Charlottesville, Christ Episcopal Church (fig. 182), was begun in 1824 and completed on 20 May 1826 on the north half of Malcolm F. Crawford's lot number 66. As early as 1857 Bishop William Meade attributed the design to Thomas Jefferson. A letter written by the rector of Fredericksville Parish in 1824, however, suggests that John M. Perry was the builder. In 1838 William B. Phillips enclosed the churchyard with a brick wall costing $500. George Wilson Spooner Jr. attached a distyle-in-muris to the facade similar to the one added to the 1834 Saint Thomas's Church in Orange, both in 1853. Originally the front of the church simply had two doors in a plain brick facade. Inside, Spooner also built side galleries that were

Fig. 182. Christ Episcopal Church, Charlottesville, 1824–26

Fig. 183. Interior of Christ Episcopal Church, Charlottesville, 1824–26

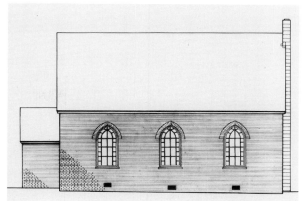

Fig. 184. (left) Cove Presbyterian Church, 1809

Fig. 185. (above) South Plains Presbyterian Church, 1828, elevation

to be supported with Ionic columns, but in the only extant photograph of the interior (fig. 183), the columns appear to have been modeled after those at the Tower of the Winds. Five years later a chancel with cruciform wings was added, and William A. Pratt submitted drawings for a new steeple to the vestry; it was built but collapsed in a windstorm eleven years later. In 1873 a belfry was added to the roof and a new bell installed. The original 35-foot-wide stone foundation still exists within the present church cellar.[95]

The Presbyterian Church

The current Cove Church (fig. 184), built of brick in 1809 at Covesville, is the oldest standing Presbyterian church in the county. The South Plains Presbyterian Church (fig. 185) congregation was established in 1820, and the present brick church here dates from about 1828. In 1819 James Dinsmore purchased Charlottesville town lot number 22, and in 1827 he deeded a part of it at the southwest corner of Second and Market Streets to build a Presbyterian church. John M. Perry and George Wilson Spooner Jr. completed the church here in 1828 for $2,080, for the second denomination to appear in Charlottesville. This church was used until 1856, when a second (fig. 186) was built on that site. It later became a YMCA, and its bell was sold to Mount Zion Church on Ridge Street after a third church was designed by Charles W. Read Jr. of Richmond and constructed across the street on the southwest corner in 1898 at a cost of $30,000. The YMCA was razed in 1909. In 1955 the firm of Stainback and Scribner, with Raymond Hiroux Julian as consulting architect, designed the fourth

First Presbyterian Church on Park Street, when the older church was razed.[96]

The Baptist Church

No longer extant, the Hephzibah Baptist Church was formed in 1802. Preddy's Creek Baptist Church became the mother church for several mission churches. One of them, Liberty Baptist Church, was built in 1829 on the land of Dr. John Gilmer of Edgmont and was similar in form to Preddy's Creek.[97]

The Methodist Church

In 1808 Bland Ballard donated land for the Ivy Creek Methodist Church, now replaced by a twentieth-century stone edifice on Hydraulic Road. Temple Hill Methodist Church was built about 1820 on present-day Route 613 about nine miles south of Charlottesville and was razed by the 1930s. It was a rectangular, Flemish-bond brick structure with nine-over-six windows. Hammock's Gap Methodist Church was constructed in 1825, Mount Zion Methodist Church in 1828, Buck Island Methodist Church in 1831, Shiloh Methodist Church and Scottsville Methodist Church in 1832, and Wesley Methodist Chapel in 1833. Only the last two still stand.[98]

MANUFACTURING BUILDINGS

Mills

Several frame mills were built in Albemarle around the turn of the nineteenth century, reflecting the agricultural shift from tobacco to grain. The one-story Hydraulic millhouse

Fig. 186. First Presbyterian Church, 1856

(fig. 187) on the Rivanna River, dating to about 1800, was acquired by Nathaniel Burnley in 1829. The Hydraulic Mills complex included gristmills for corn and wheat and a sawmill as well as a blacksmith shop, a cooper shop, a store, a silkworm industry, several dwellings, and a wharf. Jeremiah and Joel Yancey operated the 1820 Crozet Mill (fig. 188) on Lickinghole Creek. Also in 1820, Joseph Bishop announced in a newspaper advertisement that his rebuilt mill would operate "by either wind or water." Maupin's mill (fig. 189) on Moorman's River dated to the early nineteenth century; it was a two-story frame structure on a stone foundation. A two-story log house with a stone chimney remains on the property. The two-story Ivy Mill (fig. 190) on Ivy Creek, built about 1830, rested on a stone foundation into which was mortared a millstone from an earlier mill. Patterson's mill (fig. 191) was built on Stockton's Creek, perhaps on the site of the county's first mill. The last frame mill on the site was erected in the mid–nineteenth century.[99]

Several brick mills were constructed in Albemarle during the nineteenth century. The complex built at Pireus, later known as the Charlottesville Woolen Mills, was the largest. Wool, cotton, flour, and timber were milled at this assemblage of buildings constructed on the Rivanna River at Moore's Creek about 1820 by William D. Meriwether. In 1827 the Albemarle County Court authorized Meriwether to build a toll bridge over Moore's Creek at the Three Notch'd Road, and two years later it granted him permission to dam the Rivanna River to power the mills. At various times Pireus included a gristmill, plaster mill, sawmill, cotton mill, dye house, blacksmith shop, and brass factory. In 1865 the mill complex and an adjacent railroad bridge were burned by Union troops. Henry Clay Marchant rebuilt the mill three years later, but it suffered from a severe flood in 1870, a break in the millrace in 1873, and a financial panic the same year; a second fire in 1882 finally destroyed it. George Wallace Spooner then designed and built a new four-story, 60-by-120-foot brick mill (fig. 192). The Charlottesville Woolen Mills was Albemarle's first big industry, manufacturing uniform fabric for both the U.S. Military Academy at West Point and the Confederate States of America, at different times, for Philadelphia mail carriers in 1887, and for guards at the 1893 Columbian Exposition in Chicago. At one time the company had its own two-room school, a store, a chapel, and

Fig. 187. (above left) Hydraulic millhouse, c. 1800

Fig. 188. (above) Crozet Mill, 1820

Fig. 189. (left) Maupin's mill, E19C

Fig. 190. Ivy Mill, c. 1830

Fig. 191. Patterson's mill, M19C

Fig. 192. Charlottesville Woolen Mills, c. 1820, 1880s

Fig. 193. Woolen Mills president's house, Charlottesville, L19C

for its president the largest house (fig. 193) in town. It employed 150 workers at its peak. Today its records are preserved in the Merrimack Valley Textile Museum in North Andover, Massachusetts.[100]

Several other brick mills besides those at Pireus once were located in the county. Peter Field Jefferson, the grandnephew of Thomas Jefferson, owned a two-story, three-bay Flemish-bond mill (fig. 194) on the Hardware River in 1820. It has been tastefully converted into a residence. The two-story brick Hatton Grange Mill (figs. 195, 196) on the James River was rebuilt in 1868 after an earlier structure was burned during the Civil War. It retains its metal mill wheel and interior machinery.[101]

Sawmills were not reported in the county record books until 1801, when first George West's sawmill on the "old Wood's Gap road" and then Jonathan Barksdale's sawmill were mentioned. According to insurance records, many others were standing by the turn of the nineteenth century: by 1803, William Brockman's one-story frame 14-by-40-foot sawmill; by 1805, James Walker's 12-by-50-foot sawmill and joiner's shop; by 1812, James Dinsmore's and John H. Craven's 14-by-40-foot frame Pen Park Sawmill; by 1813, Thomas Jefferson's sawmill at Shadwell; by 1815, Benjamin Davis's sawmill; and by 1816, Joseph Coffman's Hardware Sawmill. From 1819 until 1834 John

M. Perry, Jefferson's builder, owned Hydraulic Mills, which produced 100,000 feet of reciprocating-sawed lumber annually. Rio Mills, rebuilt after the Civil War by W. R. Burnley and F. M. Wills, produced as much as 6,000 feet of circular-sawed lumber a day.[102]

These water- and steam-powered sawmills (fig. 197), which were one story high and about twice the length of the longest log sawed, replaced the older method of hand pit-sawing first with the reciprocating or up-and-down saw and later with the circular saw. The saw itself was positioned about midway the length of the mill. The first steam-powered circular sawmill in the county, built in the mid-nineteenth century on the Findowrie property of Joseph W. Campbell, supplied crossties for the newly arrived Virginia Central Railroad.[103]

In the early 1800s some forty-eight mills, factories, and manufacturing establishments stood in Albemarle County. By 1815 tax records reported forty gristmills as well as five sawmills. But in 1820 seventeen sawmills and twelve flour mills were identified in the county. The rise in the number of sawmills probably was due to increased local construction spurred in part by the popularity and cheapness of wood products, manufactured in such cities as Baltimore, as well as by general prosperity. The decline in the number of gristmills may have resulted from the

Fig. 194. Peter Field
Jefferson's mill, 1820

Fig. 195. Hatton Grange Mill, 1868

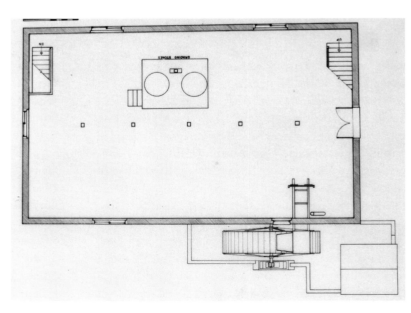

Fig. 196. Hatton Grange Mill, 1868, plan

Fig. 197. Albemarle County sawmill, L19C

erection of a few large new mills that featured the latest technological advances and thus dominated the market. As the county's farms increased grain production during the antebellum period, however, the number of gristmills likewise grew dramatically.[104]

Factories

Several tobacco-related buildings once were located in Albemarle, such as Benjamin Harden's Morgantown tobacco factory, which he constructed by 1814. Harden had owned the Hardendale Tavern here; its outbuildings included a 32-by-48-foot one-story stable and a frame dairy with a smokehouse over it. As late as the 1870s, C. C. Wertenbaker operated the Monticello Cigar Factory in Charlottesville.[105]

COMMERCIAL BUILDINGS

Taverns and Hotels

The county court issued nine ordinary licenses in 1800, and the personal property tax book listed Captain Edward Moore of Crutchfield as the wealthiest innkeeper. It was during this period that the provocatively named Pinch'em-slyly Tavern was located in the community of Barterbrook on Coursey's Road. The White Hall Inn on Buck Mountain Road dates to the turn of the nineteenth century. The two-story frame building probably was built by the Maupin family and is one of the oldest structures in the village. Other turn-of-the-century taverns abounded in the county. Jacob Gitt's Pleasant Grove Tavern on Wheeler's Road in the community of Travellers' Grove dated to about 1801. It was a 20-by-40-foot, one-story frame building that was razed about 1925. Nathaniel Garland's 1802 tavern (fig. 198) is at the junction of the Lynchburg Road and what became the Staunton and James River Turnpike. A ballroom and dumbwaiter added to the building's amenities. It also served as a tollgate for the turnpike, and records kept here reveal that in 1831 a wagon hauling wheat was charged forty-six cents to pass through the gate.[106]

By 1815, when Charles Yancey's Cedars Tavern on the Rockfish Gap Turnpike west of Yancey's mills (Hillsboro) was listed in the land tax book with an assessed value of $2,500, the county court had issued twice as many

Fig. 198. Nathaniel Garland's tavern, 1802

licenses as in 1800. Five years later the number of ordinary licenses had increased to twenty-one, of which seven were for "Houses of Private Entertainment." That year, the county land tax books showed an increase in the value of Charles Yancey and Elijah May's Cedars Tavern to $11,000. Thomas Wells's Eagle Tavern in Charlottesville was assessed at about $4,000. By 1830 the county land tax records listed only seventeen taverns.[107]

Bentivoglio Tavern, which Mann and Judith Walker Page owned on the road to Fredericksburg in 1816, was an 18-by-36-foot one-story frame structure with a portico. The Green Teapot Inn at Yancey's mills dated to the first half of the nineteenth century; by the early twentieth century it became a resort hotel. The frame tavern on Wheeler's Road at Crossroads, built about 1810 by the Morris family, was razed in 1991. The Locust Grove Tavern (fig. 199) in Milton is one of only a few buildings remaining here. Isham Chesholm erected the one-story frame hall-parlor section about 1812; its foundation is recessed into a hill, and a jail formerly occupied the cellar. About 1857 a frame I-house was attached to the northern gable end. The four-story frame Midway Hotel was built in 1818 at a favorable location at the intersection of the Three Notch'd Road (West Main Street) and the Lynchburg Road (Ridge Street) and contained thirty rooms, each with its own

fireplace. On its grounds were an icehouse, a summer kitchen, dairy, smokehouse, forty-stall stable, and a separate 20-by-52-foot dining room heated by three fireplaces.[108]

Stone and brick taverns as well as those of frame were constructed in the late eighteenth and early nineteenth centuries. Two stone taverns were located in the county. George Nicholas, the son of Robert Carter Nicholas, built the first one as a dwelling on lots 17 and 18 on Market Street in Charlottesville about 1782. In 1790 James Monroe bought the property and lived here but a short time before moving to Monroe Hill. When he sold the house to Peter Marks that year, Monroe reserved the right for his family and furniture to remain here until his new farmhouse was ready. The dwelling was used as a tavern by 1824, when Lafayette was received here by townspeople as he rode from Monticello to the university in a landau with Jefferson and Madison. At different times called the Central Hotel, Stone Tavern, and Monticello House, the building burned about 1852 and finally collapsed in 1940; its stones were reused by the Charlottesville Milling Company. The other stone tavern stood in Warren. The two-story, 32-by-34-foot Warren Tavern (fig. 200) probably was built by George Nicholas's brother, Wilson Cary Nicholas, in 1804. It was razed about 1970.[109]

Fig. 199. Locust Grove Tavern, c. 1812, c. 1857

Fig. 200. Warren Tavern, 1804

Taverns built of brick became more numerous than those of wood by the second quarter of the nineteenth century. The earliest, the Hardendale Tavern, was a two-story, double-pile brick building with a Roman Ionic tetrastyle portico in front and a piazza in back. Built for Benjamin Harden at the turn of the nineteenth century, it formed the nucleus of the community of Morgantown. Originally called the Albemarle Hotel, it was sold to carpenter James Oldham in 1828, and he maintained a tavern here. The building and its large barn burned in the late 1920s. Another brick tavern of the same vintage, the two-story Brooksville Tavern (fig. 201), was built for James Hays, the planner of the community called New York that was constructed in the western part of the county near the mountains. The hostelry is named for Robert Brooks, who married Hays's daughter and acquired the tavern, which in 1808 included a brick summer kitchen and brick smokehouse.[110]

The Locustdale Inn, a 19-by-38-foot two-story, hall-parlor brick tavern, was built in the early nineteenth century near the Blue Ridge Mountains on the road to Rockfish Gap. About 1858 a frame addition was erected to the south and a hipped roof with lantern placed on top. The Browning-Dettor tavern in Brownsville was built in three parts, the oldest part being frame. A two-story brick

Fig. 201. Brooksville Tavern, c. 1800

hall-parlor section dates to the 1820s, and an attached two-story brick wing was added not long before the Civil War. Crossroads Tavern (figs. 202, 203) was constructed by the Morris family about 1820 on the Staunton and James River Turnpike. It features five-course American-bond brick with Flemish variant and a long two-tier porch. The interior contains two separate stairs leading to the upper level and a wine cellar and stable on the lower level. A two-level bank building contained a summer kitchen with a smokehouse below and still survives as a dependency about eighty feet north of the tavern. The old tavern now serves as a bed-and-breakfast inn.[111]

The two-story Castiglione Tavern (figs. 204, 205) is in the southern part of the county near the Nelson County line on the road to Lynchburg. John T. Hamner constructed it in the 1820s in Flemish-bond brick with a molded-brick cornice. Tavern license receipts dating from 1830 to 1843 and coach registers from 1853 have been found in the attic. The Scottsville Tavern on Valley Street dates to the second quarter of the nineteenth century. It consists of two brick buildings, one single-story and the other two-story.[112]

The three-story brick Jefferson Hotel (fig. 206) was built within a year of Jefferson's death in 1826 just to the east of the Eagle Tavern on town lot number 2 in Charlottesville.

George Garrett advertised that the "apartments are commodius and from many a delightful prospect of landscape scenery [offer a] view of the mountain of Monticello." The next year John Winn proclaimed that "this house, 95 by 40 feet . . . [included] every necessary out convenience — a brick kitchen, . . . brick smoke house; a good ice house; a well of most excellent water . . . and a brick stable 103 by 30 feet containing 44 stalls. . . . A carriage house large enough to contain 8 or 10 carriages will be put up as soon as it may be wanted." The first floor of the hotel housed a post office and shops owned by postmaster John Winn of Belmont. About a century later, in 1926, the nine-story brick Monticello Hotel designed by Lynchburg architect Stanhope Johnson replaced the earlier buildings. The next year a giant searchlight was installed on the roof; supposedly the world's most powerful, its beam could be seen from many miles away. The hotel's elegant Tea Room offered its visitors fine dining.[113]

Stores

The county court order books contain some of the first mentions of stores in notations about road construction, lawsuits, and the like. Staples's store, for example, appeared among the court orders in 1785, Hart's in 1791, and Dyer's in 1792. Other sources for descriptions of early stores

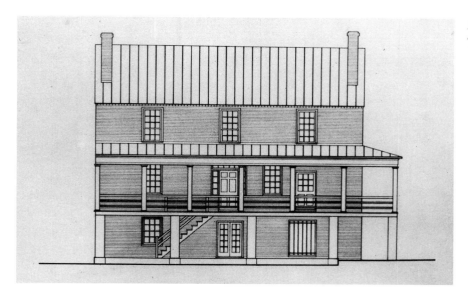

Fig. 202. Crossroads
Tavern, c. 1820, elevation

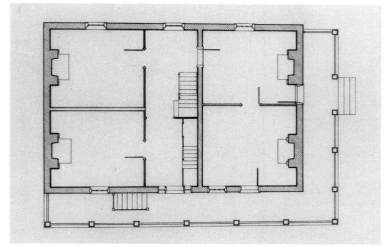

Fig. 203. Crossroads
Tavern, c. 1820, plan

Fig. 204. Castiglione Tavern,
1820s

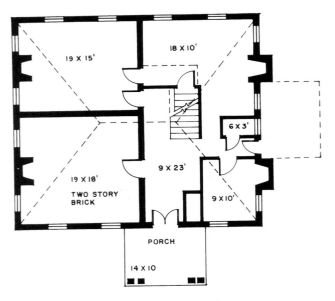

Fig. 205. Castiglione Tavern, 1820s, plan

The area around Court Square in Charlottesville remained the primary commercial district of the town until the mid–nineteenth century. A wide variety of stores and shops occupied the McKee block (figs. 207, 208) on lot number 58 just west of the courthouse at different times. They included dry goods stores, a hatter's shop, a post office, a tailor shop, a hotel, a jewelry store, a grocery, a bank, and a printing shop. The entire block was razed before 1921 to construct Jackson Park. The earliest extant store in old downtown is the two-story brick Number Nothing (fig. 209) that is southeast of Court Square. Various reasons have been suggested for why the building was not assigned a number; it may have been because it served as an auction lot for slaves as well as for goods. The building was constructed in the 1820s, and by 1829 Opie Norris and John C. Ragland had purchased it to use as an auction house.[114]

TRANSPORTATION BUILDINGS: TOLLHOUSES

include the records of the Mutual Assurance Society of Virginia. The 1803 policy for William Walker's retail store, for instance, described it as a two-story frame building, 18 by 34 feet. One of the oldest stores still standing in the county is the 1853 frame Piedmont Store at White Hall.

In the first half of the nineteenth century, several eighteenth-century roads were improved by joint-stock companies and became turnpikes that charged tolls. Some were macadamized, or hard-surfaced with layers of increasingly fine gravel, while others were built of squared

Fig. 206. Jefferson Hotel, 1827

Fig. 207. McKee block, Charlottesville, 19c

Fig. 208. McKee block, Charlottesville, 19c, plan

Fig. 209. Number Nothing, 1820s

logs laid perpendicular to the line of traffic; their nickname, corduroy roads, referred to their bumpy surface. In 1827 William Hunter Meriwether received permission from the county court and then built a toll bridge across the Rivanna River at Moore's Creek. The Rivanna and Rockfish Gap Turnpike, chartered in 1828, constructed its first tollgate just west of Charlottesville "opposite the large oak tree on Jesse Pitman Lewis's place, under which General George Washington is said once to have lunched." What is believed to be the first tollhouse still stands near that spot on old Ivy Road just west of Charlottesville.[11]

IV

The Greek Revival (1830–1860)

BACKGROUND

The Greek Revival followed the Roman Revival in America, the reverse of the sequence in antiquity. Americans identified with the Greek War of 1821–27 for independence from the Turks and equated it with their own struggle for democracy. Through James Stuart and Nicholas Revett's *The Antiquities of Athens*, a folio of measured drawings from Greek examples that was published in three volumes between 1763 and 1795, and from the treasures discovered and publicized by archaeologists, Americans learned that classical forms had their origin in Greece. Asher Benjamin revised the 1827 edition of his popular pattern book, *The American Builder's Companion*, to include the details of Greek architecture. In the first edition of Benjamin's fourth pattern book, published in 1830, he illustrated symmetrical architrave trim and stated in the preface that "since my last publication, the Roman school of architecture has been entirely changed for the Grecian."[1] Three years later Minard Lafever published *The Modern Builder's Guide*, in which he further disseminated these new ideas.

Earlier, architect Charles Bulfinch had introduced the Greek Revival style to New England after touring Europe between 1785 and 1787, although he did not strictly adhere to the style later. Although B. Henry Latrobe had incorporated Greek Ionic porticoes on his Bank of Pennsylvania in Philadelphia as early as 1798, the first completely Greek Revival–style building was William Strickland's Second Bank of the United States, begun in 1818 in the same city. It preceded European versions of the Parthenon, on which it was based, by ten years. Athenian monuments, such as the Choragic Monument of Lysicrates, the Temple of Illisus, and the Tower of the Winds, became paradigms for American buildings. The popularity of the Greek Revival resulted in its being dubbed America's "National Style."

The new style featured bilateral symmetry with little ornament, smooth wall surfaces painted white, and low-pitched roofs. Pilasters became commonplace. True Greek Doric columns were squatter (5½:1 proportion) than their Roman counterparts (8:1), with the true Greek columns being fluted and without bases. The Ionic Greek versions had volutes parallel to the facade rather than at forty-five degrees as in most Roman examples.

Among the characteristic details of the style in America were Flemish-bond brick facades with five-course American bond (and Flemish variant) on the remaining walls and below the water table. Doorways were trabeated, or built with flat lintels, with an overhead transom and flanking sidelights. The doors contained four panels between the rails and stiles and separate applied moldings. The door surrounds were composed of triangulated lintels, symmetrical moldings with rondel blocks, and flat cyma curves. The Greek Revival mantel was usually plainer than its Federal predecessor, with a thick, straight mantel shelf. The mantel sometimes incorporated a frieze decorated with a Greek fret or meander (fig. 210).

Beginning in the 1830s, certain other features were widely accepted. Among the new window treatments were tripartite windows, which consisted of a wide double-hung window flanked by two narrower ones (fig. 211). Such windows became popular after 1810 and were a favorite motif of the architect B. Henry Latrobe. Often a device held the center window blinds at ninety degrees to the windows in order not to close over the side windows. Dual windows — coupled or paired groupings of windows that brought more light to interior rooms (fig. 212) — also became popular. Entrance doorways also received changes, with Federal fanlights being replaced by flat transoms, and the

Fig. 210. Greek Revival mantel at Hillcrest Farm, c. 1837

New brickwork motifs included crow-stepped brick gables that formed a parapet wall above the roof level. When buildings adjoined or shared common walls, as in abutting town houses, such gables could help prevent fires from spreading to adjacent buildings (fig. 215). Brick cornices that formed modillions or dentils replaced the mousetooth cornice in popularity during the Greek Revival period (fig. 216). In addition, the column was a prominent feature of the Greek Revival style. One-story porticoes with coupled or paired columns (often square with recessed panels) were common features of the period. Also, flat wall-and-corner pilasters adorned exterior walls (fig. 217).

During the height of the Greek Revival style, the construction trades benefited from several technical improvements. Cut nails with stamped heads were introduced about 1825. After 1840 steam-powered circular-sawed lumber came into use, as did mass-produced, narrower hardwood flooring with tongue-and-groove joints. Mass-produced two-by-fours also became common and were used in the balloon-framing system. Joseph W. Campbell installed Albemarle County's first steam-powered sawmill at Findowrie by 1848 to make wooden rails for the new railroad track nearby. After 1850 sawed-wood lath replaced hand-split rivens, and manufactured carpeting also became affordable.[2]

Foreshadowed by the Jeffersonian influence, the Greek Revival in Albemarle County took the form of symmetrical brick buildings with pilasters and hipped roofs. Most of them also exhibited trabeated transom doorways and symmetrical moldings. Among the better examples of the style are such fine public buildings as the privately constructed 1851 Charlottesville Town Hall; many pilastered churches, such as the First Baptist Church on Jefferson

addition of sidelights (often with scroll brackets) that admitted even more light into the passages (fig. 213). Alternatively, sometimes wooden panels (or simply the wall itself) were substituted for the two top corner glasses of the sidelights (fig. 214).

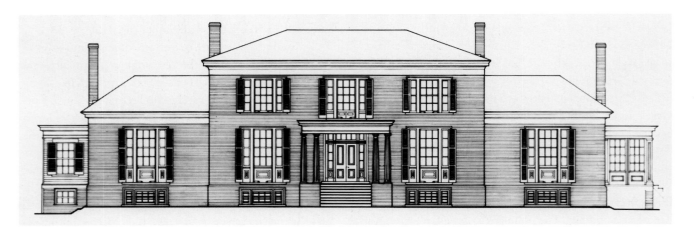

Fig. 211. Tripartite windows at Enniscorthy, 1850, elevation

Fig. 212. Dual windows at Bonahora, 1858

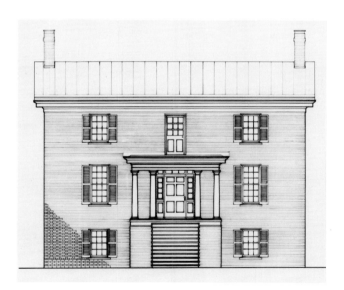

Fig. 213. (above) Transom with sidelights at Tipton-Blair house, c. 1844, elevation

Fig. 214. (right) Transom with sidelights and corner panels at Dr. John C. Hughes house, c. 1853

Fig. 215. Crow-stepped brick gables at Bibb-Wolfe house, 1845

Fig. 216. Brick dentil cornice at Heiskell-Livers town house, 1842

Fig. 217. Pilasters at Fairmount, c. 1840

Street in Charlottesville built by George Wilson Spooner Jr. in 1852; and such exquisite houses as the Abell-Gleason house on First Street in Charlottesville and Glenmore in the eastern part of the county.

In 1830, just four years after Jefferson completed his use of Welsh tin on the university's roofs, Peter U. Ware, a metal-plate worker, advertised that he would clad houses using Richard S. Tildon's patent. This "new and highly approved method of covering houses with tin" supposedly exposed no nails to the weather, and its installation method compensated for the shrinkage of roofing planks.[3]

The highest-taxed Albemarle County estate in 1830 was Redlands, followed by John Coles III's Estouteville, which included more than 3,000 acres, fifty-seven slaves, and coaches valued at $400. Next came George Divers, with about 2,700 acres of land; he also claimed the largest number of slaves (eighty-six), the highest-valued personal property, and by far the most expensive dwelling, Farmington, valued at $22,300. The next wealthiest was Dr. Mann Page of Keswick, who had forty-five slaves and twenty-seven horses, as well as a carriage and a gig.[4]

An 1835 gazetteer noted that in addition to four churches, Charlottesville had three hotels, one tavern, one female academy, one male elementary school, a library, a newspaper office, a fire company, and 200 "mostly brick" dwellings. It further mentioned "about twenty mercantile establishments," including two bookstores, two drugstores, and four tailor shops, as well as six attorneys, six physicians, three "surgeon dentists," two jewelers, a hatter, two confectioners, two bookbinders, three saddlers, a tin plater, two cabinetmakers, several carpenters and bricklayers, three wheelwrights, a chairmaker, a house-and-sign painter, two coach-and-gig factories, two boot-and-shoe factories, one brickyard, and three tanyards.[5]

The area around the university prospered, and fine residences arose nearby. Morea, built in 1835 for Professor John Patton Emmet, and the 1856 Rugby, later the home of Major General Thomas Lafayette Rosser, accounted for the subsequent naming of Emmet Street, Rugby Road, and Rosser Lane. The vernacular Maury house, Piedmont, was erected about 1806 southwest of the university, while the building now known as Faulkner House was constructed to the west in 1855. Wyndhurst was built in 1857 north of the university. Other estates sprang up around the town in the mid–nineteenth century, including Enderly and Branchlands to the north and Willoughby to the south. Elsewhere, Locust Grove was built about 1840 and lent its name to Locust Avenue. In the 1850s the increasing importance of Charlottesville as a rail center brought industrial development and contributed to the town's rise as a commercial center. Meanwhile, gas service had become available in some areas, and by 1860 the telegraph had reached the city. Further annexation had occurred around the town center as well.[6]

Several events of note affected Albemarle during the antebellum period. On 27 August 1833 the most severe earthquake to date rumbled through the county.[7] Four years later a financial panic struck the entire country, and several years passed before industry recovered. In the following decade the Mexican War took place between 1846 and 1848, and in the latter year the railroad first reached the county.

Mid-nineteenth-century censuses and tax records reveal much about Albemarle County. The 1840 census showed Albemarle fifth among Virginia counties in wheat production, third in corn. While in that year Thomas Jefferson Randolph's Edgehill had the highest real estate value at $54,114, John Timberlake and John Bowie Magruder's Shadwell Mills had a building value alone of $15,800. John Winn's downtown Jefferson Hotel had the next-highest building value at $12,000, followed by John Coles III's Estouteville at $10,000. Isaac White's Farmington, on 815 acres on Ivy Creek, was the only property in the county valued in the $7,000 range.[8]

The 1850 census indicated that only 213 of the 25,000 county residents had been born outside Virginia, and that 31 people each owned total real estate (both land and buildings) valued at $25,000 or more. Tucker Coles of Tallwood led the list with property valued at $92,000, including 121 slaves. Selina Skipwith Coles's Estouteville was assessed the highest value for a dwelling, $10,000, followed by Farmington, now owned by John Coles Carter, at $7,000. The county livestock consisted of about 5,000 horses, 14,000 cattle, 20,000 sheep, and 34,000 swine. The major crops were still wheat, tobacco, Indian corn, and oats, but potatoes, peas, beans, rye, flax, hay, and clover also were grown.[9]

In 1855–56 a smallpox epidemic plagued Virginia, followed by a financial panic the next year. The panic's effects were short-lived, however, for by 1859 there were four banks, a telegraph, and two hotels in the county. In that year the engineering firm of Wirt and Ford advertised their surveying services from their office on the public square in Charlottesville, suggesting that business was brisk.[10]

The 1860 census revealed that 107 county residents owned real estate and personal property valued at more than

$50,000. The wealthiest individual was William P. Farish of Hillcrest Farm, with an estate valued at $309,760 including 131 slaves. The Coles family owned combined real and personal property worth more than $800,000, while the Rives clan was worth about $641,000. William Cabell Rives of Castle Hill owned an estate worth $165,000 with 77 slaves. The highest building value listed, $9,900, was for Benjamin C. Flannagan and Company's factory at Buck Island; William and Tyree Rodes's Midway was the most valuable dwelling at $8,800. Next were Dr. Charles D. Everett's Belmont near Keswick and Selina Coles's Estouteville, both valued at $8,000.[11]

LOG DWELLINGS

Although milled wood for frame dwellings had become widely available and affordable, some owners continued to build log houses during the antebellum period.

One-Story Log Hall-Parlor Dwellings

Springdale (fig. 218), constructed for the Winston family in 1845 on Route 729 in eastern Albemarle, is a one-story, V-notched log house with a hall-parlor plan, external gable-end brick chimneys in five-course American bond, and two four-panel front doors. According to local tradition, this farm supplied some of the best whiskey to the Jefferson Hotel in Charlottesville during Prohibition.[12]

Two-Story Log Dwellings

The Moon house in Batesville is a two-story antebellum log dwelling on a stone bank foundation with a stone

chimney. The Jarman-Walker house (fig. 219) in Jarman's Gap, where the Three-Notch'd Road crosses the Blue Ridge Mountains into the Shenandoah Valley, began as a two-story, single-cell log house, now sheathed in weatherboards, with a stone chimney, and was built about 1835.[13]

ONE-STORY FRAME DWELLINGS

One-Story Frame Hall-Parlor Dwellings

The Scotch-Irish primitive-portrait painter John Toole arrived in the county at age eleven in 1827. Some twenty years later he built his hall-parlor frame house Church Hill at Crossroads. Certain features, however, suggest that the house may predate 1847: beaded siding, beaded joists in a high ceiling, a Flemish-bond chimney with English-bond sides, and English-bond underpinning. After Toole's death from tuberculosis in 1860, a subsequent owner attached a cat-slide addition to the eastern end of the house.[14]

When William Hunter Meriwether purchased 148 acres in 1825 at the future Woolen Mills site from Molly Miller, daughter of Nicholas Lewis, there were no buildings on the property. In the 1830s Meriwether built the Pireus house here on East Market Street. Relocated around the corner to a lot on Riverside Avenue in the late nineteenth century, the one-story, hall-parlor frame house features a gambrel roof with clipped gables. Thornton Bowen constructed the one-story frame house called Tarry on Route 810 east of Doyle's River about 1836. He probably built it with a hall-parlor plan, then later expanded it to double-pile. In 1919 Massie Tarry bought the house.

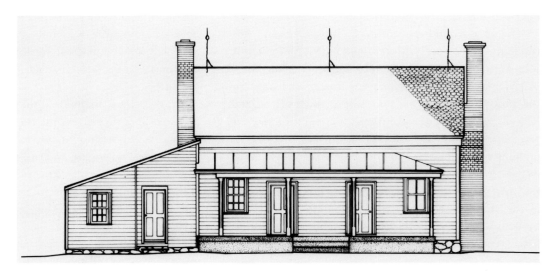

Fig. 218. Springdale, 1845, elevation

Fig. 219. Jarman-Walker house, c. 1835

Tarry, born in 1883, was the son of a former slave who had remained on the property after the Civil War.[15]

Christmas Hill (fig. 220), erected as a hall-parlor-plan house but with a stone chimney, was west of Keene on Route 713. Shadrack Lively probably built it in the mid–nineteenth century. Later acquiring a center passage, the house was abandoned for years, burned in 1991, and then was razed. Also in the 1850s the one-story frame house at Lindsay was constructed, but with brick five-course American-bond chimneys with single washes rather than stone. Another such house, also built with five-course American-bond chimneys and a cellar, but with beaded siding, was Horse-shoe Retreat on Route 631 on Gay Mountain.[16]

One-Story Frame Double-Pile Dwellings

Round Top (fig. 221) was erected on the western slope of Carter's Mountain at the time of the 1834 marriage of Dr. Benjamin Franklin Randolph, grandson of Thomas Jefferson, to Sallie Champe Carter, daughter of Robert and Mary Eliza (Polly) Coles Carter of Redlands. Round Top is a double-pile frame house built into the mountainside

Fig. 220. Christmas Hill, M19C

Fig. 221. Round Top, 1834

atop a five-course American-bond brick foundation. Its six-column, two-story veranda replaced a smaller upper-level entrance portico. The frame kitchen and slave quarters remain on the property. In 1884 the Randolphs' son Robert Mann Randolph acquired the property and then sold it in 1902 to Joseph and William N. Wilmer.[17]

Two-Story Frame Dwellings

The two-story frame Stapleton C. Sneed house in Charlottesville was built in 1846. It had one-story wings and a T-plan.[18]

Two-Story Frame Hall-Parlor Dwellings

The Dunkum-Spooner house at 409 Ridge Street was constructed in 1842 for Elijah Dunkum, son of master carpenter William Dunkum, as a two-story, hall-parlor frame house. The following year the younger Dunkum built a large two-story brick house a block away that has since been razed for commercial property. In 1861 Dunkum's frame house was expanded and Victorianized by carpenter George Wallace Spooner, son of Jefferson's builder George Wilson Spooner Jr. In 1994 a large oak tree fell on

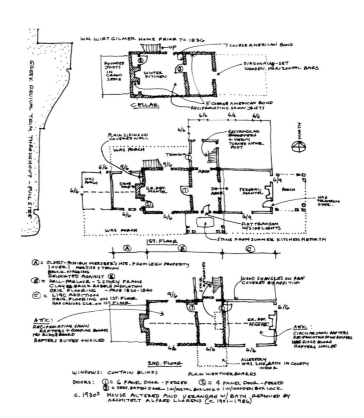

Fig. 222. West Leigh, 1836, field notes

the house and demolished it. Only its brick kitchen dependency with mousetooth cornice remains.[19]

The house at West Leigh (fig. 222) northeast of Ivy was built for William Wirt Gilmer in 1836 as a two-story frame hall-parlor dwelling that was later expanded into an I-house plan. Its features include a flat transom with sidelights, Greek Revival mantels, flat cyma architrave trim, and reciprocating-saw marks. Attached to the western end of the house is a one-over-one frame dwelling with mortise-and-tenon joinery, L-corner posts, pit-sawed marks, and brick nogging. This west wing could well have been an earlier overseer's house built on what was then the Leigh property.[20]

The Frame I-House

Three-bay frame I-houses continued to dominate domestic architecture in the countryside. The eighteenth-century Moore's tavern, later the Cottage rectory and school of the Reverend Ebenezer Boyden, was located near Cismont. Elsewhere on this land, a builder named McMullen constructed a frame I-house called Cismont Manor in 1836–37 for Peter Minor Meriwether. At the same time he relocated the old Clark house from Ben-Coolyn to serve as Cismont Manor's kitchen, and in 1847 Meriwether added a T-wing to the main house. In 1860 the old tavern was razed. Twenty-four years later George G. Randolph inherited Cismont Manor, but it was not until

1894 that the property acquired its H-plan after its purchase by Colonel H. W. Fuller.[21]

Johnson Rowe sold Glenmore, which then had a 1795 stone house on the property, to Thomas Eston Randolph in 1805 but retained the rights to the slate quarry here. In 1813 Louis H. Girardin, editor of *Burk's History of Virginia*, purchased the property. The Reverend Walker Timberlake later owned it for a time. Another of Jefferson's physicians, Dr. Thomas G. Watkins, succeeded him, and then Colonel Benjamin Henry Magruder acquired it in 1843. Magruder, one of the first law graduates of the University of Virginia, substantially remodeled the house with Greek Revival–style details, added a larger frame house to the smaller stone dwelling, and constructed a law office on the property.[22]

Another three-bay frame I-house, the antebellum Clermont (fig. 223) with a central gable and triangulated lintels, burned in 1922. It was razed to make way for McIntire Park. White Hall Farm on Route 795 probably was built by the Tompkins family in the mid–nineteenth century. The northern portion, a two-story frame I-house, was constructed first, with its T-wing added to the south facade shortly thereafter. At one time the property was called Sunny Hill, and legend has it that an Indian chief was buried near the entrance. Built by Matthew F. Jarman about 1860, the Jarman-Cree house on the old Three Notch'd Road near Crozet formed a magnificent setting

Fig. 223. Clermont, M19C

with its farm road and outbuildings. It remains one of the most intact post–Civil War farm complexes in the county and includes a family cemetery, icehouse, smokehouse, carriage house, and apple storage houses.[23]

Larger five-bay frame I-houses also were built during the antebellum period. The first house at Mount Fair in Brown's Cove, erected by Captain Bezaleel Brown Sr., burned in 1846. It was rebuilt in 1848 as an I-house with a lantern atop its roof by some former Jefferson builders for Brown's son William T. Brown. From 1930 to 1950 it served as the residence of Edmund S. Campbell, head of the university's School of Architecture. Seven Oaks Farm at Yancey Mills contains an octagonal icehouse as well as more than a dozen other nineteenth-century frame buildings. The 1847–48 main house built for Dr. John Bolling Garrett, son of university bursar Alexander Garrett, is a five-bay frame I-house with Greek Revival mantels. In 1906 a fluted Ionic-columned tetrastyle portico with a lunette in its tympanum was added to the façade. After the sale of Mirador by the Langhorne family, Nancy Langhorne Astor, Viscountess Astor, occupied Seven Oaks Farm during her Virginia visits. Piedmont, another five-bay frame I-house, was constructed at White Hall for J. J. Pace about 1853; the nearby frame family store probably was built at the same time. An uniden-

tified house (fig. 224) with one-story frame wings and a wonderful latticework porch is another example of the type.[24]

Two-Story Frame Double-Pile Dwellings

Double-pile, two-story frame houses were less common than the single-pile variety. The Oaks, built for Stephen Sampson about 1834 near Keswick, lacks a center passage; it originally had two front doors opening into its two front rooms. Its interior features a spiral staircase.[25] The 1840s Allwood house, relocated from the vicinity of Crozet, contained a diagonally set chimney to serve two rooms. A two-tier porch with an upper-balcony railing in a latticework pattern sheltered the front entrance.

Francis Kinloch Nelson in 1845 became the second husband of Margaret Douglas Meriwether of Clover Fields, where he found "all the buildings necessary for farming purposes wanting" and the estate "ragged, bushy, and briery." He proceeded to have a master carpenter by the name of Clarke as well as a brickmason named McMullen and his son William build the "Big House" (fig. 225) here in 1847–48. An incised brick contains the name "Nelson." The following year he made further improvements valued at $2,500. Here too he built a one-story log medical office for Dr. Thomas Walker Meriwether in 1846.[26]

Fig. 224. Unidentified house, 19c

In 1857 Sally Ann McCoy constructed Wyndhurst north of the university and east of Rugby Road. What might possibly be an even-earlier frame kitchen stands next door. In 1863 Colonel Thomas L. Preston purchased Wyndhurst. From 1930 until 1970 Charity S. Pitts operated a popular boardinghouse here for university students. The midcentury Coniston features two-over-two sash in its five-bay facade. It also has a hipped roof, widow's walk, and four exterior wall chimneys. Little Keswick, another double-pile, two-story frame house, was built with two internal chimneys to serve its four rooms. The Rogers family constructed it at midcentury on Route 731 at Keswick. Old Paradise, at Greenwood, is a two-story, double-pile frame house with internal chimneys and a hipped roof. Its four-bay facade was originally five bays with a center passage.[27]

Fig. 225. Clover Fields, 1847–48

Two-Story Stucco Dwellings

During the antebellum period houses often were finished with stucco scored to resemble ashlar masonry and painted white. About 1850 Judge William J. Robertson built such a scored stucco house with marble mantels at 705 Park Street. Robertson sat on the Virginia Supreme Court of Appeals. After the Civil War he participated as an attorney in the futile attempt by the Lee family to recover Arlington House, the home of General Robert E. Lee's wife, Mary Custis Lee; the estate eventually became Arlington National Cemetery.

ONE-STORY BRICK DOUBLE-PILE DWELLINGS

The double-pile configuration was a somewhat larger version of the one-story brick house. James B. Hart probably built the Jeffries-Bruce house (figs. 226, 227) about 1838 on Harrison Street at Bird Street in Scottsville. The five-bay house has a one-story paired-column portico, a two-leaf doorway, a flat transom and sidelights, a Flemish-bond facade with five-course American-bond sides, nine-over-nine sash windows, and symmetrical trim with rondel blocks on the interior.[28]

Two-Story Brick Dwellings

Several two-story brick dwellings exhibited unusual floor plans. The lovely Old Hall (figs. 228, 229) on Harrison Street in Scottsville was built in 1830 by Benjamin Magruder for James W. Mason. Its I-house floor plan contains a rear T-wing to enclose its stair. Its three-bay facade features tripartite windows, a one-story paired-column Doric portico with fluted columns, and a double-leaf doorway with flat transom and sidelights. The mantel in the south room is an especially handsome piece, with coupled fluted Doric colonnettes and richly molded end blocks.[29] Sherwood, a two-story Flemish-bond brick house located east of Carter's Bridge and razed in 1953, was built about the same time. Its two-story brick school and office still stand.

Morea (fig. 230), on Sprigg Lane in Charlottesville, possesses an unusual plan. The house was built about 1835 for the university's first professor of natural history, John Patton Emmet, on land previously owned by university builder John M. Perry. Emmet wrote fondly of the house: "Although contrived by myself, I may venture to assert that a more comfortable country house does not exist in these parts for the same cost." Morea's second-floor plan resembles a two-thirds Georgian plan with double-pile bedchambers and a side passage. The first floor is unique, with a front entry under a roof garden, behind which a three-bay brick arcade leads to another passage, then into a room with a hidden stair to the side. The name Morea is

Fig. 226. Jeffries-Bruce house, c. 1838

Fig. 227. Jeffries-Bruce house, c. 1838, plan

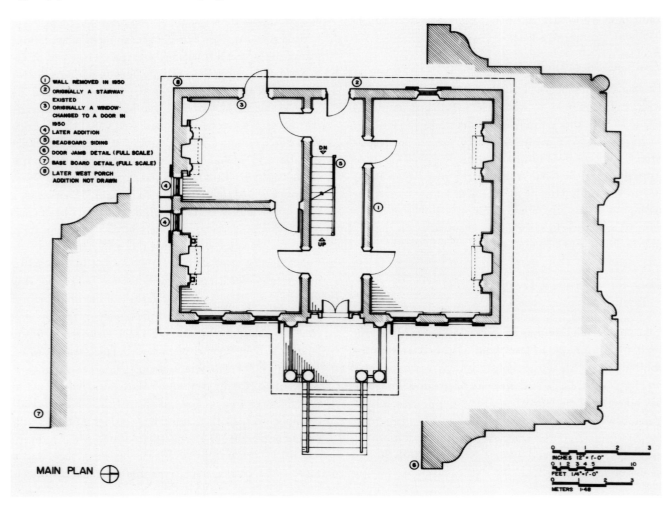

1. WALL REMOVED IN 1950
2. ORIGINALLY A STAIRWAY EXISTED
3. ORIGINALLY A WINDOW CHANGED TO A DOOR IN 1950
4. LATER ADDITION
5. BEADBOARD SIDING
6. DOOR JAMB DETAIL (FULL SCALE)
7. BASE BOARD DETAIL (FULL SCALE)
8. LATER WEST PORCH ADDITION NOT DRAWN

MAIN PLAN

INCHES 12" = 1'-0"
FEET 1/4" = 1'-0"
METERS 1:48

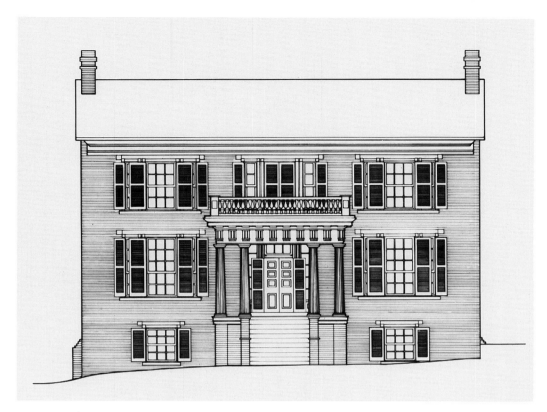

Fig. 228. Old Hall, 1830, elevation

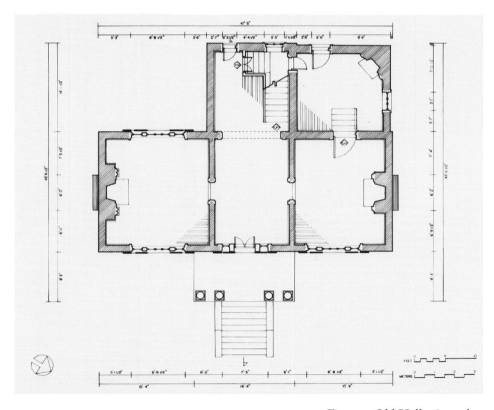

Fig. 229. Old Hall, 1830, plan

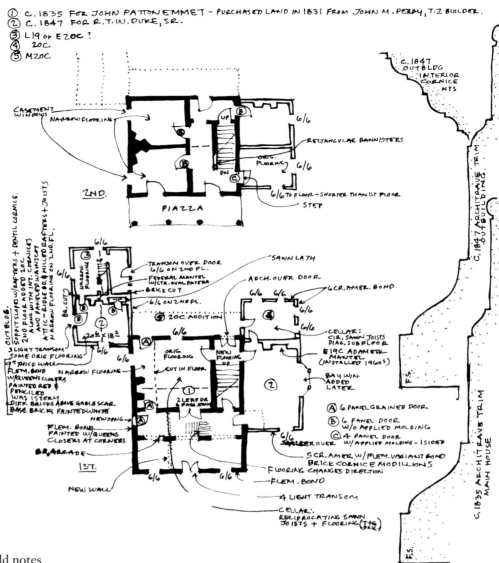

Fig. 230. Morea, c. 1835, field notes

derived from *Morus multicaulis*, the Chinese mulberry tree that Emmet grew here while experimenting with silkworm culture. About 1847 Richard T. W. Duke Sr. added Little Morea to the southwest corner of the house.[30]

The Anne C. Morris house was built in Charlottesville before 1845 as a two-story brick dwelling with two-story brick wings. Interestingly, a one-story brick orangery was located to the south of the center pavilion.[31] Rutledge, constructed for the Farish family at midcentury on present-day Route 743, presents another unusual two-story plan. The house was erected on a T-plan, and the main entry is sheltered by a porch in the wing at its junction with the other building block.

The second house at Belmont near Keswick was built in 1858 for Dr. Charles D. Everett on the site of the first Bel-mont, which was moved to the rear. Everett had inherited the property in 1849 from his uncle, who had founded Everettsville nearby. He had graduated in medicine from the University of Pennsylvania in 1836 and earlier lived in the first Belmont. The new house, erected six years after his marriage, was under construction for three years at a cost of $17,500 and was one of the finest in the county. The two-story, 45-by-60-foot brick building was stuccoed and scored to resemble stone. It featured a very high raised basement with double "welcoming arms" granite stairs that led to its piano nobile or first floor. At the top of the stairs, which were flanked by parterres of flowering plants, was a paired-column portico with cast-iron Corinthian capitals. The facade featured iron-framed windows that extended two full stories and ended in semicircular tops. Above, a hipped roof culminated in a widow's walk. Behind the windows, inside the house, were a gallery for musicians with a marble water fountain and a grand hall for dancing that was 20 feet wide, 46 feet long, and 25 feet in height. The lower level of the house contained a winter kitchen, bathroom, library, and dining and dessert rooms. A large tank in the attic held 1,500 gallons of water, drawn from a pond almost a mile away by a mechanical ram, a device that pumped water uphill and was operated by the flow of the water itself. Everett died in 1877, and the house was destroyed by fire in 1883.[32]

The Brick I-House

Three-bay versions dominated the brick I-house forms. Hatton Grange (fig. 231), constructed for Dr. Joseph B. Glover in 1831 on the James River at Hatton, is a case in point. It was erected with a Flemish-bond facade and five-course American bond elsewhere, a one-story paired-column portico, a doorway with a flat transom and sidelights, and a tripartite window above the portico — all typical of the period. The property also contained a brick gristmill, distillery, corncrib, blacksmith's shop, brick pyramidal-roofed smokehouse, and two-story brick kitchen that later housed a girls school. In 1847 the house passed to Glover's daughter who had married James Mason of Hanover County.[33]

William Lewis Dunkum, son of builder William Dunkum, built Tudor Grove on Route 631 south of Charlottesville shortly after his marriage in 1832 to his second cousin Elizabeth Bradley. The brick house features gable-end walls with parapets and brick mousetooth cornices. A one-story log outbuilding with a stone chimney, a brick outbuilding with a mousetooth cornice, and a circular stone icehouse also stand on the property. Tudor Grove later became the boyhood home of Colonel John Singleton Mosby of Civil War fame and, after the war, the home of Confederate commissary general Lucius B. Northrop.[34]

In the second quarter of the nineteenth century, Thomas Seldon Macon of New Kent County built a brick I-house at Tufton near Simeon. It features a hipped roof, a paired-square-column portico, and a four-panel entry door with a flat transom and sidelights containing decorative tracery similar to that at Wertland and Bloomfield. Tufton was connected to the early nineteenth-century stone house built for Thomas Jefferson Randolph by a late eighteenth-century log house that was razed in the 1950s. Canaan, a brick I-house near Warren, was built for Matthew M. Harris in the first half of the nineteenth century. It features a Flemish-bond facade, five-course American-bond brickwork elsewhere, dual windows, and a two-tier portico.[35]

Westcote, also known as Summer Hill, is on the Rock-

Fig. 231. Hatton Grange, 1831

Fig. 232. Cliffside, 1835

fish River at its confluence with the James River, on the original 400-acre Westcote tract patented by Major Allen Howard, founder of Howardsville. The present brick I-house, built in the 1830s, has penciled Flemish-bond brick on two sides with five-course American bond on the other two. Its exterior wooden cornice exhibits rope-and-bead moldings, and its mantelpiece resembles ones at Cliffside and Glendower. The vertical two-story paired-column portico could have been added later.[36]

Cliffside (fig. 232), atop a bluff overlooking the town of Scottsville, was built in 1835 for Dr. Gilly M. Lewis, who also owned Albemarle Mill on the Hardware River. Its square-columned portico shelters a doorway with a magnificent elliptical fanlight and sidelights. The extrados, or outer curve of the fanlight arch, is enriched by a band of turned pendants. Above the portico a tripartite second-floor window is centered under a central roof gable. Cliffside's Flemish-bond facade changes to five-course American bond on the gable ends and in its L-addition. The interior contains highly individualized mantels. The only surviving early outbuilding, the Ginger House, is a

one-story frame office and school erected in the mid–nineteenth century; it features Gothic Revival detailing such as board-and-batten walls and scalloped eaves. In 1836 Dr. William George Rogers, son of Dr. James B. Rogers who lived nearby, built Bleak House on present-day Route 662 in the northwest part of the county. This three-bay I-house with a center gable, bracketed cornice, and T-plan features a transom with sidelights and once had a two-tier portico.[37]

In 1813 General William Fitzhugh Gordon married as his second wife Elizabeth Lindsay, daughter of Reuben Lindsay of Springfield, and the couple resided at the old glebe of Fredericksville Parish. In 1835, while Gordon was in Washington, D.C., as a member of Congress, Mrs. Gordon wrote to him from Springfield: "And now, my dear husband, when I tell you your manuscript papers and books are safe, I hope you will not suffer yourself to be much agitated, when I add that our house is burned." Two years later he had the Flemish-bond brick I-house Edgeworth erected on the property by the brickmason McMullen who several years later worked on the main house at

Clover Fields. Among its features were mantels that incorporated Ionic colonnettes, structural timbers with Roman numerals, and a brick inscribed "WFG." In 1859 Dr. Charles Hancock added a frame T-wing to the rear of the house. In 1933, during Florence M. Smith's ownership, the T-wing was brick-veneered and raised to two stories, seven-course American-bond wings were added to each side of the house, and a two-tier portico replaced a single-story one — thereby creating one of the largest remodeled antebellum houses in the county.[38]

Auburn Hill was built for John Edward Timberlake after his acquisition of the property in 1842. Timberlake had owned the Jefferson mill and Shadwell tract across the Rivanna River to the north. Auburn Hill is a three-bay I-house with a hipped roof, paired-square-column portico, brick dentil cornice, and five-course American bond. A one-story brick kitchen is located behind the house; it features the same brick bond and cornice. A suspended pedestrian bridge once crossed the Rivanna River to Shadwell Depot, and an early twentieth-century chicken house served the property.[39] Another brick I-house, Woodlands, was built near Hydraulic in the same year for Richard Woods Wingfield by carpenter Patrick Martin and brickmason James H. Ward. The house was expanded in the 1890s by the addition of a large rear ell with two-tier galleries.

Woodlands was the home of John Richard Wingfield, who served as consul to Costa Rica from 1886 to 1889. The house remains in the Wingfield family to this day.

William Adams built the brick I-house Blair house about 1844 on Harrison Street in Scottsville. It features a one-story paired-column portico, a doorway with a transom and sidelights, and a Flemish-bond facade with five-course American-bond brick with Flemish variant on the sides. In 1875 Martha M. Blair acquired the property. The Bibb-Wolfe house, a brick I-house with stepped gables, is at 505 Ridge Street. It was built in 1845 for John H. Bibb, first cashier of the Charlottesville Savings Bank. In 1852 it became the home of Ezra M. Wolfe; later, Walter Everett Fowler lived here.[40]

Paul H. Goodloe of Louisiana built Bloomfield, a brick I-house with a center gable, in 1849 near Ivy. The house has a hipped roof and a one-story paired-column portico; the columns are made of pie-shaped bricks. In the 1850s W. LeRoy Broun and W. Willoughby Tebbs conducted Bloomfield Academy, a successful school for boys, on the property. Bloomfield was long the home of J. Tatnall Lea of Philadelphia, who first saw it while a prisoner during the Civil War. To the side of the house stands a one-story frame slave quarters. Architect Charles Baker made extensive alterations, including the addition of demioctagonal wings,

Fig. 233. High Mowing, 1856

about 1920. Henry Canter Moore built his three-bay brick I-house, Mooreland, in 1850 on Wheeler's Road, present-day U.S. Route 29, south of Charlottesville. The house features a Flemish-bond facade, brick dentil cornice, five-course American bond on the rear, and gable ends with the Flemish variant.[41]

Jefferson's brickmason William B. Phillips built a brick I-house on Ridge Street that he sold to Colonel John Bowie Strange in 1856. Strange operated the Albemarle Military Academy here until it closed at the outbreak of the Civil War. A graduate of the Virginia Military Institute, Strange assumed command of Colonel Philip St. George Cocke's 19th Virginia Infantry Regiment after Cocke committed suicide on 26 December 1861. Strange himself was mortally wounded the following year at Boonsborough, Maryland, during the Antietam campaign.[42]

Jeremy Wood constructed his brick I-house, High Mowing (fig. 233), in 1856 on Stillhouse Road near Batesville. The house has a hipped roof, a portico with paired, square, paneled columns, and a doorway with sidelights and a flat transom above. The facade is constructed in the then-new running bond (all stretchers, but with each row offset from the next one) while the remaining three walls were in penciled five-course American bond.[43] The Horseshoe was built in the mid–nineteenth century where John Michie had resided at the junction of Mechum's and Moorman's Rivers in the late eighteenth century. The three-bay brick I-house features a hipped roof and a flat transom with sidelights. Architects Marshall Wells, Henderson Heyward, and Milton Grigg extensively renovated and enlarged The Horseshoe in the mid–twentieth century. Enderly, built in 1859–60 for Mrs. William Fitzhugh Gordon Jr., is at 603 Watson Avenue in the northern part of Charlottesville. It has a Flemish-bond facade with five-course American bond on the other elevations, a hipped roof, and rear-elevation chimneys that also serve a one-story brick wing that extends across the rear of the house.

Several three-bay I-houses exhibited Greek Revival–style brick pilasters. Dr. A. G. Dulaney (1819–1889), for example, built his pilastered Fairmount near Stony Point about 1840. The house has a hipped roof, a paired-square-column portico with a jib window above, and a two-leaf doorway with a transom, sidelights, and wooden corner panels. The Dr. Joseph Norris house at Third and East High Streets was built about 1850. This three-bay pilastered I-house featured a hipped roof, tripartite window, and one-story paired-square-column portico. A similar Charlottesville dwelling, the Dr. John C. Hughes house (fig. 234), was constructed about 1853 at 307 East Market Street. Its paired, fluted, Ionic-columned portico originally was reached by spiral staircases on each side. The entrance doorway has a flat transom, sidelights, and wooden corner blocks, a tripartite window over the portico, and a hipped roof. As at Fairmount, the Hughes house has a running-bond facade and five-course American bond with Flemish variant sides. On the interior are mantels patterned after those in Edward Shaw's *Civil Architecture* (1836); the doors and windows have symmetrical architrave trim with rondel blocks at the corners. The Hodges-Gleason house at 510 Ridge Street in Charlottesville was built in 1857 for James M. Hodges. Like the others, it was constructed with a hipped roof, a doorway with a transom and sidelights, and a tripartite window, but with seven-course American bond with Flemish variant. Hodges had apprenticed as a brickmason under Allen W. Hawkins and is known to have built at least two houses in Goochland County.[44]

Most brick I-houses had three-bay facades, but a few had

Fig. 234. Dr. John C. Hughes house, c. 1853

five bays. One such example, the Lipop house at 426 Second Street, was built for Mary Railey about 1838 and featured a one-story paired-square-column portico, mousetooth cornice, and Flemish-bond facade. Another example, the Trice-Towe house, was constructed for Robert Trice about 1850 at 211 East High Street. In 1919 W. R. Wilson stuccoed it.

Two-Story Brick Double-Pile Dwellings

The prototypical Georgian house plan—two-story, double-pile, and center-passage—most often appeared in a three-bay house form. In 1833 Jefferson brickmason William B. Phillips purchased 346 acres of what had been the Philip Mazzei estate near Monticello and with additional purchases amassed over 500 acres. Here he built his country house, later called Sunnyfields, with a mousetooth cornice and a hipped roof that culminated in a glazed monitor. A brick kitchen–slave quarters remains on the property. Sunnyfields served as Phillips's home until 1856, five years before he died, when he sold it to Gessner Harrison, a professor at the University of Virginia. One of the recent owners was Lucius P. Battle, deputy secretary to NATO in 1955–56 and ambassador to Egypt in 1966–67.[45]

Hillcrest Farm, on Route 20 south of Charlottesville, has undergone many exterior transformations over the years. Built on the earlier Verdant Lawn site about 1840 for William P. Farish, it is a three-bay Greek Revival–style dwelling with chimney curtains, a one-story paired-square-column portico, symmetrical trim with rondel blocks, and exquisite mantels with Greek Doric fluted columns and fretwork. Its extant kitchen-laundry contains a mousetooth cornice. About 1903 Dr. Paul Brandon Barringer of the university established a sanitarium here. It is now the home of Tandem Friends School.[46]

New Shadwell was built in 1841 on U.S. Route 250 East near Shadwell for Colonel Frank G. Ruffin, who was the son-in-law of Thomas Jefferson Randolph and the son of the editor of the influential *Farmers' Register*. The house's floor plan closely resembles that of the frame 1846 Clover Fields; its rear double-pile rooms are without chimneys or fireplaces, and one contains a stair to the side. Because its land was conveyed in 1736 to Peter Jefferson for "Henry Weatherbourn's biggest bowl of Arrack punch," it was often referred to as the Punch Bowl Farm. After the death of Colonel Ruffin, Major Thomas Jefferson Randolph Jr. acquired the property and resided here until his accidental death in 1870 while attending to a C&O Railway construction project in West Virginia. The interior burned in 1923.[47]

Ellerslie (fig. 235), at Overton, was built for John O. Harris of Louisa County in 1842. His son-in-law Captain Richard J. Hancock established the famous Ellerslie stud line here. The five-bay brick house has a hipped roof and gable-end chimneys. The outbuildings included a kitchen, school, and smokehouse. One brick outbuilding featured a mousetooth cornice, and another had brick diapering for ventilation. In 1976 Ellerslie's frame barn was relocated and converted into a residence called Three Rivers. William Dunkum probably built the Dunkum-Dice house on Ridge Street in Charlottesville for his son Elijah in 1843. It had chimney curtains, a roof monitor, and a transom with sidelights under a one-story paired-column portico. It was later the home of Dr. R. B. Dice and of Brigadier General Fitzhugh Lee, who was elected governor of Virginia in 1885 and became consul general to Cuba in 1896.[48]

Enniscorthy, the third house on the site on Green Mountain Road, was built in 1850 for Julianna Stricker Coles. It features tripartite windows, a hipped roof, and a one-story paired-column portico that shelters a doorway with a flat transom and sidelights. Tucker Skipwith Coles and other family members added to it twice by 1904. The house remained in the Coles family until 1926. Its collection of eighteenth-century outbuildings, which included a bank barn and square-plan structures with pyramidal roofs, was among the earliest in the county. In 1993 the barn was razed and burned, and the outbuildings were relocated.[49]

About 1853 Edward Coles, son of Walter Coles Sr. of Woodville, built Richland on Biscuit Run some five miles south of Charlottesville. It is a two-story, double-pile brick house with a center passage, a hipped roof, and a one-story paired-square-column portico covering a doorway with a flat transom and sidelights.[50] Another three-bay, double-pile brick house with hipped roof but with a brick dentil cornice is the 1858 William Jeffries house on West Main Street in Charlottesville.

Several three-bay, double-pile, two-story brick houses featured four Greek Revival pilasters on the facade, as well as a hipped roof and internal chimneys. A case in point is Monticola (fig. 236), built in the early 1840s for Daniel James Hartsook, a merchant, banker, and planter who made a fortune in the Howardsville community because of its proximity to the James River and Kanawha Canal. Monticola's two-tier square-columned portico covered a recessed entrance on one facade while the opposite facade had a one-story paired-column portico that in 1900 was replaced by a circular, Ionic-columned two-story portico from the Richmond Exchange Hotel. The roof of the house was

Fig. 235. Ellerslie, 1842

topped with a belvedere. Two classical brick outbuildings flanked the main house. In 1887 Emil Otto Nolting purchased the property. He was a successful merchant, the president of two banks, and a director of the Virginia Steamboat Company. Three years before his purchase, he had been knighted by the king of Belgium for his service as consul to that country. In 1940 part of the motion picture *Virginia* was filmed on the Monticola estate. The eighteenth-century Fowles tavern once occupied the site.[51]

Another pilastered brick house with a recessed entry is the Word-Wertenbaker house (fig. 237) on South Street in Charlottesville. By 1841 James H. Word of Richmond had purchased land from Alexander Garrett, the first bursar of the university, who lived nearby at Oak Hill. The South Street part of Garrett's land was cut off by the Louisa Railroad tracks that were completed in January 1849. That year Word advertised his two-story brick residence and three vacant lots for sale. He did not sell the property, however, until 1857, when one of the town's first aldermen, William M. Keblinger, acquired it. The following year Thomas Jefferson Wertenbaker, son of the university's second librarian and himself a tailor and clothier, bought the house. From 1884 to 1897 Robert P. Valentine of Richmond, who became general manager of Charlottesville's first

streetcar company, occupied the house. A two-story brick kitchen was located on the property, and about the turn of the century a wraparound porch was added to the main house.[52]

Tall Oaks near Keswick, originally called Cedar Hill, was built for Dr. A. S. Hart in 1852. In the early nineteenth century, a small frame house had occupied the site and served as a store for a Mr. DeFoe. Tall Oaks has a three-bay facade with four pilasters, a hipped roof, internal chimneys, and a one-story paired-column portico that shelters a doorway with a flat transom and sidelights. Bonahora, at 610 Lyons Court, was built by John Timberlake for Benjamin Collins Flannagan and his wife, Ann (Nannie) Virginia Timberlake Flannagan, in 1858. Flannagan, son-in-law of the Reverend Walker Timberlake, was a cashier in the Monticello Bank and owned a brick factory at Buck Island. During the Civil War he concealed some of the bank's money in the house; afterwards, he stood trial for removing it but was acquitted. From 1891 to 1928 Bonahora was the home of Judge Thomas Barton Lyons who had moved here from Birmingham, Alabama. The house features brick pilasters, dual windows, a tripartite window above the turn-of-the-century porch with Ionic columns, an entrance doorway with a flat transom and sidelights, eave brackets, a hipped roof, and internal chimneys. The attic

Fig. 236. Monticola, E1840s

contains a 4,000-gallon water tank. In addition, a brick carriage house with a mousetooth cornice and stepped gables still stands on the property.[53]

The Abell-Gleason house (fig. 238) on First Street in Charlottesville was built for Alexander Pope Abell in 1859. A female academy had occupied the site, of which builder William B. Phillips was one of many joint owners. Abell was the president of the Monticello Bank. During the Civil War some of its money was buried on Barracks Road to protect it from Federal cavalry. After the war, when the site was excavated, it was found to be empty, and Abell was forced to sell his property in 1888 to satisfy creditors. The Abell-Gleason house features brick pilasters, dual windows, a tripartite window over a square-columned portico, and brackets in the eaves.[54]

Most two-story, double-pile brick dwellings built in the Greek Revival style contained three bays, but larger five-bay versions were also constructed. For example, The

Hill, on what is now Altamont Circle, was erected with internal chimneys in 1831 by William B. Phillips. Owner John H. Craven of Pen Park sold it to future governor Thomas Walker Gilmer in 1836. In 1874 John T. Antrim Sr. acquired and removed Billie Summerson's frame house to the south to create a lawn that extended to High Street. At the turn of the century, a tetrastyle portico with a suspended balcony was added to the facade. In 1904 the house was razed.[55]

Fig. 237. Word-Wertenbaker house, 1840s, sketch

Fig. 238. Abell-Gleason house, 1859

In the early 1840s the hipped roof, five-bay Locust Grove was built for George Sinclair on what became Locust Avenue. It contains blind windows and chimneys in its gable-end walls. The eighteenth-century Thomas Walker Lewis house here had burned before Sinclair's purchase of the property from Dr. Thomas Walker Meriwether in 1839. A brick kitchen and an altered pre-1840s dwelling still stand on the property. Judge John M. White purchased Locust Grove in 1893, and in 1923 it was acquired by Judge Lemuel F. Smith, a justice of the Virginia Supreme Court of Appeals.[56]

Mirador (fig. 239), on U.S. Route 250 south of Greenwood, was built in 1842 for James M. Bowen, a prosperous miller. The front facade had fanlight doorways over as

Fig. 239. Mirador, 1842

well as under the one-story paired-column portico (a window replaced the upper doorway in a later remodeling); the original plaster panels between the first- and second-floor windows remain. Chiswell Dabney Langhorne added one-story brick wings on the east and west ends in 1897. His daughter Nancy (1879–1964), better known as Lady Astor, succeeded her husband Waldorf Astor in the British House of Commons and thereby became the first woman member of Parliament. Another daughter, Irene, achieved widespread fame as the inspiration for the "Gibson Girl," the prototype of beauty and fashion created by her future husband, illustrator Charles Dana Gibson. In 1921 architect William Adams Delano extensively renovated Mirador for Lady Astor's niece, Nancy Tree (later Nancy Lancaster). He extended the rear wall by fifteen feet above an arcaded cellar, added a spiral staircase inside the house, and constructed a stable on the property. The woodwork and mantel in the music room were taken for the renovation from Soldier's Joy in Nelson County, constructed by Jefferson builder James Oldham. Bricks and other materials for the renovation were removed from the Bernard Brown Jr. house, Pleasant Retreat, built in 1816 in Brown's Cove.[57]

Late in the eighteenth century, Charles Lilburn Lewis, who had married a sister of Thomas Jefferson, built a frame house on present-day Route 53 south of the Rivanna River near the Fluvanna County line. In 1803 Lewis's son-in-law Craven Peyton bought the property; in 1838 Robert Gentry acquired it and built the present two-story, five-bay brick Mount Eagle here about 1846.[58]

On land near Cismont where John Davidson had constructed a house and store in 1803, William Cowherd built Windsor Hill about 1848. The house is a five-bay, double-pile Greek Revival–style dwelling with a hipped roof and gable-end chimneys. At the turn of the century, Windsor Hill was the home of James Gavin Field, attorney general of Virginia in 1877–82.[59]

William Cabell Rives Jr. of Newport, Rhode Island, married Grace Winthrop Sears of Boston in 1849. Some six years later he built his summer residence, Cobham Park (fig. 240), as the centerpiece of a 2,500-acre park that contains formal gardens designed in 1924 by the Olmsted Brothers' landscape-architecture firm. The English master carpenter E. S. McSparren, who executed the interior of Grace Church after its fire, was also responsible for Cobham Park's interior, which contains a flying spiral staircase similar to the Montmorenci stair at the Henry Francis du Pont Winterthur Museum. Architect Stanford White resided at Cobham Park in the late 1890s while supervising the reconstruction of the Rotunda interior and the enclosure of the Lawn with new buildings at the university. During the early part of the twentieth century, the estate became the country home of the Peter family of Tudor Place, Washington, D.C.[60]

Some double-pile, two-story brick houses deviate from the prototypical Georgian plan in that their center passages do not continue from the front to the back of the house. The Richard Matthews house at 222–24 Court Square in downtown Charlottesville was built about 1836 on the site of the frame Lewis Leschot jewelry-and-watch shop and the frame town library. It has a mousetooth cornice and probably was derived from a brick I-house. The two-story brick Rugby (fig. 241), north of the university, probably was constructed about 1850 by Andrew Farish. In 1856 Andrew J. Brown operated a school for boys here. After Major General Thomas Lafayette Rosser acquired the property in 1885, he had it extensively remodeled in the shingle style by a Minneapolis architect. Rosser had attended West Point until the outbreak of the Civil War, when he returned to serve the Southern cause in which he was wounded three times. After the war he became the city engineer of Minneapolis and was chief engineer of the Canadian Pacific Railroad. In 1890 Rosser developed a plan for the new town of Minneapolis in Russell County, Virginia. From 1905 to 1910 he was postmaster of Charlottesville. The house served as a boardinghouse for university students as well as a dairy and chicken farm.[61]

Fig. 240. Cobham Park, 1855

Fig. 241. Rugby, c. 1850

The Brick Town House (Two-thirds Georgian)

The two-thirds Georgian brick town house, with its double-pile side-passage plan, remained popular in towns throughout the Greek Revival period. Several fine examples survive in Charlottesville. Located on Park Street across from the courthouse on the site of the eighteenth-century Swan Tavern, Edward Valentine's double-pile side-passage house was constructed in 1832 with a mouse-tooth cornice and a chimney curtain. A one-story brick kitchen was situated beside it. Five years later Samuel Leitch Jr. acquired the property, and in 1905 it became the private Redland Club.[62] The Heiskell-Livers town house at 1213 West Main Street was built in 1842 for newspaper editor Clement P. McKennie as an addition to the house at 1211 West Main Street. It features a brick dentil cornice, two front doors, and an arched passage to the rear. The Dr. Robert B. Nelson house (fig. 242) on East High Street was built with a double-pile, side-passage plan shortly after he bought the lot in 1857.

THREE-STORY BRICK DWELLINGS

Practically all brick houses were one or two stories high, although some were elevated even more by raised cellars. The mid-nineteenth-century three-story brick Barksdale house (fig. 243) at 710 Ridge Street was an exception. It was a three-bay structure constructed in five-course American bond with Flemish-bond variant and a hipped roof topped with a light monitor. This was one of three major buildings of the Albemarle Military Academy.

BRICK TRIPARTITE DWELLINGS

In 1833 Minard Lefever's *Modern Builder's Guide* popularized the tripartite house form in America but with square columns instead of round. Between 1832 and 1835 John Simpson Jr. built a house on the southeastern corner of East Jefferson and Tenth Streets facing Market. By 1837, when Anderson Wingfield sold it to John Timberlake, it had evolved into a brick tripartite dwelling (fig. 244) that was

Fig. 242. Dr. Robert B. Nelson house, 1857

Fig. 243. Barksdale house, M19C

Fig. 244. John Simpson Jr. house, E1830s

double-pile in its two-story center section with a hipped roof culminating in a widow's walk. Rather than using the then-popular one-story paired-square-column portico, the builder employed columns that were rounded and fluted. In 1841 Timberlake and brickmason William B. Phillips sold the house to Phillips's brother-in-law John Vowles. From that time until his death in 1871, it remained Vowles's home, after which it became the Episcopal parsonage for Christ Church. It was razed late in the 1960s.[63]

PORTICOED DWELLINGS

Tetrastyle Porticoes

Tetrastyle, or four-columned, porticoes are among the most obvious features of Greek Revival–style dwellings constructed during the antebellum period. Several houses with such porticoes already have been noted. About 1800 Benjamin Gentry occupied a house just south of Charlottesville where Biscuit Run joined Moore's Creek. In 1850 Captain Eugene Davis, son of John A. G. Davis of The Farm and later the mayor of Charlottesville, built Willoughby on the property. The house had tripartite windows and a tetrastyle portico of square columns with inset panels. The pediment of the portico was altered in later years, and the long-abandoned house was destroyed by fire on Halloween night in 1991.[64]

David Lewis and his brother-in-law Joel Terrell acquired 3,000 acres just west of the university in 1734, on present-day U.S. Route 250. The first Lewis house here burned in 1815 and was rebuilt the following year for Lewis's grandson, Jesse Pitman Lewis. In 1855–56, the present two-story brick house with tetrastyle parged-brick (plaster-

covered) columns on the north facade was erected for Addison Maupin, a hotelkeeper at the university. The house was constructed as two back-to-back I-houses with tetrastyle porticoes. Both sections display five-course American bond with Flemish variant, have circular-saw marks throughout, and exhibit the same asymmetrical cyma reversa exterior-window trim. But the southern section evinces an overhang for a box cornice on its northern wall and is longer than the northern section, thereby suggesting that one section was erected in 1855–56 and the other a few years later, rather than both being constructed simultaneously. In 1907 Washington, D.C., architect Waddy Wood remodeled the house for U.S. senator Thomas Staples Martin. Wood added wings on each side, created an elliptical interior arch and a cross passage to the east wing, relocated the stair, expanded the three-bay southern facade to five, built a tetrastyle portico on the south facade, added a wooden belt course, and painted all the brick walls red with penciled mortar joints. The attic contained a large water tank. In 1963 the University of Virginia acquired the property and named it Faulkner House (fig. 245) in memory of William Faulkner, Nobel Prize winner and writer-in-residence from 1957 to 1958. In 1991 the classical architect Allan Greenberg designed additions.[65]

William D. Grayson bought land on present-day Route 692 northwest of Batesville from James Durrett of Alton Park, on which he built Wavertree Farm in 1859. The house features a Doric tetrastyle portico that may have been rebuilt by subsequent owners, perhaps after 1913 by Quincy Adams Shaw II, a brother-in-law of Lady Astor, or after 1921 by Colonel Herman Danforth Newcomb, who made additions to the house. A tunnel beneath the main house provides access to the outdoors. The site is extensively landscaped and contains a large collection of service and agricultural outbuildings — the oldest being a one-story log slave quarters with center stone chimney.[66]

Two-Tier Porticoes

Two-tier porticoes remained popular throughout the Greek Revival period, and several fine examples exist today in Albemarle County. A portico with square columns and Chinese railings adorns Hopewell, which the photographer Frances Benjamin Johnston captured on film in the 1930s. Grassmere, a frame I-house that has a two-tier portico with square columns and a doorway with a flat transom and sidelights, was built about 1830

Fig. 245. Faulkner House, 1855–56

near Ivy for Francis McGehee, who operated Harden's tavern nearby. John Wiant resided in Brown's Cove at Pleasant Retreat (fig. 246), a dwelling with two front doors and a two-tier portico with square columns and Chinese railings. The house may have been derived from the 1816 home of Bernard Brown Jr. Pleasant Retreat was razed in 1930 and its bricks reused at Mirador. About 1830 Creek Dave Maupin built a two-story, double-pile frame house about a mile east of Free Union on present-day Route 665. The Maupin house is a five-bay dwelling with a hipped roof and a two-tier portico. A pyramidal smokehouse also is located on the property.[67]

The first house at Kenwood, called Fancy Hill, was built about 1836 for Benjamin N. Snead. In 1868 John Warren Porter added the south wing. Fancy Hill was a five-bay frame I-house with a two-tier portico, and the farm included slave quarters, office, icehouse, dairy, smokehouse, well house, and kitchen. The house and its outbuildings were razed in 1938 to make way for the present house designed by architect William Adams Delano for General Edwin M. Watson, secretary to President Franklin Delano Roosevelt.[68]

The Cedars (fig. 247) is another double-pile, five-bay house with a two-tier portico, square columns instead of round, and Chinese railings. It is just west of Yancey Mills on U.S. Route 250. This brick house was built about 1855 for John S. Cocke. As early as 1827, Cocke had purchased from Elijah May a tavern here that became "widely celebrated for its admirable fare among throngs journeying to the Virginia springs." After the Civil War, Cocke operated a boys school, utilizing the nearby Long house tavern as a dormitory. In 1878 he relinquished the property to satisfy a gambling debt. By 1902 Chiswell Dabney Langhorne of Mirador used the house, then called The Casino, for gambling. To the east is a brick two-story, galleried kitchen–slave quarters.[69]

PUBLIC ARCHITECTURE

Opera House and Town Halls

The first facility in Charlottesville constructed as an auditorium for cultural events (fig. 248) was privately owned. It was built in 1851–52 near the courthouse on Court Square, on what had been the battery or commons, and

Fig. 246. Pleasant Retreat, 1816

Fig. 247. The Cedars, c. 1855

Fig. 248. Levy Opera House, 1851–52

George Wilson Spooner Jr. probably designed it. Originally the pilastered Greek Revival–style building had a pedimented gable. In 1887–88 it was converted into an opera house by Jefferson Monroe Levy, who had inherited Monticello from his uncle Commodore Uriah Phillips Levy. In the heyday of the Levy Opera House, some of the finest entertainers of the time performed here. In 1981 the building was again remodeled; this time architect Henderson Heyward converted it into office space. It is often referred to as the "Town Hall."[70]

In 1887 the town of Charlottesville purchased a building at Market and Fifth Streets that had been constructed in 1852 to house the Farmers' Bank of Virginia. It subsequently had been used as a residence. Here the town offices were established, and when Charlottesville was incorporated as a city the next year, it became the first city hall (fig. 249). The two-story pilastered brick structure had a hipped roof that culminated in a light monitor; a two-

story wing had been attached to it about 1871. In 1967 Grigg, Wood, and Browne designed the present city hall on the eastern end of the Main Street pedestrian mall downtown, and two years later the old city hall was razed to make way for a parking garage.

Fig. 249. Charlottesville City Hall, 1852

Firehouses

George Wallace Spooner added a columned portico to Charlottesville's first firehouse, which had been built on the west side of Court Square in 1855. That structure and the 1906 Water Street Firehouse (fig. 250) in Vinegar Hill have since been razed.

ECCLESIASTICAL BUILDINGS

Churches

THE EPISCOPAL CHURCH Although many Episcopal congregations withered after the disestablishment of the Anglican Church in 1786 and because of conversions to other denominations, some took root and grew instead. After Samuel Dyer of Plain Dealing sold land to the congregation for $25, an agreement for the construction of Christ Church Glendower (fig. 251) east of Keene was signed on 31 August 1831 between Tucker Coles of Tallwood, John Coles II of Estouteville, and Dr. Charles Cocke of Esmont, as agents of the church, and James Walker and James W. Widderfield, carpenters. The work was to be done to keep pace with the work of William B. Phillips, the brickmason; one C. Brown was the plasterer. An exterior Tuscan entablature was called for, but an exquisite Doric entablature with triglyphs was built instead and survives today. The church was constructed with three eight-over-eight sash windows on each side and two on the rear, as well as two lunettes with fanlights to light the gallery. In 1848 a frame vestry was added, and a frame rectory enveloped the Plain Dealing Store nearby.[71]

The first Emmanuel Episcopal Church near Mirador was built as a rectangular edifice in 1862–63 at a cost of $2,500. This brick church resembled both the Mount Ed Baptist and the Batesville Methodist Churches (fig. 252).

Fig. 250. Water Street Firehouse, 1906

Fig. 251. Christ Episcopal Church, Glendower, 1831–32

Fig. 252. Batesville Methodist Church, 1860–61

About 1890 a massive oak reredos, a vaulted oak ceiling, and a baptismal font were added to the sanctuary. In 1905 a bell tower, donated by Nancy Langhorne (later Lady Astor) and her sister Phyllis Langhorne Brooks of nearby Mirador, was placed over the entrance, and the two front doors were replaced with one. The Langhorne family commissioned Waddy Wood to renovate the interior, add a larger bell tower, and design the parish house between 1911 and 1914. Wood's use of rounded window fenestration and a Palladian window were reminiscent of eighteenth-century Christ Church in Alexandria. In the mid–twentieth century, Milton Grigg renovated the church after a fire and enlarged the parish hall. Outside the church cemetery is the classical Owsley mausoleum, built in the 1930s for the owners of nearby Tiverton. The church complex is an outstanding example of early twentieth-century Georgian Revival–style ecclesiastical architecture in Albemarle County.[72]

THE PRESBYTERIAN CHURCH Several Presbyterian churches were built in the nineteenth century, both in rural Albemarle and in Charlottesville. The Presbyterian Church of Scottsville was organized at Warren in 1827, and the brick church (fig. 253) in Scottsville was completed about 1832. An added exterior gable-end stair that led to the slave gallery was removed before 1890. The nearby manse was destroyed by fire in 1901. The pilastered Lebanon Presbyterian Church on U.S. Route 250 West was built in the mid–nineteenth century of five-course American-bond brick with Flemish variant. The congregation is said to have been established a hundred years before the church was constructed. As early as 1853 Tabor Presbyterian

Fig. 253. Presbyterian Church, Scottsville, c. 1832

Church was located in the county, but it was sold as a residence in 1915 when the congregation moved into a new frame structure still standing in Crozet. The brick Mountain Plains Presbyterian Church, built about 1855, today serves a Baptist congregation.[73]

THE BAPTIST CHURCH The Baptists were the third denomination to appear in Charlottesville. In 1833 they built the First Baptist Church on the north half of lot number 5 on the southwest corner of East Jefferson and Fourth Streets.[74] Charlotte Digges Moon, a Baptist heroine known as Lottie Moon, became associated with the Charlottesville church. She was born at Viewmont and graduated with a degree in French from what is now Hollins College. In 1858 she was converted at a revival in Charlottesville's second First Baptist Church (fig. 254), a pilastered brick building built just six years earlier by George Wilson Spooner Jr. on the northeast corner of East Jefferson and Second Streets Northeast. She later served as a missionary in China for thirty-nine years. In 1904 that First Baptist Church was razed, and the third First Baptist Church (figs. 255, 256) was built of brick in the Romanesque Revival style, positioned diagonally on the corner to respond to what became Lee Park. The congregation had already begun work on its new church on Park Street when fire destroyed the Romanesque building in 1977. About a decade later the Queen Charlotte Square Apartments were built on the site.

Mount Ed Baptist Church, or Whiteside's Creek Church, was founded in 1788 by Benjamin Burgher, its first pastor. The present Greek Revival–style brick church (figs. 257, 258) dating from 1856–57 was built for $3,500. Its pilastered facade is similar to Batesville Methodist Church (1860–61; see fig. 252), Emmanuel Episcopal Church (about 1862), and Adiel Baptist Church (about 1854) in Nelson County. A frame church, Slate Hill Baptist, dates to the period of the Civil War and first served as a union church (used by more than one denomination). Free Union Baptist Church is a brick union church of four-course American bond that was built in 1837 on land owned by Dickerson Burrus. Another brick church, but in Flemish and five-course American bond, is Scottsville Baptist Church (fig. 259), built three years after Free Union.[75]

THE METHODIST CHURCH The first record of a Methodist church in the county was a 1788 deed that mentioned two acres on which "the Methodist Episcopal Church stands." This building, Maupin's meetinghouse, was the predecessor of the present pilastered Mount Moriah

Fig. 254. First Baptist Church, Charlottesville, 1852

Fig. 255. First Baptist Church, Charlottesville, 1904

Fig. 256. First Baptist Church, Charlottesville, interior, 1904

Fig. 257. Mount Ed Baptist Church, 1856–57

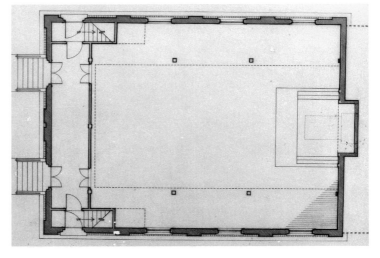

Fig. 258. Mount Ed Baptist Church, 1856–57, plan

Fig. 259. Baptist Church, Scottsville, 1840

Fig. 260. Mount Moriah Methodist Church, 1834, 1854

Methodist Church (fig. 260) at White Hall, built in 1834 and enlarged in 1854. Another early Methodist church, the frame vernacular Centenary Methodist Church South on Route 721 west of Damon, was built in 1840 and altered in 1907. Originally Key's meetinghouse, later it was known as Finnell's chapel at Heard's and was replaced by Bethel Methodist Church.[76]

The pilastered brick Howardsville Methodist Church (fig. 261) dates from the town's heyday as a port on the James River and the terminus of the Howardsville Turnpike from the Shenandoah Valley. The church was constructed in 1854 adjacent to the 1846 Masonic lodge on the land of Drury W. Kendrick and Washington C. Kendrick.[77]

The Charlottesville First Methodist Episcopal Church was constructed by the fourth denomination to appear in Charlottesville. James Lobban built the first

church (fig. 262) of brick in 1834 on the north half of lot number 55 on the southeast corner of Water and Second Streets.[78] The second church (fig. 263), also brick, was built by George Wilson Spooner Jr. in 1859 on the southwest corner of Water and First Streets on lot number 53. Mrs. Malcolm Crawford, the wife of another Jefferson builder, was an early member of the church.

THE DISCIPLES OF CHRIST CHURCH (CHRISTIAN CHURCH) The Disciples of Christ, the fifth denomination to appear in Charlottesville, was founded in 1832 as a Baptist reform group led by Alexander Campbell. Just a few years later, the brick Disciples of Christ Church (fig. 264) was built in 1836 on the north half of lot number 25, the southwest corner of Market and First Streets. The present brick church, the First Christian Church, was built in 1897 on the same site. Its stained-glass windows were made at the Hefferman Art Glass Works in Washington, D.C. The Scottsville Disciples of Christ Church (fig. 265) was built in 1846 on town lot number 30 largely through the efforts of Dr. James Turner Barclay, who was reared at Viewmont and in 1831–36 owned Monticello. The brick building now serves as the Scottsville Museum.[79]

NONDENOMINATIONAL CHURCHES Several nondenominational or union churches were constructed in Albemarle County, and the 1803 courthouse served as a common house of worship before church buildings were

Fig. 261. Methodist Church, Howardsville, 1854

Fig. 262. First Methodist Church, Charlottesville, 1834

Fig. 263. First Methodist Church, Charlottesville, 1859

Fig. 264. Disciples of Christ Church, Charlottesville, 1836

Fig. 265. Disciples of Christ Church, Scottsville, 1846

erected in Charlottesville. The frame Earlysville Free Union Church (fig. 266) of 1833 is an example of an early church building that served several denominations, including Baptists, Presbyterians, and Methodists.[80]

Rectories and Manses

THE EPISCOPAL CHURCH After the Revolution, Episcopalians referred to ministers' residences as rectories and manses. Three dwellings in Charlottesville served as manses for Christ Church. A brick I-house, Meadelands (fig. 267), was built about 1844 on Park Street as the manse for the Reverend R. K. Meade. It was later the residence of Dr. Halstead Hedges. Originally built in the 1830s for John Simpson Jr., the tripartite house on the southeast corner of Jefferson and Tenth Streets near the Rawlings Institute was acquired by the church in 1871 for an Episcopal manse. In 1919 Judge Egbert R. Watson's house on Park Street became the Episcopal rectory. The two-story brick house was sold by the church in 1971.[81]

Fig. 267. Meadelands, Episcopal manse, Charlottesville, 1844

In Albemarle County, The Rectory near Keene served as the residence for the Reverend Joseph Wilmer of Christ Church Glendower. It is an 1848 frame enlargement of Samuel Dyer's 1787 Plain Dealing Store, whose foundation can still be seen in its cellar.[82] Verdant Lawn Rectory near Ivy was built at the end of the Civil War to serve the Ivy Parish on land donated by William Wirt Gilmer and William H. Southall.

BAPTIST AND PRESBYTERIAN MANSES A Charlottesville manse served both Baptist and Presbyterian ministers and later became the Charlottesville Female Academy. The brick Old Manse (fig. 268) of 1839 is at 422 Second Street Northeast.

MANUFACTURING BUILDINGS

Quarries

Lime not only had important agricultural and industrial applications but also served as a component of the mortar used in masonry construction. The Shenandoah Valley's prolific limestone belt did not extend east of the Blue Ridge and into Albemarle County, except for a few isolated pockets. Lime for the mortar used at Monticello and the University of Virginia was produced at a limekiln on James Monroe's Limestone Farm. Two other quarries were operated in the county during the nineteenth century: Campbell Lime Quarry near Findowrie and the Garland Lime Quarry, which functioned from 1838 to 1870.[83]

Fig. 266. Free Union Church, Earlysville, 1833

Fig. 268. Old Manse, Baptist and Presbyterian, Charlottesville, 1839

Other minerals used in building construction were quarried in Albemarle County. In 1846 a good grade of granite was located at Rougemont and used at Grace Episcopal Church. Greenstone was mined at the Peter's Mountain Quarry. Although slate for shingles was being cut in Buckingham County by 1790, a slate quarry was located in Albemarle County and its products were advertised as late as 1860. Other county slate quarries included Esmont Quarry, Buck Island Quarry, Slate Hill Quarries, and Blue Ridge Quarry. In 1917–20 the Ohio Sulphur Mining Company extracted pyrites a mile northwest of Proffit.[84]

Factories

During the eighteenth and nineteenth centuries, the manufacture and firing of brick in kilns often occurred on the building site. For example, the University of Virginia erected a kiln just west of Hotel A, and university builder William B. Phillips also operated one nearby in the south of town. As the means of shipping large amounts of brick became available, however, brick factories were built and their products were sold nationwide. Later in the nineteenth century, Benjamin C. Flannagan constructed the Buck Island Brick Factory on the south side of the Rivanna River at Buck Island Creek. The Scottsville Factory, built about 1835, stands on a one-story stone base over which are two

floors of five-course American-bond brick. At one time the factory manufactured textiles, and at another time it served as a tobacco factory.[85]

Mills

Martin Dawson, who had purchased Bellair near Carter's Bridge from Charles Wingfield Jr. in 1822, engaged Martin Thacker of Cedar Grove to build the Eolus Gristmill (fig. 269) on Dawson's property in 1854. The mill had two wheels, one for corn and one for wheat.[86] Its huge wooden shear blocks, columns, and beams were typical of mill construction; some of the components were later incorporated into the Old Mill Room at the Boar's Head Inn.

In 1840 the buildings alone at John Timberlake and John Bowie Magruder's Shadwell Mills (formerly Jefferson's mill) on the Rivanna River were assessed at $15,800, which included $7,800 worth of improvements made within the preceding year. Mills in the $6,000 range included Dr. Gilly M. Lewis's Albemarle Mills (formerly Peter Field Jefferson's mill) on the Hardware River, and Rice W. Woods and Nathaniel Burnley's Hydraulic Mills on Ivy Creek. Among those in the $5,000 range were Tucker Coles's mill on the Hardware River and Richard Duke's Rivanna Mills (later called Burnt Mills) on the Rivanna River. Buck Island Mills was valued at about $4,000.[87]

Albemarle's forty gristmills, four cotton and woolen

Fig. 269. Eolus Gristmill, 1854

mills, and thirteen sawmills again constituted some of the highest-valued buildings in the county in 1850. John Timberlake and John Bowie Magruder's Shadwell Mills were still valued at $15,800. Walker Timberlake's Eolus Mill on the Hardware River followed at $8,000, Nathaniel Burnley's and the Rice W. Woods estate's Hydraulic Mills on the Rivanna River at $6,900, the Dr. Gilly M. Lewis estate's Albemarle Mills on the Hardware River at $6,440, Southall and Minor's Rio Mills at the intersection of Ivy Creek and the south fork of the Rivanna River at $6,000, John Cochran's mill on Meadow Creek at $6,000, and Tucker Coles's mill on the Hardware River at $5,600.[88]

Warehouses

Peter Field Jefferson's tobacco warehouse (fig. 270), built in Scottsville in 1834, is the only one of its kind remaining in the county. A two-story, five-course American-bond brick building with two attics and huge wooden shear

blocks mounted atop its structural columns, it is located on the James River and Kanawha Canal. The warehouse also was called a "lumber house," or a building for the storage of miscellaneous items including lumber. Although the heyday of tobacco warehouse construction ended before the Civil War, in more recent years many other warehouses were constructed for a multitude of functions. Charles King's warehouses on Water Street in Charlottesville, for example, were designed by the well-known architectural firm of Alfred B. Mullett in 1897 and were used for wholesale grocery storage.[89]

COMMERCIAL BUILDINGS

Taverns and Hotels

The Woolen Mills Tavern was built of Flemish-bond and five-course American-bond brick in the late 1830s on East Market Street in Charlottesville. It was part of the Charlottesville Woolen Mills complex. In 1854 William P. Farish constructed the Farish House hotel (fig. 271) on the Eagle Tavern site. It still survives, a three-story brick building with recessed balconies and pilasters in the Greek Revival style. In 1861 George L. Peyton, then the proprietor, advertised that "his table servants and attention to the wants of his visitors shall be everything that the most fastidious may desire." Yancey's tavern on the Rockfish Gap Turnpike at Yancey's mills is a two-story log hall-parlor building constructed about 1835. In that year James P. Henderson of Blair Park, a grandson of U.S. Supreme Court justice John Blair, committed suicide there.[90]

The Long house tavern, across the Rockfish Gap Turn-

Fig. 270. Peter Field Jefferson's tobacco warehouse, 1834, elevation

Fig. 271. Farish House hotel, 1854

pike from the Cedars Tavern, served as a dormitory for the Cedars Preparatory School for Boys after the Civil War. Mantels removed from the Jessup house on High Street and Dr. Fishburn's house at 801 High Street were installed in the building during the twentieth century. The Garland A. Garth tavern on the Rockfish Gap Turnpike in Brownsville has evolved from a two-story, hall-parlor frame building constructed about 1838. It contains beaded interior joists, cellar joists bearing reciprocating-saw marks, and beaded weatherboards. By 1860 the county court licensed some seventeen taverns throughout Albemarle County.[91]

The arrival of the railroad in Albemarle County in the mid–nineteenth century encouraged the construction of hotels at depots to accommodate rail travelers. One of the earliest, Price's Hotel, was built about 1850 at the Mechum's River station on the Virginia Central Railroad where its huge truss bridge spans the highway. The hotel was built for William Graves and purchased by Charles H. Price in 1855.[92]

Banks

Charlottesville's first bank, Savings Bank of Charlottesville, opened in the 1830s with John H. Bibb as cashier. In 1840 a branch of the Farmers' Bank of Virginia was established on the west side of Court Square. In 1852 the bank was relocated to the corner of Market and Fifth Streets in a building that later served as the city hall. John Bibb's uncle, William A. Bibb, was the cashier. A third bank, the Italianate-style Monticello Bank (fig. 272), was built in 1854 at 323 East Main Street.[93] After the financial panic of 1857, the growth of banks came to a virtual halt in Virginia and did not resume until after the Civil War. In 1859, however, banks opened at Howardsville and Scottsville.

MEDICAL BUILDINGS

Two of the first eighteenth-century physicians in the region were Dr. Thomas Walker of Castle Hill and Dr. William Cabell, who lived in what is now Nelson County. Walker's daughter Lucy married Dr. George Gilmer, whose father was a Williamsburg doctor. Young Gilmer purchased Pen Park and became Thomas Jefferson's physician. Walker had spent his childhood in the household of the elder Dr. George Gilmer, who was also his uncle and with whom he apprenticed. By 1835 six physicians served Charlottesville.[94]

The plantations owned by physicians usually included

Fig. 272. Monticello Bank, 1854

a doctor's office as one of the outbuildings. The 1846 log office (fig. 273) of Dr. Thomas Walker Meriwether, for example, remains at Clover Fields and is known as Sunset Cabin. The mid-nineteenth-century office of Dr. John Bolling Garrett, the son of Alexander Garrett, proctor of

Central College and — from 1825 to 1851 — bursar of the University of Virginia, was located at Seven Oaks. Dr. Edward F. Birckhead (1820–1907) and Dr. Edward H. Birckhead (1859–1907) also maintained an office at their farm, Morven, near Earlysville. After the Civil War, Dr. Thomas Martin Dunn maintained an office, now in ruins, on his farm on present-day Route 609 near Free Union.[95]

EDUCATIONAL BUILDINGS

In 1811 the General Assembly established the Literary Fund to help educate the poor. By 1840 about forty public schools operated in Albemarle County. But many private schools, especially for boys, were established in the nineteenth century to provide a classical education and prepare students for college. Often classes were conducted in private homes. Franklin Minor operated a private school at Ridgway, and others were run by Dr. Charles Minor at Brookhill, Samuel O. Minor at The Farm, Gessner Harrison at Cocke's tavern, and Broun and Tebbs at Bloomfield Academy (fig. 274), built in 1849. Major Horace W. Jones's School for Boys was founded in 1857 and continued until 1903. It was first located on the site of the later McGuffey Elementary School in Charlottesville, then in a frame building at Market and Eighth Streets. Charlottesville's other classical schools included George Carr and Thomas W. Maury's school (fig. 275); Jefferson School for Boys (fig. 276), which was razed for the

Fig. 273. Office of Dr. Thomas Walker Meriwether at Clover Fields, 1846

Fig. 274. Bloomfield Academy, 1849, engraving

Fig. 275. George Carr and Thomas W. Maury's school, 19c

Fig. 276. Jefferson School for Boys, 19C

city hall addition; and Colonel Watson's School for Boys (fig. 277) at the corner of Market and Fifth Streets.[96]

Other nineteenth-century schools were established specifically for women. The Edgehill School for Young Ladies was founded in 1829 to raise income to pay the debts inherited by the estates of Thomas Jefferson and Thomas Mann Randolph Jr. A dormitory was added to the Edgehill house to accommodate increased enrollment, and a stone chapel was built in the late nineteenth century. Other girls schools included Charlottesville Female Academy, which operated from about 1820 to 1830 in the Maupin-Bibb house in Charlottesville; Piedmont Female Academy at Cobham; Rockland Home School for Girls and Young Ladies on present-day U.S. Route 29 South, which was established about 1880 by J. N. Faris; and Albemarle College (fig. 278), begun in 1898 on Park Street in Charlottesville. Founded in 1857, Albemarle Female Institute eventually became the Rawlings Institute and relocated to Tenth and East Jefferson Streets in a building designed by

architect Charles Henry Ford. In 1910 Saint Anne's School began here; the building was razed in 1972. In 1939 the present Saint Anne's was built near U.S. Route 250 West, now within the Charlottesville city limits, from designs by architect Eugene Bradbury.[97]

TRANSPORTATION BUILDINGS: RAILROAD DEPOTS

With the aid of several hundred Irish workmen, the Virginia Central Railroad tracks were extended from Gordonsville to Cobham in 1848. Francis Kinloch Nelson of Clover Fields helped the railroad president and his committee select a site for a depot in the Keswick-Cismont area on 17 February 1848, and Joseph W. Campbell of Findowrie supplied railroad ties from his sawmill. At midcentury the area between downtown and the university was further invigorated with the junction of two major railroads: the Virginia Central Railroad (later the Chesapeake and Ohio) in

Fig. 277. Colonel Watson's School for Boys, 19c

Fig. 278. Albemarle College, 1898

1849 and the Orange and Alexandria (now the Southern Railway) in 1863. Although temporary tracks around construction existed earlier, in 1858 the Virginia Central was connected with the Shenandoah Valley through four tunnels (fig. 279) dug seven miles through the Blue Ridge, a remarkable feat accomplished by the French-born civil engineer Claudius Crozet. One of the tunnels, the Blue Ridge Tunnel, was the longest (4,273 feet) in America when it opened in 1856. Among the more spectacular bridges on the C&O line is the metal truss span at Mechum's River that was built in 1924.[98]

Because of reduced railroad passenger service, in recent years many depots have been razed or abandoned. Perhaps the oldest extant depot, no longer in use, is that at Keswick. The oldest section (figs. 280, 281), dating to about 1850, was burned in the Civil War, and an addition was constructed in 1909. Among C&O depots no longer extant are the 1915 frame Shadwell Depot; the 1900 frame Warren Depot; the 1890 frame Crozet Depot (fig. 282), which was replaced by a brick building in 1923; and the 1860 frame Scottsville Depot, which was replaced by a brick depot in 1915. An example of a rural depot's privy (fig. 283) was once located at Lindsay.[99]

Fig. 279. C&O Railroad tunnel entrance at Greenwood, LI850s

Fig. 280. Railroad depot at Keswick, c. 1850, c.1865

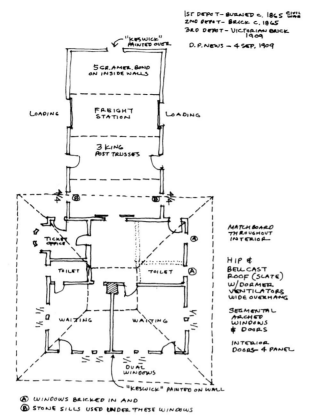

Fig. 281. *(left)* Railroad depot at Keswick, c. 1865, 1909, field notes

Fig. 282. *(below)* Railroad depot at Crozet, 1890

Fig. 283. *(above)* Railroad depot privy at Lindsay, E20C

V

Beyond the Classical Revival

AFRICAN AMERICANS

The first African Americans in Albemarle County doubtless came as slaves to clear and farm their owners' new land. Slavery's roots in English America extended back to at least 1619, when some of the first Africans in the British colonies arrived at the mouth of the James River in a Dutch ship, perhaps as quasi-indentured servants, although their precise status remains unknown. The institution of slavery evolved over the next hundred years, slowly becoming codified as custom and as law, culminating in 1705 in an act of the General Assembly that consolidated all previous legislation into one systematic "slave code." Slaveholding in Virginia increased with the demand for tobacco, that most labor-intensive of crops to cultivate, at the same time that indentured white servitude declined due to a general improvement of conditions in England. By the early eighteenth century, slavery was entrenched in the colonies.

In 1749 Albemarle County's white population approached 1,725. Six years later 3,100 people lived in the county, with slaves slightly outnumbering whites. By 1782, when the county's land area was reduced to its present size, the population had reached 5,300. The term *slaves* was used in the early tax records, but interestingly the more recent term *blacks* was used in these records in 1786. The first two federal population censuses, in 1790 and 1800, showed whites slightly outnumbering blacks. Total population figures for those two censuses were approximately 13,000 and 16,000 persons respectively, indicating a ninefold increase over population estimates for the county fifty years before.[1]

Albemarle had at least five black Revolutionary War soldiers: David Barnett, Shadrack Battles, Stephen Bowles, Sherard Goings, and Johnson Smith. Free blacks numbered about 171 in 1790 and 606 by 1860, but even they had restrictions: a Virginia law of 1806 required that freed slaves depart the state within twelve months of manumission or risk reenslavement. And free blacks often were treated severely, as noted in 1864: "Lizzie Burns, a free negress, waiting-maid on the Central Railroad, was arrested yesterday, for using insulting and provoking language to a gentleman. She was carried before Justice Lobban, who ordered thirty stripes on her bare back."[2]

After the Civil War freed blacks established separate communities in the county; one of those was Egypt, later called Bethel, and now Proffit. Others were the "Free State" at Dunlora and Kellytown off Preston Avenue in Charlottesville where the Alexander Kelly house and the Albert Brooks frame I-house still exist. Part of Cismont Manor near Keswick was transferred to black tenant farmers and former slaves by the widow of Peter Minor Meriwether in 1882. On one parcel the black housewright Albert Johnson built Breezy Oaks, which began as a two-story frame hall-parlor and later was enlarged. And after the war Hugh F. Carr (1843–1914) built his frame I-house with L-shaped plan near Hydraulic where he had been a slave on the Richard Woods Wingfield property, Woodlands. The property is now the site of the Ivy Creek Natural Area.[3]

Compassion for slaves varied with the outlook of the time. Walker Timberlake, who had thirty-two slaves in 1850, expressed in his will his desire that "all my children will bear in mind what they know to be my feelings of clemency and humanity towards my slaves, and that they will as far as practicable extend a corresponding treatment towards them, especially the oldest ones." He wished his executors to "exchange such men with the owners of their wives" in order to reunite families, but the exchanges were only to be "for servants of equal value" and "provided such sales can be made without unreasonable sacrifice." Persons such as General John Hartwell Cocke of Bremo were members of the American Colonization Society founded in 1817 with the notion of transporting freed slaves from America to Liberia in Africa. The society aid helped them resist European powers and threatening tribes, but only about 12,000 took the offer. Liberia, founded in 1822 for this purpose, declared its independence in 1847. The following year Dr. Charles D. Everett of Belmont requested in his will that his plantation be sold five years after his death with the proceeds used to send his slaves to Africa "for the enjoyment of their liberty." But his executor sent them to Mercer County, Pennsylvania, because he was "convinced that the wilds of Africa were unsuited as a home for these helpless, ignorant people."[4]

An 1824 newspaper ad indicated an ironic compassion in announcing that Frank Carr would sell about twenty slaves at public auction before the door of the Swan Tavern but "they will be sold in families." Others were direct in their support for freedom of slaves. When John Coles II of Enniscorthy died in 1808, his youngest son, Edward, private secretary to President Madison, received slaves as part of his inheritance. In the spring of 1819, he took his slaves to Illinois and freed them, then spent two terms as governor of that state. Ironically his second son, Roberts, moved back to Albemarle County and, as a Confederate captain, was killed in 1862 in the battle of Roanoke Island.[5]

In 1810 Albemarle County's population was about 18,000. By 1830 there were approximately 12,000 blacks to 10,000 whites. The 1850 census identified about 13,000 slaves, 600 "free colored," and 12,000 whites in the county residing on 2,000 plantations. By 1880 the county's population had grown to 32,000, with blacks outnumbering whites, after which time freed blacks migrated to the Norfolk area and the urban North. From 1810 to 1880 Charlottesville experienced tenfold growth from 260 people to about 2,700. By the turn of the twentieth century, the county had a population of about 35,000, and Charlottesville had 6,500 residents; in both town and county, whites now outnumbered blacks by two to one.[6]

By 1920, due largely to annexation, Charlottesville's population had nearly doubled to 11,000. Just 29 percent of the county's population was black, and fifty years later the county recorded about 14 percent black, with the city of Charlottesville about 16 percent.[7]

Little is known about the building crafts and skills of slaves. Many blacks were obviously skilled workmen as indicated in 1752 by an ad for the return to Colonels Fry or Harvie in Albemarle County of a runaway "servant . . . by trade a joiner" belonging to the Reverend Robert Rose. The reward was four pistoles, "besides what the Law allows." A list of more than forty slaves from the late Dabney Minor's Carrsbrook estate advertised for hire at Brice Edwards's tavern includes two blacksmiths with tools, a stonemason, a carpenter, and several wagoners. The recent archaeological investigations by Jeffrey L. Hantman and Drake Patten at the Foster house near the University of Virginia have shed light on the everyday lives of freed blacks. In addition, researchers Lucia C. Stanton and Dianne Swann-Wright of the Thomas Jefferson Memorial Foundation have uncovered new information on the slaves at Monticello, and Ashlin Smith's oral history project, sponsored by Preservation Piedmont, has revealed much about the social history of the black community. In his lifetime Jefferson owned more than 400 slaves, including cabinetmakers, carpenters, brickmasons, and blacksmiths; perhaps the best known was the carpenter John Hemings. James Oldham, who worked for Jefferson at the university, owned slaves valued at $5,500; two of them were carpenters. Another Jefferson builder, John M. Perry, obviously owned skilled slaves too, because he advertised for the return of a runaway "first-rate House Joiner."[8]

The Civil War (1861–1865)

During the American Civil War, Virginia suffered more damage than any other state. Although military activity in Albemarle County was limited, the war brought about the destruction of a number of buildings, bridges, and canals. On 29 February 1864 a skirmish at Rio Hill involving Brigadier General George Armstrong Custer resulted in the burning of the frame bridge over the Rivanna River on the Earlysville Road as well as the Rio Flour Mills beside it. Custer had been assigned to destroy a railroad bridge over that river to the east but thought it too heavily guarded by Confederate infantry, cavalry, and artillery, and destroyed the Earlysville Road bridge instead.[9]

In 1865 then Brevet Major General Custer, under Major General Philip H. Sheridan, arrived in Charlottesville at 4:00 P.M. on 3 March. The day before, his men had destroyed the Brooksville tannery and the depot, railroad cars, and warehouses at Greenwood. At Ivy they destroyed the depot and its water tanks as well as warehouses filled with tobacco and Confederate government supplies. Arriving in Charlottesville from Staunton, the Union forces methodically demolished the Virginia Central Railroad (later Chesapeake and Ohio) tracks, depots, and bridges as they advanced, including the large wooden railroad bridge over Mechum's River.

In Charlottesville, Union soldiers burned a tannery and the iron railroad bridge as well as a new county bridge over the Rivanna along with Marchant's Woolen Mills. The devastation of war probably would have been worse except that the mayor and Charlottesville council members met Custer in the county and formally surrendered the town. Included in this group were the rector and other representatives from the university. Custer assured the delegation that as long as his men were not attacked, they would spare and protect the buildings of no military value.[10]

South of town, the Orange and Alexandria Railroad (later Southern Railway) was devastated. Ties were piled up and burned to heat, bend, and twist the rails. At North Garden the Union forces destroyed the depot, freight station, water tanks, and two culverts. The depot at Covesville was also destroyed. Two "fine wooden bridges over the north and south fork of the Hardware River, each about 200 feet in length" were demolished as was the "large railroad bridge over the Rockfish River" just over the county line in Nelson County. At Scottsville a large cloth mill was burned as were a five-story flour mill, a candle factory, a machine shop, tobacco warehouses, and the canal lock, as well as three canalboats loaded with shells, tobacco, and government supplies. Brigadier General Alfred Gibbs later reported, "I regret that a few private dwellings, close to the mill, were more or less charred by the intense heat."

On the James River and Kanawha Canal east to Columbia and west to New Market, all of the large flour mills, woolen factories, and manufacturing establishments, as well as the canal itself, were destroyed. The Totier Creek aqueduct was damaged as were all the locks. At Warren the raiders burned the Hatton Grange Mill and another large mill. At Howardsville they demolished a manufacturing plant of government saddletrees, a large wagon and plow factory, a wagon shop, a forge, two tobacco warehouses, and a canal aqueduct. The cavalrymen also confiscated a boatload of butter, bacon, flour, and molasses for Federal use.[11]

No doubt more buildings were destroyed than were officially recorded. According to local tradition, Buck Island Mill on Buck Island Creek at the Rivanna River, Keswick Depot, Pounding Brook Farm on Mechum's River, and Scotland, off Totier Creek, were all burned. At

River Lawn, Sheridan's cavalrymen destroyed stock and colts, and at The Riggory they burned the slave quarters. They also raided Dunlora, Estouteville, Midmont, and Wyndhurst. At Farmington, Sheridan's troops drank many of the 5,000 bottles of wine that had been imported from England and stored in the vaulted cellar and then broke what they could not consume.

The local newspapers of 1865 carried appeals by General Robert E. Lee for citizens to donate "carbines, muskets, pistols, sabres, and bayonets" to the war effort. In addition, a local auction of Confederate horses, mules, and wagons was held to raise funds for the Southern effort.[12]

Charlottesville, designated as a general hospital, served almost 23,000 wounded or sick soldiers during the war. Some 1,200 died and were interred in the university cemetery. Not only did the university's Range rooms serve as hospitals, so too did the brick Delevan Hotel building as well as three one-story buildings on the Southern Railroad Depot site, Smith's Central Hotel, the Midway Hotel at Ridge and West Main Streets, and the Stone Tavern on Market Street. The depot buildings were razed after the war by George Sidney Ford. Many homes in the county and the town were opened to convalescing soldiers, including Headquarters, Morea, Redlands, Wertland, The Cedars, and Piedmont at White Hall, as well as Scottsville's Baptist Church. Thomas H. Brown, a cabinetmaker at Headquarters, made artificial limbs for Confederate soldiers. Allegedly, ammunition was stored in Preddy's Creek Baptist Church, and Confederate uniforms were tailored in the Charlottesville Town Hall.

Both armies camped and bivouacked in the county. In 1862 Major General Thomas J. "Stonewall" Jackson and part of his Valley Army had bivouacked near Shadwell. With the arrival of Generals Sheridan and Custer in the area in 1864 and 1865, Union camps were established at The Riggory, Mount Armour, Seymour (Faulkner House), the Maury house (Piedmont), and the McCoy house (Chancellor-Cocke house) on the site of the present Saint Paul's Memorial Episcopal Church. In Charlottesville, Judge Watson's house on Park Street was occupied by Union soldiers, and Sheridan slept at the Tower House on the same street and Custer at The Farm, while near Keswick in March 1865, Lieutenant General Jubal A. Early set up temporary Confederate headquarters at Belmont. In Scottsville a Union encampment was located at Chester, Sheridan and Custer occupied Cliffside, and Brigadier General Wesley Merritt spent some time at Old Hall.[13]

Although little damage was done in the area compared

to other parts of Virginia, the memory of the war's hardships affected the lives of local citizens for years to come. Five generals are buried in Charlottesville: Major General Thomas Lafayette Rosser in Riverview Cemetery; Jefferson's grandson Brigadier General George Wythe Randolph, who served as secretary of war, in the family cemetery at Monticello; Brigadier Generals John Marshall Jones and Armistead Lindsay Long in Maplewood Cemetery; and Brigadier General Carnot Posey in the university cemetery.[14]

The Gothic Revival (1830–1860)

In England taste shifted during the fourth decade of the nineteenth century from the classical to the Gothic, as promulgated by the Cambridge Camden Society and the publication of *The Ecclesiologist*. Augustus Charles Pugin's books on Gothic architecture were reprinted by his son several times after his death in 1832. In the United States the use of the Gothic Revival style in house design was popularized through such publications as *Rural Residences* (1837) by architect Alexander Jackson Davis, *Cottage Residences* (1842) and *Architecture of Country Houses* (1850) by his landscape-architect friend Andrew Jackson Downing, and Richard Upjohn's *Rural Architecture* (1852). In addition to a wooden, board-and-batten framework that resulted in the lasting contribution to housing of the open plan, the

characteristics of the style included pointed-arch windows, steeply pitched roofs, and decorated vergeboards. Downing enthusiastically promoted the use of such decoration: "Take for example, the vergeboard of a rural Gothic gable. As part of a well-built villa, this verge board is carefully carved in thick and solid plank, so as to exhibit all the details of outline and tracery boldly to the eye, and so as to endure as long as the house itself."[15]

In America the Gothic Revival paralleled the Greek Revival period and was overshadowed by the classical style. Because of the influence of Jefferson and his master builders, as well as the strong resurgence of classical forms in the area at the turn of the twentieth century, the multiplicity of Victorian styles—especially the Gothic Revival—had little effect on the architecture of Albemarle County. The county can boast, however, of having Grace Episcopal Church, the only known building in Virginia designed by the nationally renowned architect William Strickland, which was constructed in 1847 at Cismont in the Gothic Revival style. Also, after the first house at Blenheim burned, Andrew Stevenson (Speaker of the House of Representatives, minister to England, and rector of the University of Virginia) purchased the property in 1846 and built the second Blenheim (fig. 284) as a one-story frame dwelling with pointed windows in the Gothic Revival style. An assortment of outbuildings grace the property, including a school-chapel, smokehouse, pyramidal-

Fig. 284. Blenheim, 1846

Fig. 285. Sunnyside, c. 1800, c. 1858

roofed kitchen-laundry, classical library, and an eighteenth-century one-story frame overseer's house believed to have been a claim house.[16]

The Gothic Revival style was particularly applicable to small, picturesque cottages, resulting in the construction of several A. J. Downing and A. J. Davis–inspired "gothick" cottages in the area. In the mid–nineteenth century, for instance, Thomas Walker Gilmer built the Perkins house on North First Street in Charlottesville. It features a steep gable with sawed vergeboards and pendants as well as pointed windows. In 1863 it was sold to Charles Meriwether for 24,910 inflated Confederate dollars; George Perkins bought it in 1880 for $800. Another Gothic Revival cottage once stood next to this house.

About 1800 Blake Harris built a one-story log hall-parlor house with a stone chimney on Barracks Road just on the western edge of Charlottesville. In 1858 William Carroll purchased this property, called Sunnyside (fig. 285), after it had been remodeled with sculptured, sawed vergeboards in the Gothic Revival style of Washington Irving's Sunnyside in Tarrytown, New York. It was at this time too that a frame dining room with a bedchamber above was added to the house on the south. In 1863 Colonel Richard Thomas Walker Duke Sr. acquired the property and enlarged a small bedchamber attached to the western side of

the log portion. Another two-story frame section was added to the southern part of the house in 1894. Many other outbuildings completed the plantation setting, including a log kitchen, log stable, octagonal office, slave quarters, and icehouse. After the University of Virginia acquired the property in 1963, it served until 1982 as the home of Frederick Doveton Nichols, the first Cary D. Langhorne Professor of Architecture and chairman of both the Division of Architecture and the Division of Architectural History.[17]

During the Civil War, in 1863, Charles E. Bailey built the Fowler house at the corner of Ridge and Garrett Streets of wood rusticated to resemble ashlar masonry, a variegated slate roof, scalloped-eave vergeboards, and pendant loops at the corner and at the gable peak. That same year William I. Parrott acquired the property and added the bay window. After Parrott's death, D. W. Fowler bought the house in 1894.[18]

THE VICTORIAN ERA (1860–1900)

In the Victorian period asymmetrical romantic buildings proliferated in a variety of architectural styles. They included "carpenter Gothic," Queen Anne, Second Empire, Romanesque Revival, Italianate, Edwardian, Eastlake, and Jacobean Revival, to name a few. Collectively, they are known as Victorian, and most of them rose to national popularity after the Civil War.

Just before the war, Albemarle County had been at the forefront of livestock breeding and production in the state. By the late nineteenth century, increased wheat production in the Great Plains states resulted in a decline in wheat production in the county. Land was used instead for the raising of livestock and the cultivation of orchards and vineyards. But the 1907 Massie map of the county identified more than forty-eight working mills, indicating that wheat was still a vital commodity.

Building activity, which had slowed after the 1857 depression, did not fully resume until 1866. Between then and 1885 many of the great fortunes that exist today in America began to be accumulated. The real estate tax assessment of 1865 revealed that John Vowles owned the most expensive building in the county, the John Simpson Jr. tripartite brick house on the southeast corner of Tenth and East Jefferson Streets, valued at $14,000. William P. Farish's double brick grocery and dry goods store (lots 23 and 24) at 101 East Main Street, assessed at $13,500, was the next most valuable building. Benjamin C. Flannagan's Buck Island Brick Factory and the Scottsville Manufacturing Company were assessed at almost $10,000 each. Several buildings were valued in the $8,000 range, including the Farmers' Bank of Virginia in Charlottesville, John D. Ryland and Tyree Rodes's Midway, William P. Farish's Monticello House on Main Street (lots 17 and 18), Dr. Charles D. Everett's Belmont, and Peyton Skipwith Coles's Estouteville. The economic depression that followed the war, the collapse of the plantation system, and an increase in the number of bankruptcies resulted in the doubling of the number of small farms between 1870 and 1880.[19]

The use of balloon-frame construction and the availability of inexpensive factory-made building parts established the I-house with new Victorian trim as the prototypical dwelling of the period. The kitchen was moved from an outbuilding into the cellar or a rear ell of the main house. Chimneys shrank in size and frequently were positioned in the interior of the house rather than on the gable ends. The use of wood- and coal-burning cast-iron stoves increased, especially after the opening of the Pocahontas coalfields in southern West Virginia in the 1880s made inexpensive, smokeless coal available for use in the home as well as in factories. Builders and homeowners alike referred to a multitude of pattern books and magazines that featured house plans.[20]

Largely because of the emancipation of the slaves, by the time of the 1870 census overall wealth in the county had declined, yet four estates had real and personal property valued at more than $100,000: Samuel Overton Moon of Westbury ($190,000), Peyton Skipwith Coles of Estouteville ($150,000), Mary A. Harper of Farmington ($144,000), and Tucker Skipwith Coles of Enniscorthy ($106,560). Also in 1870, land tax records revealed that the highest assessed building value, other than the mills at Charlottesville, remained John Vowles's Tenth Street house at $14,000.[21]

The simultaneous expansion of Charlottesville and the University of Virginia during the nineteenth century was not without turbulence. With the addition of land to the north in 1818, the town actually increased five times in population in eight years and extended toward what is now Hedge Street. The growing population disrupted the community's peace and quiet. In that same year a traveling minister, Dr. Conrad Speece, exclaimed after an uneasy night in town: "When Satan promised all the Kingdoms of the world to Christ, he laid his thumb on Charlottesville and whispered, 'except this place, which I reserve for my own especial use.'" Two years later Charlottesville's first newspaper, the newly founded *Central Gazette*, advertised "to let the repair of gaol and erect whipping post, stocks, and pilory" for the "especial use" of unruly citizens. In the mid–nineteenth century, rental dormitories were built on the south side of West Main Street between the university and downtown to house the growing student population. General John Hartwell Cocke of Bremo built the Delevan or Mudwall Hotel surrounded by a rammed-earth fence, and Chiles M. Brand built additional brick dormitories nearby.[22]

Charlottesville continued to grow throughout the remainder of the century. In 1873 the town annexed more land to the east, and five years later the Woolen Mills installed Charlottesville's first telephone system. A horse-drawn omnibus began scheduled routes in 1883, and by 1887 the first street railway cars traveled between the university and downtown. A year earlier a town water system had been installed. More urban amenities became available after the town acquired city status in 1888. Two years later horse-drawn fire engines were introduced, and in 1894 electric- or steam-powered railways replaced streetcars drawn by horse or mule. In 1895 the Albemarle Telephone Company was established, a sewage system was installed, and Main Street was macadamized.

Charlottesville was incorporated as a city in 1888 after it had increased its population to the requisite 5,000 people by annexing a surrounding ring of land, thereby expanding its area to 781 acres and extending its boundaries westward to The Corner at the university. A boom period began the next year in real estate, industry, transportation, and resort hotels, with as many as five land-improvement companies promoting industry and housing through suburban land developments adjacent to the city. Fry's Spring, named for J. Frank Fry who had carved his name on a stone near the spring here in 1852, was one such development; the subdivision of the Belmont estate created an even larger development. In industry, the Armstrong Knitting Factory on Harris Street opened during this period in one of the few Second Empire buildings in the city.

The city's first directory, published in 1888, listed five private schools, three hotels, two restaurants, twenty saloons, two breweries, a winery, a gristmill, two newspapers, nine barbers, three cigar manufacturers, eight tailors, seventeen dressmakers, seventeen shoemakers, three carriage makers, two harness makers, eight blacksmiths, and four livery stables. The town had no paved streets, although Main Street had sidewalks and flat paving stones at street-corner crossings.[23]

On the death of his builder father in 1865, George Wallace Spooner (1820–1904), the "architect" son whose office was on town lot number 48, obtained the elder Spooner's mortise machine. Young Spooner married Dorothy "Dolly" Ann Durrett in 1853, and they had ten children. A city directory listing "G. W. Spooner & Son, Architect and Builder" suggests that Spooner and one of his sons were working together by the time of the city's incorporation in 1888. Spooner lived just south of Mount Zion Baptist Church at 409 Ridge Street in a frame house that evolved into a tripartite form. About 1892 Spooner became the city manager of Charlottesville. During his lifetime he designed and built several churches and public buildings in the city.[24]

Two sons whose parents, Charles Henry and Martha Harriett Ford, were natives of England worked in the area from about 1853 until after the Civil War: Charles Henry Ford was an architect for the Rawlings Institute, and George Sidney Ford, born in 1837, worked for Hudson and Lushbaugh, Staunton contractors for the Robert Mills–designed Annex to the Rotunda. George Ford and his wife, Anne E. Bowyer Ford, are buried at Saint Paul's Church in Ivy. Among local architects and craftsmen, Charlottesville's first city directory listed R. C. Vandegrift as a builder as well as Spooner. W. P. Connell and Son was listed among white carpenters, and three black carpenters, Joseph Cash, John Coles, and Charles Goodloe, were listed.[25]

William P. Connell was born in West Virginia in 1827

and married Sarah E. Bowyer, the sister of Anne Bowyer Ford, in Albemarle County in 1852. Their carpenter son, George E. Connell, who was born in 1858, was thrice married. The Connells, like George Ford, apparently were associated with the university. In 1888 they designed a house for J. Ben Key on Nalle Street in the city; L. C. Anderson was the builder. The 1890–91 city directory added builders J. D. Nimmo and B. F. Wingfield and Son, as well as two more black carpenters, John Dickinson and Charles E. Coles. The latter owned the largest building in the Vinegar Hill section of Charlottesville; it contained seven businesses. Other architects were named in subsequent directories, including W. T. Vandegrift and Edward L. Melborne in 1898 and William W. Keenan in 1902.[26]

Robert Carson Vandegrift Sr. was born in 1832 to David and Ann Wertenbaker Vandegrift, who had been married in Albemarle County in 1820. He apprenticed under his father as a carpenter and before the Civil War was a partner with Benjamin F. Wingfield. In 1888 he became a member of Charlottesville's first city council. Earlier, in 1859, he had married Catherine Elizabeth Johnson; on his death in 1921 he was buried beside her in Oakwood Cemetery. Their son, William T. Vandegrift (1860–1935), carried on the family's carpenter tradition in Charlottesville. In 1894 he built the Marshall-Rucker house on Park Street, while S. Burrage Reed was the architect for the 1884 Duke house next door. Vandegrift and his wife Sarah Agnes Archer Vandegrift moved to Dallas, Texas, by 1921, but they subsequently returned to Charlottesville and were also buried in Oakwood Cemetery.[27]

Victorian has become a catchall term applied to the multitude of styles that evolved primarily between the Civil War and the turn of the twentieth century, although certain Victorian styles such as the Italianate were established well before the war during the earlier years of Queen Victoria's long reign. Many asymmetrical two-story frame houses in Albemarle County exhibit typical later Victorian features. In 1871, for example, Captain H. Clay Michie purchased the Carr property on Meadow Creek just north of Charlottesville and altered an existing L-shaped house here into a two-story frame house he called The Meadows. He added such stylistic details as a bay window, decorative sawed brackets, and two-over-two sash windows. The Meadows was dismantled in 1992 for reassembly at North Garden to make way for Seminole Square Shopping Center. Another such frame Victorian house was Belle Haven, built about 1880 on a site overlooking the James River at Scottsville. The home of J. L. Pitts, it included richly decorated vergeboards in its gables and Tiffany-designed stained-glass windows. About this same time a Victorian addition with a bay window was made to Stonefield, at the intersection of Rugby and Barracks Roads in Charlottesville, for owner Mason Gordon. Gordon had purchased the property in 1869; it included a two-story board-and-batten house built for Schuyler T. Rhodes eight years earlier. In 1915 Gordon's daughter, Nancy Burr Gordon, moved her school into the remodeled house. The tract also included brick dependencies and a carriage house. Another example is on the Green Mountain Road, where either Colonel Charles P. Shaw or the sisters Misses Sally Logan Coles and Elizabeth Cocke Coles built New Woodville about 1892. The sisters operated a summer hotel in the house. In 1989 it was renovated as the home of Jaquelin T. Robertson, dean of the university's School of Architecture.[28]

Brick versions of the Victorian modes included the three-bay, two-story Judge Egbert R. Watson house on Park Street, which became an Episcopal rectory in 1919. It was built in 1861 with segmental-arched windows and a center gable. The brick two-story Key West was built about 1872 on the Rivanna River northeast of Charlottesville for Captain Bryan, son-in-law of Peter Minor, on land once owned in the mid–eighteenth century by John Key. It featured decorative brackets, triangular lintels, and a water tank in the attic. The fifty-room brick Nydrie (fig. 286) on Green Mountain was perhaps the grandest Victorian house in the Piedmont. It probably was designed by architect D. Wiley Anderson in 1898 for Harry Douglas Forsyth of New Orleans, who had made a fortune in sugar and banking. Patterned after a Scottish baronial castle, the main dwelling was 68 by 175 feet with brownstone trim and slate roof. Its 22-by-61-foot two-story entrance hall served as a ballroom, above which was a music gallery. Other features included a walnut library, drawing room, dining room, greenhouse with a swimming pool, quartered-oak staircase, an ash billiard room, and window-label molds. Water tanks were enclosed in castellated towers. In 1928 the house passed to the Van Clief family and was renovated by carpenter Ernest Hoover from designs by Anderson, his father-in-law. Nydrie was razed in 1978.[29]

Although several of the Victorian styles were hugely popular in various parts of the United States, they never reached the same level of acceptance in Albemarle County. Of the relative handful that were built here, however, several of them are gems.

Dwellings

ITALIANATE The Italianate style, which employed such features as square towers, wide bracketed eaves, and

Fig. 286. Nydrie, 1898

rounded dual windows, appeared by the mid–nineteenth century and continued to be popular in many parts of the country after the Civil War. It was less popular in Albemarle County, but even so, Ernscliff, a fine example, was constructed here. Built for J. O. Pendleton at Overton in the 1850s, Ernscliff was a two-story Italianate brick house that featured interior chimneys between its double-pile rooms, rounded dual windows, and a center gable with a bull's-eye window. It was demolished in 1991. The pilastered Tower House on Park Street in Charlottesville, built in the late 1850s for John Wood Jr., employs an unusual plan that does not contain a center passage. One instead enters directly into one of the four first-floor rooms that adjoins a square Italianate tower with rounded dual windows and brackets. The Edward M. Antrim house on East High Street, built in the mid-1880s, contained paired segmental-arched windows, trefoil gable windows, Eastlake fan-shaped cornice stops, a bracketed cornice, a projecting bay window, and a veranda. It was razed after the First Baptist Church burned in 1977 to make the entire block available for redevelopment.[30]

CARPENTER GOTHIC The so-called carpenter Gothic style was characterized by frame buildings with an abun-

dance of decorative scroll-sawed brackets and lathe-turned spindles. Such "gingerbread" houses were constructed throughout America but were not as popular in Albemarle County. In 1886 Alexander Pope Abell sold the north garden plot of his house on North First Street to H. M. Gleason, who built the Gleason-Pendleton house (fig. 287) here three years later. In 1904 Corrine D. Pendleton acquired it. The frame I-house contains eave brackets, dual circular-headed vents in its center gable, a scroll-sawed porch with a spool frieze and a loop balustrade, internal chimneys and coal-burning fireplaces, and two-over-two sash windows in its three-bay facade.

QUEEN ANNE The Queen Anne style was created in the mid–nineteenth century by English architect Richard Norman Shaw, who borrowed from the craftsmanship of the days of Queen Anne in England 150 years earlier, as well as from the medieval period. This romantic style, which also borrowed elements from other Victorian styles, was popularized in the United States at the Centennial Exposition in Philadelphia in 1876. Round, square, or polygonal towers and turrets were common features of the Queen Anne style. Bay windows projected from the walls, and windows

Fig. 287. Gleason-Pendleton house, 1889

and doors sometimes were inset behind transparent arches to reflect the layering of space within and without. Verandas surrounded the house and frequently featured porch gazebos. Contrasting materials often were employed in wall surfaces, and brick chimneys likewise were patterned. Gables frequently featured decorative sawed brackets and other ornaments such as pendants.

In 1884 Charlottesville's first judge, Richard Thomas Walker Duke Jr., built the Duke house on Park Street from a design by New York City architect S. Burrage Reed. The frame two-story asymmetrical house contains a pedimented gable on its projecting pavilion, a balcony over its entrance, a bay window, and a handsome veranda with segmental frieze, turned Victorian columns, and a porch gazebo. Stephen Price Maury built his shingled house, White Cross, at 152 Stribling Avenue in 1891. It features a circular stone tower that contains a belvedere on top. For more than a decade, Charlottesville School for Boys, founded by Robert S. Osburn in 1932, was located here.

An even more lavish brick house (fig. 288) was constructed in 1894 just to the north of the Duke house for Carrie Marshall by builder William T. Vandegrift. In 1913 wealthy philanthropist William J. Rucker acquired it, and

it thus became known as the Marshall-Rucker house. He added a wing to the south facade about 1930 that contains a solarium with a paneled library above. The house's octagonal tower is juxtaposed with a wide gable that contains an open Romanesque arcade. A three-story dogleg stair arises behind a walnut entrance arch on the first floor, which also contains double parlors with carved walnut mantels and mirrored overmantels.[31]

Kirklea, a frame Queen Anne–style house at Ivy, was built about 1896 as the residence of Episcopal archdeacon Frederick William Neve (1855–1948), a graduate of Merton College in Oxford, England. The house is another of the fine examples of the Queen Anne style in Albemarle. Its picturesque setting, the wealth of original interior fabric and exterior detail, and its association with the Reverend Mr. Neve make it an important contribution to the county's material culture.[32]

Dr. Paul Brandon Barringer, chairman of the faculty at the university from 1896 to 1903, inspired the creation of the University of Virginia Hospital; he later became president of Virginia Polytechnic Institute. In 1896 he built at 1404 Jefferson Park Avenue the Barringer mansion (fig. 289), perhaps the most lavish Queen Anne–style house in

Fig. 288. Marshall-Rucker house, 1894

Fig. 289. Barringer mansion, 1896

Albemarle County and Charlottesville. The two-story brick house incorporates an octagonal tower, tall pointed gables, decorated brick chimneys, fine interior woodwork, glazed fireplace tiles, and a molded-brick Romanesque Revival–style entrance doorway with Corinthian pilasters. Threatened with demolition, it was converted into the university's French House in 1985 by local architect Robert Moje.

Two frame two-story country houses built in the 1890s shared similar plans. James Gibbon Carter built Crestwood on old Ivy Road just west of Charlottesville, and New York City architect C. Wellesley Smith designed a "mirror-image" copy of Crestwood to serve as the 1899 Alberene Soapstone Company's president's house (fig. 290) commissioned by James H. Serene. Both dwellings featured three-story octagonal towers, hipped roofs, and widow's walks at the roof peaks. Crestwood was razed in 1990.[33]

SECOND EMPIRE The additions to the Louvre in Paris made between 1852 to 1857 by Louis-Tullius-Joachim Visconti and Hector-Martin Lefuel popularized the Second Empire style in Europe. In America, Alfred B. Mullett, the supervising architect for the U.S. Treasury Department, designed several government buildings in the style after the

Civil War. Largely because of Mullett's influence, during the administration of President Ulysses S. Grant especially, the Second Empire style spread throughout the country. Its hallmark was a high mansard roof that was sometimes covered with imbricated or patterned shingles and often featured cast-iron crestings and massive eave brackets. Only a few examples can be found in Albemarle.

About 1839 Nancy Price built a one-story brick house, the Price-Poore house, on Park Street a block north of the courthouse. In 1851 Mrs. Ann E. Poore purchased the property, where she conducted a school for small children. Probably shortly after the Civil War, the house was enlarged to two stories and given a bellcast mansard roof (fig. 291). A mansard roof originally topped the five-bay, two-story brick dwelling at Blue Ridge Farm built about 1870 for William B. Smith. In 1899 Dr. Frederick D. Owsley bought the property. Between 1923 and 1927 the architect William Lawrence Bottomley completely renovated the interior of the house in the Georgian Revival style and changed the roof as well for a subsequent owner, Randolph Ortman. Charles Gillette designed the expansive English-style landscaping, thereby transforming Blue Ridge Farm into one of Virginia's most beautiful estates.[34]

Fig. 290. (top) Alberene Soapstone Company, president's house, 1899

Fig. 291. (bottom) Price-Poore house, c. 1839, L19C, elevation

ROMANESQUE REVIVAL The Romanesque Revival style was first used in the United States by architects Richard Upjohn and James Renwick. Usually rendered in brick, light-colored stone, or brownstone, such buildings typically featured medieval-type round arches. Because of its employment by Boston architect Henry Hobson Richardson, this style is often referred to as "Richardsonian Romanesque." Although some houses such as the Marshall-Rucker house feature arches, very few pure Romanesque Revival houses were built in Albemarle County. A Gothic Revival cottage was located until 1973 on North First Street next to the Perkins house. In 1889 Edward M. Antrim had a duplex built on part of the same property. It exhibited an unusual almost flat roof and such Romanesque features as large Diocletian therm windows, with large lunettes and two vertical mullions, at the second-floor level and label molds, or raised drip molding, over the windows.

Public Architecture: Jails

The fifth Albemarle County Jail (figs. 292, 293), north of High Street, was completed in 1876 by architect George Wallace Spooner, stonemason J. J. Gleason, and ironworker Randolph Frank Harris. It stands two stories high with three-foot-thick stone walls, a rough flagstone floor, a hipped roof with slate shingles, and two internal brick chimneys. In 1880 Spooner added a two-story section to the east that had eighteen-inch brick walls and an outside brick wall that formed a courtyard around the entire complex. The first floor of this addition contains a steel cage with six cells made by the Stewart Iron Works of Cincinnati, Ohio, which also made the iron cemetery gates for

Fig. 292. Albemarle County Jail and Jailer's House, 1875–76, 1886

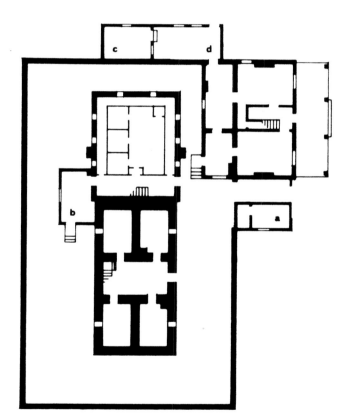

Fig. 293. Albemarle County Jail and Jailer's House, 1875–76, 1886, plan

Morven, the Birckhead property near Earlysville. In 1886 Spooner designed a two-story brick jailer's house that is attached to the jail. The jail was in use until 1974, when the county's sixth jail was constructed south of town. The northwest corner of the fifth jail's courtyard was the scene of the last public hanging in Albemarle County when the town's former mayor J. Samuel McCue was executed for the 1904 murder of his wife.[35]

Ecclesiastical Buildings

CHURCHES

The Episcopal Church In April 1847 a foundation and cornerstone were laid for Grace Episcopal Church (fig. 294) north of Cismont, to replace Walker's Church. Commissioned by Judith Walker Rives of Castle Hill, it was designed in the Gothic Revival style and constructed of granite quarried at the convenient Rougemont estate. It is the only building in Virginia known to have been designed by architect William Strickland, who was trained by B. Henry Latrobe and designed such Greek Revival–style buildings as the Exchange, the Independence Hall steeple, and the Second Bank of United States, all in Philadelphia, and the Tennessee State Capitol in Nashville.

An English carpenter, E. S. McSparren, built the interior of Grace Episcopal Church and, later, the Riveses' nearby summerhouse, Cobham Park. In 1854 a bell was installed that was donated by David Sears, the father of Grace Rives (Mrs. William Cabell Rives Jr. of Cobham

Fig. 294. Grace Episcopal Church, Cismont, 1847, 1896

Park) for whom the church is named. A fire gutted the building in 1895, and the following year the interior was restored and a chancel added. The "blessing of the hounds" at Grace Church, which continues to this day, is an annual foxhunting ritual. Dr. Thomas Walker of nearby Castle Hill introduced the Walker strain of foxhounds to Virginia in the eighteenth century and popularized foxhunting in Albemarle.[36]

Saint Paul's Episcopal Church in Ivy was built in 1869–70 for about $1,750, supposedly using salvaged timbers from the earlier 1836 church at Mechum's River. The church is a rectangular brick structure with three Gothic-style windows on the lateral sides. In 1892–93 a Mr. Caldbeck remodeled and enlarged it with a Stick-style interior truss system and belfry. In the early twentieth century, a brick narthex and vestry were added, as were many more accretions into midcentury. The Reverend Frederick William Neve, who was born in Great Britain, became rector of Saint Paul's in 1888 and held that post for thirty-five years. He was long a friend of Lady Astor and established

chapels of ease and schools in the remote areas of the county. Thirty-nine mountain missions were built from Albemarle County to Luray in Page County under Neve's auspices as archdeacon of the Blue Ridge; several of these picturesque chapels are of uncoursed stone. A dynamic and influential clergyman, Neve was among the first to extend formal education to the mountain people in Virginia.[37]

In 1895 George Wallace Spooner tore down the old Christ Episcopal Church and built a larger one of stone on the same site. It contains hammer beams, a large rose window, and Gothic-style stained-glass windows, some by Louis Comfort Tiffany. Spooner's partner in the project was Harry P. McDonald (1848–1904), a Louisville, Kentucky, architect who had studied civil engineering at Washington College (now Washington and Lee University) and designed the Kansas State Capitol in Topeka. Later that same year the Rotunda Annex and the Rotunda interior were destroyed by fire. Spooner and McDonald were commissioned for the reconstruction project; but when construction problems developed, they lost the job, and it was ultimately completed between 1896 and 1898 by New York architect Stanford White.[38]

The stone Edgehill Chapel, which had a false hammer-beam ceiling and Gothic windows, was built in 1880 to serve Edgehill School, the private school for young women that had opened in 1829 on the Edgehill property. The chapel was razed about 1960.

Other Episcopal churches were of frame construction. Saint John's Episcopal Church (fig. 295) was built in Scottsville in 1875, the second church in Saint Anne's Parish. This board-and-batten church with Gothic windows and a scrollwork vergeboard is a picturesque example of carpenter Gothic architecture. Saint Luke's Episcopal Mission Chapel, built in 1892 at Simeon, contains elements of the Gothic, Queen Anne, and Stick styles. Its projecting front gable is pierced with a pointed arch, and its interior contains scissors trusses. The stained-glass windows are some of the finest in the county. The frame Gothic Revival–style Saint James's Episcopal Mission Chapel on Garth Road has connections with the Garth family. The earliest legible inscribed gravestone is that of Willis Garth, who died in January 1851. The church dates to about 1897.[39]

African Americans, who earlier could attend white Episcopal churches where they usually were relegated to the "coachman's gallery," established their own congregations after the Civil War. The frame Trinity Episcopal Church (fig. 296) was built in 1910 as the Church of the Ascension by bridge builder C. Chastain Cocke in Palmyra

Fig. 295. Saint John's Episcopal Church, Scottsville, 1875

in Fluvanna County. The projecting front gable pierced with a pointed arch is similar to that of Saint Luke's Chapel. In 1939 the building was dismantled and moved to its present site at Grady and Tenth Streets to serve black Episcopalians whose chapel had been razed to make way for Lane High School. In 1974 the original congregation moved to a new church nearby; the old church serves as a Pentecostal Assembly.[40]

The Methodist Church The Batesville Methodist Church, which dates from 1860–61, is similar to the nearby Mount Ed Baptist Church, another brick pilastered church. Carpenters James H. Shepherd and John Via built the structure using materials from the razed Midway Church, which had been constructed in 1830 on Shepherd land. The Beaver Creek Methodist congregation erected the frame Crozet Methodist Church in 1889.[41]

Fig. 296. Trinity Episcopal Church, Charlottesville, 1910

The Lutheran Church The community of New York at the foot of the Blue Ridge near Greenwood was inhabited in the early nineteenth century by Germans from Pennsylvania who brought to the area the Lutheran denomination. A church was established here, and in 1871 a Lutheran chapel was built east of Ridge Street in Charlottesville. In 1908 a congregation that had been founded in 1869 constructed a frame Lutheran church (fig. 297) with clipped gables and Gothic windows on West Main Street just west of the Southern Depot. When the depot was expanded in 1916, the church was relocated to the north of the street and then demolished in 1953; a new church was built on Jefferson Park Avenue.[42]

The Baptist Church In 1805 the General Assembly amended an act passed the previous year that prohibited slaves from meeting at night for any purpose, to permit them to attend church services with their masters. Frequently, black Baptists outnumbered whites in congregations because white members often brought their slaves to church with them. By 1848 even free blacks were permitted to attend religious services only if a white minister conducted them. Despite the restrictions, according to a county map drawn in 1864, of the thirty-three churches outside Charlottesville, two were "African": one near Forge Church at Carter's Bridge and the other near Brookhill on present-day Route 20 South. The same two churches also appear on an 1866 map. After the Civil War blacks formed their own churches, often on land donated by whites.[43]

Neither of the two Civil War–era black churches exists today. The prototypical rural church of frame construction and rectangular plan, with a symmetrical entrance bell tower, is ubiquitous in the countryside. Mount Zion Baptist Church, just south of the Greene County line on Route 743, dates to about 1870 and is one of the earlier houses of worship still standing. Because the congregation first met in a forest clearing before it constructed the church building, Mount Zion and other churches of the period often are referred to as "arbor" churches. The Oak Union Baptist Church congregation, founded in 1875 near Owensville, built another of these early frame churches in 1880. Its entrance doors were placed on either side of the bell tower, and the building was stuccoed in 1918.[44]

The frame prototype church proliferated throughout the county in the late nineteenth and early twentieth centuries, many with black congregations. Mount Sinai Baptist Church near Earlysville was built about 1890 on land

donated by J. S. Richards in 1874 with the stipulation that two of its five trustees be white. Evergreen Baptist Church is another example of the type, founded in 1888 and built about 1891 in the freed black community that became Proffit. Other church specimens include Union Ridge Baptist Church on Hydraulic Road, built about 1900, and Mount Calvary Baptist Church in Ivy, which was constructed about 1890 to replace an earlier church. Mount Calvary is remarkable for its exterior decorative details: atop its spire a wooden finger points toward heaven, and on its bell tower are silhouetted tearful African faces. The land for this church was given by a local black landowner, Mr. Kinney, who also built the church.[45]

Orson Squire Fowler, in his book *A Home for All; or, The Gravel Wall and Octagonal Mode of Building*, first published in 1848, suggested that people's lives would be much enhanced if they lived, worked, and worshiped in multisided buildings. His recommendations increased the popularity of octagonal and other nonorthogonal structures. As late as 1871 Zion Baptist Church (fig. 298), a black congregation, built its frame decahedron church at Crossroads. This unique building was razed in 1975 and replaced by a concrete-block edifice.[46]

White Southern Baptists also constructed frame

Fig. 297. Lutheran Church, Charlottesville, 1908

Fig. 298. Zion Baptist Church, Crossroads, 1871

churches in rural Albemarle County. In 1879, for example, a congregation built the frame Chestnut Grove Baptist Church northwest of Earlysville at the junction of Routes 663 and 665.[47]

The Mount Zion Baptist Church in Charlottesville is a brick version of the typical rectangular frame church. The congregation was founded in 1867 by black members (both freeborn and former slaves) of Charlottesville's white First Baptist Church who had first petitioned the white church in 1864 for dismissal to form their own congregation. About 1875 the members built a frame church on Ridge Street that they called the Mount Zion First African Baptist Church of Charlottesville. In 1883 the frame church was razed, and by 1884 it was replaced with a brick edifice (fig. 299) designed by George Wallace Spooner with George A. Sinclair as brickmason. During the 1890s the steeple, stained-glass windows, and pipe organ were added.[48]

Delevan Baptist Church on West Main Street in Charlottesville is another urban brick black church. This congregation was formed in 1864 from the white First Baptist Church as well, and in 1868 it purchased and occupied the cellar of a three-story brick student boardinghouse constructed by General John Hartwell Cocke of Bremo in

Fig. 299. Mount Zion Baptist Church, Charlottesville, 1884

Fluvanna County. The building, called the Delevan Hotel, was surrounded by a pisé wall of rammed earth, which gave the property its soubriquet, Mudwall. The hotel was razed in 1876, and the cornerstone for the new church was laid the following year. But it was not until 1883 that John C. Sinclair finished the brick church (fig. 300) at a cost of a little more than $6,000. The next year, the first services were held, and the congregation changed its name to the First Colored Baptist Church of Charlottesville.[49]

Ebenezer Baptist Church, also in Charlottesville, was built in 1894 by a congregation founded two years earlier. Robert C. Vandegrift and Sons constructed the brick building. On Thanksgiving Day in 1907, the interior burned; it was rebuilt the next year.[50]

The Roman Catholic Church The earliest-known Catholic church in the county was a log structure built about 1825. The first one in Charlottesville, the brick Church of the Holy Paraclete, later called Holy Comforter Catholic Church (fig.

Fig. 300. Delevan Baptist Church, Charlottesville, 1883

301), was built in 1880 on the southwest corner of Second and East Jefferson Streets. In 1925 it was replaced by the present church designed by Stanislaw Makielski and based on Alberti's San Andrea in Mantua, Italy. Local architect Jack Rinehart, a graduate of the University of Virginia, designed an addition in the 1970s. The most recent Catholic chapel built in the county is at Albemarle House; it was designed about 1985 by David Easton of New York for Patricia Kluge.

The Jewish Synagogue The earliest record of Jews in Albemarle County is a patent issued to Michael and Sarah Israel in 1757 for eighty acres between North Garden and Batesville; to this day the land features here are called Israel's Gap and Israel's Mountain. Isaiah Isaacs moved to Charlottesville from Richmond before 1800, and another Jew, Commodore Uriah Phillips Levy, purchased Monticello from Dr. James Turner Barclay in 1836. Despite the existence of a growing Jewish community, it was not until 1882, largely through the efforts of the Leterman family, that George Wallace Spooner built the first brick Beth Israel Synagogue at Market Street and Second Street Northeast in Charlottesville. In 1904, to build the federal court and post office, it was dismantled and reassembled (fig. 302), reusing some of the original fabric, on its present site on the northeast corner of Third and East Jefferson Streets.[51]

Nondenominational Churches Several union and nondenominational churches were built in Albemarle County early in the nineteenth century. Later, in 1887, Henry Clay Marchant, president of the Charlottesville Woolen Mills, built a nondenominational chapel (fig. 303) for his employees and the community.[52]

Jefferson once wrote that he had "recently been examining all the known superstitions of the world, and do not find in our particular superstition [Christianity] one redeeming feature. They are all alike, founded upon fables and mythologies." In *Notes on the State of Virginia*, he asserted that "it does me no injury for my neighbour to say there are twenty gods, or no god. It neither picks my pocket nor breaks my leg."[53] As Marie Kimball later observed in her biography of Jefferson, this statement probably caused him more difficulty than anything else he said or wrote in his lifetime.

When he established his university, Jefferson deviated from the usual scheme of affiliating a college with a religious denomination and placing the chapel at the physical center of the institution. Instead, the University of

Fig. 301. Holy Comforter Catholic Church, Charlottesville, 1880

Fig. 302. Beth Israel Synagogue, Charlottesville, 1904

Fig. 303. Woolen Mills Chapel,
Charlottesville, 1887

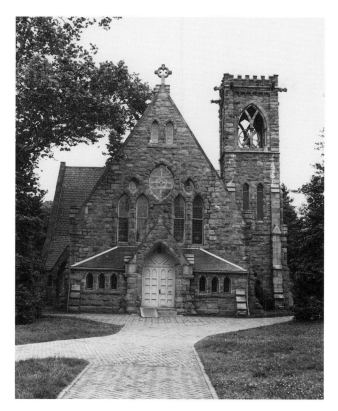

Fig. 304. University of Virginia Chapel, 1885–90

Virginia's visual center was the library, a focus of knowledge and learning divorced from religion. However, some students, many of them scions of Episcopal Virginia families, quickly complained about the lack of a chapel. Beginning in 1835 and continuing for the next fifty-five years, four different designs for a chapel were proposed. As early as 1841, the east gymnasium wing at the Rotunda was enclosed and used for religious purposes, and what is now the Luther P. Jackson House in Dawson's Row became a parsonage. But it was not until 1885 that the present stone Gothic Revival–style University Chapel (fig. 304) was begun. It was completed in 1890 from designs by Charles E. Cassell of Baltimore.[54]

PARSONAGES

Methodist The frame Scottsville Methodist Church parsonage on Jackson Street dates to the mid–nineteenth century, and the 1872–73 Batesville Methodist parsonage is a three-bay brick I-house with a center gable. The Queen Anne–style Elder's House, built about 1891 at 401 Ridge Street in Charlottesville, served as the residence of the presiding elder or district superintendent for the Methodist Church for more than a century.[55]

Baptist Charlottesville's First Baptist Church offered its clergy the brick Baptist parsonage, also known as the Jessup house, which was built about 1885 at 614 East High, as well as the stuccoed early twentieth-century Park Hill parsonage.

Manufacturing Buildings

QUARRIES During the Civil War, James H. Serene, who served in Albemarle County in Major General Philip H. Sheridan's cavalry, noticed large soapstone deposits near South Garden, where the mineral had been mined as early as the Late Archaic period (2500–1200 B.C.). In January 1883 Serene, John G. Porter, and Mrs. Selina A. Carroll purchased 1,955 acres from A. Harris and W. D. Schutz. Their company, the Alberene Soapstone Company, took its name from a combination of Albemarle and Serene. The company built a self-sufficient "company town" named Alberene as well as a railroad line to its other quarries at Schuyler in Nelson County. In 1899 Serene developed an executive row at Alberene that included the Queen Anne–style president's house designed by New York architect C. Wellesley Smith and a dwelling each for the company vice president (Serene himself), the treasurer, and a tenant farmer. The streets of the town were lined with frame company workers' houses, a livery, a general store, and a depot. In 1916 the company moved all of its operations to Schuyler.[56]

MILLS In 1860 the county census identified thirty-four gristmills and sixteen sawmills. Even during the Civil War a map of the county drawn in 1864 under the direction of Major General Jeremy F. Gilmer, chief of Confederate engineers, noted more than sixty-six mills including a steam sawmill in the vicinity of Buck Island Mills on the Rivanna River.[57]

Brigadier General George A. Custer's cavalrymen destroyed many mills in the county during the Civil War; most were rebuilt afterwards. Natural disasters also took their toll. In 1870, the year Virginia was readmitted to the Union, another devastating flood struck the county almost a century after the "Great Freshet" of 1771 and demolished many mills and bridges. Among the casualties were Pace's mill on Mechum's River and Carr's mill on the north fork of the Rivanna, as well as Hydraulic Mills, Rio Mills, North Milton Mills, Magruder Mills, and Union Mills. Earthquakes rumbled through the county in 1875, 1897, and 1907, but none was as powerful as that of 1833; there is no record that any of the earthquakes damaged the county's mills as severely as did the war and periodic floods. Nevertheless, recovery was swift; in 1870, according to the county land tax records, Charlottesville Mills, the highest-valued building in Charlottesville, was assessed at $17,800. Both Eolus Mill on the Hardware River, owned by the estate of Walker Timberlake, and the Nathaniel Burnley estate's Hydraulic Mills were valued at about $6,000.[58]

Flour milling in Albemarle County declined in the early twentieth century. The introduction of electricity and high-powered roller mills shifted the industry to the Midwest, where flour and meal could be produced at a fraction of the price charged by the older water-powered mills. The decline was registered on county maps: that published in 1875 by Green Peyton identified more than sixty-nine mills, while the map published in 1907 by Frank A. Massie noted only about forty-eight working mills. By the late twentieth century, most mills had disappeared. They were located in floodplains, and floods and fire had taken their toll. Today only a few remain, none of which are operational, and of them only four have been adapted to other uses.[59]

WINERIES After the Civil War, besides wool milling and shoe manufacturing, wine making was Charlottesville's major industry. The Monticello Wine Company, the largest in the South at that time, was on a hill at the end of Wine Street near Hedge Street, where some stone terraces allegedly from the vineyards remain. Chartered in 1873, the company processed grapes supplied by county growers including William Hotopp of Pen Park; William T. Stevens of Piedmont; and Adolph C. H. F. Russow of Bellevue Vineyards. Russow also served as superintendent of the company's operations. Prohibition put it out of business when Virginia passed legislation in 1914.[60]

FACTORIES The Charlottesville Industrial and Land Improvement Company erected the Second Empire–style Armstrong Knitting Factory (fig. 305) in Charlottesville in 1889–90. In 1913 it was renamed the Charlottesville Silk Mills.

Commercial Buildings

HOTELS In the late nineteenth century, summer resorts were established at local plantations such as Clover Fields and Hopedale, and land development companies speculated in land for housing in the suburbs around Charlottesville. Trolley-rail lines were extended to the resorts and suburbs.

One of the developments, the dream of Stephen Price Maury, became a resort on the southern edge of Char-

Fig. 305. Armstrong Knitting Factory, 1889–90

lottesville. It included the hundred-room Jefferson Park Hotel, at first named the Hotel Albemarle, built for $40,000 in 1892 near the 1890 frame Fry's Spring Clubhouse. In 1906 a dance hall was added to the resort and, later, an outdoor movie theater. Advertisements claimed that drinking from the Fry's Spring waters here would help sufferers of "Gall Stones, Rheumatism, Kidney or Bladder trouble, or general disability." The resort built its own dairy and raised its own vegetables. In 1907 a Wonderland Park built here under different ownership offered an animal menagerie, a playground, merry-go-round, roller-skating rink, billiard hall, and shooting gallery. Three years after a disastrous fire in 1910, the hotel was razed, but in 1921 J. Russell Dettor opened the Fry's Spring Beach Club at the clubhouse, featuring a ninety-meter-long swimming pool.[61]

The intersection in Charlottesville of two major railroad lines halfway between the university and downtown made it a prime area for travelers' lodging after the mid–nineteenth century. Several hotels were built on West Main Street, and other buildings were converted into hotels to satisfy this need. Many have since been razed, including the Cabell House, the Clermont Hotel, the Queen Charlotte Hotel of about 1915, and the Dolley Madison Inn, which was converted about 1920 from a house that had been built about 1850. The main portion of the Albemarle Hotel, constructed about 1896 by Michael S. Gleason, still survives, however.[62]

BANKS In 1866 the Monticello Bank reopened as the Charlottesville National Bank. A year later the Farmers' and Merchants' Bank began operations at 509 East Main while the Citizens' National Bank opened at 500 East Main. Both closed after the national panic of 1873. People's National Bank, now NationsBank, opened in 1875 at 401–3 East Market Street but relocated to 322 East Main in 1896. In 1916 it moved again into a two-story stone edifice with Corinthian columns and pilasters at 300 East Main Street that was designed by architect Eugene Bradbury. After a fire in 1909 and a renovation in 1917, the 322 East Main Street building reopened as Marshall Timberlake's drugstore. In 1882 the Bank of Albemarle began operations at 323 East Main Street, at the location of the former Monticello Bank.[63]

STORES AND SHOPS The prototypical general store, the retail and social center of many rural communities, is a two-story frame building with a two-tier porch, and many were constructed in Albemarle County. The business of the store was conducted on the main level, and the second floor was used either for storage or as living space for the storekeeper and sometimes as lodging for travelers. Like innkeepers, merchants and peddlers were licensed annually by the county courts after the Revolutionary War. By 1860 the Albemarle County Court licensed some seventy-seven retail businesses.[64]

Several prototypical stores with two-tier porches have survived from the late nineteenth and early twentieth centuries. Among them are the store at Keene (fig. 306), the Marshall-Parrish store at Nortonsville, H. I. Davis's store at Boonesville, the Foster-Layman store at Batesville, J. I. Maupin's store at Alberene, the Covesville store, Blackwell's store (fig. 307) at Doylesville, and Craig's store in the western part of the county. Other frame stores constructed with a simple one-story porch include the Carter's Bridge store (fig. 308), Heard's store (fig. 309), the Warren store, and the semicircular, false-fronted Steed's store at Esmont. A brick version of the general store is the mid-nineteenth-century Critzer's store at Ivy.[65]

About 1840 commercial buildings were erected west of downtown Charlottesville on Main Street. After the Civil War this street flourished as shops and stores stretched from downtown to the university. At the Corner near the university, a bookstore had been located on one site since 1852, for many years named Anderson Brothers' Bookstore (fig. 310), thereby surviving until recently as the oldest type of business at its original location in Charlottesville. The present metal-clad building was constructed in 1891–92 by the Vandegrift Construction Company around an 1848 structure. The J. L. Mesker Company of St. Louis manufactured this metal facade and another the same year for James Perley at 100–108 West Main Street.[66]

Fig. 306. Store at Keene, c. 1900

Fig. *307*. Blackwell's store at Doylesville, c. 1845

Fig. 308. Store at Carter's Bridge, ʟ19ᴄ

Fig. 309. Store at Heard's, c. 1900

Fig. 310. Anderson Brothers' Bookstore, 1848, 1891–92

Many commercial buildings evolved from two-story brick houses with stepped gables, in which the owner lived above the store, whose entrance was protected by a metal sidewalk canopy on the street level. The Johnson W. Pitts house (fig. 311) on West Main Street is one example. Built in 1820 on land that Pitts's father-in-law, Joseph Bishop, had purchased from John Carr in 1803, it features a Flemish-bond brick facade with a mousetooth cornice. Musgrove and Patterson operated a dry goods store here by 1853. R. A. Musgrove also conducted a tuition school for black students and helped Anna Gardner establish another such school. In 1890 George Pinkney Inge purchased the property, in which he both lived and operated a market. Inge was born a slave in Southside Virginia, attended Hampton Institute, and became a public school teacher. His college friend Booker T. Washington visited his home, which is on the corner of what were known as Random Row and Bull Alley in the Vinegar Hill area. At the time of the store's closing in 1979, it was the oldest black-owned business in the community. It was converted into a restaurant in the 1980s.[67]

Other downtown examples of commercial buildings include the brick Keller and George Jewelers' building at Third and Main Streets and the Charlottesville Hardware Store, which was constructed about 1895. Although the latter structure was rebuilt after a fire and converted to a restaurant about 1975, it still retains much of the hardware store's interior fabric.[68]

Educational Buildings

Several private schools were conducted in rural areas. They included William Dinwiddie's Greenwood School for Boys and Pantops Academy, a Presbyterian boys school established by the Reverend Edgar Woods in 1879 and closed in 1906. Samuel Miller, who was born out of wedlock and into poverty, became a wealthy merchant and endowed the University of Virginia's School of Biology. He also bequeathed almost $2 million for a school of manual labor (fig. 312) to provide a vocational and general education for the poor and orphaned boys of Albemarle County (girls were admitted in 1884 to increase the enrollment). This massive High Victorian Gothic complex, begun in 1874 near Batesville, was designed by Richmond architects

Fig. 311. J. W. Pitts house (Inge's store), 1820

Fig. 312. Miller School of Manual Labor, 1874

Albert M. Lybrock and D. Wiley Anderson as well as Edmund G. Lind of Baltimore. Lybrock had designed the Gothic Revival cast-iron tomb of James Monroe in Richmond's Hollywood Cemetery for the 1858 centennial of Monroe's birth. By 1885 the complex was generating its own electricity.[69]

After the Civil War schools were opened for African Americans by the Freedmen's Bureau. Other schools for blacks, such as the Jefferson School, existed as early as 1867. The Constitution of 1869 established a statewide public school system segregated by race. In 1870 fifty-seven schools operated in the county: thirty-eight for whites and nineteen for blacks. The first black school was on present-day Route 600 near Route 20, southeast of Stony Point on Flannigan's Branch. Some early black schools still stand, including the 1869 Glendower School (fig. 313) and Mount Alto School.[70]

School interiors, whether intended for blacks or whites, usually were simple one- or two-room spaces with wooden bench seats, two-student desks on metal frames, and a pot-bellied stove, such as the school at Proffit (fig. 314). The Earlysville School (fig. 315) was of log construction, but frame schools proliferated. Typical of these one-room schools were Buck Island School (fig. 316), a second Earlysville School, Red Hill School, and Burnley School. One-story

Fig. 313. (top) Glendower School, 1869

Fig. 314. (bottom) Interior of school at Proffit, E20C

Fig. 315. School at
Earlysville, L19C

Fig. 316. School at
Buck Island, E20C

Fig. 317. Southern Railroad
depot at Charlottesville,
1885, 1913

Fig. 318. C&O Railroad depot at Charlottesville, 1905

versions that contained more than one room included Crozet School and Covesville School. Red Hill School, a second Crozet School, and Scottsville High School were two-story examples.

In 1892 Trinity Episcopal Church at Crossroads, which had been built in 1835, became the first free public school in the Samuel Miller District. The first city public school was the one-story frame Garrett Street School, which operated from 1870 to 1890. In 1893 a new Midway High School was built on the site of Charlottesville's 1886 public school, which had been adapted from the 1818 frame Midway Hotel at the intersection of West Main and Ridge Streets. The architects for this new school were John Kevan Peebles and J. Edwin R. Carpenter, with Vandegrift and Son as contractors. The building was razed in 1973.[71]

Transportation Buildings: Railroad Depots

Although earlier depots were built in Charlottesville, two later versions still stand. The 1885 brick Southern Depot or Union Station (fig. 317) on West Main Street was remodeled in 1913 and now is used as the Amtrak station. Presently, efforts are underway to preserve the main depot and baggage room for adaptive reuse. The trainmaster's house at the depot, built in 1856 by William B. Phillips, burned in 1991. The 1905 brick Chesapeake and Ohio Depot (fig. 318) on Water Street, which had replaced an 1883 frame building, was adapted to other uses in 1990.[72]

VI

The Eclectic Era (1890–1939)

THE "AMERICAN RENAISSANCE" AT THE TURN OF the twentieth century embraced the past, adapting elements from antiquity to create a new American style. Architects studied in Europe at such institutions as the Ecole des Beaux-Arts and the Fountainbleau School of Fine Arts in France and the American Academy in Rome, where they became steeped in the classical vocabulary. The first two Americans to attend the Ecole were the later well-known architects Richard Morris Hunt and Henry Hobson Richardson. As early as 1835 houses in America had been designed in revivals of earlier styles in traditions other than the classical. Examples from the late 1830s include General John Hartwell Cocke's remodeling of Bremo Recess and his addition to Lower Bremo in Fluvanna County, Virginia, both executed in the Jacobean Revival style, and Washington Irving's Sunnyside in Tarrytown, New York, designed in the English and Dutch styles.[1]

In 1877 the renowned architectural firm of McKim, Mead and White recorded older traditional styles on the New England coast to serve as prototypes for new houses. In the 1890s Henry Chapman Mercer, curator of American archaeology at the University of Pennsylvania, collected Americana and wrote about the technical dating of buildings. During this time the English Arts and Crafts movement led by Charles F. A. Voysey influenced American architects, as did the Dutch Colonial revival at the turn of the century. Between 1911 and 1941 William Lawrence Bottomley, as well as other notable classical-style architects, designed many buildings in Virginia based on eighteenth-century Tidewater examples.

Publications and expositions had a profound influence on architecture during this period. National expositions awakened interest in America's architectural heritage and reflected its view of itself as heir to Europe's cultural legacy. The first was the Centennial Exhibition of 1876 in Philadelphia's Fairmont Park, celebrating the birth of the nation a century before. This successful exhibition was followed in 1893 by the World's Columbian Exposition in Chicago, which commemorated the discovery of America four hundred years earlier. Architect Richard Morris Hunt and planner Daniel Burnham were among the major exposition designers. Such famous earlier buildings as Independence Hall and Mount Vernon were reinterpreted by the architects of the exposition. At the Pan American Exposition in Buffalo in 1901, Beaux Arts architecture flourished. The Louisiana Purchase Exposition followed three years later in St. Louis. And in Virginia, the Jamestown Tercentennial Celebration in Norfolk in 1907, chaired by architect John Kevan Peebles, promoted the Colonial Revival (which basically draws on every "style" from the truly colonial, including the vernacular as well as the Georgian, through the Federal, Roman Revival, and Greek Revival) and had a profound effect on Virginia architecture.[2]

Early in the twentieth century, the arrival in Albemarle County of a new moneyed class with good taste inspired the creation of modern buildings of high quality. And with the advent of the University of Virginia School of Architecture under Sidney Fiske Kimball in 1919, the institution produced some of the finest Beaux Arts architects in the country who returned again to eclectic, classical motifs. Grand dwellings throughout the county competed for attention with the Jeffersonian models of a hundred years earlier.

In 1901 electric street lighting came to Charlottesville, and in 1905 a waterworks was built to supplement the city's sixteen "watering" establishments serving alcoholic beverages. In 1906 J. P. Ellington sported Charlottesville's first automobile. Ten years later the city tripled its land area through annexations extending to Emmet Street, Rugby Avenue, and Meade Avenue.[3]

TURN-OF-THE-CENTURY ECLECTIC ARCHITECTS

The recent rediscovery of historicity and classicism, neglected during the Modern movement in American architecture, has renewed interest in the diversely talented architects of this period and focused public attention on previously ignored turn-of-the-century eclectic architecture. This, in turn, has provided a counterpoint of investigation to the Modern movement and fulfilled a need for the discovery of our architectural past. The tremendous growth of industry and population in Charlottesville that occurred between the latter part of the nineteenth century and the depression of the 1930s, and the concomitant growth of the university and the establishment of its architecture school, brought employment to many local architects and builders. In addition, with the new prosperity in the South at the turn of the twentieth century and the influx of wealthy northerners into Albemarle County, architects both inside and outside the area received commissions to design houses in the countryside.[4]

David Wiley Anderson, who is believed to have designed Nydrie in 1898, was the architect for Ednam. Anderson was born in Albemarle County on 20 August 1864 and learned about architectural design while apprenticing for construction firms. He was the son of a carpenter, Captain John B. Anderson (1819–1911), whose grandfather came to Virginia from England in the eighteenth century. In 1895 D. Wiley Anderson established an architectural practice in Richmond that he maintained until his death on 7 April 1940.[5]

Other architects came from the District of Columbia. Paul J. Pelz, supervising architect for the Treasury Department, designed Castalia in 1899 and the University Hospital two years later. Another supervising architect, Alfred B. Mullett, was born in England in 1834. Mullett died in 1890; in 1902 his firm designed the Hulfish house on Park Street. It bears no resemblance to the Second Empire style that he had popularized a generation earlier and that by then was largely out of vogue. Another Washington architect, Waddy Butler Wood, designed or remodeled several area houses: an addition to Faulkner House in 1907, Edgewood in 1911 for George Barclay Rives, Ackley in Charlottesville in 1920–21, and the renovation of Spring Hill in 1925. Although born in St. Louis in 1869, he had local ties to the county as his family had moved into Spring Hill the year after his birth. He was educated at Virginia Polytechnic Institute and died in 1944.[6]

Other notable architects came to Albemarle County from New York City. Frederick Hill, who was with the firm of McKim, Mead and White, designed Guthrie Hall about 1901 for John Guthrie Hopkins. Another architect from the city was William Adams Delano, born 1874 in New York and a cousin of President Franklin Delano Roosevelt. Delano was educated at Yale and the Ecole des Beaux-Arts and worked for Carrère and Hastings. He was responsible for the 1921 renovation of Mirador, the home of Lady Astor and the Gibson Girl, the new house at Colle in 1933, and the new Kenwood in 1938.

Lynchburg architect Stanhope S. Johnson designed several houses in Albemarle County. They include Belvoir, patterned in 1928 after eighteenth-century Gunston Hall, the Georgian-influenced Gallison Hall in 1933, and Oak Forest, which resembles Jefferson's Poplar Forest, in 1933.[7]

Various Richmond firms and individual architects designed houses in the county. The magnificent stone castle called Royal Orchard was designed in 1913 for Frederic W. Scott Sr. of Richmond by Baskervill and Nolan. The firm had just designed the neighboring Afton Mountain house Swannanoa in Nelson County. In 1917 John Russell Pope of New York City designed the interior of Royal Orchard. Pope, a nationally distinguished architect, planned the National Archives, the Jefferson Memorial, and the National Gallery of Art. He was born in 1874, graduated from the City College of New York and Columbia, attended the American Academy in Rome and the Ecole des Beaux-Arts, and died in 1937. Another Richmond architect, Carl Linder, designed Tiverton in 1936–37, patterning it after the White House in Washington, D.C. Claude K. Howell, also of Richmond, designed Westover in 1915–16 and also was responsible for the design of Charlottesville's Jefferson Theater at the same time. The gifted William Lawrence Bottomley, who was born in 1883 in New York City and died in 1951, designed three houses in the county: the 1928 additions and alterations to Blue Ridge Farm, the 1930 addition to Casa Maria, and the 1930–31 Rose Hill. The equally gifted Richmond landscape architect Charles Freeman Gillette (1886–1969), with whom Bottomley often collaborated, designed at least sixteen gardens in the county, for example, those at Casa Maria, Tiverton, and Verulam.[8]

Local architects also abounded. In 1910 Hill's *Charlottesville City Directory* listed Nimrod T. Wingfield, whose name appeared for the next ten years, and Eugene Bradbury, who was listed through 1924. Nimrod Tupper Wingfield was born 1 January 1867, the son of Elizabeth Perley and Benjamin F. Wingfield, a carpenter who had himself been born in Albemarle County in 1834 and had worked for George Wilson Spooner Jr. The younger Wingfield married Nellie L. Novell, owned several properties in the Belmont area in the 1890s, and was elected a member of city council. In 1920, the year before his death, he was ordained a Baptist minister; he is buried in Oakwood Cemetery as is his father.[9]

Eugene Bradbury was one of the ablest of all the local early twentieth-century architects. He was born in Arlington, Virginia, on 22 September 1874 to Sanford and Eugenia Corbett Bradbury. After attending Virginia Military Institute and George Washington University, Bradbury worked for the talented Washington architect Waddy Wood. He also worked from 1901 to 1907 for the supervising architect of the Treasury Department, Paul J. Pelz, and for the Historic American Buildings Survey in Virginia and Charleston, South Carolina, in the 1930s and 1940s. As an architect in Charlottesville, Bradbury designed at least forty buildings in the area, among them the Brigadier General John Watts Kearney house (1909), which overlooks the university from Lewis Mountain, Four Acres (1910), Peoples' National Bank (1916), the Entrance Building at the university, Chi Phi fraternity house (1922), and several houses on University Circle and Rugby Road. In designing Saint Paul's Episcopal Church, constructed in 1925, Bradbury showed his capacity for rendering different styles in the greatest detail. Bradbury died on 3 July 1960.[10]

Hill's *Directory* added architect L. Ashley Kidd in 1916 and D. Wiley Anderson and John M. Clark in 1922. The 1927 directory listed architects K. G. Koltukian and Stanislaw Makielski. In 1931 the name Elmer E. Burruss Sr. appeared. Burruss had trained as an architect through correspondence courses and went on to design both the Hill and Irving Funeral Home and the Monticello Dairy in 1937. Two years later he and A. K. Stevens designed the Albemarle County Office Building adjacent to the historic courthouse.[11]

HOUSE STYLES

A 1909 ditty entitled "I Want A Home, That's All" reflects the increasing national demand for affordable small houses that could be maintained without the help of servants and featured modern conveniences that once were affordable only by the wealthy. At the beginning of the twentieth century, the lines between the creature comforts available to the rich, the well-to-do, and the middle class began to blur as never before when indoor plumbing, electrical appliances, central heat, multiple bedrooms, and other amenities became common features of new houses. And the houses themselves became available in an unprecedented array of sizes, floor plans, and styles designed by eclectic architects.[12]

The architectural heritage of Albemarle County and Charlottesville spans more than two hundred years. It is distinguished by the creations of Jefferson and his master builders in the first half of the nineteenth century and by the productions of talented eclectic architects in the early decades of the twentieth. This rich legacy has made Charlottesville and Albemarle County a showplace of America's finest architectural styles, especially those of the Colonial Revival.

The New Classicism

Architects trained in Europe introduced academic Beaux Arts architecture to America. Wealthy northerners who relocated to Albemarle County at the turn of the twentieth century, drawn by the scenic countryside, milder weather, and southern social life, in turn introduced a new interest in the use of classical design to the county that gave birth to the first classical revival almost a century before. Many of these new dwellings incorporated two-story classical porticoes. The first physician at the Miller School, Dr. John D. Smith, built the two-story frame Woodlea in Batesville about 1890. It featured German siding (interlocking horizontal wood siding with a concave upper edge) and a two-story portico supported by coupled Corinthian columns, a lunette in the tympanum, and a lower veranda that wrapped around three sides of the house. The interior burned in 1945.[13]

Richmond architect D. Wiley Anderson designed Ednam (fig. 319), a two-story frame dwelling just south of Farmington, about 1901 for New York City importer Edwin O. Meyer. A bachelor, Meyer resided here with fellow New Yorkers Emilie L. and Louis Borchers, an Austrian painter. Emilie Borchers, the latter's wife, inherited the house in 1908. Ednam features a tetrastyle portico with Ionic columns and a suspended balcony beneath the roof, a Palladian window, a porte cochere, a magnificent stairway, a library, a fully paneled dining room, a large drawing room, and exquisite mantels. The design of the demioctagonal southwest salon is a masterful use of the transparency of space. Here a fireplace centered on the octagonal end is framed by transparent double-leaf doors that open onto a circular covered gallery with stairs leading into the landscape beyond.[14]

John Guthrie Hopkins built Guthrie Hall (figs. 320, 321) near Esmont. The walls are of concrete imbedded with

Fig. 319. Ednam, c. 1901

Fig. 320. Guthrie Hall, c. 1901, southern front

Fig. 321. Guthrie Hall, c. 1901, northern facade

quartz stone and display a huge arch on the northern facade and a six-column portico on the southern front. Designed about 1901 by New York City architect Frederick Hill of McKim, Mead and White and engineer Fred Kennedy, the house contains 19,000 square feet of living space and thirty-six rooms. Among the rooms are a 25-by-45-foot drawing room, a mahogany-paneled library, ballroom, cinema room, bowling alley, billiard room, wine cellar, walk-in safe, conservatory, an indoor pool, and an elegantly plastered dining room. Large tree trunks cut on the property adorn the interior as ceiling beams. Outside, curving Ionic colonnades culminate in a porte cochere and a two-story kitchen and servants' quarters. Guthrie Hall also once had a private railroad depot. Hopkins, who made his fortune in Arizona copper mines, sold the property in 1906 and moved to Leesburg in Loudoun County. In 1939 a Dutch nobleman, Baron John von Liedersdorf, acquired the property. From 1968 until 1997 it was occupied by Maryann Jessup MacConochie, a pioneer woman pilot and an interpreter of Russian and French during the Nuremberg war trials.[15]

A second two-story brick Patton house was built on West Main Street in 1907 for John S. Patton, the university librarian. It features a tetrastyle portico, a suspended balcony with Chinese railings, and triple-hung sash windows. During 1953–54 it was converted into a bank.

The university purchased Carr's Hill across from the Rotunda from James Burnley in 1829 to use for additional student housing. The two-story frame boardinghouse called Blue Cottage was located here until it burned in 1867. In the mid–nineteenth century, Buckingham Palace, a one-story brick building, was also constructed for students. Mrs. Sidney S. Carr operated a boardinghouse here from 1854 to 1863, and in 1888 George Sidney Ford built several L-shaped two-story dormitories and a dining hall.

At the turn of the century, architect Stanford White was commissioned to design a house for the university president on Carr's Hill (fig. 322). A carriage house with a Diocletian therm window was built first in 1907, possibly using part of an existing dormitory, and the house was completed two years later. The architects William Kendall and William Richardson of McKim, Mead and White

Fig. 322. Carr's Hill, 1907–9

probably executed White's design. The five-bay, two-story brick house exhibits a fluted tetrastyle portico with a lunette in its tympanum and a balcony underneath, a hipped roof culminating in a widow's walk, a doorway with a fanlight and sidelights, triangulated window lintels, and a porte cochere.[16]

Carrollton Manor, a more modest house, was constructed on Jefferson Park Avenue about 1909 for Z. F. Barnum. The two-story, five-bay house is built of concrete block with rock-faced blocks used as quoins and features a tetrastyle portico with a lunette.

Architect Eugene Bradbury designed Lewis Mountain (fig. 323), erected on a hill just west of the university in 1909 for John Watts Kearney, a Union brigadier general who had passed through the area during the Civil War and returned with his Virginia bride. Kearney was the son of Major Gen-

eral Philip Kearney, a grandnephew of General Stephen Watts Kearney, and a relation of the explorer brothers William and George Rogers Clark. Constructed of local granite, the two-story, three-bay house exhibits lower wings on each end, a tetrastyle portico, a hipped roof culminating in a widow's walk, a porte cochere, Italian marble mantels, and an attic water tank. Warren H. Manning of Boston, under whom Charles Gillette trained, designed the landscaping. Four Acres, another brick house designed by Bradbury, was built the following year on Rugby Road for Melton C. Elliot. The tetrastyle portico features Ionic columns and a doorway with a fanlight. After the Second World War, Fleet Admiral William F. Halsey occupied Four Acres.[17]

George Barclay Rives, a foreign service officer who had been stationed in Germany and Brazil, built Edgewood

Fig. 323. Lewis Mountain, 1909

Fig. 324. Westover, 1915–16

across from Castle Hill in 1911. Architect Waddy Wood designed the two-story, five-bay brick dwelling, which features a tetrastyle portico with composite columns and a balcony with Chinese railings. The interior contains an Italian marble mantel and a mahogany-paneled library. To the rear of the house is a courtyard, with a water tower and stable beyond. In the 1970s singer Art Garfunkel bought the house; it has had several other owners since.[18]

Dr. William Alexander Lambeth, who was head of Buildings and Grounds at the university from 1905 to 1930 and is considered the father of the school's athletics program, built a house with classical gardens to the northeast of Carr's Hill, approximately on the site of the present Bayly Museum. In 1912 he built Villino Lambeth, a two-story brick dwelling, on Thomson Road to the west of Memorial Gymnasium. Its classical sunken gardens, now called The Dell, contained a pergola and a stone aedicule as well as statuary including a bust, sculpted by Charles Keck, of former university coach John Desalle. A man of diverse interests, Lambeth published in 1913 the first study of Jeffersonian architecture, *Jefferson as an Architect*, and he also furnished the Italian Room in Pavilion VI on the East Lawn.[19]

Another two-story brick house, Riverdale, was built as an addition to a small mid-nineteenth-century frame house on Riverdale Drive in Charlottesville for Minnie M. Barnes in 1912. The addition features rock-faced concrete-block quoins, a concrete-block foundation, and a tetrastyle portico without capitals or bases. The entire house was painted white. In 1917 the well-known horse trainer Aldretus Wilton Ward purchased Riverdale.[20]

P. H. Faulconer, president of the construction firm of Rinehart and Dennis, built Westover (fig. 324) on Garth Road just west of Charlottesville in 1915–16. It was designed by Richmond architect Claude K. Howell. The two-story, five-bay stucco house includes a Doric tetrastyle portico with a lunette, a doorway with a fanlight, and a garden pergola. The two-story brick Dunlora, built in 1828 north of Charlottesville, burned in 1916, and the owner hired Eugene Bradbury to renovate the shell. He lowered the first-floor level to the ground, constructed another one-story portico with paired columns, and reconstructed the widow's walk.[21]

Hollis Rinehart Sr. sold Birdwood in 1921. About a year later he built Kenridge, designed by Washington, D.C., architect William Johnston Marsh, just north of it across the highway. Rinehart had been a partner in the firm of Rinehart and Dennis, which built railroads as well as Camp Lee near Petersburg. In 1914 he founded the Charlottesville National Bank, served as its first president, and had Marsh design its downtown high-rise bank building. Kenridge, a five-bay, two-story brick house with two-story wings, features a one-story circular portico on the northern facade and a tetrastyle portico on the southern front with columns patterned after the ancient Tower of the Winds in Athens, Greece, and included in James Stuart and Nicholas Revett's *The Antiquities of Athens*. In 1965 Kappa Sigma Fraternity established its national headquarters in the house and painted the brick white.[22]

Just to the west of Kenridge, Rinehart built Boxwood in 1923 for his son, William Alonzo Rinehart. Designed by architect Stanislaw Makielski, Boxwood is a five-bay, two-story stucco house that features a six-column portico with Chinese railings. In 1944 Boxwood became the home of the Institute of Textile Technology. Makielski also designed in 1929–31 a three-bay, two-story brick dwelling named Su Casa on Rio Road for Harvey A. Basham of Mexico City. It included a spiral stair and a two-story circular portico with Ionic columns.[23]

Modeled on Jefferson's octagonal Bedford County country retreat Poplar Forest, Oak Forest just east of Farmington was designed about 1933 by Lynchburg architect Stanhope Johnson for E. J. Perkins. It features a tetrastyle portico over an arcade. Fiske Kimball's self-designed home, Shack Mountain (fig. 325), built northwest of Charlottesville in 1935–36, is patterned after another Jefferson house, Farmington. A masterpiece of scale, setting, and reinterpretation, Shack Mountain's name is derived from the Shackelford family, for whom the ridge on

Fig. 325. Shack Mountain, 1935–36

which it is situated was named. Shack Mountain not only is listed in the National Register of Historic Places but also been designated a National Historic Landmark.[24]

Tiverton (fig. 326), patterned after the White House, is on U.S. Route 250 West between Lebanon Church and Emmanuel Church. The house was rebuilt in 1936–37 by Richmond architect Carl Linder after its interior had burned two years earlier. An earlier large dwelling and carriage house occupied the site when Dr. Frederick D. Owsley built Tiverton on the property in 1925–26. During the 1930s rebuilding Charles Gillette was engaged to design the gardens. The house, measuring about 60 by 93 feet, is a nine-bay two-story stucco-over-brick structure with an Ionic tetrastyle portico, Ionic side pilasters, triangular window lintels, a balustrade around the edge of the hipped roof, and a spiral staircase in the oval entrance hall.[25]

In 1941 architect Marshall Wells designed the five-bay, two-story brick Verulam for Courtland Van Clief. The house features a Tower of the Winds tetrastyle portico, a doorway with a Palladian motif, and classical gardens planned by Charles Gillette. Verulam's interior features an eighteenth-century Dutch mural, an Italian marble mantel, and butternut library paneling. In 1970 its sale to John A. Ewald of New York City set a local real estate record. Architect Milton Grigg designed the poolhouse and pavilion.[26]

Also in 1941, Grigg designed Fairview Farm for Professor John L. Manahan on Route 20 South, modeling it after the tripartite William Finnie (formerly the James Semple) house in Williamsburg as a center-pavilion structure with lower side wings. The dining and living rooms are based on rooms in the reconstructed Raleigh Tavern in Williamsburg. In 1960 Grigg designed a house on University Circle in Charlottesville for Manahan's son John E. Manahan. The house is patterned on the facade Grigg had designed for Jefferson's Edgemont in the 1930s: a tetrastyle portico over an arcade, a feature that Jefferson had employed at Poplar Forest and at Pavilion VII at the university. The Manahan house is best known as the refuge of his wife Anna Anderson of Württemberg, who was engaged in a lawsuit from 1937 until her death in 1984 to establish her identity as Anastasia, daughter of Czar Nicholas II of Russia. In 1996 DNA tests proved that she was not Anastasia.[27]

Georgian-Colonial Revival

Beginning in the late nineteenth century, some eclectic architects designed buildings that were based on examples from the Georgian — often called the Colonial — period.

Fig. 326. Tiverton, 1936–37

In addition, many publications popularized the style. William Rotch Ware published *The Georgian Period* in 1898, a book in such demand that it was reprinted a quarter of a century later. From 1915 through the 1940s, the Weyerhaeuser Company printed its White Pine Series of Architectural Monographs, which contained measured drawings of historic American buildings and their architectural details. About 1918 Aymar Embury II reprinted Asher Benjamin's five pattern books. The style was further popularized by the work of the well-known firm of McKim, Mead and White. In Albemarle County examples of the style were often devoid of classical porticoes and instead had simple aedicule doorways in the Georgian manner.

About 1875 J. W. B. McAllister built the McAllister-Andrews house on Ridge Street in the Queen Anne style. J. B. Andrews purchased the house in 1890, and six years later he extensively altered it with Georgian Revival exte-

rior details that included a Palladian second-floor doorway, broken pediments over the windows, ball finials in the dormers, dentils, frieze swags, and Ionic porch columns.[28]

Ramsay, a two-story house built about 1900 for William H. Langhorne, is northwest of Emmanuel Church just across U.S. Route 250. In the late 1930s Milton Grigg heavily remodeled Ramsay for William's grandson, C. Langhorne Gibson, by adding, among other features, a tetrastyle portico and a west wing. Grigg also designed a retirement cottage on the property for Mrs. Charles Dana Gibson, wife of the famous painter who had celebrated her in her youth as the society beauty known as the Gibson Girl.[29]

In Charlottesville on University Circle, architect Eugene Bradbury designed the two-story, five-bay brick Macon-Victorius house in 1914 for Lyttleton S. Macon Jr. It features a simple two-column aedicule doorway with a flat transom and sidelights. The dwelling served as the Phi

Delta Theta fraternity house for more than thirty years before Paul B. Victorius acquired it in 1958. In 1914 Bradbury also designed the two-story frame house Whilton near Greenwood for Algernon Craven, the father of local architect Thomas Craven. In 1936 the house was brick-veneered and enlarged, and Milton Grigg added a spiral staircase for owner Gordon Buck.[30]

Architect Waddy Wood designed Ackley, a five-bay, two-story brick house with a doorway topped with a broken pediment, on Gordon Avenue in Charlottesville for Allen Wheat in 1920–21. Milton Grigg made additions to the house in 1956–57 when it was converted into Martha Jefferson House, a retirement home.[31]

Lynchburg architect Stanhope Johnson designed Belvoir (fig. 327) at the corner of Rugby Road and Barracks Road in 1928 for F. W. Twyman. The gardens of the five-part, one-story brick house were laid out by Charles Gillette. The central portion of Belvoir, with its three-dimensional Palladian-motif doorway, is patterned after Gunston Hall in Fairfax County. A year later Stanislaw Makielski designed the five-bay, two-story brick Dulaney house two doors south of Belvoir on Rugby Road. It features a Corinthian-columned doorway with a broken pediment above and an imposing front gate. According to tradition, an iron entrance gate from Swannanoa at Rockfish Gap in Nelson County, designed by the Richmond architectural firm of Baskervill and Noland in 1911, was relocated to a "Mr. Dulaney's mother's house in Charlottesville" when the gatehouse at Swannanoa was razed to make way for the Blue Ridge Parkway in the 1930s.[32]

Dr. Stephen H. Watts, who served as president of Farmington Country Club for many years, built a two-story white brick house called Broomley on Brook Road in Farmington in 1930–31. It features a spiral stair and elaborate mantels and woodwork.[33]

Just south of Emmanuel Church, Susan Bueck Massie in 1904 built a two-story frame house, Rose Hill, which burned in 1930. An eighteenth-century dwelling called Rose Cottage apparently had also existed on the property. After the fire William Lawrence Bottomley designed for the site a two-story, five-bay brick house with curving hyphens leading to wings, after the manner of the eighteenth-century Mount Airy in Richmond County. The hipped-roof house has a Palladian-type recessed entrance and limestone quoins. Orange County architect James Russell Bailey designed its library in 1968 for Henry Bradley Martin, who owned one of the finest private collections of books in the world. Born in New York in 1905, Bailey received a bachelor's degree in architecture from the University of Michigan in 1932 and then attended the Cranbrook Academy of Art in Michigan in 1932–33.[34]

In 1929 Dr. Julio Suarez-Galban, a foreign language professor at the university, purchased more than sixty-two acres in Farmington and built the five-part brick mansion Gallison Hall (fig. 328) four years later. Stanhope Johnson designed the house and Charles Gillette the gardens. Its five-bay, two-story central portion features a hipped roof and a broken-pediment doorway derived from one at Westover in Charles City County. The entrance hall contains a combination of details borrowed from several other eighteenth-century houses: the paneling and marble floor are based on those of the Nelson house in Yorktown, and the staircase and chandeliers are modeled on those at Gadsby's Tavern in Alexandria. The library is adapted from Stratford Hall, the dining room from the Baltimore Room in the Metropolitan Museum, and other mantels, chair rails, and cornices from various other Virginia houses. Its clustered, diagonally set chimney stacks are reminiscent of those at Bacon's Castle. The complex is one of the state's finest twentieth-century country estates.[35]

In 1932 local architect Mar-

Fig. 327. Belvoir, 1928

Fig. 328. Gallison Hall, 1933

shall Wells designed the five-bay, two-story brick Alderman house on Rugby Road for Mrs. Edwin Anderson Alderman, the widow of the first president of the university. The house features a segmental-arched doorway and two marble mantels selected by Mrs. Alderman while on a trip to Florence, Italy.

Tobacco executive Grover C. Dula purchased an eighteenth-century frame farmhouse on Garth Road and in 1939 had Milton Grigg design the five-part brick Jumping Branch that wraps around it. Grigg's addition contains a broken-pediment doorway and a hipped roof that culminates in a widow's walk. An interior marble mantel came from Montpelier. On Hessian Road in Charlottesville stand many houses designed by Grigg and his partner, William Newton Hale Jr. The L. Dee York house, built in 1946, is a three-bay, two-story brick dwelling with a hipped roof, a widow's walk, and a doorway that forms a Palladian motif when its louvered two-leaf doors are fully opened. Grigg built his own home as a split-level brick house with spiral stair. Hale built a house for his mother on Hessian Road about 1948, a three-bay, one-story frame dwelling with attic frieze windows and side wings. Hale's own house, a two-bay, two-story frame dwelling with a two-column portico, was built in 1949 on Meadow-

brook Road. After Hale's early death, later owners engaged Grigg to design additions to the house.[36]

Audrey Emery restored several houses in Albemarle County, including Plain Dealing and Burnley's tavern. Her first husband was Dimitri Pavlovich, first grand duke of Czarist Russia; she next married Prince Dimitri Djordjadze, a Georgian. In 1957–58 Joseph Norris, a graduate of the University of Virginia, designed for her Rivanna Farm (fig. 329), a two-story frame Georgian-style mansion at the intersection of Routes 20 and 649. Three years later landscape architect Charles Gillette was commissioned to design the gardens. Rivanna Farm's two detached frame outbuildings form a U-shaped, stone-paved courtyard suggestive on a reduced scale of those at the Château de Jossigny and the Pavillon de la Lanterne. Also on the property are remnants of the site of Gale Hill, a house built about 1770 that burned in 1932. Presently, Rivanna Farm is the residence of Swedish countess Margareta C. H. Douglas.

Other Traditional Styles

What has been described as a combination "Georgian Revival and Italian Villa style" mansion, the seven-bay, two-story stucco Villa Crawford near Keswick, was designed

Fig. 329. Rivanna Farm, 1957–58

in 1912 by architect Eugene Bradbury for Robert B. Crawford and constructed at a cost of $100,000. A hundred-column peristyle separated its stable courtyard from its formal gardens. The estate featured peacocks and two of the "smallest donkeys ever brought to this country." In 1947 it was converted into a country club, and in 1992 it became Keswick Hall, a luxury hotel. About 1912 the rambling two-story stone house called West Cairns, designed by architect R. E. Shaw, was built for H. B. Boone and Kenneth Brown. It was on the site of the present Kluge Rehabilitation Center on Route 250 just west of Charlottesville.[37]

Perhaps the most unusual of all the turn-of-the-century eclectic houses is the two-story castellated stone mansion Royal Orchard (fig. 330) built as the summer estate of Frederic W. Scott Sr. of Richmond on the eastern slope of the Blue Ridge Mountains near Afton. Designed in 1913 by Richmond architect Henry E. Baskervill, it is patterned after a Newport, Rhode Island, estate. Its arcaded facade encloses a medieval interior designed in 1917 by the renowned architect John Russell Pope and features linenfold paneling, wood carvings, painted decoration, and suits of armor. The superb wrought-iron doors were made by Samuel Yellin of Philadelphia. Two stone cottages were begun earlier, in 1905, and

a one-story frame house originally occupied the manor house site. The estate derives its name from the Albemarle Pippin apples raised here that were given in 1838 as a gift to Queen Victoria of England. She greatly adored them and for years permitted them to be imported duty-free.[38]

Casa Maria, a two-story "Spanish-Mediterranean"–style house, was begun near Emmanuel Church by Mary Williams, who died in 1920; she was the sister of Susan Bueck Massie, who owned the adjacent estate, Rose Hill. In 1922 Gordon Smith and his wife Ella, Mrs. Massie's daughter, completed the house. Casa Maria allegedly was designed by Richmond landscape architect Charles

Fig. 330. Royal Orchard, 1913

Gillette. If so, it would be his only known architectural design. In 1928 a two-story south wing with a music room was added by New York architect William Lawrence Bottomley, and Gillette designed the gardens then. After a fire in 1930, Bottomley renovated the main house. Called a "Spanish Colonial Revival" house, Recoleta on Rothery Road in Charlottesville was built in 1939–40 by local architect Charles Baker for Harry Rogers Pratt, a university music professor, and his author-wife Agnes Rothery. Standing two stories high and constructed of painted, reinforced cinder block, Recoleta features tile roofs, casement windows, Norwegian corner fireplaces, and round-arch entrance loggias leading to the gardens.[39]

Homestead

Based on dwellings constructed on the western prairies after the Civil War, the two-story, usually L-shaped Homestead-style house (fig. 331) with a side entrance porch became the prototypical simple farmhouse or suburban dwelling, not only for families who moved to the West but for new houses everywhere. Being two stories high, it provided a large amount of floor space under a simple roof and maintained its appeal through the 1920s.[40]

Dutch Colonial

About the turn of the twentieth century, the Dutch Colonial (fig. 332) style became popular; it was modeled after late seventeenth- and early eighteenth-century Dutch houses in New York and New Jersey on the Hudson River. Architect Ernest Flagg, popularizer of the Dutch Colonial,

Fig. 332. Dutch Colonial and American Foursquare styles, Locust Avenue, Charlottesville, E20C

designed his own house in that style. Its most dominant characteristic was a double-sloped gambrel roof with an almost-vertical lower roof leaf, which thus created a full additional floor from the attic space while maintaining the appearance of a one-story house for tax assessments.[41]

Bungalow

With the publication of Henry Lawrence Wilson's *The Bungalow Book* in 1908, the appeal of this cottagelike dwelling spread throughout the country. The Bungalow-style house (fig. 333), sometimes referred to as "Cape Cod," was a one-and-a-half-story dwelling with projecting roof over a front porch and often included dormers and bulky square, tapered wooden columns.[42]

Vernacular

Pine Knot (fig. 334), built as a farmworker's house near Keene in 1903 by William N. Wilmer of Plain Dealing, became the hunting lodge of Theodore Roosevelt in 1905 during his second term as the twenty-sixth president of the United States. On his last visit in 1908, Roosevelt was accompanied by naturalist John Burroughs. It is a frame I-house with a center gable and a porch with untrimmed cedar posts. It is now owned by the Theodore Roosevelt Association. Montalto (fig. 335) was built on a commanding site on

Fig. 331. Homestead style, Locust Avenue, Charlottesville, E20C

Fig. 333. Bungalow style, East High
Street, Charlottesville, E20C

Fig. 334. Pine Knot, 1903, 1905

Fig. 335. Montalto, c. 1905–15

Carter's Mountain, where Jefferson once proposed to erect a ziggurat-shaped structure from which water would emanate. The house was built with an observation deck and a stone and shingle water tower that was destroyed by a storm.[43]

American Foursquare

The American Foursquare (see fig. 332) was another style that became extremely popular in the first quarter of the twentieth century. Basically square in plan or footprint and having square two-story sides, it usually featured a hipped roof, a front porch, and an asymmetrical floor plan. It provided a considerable amount of livable space under one roof.[44]

Voysey Influence

Architect Charles F. A. Voysey expressed a new style in England's Arts and Crafts movement during the 1890s by harkening back to medieval craftsmanship. Early in the twentieth century the movement appeared in America in what was called the Craftsman style. The Voysey influence was typified by flat stucco facades with cutout openings that added to the layering or transparency of the facade. The five-bay, two-story stuccoed Archibald Randolph house (fig. 336) on Rugby Road at Barracks Road is an example of the style and was designed in 1910 by the versatile local architect Eugene Bradbury.[45]

Prefabricated

Sears, Roebuck and Company is the best known of the companies that sold prefabricated houses through their catalogs during the first part of the twentieth century. A one-story frame Sears house (fig. 337), built in 1924 for J. J. Porter, is on Farish Street in Charlottesville.[46]

Modern

In 1932 the Museum of Modern Art in New York City held its first architectural exhibit. It was titled "Modern Architecture" and featured the work of architects from around the world in what was soon called the "International

Fig. 336. (top) Archibald Randolph house, 1910

Fig. 337. (bottom) Sears, Roebuck prefabricated house, 1924

Style." In conjunction with that exhibit, Henry-Russell Hitchcock and Philip Johnson published their influential study *The International Style: Architecture since 1922*. The German Bauhaus school produced many artists and architects who perpetuated the Modernist movement. Walter Gropius, for example, went to teach at Harvard, and Ludwig Mies van der Rohe lectured at the Illinois Institute of Technology. The Bauhaus school presented architecture's version of Aldous Huxley's *Brave New World*, replete with such pronouncements as "Less is more" and "Simplicity is the essence of beauty." Borrowing from the Art Moderne and the Art Deco styles, the promoters of the International Style proclaimed it the indisputable

final answer to the problems of ever-changeable "style." It could be constructed anywhere, they said, and would last forever, never going out of style. Most architects educated after the Second World War were trained as Internationalists. An early example of the International Style is the brick house (fig. 338) on Bollingwood Road in Charlottesville designed for Mrs. James A. Cole in 1934 by Philadelphia architect Kenneth Day. It features a living room with rounded corners, flat roofs, a roof sundeck, horizontal window units with sun trellises above them, and a sloping stair roof. It is not only the first Modern house in the county but a very early one in America's Modern movement.[47]

PUBLIC ARCHITECTURE

Post Offices

Post offices often were located in the postmasters' houses or in country stores. After 1850 post offices also became associated with railroad depots, such as those at Cobham, Gilbert, Howardsville, Earlysville, Crozet, and Charlottesville. In the 1920s, however, rural free delivery accelerated the decline of many of these country post offices. A supervising architect of the U.S. Treasury Department, Percy Ash (1865–1933), later the chair of architecture at Pennsylvania State University, designed the classical post office in downtown Charlottesville in 1904. When that same structure was enlarged (fig. 339) thirty-two years later, another supervising architect, Louis Adolphe Simon, who was born in Baltimore and educated at the Massachusetts Institute of Technology, directed the recentering of its stone portico.

Fig. 338. Mrs. James A. Cole house, 1934

Fig. 339. Charlottesville Post Office, 1904, 1936

Statues

In conjunction with the "City Beautiful" movement in America in the early years of the twentieth century, several statues and monuments were unveiled in the city and on the university grounds. Many of them were funded by Paul Goodloe McIntire. The first such monument (fig. 340) was erected in 1906 by the Ladies Confederate Memorial Association to honor Confederates buried in the university cemetery. It had been cast in 1893 by the Henry-Bonnard Bronze Company in New York from the design of sculptor Caspar Buberl. Born in Bohemia to a prominent sculptor, Buberl immigrated at the age of twenty to New York City in 1854; he maintained his studio there until his death in 1899. The second Civil War monument was erected on Court Square in 1909 by the United Daughters of the Confederacy in cooperation with the city government. Cast by the American Bronze Company of Illinois, the bronze Confederate infantryman is mounted on an

Fig. 340. Confederate Monument, University of Virginia Cemetery, 1893, 1906

inscribed Vermont granite plinth with bronze tablets; the entire monument is flanked by two cannon. In 1909 the United Daughters of the Confederacy put up an iron fence manufactured by the Stewart Iron Company of Cincinnati around the unmarked graves of some forty soldiers in Scottsville. Five years later the group erected a granite Confederate monument here to honor the soldiers.[48]

Two statues at the university were designed by Sir Moses Ezekiel (1844–1917). The first, of Homer, was erected in 1907 on the south Lawn, and the second, of Thomas Jefferson, was placed on the north side of the Rotunda in 1910. Ezekiel was born in Richmond, fought as a cadet in the battle of New Market in 1864, and graduated from Virginia Military Institute in 1866. He later received his art education at the Royal Academy of Art in Berlin and maintained a studio in the Baths of Diocletian in Rome. Ezekiel also was knighted by the king of Italy. He sculpted the allegorical figure *Virginia Mourning Her Dead* and a statue of Stonewall Jackson, both at Virginia Military Institute. Ezekiel died in Rome and was buried in Arlington Cemetery.[49]

Three other notable statues are located on the grounds of the university. Karl Bitter (1867–1915) sculpted the statue of Jefferson that is on the west Lawn in 1915, the year Bitter was killed by an automobile while leaving the Metropolitan Opera in New York. Bitter was a graduate

Fig. 342. Lewis and Clark statue, 1921

Fig. 341. James Rogers McConnell Memorial, University Of Virginia, 1919

of the Vienna Academy of Fine Art and the director of sculpture for national expositions at Buffalo, St. Louis, and San Francisco. His Jefferson faces a copy of Houdon's statue of George Washington commissioned by Jefferson for the Virginia State Capitol in Richmond. In 1919 Gutzon Borglum (1871–1941), the sculptor of Mount Rushmore, created the James Rogers McConnell memorial (fig. 341), to the side of the Alderman Library, which honors a pilot in the Lafayette Escadrille who was killed in World War I.[50]

Charles Keck, who was born in New York City in 1875 and died in 1951, sculpted two of the statues that stand in Charlottesville. One, *The First View of the Pacific*, was created in 1919 and depicts Meriwether Lewis and William Clark (fig. 342), explorers of the Louisiana Territory, and their Shoshone Indian guide Sacagawea. The other, sculpted in 1921, portrays General Thomas Jonathan "Stonewall" Jackson (fig. 343) riding into battle on Little Sorrel. This statue, in Jackson Park, was judged by a jury of sculptors to be the finest equestrian statue in the United States and one of the three best in the world. General George Rogers Clark, the Revolutionary War hero of the Northwest Territory, is commemorated by a statue executed by Robert Ingersoll Aitken in 1921. Aitken, who was born in 1878, designed the $50 U.S. gold coin in 1915.

Fig. 343. Stonewall Jackson statue, 1919

Fig. 344. Robert E. Lee statue, 1924

The bronze equestrian statue of General Robert E. Lee (fig. 344) was unveiled in 1924 in Lee Park. Sculptor Henry Mervin Shrady (1871–1922) of New York City, began the statue, and Leo Lentelli (1879–1962) of Italy, completed it. Architect Walter Dabney Blair designed the stone base.[51]

Libraries

Early in the twentieth century, Charlottesville-born Paul Goodloe McIntire, who made his fortune in stocks and bonds in Chicago and New York, donated more than a million dollars to Charlottesville to finance parks, statuary, the arts, health facilities and research, the university amphitheater, and McIntire Public Library (fig. 345). McIntire's generosity funded the classical library facing Lee Park that was designed by architect Walter Dabney Blair and completed in 1922. Presently, it is the home of the Albemarle County Historical Society, founded on 4 April 1940. A nineteenth-century town library was located in a frame house on Court Square. It was founded by Charles Harper of Spring Hill and Valentine W. Southall, whose home was later razed for Lee Park.[52]

Fig. 345. McIntire Public Library, 1922

The Episcopal Church

The Church of the Good Shepherd on U.S. Route 29 south of Charlottesville was built as a rectangular stone church in 1905. In 1959–62 Milton Grigg added stone wings, thus creating a T-shaped plan. The Church of Our Savior (Rock Church of Rio), built on Rio Road just north of Charlottesville between 1905 and 1906, was designed by New York architect G. R. Bolton, whose Albemarle County relative was a patron of the church. The church is asymmetrical with a square bell tower and a red-clay tile roof. The stone foundation for a parish house was completed in 1921, but the project was abandoned. Another of these stone missions, Saint John the Baptist Episcopal Church, was built about 1920 on Route 637 near Taylor's Mountain. It has a castellated square bell tower.[53]

In 1910 a second Episcopal church, Saint Paul's Memorial Church, was built in Charlottesville just down the street from Jefferson's Rotunda. In 1925 this frame church was replaced with a Georgian Revival–style brick church. Eugene Bradbury, the architect, had submitted two sets of drawings to the vestry, which chose the Georgian Revival–style plan over a medieval one. A brick hall-parlor-plan house, once the residence of the Chancellor and Alderman families, was razed for the original church. In 1914 Saint Stephen's Episcopal Church was built by Marmaduke Brown in Esmont as the third church in Saint Anne's Parish. The frame building features Gothic windows and an asymmetrically set belfry above the entrance.[54]

The Presbyterian Church

Architect Marshall Wells designed the brick Westminster Presbyterian Church on Rugby Road in Charlottesville in 1939, patterning it after the 1755 Abingdon Church in Gloucester Point, Virginia. Molded and rubbed brick define its aedicule doorway.[55]

The Methodist Church

The present brick First Methodist Church, on the northeast corner of First and Jefferson Streets across from Lee Park in Charlottesville, was designed in 1924 by architect Joseph Hudnut. An African Methodist Episcopal Church formerly stood at the corner of Commerce and Fourth Streets in Charlottesville, but it was razed before 1910 because with the popularity of the Baptists, the congregation could not sustain itself.[56]

The Baptist Church

High Street Baptist Church was built in 1901 on the northwest corner of High and Seventh Streets in Charlottesville, but the congregation later relocated closer to the university to provide a church for students. In 1928–29 the former church was partially razed, and an office building was constructed that incorporated the buttressed brick walls. The congregation then built the six-columned brick University Baptist Church on West Main Street from designs by Richmond architect Herbert Levi Cain. He was born in Delaware in 1888 and had worked for D. Wiley Anderson in 1909–10.[57]

Among early twentieth-century Baptist churches are the brick Hillsboro Baptist Church, erected in 1905 for a congregation that was founded in 1839, and the frame Alberene Baptist Church. The latter church was constructed in 1902–3 on land donated by the Alberene Soapstone Company.[58]

The First Church of Christ, Scientist

Raymond Hiroux Julian, a Long Island architect, designed the brick Christian Science Church on Gordon Avenue in 1958. The church is an interesting eclectic mixture of architectural elements. They include Ionic pilasters, quoins, a recessed-arch entry with keystones, a bell-cast mansard roof, and a spire.

Nondenominational Churches

Funds raised over a period of four years resulted in 1925 in the construction of the stone Blue Ridge Sanitorium Chapel at the intersection of Routes 20 South and 53. It exhibits a demioctagonal apse, buttresses, Gothic windows, and a circular window. It resembles the Catawba Tuberculosis Chapel in Roanoke.

Episcopal Rectories

Neve Hall, which features an open bell tower, was built on Wheeler's Road south of Charlottesville in 1927 and contains a cornerstone in its stone facade that identifies its architect, Eugene Bradbury. Originally, Neve Hall served as a manse for the Reverend Mr. Neve's Diocesan Missionary Society of Virginia. About 1940 architect Stanislaw Makielski designed Spruce Hill Rectory near Cismont for the Reverend Frank Robinson of Grace Episcopal Church.[59]

COMMERCIAL BUILDINGS

Hotels

By the mid–twentieth century the increase in tourism and the growth of the university prompted the construction of several fine hotels and motels. The Thomas Jefferson Inn, an elegant facility designed by architect Milton Grigg and built on Emmet Street in 1951, is now the Federal Executive Institute. In the 1950s Stanislaw Makielski designed the Town and Country Motor Lodge, an interesting motel of the period at Charlottesville's eastern entrance that features a curving facade and a restaurant that borrows its appearance from Monticello's dome, which can be seen from the site. The firm of Johnson, Craven and Gibson designed the nationally known Boar's Head Inn, built in 1964 west of town near Farmington for John Rogan. Recently, the Virginia Society of the American Institute of Architects honored the inn with a "Test of Time Award" for its "lasting value of good architectural design."

Stores and Shops

Several architecturally interesting commercial buildings are located in Charlottesville, including the J. S. Young Company building on Carlton Avenue, built in 1916 with Jacobean Revival gables and brick quoins. In 1936 the Monticello Dairy purchased sixteen lots south of Preston Avenue, and the following year it built a structure with six distinctive Tuscan columns that was designed by Elmer Burruss. Nearby, the Art Deco–style Coca Cola Bottling Plant was erected in 1939. Except for this building, two gasoline service stations, the W. A. Hartman Memorials building at 1301 East Market Street, and the Ben Franklin Store on West Main Street, almost no Art Deco structures were built in the city or county.[60]

By the 1920s good roads and trucks enabled goods and people to travel longer distances, resulting in the decline of the country store. Rural shoppers flocked to urban downtowns to visit the new department stores and "five and dimes." The country store's function as a post of-fice also declined at this time with the advent of rural free delivery. In 1916 McCrory's opened as Charlottesville's first five-and-ten chain store. In 1958 Barracks Road Shopping Center became the first regional shopping center; it was built on the site of the old "duck pond" that was the remnant of the swamp that once had extended to the university. Nearby on the corner of Emmet Street and Barracks Road was located the legendary Carroll's Tea Room, a beer tavern constructed in 1937 as an Amoco gas station, which had as its slogan "No Carroll's, No Tea, No Room."[61]

Gas Stations

In the 1930s the first automobile service stations were built in the county, many of them as appendages of existing general stores. Robert Nicholas Estes's gas station on U.S. Route 29 North was added to an 1890s store. It was demolished in a car crash in 1985, but Estes's frame I-house with a two-tier portico is nearby. Other one-story frame gas stations include the no-longer-extant Crossroads Store and Gas Station (fig. 346) on U.S. Route 29 South and an abandoned station on Route 681 at Route 631 in the southwestern part of the county. A handsome classical-style brick example in Charlottesville is Fry's Spring Gas Station (fig. 347), constructed about 1932 on Jefferson Park Avenue; even the exposed light bulbs form part of the modillion decoration. The garage section was added about 1939. The Colle Gas Station, built of stone about 1933 by Simpson Wickline for Frank Mehring at Simeon, was one of the county's more substantial early service stations. The

Fig. 346. Store and gas station at Crossroads, E2OC

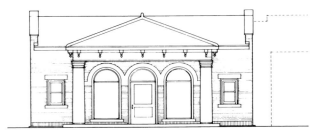

Fig. 347. Fry's Spring Gas Station, c. 1932, elevation

mid-twentieth-century Texaco Gas Station in Barracks Road Shopping Center is one of the finest examples of the later Georgian Revival–style stations.[62]

Entertainment

In 1888 Jefferson Monroe Levy converted the 1851–52 Town Hall into an opera house seating 500 persons. In 1896 a larger auditorium with better lighting was built on the second floor of a new store on Main Street. This building, the Jefferson Opera House, burned in 1915 and was rebuilt (fig. 348) to seat 1,200. Its owners also erected the Lafayette Theater on Main Street in 1921; it seated 1,000 and was specifically designed for motion picture presentations.[63]

Vaudeville reached its heyday in Charlottesville in the early twentieth century. In 1912 F. W. Twyman opened his 1,000-seat Jefferson Theater in the 1901 Jefferson Bank building, which he had renovated at a cost of $40,000. In 1915 a balcony patron's lit cigar started a fire that burned down the theater. It was rebuilt that same year by Richmond architect Claude K. Howell, who had designed Richmond's Lyric Theater. The interior plasterwork was again executed by Victor Pierrel. Richmond architect D. Wiley Anderson designed Victory Hall (fig. 349) in Scottsville for vaudeville. The two-story building, constructed between 1918 and 1920, features a large semicircular entry arch.[64]

John Armstrong Chaloner was an Astor family heir who was married to Amélie Rives of Castle Hill for a short time. Later, with the help of architect Stanford White, his family committed him to a New York mental asylum, but he escaped. After his return to Albemarle County, he shot and killed a neighbor in March 1909, supposedly in self-defense. Despite Chaloner's eccentricity, he was much interested in film and was a benefactor of the poor and needy. In 1920 he converted his Merrie Mill barn near Cismont into a motion picture theater and dance hall and opened it free to the community.[65]

By 1930 the motion picture had replaced vaudeville. The Paramount Theater, which seated 1,300, opened its doors on Thanksgiving Eve, 1931. The well-known theater firm Rapp and Rapp had designed it. As in other theaters, sep-

Fig. 348. Jefferson Opera House, 1915

Fig. 349. Victory Hall, 1918–20

Fig. 350. Marguerite de Crescioli's bordello, E20C

arate toilets, concessions, and seating areas served black patrons, but the Paramount also had a separate box office and entrance; it was desegregated in 1963. Eleven years later the owners closed the Paramount and opened another theater in a more convenient suburban shopping center. Entertainment was not limited to urban areas. The community of Ivy had its Ivy Hall around the turn of the century, and country stores offered dances. Allen's store on Route 53, for example, featured Woody's Dance Hall in the 1930s.[66]

The city also had its brothels. In 1922 Marguerite de Crescioli's bordello (fig. 350) was established at 303 Fifth Street Southeast in Charlottesville in a two-story brick house with Ionic columns and porte cochere. This notable landmark was razed in 1972 to make way for the urban renewal of Garrett Street.[67]

Banks

The Jefferson National Bank (not related to the later bank of the same name) at 108 East Main Street was designed by W. T. Vandergrift in 1901; in 1912 it was converted into the Jefferson Theater. In 1920 Washington, D.C., architect William Johnston Marsh designed the eight-story Charlottesville National Bank and Trust (fig. 351) on Main Street for Hollis Rinehart Sr. By then Charlottesville had four banks, and three others were located at Scottsville, Crozet, and Esmont. The financial crash of 1929 eventually produced widespread bank closings.[68]

Fig. 351. Charlottesville National Bank and Trust, 1920, artist's rendering

MEDICAL BUILDINGS

In 1886 Piedmont Hospital, known as The Cottage, was established in a brick building at 232 Fifth Street Northwest. Nine years later Dr. Robert B. Nelson established a sanitarium in the brick I-house built for Martha Minor in 1835 at 201 East High Street in Charlottesville. In 1899 Dr. Edward May Magruder erected his private sanitarium (fig. 352) at 100 West Jefferson Street. Dr. Magruder shortly thereafter joined the University Hospital staff and later headed Martha Jefferson Hospital. In 1902 the Magruder family moved into the sanitarium, where his daughter, Evelina, still resides.[69]

In 1889 Paul Brandon Barringer returned to his alma mater, the University of Virginia, as professor of physiology and surgery and later became chairman of the faculty. Largely through his efforts, the Board of Visitors allocated funds for the construction between 1901 and 1904 of the University Hospital (fig. 353), designed by the well-known architect Paul J. Pelz. In 1903 a group of doctors founded Martha Jefferson Hospital and Sanitorium (fig. 354), replaced in 1928–29 with a structure designed by architect Stanhope Johnson. The first building was razed in 1972. In 1914 a facility for the mentally ill was founded near Monticello. Five years later it became Blue Ridge Sanitorium and treated tuberculosis patients.[70]

Fig. 352. Sanitarium of Dr. Edward
May Magruder, 1899

Fig. 353. (above) University of Virginia
Hospital, 1901–4

Fig. 354. (left) Martha Jefferson Hospital and
Sanitorium, 1903

Educational Buildings

In 1916 the William Holmes McGuffey Elementary School (fig. 355), named for the University of Virginia professor who wrote the famous *McGuffey Readers*, was designed by the Norfolk architectural firm of Finley Forbes Ferguson, Charles J. Calrow, and Harold H. Wrenn; it is now the McGuffey Art Center. The same firm designed Venable Elementary School, named for university professor Charles Scott Venable and erected on Fourteenth Street in 1924, the year before buses began operation for white students. In 1926 Jefferson High School was erected for black students at Commerce and Fourth Streets; the Norfolk firm, by then without its senior partner Ferguson, also designed this building. George Rogers Clark Elementary School was built on Belmont Avenue in 1930–31 from the design of Norfolk architect Thomas David Fitz-Gibbon, who was born in 1892 and attended Carnegie Institute of Technology in Pittsburgh. As a 1936–37 Works Progress Administration project, the county's McIntire High School was constructed opposite McIntire Park. During 1939–40 Lynchburg architect Pendleton Scott Clark, who had graduated from the University of Pennsylvania in 1917, designed Lane High School in downtown Charlottesville. As recently as 1949 Jackson P. Burley High School was built in Charlottesville solely for black students.[71]

Transportation Structures and Buildings

Road Bridges

With the advent of the automobile and the proliferation of roads in the early twentieth century, many new bridges were constructed. Among them were the Hydraulic Mills

Fig. 355. William Holmes McGuffey Elementary School, 1916

bridge over the Rivanna River and those over the Hardware River at Carter's Bridge, which were often replaced due to flooding. One of the few metal truss bridges remaining in the county is Advance Mills Bridge over the north fork of the Rivanna River, relocated here in 1943. The metal truss Millington Bridge over the Moormans River, relocated here in 1924, was razed in 1995.

Airports

In 1929 Dixie Flying Service opened an airport on Garth Road that offered passenger service and a flight school. In 1939 the University of Virginia's Aviation Club established University Airport on the Rivanna River near Milton. It served as a commercial airfield through 1971. Just west of U.S. Route 29 north of Charlottesville, the Charlottesville-Albemarle Airport opened for commercial flights in 1954; the facility was vastly expanded in 1988 by Obrien and Atkins Associates of North Carolina. It reopened for passenger flights after the expansion was completed in 1991.[72]

Fig. 356. George Masonic Lodge No. 32 at Howardsville, 1846

Fig. 357. Benevolent Order of Elks, 1902–3

SOCIAL AND CIVIC ORGANIZATIONS

In addition to the many farm, social, civic, fraternal, and athletic clubs, the county had eleven Masonic lodges at different times. The oldest extant Masonic building is the 1846 brick George Lodge No. 32 (fig. 356) at Howardsville; the lodge had earlier been chartered in Amherst County on 14 April 1791. Other lodges still functioning in the county include the Widow's Sons' Lodge No. 60, chartered at Milton in 1799 and relocated to Charlottesville in 1815; Scottsville Lodge No. 45, established in 1850; King Solomon's Lodge No. 194 at Yancey's mills, chartered in 1864; and Alberene Lodge No. 277, chartered in 1900. Masonic lodges that are no longer extant include Warren Lodge No. 33, which was chartered 29 October 1791 and became extinct in 1848; Door to Virtue Lodge No. 44 in Charlottesville, 1794–1811; Charlottesville Lodge No. 90, 1811–48; James River Lodge No. 147 at Scottsville, 1868–73; and Charlottesville Lodge No. 55, 1873–1990.[73]

In 1902–3 the Benevolent Order of Elks (fig. 357) built its lodge to the north of the courthouse. After a fire in the late 1940s, its tetrastyle portico was removed as well as the elk's head in the tympanum of its pediment. Today it serves as a juvenile court. The private Redland Club has occupied the 1832 brick dwelling to the east of the courthouse since 1905.[74]

In 1914 the Charlottesville Country Club was organized at the end of Rugby Road in a stone building designed by architect Eugene Bradbury, who was also a club founder. In 1927 Farmington Country Club made its debut on the Jefferson-designed Farmington estate. In 1947 the 1912 Villa Crawford, also designed by Bradbury, became the Keswick Country Club. It closed in the early seventies and reopened in 1992 as Keswick Hall, a luxury hotel.[75]

The Keswick Hunt Club, formed in 1896, erected its clubhouse two years later; Murray Boocock of Castalia was its principal benefactor. The Farmington Hunt Club was founded in 1929 as an outgrowth of the Farmington Country Club.[76]

VII

The University of Virginia and the Jeffersonian Legacy

THE UNIVERSITY OF VIRGINIA SCHOOL OF ARCHITECTURE

In 1782 Thomas Jefferson had stated in his *Notes on the State of Virginia*: "Architecture being one of the fine arts, and as such within the department of a professor of the college, according to the new arrangement, perhaps a spark may fall on some young subjects of natural taste, kindle up their genius, and produce a reformation in this elegant and useful art." When Jefferson formulated an educational program for the commonwealth of Virginia in 1814, he included architecture and the fine arts as professional components. In 1818 he incorporated these courses of study into the curriculum for the University of Virginia. He also designed the Lawn and its buildings "to be of various forms, models of chaste architecture, as examples for the school of architecture to be formed on," in which students would observe and learn about "that most noble adornment." As Jefferson wrote, the pavilions were to be "chaste models of the orders of architecture taken from the finest remains of antiquity." But modifications imposed on the curriculum placed military and civil architecture courses of study in the School of Mathematics, probably under Thomas Hewitt Key, in 1825. By 1832 William Barton Rogers, the noted geologist, was teaching courses in architectural drawing and construction. It was not until the close of World War I, when a gift from the late Paul Goodloe McIntire made it possible to establish the McIntire School of Fine Arts, that a formal curriculum in architecture at last was established.[1]

The centennial anniversary in 1919 of the founding of the University of Virginia also marked the advent of Fiske Kimball as the head of the University of Virginia's architectural curriculum. Under his guidance the faculty of the architecture school began to influence building design in Charlottesville and Albemarle County just as Jefferson and his master builders had done a century before. In September 1919 the school's first class contained but eleven students. The number increased to twenty the next year, and classes met in an expanded Hotel E on West Range. Alpha Rho Chi Architectural Fraternity was established in 1922, and in June 1923 the school graduated its first students. In 1924–25 Fayerweather Hall Gymnasium was converted into the School of Architecture. During the 1920s a frame "drafting barn" (fig. 358) with a shed monitor for north light was constructed on Carr's Hill; it was razed about 1940.

Fig. 358. School of Architecture drafting barn, 1920s

Sidney Fiske Kimball, known as the dean of architectural history in America and an authority on Jeffersonian architecture, was born in Brighton, Massachusetts, in 1888. He graduated summa cum laude from Harvard University in 1909 and took his Master of Architecture degree there three years later. He joined the University of Illinois faculty for a year and then taught at the University of Michigan before coming to Charlottesville and the university in 1919. Kimball was a pioneer in the restoration of historic sites and buildings; his projects include Colonial Williamsburg, Monticello, Stratford Hall, and Gunston Hall. In 1923 he became head of fine arts at New York University and then director of the Philadelphia Museum of Fine Art. His own retirement home, Shack Mountain, built in 1935–36, is testimony to his understanding of and ability to assimilate Jefferson's design principles. During his time at the university, Kimball designed the Faculty Apartments (1917) at Beta Bridge, the university amphitheater (1921), and, with the help of Stanislaw Makielski, Memorial Gymnasium (1922–24). Kimball died in 1955 and was buried in Monticello Memory Gardens.

Stanislaw John Makielski (1893–1969), who was born of Polish heritage and briefly attended the University of Notre Dame, took his degree in architecture from the University of Virginia in 1922. From 1919, when still a student at the university, until 1965, he served as a member of the architecture faculty. Among the buildings he designed were the Phi Kappa Psi fraternity house on an axis with Madison Hall in 1928, the Beta Theta Pi house (now Delta Upsilon) and the Dulaney house on Rugby Road in 1929, and the Unitarian Church on Rugby Road and the Earl C. Leake house on Todd Avenue in 1950.[2]

The second faculty member hired by Kimball was Louis F. Voorhees, who was born in Michigan in 1892, received a Bachelor of Architecture degree from the University of Michigan in 1916, and the next year took his Master of Architecture degree there. In 1921–22 he worked for Eugene Bradbury and Fiske Kimball and then served as an instructor at the University of Virginia for a year before studying with Hugh Breckenridge at the School of Art in Massachusetts. He next organized his own firm in High Point, North Carolina. In Charlottesville he designed the Zeta Psi fraternity house (1926), which has features similar to Farmington and Monticello and was a precursor of Kimball's own house, Shack Mountain.

Joseph Hudnut (1886–1968), who had taught art history courses during the university's summer session in 1920, succeeded Kimball at the university in 1923. During his tenure the architecture school was moved from Hotel E to Fayerweather Hall. Hudnut graduated from the University of Michigan in 1912 and from Columbia University four years later. During his subsequent career he became dean of architecture at Harvard University and brought Bauhaus architect Walter Gropius and the Modern movement to America in 1937. While he was at the University of Virginia, Hudnut designed the First Methodist Church in downtown Charlottesville in 1924.

In 1926 Alfred Lawrence Kocher, head of architecture at Pennsylvania State University since 1918, succeeded Hudnut at the University of Virginia. Kocher (1885–1969), born in San Jose, California, graduated from Stanford University in 1909 and received a Master of Architecture degree from Pennsylvania State University in 1916. He also attended the Bauhaus in Germany. After his tenure at the University of Virginia, Kocher served for ten years as the editor of *Architectural Record* and then as a professor at the Carnegie Institute of Technology in Pittsburgh. He also wrote, and he sat on the first Advisory Committee of Architects for Colonial Williamsburg, where his library of more than 450 volumes became part of the research library after his death in 1969.[3]

The fourth scholar to direct the university's program in architectural studies was Edmund Schureman Campbell (1884–1950), who received his bachelor's and master's degrees from the Massachusetts Institute of Technology, attended the Ecole des Beaux-Arts in Paris, and was dean of the Beaux Arts Institute of Design in New York before his arrival in Charlottesville. He, like Kimball, was knowledgeable about Jefferson and nineteenth-century Virginia architecture, and he was also on the Advisory Committee of Architects for Colonial Williamsburg. Campbell designed the Bayly Museum in 1934 and the Lady Astor Squash Courts at the University of Virginia in 1937.[4]

Graduates of the university's architecture program also had an effect on the architecture of Charlottesville and Albemarle County. Marshall Swain Wells (1900–1974), a member of the university's first architecture class who studied under both Kimball and Hudnut, was born in Chattanooga, Tennessee. After working with Thomas Harlan Ellett in New York, Wells designed many buildings in the Charlottesville area on his own. Among them were the home of former university president E. A. Alderman's widow on Rugby Road in 1932, the Mrs. William Goodwin house (now the University Press of Virginia) on Sprigg Lane in the 1930s, and the Westminster Presbyterian Church in 1939.[5]

University graduate Arthur C. Barlow (1906–1944) worked for Wells immediately after he graduated in 1930.

About 1941, while in private practice, he renovated interiors and the guest cottage at Birdwood, just west of Charlottesville. Another university alumnus, Clarence W. Wenger (1899–1982), was born in Edom, Virginia. He worked for McKim, Mead and White in New York in 1925–27 and with Shreve, Lamb and Harmon, also a New York firm, in 1930–31. From 1933 to 1961 Wenger maintained his office in Harrisonburg; thereafter, he was located in Charlottesville. Among his numerous projects in Charlottesville and around the state were the Angus Barn Restaurants.[6]

Milton LaTour Grigg (1905–1982), who was born in Alexandria, Virginia, attended the architecture school at the university in 1924–29. He worked for Perry, Shaw and Hepburn on the restoration of Colonial Williamsburg until 1933, the year he established his own firm in Charlottesville. From 1937 to 1940 he was in partnership with Floyd Johnson; both men afterward became fellows of the American Institute of Architects. Later, Grigg was associated with William Newton Hale Jr. (1920–1954), who was born in Salem, Virginia, and graduated from the university's architecture school in 1943. Hale and Grigg designed many houses on Hessian Road in Charlottesville. As a leading restoration architect, Grigg restored Monticello in 1936, Edgemont in 1939, and many other historic buildings thereafter. Among his projects was the renovation of the Albemarle County Courthouse (1938); he also designed the Thomas Jefferson Inn (1951), now known as the Federal Executive Institute, and the Virginia Angus Association building (1952), both in Charlottesville. Grigg's residential work had a very personal touch that produced a lower, more intimate scale.[7]

Floyd Elmer Johnson, also a leading restoration architect, was born in Charlottesville in 1909 and was graduated in architecture from the university in 1934. His partners too were university graduates: David Jameson Gibson in 1937 and Thomas W. S. Craven in 1941. Johnson's first building after his association with Grigg had ended was the Conduff house, built in 1941 at the corner of Lyons Avenue and Cargil Lane. His restoration and renovation work included Monticello, where he and Grigg first reconstructed the stables, Farmington, Shadwell (Jefferson's birthplace), the Albemarle County Courthouse, and such county estates as Cherry Hill and Windsor Hill, both about 1946. In 1989 Johnson received the Ross Award from the Classical America Society.[8]

Louie Lorraine Scribner, born in Raleigh, North Carolina, in 1906, attended the university's architecture school in 1925–30. He worked first for Marshall Wells, then for Stanislaw Makielski, and finally operated the Charlottesville branch office of the New York firm of Pruitt and Brown until he became a registered architect. Scribner was also active in Democratic party politics and served as mayor of Charlottesville in 1960–62. His partner, William Edward Stainback (1906–1965), another North Carolina native, received his architecture degree from the university in 1928. He then worked for Makielski before joining the New York State Architect's Office from 1930 to 1933. In 1955 the firm Stainback and Scribner, with Raymond Hiroux Julian as consulting architect, designed the First Presbyterian Church on Park Street. Julian, who was born in 1902 in Kentucky and attended Yale University and Columbia University, also worked for Otto R. Eggers and Daniel Paul Higgins. In addition to his consulting work, he designed the Christian Science Church on Gordon Avenue in Charlottesville in 1958 while maintaining his Long Island office.[9]

Ben Henderson Heyward, born in Memphis, Tennessee, in 1913, was graduated from the university's architecture school in 1935. He subsequently worked for Pruitt and Brown and the famous architect William Lawrence Bottomley who undertook so many commissions in Virginia. Heyward also drew many of the county house sketches that were published in Mary Rawlings's *Antebellum Albemarle* in 1935. His partners were Baker and Llorens. Benjamin Charles Baker (1884–1955), a graduate of the Massachusetts Institute of Technology, Brown University, and the Ecole des Beaux-Arts, also worked for McKim, Mead and White. Alfred Llorens (1901–1986) was born in Puerto Rico of Spanish parents. He won a scholarship to Syracuse University and worked for Bottomley before joining the Charlottesville firm. That firm designed several city schools and renovated the eighteenth-century The Farm in 1949–50 and the Levy Opera House in 1981.[10]

In 1935, the year Heyward graduated, Kimball built his own retirement house, Shack Mountain, a reduced version of Farmington, on the edge of town. At the same time Kenneth Day constructed the city's first International Style house for Mrs. James A. Cole on Bollingwood Road. Day, born in 1901 in Philadelphia and a University of Pennsylvania graduate, worked for the eclectic firm of McKim, Mead and White and later for the Modernist Louis I. Kahn. The contrasting dwellings by Kimball and Day, both competent within their own idiom, epitomized the architectural struggles to come—the Jeffersonian classicism interpreted by Kimball and the early Modern movement in American architecture that Day's work represented.

In 1919 women were admitted to the graduate and professional schools at the university. The first woman graduated in architecture from the University of Virginia, however, Evelina Magruder, took her degree in 1935. She was the great-granddaughter of John Bowie Magruder, whom Jefferson listed in his account books as supplying plank for Monticello. Born on 19 April 1898, Evelina Magruder studied interior design at the Parsons School in the 1920s, worked in that field in New York City, and then made a fourteen-month tour around the world by land and by sea. Among her architectural works was the redesign as a law office of the stable at the corner of Market and Sixth Streets about 1938.[11]

The School of Architecture remained in Fayerweather Hall until 1970 when the present school, designed by Pietro Belluschi, was built. Also in 1970, the first women matriculated as first-year undergraduate students at the university, and two women received master's degrees from the School of Architecture: Anne Carter Lee in architectural history and Virginia B. Overton McLean in planning. In 1973 two women who transferred from other colleges received bachelor's degrees from the school: Kathy Auth in architectural history and Susan S. Nelson in landscape architecture. The following year seven more women received bachelor's degrees, six in architecture and one in landscape architecture. Of those 1974 graduates, only one, Joan Kennedy, had begun as a first-year University of Virginia architecture student; the other six had transferred into the program from other programs at the university.

In 1968, eighteen years after the first black student was admitted to the university,[12] Edward Wayne Barnett was admitted as the first black student to the School of Architecture. He earned a Bachelor of Science in Architecture degree in 1972, and Harvard later awarded him a master's degree.

THE NON-JEFFERSONIAN BUILDINGS

Thomas Jefferson's university, like Albemarle County generally, did not escape an influx of outsiders who competed for architectural commissions here with local and University of Virginia–trained architects. The university's expansion that began in the late nineteenth century necessitated the construction of dozens of new buildings (fig. 359). In 1893 Carpenter and Peebles of Norfolk designed Fayerweather Hall to serve as the university's gymnasium. It inaugurated the recurrence of classical forms at the university after the construction of John R. Thomas's

Victorian Brooks Museum in 1876 and Charles E. Cassell's Gothic Revival chapel in 1890. The "dialogue with Jefferson" in the form of red brick and white columns returned with the resurgence of classicism and other traditional historic building styles executed by these talented architects. Until late in the twentieth century, few of the buildings constructed at the university were in any style other than the classical.[13]

The most important "non-Jeffersonian" building at the university was, ironically, the great Rotunda itself, which was reduced to a brick shell by fire on 27 October 1895 and then was remodeled by Stanford White. In renovating the Rotunda, White omitted one of Jefferson's floors, added a north portico, and continued an arcade around the drum of the building to enclose gardens. As an additional fireproofing measure, Rafael Guastavino designed thin-shell concrete vaulting for the main floor and for its dome. Some seventy years later White's work was removed and the Rotunda was returned to Jefferson's vision, but not without some controversy over the obliteration of White's design, as he had become renowned in his own right. Many other White-designed buildings still stand on the grounds, however, and the influence of his classical compositions on the architecture of the university and on Albemarle County was almost as great as that of Jefferson's style.[14]

The university's principal athletic field was built on twenty-one acres between 1901 and 1903 and named in honor of Dr. William Alexander Lambeth (1867–1944), a physician who was head of Buildings and Grounds from 1905 to 1930. It required the removal of 48,000 cubic yards of earth. By 1913 a classical segmental stadium for seating fans, the Colonnades (fig. 360; no. 1 on fig. 359), was built from the design of architect Robert E. Lee Taylor (1882–1953) of Baltimore at a cost of $35,000. Born in Norfolk, the godson of Robert E. Lee, he graduated from the University of Virginia in 1901 and then from the Massachusetts Institute of Technology. Taylor later was part of the university's architectural commission, consisting also of Walter Dabney Blair, Edmund S. Campbell, and John Kevan Peebles, a team responsible for the design of several university buildings. Behind the Colonnades on Rugby Road are the 1917 Faculty Apartments (no. 2) designed by Kimball with a Greek Ionic tetrastyle portico.[15]

The cast-iron capital (no. 3 on fig. 359) outside the Bayly Museum is one of several magnificent capitals salvaged from the Rotunda Annex designed by Robert Mills and completed in 1853. As the first natively trained Amer-

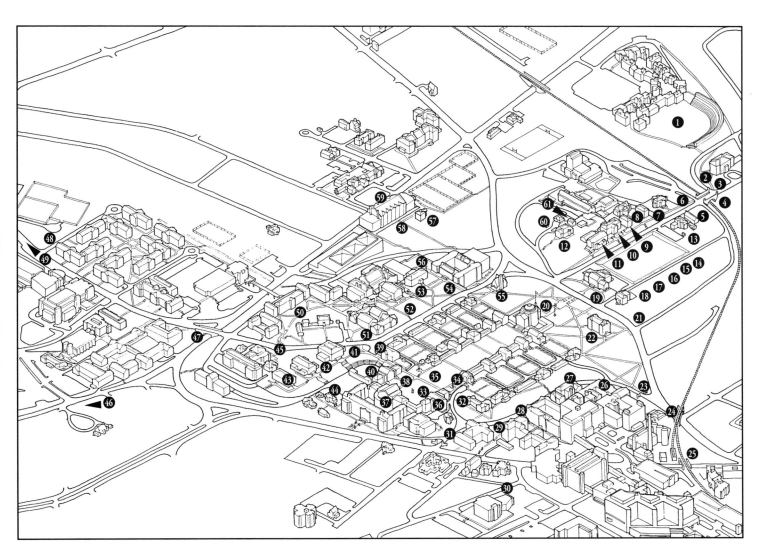

Fig. 359. University of Virginia plat of non-Jeffersonian buildings, L19C, E20C

ican architect and a Jefferson protégé, Mills is best known for designing the Washington Monument in the District of Columbia and Monumental Church in Richmond. The Rotunda Annex contained seating for 1,200 persons and had several classrooms. Other surviving capitals are located behind Hotel E, at Monroe Hill and Carr's Hill, elsewhere around the university grounds, and at several county plantations.

Westminster Presbyterian Church (no. 4 on fig. 359) was erected in 1939 from designs by Marshall Wells. In 1929 Stanislaw Makielski designed the Georgian-Colonial Revival Beta Theta Pi (Delta Upsilon) fraternity house (no. 5), one of a number of fine fraternity houses built in the Rugby Road neighborhood during the early twentieth century. Two other of his projects are located north of the fraternity house on Rugby Road: the Dulaney house (1929) and the Unitarian Church (1950). The Zeta Psi house (no. 6), which exhibits features similar to Monticello, was built in 1926 from plans by architect Louis F. Voorhees. Julius Gregory (c. 1875–1955) of New York designed the interior. Attributed to James J. Burley of New York, the Kappa Sigma fraternity house (no. 7) was built in 1911. This fraternity and nearby Chi Phi exhibit both Greek and Roman Ionic capitals. The house for Delta Tau Delta (Sigma Phi) (no. 8) also dates to 1911 and has been attributed to the firm of McKim, Mead and White. Eugene Bradbury of Charlottesville designed the classical Chi Phi (no. 9), built in 1922. He designed at least forty

Fig. 360. Lambeth Field Colonnades, 1901–3, c. 1913

buildings in Charlottesville, many of which are located on Rugby Road and University Circle to the north of the university.

The Bayly Art Museum (no. 10 on fig. 359) was constructed in 1934–35 from funds provided both by a private bequest and by a grant from the Public Works Administration. It is named in honor of Thomas Henry Bayly (1810–1856), a graduate of the university's law school and a member of the Virginia General Assembly. Designed by Edmund S. Campbell, the five-bay brick museum displays a Palladian-motif entrance portico.

Fayerweather Hall (fig. 361; no. 11 on fig. 359), the first classical building built at the university after Jefferson's time, was at the time the largest gymnasium in the South. J. Edwin R. Carpenter (1867–1932) and John Kevan Peebles (1866–1934) of Norfolk were its architects. Erected in 1892–93, it is now the home of the art department, having housed the School of Architecture from the 1920s until 1970. Peebles, born in Norfolk, was the restoration architect for Jefferson's Virginia State Capitol in 1902–3 and chairman of the influential Jamestown Tercentennial Cele-

bration of 1907. Having written about Jefferson, he was instrumental in securing the Colonial Revival firm of McKim, Mead and White to undertake the massive building program at the university at the turn of the century. His partner, Carpenter, was born in Columbia, Tennessee, attended the Massachusetts Institute of Technology and the Ecole des Beaux-Arts, and became an American Institute of Architects Gold Medalist in New York in 1916.

The university president's house, Carr's Hill (no. 12 on fig. 359), was a product of McKim, Mead and White's activity. The prestigious New York firm had previously designed such landmarks as New York's Metropolitan Club and Madison Square Garden. Carr's Hill was built between 1906–9 and probably was designed by Stanford White (1853–1906), although it was completed after White's demise at the hands of his mistress's wealthy, irate husband, Harry K. Thaw, in the roof garden of Madison Square Garden. Behind Carr's Hill is a carriage house of the same period and a portion of a nineteenth-century dormitory. To the west of the house is Bucking-

Fig. 361. Fayerweather Hall Gymnasium, 1892–93

ham Palace, a one-story brick mid-nineteenth-century house built for use by students.

Several fraternity houses flank Madison Bowl north of Madison Hall. In 1928 Stanislaw Makielski designed Phi Kappa Psi (no. 13 on fig. 359). Elliston Perot Bissell (1873–1944), John Penn Brock Sinkler (b. 1875), and possibly Fiske Kimball were responsible for the Phi Kappa Sigma (no. 14) house, constructed in 1911 and then rebuilt about 1922 after fire destroyed the first building. Bissell and Sinkler were graduates of the University of Pennsylvania and were the designers of Battle Abbey in Richmond. Delta Psi (Saint Anthony Hall) (no. 15), built in 1900, is the oldest extant fraternity house at the university, perhaps designed by the firm of Parker, Thomas and Rice. Sigma Phi Epsilon (no. 16) dates to 1925, while Delta Phi (Saint Elmo Hall) (no. 17) and Phi Gamma Delta (no. 18) both were constructed in 1913.[16]

Originally built in 1905 for the university's YMCA, the classical Madison Hall (no. 19 on fig. 359) now houses the office of the president of the university. It was designed by Wainright Parrish (1867–1941) and J. Langdon Schroeder of New York. Partners for more than three decades, Parrish and Schroeder were the architects for the 57th Street

YMCA in New York City. Parrish was a graduate of Rensselaer Polytechnic Institute.

Sir Moses Ezekiel sculpted the 1910 statue of Jefferson atop a bell (no. 20 on fig. 359) that stands on the north side of the Rotunda on a terrace once occupied by Mills's Rotunda Annex.[17]

In 1925 Eugene Bradbury designed a new building for Saint Paul's Memorial Episcopal Church (no. 21 on fig. 359), across University Avenue from the university grounds. Bradbury presented designs for this church in two different styles, a typical practice of the architects of his day. A medieval design was rejected in favor of the classical one that was built.

The Victorian Brooks Museum (fig. 362; no. 22 on fig. 359) was built in 1875–76 from plans drawn by John R. Thomas (1848–1901) of Rochester, New York. Thomas was said to have designed more buildings in New York City in the late nineteenth century than any other architect. Another New York architect, Henry Bacon (1866–1924), designed the Entrance Gateway (no. 23) at the university in 1915. Eugene Bradbury had entered the design competition for these gates, but the project went to Bacon, an American Institute of Architects gold medalist who had

Fig. 362. Brooks Museum, 1875–76

Fig. 363. University of Virginia Entrance Building, c. 1920

worked for Stanford White and designed the Lincoln Memorial in Washington, D.C. A few years later Bradbury was more successful, gaining the opportunity to design the Entrance Building (fig. 363; no. 24 on fig. 359) that was built about 1920 next to the gates. This lovely building, which was moved a short distance from its original site, has served several purposes over the years and now contains the Women's Center.

In 1921 Robert Ingersoll Aitken of New York sculpted the George Rogers Clark monument (no. 25 on fig. 359) as a gift to the university from local philanthropist Paul Goodloe McIntire.

The first building for the University of Virginia Hospital (no. 26 on fig. 359), designed by Paul J. Pelz (1841–1918) of Washington, D.C., was built in the classical style between 1901 and 1904, with wings added in 1906 and 1908 that followed his original scheme. The hospital's Barringer Wing (no. 27) of 1939–41 owes its form to Robert E. Lee Taylor and D. K. Este Fisher Jr. (b. 1892) of Baltimore. Fisher was a graduate of Princeton and the Massachusetts Institute of Technology. Taylor had earlier designed McKim Hall (no. 28) in 1930–31; it originally housed the nursing school.

Walter Dabney Blair (b. 1877), who graduated from the university in 1896 and then studied architecture at the University of Pennsylvania and the Ecole des Beaux-Arts, drew the plans for the 1916–17 Cobb Chemical Laboratory (no. 29 on fig. 359). He was born in Amelia County, Virginia, but practiced in New York. He spent a year on the architecture faculty at Cornell University. Two years after designing this laboratory, he designed the McIntire Public Library in downtown Charlottesville.

The Barringer mansion (no. 30 on fig. 359) at 1404 Jefferson Park Avenue, the home of Dr. Paul Brandon Barringer, presently serves as the French House. Varsity Hall (no. 31), built in 1857, was the university's first infirmary and contains an early, unique mechanical system. It is now the Air Force Reserve Officers Training Corps headquarters. Nearby Randall Hall (no. 32), constructed in 1898–99, was also the creation of Paul J. Pelz.

At the south end of the Lawn is Ezekiel's statue of Homer (no. 33 on fig. 359), which dates to 1907. Looking toward the Rotunda from this point, the original entrance to the Lawn, one is captivated by the illusion of deeper perspective by the use of parterres (land terraces) and the increasing number of student rooms between pavilions. The George Washington statue (no. 34) is a copy of the statue by Jean Antoine Houdon (1741–1828) commis-

Fig. 364. Cabell Hall, 1899

sioned by Jefferson for his Capitol in Richmond. Karl Bitter created the Thomas Jefferson statue (no. 35) of 1915.

Besides reconstructing the Rotunda after the fire of 27 October 1895, McKim, Mead and White added three classical buildings in 1899 at the south end of the Lawn to replace the classroom space lost in the Rotunda Annex fire. The centerpiece, Cabell Hall (fig. 364; no. 37 on fig. 359), includes an auditorium originally built to seat 1,500 that contains the university's second copy of Raphael's sixteenth-century *School of Athens.* Executed in 1902 by George W. Breck of the American Academy in Rome, it replaced the first copy destroyed in the Annex fire. Cabell Hall's interior Doric columns, which support the balcony, are based on the Cancelleria Palace in Rome. To execute the pediment sculpture, Hungarian George Julian Zolnay used local female models from "Aunt Mat's Bordello." Rouss Hall (no.

36) and Cocke Hall (no. 38) complete the building group. These three buildings closed off the view from Jefferson's Lawn terraces, for which Stanford White has often been criticized. Yet he proposed an alternate plan that would have preserved the view by placing the new buildings east of and perpendicular to the Lawn axis; the Board of Visitors, however, chose the former plan.[18]

Just west of the south end of the Lawn is Garrett Hall (no. 39 on fig. 359), another building by McKim, Mead and White, erected between 1906 and 1908 as a dining hall called the Commons. It exhibits a fine interior plaster ceiling. Garrett Hall faces McIntire Amphitheater (fig. 365; no. 40 on fig. 359), which was earlier designed by Warren H. Manning (1860–1938) of Boston and finally built by Fiske Kimball in 1921. Manning was an assistant landscape architect for the 1893 Columbian Exposition in Chicago and landscape architect for the 1907 Jamestown Tercentennial Celebration. He also worked at Biltmore, the Vanderbilt estate in Asheville, N.C. Just after the turn of the century, he was associated with site planning at the university. Allegedly, the amphitheater was constructed in a

borrow pit from which earth had been excavated earlier to build the parterre for Stanford White's building group at the southern end of the Lawn. Minor Hall (no. 41), constructed as the first law school building in 1911, is on the west side of the amphitheater. Manning and John Kevan Peebles were the architects.

Robert E. Lee Taylor and D. K. Este Fisher Jr. designed both Maury Hall (no. 42 on fig. 359), which dates to 1941–42 and houses the Naval Reserve Officers Training Corps, and Halsey Hall (no. 43), which was built between 1945 and 1947 and serves as the Naval Armory. Dawson's Row (fig. 366; no. 44 on fig. 359), a series of mid-nineteenth-century dwellings, was located on a curving road here. Only one, which was built in 1859 and features a portico added about 1912, now remains. Now called the Luther P. Jackson House, it houses the Office of African-American Affairs.[19]

In 1931–32 a team of four architects planned the second building for the law school, Clark Memorial Hall (fig. 367; no. 45 on fig. 359). John Kevan Peebles (chairman), Walter Dabney Blair, Edmund S. Campbell, and Robert E. Lee

Fig. 365. McIntire Amphitheater, 1921

Fig. 366. Dawson's Row, 1859, c. 1912

Taylor collaborated on several other buildings at the university as well, including Thornton Hall (no. 47) in 1935 to house the engineering school. Allyn Cox (1896–1982), who also painted murals in the U.S. Capitol, executed the murals inside Clark Hall. Also in 1931, Scott Stadium (no.

46) was built on Alderman Road at Whitehead Road.

The university cemetery, filled with interesting epitaphs to the faculty, is on the northeast corner of McCormick and Alderman Roads. Charlottesville was designated as a general hospital during the Civil War and almost 23,000 wounded or sick soldiers were brought here from nearby battlefields for care. Interred in the university cemetery are more than 1,000 who died. It is a fitting location for the Civil War monument (no. 48 on fig. 359) by New York sculptor Caspar Buberl, which was unveiled in 1893. On Observatory Road on the little mountain to the west, then called Mount Jefferson, the Leander-McCormick Observatory (fig. 368; no. 49 on fig. 359) was the largest refracting telescope in America when it was built in 1884.[20]

The Monroe Hill Dormitories (no. 50 on fig. 359), built in 1928–29, and Monroe Hall, constructed in 1929–30 (no. 51), were the results of collaborations by Peebles, Blair,

Fig. 367. Clark Memorial Hall, 1931–32, elevation

Fig. 368. Leander-McCormick Observatory, 1884

Campbell, and Taylor. A classical-style addition to Monroe Hall was completed in 1987 by the Washington, D.C., architectural firm of Hartman-Cox.

Peabody Hall (no. 52 on fig. 359), built in 1912, housed the university's first education school. A team of architects that included Finley Forbes Ferguson (1875–1936), Charles J. Calrow (1877–1938), and Robert E. Lee Taylor of Norfolk designed it. Calrow began the study of architecture at the age of sixteen in the office of J. Edwin R. Carpenter. Ferguson was a graduate of the Massachusetts Institute of Technology and later served on the advisory board of Colonial Williamsburg. The original building on the site of Miller Hall (no. 53) dated to 1868–69, but it burned in the 1920s. It was rebuilt, incorporating the existing brick walls, from drawings by Eugene Bradbury, who added a second story. Now the Office of Admissions, it once served as a chemistry lab, then as Peabody Annex.

Alderman Library (no. 54 on fig. 359) dates to 1938 and was the work of Robert E. Lee Taylor and D. K. Este Fisher Jr. Jefferson's Anatomical Hall was razed to make way for

Fig. 369. Memorial Gymnasium, 1922–24

the library, though it in no way impinged on the library foundation itself. Except for a student room, it is the only Jeffersonian building at the university to have been demolished. Charles E. Cassell of Baltimore designed the Gothic Revival–style University Chapel (no. 55), erected in 1885–90. The sculptor of Mount Rushmore, Gutzon Borglum, created the Aviator statue (no. 56), a 1919 memorial erected in memory of university alumnus James Rogers McConnell.

Edmund S. Campbell designed the Lady Astor Squash Courts (no. 57 on fig. 359) in the early years of the twentieth century. The building was moved to its present location in 1992 from a site nearby to make way for a new parking garage. Memorial Gymnasium (fig. 369; no. 58 on fig. 359) was built in 1922–24 just west of a large reflecting pond no longer extant. Fiske Kimball and Stanislaw Makielski were the architects. Built as a private residence about 1915, Alumni Hall (no. 59) later became a fraternity house associated with Zeta Beta Tau and Phi Sigma Kappa. It has been greatly enlarged since it was purchased for the Alumni Association in 1936.

Sigma Nu (no. 60 on fig. 359) was built in 1928 from a design by Louis Justement of Washington, D.C. Justement, born in 1891, graduated from George Washington University in 1911. Delta Kappa Epsilon (no. 61) claims to be the first social fraternity established at the university, meeting secretly after its petition for approval was rejected by the faculty in 1852. In 1899 it built its first fraternity house, which is no longer extant. The present house dates from 1914.[21]

CONCLUSION

Although this study was derived from a survey of more than 2,300 buildings in Charlottesville and Albemarle County, it is but a sampling of the many that once existed in Jefferson country, which yet remains rich in historic buildings that represent many national architectural styles. The city and county, then, are a microcosm of our country's architectural history, but through Jefferson and his influence it not only holds a significant collection of his work and that of his master builders, it is also unique in the United States. Later, because of the county's appeal to wealthy northerners as the ideal place for their retirement and second residences, and because of the influence of the University of Virginia School of Architecture, the area was further enriched with early twentieth-century architectural creations.

It is hoped that this study will provide resident and visitor alike with a detailed overview of the city and county's architectural heritage and will promote its active preservation for generations to come.

Appendix Tables

APPENDIX TABLE 1. *Albemarle County Landmarks with Historic Designations* (as of April 1999)

World Heritage List
    Monticello
    University of Virginia

National Historic Landmarks
    Monticello
    University of Virginia Historic District
    University of Virginia Rotunda
    Shack Mountain

National Register of Historic Places and Virginia Landmarks Register Districts
    Charlottesville and Albemarle County Courthouse
    Rugby Road–University Corner
    Scottsville
    Skyline Drive (in Shenandoah National Park)
    Southwest Mountains
    University of Virginia (including the Lawn, Rotunda, and Brooks Hall)
    Wertland Street

Virginia Landmarks Register District
    Proffit

National Register of Historic Places and Virginia Landmarks Register individual properties
    Arrowhead
    Ash Lawn (Highland)
    Ballard-Maupin house (Plainview Farm)
    Bellair
    Blenheim
    Blue Ridge Farm
    Brooks Hall (included with University of Virginia Historic District National Historic Landmark)
    Carrsbrook
    Casa Maria
    Castle Hill
    The Cedars

Christ Church Glendower
Cliffside
Clifton
Cobham Park
Cocke's millhouse (Tsuquatania) and mill site
Cove Presbyterian Church
Crossroads Tavern
D. S. Tavern
Edgehill
Edgemont (Cocke farm)
Ednam
Emmanuel Church
Esmont
Estouteville
The Farm (John A. G. Davis house)
Farmington
Faulkner House
Four monumental outdoor sculptures donated by Paul Goodloe McIntire to the city of Charlottesville: George Rogers Clark, Robert Edward Lee, Thomas Jonathan Jackson, and *Their First View of the Pacific* (Lewis and Clark)
Gallison Hall
Grace Church
Guthrie Hall
High Meadows
Longwood
Malvern
Midway (Riverdale Farm)
Miller School of Albemarle
Mirador
Monticello
Monticola
Morea
Morven
Mount Fair
Mount Zion Baptist Church
Mountain Grove

National Register of Historic Places and Virginia Landmarks Register individual properties (cont.)

Oak Lawn
Piedmont
Pine Knot
Plain Dealing
The Rectory
Red Hills
Redlands
Seven Oaks Farm and Black's tavern
Shack Mountain
Spring Hill
Sunny Bank
Sunnyfields
University of Virginia Rotunda
John Vowles house
William Walker house
Wavertree Hall Farm
Woodlands
Woodstock Hall Tavern

Virginia Landmarks Register only

Buck Mountain Church
Earlysville Union Church (listing on National Register pending)
East Belmont (listing on National Register pending)

Marshall-Rucker house (listing on National Register pending)
Michie Tavern

National Register of Historic Places only

Charlottesville Multiple Resource Area: Anderson Brothers' Bookstore, Armstrong Knitting Factory, Barringer mansion, Belmont, Carter-Gilmer house, Dabney-Thompson house, Delevan Baptist Church, Enderly, Ficklin-Crawford cottage, Four Acres, Gardner-Mays cottage, Hard Bargain, Hotel Gleason/Albemarle Hotel/Imperial Cafe, house at Pireus, King Lumber Company warehouse, King-Runkle house, Locust Grove, McConnell-Neve house, Patton mansion, Paxton Place, Peyton-Ellington building, Pireus store, Johnson W. Pitts house and Inge's store, Ridge Street Historic District, Rose Cottage/Peyton house, Stonefield, Timberlake-Branham house, Benjamin Tonsler house, Turner–La Rowe house, Robert L. Updike house, White Cross–Huntley Hall, Woolen Mills Chapel, Wyndhurst, Young building

National Civil Engineering Landmark

Crozet railroad tunnel through Afton Mountain

APPENDIX TABLE 2. *Architectural periods and significant events in Albemarle County*

Georgian, 1719–1800

1719	First settlers arrive in county
1720s	Mountain Anglican chapel built
1726	First road enters county
1727	First patent for land in county
1730s	Findowrie built
1731	River road enters county
1732	Martin King's Road in county
1733	Old Mountain Road enters county
1734	Scotch-Irish enter county
1737	Shadwell built
1739	First bridge over Mechunk Creek
1740s	Viewmont built
c. 1740	First Enniscorthy built
1741	D.S. Presbyterian Church built
1742	St. Anne's Parish established
1742	First gristmill on Preddy's Creek
1743	Thomas Jefferson born at Shadwell
1744	Albemarle County established
1745	Walker Anglican Church built
1745	Belle Grove built
c. 1746	Belvoir Anglican Church built
1747	Buck Mountain Anglican Church built
1747	First Meriwether house built
1750s	Maury Classical School established
1751	Fry/Jefferson Map of Virginia published
1754–63	French and Indian War
1756	North Garden Presbyterian Church built
1758	Earthquake
c. 1760	Clover Fields built
1761, 1789	Plain Dealing built
1762	Charlottesville established
1764	First Castle Hill frame house built
c. 1764	First Belvoir built
c. 1764	First Keswick built
1768–1809	Monticello built
1769	Old Forge built
1769	Cove Presbyterian Church built
1771	Devastating flood
1771	Bateaux introduced
1773	Lewis's Baptist Church built
1775	Totier Baptist Church built
1775	Ballenger's Creek Baptist Church built
1775	Earthquake

Georgian, 1719–1800 (cont.)

1775–83	Revolutionary War
1776	Virginia declares Independence
L18c	Ballenger's Anglican Church built
L18c	Forge Anglican Church built
L18c	Garden Anglican Church built
1780s	First Spring Hill built
1781	Jack Jouett's ride
1784	Preddy's Creek Baptist Church built
1784–89	Jefferson minister to France
1788	Whitesides Baptist Church built
1788	Mount Moriah Methodist Church built
1788	Virginia becomes tenth state
1789	Washington elected president
1789	Milton established
1789–1813	Redlands built
1790	Monroe Hill built
1790s	Limestone Farm built
1793	Edgemont built
c. 1793	Warren established
1794	Bellair built
1795	Bingham's Methodist Church built
1796	Woodville built
c. 1797	Sunny Bank built
1798	Arrival of James Dinsmore
1799	Edgehill built
c. 1799	Highlands (Ash Lawn) built

Federal, 1800–1830

c. 1800	Arrowhead built
1801–9	Jefferson third president
1802	Farmington built
1803	Louisiana Purchase
c. 1803	Tallwood built
1803	Mountain Grove built
1803	Third courthouse built
1803	Walker house built
1804–6	Lewis and Clark expedition
1804	Arrival of John Neilson
1807	Midway built
1809–23	Poplar Forest built
1809–17	Madison fourth president
c. 1810	Clifton built
1812	Carrsbrook built
1812–15	War of 1812
1817–25	Monroe fifth president
1817–26	University of Virginia built
1818	Charlottesville annexation
1819	Financial panic
1819	Birdwood built
c. 1820	Morven built
1820s	Bentivar rebuilt
1822	Oak Lawn built

1824	Christ Church, Charlottesville, built
1826	Death of Thomas Jefferson
1827–30	Estouteville built
1828	Second Edgehill built
1828	Dunlora built
1829–33	High Meadows built

Greek Revival and Gothic Revival, 1830–60

1830	Old Hall built
1832	Cholera epidemic
1832	Christ Church Glendower built
1835	Cliffside built
1837	Financial panic
1839	Walker's Episcopal Church built
1840s	Monticola built
1842	Mirador built
1842	Woodlands built
1845	Mount Fair built
c. 1845	Auburn Hill built
1846–48	Mexican War
1847	Seven Oaks built
1847	Grace Church by Strickland built
1848	Railroad enters the county
1849	Cholera epidemic
1849	Bloomfield built
1850	Rugby built
1850	Word-Wertenbaker house built
1850	Third Enniscorthy built
c. 1855	Faulkner House built
c. 1855	The Cedars built
1855–56	Smallpox epidemic in Virginia
c. 1856	Cobham Park built
1857	Financial panic
1859	Wavertree Hall built
1859	Abell-Gleason house built

Victorian, 1860–1900

1860	Charlottesville annexation
1861	Virginia secedes from the Union
1861–65	Civil War
1864	Gilmer map of Albemarle County published
1866	Hotchkiss map of Albemarle County published
1870	Devastating flood
1870	Virginia readmitted to the Union
1873	Financial panic
1873	Charlottesville annexation
1874–83	Miller School built
1875	Peyton map of Albemarle County published
1877	Gray map of Charlottesville published
1884	Financial depression
1886	Charlottesville water system established
1888	Charlottesville incorporated

Eclectic, 1890–1939

1893	Midway School built
1893	Fayerweather Hall built at UVA
1893	Financial panic
1895	Charlottesville sewer system established
1895	Rotunda burns at UVA
1898	Spanish-American War
1901	Charlottesville electric lights established
c. 1901	Guthrie Hall built
1904–21	Casa Maria built
c. 1905	Ednam built
c. 1905	Pine Knot built
1907	Financial panic
1907	Jamestown Tercentennial
1907	Massie map of Albemarle County published
1909	Kearney mansion built
1914–18	World War I
1916	Charlottesville annexation
1918	Influenza epidemic
1919	UVA School of Architecture established
1925	Tiverton built
1927	Farmington Country Club established
1928	Charlottesville building permits established
1928	Blue Ridge Farm built
1929	Stock market crash
1929	Great Depression
1931	Gallison Hall built
1935	Shack Mountain built

Modern, 1935–Present

1935	Cole house built, first modern house
1938	Charlottesville annexation
1939–45	World War II

APPENDIX TABLE 3. *Albemarle County time periods*

	1600–1699	1700–1749	1750–1799	1800–1849	1850–1899	1900–1949	1950–Present
Styles	Pre-Georgian 1607–1700 No white settlement in Albemarle County during this period	Georgian 1719–1800 Beginning of white settlement in Albemarle County		Federal 1800–1830	Greek & Gothic Revival 1830–1860 Victorian 1860–1900	Eclectic 1890–1939	Modern 1935 on
Brick bonds	English bond 1607 on	Flemish bond 1719 on	American bond 3-course 1780 on	5-course (& Flemish variant) 1820 on	American bond 7-course 1860 on		
Doors			6-panel 1780 on	4-panel with applied moldings 1820 on	2-panel 1860 on		
Ridge boards		None 1700 on			Ridge boards 1860 on		
Saw marks		Pit sawn 1700 on		Reciprocating sawn 1800 on	Circular sawn 1840 on		
Nails		Wrought iron roseheads 1700 on		Cut w/ roseheads 1796 on	Cut w/o roseheads 1825 on	Wire 1875 on	

299

Notes

ABBREVIATIONS

AC   Albemarle County

ACHS   Albemarle County Historical Society

AIV ser.   Architecture in Virginia series, for Prof. K. Edward Lay, Fiske Kimball Fine Arts Library, University of Virginia

DP   Charlottesville *Daily Progress*

LVA   Library of Virginia, Richmond

MACH   *Magazine of Albemarle County History*

NRHP   National Register of Historic Places

SC-VIU   Special Collections, University of Virginia Library

study for Nichols   architectural history study for Prof. Frederick D. Nichols, Fiske Kimball Fine Arts Library, University of Virginia

study for Kayhoe   architectural history study for Prof. Matthias E. Kayhoe, Fiske Kimball Fine Arts Library, University of Virginia

SVA ser.   Studies in Vernacular Architecture series, for Prof. K. Edward Lay, Fiske Kimball Fine Arts Library, University of Virginia

UVA   University of Virginia

VDHR   Virginia Department of Historic Resources, Richmond

VRT ser.   Virginia Road Traces series, for Prof. K. Edward Lay, Fiske Kimball Fine Arts Library, University of Virginia

WPA   Works Progress Administration

I. THE GEORGIAN PERIOD

1. Nathaniel Mason Pawlett, *Historic Roads of Virginia: Albemarle County Roads, 1725–1816* (Charlottesville, Va., 1981), 2–3, 5–6.

2. Jim Denery, *DP*, 25 Feb. 1994, 18; Pawlett, *Albemarle County Roads*, 8, 16.

3. The memory of the Three Notch'd Road can be seen today in the jagged street pattern in the center of Belmont and in the angled building on the southeastern end of the Main Street pedestrian mall, a reflection of the road's entering there from Belmont. For a general discussion of native Americans in the area, see Garrow & Associates, Inc., "From the Monacans to Monticello and Beyond," VDHR, May 1995.

4. John Hammond Moore, *Albemarle: Jefferson's County, 1727–1976* (Charlottesville, Va., 1976), 43.

5. The Scotch-Irish are sometimes referred to as the Scots-Irish or Ulster Scots today.

6. Nicholas Meriwether proceedings for a land grant in present-day Albemarle County, Hanover County Court Records, 1719 and 1722 (as early as 1720 the Mountain Anglican Chapel was established on the Three Notch'd Road, or Old Mountain Road); Dr. George Nicholas (c. 1695–1734) married Elizabeth Carter Burwell, daughter of Robert "King" Carter (1663–1732) of Corotoman in Lancaster County; Moore, *Albemarle*, 25 (ironically, although Howard had slit and cropped ears in the manner of persons with an unsavory past, and Nicholas had fled England in 1722 to avoid charges of forgery, both acquired wealth and respect in the community, with Nicholas becoming the treasurer of Virginia); John Carter, who died in 1742, was eldest son of Robert "King" Carter; C. W. Watts, "Colonial Albemarle: The Social and Economic History of a Piedmont Virginia County, 1772–1775" (M.A. thesis, UVA, 1948), app. 3.

7. Clifford Dowdy, *The Virginia Dynasties* (Boston, 1969), 379; Joan Clifford Hutter, *DP*, 25 Feb 1994, 11; David Hackett Fischer, *Albion's Seed* (New York, 1989), 381; S. Edward Ayres, *DP*, 25 Feb. 1994, 1.

8. Moore, *Albemarle*, 35. In the 1980s during excavation for high-rise buildings in Richmond, bateaux were discovered in the mud of the James River and Kanawha Canal turning basin, thereby revealing the exact forms and measurements of the boats and enabling the accurate construction of new bateaux for the annual races on the James River. In 1994 another bateau was unearthed in Albemarle County at Milton.

9. Ibid., 89–90, 165–66.

10. *Virginia Advocate*, 14 Jan. 1831, 3.

11. The Sanborn maps, as they are popularly known, are available in several repositories. The complete series for the entire country is located in the Library of Congress. The Library of Virginia in Richmond possesses a microfilm copy of the series as well as the maps themselves for Virginia. The maps for Albemarle County are available (through 1964) in Charlottesville's Department of Community Development.

12. Shadwell is where Jefferson's parents, Peter Jefferson (1708–1757) and Jane Randolph Jefferson, had patented land in 1737; list of county officials in Edgar Woods, *Albemarle County in Virginia* (1900; rept., Harrisonburg, Va., 1972), 8–9, 375–76; Joshua Fry was also designated as surveyor; Joseph Thompson was also designated as sheriff; list of members of House of Burgesses in William Glover Stanard, *The Colonial Virginia Register* (Albany, 1902); William Cabell (1730–1798) resided at Union Hill in Nelson County, then a part of Albemarle; *DP*, 25 Feb. 1994, 25.

13. Angelika S. Powell lecture for ACHS meeting, 13 Nov. 1994; Bryan McKenzie, *DP*, 12 Nov. 1994.

14. W. J. Bell, "Thomas Anbury's Travels in America," *Papers of the Bibliographical Society of America* 37 (1942): 23–36 (quote); Jedediah Morse, *American Gazetteer* (1797), noted in Moore, *Albemarle*, 92.

15. U.S. Census, Schedule of Inhabitants, Albemarle County, Va., 1810; AC Deed Books 10:172, 346, 366, 370, 11:173, 222, 239, 271–72, 274, 282–83, 287–88, 347, 407, 12:524, 13:430, 15:57, 18:25; Woods, *Albemarle*, 57–58; James Green, *Richmond Times-Dispatch*, 11 Apr. 1965; [Malcolm H. Harris, M.D.], "The Highways and Byways of Fluvanna County," *Bulletin of the Fluvanna County Historical Society* 12 (Apr. 1971): 21. In the late eighteenth century, lots were sold to George Bruce, Edward Butler, William Clark, John Gambill, John Henderson, William D. Hunt, James Key, John Key, Howell Lewis, Randolph Lewis, Joseph J. Monroe, Jacob Oglesby, Richard Price, Robert Snelson, Joel Shiflett, William Sutton, Charles Terrell, James Usher, and Christian Wertenbaker.

16. AC Order Book, 11 July, 12 Sept. 1793 (Nicholas's tobacco inspection warehouse contained a stove 10 feet high and 4 feet in diameter); Elinor J. Weeder, "Wilson Cary Nicholas, Jefferson's Lieutenant" (M.A. thesis, UVA, 1946); William Minor Dabney, "Jefferson's Albemarle: History of Albemarle County, 1727–1819" (Ph.D. diss., UVA, 1951), 96; Victor Dennis Golladay, "The Nicholas Family of Virginia, 1722–1820" (Ph.D. diss., UVA, 1973); Golladay, "The Nicholas Family and Albemarle County Political Leadership, 1782–1790," *MACH* 35–36 (1977–78): 123–56; Mutual Assurance Society Policies, Albemarle County, 1812, Microforms Room, VIU (Oakland, later called Donegal, consisted of a 46-by-43-foot two-story brick house containing a brick-paved cellar with winter kitchen, a 34-by-18-foot one-story brick office, a 22-by-32-foot one-story brick slave quarters, and a 92-by-18-foot one-story brick stable); Jason Boroughs, Dawn Chapman, and LeNora King, "James River Road Survey," bldg. no. 10, VRT

ser., 1996; Peter Hodson, *The Design and Building of Bremo, 1815–1820* (Birmingham, Ala., 1968) (Patterson connection brought to my attention by Don Swofford); 21 June 1814, George Carr Papers, SC-ViU; Joseph Carroll Vance, "Thomas Jefferson Randolph" (Ph.D. diss., UVA, 1957), 36–37; Malone, *Jefferson* 6:app. 1.

17. Dr. William Bache was the grandson of Benjamin Franklin; Edward Garland married Sarah Old, the daughter of John Old, of Old's Forge.

18. AC Deed Books 13:430, 14:9, 165, 386, 15:467–69, 474, 20:214; Woods, *Albemarle*, 57–61; Moore, *Albemarle*, 93.

19. Thomas Jefferson's father, Peter Jefferson, built his house Shadwell in 1737. It burned in 1770. In 1991 archaeologist William Kelso uncovered two cellar foundations there, one of which could indicate the site of the main house. *DP*, 25 June 1898; Edward C. Mead, *Historic Homes of the South-West Mountains Virginia* (1898; rept., Harrisonburg, Va., 1978), 59; Melinda B. Frierson and Geoffrey B. Henry, "An Architectural Survey of Albemarle Villages," lecture, ACHS, 12 Nov. 1995; Dames & Moore, "Historical Architectural Survey of Albemarle County Villages [Advance Mills, Batesville, Covesville, Crossroads, Crozet, Free Union, Greenwood, Ivy, Milton, Proffit, White Hall, and Yancey Mills]," submitted to the VDHR, prepared for the Albemarle County Department of Planning and Community Development, Oct. 1995.

20. Quoting Thaddeus M. Harris in K. Edward Lay, "European Antecedents of Seventeenth and Eighteenth Century Germanic and Scots-Irish Architecture in America," *Pennsylvania Folklife* 32 (Autumn 1982): 15, n.135.

21. Lay, "European Antecedents," 15–18; Henry H. Glassie, *Pattern in the Material Folk Culture of the Eastern United States* (Philadelphia, 1969), 104–6.

22. Richard H. Hulan, "The Dogtrot House and Its Pennsylvania Associations," *Pennsylvania Folklife* 26, 4 (1977): 25–32; Vera V. Via, *DP*, 8 Mar. 1956.

23. Terry G. Jordan, "The 'Saddlebag' House Type and Pennsylvania Extended," *Pennsylvania Folklife* 44, 1 (1994): 36–48.

24. William Waller Hening, comp., *Statutes at Large . . .* (New York, etc., 1809–23), 4:37, 39 (quote). Extant houses that tradition suggests were claim houses are located at Blenheim (Whitchris), Castalia, Cedar Grove, Dunlora, D. S. Tavern, Glendower, Old Longwood, and Spring Hill.

25. Thomas Jefferson, *Notes on the State of Virginia*, ed. William Peden (rept. New York, 1974), 152, 154; Frederick Doveton Nichols and Ralph E. Griswold, *Thomas Jefferson, Landscape Architect* (Charlottesville, Va., 1978), 37.

26. Mead, *Historic Homes*, 129–38; WPA of Virginia Historical Inventory Project 1935–39, LVA; Mary Rawlings, *Ante-bellum Albemarle* (Charlottesville, Va., 1974), 76; *DP*, 11 Feb. 1973.

27. Woods, *Albemarle*, 324–25; correspondence with Margaret Fowler Clark, 22 Feb. 1983.

28. Woods, *Albemarle*, 310, 360; Richard Cecil Garlick Jr.,

Philip Mazzei, Friend of Jefferson: His Life and Letters (Baltimore, 1933); Ralph S. Walker, "Philip Mazzei, Cosmopolitan Virginian," *Iron Worker* 39, 3 (Autumn 1975): 2–15; *Piedmont*, supplement to the *Daily Progress*, 9 Oct. 1976; Margherita Marchione, "Philip Mazzei, Albemarle's Naturalized Patriot," *MACH* 37–38 (1979–80): 18–65.

29. Woods, *Albemarle*, 207; Rawlings, *Ante-bellum Albemarle*, 49.

30. Mutual Assurance Society Policies, Aug. 1800, July 1809, 5 Nov. 1816; Sale of Property, *Virginia Advocate*, 7 June 1828, 24 Dec. 1830; *DP*, 20 Oct. 1898, 10 Feb., 28 Apr. 1930; Woods, *Albemarle*, 279–81; Rawlings, *Ante-bellum Albemarle*, 6; Elizabeth Howard, *DP*, 31 Oct. 1973; David Allen Edwards, Mark Randolph Wenger, and George Humphrey Yetter, "Secretary's Road Survey," bldg. no. 58, VRT ser., 1977; Margaret G. Davis, Ann R. Fair, Kathryn M. Kuranda, and Stuart N. Siegel, "Staunton and James River Turnpike Survey," bldg. no. 51, VRT ser., 1979; Francis A. LaPoll, "Highland," study for Nichols, 1980; Robert Brickhouse, *DP*, 20 Mar. 1983; Harry Ammon, *James Monroe: The Quest for National Identity* (Charlottesville, Va., 1990).

31. William T. Stevens, *Virginia House Tour* (Charlottesville, Va., 1962), 116; Rawlings, *Ante-bellum Albemarle*, 62; Malcolm Ward Hill and Patricia Anne Murphy, "Coursey's Road Survey," bldg. no. 5, VRT ser., 1978.

32. Cynthia Ann MacLeod and Mark James Wenger, "Buck Mountain Road Survey," bldg. no. 78, VRT ser., 1976.

33. Elena Kaplan, "Cedar Grove, Wingfield House, and Other Ghost Homes in Albemarle County," no. 134, AIV ser., 1992, 17–31; Boroughs, Chapman, and King, "James River Road Survey," bldg. no. 11.

34. MacLeod and Wenger, "Buck Mountain Road Survey," bldg. no. 29; WPA Inventory; *DP*: Boyce Loving, 28 May 1958, Dan Friedman, 23 Oct. 1977; Cathleen Ganzel, "Solitude," no. 68, SVA ser., 1982; Gina Haney, NRHP nomination, 30 Apr. 1991, VDHR.

35. Rick Kniesler, "Morven and Verulam," study for Nichols, 1976; Edwards, Wenger, and Yetter, "Secretary's Road Survey," bldg. no. 57; Lucia C. Stanton, "Thomas Jefferson and Morven," Nov. 1986, Thomas Jefferson Memorial Foundation.

36. Rawlings, *Ante-bellum Albemarle*, 29; Stevens, *House Tour*, 84–85; Dan Friedman, *DP*, 28 Aug. 1977. Hugh Morris donated land in North Garden to his son's Episcopal congregation.

37. Rawlings, *Ante-bellum Albemarle*, 91; Emily Billheimer and Susannah Wood, "Glentivar," no. 178, AIV ser., 1997.

38. For more definitive studies of house space relative to use, see: Dell Upton, "Vernacular Domestic Architecture in Eighteenth-Century Virginia," *Winterthur Portfolio* 17, 2–3 (Summer–Autumn 1982): 95–119; Mark R. Wenger, "The Central Passage in Virginia: Evolution of an Eighteenth-Century Living Space," *Perspectives in Vernacular Architecture* 2 (1986): 137–49; Wenger, "The Dining Room in Early Virginia," ibid.,

3 (1989): 149–59; Elisabeth Donaghy Garrett, *At Home: The American Family, 1750–1870* (New York, 1990); Marcus Whiffen, *The Eighteenth-Century Houses of Williamsburg* (Williamsburg, Va., 1960), xviii; lecture by Mark R. Wenger, Colleagues' Weekend, Colonial Williamsburg, 22 Sept. 1997.

39. The punkah that originally hung in Tallwood, in Albemarle County, still exists but is now in another place. Mutual Assurance Society Policies, 12 Jan. 1803, 1805, 1816; Mead, *Historic Homes*, 249–51; Woods, *Albemarle*, 149, 310–11; Rawlings, *Ante-bellum Albemarle*, 82; WPA Inventory; Ann L. Brush and A. James Siracuse, "Fredericksburg Road Survey," bldg. no. 17, VRT ser., 1978; Jeff O'Dell to Douglas Gilpin, 19 July 1991, private collection; John E. Wells to J. Timothy Keller, 30 Dec. 1993, private collection; Marcia Joseph, "Findowrie," no. 161, AIV ser., 1994.

40. *DP*, 18 Oct. 1897, 28 Oct. 1929; Woods, *Albemarle*, 198, 222–23; Rawlings, *Ante-bellum Albemarle*, 30; notes of Stella Pitts Puett, 1960s–1970s, Valmont file, VDHR; Robert E. Troxell, "Valmont," no. 26, SVA ser., 1975; Dan Friedman, *DP*, 25 Aug. 1977; Boroughs, Chapman, and King, "James River Road Survey," bldg. no. 2.

41. Stevens, *House Tour*, 88; Hornor Davis, Peter Flagg Maxon, and Duncan J. McCrea, "Mount Walla," no. 10, SVA ser., 1974; Dan Friedman, *DP*, 2 Feb. 1978.

42. Mead, *Historic Homes*, 167–78; Rawlings, *Ante-bellum Albemarle*, 78; Stevens, *House Tour*, 57; Brush and Siracuse, "Fredericksburg Road Survey," bldg. no. 26.

43. Woods, *Albemarle*, 277–79; Lori Feldman, Margaret Pearson Mickler, and Martin Perdue, "Buck Mountain Road Survey," bldg. no. 85, VRT ser., 1977.

44. Woods, *Albemarle*, 285; WPA Inventory, 1938; "The Moore's of Central Virginia," *Central Virginia Heritage* 3, 3 (Fall 1985): 2.

45. WPA Inventory; Davis et al., "Staunton and James River Turnpike Survey," bldg. no. 3.

46. Margaret McClung Dudley and Osborne Phinizy Mackie, "Staunton and James River Turnpike Survey," bldg. no. 47, VRT ser., 1980.

47. Rawlings, *Ante-bellum Albemarle*, 39; MacLeod and Wenger, "Buck Mountain Road Survey," bldg. no. 77; Gina Baylon, "Wakefield," no. 177, AIV ser., 1996.

48. Guy M. Lapsley and Richard P. Thomsen Jr., "Three Notch'dRoad Survey," bldg. no. 18, VRT ser., 1976; Wayne Kille and Richard P. Thomsen Jr., "Brown-Parrott House," no. 40, SVA ser., 1977; F. H. Boyd Coons, "Benjamin Brown Sr., of Brown's Cove," no. 24, AIV ser., 1984.

49. Woods, *Albemarle*, 247–48; Rawlings, *Ante-bellum Albemarle*, 88; Lapsley and Thomsen, "Three Notch'd Road Survey," bldg. no. 28; Dan Friedman, *DP*, 24 Dec. 1977.

50. Thomas Jefferson to William Bache, 2 Feb. 1800, Jefferson Papers, SC-ViU; *DP*, 27 Aug. 1895, 26 May 1903.

51. William and Mary Center for Archaeological Research, "Archaeological and Architectural Investigations, the Dawson House, Albemarle County, Virginia," 11 Mar. 1996.

Frazier Associates of Staunton supervised the relocation of Mount Ida.

52. Feldman, Mickler, and Perdue, "Buck Mountain Road Survey," bldg. no. 99.

53. Rawlings, *Ante-bellum Albemarle*, 31; Anna Mary Moon, *Sketches of the Moon and Barclay Families* (Chattanooga, 1939), 89; Margaret A. Pennington and Lorna S. Scott, *The Courthouse Burned: Book II* (Waynesboro, Va, 1986), 88.

54. Mead, *Historic Homes*, 159–66; Rawlings, *Ante-bellum Albemarle*, 83; Stevens, *House Tour*, 54; Brush and Siracuse, "Fredericksburg Road Survey," bldg. no. 18.

55. Mutual Assurance Society Policies, 4 May 1799, 9 Dec. 1816.

56. WPA Inventory; Woods, *Albemarle*, 347–50.

57. Property of Michie sons brought to my attention by Cindy Conte and Eugenia Bibb, 1991; Woods, *Albemarle*, 274–76; MacLeod and Wenger, "Buck Mountain Road Survey," bldg. no. 58; Dan Friedman, *DP*, 5 Jan. 1978; information from Eugenia Bibb raises questions as to the builder of Longwood, 16 Mar. 1996.

58. Rawlings, *Ante-bellum Albemarle*, 33.

59. Mary S. Cerrone and Kevin L. Wagstaff, "Rockfish Gap Turnpike Survey," bldg. no. 29, VRT ser., 1986.

60. Stevens, *House Tour*, 80; Rawlings, *Ante-bellum Albemarle*, 11.

61. *Central Gazette*, 22 Jan. 1825; *Virginia Advocate*, 16 Feb. 1828.

62. AC Will Book 2:59–63 (1754), 300 (1758); Mutual Assurance Society Policies, 6 June 1805, 24 May 1809, 11 Oct. 1816; Woods, *Albemarle*, 197–98, 356–57; *Architectural Record*, Jan. 1928, 81–83; Historic American Buildings Survey, Dept. of Interior, National Park Service, 4 Sheets for Viewmont, Survey 11–12, Feb. 1934, Library of Congress, Washington, D.C.; Moon, *Sketches*, 39–44, 84–85; Thomas Martin Thacker Papers, courtesy of William Thacker; Rawlings, *Ante-bellum Albemarle*, 13, errata (1957); Stevens, *House Tour*, 73–75; *DP*: 11 Aug. 1949, Vera V. Via, 24 Nov. 1952; George W. Fry, *Colonel Joshua Fry of Virginia* (Cincinnati, 1966), 53–59 (Fry inventory); Ruth H. McConathy, *The House of Cravens* (Charlottesville, Va., 1972), 296–98.

63. Mutual Assurance Society Policies, 1799, 1806, 1810; Woods, *Albemarle*, 172; Rawlings, *Ante-bellum Albemarle*, 115; *DP*, 17 Apr. 1973; Thomas Dolan, "Woodville," no. 91, SVA ser., 1983; Elizabeth Langhorne, K. Edward Lay, William D. Rieley, *A Virginia Family and its Plantation Houses* (Charlottesville, Va., 1987), 45–52.

64. Vera V. Via, *DP*, 18 Sept. 1958; information from Eugenia Bibb raises questions about for whom Chestnut Avenue was built, 16 Mar. 1996.

65. Rawlings, *Ante-bellum Albemarle*, 62, 67; Stevens, *House Tour*, 112–13; Feldman, Mickler, and Perdue, "Buck Mountain Road Survey," bldg. no. 83; *DP*: Dan Friedman, 29 Dec. 1977, Lenny Granger, 8 Oct. 1978; Virginia Moore, *Scottsville on the James: An Informal History* (Charlottesville, Va., 1969), 3; Davis

et al., "Staunton and James River Turnpike Survey," bldg. no. 31.

66. Mutual Assurance Society Policy, vol. 31-1, no. 19, reel 3; *Charlottesville Gazette*, 25 Dec. 1824; *Central Gazette*, 8 Jan. 1825; *Virginia Advocate*, 12 Dec. 1840; Rawlings, *Ante-bellum Albemarle*, 51; Stevens, *House Tour*, 123; John Cook Wyllie, "Daniel Boone's Adventures in Charlottesville in 1781," *MACH* 19 (1960–61): 17; Francis A. LaPoll, "The Nicholas Lewis House," study for Nichols, 1980; Coy Barefoot, *C-ville Weekly*, 20–26 May 1997; *DP*: Patrick Hickerson, 23 May 1997, Michael Bednar, letter to the editor, 24 June 1997.

67. WPA Inventory; Dudley and Mackie, "Staunton and James River Turnpike," bldg. no. 41A; Susan Hastings Barto, "Glen Esk," no. 162, AIV ser., 1994.

68. Conjectural sketch of Carrsgrove by Bronislaw A. Makielski; tape-recorded conversation with Horace Burr, 3 Aug. 1992; Dan Friedman, *DP*, 6 Oct. 1977; Cerrone and Wagstaff, "Rockfish Gap Turnpike Survey," bldg. no. 25; Rawlings, *Ante-bellum Albemarle*, 73; Edwards, Wenger, and Yetter, "Secretary's Road Survey," bldg. no. 60.

69. Dan Friedman, *DP*, 12 Feb. 1978; David A. Dashiell III and David D. McKinney, "Rockfish Gap Turnpike Survey," bldg. no. 5, VRT ser., 1982.

70. Woods, *Albemarle*, 151–54; Rawlings, *Ante-bellum Albemarle*, 48; *DP*: Vera V. Via, 16 Sept. 1954, Boyce Loving, 21 June 1956, John Blake, 13 Oct. 1976; Coons, " Brown," 93–98; correspondence with Eugenia Bibb, 12 Jan. 1990, 3, 25 June 1991; David A. Maurer, *DP*, 3 Dec. 1995.

71. Lapsley and Thomsen, "Three Notch'd Road Survey," bldg. no. 46.

72. "Early Memories of Spring Hill," VDHR; *DP*, 26 July 1929; Rawlings, *Ante-bellum Albemarle*, 87; Stevens, *House Tour*, 230; Robert Estill O'Neill, "Spring Hill House," architectural history study, UVA, n.d.; Lapsley and Thomsen, "Three Notch'd Road Survey," bldg. no. 40; Dan Friedman, *DP*, 23 Feb. 1978; William R. Martin Jr., "Spring Hill Farm," study for Nichols, 1980. Derived from a 1735 patent by Charles Hudson, the Spring Hill Farm tract had been acquired in 1814 by Charles Harper, cofounder of Charlottesville's first circulating library, from Thomas Wells, who was proprietor of the Eagle Tavern in Charlottesville and a trustee with Thomas Jefferson to oversee the founding of Albemarle Academy.

73. Lapsley and Thomsen, "Three Notch'd Road Survey," bldg. no. 7.

74. U.S. Patent Office Records, 21 May 1814 ; Vera V. Via, *DP*, 7 Sept. 1949; Coons, "Brown," 83–90.

75. William B. O'Neal, *Pictorial History of the University of Virginia* (Charlottesville, Va., 1968), 44.

76. Charles E. Brownell, Calder Loth, William M. S. Rasmussen, and Richard Guy Wilson, *The Making of Virginia Architecture* (Charlottesville, Va., 1992), 19.

77. Mutual Assurance Society Policy, 22 May 1799; *Virginia Advocate*, 12 Dec. 1840.

78. Mutual Assurance Society Policies, 15 Aug. 1800, 6

June 1805, 28 Oct. 1816; Woods, *Albemarle*, 185–86; *DP*, 11 Jan. 1905; Rawlings, *Ante-bellum Albemarle*, 16; Stevens, *House Tour*, 81; Dan Friedman, *DP*, 13 Oct. 1977; Davis et al., "Staunton and James River Turnpike Survey," bldg. no. 35; John Pearce, "Plain Dealing, Keene, Albemarle County, Virginia," *Chesapeake Country Life*, Sept. 1983, 28–32; H. W. Hugh Darville, "Plain Dealing," no. 147, AIV ser., 1994.

79. Mead, *Historic Homes*, 216–30; Woods, *Albemarle*, 293; Rawlings, *Ante-bellum Albemarle*, 81; Brush and Siracuse, "Fredericksburg Road Survey," bldg. no. 5; Feldman, Mickler, and Perdue, "Buck Mountain Road Survey," bldg. no. 92; Diane Crowley, "Old Keswick," study for Nichols, n.d.; Golladay, "Nicholas Family"; S. Allen Chambers Jr., *Poplar Forest and Thomas Jefferson* (Little Compton, R.I., 1993), 139–40; Boroughs, Chapman, and King, "James River Road Survey," bldg. no. 9; Mutual Assurance Society Policies, 10, 13, 15 Jan. 1803, 16 July 1805, 12 Oct. 1816, 17 June 1823, 2 Dec. 1840, 25 Nov. 1846, 15 Dec. 1853, 6 Oct. 1860.

80. Rawlings, *Ante-bellum Albemarle*, 68; Hill and Murphy, "Coursey's Road Survey," bldg. no. 9; Caroline Meta Kurrus, "Edgmont," no. 146, AIV ser., 1994; Thomas R. Blackburn brought to my attention by John Wells, 25 Sept. 1998.

81. K. Edward Lay and Martha Tuzson Stockton, "Castle Hill: The Walker Family Estate," *MACH* 52 (1994): 38–64.

82. Natalie J. Disbrow, "Thomas Walker of Albemarle," ibid., 1 (1940–41): 11; William W. Reynolds, "An Account of the Albemarle Iron Works," ibid., 50 (1992): 46; AC Tax Lists, 1782, 1787, SC-ViU.

83. Thomas and Mildred Walker had twelve children. Their eldest child, Mary, married Nicholas Lewis (1728–1807), who inherited the 1,020-acre 1735 land patent known as The Farm, now in the east part of Charlottesville. The oldest son, John, who married Elizabeth Moore, granddaughter of Governor Alexander Spotswood, inherited Belvoir near Cismont. John was an aide to General Washington, a member of the House of Burgesses, a commonwealth's attorney, and a U.S. senator. Their granddaughter, in turn, married Hugh Nelson, minister to Spain and son of Governor Thomas Nelson. Other of Thomas and Mildred Walker's children were Susan (b. 1746), who married Henry Fry (1738–1823), the deputy county clerk; Captain Thomas (1748–1798), who married Margaret Hoops and resided at Indian Fields; Lucy (b. 1751), who married Dr. George Gilmer (d. 1836) and resided at Pen Park; Elizabeth (b. 1753), who married the Reverend Matthew Maury (d. 1808) and resided at Edgeworth, the location of Maury's school; Mildred (b. 1755), who married Joseph Hornsby; Sarah (b. 1758), who married Reuben Lindsay (d. 1831) and resided at Springfield; Martha (b. 1760), who married George Divers (d. 1830) and resided at Farmington; Reuben (1762–1765); and Peachy (b. 1767), who married Joshua Fry, county magistrate, member of the House of Burgesses, and grandson of Col. Joshua Fry, who published the 1751 map of Virginia with Peter Jefferson. AC Personal Property Tax Lists, 1800, 1815.

84. Judith Page Walker Rives, *Home and the World* (New York, 1857), 17–18, 29, 41; AC Land and Personal Property Tax Lists, 1820, 1821, 1830, 1840, 1850, 1860, 1870.

85. Articles of agreement between William C. Rives and John Perry, 10 Aug. 1823, William C. Rives Collection, Library of Congress.

86. Moore, *Albemarle*, 150; AC Tax Lists, 1870; Martha M. Tuzson, "Castle Hill," no. 111, AIV ser., 1991; Lay and Stockton, "Castle Hill"; *C-ville Weekly*, 22–28 July 1997; McDavid Stilwell, *DP*, 24 July 1997.

87. AC Deed Books 1:352 (1751), 6:514 (1776), 8:55 (1777), 9:309 (1787), 18:522 (1814), 21:358 (1819), 42:521 (1845); *DP*, 12 Aug. 1899, 30 Apr. 1900, 6 June 1903, 25 Feb., 7 June 1904; Woods, *Albemarle*, 173–74, 258–59; Charlotte Tucker, *Jefferson Journal*, 13 Jan. 1972; Moore, *Albemarle*, 249.

88. Mutual Assurance Society Policies, 1803, 1809; Rawlings, *Ante-bellum Albemarle*, 65; Hill and Murphy, "Coursey's Road Survey," bldg. no. 15.

89. Mead, *Historic Homes*, 192–200; Rawlings, *Ante-bellum Albemarle*, 79; Roy Wheeler Realty Company, *Historic Virginia: A Volume of Estates Reminiscent of Old and Historic Virginia in Photographs* . . . (Richmond, 1949), 165; Brush and Siracuse, "Fredericksburg Road Survey," bldg. no. 28; Melanie Arndt, "Valmontis," no. 175, AIV ser., 1996.

90. Feldman, Mickler, and Perdue, "Buck Mountain Road Survey," bldg. no. 81; Ruth Ewers-Self, *Charlottesville Albemarle Observer*, 13–19 June 1985; *Observer*, 22–28 May 1986; Kathy Hoke, *DP*, 23 June 1986; Susie Hurst and Susan Scott, *Cavalier Daily*, 12 Nov. 1986; Linda C. Feltman, *Keystone Gazette*, 11 May 1990; Kristen Kaiser, "High Meadows," no. 169, AIV ser., 1995; Woods, *Albemarle*, 306–7; Ruth Lynn Rodes Culpepper, *My Heritage: The Ancestors and Descendants of Mary Alberta Coiner and Edward Thomas Rodes* (Harrisonburg, Va., 1982), 90–99.

91. Woods, *Albemarle*, 39.

92. Camille Wells lecture at the University of Virginia on "Houses and Rural Landscapes in 18th-Century Virginia," 24 Feb. 1993; Wells, "The Planter's Prospect: Houses, Outbuildings, and Rural Landscapes in Eighteenth-Century Virginia," *Winterthur Portfolio* 28, 1 (Spring 1993): 15ff.; Milton L. Grigg, personal interview, 1980s.

93. Eighteenth-century advertisements in *Virginia Gazette* brought to my attention by Camille Wells, 8 Aug. 1991.

94. P. J. Gaesser, "Barns in Albemarle County," folklore study for Prof. Charles Perdue, UVA, 1974; *DP*, 6 Dec. 1970; Dudley and Mackie, "Staunton and James River Turnpike," bldg. no. 50; Kristie Struble, "Sutherland Barn," no. 67, SVA ser., 1982; George B. Chandler and Mark A. Thompson, "Stockton Creek Barn," no. 3, SVA ser., 1973; Belinda Grosskopf, Jennifer Thaler, and Jill Trischman-Marks, "Rockfish Gap Turnpike Survey," bldg. no. 1, VRT ser., 1991; Roulhac Toledano, *Charlottesville Observer*, 11 Nov. 1993; Anthony O. James and Steven C. Meixner, "The Wilhoit Farm," no. 5, SVA ser., 1973; David W. Amundson, "A Blend of Building Tradi-

tions in Albemarle County Barns," no. 14, AIV ser., 1983; Thacker Papers.

95. Brush and Siracuse, "Fredericksburg Road Survey," bldg. no. 9.

96. Mutual Assurance Society Policy, 28 Oct. 1812; Karen McIntyre, "Horse Barns," no. 140, AIV ser., 1993; *Real Estate Weekly*, 16–22 Mar. 1994; *DP*, 28 Apr. 1994.

97. Maura Singleton, *DP*, 27 Oct. 1996; correspondence with Thomas S. George Jr., 25 May 1995, brought to my attention the distinction he gleaned from his mentors Henry Chandlee Forman and Thomas Tileston Waterman between "dependency," a building near the main house for use by persons involved in the house and its immediate surroundings, and "outbuilding," one far from the main house used by persons involved in the outer reaches of the plantation.

98. Moore, *Albemarle*, 115; Charlotte D. Buttrick and Tamara A. Vance, *Southwest Mountains Area Natural Resource and Historic Preservation Study* (Charlottesville, Va., 1989), 58; Clover Fields farm journals brought to my attention by Sara Lee Barnes.

99. Lay and Stockton, "Castle Hill," 47–49.

100. AC Surveyors' Book 1:12, 86; AC Order Books, 28 Feb. 1745: 3, 25 Apr. 1745: 10, 12, 20, 27 June 1745: 22, 23, 25 July 1745: 33, 10 July 1746: 139, 13 Mar. 1747: 245. R. E. Hannum, "Albemarle County, 1936," WPA Inventory; *DP*, 22 Aug., 3 Sept. 1896, 30 Apr. 1929; Bernard P. Chamberlain, "The Albemarle County Court House," *MACH* 21 (1962–63): 65–70; W. Sam Burnley, *The Court House of Albemarle County in Old Virginia* (n.p., 1939); Steven G. Meeks, "Virginia's Courthouses: Albemarle County," *Central Virginia Heritage* 5, 4 (Winter 1987): 4–6; Floyd Johnson, Apr. 1991, and Shockey Massie, 2 Mar. 1992, personal telephone interviews.

101. Moore, *Scottsville*, 14–17; Edmund Berkeley Jr., "New Light on Albemarle County Courthouse," *MACH* 29 (1971): 65–66; Woods, *Albemarle*, 80, mentions that it had a portico by 1800.

102. AC Surveyors' Book 1:12, 86; AC Order Book, 1744–48: (28 Feb. 1745): 3, (25 Apr. 1745): 10, 12, 20, (27 June 1745): 22, 23, (25 July 1745): 33, (10 July 1746): 139, (13 Mar. 1747): 245; WPA Inventory, 1936; Woods, *Albemarle*, 80; Burnley, *Court House*, 3–9; Woods, *Albemarle*, 80–83; Chamberlain, "The Albemarle County Court House"; Berkeley, "New Light on Albemarle County Courthouse"; Jonathan C. Bohm and Matthew T. Lowry, "Albemarle County Courthouse," no. 31, SVA ser., 1976; AC Minute Book, 1875–77, 9 Apr. 1875, 23:123. The first recorded instance of capital punishment in the court records involved Aaron, Hugh Rice Morris's slave, who was convicted of breaking into a store and stealing seven sides of leather. In accordance with the laws of the time, he was hanged on the second Friday of February 1801.

103. Rosalie Edith Davis, *Fredericksville Parish Vestry Book, 1742–1787*, 2 vols. (Manchester, Mo., 1981); Charles Francis Cocke, *Parish Lines: Diocese of Virginia* (Richmond, 1967); Melinda B. Frierson, "A Study of Five Episcopal Churches in Albemarle County," no. 17, AIV ser., 1983; Moore, *Albemarle*, 78.

104. Vestry Book of Fredericksville Parish, Louisa County, 1742–87, p. 14, LVA. Strangely, the marker is not on the Edgehill property. This is confusing at best. Perhaps there were two mountain chapel locations.

105. William Meade, *Old Churches, Ministers, and Families of Virginia* (Philadelphia, 1857) 2:41, 47; James Scott Rawlings, *Virginia's Colonial Churches: An Architectural Guide* (Richmond, 1963), 175; Vera V. Via, *DP*, 5 May 1958; William Newman and Camille Wells, "Buck Mountain Church," no. 20, SVA ser., 1974; Frierson, "Five Episcopal Churches"; Lisa Tucker, "Virginia's Colonial Churches," no. 34, AIV ser., 1986; *DP*, 24 July 1997; Vestry Book of Fredericksville Parish, Louisa County, 1742–87, p. 26, LVA; the Reverend F. L. Robinson, *The Buck Mountain Church* ([Charlottesville, Va.], 1928), 3–8; papers of Dr. Edward F. Birckhead, given to me by the Birckhead family and deposited with SC-VIU.

106. Vestry Book of Fredericksville Parish, Louisa County, 1742–87, pp. 13–14, LVA; AC Deed Books 5:520 (1772), 24:236 (1824), 32:529 (1835), 97:316 (16 Feb. 1892), 421:55 (1966), 666: 302 (1979); WPA Inventory, Jan. 1938.

107. The Reverend G. Maclaren Brydon, of the Richmond Diocese, to Douglas Forsyth, 25 Feb. 1931, private collection, mentions that Ballenger Church was built about 1745 but was in ruins in 1820.

108. Russell Scott and Jay Wyper, "Christ Church Glendower," no. 14, SVA ser., 1973, p. 3.

109. Jay Wesley Worrall Jr., "The Albemarle Quakers, 1742–1754," *MACH* 40 (1982): 25–44; Worrall, *The Friendly Virginians* (Athens, Ga., 1994); Worrall lecture, ACHS meeting, 26 Feb. 1995.

110. Deborah Kay Cannan, "Some Presbyterian Churches in Albemarle County," no. 18, AIV ser., 1983.

111. Home Mission Messenger of West Hanover Presbytery, "History of the Cove Church at Covesville, Virginia," Sept. 1927, SC-VIU; WPA Inventory, "Covesville Presbyterian Church Cemetery"; Ash Nichols, "Church Retains History," *DP*, 12 Feb. 1975; M. Tabb Lynn and Charles M. Watts, "Cove Presbyterian Church," no. 45, SVA ser., 1978; Cannan, "Some Presbyterian Churches"; Robert Boucheron, "Cove Presbyterian Church," *ACHS Bulletin* 11, 4 (Oct.–Nov. 1991): 3–4.

112. Joseph Hathaway Cosby, "A Survey of the Rural Baptist Churches of Albemarle County" (M.A. thesis, UVA, 1937); Vera V. Via, *DP*, 2 June 1955; *DP*, 28 July 1973; MacLeod and Wenger, "Buck Mountain Road Survey," bldg. no. 59.; *DP*, 20 June 1973; Hill and Murphy, "Coursey's Road Survey," bldg. no. 19.

113. LeAnn Pegram, "Vernacular Victorian Churches in Albemarle County," no. 33, AIV ser., 1986.

114. Armistead C. Gordon, *William Fitzhugh Gordon* (New York, 1909), 58–63.

115. For a general discussion of mills, see: Edward P. Hamilton, *The Village Mill in New England*, Old Sturbridge Village Booklet Series, no. 18 (Sturbridge, Mass., 1964); K. Edward Lay, "Mills in the Central Piedmont Region of Virginia," *Echoes of History* 4, 4 (July 1974): 57–64; William Fox, *The Mill* (Boston, 1976); Elmer L. Smith, *Grist Mills* (Lebanon, Pa., 1978); AIV ser.: Craig Farnsworth, "Grinding to a Halt: The Lives of Two Grist Mills in Madison County," no. 63, 1987, Tina Moon, "Woodson's Mill, Lowesville, Nelson County," no. 76, 1988, Dana Heiburg, "Colvin Run Mill," no. 84, 1988, and Silvia Sabadell-Johnson, "Two Mills in Northern Virginia," no. 94, 1988; James Rose and Thomas Taylor, "A. J. Long Mill, Greene County," no. 8, 1973, SVA ser.

116. Edwin Morris Betts, ed., *Thomas Jefferson's Farm Book* (Charlottesville, Va., 1976), 369.

117. Moore, *Albemarle*, 36; AC Order Book, 1744–48: (27 June 1745): 25, (22 Aug. 1745): 45, (26 Sept. 1745): 65, (16 Aug. 1746): 164.

118. William E. Trout III, *The Rivanna Scenic River Atlas* (Lexington, Va., 1992); "Jefferson's Toll Mill," Thacker Papers; Mark E. Reinberger and DeTeel P. Tiller, "Three Notched Road Survey," bldg. no. 111, VRT ser., 1976; Robert L. Hiller, "Jefferson's Shadwell Mill Complex," architectural history study for Prof. William Kelso, UVA, 1981; Amy Elizabeth Bennett, "Jefferson's Manufacturing, Toll Mill and Canal" (Master of Landscape Architecture thesis, UVA, 1981); Robert Weise, "Shadwell Mills," study for Prof. Charles Perdue, UVA, 1991; Beth Ann Cates, "Shadwell Mill," no. 138, AIV ser., 1993.

119. Mutual Assurance Society Policy, John H. Craven and James Dinsmore, 19 Oct. 1812; Feldman, Mickler, and Perdue, "Buck Mountain Road Survey," bldg. no. 97; Brush and Siracuse, "Fredericksburg Road Survey," bldg. no. 25.

120. Jennifer Kramer, "New Life at Walker's Mill," *Architectural Digest* 54 (June 1997): 158–63, 223–24 (in 1995 the conversion of the mill to a personal residence by architect Henry J. Browne garnered a preservation award from the Thomas Jefferson Chapter of the Association for the Preservation of Virginia Antiquities); Ann L. Brush, "Fredericksburg Road Survey," bldg. nos. 35 and 36, VRT ser., 1979; Hill and Murphy, "Coursey's Road Survey," bldg. no. 2; Davis et al., "Staunton and James River Turnpike Survey," bldg. no. 29; Mutual Assurance Society Policies, 6 June 1805, 20 Oct. 1810; Rawlings, *Ante-bellum Albemarle*, 23; Lapsley and Thomsen, "Three Notch'd Road Survey," bldg. no. 24; Jennet E. Dame and Silvia Sabadell, "Brown's Gap Turnpike Survey," bldg. no. 1, VRT ser., 1980.

121. Mutual Assurance Society Policies, 31 Dec. 1801, 24 May 1809, 9 Oct. 1816; Boroughs, Chapman, and King, "James River Road Survey," bldg. no. 15.

122. Mutual Assurance Society Policy, 4 May 1799, 2 Apr. 1803, 15 July 1805, 12 June 1823, 9 May 1833.

123. For a general discussion of ironworks, see Robert A. Rutland, "Men and Iron in the Making of Virginia," *Iron Worker* 40 (Summer 1976): 2–17; Reynolds, "An Account of the Albemarle Ironworks," 38–65; Kay Collins Chretien, *Charlottesville Home*, 13 Jan. 1994; my field research with Thomas T. Brady and William W. Reynolds, 17 Nov. 1990.

124. Elsie Lathrop, "Early American Inns and Taverns," in *An English Traveler in Virginia* (n.p., 1937), 217 (first quote); Woods, *Albemarle*, 39 (second quote).

125. *The Revised Code of the Laws of Virginia* (Richmond, , 1819), 2:279–84.

126. Nathaniel Mason Pawlett, *Historic Roads of Virginia: Albemarle County Road Orders, 1744–1748* (Charlottesville, Va., 1975), 9; Moore, *Albemarle*, 39–40.

127. Mutual Assurance Society Policies, 30 July 1805, 17 Nov. 1810; Carolyn Welton, *Richmond News Leader*, 10 Apr. 1974; Hill and Murphy, "Coursey's Road Survey," bldg. no. 16.

128. Woods, *Albemarle*, 144–45; Rawlings, *Ante-bellum Albemarle*, 90; Wagstaff and Cerrone, "Rockfish Gap Turnpike Survey," bldg. no. 32.

129. Woods, *Albemarle*, 320; Moore, *Albemarle*, 78; Lapsley and Thomsen, "Three Notch'd Road Survey," bldg. no. 59; Jane E. Kimball, "D. S. Tavern," bldg. no. 53, VRT ser., 1979; DP: Richard Prior, 19 Aug. 1979, Rita McWilliams, 28 Aug. 1983.

130. François, duc de La Rochefoucauld-Liancourt, *Travels through the United States of North America* (London, 1799) (quote); Mutual Assurance Society Policies, 1799, 19 July 1805; AC Tax List, 1805; Charles Meredith Rhinelander, "Dick Woods's Road Survey," bldg. no. 21, VRT ser., 1978; Marlene E. Heck and Richard P. Thomsen Jr., NRHP Nomination Form, VDHR.

131. DP, 22 Oct. 1927, 14 Jan. 1928; Rawlings, *Ante-bellum Albemarle*, 4; David A. Maurer, DP, 25 Feb. 1990, 22 Oct. 1927, 14 Jan. 1928; NRHP Nomination Form, VDHR; *Historic Michie Tavern Museum, "A Famous Tavern of the 1700's": Cooking Treasures of the Past* (Charlottesville, Va., 1976); David A. Maurer, DP, 21 Nov. 1996, quoting from Julie L. Horan, *The Porcelain God: A Social History of the Toilet* (Secaucus, N.J., 1996); Chris Kness and Chris Redmann, "Michie Tavern," no. 110, SVA ser., 1997.

132. *Virginia Herald*, 15 Nov. 1824; Robert D. Ward, *An Account of General Lafayette's Visit to Virginia in the Year 1824–25* (Richmond, 1881), 94; Edgar Ewing Brandon, *Lafayette, Guest of the Nation* (Oxford, Ohio, 1957), 3:131; Reinberger and Tiller, "Three Notched Road Survey," bldg. no. 119.

133. Mead, *Historic Homes*, 267–70; DP, 31 Oct. 1903, 25 May 1907; WPA Inventory; Reinberger and Tiller, "Three Notched Road Survey," bldg. no. 117; Brush and Siracuse, "Fredericksburg Road Survey," bldg. no. 1.

134. *Charlottesville Central Gazette*, 4 Jan. 1822; Bell, "Travels in America," 23–36; AC Tax Lists, 1805; Woods, *Albemarle*, 240–42; Edward O. McCue II, "A Jouett Miscellany," MACH

39 (1981): 9–11; Albert E. Walker, ed., *The Daily Progress, Historical and Industrial Magazine* (Charlottesville, Va., 1906), 6.

135. Farm Sale, *Virginia Advocate*, 25 Aug. 1827; Mutual Assurance Society Policies, 16 June 1823, 2 Dec. 1840, 25 Nov. 1846; Woods, *Albemarle*, 194–95.

136. Woods, *Albemarle*, 88; Harold Mopsik, "A History of Private Secondary Education in Charlottesville" (M.A. thesis, UVA, 1936); DP, 23 Jan. 1940, 15 Mar. 1955; Moore, *Albemarle*, 258–61, 319–22, 432–37; David Kessler, DP, 3 May 1987.

137. Gordon, *William Fitzhugh Gordon*, 56–63; Moore, *Albemarle*, 78, 82.

138. John Hammond Moore, "The Ferries of Albemarle," MACH 42 (1984): 1–22; Hening, *Statutes* 5:249, 365; AC Order Books, 25 July, 22 Aug. 1745; Boroughs, Chapman, and King, "James River Road Survey," bldg. no. 8; *Jefferson Journal*, 15 Feb. 1973; DP: Robert Brickhouse, 1 June 1980, Jim Ketcham-Colwill, 11 Mar. 1984.

139. Pawlett, *Albemarle County Roads*, 16; AC Order Book, 22 Oct. 1783.

140. Moore, *Albemarle*, 181, 187; Trout, *Rivanna Scenic River Atlas*; Ronald J. Hansen, DP, 12 Sept. 1994.

141. Boroughs, Chapman, and King, "James River Road Survey," bldg. no. 19; Moore, *Albemarle*, 180–89; Robert Brickhouse, DP, 2 Jan. 1983; T. G. Hobbs Jr., "The James River and Kanawha Canal—Earliest Predecessor of the C.&O.," in Randolph Kean, ed., *The C and O in Central Virginia* (Alderson, W.Va., 1979), 1–2.

II. Thomas Jefferson and His Builders

1. James Parton, *Life of Thomas Jefferson, Third President of the United States* (Boston, 1874), 164–65; *Public Papers of the Presidents of the United States: John F. Kennedy* (Washington, D.C., 1962), 666, quote by John F. Kennedy on receiving an honorary degree at the University of North Carolina, 12 Oct. 1961 (brought to my attention by Ruth Balthaser and source located by Lucia C. Stanton); George Will on PBS series, "Thomas Jefferson," by Ken Burns, 19 Feb. 1997 (quote about Jefferson); Lucia Stanton, DP, 25 Feb. 1994, 9; conversation with Frederick D. Nichols.

2. Karen Lang Kummer, "The Evolution of the Virginia State Capitol, 1779–1965" (Master of Architectural History thesis, UVA, 1981) ; Calder Loth, lecture, UVA, 4 Nov. 1995; Frederick Doveton Nichols and Ralph E. Griswold, *Thomas Jefferson, Landscape Architect* (Charlottesville, Va., 1978), 168 (quote about Maison Carrée); Merrill D. Peterson, *Thomas Jefferson and the New Nation: A Biography* (London, 1970), 341 (quote about "best morsel"); Paul Leicester Ford, ed., *The Writings of Thomas Jefferson* (New York, 1892–94), 1:63–64 (quote about change of order).

3. William Beiswanger, lecture, UVA, 4 Nov. 1995; John F. Kennedy, 1962; James A. Bear Jr., *Jefferson at Monticello* (Charlottesville, Va., 1967), 51 (Jefferson's holdings in Albe-marle County totaled more than 10,000 acres and included four farms: Tufton, Lego, Shadwell, and Pantops).

4. Ford, *Jefferson* 1:64 (quote about Hôtel de Salm); Nichols and Griswold, *Thomas Jefferson*, 168; "First dome" brought to my attention by William Beiswanger, 17 Dec. 1997; James A. Bear Jr., DP, 8 Apr. 1973; Malone, *Jefferson* 3:222 (quote about architecture); Calder Loth, ed., *The Virginia Landmarks Register*, 3d ed. (Charlottesville, Va., 1986), 16.

5. Theresa Stanley and Al Cheatham, "Poplar Forest," no. 12, SVA ser., 1973; Travis McDonald, lecture, UVA, 4 Nov. 1995. For more about Poplar Forest, see Chambers, *Poplar Forest*; Malone, *Jefferson* 6:15.

6. Site plan research by Allan Brown.

7. *Jefferson Himself: The Personal Narrative of a Many-Sided American*, ed. Bernard Mayo (1942; rept. Charlottesville, Va., 1970), 345 (quotes from Jefferson's epitaph); Bicentennial poll of the American Institute of Architects in *AIA Journal* 65 (July 1976): 91 (second quote); Thomas Jefferson to Destutt de Tracy, 26 Dec. 1820, Jefferson Papers (third quote); Thomas Jefferson to J. Correa de Serra, 24 Oct. 1820, ibid. (fourth quote, brought to my attention by Jennings L. Wagoner Jr. at his ODK lecture at UVA, 12 Nov. 1993); Thomas Jefferson to trustees of East Tennessee College, 6 May 1810, ibid. (fifth quote); Peterson, *Thomas Jefferson*, 987 (sixth quote); Thomas Jefferson to Littleton W. Tazewell, 5 Jan. 1805, Jefferson Papers (seventh quote); Thomas Jefferson to Col. Yancey, 6 Jan. 1816 (eighth quote), ibid.

8. Philip Edwards, "Additions and Alternations to the Pavilions of the University of Virginia," study for Nichols, 1984.

9. Isaac Coles to Gen. John Hartwell Cocke, 23 Feb. 1816, Cocke Papers, SC-ViU.

10. Nichols and Griswold, *Thomas Jefferson*, 148–51, 180; Thomas Jefferson to trustees of East Tennessee College, 6 May 1810, Jefferson Papers.

11. Malone, *Jefferson* 6:255; Bear, *Jefferson at Monticello*, 31; Robert E. Simpson, "The Cornerstone Laying of Central College, October 6th, 1817," *Virginia Masonic Herald*, Feb. 1977, 8–9, 13–14.

12. Russell Martin, "Thomas Jefferson and Edmund Bacon: Two American Farmers," MACH 50 (1992): 1–27; Bear, *Jefferson*, 32–33, 70 (quotes).

13. *Fredericksburg Virginia Herald*, 15 Nov. 1824; Ward, *Lafayette's Visit to Virginia*, 94; Brandon, *Lafayette, Guest of the Nation*, 3:131; Malone, *Jefferson* 6:408.

14. J. Murray Howard, lecture, UVA, 4 Nov. 1995.

15. Kenny Lucas, DP, 30 May 1998.

16. Recollections of Prof. John A. G. Davis as recalled by his son, Rev. Dabney C. T. Davis, in the *Alumni Bulletin* 4, 4 (Feb. 1898): 115, SC-ViU.

17. Recent discoveries brought to my attention by the architect for the Lawn, Murray Howard, 26 Aug. 1996; *Envision: The Campaign for the University of Virginia* 4, 1 (Spring 1997): 1;

Jefferson to B. Henry Latrobe, 28 Feb. 1804, quoted in Chambers, *Poplar Forest*, 47–48.

18. At graduation ceremonies on 18 May 1997, the suspended balcony of Pavilion I collapsed, killing one person and injuring eighteen. In 1870 the court floor of Jefferson's Richmond Capitol collapsed into the assembly hall below, killing sixty-two people. Ian Zack and Patrick Hickerson, *DP*, 19, 20 May 1997; Dan Heuchert, *Inside UVA*, 30 May 1997, 1–2; *C-ville Weekly*, 20–26 May 1997.

19. For a general discussion of Jefferson's workmen, see: William B. O'Neal and Frederick D. Nichols, "An Architectural History of the First University Pavilion," *MACH* 15 (1955–56): 36–43; William B. O'Neal, "The Workmen at the University of Virginia, 1817–1826," ibid., 17 (1958–59): 5–48; William B. O'Neal, *Jefferson's Buildings at the University of Virginia: The Rotunda* (Charlottesville, Va., 1960); Richard Charles Cote, "The Architectural Workmen of Thomas Jefferson in Virginia" (Ph.D. diss., Boston University, 1986); K. Edward Lay, "Charlottesville's Architectural Legacy," *MACH* 46 (May 1988): 31–53; K. Edward Lay, "Dinsmore and Neilson: Jefferson's Master Builders," *Colonnade: The News Journal of the University of Virginia School of Architecture* 6 (Spring 1991): 9–13; K. Edward Lay, "Jefferson's Master Builders," *UVA Alumni News* 80 (Oct. 1991): 16–19; Frank E. Grizzard Jr., "Documentary History of the Construction of the University of Virginia, 1817–1828" (electronic diss., UVA, 1996).

20. Edwin Morris Betts, *Thomas Jefferson's Garden Book, 1766–1824* (1944; rept. Philadelphia, 1981), 245; James Dinsmore to Thomas Jefferson, 27 Mar. 1819, Jefferson Papers; Proctor's Papers, 21 Aug. 1821 (box 2), SC-ViU (such concerns continued in the 1820s, when a blacksmith was recommended to the university's proctor "provided he doesn't indulge himself with the Stager weed" [D. C. Hutchinson to Brockenbrough, 21 Aug. 1821, ibid., recommending a Mr. Leonard]); Thomas Jefferson to nephew Peter Carr, 7 Sept. 1814, Jefferson Papers.

21. John Parham to Nelson Barksdale, 23 Mar. 1819, and E. W. Hudnall to Thomas Jefferson, 26 Mar. 1819, Jefferson Papers; advertisement bills, 1819, Proctor's Papers (box 1); Thomas Jefferson and John Hartwell Cocke to Thomas Cooper, 15 Oct. 1819, Jefferson Papers.

22. Thomas Jefferson to James Dinsmore, 13 Apr. 1817, Jefferson Papers.

23. WPA, Pennsylvania Historical Commission, *Index to Records of Aliens' Declarations and/or Oaths of Allegiance, 1789–1880* (n.p., 1941), 107; *Virginia Advocate*, 14 May 1830; Jefferson Account Books, 13 June 1798, 24 Oct. 1798, SC-ViU; Thomas Jefferson to Benjamin H. Latrobe, 11 May 1815, Jefferson Papers; Thomas Jefferson and James Dinsmore, 1806–10, passim, ibid.; Mesick, Cohen, and Waite, "Report on Poplar Forest, Phase III," July 1994; Thomas Jefferson to James Madison, 19 Apr. 1809, Jefferson Papers; Conover Hunt-Jones, *Dolley and the "Great Little Madison"* (Washington,

D.C., 1977), 59–74; according to Ann L. B. Miller, 17 Nov. 1992, personal interview, a painting of the house and tempietto by Dr. William Thornton exists, suggesting that Thornton probably designed the garden temple at Montpelier with Dinsmore and Neilson, the builders; Mutual Assurance Society Policy, 1812; AC Deed Books 17:359, 19:444.

24. Thomas Jefferson to B. Henry Latrobe, 11 May 1815 (first quote), Latrobe to Jefferson, 12 July 1815 (second quote, brought to my attention by Charles E. Brownell), James Dinsmore to Thomas Jefferson, 22 Apr. 1817 (brought to my attention by James E. Wootten), Jefferson Papers.

25. AC Deed Books 21:222, 533, 23:235, 342ff., 24:405, 25:42ff., 73, 206, 254, 303, 358, 29:86; old photograph of Peter Heiskell house brought to my attention by Howard Newlon; AC Deed Books 21:302, 26:381; Mary Rawlings, *Early Charlottesville: Recollections of James Alexander, 1828–1874* (Charlottesville, Va., 1942), 78; AC Deed Books 24:16, 29:86.

26. "Oak Lawn," paper by students for Prof. Matthias E. Kayhoe, UVA, 1979; Proctor's Ledgers, SC-ViU; Langhorne, Lay, and Rieley, *Virginia Family*, 74–93; AC, Chancery Court, 1830, possible courthouse connection brought to my attention by Don Swofford, 5 Apr. 1998.

27. *Virginia Advocate*, 14 and 28 May 1830, which describe Andrew's suicide in explicit, lurid detail; Rawlings, *Early Charlottesville*, 78, writes that he drowned at Orange Dale; M. F. Clark noted in Jan. 1986 that an account also appeared in *Virginia Advocate*, 29 Oct. 1830 (no known copy exists); Leonard Allison Morrison, *Dinsmoor-Dinsmore Family* (Lowell, Mass., 1891), 3–4, 13–16, brought to my attention by Robert S. Dinsmore, Sacramento, Calif., 1993.

28. AC Will Books 10:109, 12:191; AC Deed Book 29:76; Rawlings, *Early Charlottesville*, 78. John Dinsmore, a naturalized citizen, was a surveyor in Opelousas, Louisiana Territory, probably in connection with the Louisiana Purchase. James Dinsmore had five sisters: Mrs. James Neil, Margaret Hays, and Hannah McElhose, all of Northern Ireland; Rachael Hunter of Pennsylvania; and Jane Small of Ohio (Andrew Leitch to Samuel Dinsmore, 23 Feb. 1831, George Carr Papers, SC-ViU).

29. *Virginia Advocate*, 1 Oct. 1830, 3.

30. Mesick, Cohen, and Waite, "Poplar Forest."

31. U.S. Census, Schedule of Inhabitants, AC, 1820; WPA, *Index to Records of Aliens' Declarations*, 20; Richard R. Madden, *The United Irishmen: Their Lives and Times*, 2d ser. (Dublin, 1858), 1:336–38, cited in Michael Durey, *Transatlantic Radicals and the Early American Republic* (Lawrence, Kans., 1997), 171, 200 (brought to my attention by Kevin Donleavy, 16 Jan. and 19 Aug. 1998); Thomas Jefferson to B. Henry Latrobe, 11 May 1815, to James Madison, 19 Apr. 1809 (Jefferson wrote that Neilson could help Dolley Madison in "anything there which interests her in the gardening way. He is a gardener by nature and extremely attached to it"), Jefferson Papers; Peter Hodson, "The Design and Building of Bremo, 1815–1820" (Master

of Architectural History thesis, UVA, 1967), 26 n.119. A cornerstone document credits him as "John Neilson of Albemarle Architect."

32. Stephen William Johnson, *Rural Economy* (New Brunswick, N.J., 1806).

33. Proctor's Ledgers; Margaret Fowler Clark, "Albemarle Anecdotes, XVI: The John Neilson House," *[Crozet] Bulletin* 4, 47 (8–14 Sept. 1982): 3; AC Deed Book 27:43, 62, 67.

34. Woods, *Albemarle*, 294ff.; AC Deed Books 25:65, 27:183; Andrew Leitch to Mary Ann McCracken, 7 July 1827, and to Thomas Neilson, 29 Aug. 1827, George Carr Papers, estate settlement accounts brought to my attention by Margaret Fowler Clark.

35. AC Will Book 9:205 (Neilson's friend Mary Ann McCracken; Kevin Donleavy, in a communication with me on 3 Oct. 1997, stated that she was the sister of Henry McCracken, who was hanged during the 1798 rebellion in Ulster); AC Inventory Book 9:269; Andrew Leitch to Thomas Neilson, 29 Aug. 1827, George Carr Papers.

36. Probably Latrobe's original drawings, the one of the Capitol (1806) now located in the Library of Congress, brought to my attention by Charles E. Brownell, 18 Mar. 1991; Andrew Leitch to Mary Neilson, 20 Apr. 1830, and to Thomas Neilson, 29 Aug. 1827, George Carr Papers. In 1830 the portrait was sent through Roseanna Gorman, widow of the university stonemason, Irishman John Gorman, to Neilson's widow, then living in Belfast.

37. Richard Cote also noted that the renderings attributed to Randolph were in fact executed by Neilson in D. Penrice, "Jeffersonian Architecture," *Bostonia*, July–Aug. 1985: 33; Hodson, "Bremo," 26.

38. The original study for the Maverick engraving is probably the "ground plans" listed in Neilson's inventory and noted by Frederick D. Nichols in William Howard Adams, ed., *The Eye of Jefferson* (Washington, D.C., 1976), 285; Joseph C. Cabell to Thomas Jefferson, 18 July, 6 Aug. 1823, John Neilson to Thomas Jefferson, 5 May 1823 (quote), Jefferson Papers; John Neilson to Gen. John Hartwell Cocke, 22 Feb. 1823, Cocke Papers (brought to my attention by C. Allan Brown, 18 July 1988); Proctor's Papers, 1822, box 3 (modillion sketch).

39. U.S. Census, Schedule of Inhabitants, Botetourt County, 1810; AC Order Book, 7 May 1821: 424; Mesick, Cohen, and Waite, "Poplar Forest"; Jefferson Account Books; Thomas Jefferson to Hugh Chisholm, 31 Aug. 1817 (Jefferson had noted earlier that Lynchburg had better workmen than Charlottesville), to Arthur Brockenbrough, 17 Aug. 1819, Jefferson Papers; Proctor's Papers, 17 July 1826 (Gorman apparently had his problems, however; the proctor suggested, "If Gorman does not keep sober discharge him promptly"); Proctor's Ledgers.

40. AC Order Book, 7 May 1821: 424; AC Deed Books, 21:222 (1818), 25:73, 77 (1825), 40:241 (1842); *Virginia Advocate*, 25 Aug. 1827, 16 Feb. 1828, 10 Sept. 1830.

41. U.S. Census, Schedule of Inhabitants, AC, 1810, 1820; Mesick, Cohen, and Waite, "Poplar Forest"; Marshall Bullock to S. Allen Chambers Jr., 15 Apr. 1994, in my collection; inventory brought to my attention by S. Allen Chambers Jr., Thomas Ledford, and Travis McDonald in 1993 and 24 Jan. 1995.

42. Woods, *Albemarle*, 294; AC Tax Lists, 1816; N. B. Jones, "A List of Manufacturers," *MACH* 10 (1950): 25; Philip Alexander Bruce, *History of the University of Virginia*, 5 vols. (New York, 1920), 1:171ff.; U.S. Census, Schedule of Inhabitants, AC, 1820; James Leitch Store Day Book, SC-ViU.

43. Malone, *Jefferson* 6:262; correspondence between Thomas Jefferson and James Dinsmore, 13, 22 Apr. and 25 June 1817, SC-ViU; Cote, "Workmen," 148 (a contract for the brickwork of a pavilion and other university buildings was included in Perry's sale agreement for Monroe Hill); George Wilson Spooner Jr. to Arthur S. Brockenbrough, 13 Aug. 1819, Charles E. Moran Jr. private papers (Perry diverted several windowpanes from the university to Montebello); Proctor's Ledgers.

44. P. P. Barbour Papers and Account Books, Virginia Historical Society, Richmond; Woods, *Albemarle*, 294 (the church contract was made on 1 Dec. 1827, according to church historian Robert E. Simpson); AC Deed Book 32:459; Woods, *Albemarle*, 295; Thomas Jefferson's Inventory, 7 Aug. 1826, Jefferson Papers, SC-ViU; WPA Inventory; Workers of the Writer's Program of the WPA in the State of Virginia, comp., *Jefferson's Albemarle: A Guide to Albemarle County and to the City of Charlottesville, Virginia* (Charlottesville, Va., 1941), 96–97.

45. Proctor's Ledgers; Bruce, *History* 1:253. Carter, who was born c. 1779, had at least two sons and five daughters and in 1850 was married to Fannie A. Carter, twenty-six years his junior. He had been married at least once and perhaps twice before: U.S. Census, Schedule of Inhabitants, Henrico County, 1850; Michael E. Pollock, comp., *Marriage Bonds of Henrico County, Virginia, 1782–1853* (Baltimore, 1984), 31, 80, 134, 141, 176.

46. U.S. Census, Schedule of Inhabitants, AC, 1820; Jefferson Account Books; Thomas Jefferson and Hugh Chisholm, 1806–18, Jefferson Papers; Hunt-Jones, *Dolley*, 59–74; Mesick, Cohen, and Waite, "Poplar Forest"; AC Deed Book 21:154; Proctor's Papers, 8 Mar. 1823.

47. Proctor's Papers, 22 June 1819, box 1; Robert Mills to Thomas Jefferson, 20 Mar. 1819, Thomas Cooper to Thomas Jefferson, 18 Apr. 1819, Thomas Jefferson to Proctor, 17 May 1819, Thomas Jefferson and John H. Cocke to Thomas Cooper, 15 Oct. 1819, Jefferson Papers; Proctor's Ledgers.

48. U.S. Census, Schedule of Inhabitants, AC, 1850; AC Deed Book 23:87; "King George County Marriages," *Virginia Magazine of History and Biography* 22 (1914): 311; Proctor's Papers, 9 and 13 Aug. 1819, box 1; William Lindsay Norford, *Marriages of Albemarle County, 1781–1929* (Charlottesville, Va., 1956); Woods, *Albemarle*, 295; Department of Community

Development, *Historic Landmark Study [Charlottesville]* (Charlottesville, Va., 1976), 176; Bruce, *History* 1:171, 253, 3:27, 193; Proctor's Ledgers; O'Neal, *Pictorial History*, 54.

49. Vestry Minutes, 1838–95, Christ Church, Charlottesville, sc-viu; Burnley, *Court House*, 9; Lane, *Virginia*, 217; ac Tax Lists, 1837; ac Deed Books 28:269, 36:326; U.S. Census, Schedule of Inhabitants, ac, 1860.

50. U.S. Census, Schedule of Inhabitants, ac, 1850; gravestone inscription, Maplewood Cemetery, Charlottesville; Turner to "Whom It May Concern," 31 Aug. 1818, Jefferson Papers (Phillips had also lived in Charlottesville briefly, from 1802 to 1804); Proctor's Ledgers, 1817–22, 142, 145; Thomas Jefferson's recommendation for William B. Phillips, 16 Dec. 1823, Jefferson Papers.

51. Scott and Wyper, "Christ Church Glendower," 4; Ann L. Miller, *Antebellum Orange* (Orange, Va., 1988), 119–20; *Orange Observer*, 20 July 1888 (brought to my attention by Ann L. B. Miller, 22 Feb. 1996); Phillips's work at Sweet Springs brought to my attention by Calder Loth and S. Allen Chambers Jr. from information uncovered by Agnes E. Gish; *DP*, 13 Nov. 1994; John Kelley, 5 Apr. 1830, Bishop John Early Papers, Randolph-Macon College Archives, Ashland, Va.

52. ac Tax Lists, 1825, 1837, 1840; ac Deed Books 27:92, 28:245, 410, 29:388, 36:38, 41:230, 50:476, 51:535 (Phillips owned lots 11, 12, 13, 14, 20, 22, 29, 43, 44, 47, 77, 78); *Virginia Advocate*, 9 July 1830, 3, 5 Nov. 1830, 3; Woods, *Albemarle*, 296; U.S. Census, Schedule of Inhabitants, ac, 1850; ac, Miscellaneous Papers Index, 1861, Albemarle County Circuit Clerk's Office, Charlottesville. Phillips died 24 Apr. 1861. His gravestone inscription reads: "His mortal remains here lie buried by the side of his beloved wife who preceded him only a few years to the [*illegible word*] of spirits. An affectionate husband, a kind father, an upright citizen, and a consistent Christian, he passed from Earth and calmly fell asleep in Jesus in the hope of a blissful Immortality." Nothing is said of his work at the university or throughout the state.

53. U.S. Census, Schedule of Inhabitants, ac, 1850; Norford, *Marriages*; ac Miscellaneous Papers Index, 1862, Albemarle County Circuit Clerk's Office. A John Toole portrait of Widderfield in his carpenter's shop was recently acquired from 1740 Antiques (brought to my attention by Sara Lee Barnes, Jan. 1995).

54. U.S. Census, Schedule of Inhabitants, ac, 1850; Proctor's Ledgers; Proctor Brockenbrough to Joseph C. Cabell, 1822, Jefferson Papers, brought to my attention by Robert Self, 1993; Crawford owned town lot 66 in 1823, ac Deed Book; Woods, *Albemarle*, 261; William Wallace Scott, *A History of Orange County, Virginia, from Its Formation in 1734 to the End of Reconstruction in 1870* (Richmond, 1907), 204f; U.S. Census, Schedule of Inhabitants, Orange County, 1850; Jefferson Account Books, 20 Aug. 1802; Scott, *History of Orange County, Virginia*, 204–5.

55. U.S. Census, Schedule of Inhabitants, New Kent County, 1820; ac Marriage Record, 14 July 1825; ac Will Book 17:37; ac Miscellaneous Papers Index, c. 1845, Albemarle County Circuit Clerk's Office; ac Deed Books 23:235, 25:358, 58:565; ac Tax Lists, 1825; U.S. Census, Schedule of Inhabitants, ac, 1850.

56. Thomas Jefferson to Col. John Harvie, 27 Sept. 1804, correspondence between Thomas Jefferson and James Oldham, 17 and 24 Dec. 1804, 11 Jan. 1805, 15 June 1818, Jefferson Papers; William P. Palmer, ed., *Calendar of State Papers and Other Manuscripts Preserved in the Capitol at Richmond*, 11 vols. (1875–93; rept. New York, 1968), 10:60; Cote, "The Architectural Workmen," 104–5; Proctor's Ledgers.

57. Bruce, *History* 1:277ff.; Thomas Jefferson to Joseph C. Cabell, 4 Feb. 1823, Jefferson Papers (quote); see also Board of Visitors Minutes, 7 Apr. 1823, sc-viu; Woods, *Albemarle*, 292; Grizzard, "Documentary History of the Construction of the Buildings at the University of Virginia"; W. Mac. Jones, comp., "Marriage Bonds from Records of Hustings Court, Richmond, Va.," *Virginia Magazine of History and Biography* 34 (1928): 169; Woods, *Albemarle*, 292; *Virginia Advocate*, 14 May 1829. Some years after his employment by Jefferson, while operating Oldham's Ordinary, Oldham shot a neighbor's son, but he was vindicated.

58. Correspondence with Marshall Bullock, Chapel Hill, N.C., 22 Apr. 1985; Dabney Cosby Account Book, Virginia Historical Society; J. S. Carpenter, "History of the Cosby Family," 1860, manuscript in private hands brought to my attention by James Cosby; U.S. Census, Schedule of Inhabitants, Augusta County, 1810, 1820, Prince Edward County, 1830; Proctor's Ledgers; Proctor's Papers.

59. Proctor's Papers, 8 Feb. and 31 Mar.; Carpenter, "Cosby"; U.S. Census, Schedule of Inhabitants, Augusta County, 1820.

60. Dabney Cosby Account Book, Virginia Historical Society; U.S. Census, Schedule of Inhabitants, Prince Edward County, 1830; Catherine W. Bishir et al., *Architects and Builders in North Carolina* (Chapel Hill, N.C., 1990), 147–51, 158–63, 179–85; Bishir, *North Carolina Architecture* (Chapel Hill, N.C., 1990), 195, 242, 244.

61. Jefferson Account Books, 4 Sept. 1819; Proctor's Ledgers.

62. Correspondence with Brian R. Bricknell of England, 20 June 1987; Brian R. Bricknell, "William John Coffee, 1773–c.1846, Modeller, Sculptor, Painter, and Ornamentalist: His Career in America, 1817–c.1846," 17 Aug. 1993, copy in my possession; Jefferson Account Books, 1823, p. 929; correspondence between Thomas Jefferson and William J. Coffee, 1823, Jefferson Papers; Proctor's Papers, 19 Apr. 1823.

63. Proctor's Ledgers.

64. Lester J. Cappon, "Lucy Selina's Charcoal Era," *Virginia Cavalcade* 7 (Autumn 1957): 31–39; L. M. Sims, "John Jordan, Builder and Entrepreneur," ibid., 23 (Summer 1973): 19–29; Patricia Sherwood, "John Jordan," no. 78, aiv ser.,

1988; U.S. Census, Schedule of Inhabitants, Rockbridge County, 1850; Sims, "John Jordan," 20, 29; Jefferson Account Books; James Dinsmore to Thomas Jefferson, 3 Jan. 1806, Jefferson to Dinsmore, 31 May 1807, Jefferson Papers,; AC Order Book, 1803: 226, 233.

65. Cappon, "Lucy Selina's Charcoal Era," 31–39; Sims, "John Jordan," 19–29; Thomas Dolan, personal research and observations on Belmont, Charlottesville, 1985.

66. Woods, *Albemarle*, 182–83; correspondence with Ruby Talley Smith, Baltimore, 1985–94; correspondence with Marilyn B. Roberts, Davis, Calif., 1992–94; AC Will Book 23:370; AC Inventory Book, 10 Aug. 1855. John Dunkum's first wife was Elizabeth Brown Dunkum, whom he married on 15 Dec. 1806. They had the following children: Elizabeth B.; Jane B., who married Theodore Norton Sellars and lived in Rockingham; James D.; Martha, who married William Pitts; Mary S., who married Chester Ballard; Sarah Ann, who married Philip Edge of Bundoran Farm; and John.

67. Woods, *Albemarle*, 182–83; correspondence with Ruby Talley Smith, Baltimore, 1985–94; correspondence with Marilyn B. Roberts, Davis, Calif., 1992–94; Rawlings, *Early Charlottesville*, 35–36; AC Will Book 17:445, Inventory Book, 20 Aug. 1846; William B. O'Neal, *Primitive into Painter* (Charlottesville, Va., 1960). William Dunkum's first wife was Phebe Anderson, whom he married in 1805. They had the following children: John Anderson; William Lewis; Chesley, who married Amelia Drusilla Wallace; Elijah, who married Elizabeth Ficklin; James T.; Frances E., who married Jesse L. Fry; Martha Catharine, who married John H. Barksdale of Pleasant Hill; Mary Ann, who married Lewis Sowell; Mary J., who married William Hines Durrett; Susan A., who married James Ralls Abell; and Elizabeth, who married Philip Edge (his second wife). The Thacker house, built on Wingfield property, first was called Midvale (brought to my attention by Joanne Thacker, 26 June 1998).

68. Sarah L. Favrao, Peter Sanbeck, and Louise D. Weller, "117 Cream Street," no. 25, SVA ser., 1975; Kevin Murphy and Peter Sanbeck, "117 Cream Street," study for Kayhoe, 1975.

III. THE ROMAN REVIVAL (1800–1830)

1. Calder Loth, "Jefferson's Failure to Overcome Pain," lecture at Architectural History Symposium, School of Architecture, UVA, 1993. Publications of William Pain (1730–1790) included *Carpenter's and Joiner's Repository*, *Practical House Carpenter*, and *British Palladio*.

2. Elisabeth Donaghy Garrett, "The American Home: Part I," *Antiques* 123 (Jan. 1983): pl. 8 and n. 57.

3. Langhorne, Lay, and Rieley, *Virginia Family*, 32.

4. Dwellings with molded-brick cornices include Bentivar, Brookhill, Butler-Norris town house, Cherry Valley, Headquarters, Linden Farm, Mount Armour, Piedmont (Wallace house), Pomegranate, and Valley Point Farm, as well as Castiglione Tavern.

5. Moore, *Albemarle*, 36; Pawlett, *Albemarle County Roads*, 104.

6. Frederick D. Nichols, "Jefferson: The Making of an Architect," in *Jefferson and the Arts: An Extended View*, ed. William Howard Adams (Washington, D.C., 1976), 171.

7. Parke Rouse, *Planters and Pioneers* (New York, 1988), 127; Jackson T. Main, "The One Hundred," *William and Mary Quarterly*, 3d ser., 11 (July 1954): 355–84. AC Tax Lists, 1782. Carter controlled the largest acreage with 9,700 acres, followed by Nicholas with 7,500. Carter also had the most slaves, 242, followed by Jefferson with 129 and Nicholas with 120. All the rest had fewer than 100 slaves, but there was not a single personal property tithable that did not own at least one slave. Carter, too, had the most head of cattle, 198, while Jefferson was next with 106. And Carter boasted the most horses and mules with 62, while John Coles II was next with 45. But Jefferson had the most carriage wheels, with only eight others claiming any at all, while no one admitted to owning a billiard table. John Scott, the son of Edward Scott, married Margaret, daughter of Col. Joshua Fry. Col. John Walker married Elizabeth, daughter of Bernard Moore and granddaughter of Governor Spotswood. Margaret Douglass Meriwether was the daughter of the Rev. William Douglass. She later married Charles Terrill. Moore, *Albemarle*, 84.

8. *MACH* 1:11; AC Tax Lists, 1787. John Wilkinson, an absentee landlord, was next in acreage, followed by the Robert Carter Nicholas estate at Warren and Dr. Thomas Walker of Castle Hill. Wilkinson, as manager, together with Walker, Edward Carter, William Cabell, and Alexander Trent, had established the Albemarle Iron Works in 1770. Jefferson of Monticello had the next highest number of slaves, 80, followed by Walker and John Coles of Enniscorthy with 75 each. William Marks and William Michie (son of John Michie, who purchased the land from Maj. John Henry, father of Patrick Henry) on Buck Mountain Road each had ordinary licenses, while two were physicians: James Hopkins (son of Dr. Arthur Hopkins), who eventually settled in Nelson County and was murdered in 1803, and Walker of Castle Hill. Wilson Cary Nicholas was governor of Virginia from 1814 to 1816. AC Tax Lists, 1800: John Coles II was closely followed by Maj. Francis Walker of Castle Hill with 63 slaves and 6,522 acres. John Scott of Belle Grove was the fourth-wealthiest person but with about half the wealth of the last two. He did have the second highest number of horses with 35 and the fifth-highest number of slaves at 44. But Capt. Thomas Walker of Keswick boasted the highest-valued real estate. Jefferson of Monticello with the second most slaves at 64 was the fifth-wealthiest person, largely from his personal property value. These wealthiest men were followed by George Divers of Farmington, Col. John Walker of Belvoir, and John Henderson of Glenmore. Nine ordinary licenses were issued in the county in 1800 with

Capt. Edward Moore of Crutchfield listed as the wealthiest tavern keeper. Information about real estate value was brought to my attention by Robert Carter Jr. of Redlands, 16 Apr. 1994.

9. AC Tax Lists, 1805, 1815. In 1815, of the 6,288 slaves in the county, Jefferson had the most with 102, followed by John Harris (son of William and Mary Netherland Harris) of Viewmont with 77, Hugh Nelson (minister to Spain, son of Gov. Thomas Nelson, grandson of Pres. William Nelson, and husband of Elizabeth, daughter of Francis Kinloch) of Belvoir with 73, George Divers of Farmington with 64, and Mary Eliza Coles Carter (1776–1856) of Redlands with 61. Only thirty-five African Americans were "free Negroes." The county listed 4,665 horses and 11,198 head of cattle. John Harris of Viewmont recorded the highest number of horses with 39 and the most head of cattle, 138. The next highest numbers of head of cattle were the Francis Walker estate and Daniel Scott's Belle Grove with 105 each, followed by Dabney Minor's Brookhill at Hydraulic with 104. Both James Old and James Powell Cocke operated toll bridges, Jefferson had a private bridge, and Joseph Bishop operated a tanyard in Vinegar Hill just west of Charlottesville. Farmington had the highest house value, $9,000 (but for six buildings); with Monticello next at $7,500, followed by John Patterson's Oakland (Donegal) at $5,000, Carrsbrook at $4,000, Belvoir and Redlands each at $3,500, and Reuben Lindsay's Springfield at $3,100 (for two dwellings). Valued at $3,000 were Samuel Dyer's Plain Dealing, John Watson's Little Mountain, James Powell Cocke's Edgemont, Rebecca Elizabeth Tucker Coles's Enniscorthy, Benjamin Harris's Mountain Grove, and William Morris's Stony Point. In the $2,000 range were Charles Yancey's Cedars Tavern, James Ross's Blenheim, Tucker Coles's Tallwood, Lewis Nicholas's Alta Vista, William Woods's Woodville (could be Woodstock Hall), and Craven Peyton's Mount Eagle.

10. Elizabeth Coles Langhorne, *Monticello: A Family Story* (Chapel Hill, N.C., 1987), 6; AC Tax Lists, 1815. Nathaniel Anderson married Sarah, sister of Dabney Carr, who married Jefferson's sister. According to the Thomas Jefferson Memorial Foundation, Monticello comprised 960 acres out of Jefferson's total of 5,000 acres on his five farms, as well as 100 slaves, in 1809.

11. AC Tax List, 1820. Elijah May's tavern was followed by James Powell Cocke's Edgemont at $10,000, Dr. Charles Cocke's Esmont at $8,700, and Robert Rives's Boiling Springs at $8,000. Valued in the $6,000 range were John H. Craven's Pen Park, Jesse Joplin's River Lawn at Warren, William Moon's Stony Point near Scottsville, and Nelson Nicholas's Mount Warren. In the $5,000 range were Hugh Nelson's Belvoir, William Cabell Rives's Castle Hill, Samuel Dyer's Plain Dealing, and Bernard Brown Jr.'s Pleasant Retreat in Brown's Cove. Four were in the $4,000 range: Joseph Bishop's two-story dwelling with portico built by William Dunkum

after 1803, the first brick house on Vinegar Hill in Charlottesville; Reuben Lindsay's Springfield; Mary Eliza Coles Carter's Redlands; and Andrew Hart's Sunny Bank. See also Woods, *Albemarle*, 144; Rawlings, *Early Charlottesville*, 95. Bishop married Jane Terrill, daughter of Edmund and Margaret Willis Terrill, granddaughter of the founder of Fredericksburg, and a descendant of the Washington family.

12. Rawlings, *Ante-bellum Albemarle*, 40; Barbara Hume Church, Michael Francis Conner, and Drucilla Gatewood Haley, "Secretary's Road Survey," bldg. no. 47, VRT ser., 1976.

13. Mutual Assurance Society Policies, 1802, 1805; Gillian Meredith Goodwin, "Piedmont and Meadowbrook," no. 145, AIV ser., 1994.

14. Lapsley and Thomsen, "Three Notch'd Road Survey," bldg. no. 31; Rawlings, *Ante-bellum Albemarle*, 69; Feldman, Mickler, and Perdue, "Buck Mountain Road Survey," bldg. no. 88.

15. Woods, *Albemarle*, 318; WPA Inventory; Claire Welch, "Road to Secretary's Mill," bldg. no. 10, VRT ser., 1979; Anne Richardson, *DP*, 2 Sept. 1979; Rhinelander, "Dick Woods's Road Survey," bldg. no. 16.

16. Lapsley and Thomsen, "Three Notch'd Road Survey," bldg. no. 51; Cornelius Means, "Fielding Historical Data" and "Abstract of Title," 1976, private collection.

17. George Sheldon Wallace, *Wallace: Genealogical Data* (Charlottesville, Va., 1927); Papers of the Wallace Family, 1780–1888, MSS 38–150, SC-VIU; Rawlings, *Ante-bellum Albemarle*, 92; Geoffrey Henry, NRHP Nomination Form, VDHR; Goodwin, "Piedmont and Meadowbrook"; Eugenia Bibb, "Charlottesville Landmark Survey," Department of Community Development, Charlottesville.

18. Mutual Assurance Society Policies, 1802, 1816, 1823; Victoria LaFon Ballard, "Edgehill," no. 144, AIV ser., 1994; Davis et al., "Staunton and James River Turnpike Survey," bldg. no. 4.

19. Davis et al., "Staunton and James River Turnpike Survey," bldg. no. 2; Stevens, *House Tour*, 118; Hill and Murphy, "Coursey's Road Survey," bldg. no. 12.

20. Dan Friedman, *DP*, 27 Nov. 1977; Woods, *Albemarle*, 180–81.

21. Woods, *Albemarle*, 178.

22. *DP*, 17 Dec. 1906; Rawlings, *Ante-bellum Albemarle*, 20; Dan Friedman, *DP*, 19 Feb. 1978; Woods, *Albemarle*, 155–56.

23. Woods, *Albemarle*, 198; WPA Inventory; Dudley and Mackie, "Staunton and James River Turnpike Survey," bldg. no. 46; Robert Kuhlthau, "Gantt-Sutherland History," 1 Nov. 1990, private collection; Ian Zack, *DP*, 14 Nov. 1993.

24. *Map of Albemarle*, Maj. Gen. J. F. Gilmer, Chief Engineer, 1864, Map, Jeremy Francis Gilmer Collection, Virginia Historical Society; *Map of Albemarle County, Virginia*, Jedediah Hotchkiss, Topographical Engineer, Staunton, Nov. 1866, Map, LVA; Woods, *Albemarle*, 318; *DP*, 8 Oct. 1977;

Martha Crabill and Kathryn Kuranda, "Sowell House," no. 50, SVA ser., 1979; correspondence with Cynthia M. Conte, 12, 16 Sept. 1993, 6 May 1994; Christine Jones, "Building Stages of Sowell House," draft, Apr. 1994; correspondence with W. Douglas Gilpin, 3 June 1994.

25. WPA Inventory; Woods, *Albemarle*, 203–4; Rawlings, *Ante-bellum Albemarle*, 45; Wheeler, *Historic Virginia*, 329; Stevens, *House Tour*, 238; Leslie Kuhl and Louise Jones McPhillips, "Darby's Folly," no. 46, SVA ser., 1978.

26. Woods, *Albemarle*, 339; WPA Inventory; Wheeler, *Historic Virginia*, 185–86; C. Alphonso Smith, Mamie A. Richardson, and Mary Rawlins, *Annals of an American Family: . . . the Richardson and Smith Families* (Greensboro, N.C., 1953); Stevens, *House Tour*, 45; Robert Kuhlthau, "Summary of Forest Hill Ownership," 23 Sept. 1986, private collection.

27. Mutual Assurance Society Policies, June 1823, 9 May 1833, 9 Dec. 1853; WPA Inventory.

28. James and Meixner, "Wilhoit Farm."

29. Mutual Assurance Society Policy, 16 June 1823; Woods, *Albemarle*, 358–59; Walker, *The Daily Progress, Historical and Industrial Magazine*, 6; Katherine Kilmer Mahood, "220 Court Square," no. 75, SVA ser., 1982; David A. Maurer, *DP*, 10 Dec. 1995.

30. Rawlings, *Ante-bellum Albemarle*, 57; *DP*: Lisa Gilley, 20 Jan. 1989, Thomas Pelton, 11 Nov. 1989.

31. WPA Inventory.

32. Coons, "Brown"; Rosalie Edith Davis, *The Garth Family: Descendants of John Garth of Virginia, 1734–1986* (Dexter, Mich., 1988); correspondence with Elizabeth Hamilton, May 1997.

33. Moon, "Sketches," 58–59; Davis et al., "Staunton and James River Turnpike Survey," bldg. no. 10; Jeff Seager, *DP*, 15 Nov. 1989; *DP*, 17 Apr. 1991; Timothy and Sandra Small, "Riverview," c. 1991, private collection; Phillip Gregory Russell, "Riverview," no. 139, AIV ser., 1993.

34. WPA Inventory; Carolee Williams, "Wheeler's Road Survey," bldg. no. 13, SVA ser., 1982.

35. *Washington Post*, 22 Dec. 1974; Don A. Swofford, "William Walker House" (Master of Architectural History thesis, UVA, 1976); NRHP Nomination Form, 1990, VDHR; Thomas Pelton, *DP*, 5 Mar. 1990; Boroughs, Chapman, and King, "James River Road Survey," bldg. no. 12.

36. Woods, *Albemarle*, 159–63; Marion Gordon Shaw, "Dabney/Carr Genealogy," brought to my attention by Angela Horan; Mary Winn to Martha Davis, 28 Apr. 1830, Minor-Winston Family Papers, MSS 3750–a, SC-ViU, brought to my attention by Melinda Frierson, 5 Oct. 1995; *DP*, 30 Oct. 1906; Rawlings, *Ante-bellum Albemarle*, 66; Dan Friedman, *DP*, 4 Dec. 1977.

37. First-floor plan dimensions were similar, Bentivar's being 44 by 36 feet while Dunlora was 48 by 40 feet. Mason Bazil Moon, "Dunlora," 1929, private collection; Anna Mary Moon, "Sketches of Moon Family," 1939, pp. 10–11, private collection; *DP*, 21 Apr. 1960; Mary Beverly Dabney and William Minor Dabney, "Memoirs of James Cabell Dabney," *MACH* 48 (1990): 58–105; Tina Eshleman and Sherri Nee, *DP*, 13 Dec. 1993; a drawing indicating Thomas R. Blackburn and William B. Phillips were the builders was brought to my attention by John Wells on 25 Sept. 1998.

38. Tina Papamichael, Hampton Tucker, and Virgilia Whitehead, "Staunton and James River Turnpike Survey," bldg. no. 52, VRT ser., 1991.

39. Woods, *Albemarle*, 306–8; Rawlings, *Ante-bellum Albemarle*, 46; Wheeler, *Historic Virginia*, 336; Stevens, *House Tour*, 244–45; NRHP Nomination Form, VDHR; *DP*: 8 Aug. 1971, 12 Oct. 1978, Dan Friedman, 1 Dec. 1977.

40. MacLeod and Wenger, "Buck Mountain Road Survey," bldg. no. 7; deed search by Richard P. Thomsen Jr. for owner of Rose Valley, private collection; correspondence with S. R. Gay, 16 Nov. 1973.

41. Feldman, Mickler, and Perdue, "Buck Mountain Road Survey," bldg. no. 82; Phillip Neuberg, "Munday House," architectural history study for Prof. Dell Upton, UVA, 1979; Marilyn Muse, *DP*, 24 Feb. 1985; *Albemarle* 28 (June–July 1992): 33–35; Theresa Reynolds, *Charlottesville Home*, 4 Nov. 1993, 10–12; Rhinelander, "Dick Woods's Road Survey," bldg. no. 40; Lapsley and Thomsen, "Three Notch'd Road Survey," bldg. no. 54.

42. Woods, *Albemarle*, 343–44; *DP*, 29 Sept. 1930; WPA Inventory; John W. Williams III, "The White Family in Albemarle County," July 1977, ACHS; Traci Ann Neenan, "Anchorage Farm," no. 159, AIV ser., 1994; Moon, *Sketches*, 17–48; Wheeler, *Historic Virginia*, 352; Neil Lee, *DP*, 18 Nov. 1979; *DP*, 29 June 1993; William Henry Harris III and Ayres Morrison Jr., "Walters-Page House," no. 15, SVA ser., 1973; Papamichael, Tucker, and Whitehead, "Staunton and James River Turnpike Survey," bldg. nos. 61, 61A.

43. Woods, *Albemarle*, 161; Stevens, *House Tour*, 103; Edward W. Hase II and Robert M. Hubbard, "Adolph Russow and the Monticello Wine Company," *MACH* 46 (1988): 19–20; Chris Redmann, "Red Hills," no. 176, AIV ser., 1996.

44. *DP*, 1 Aug. 1930; Coons, "Brown," 47–51; Wheeler, *Historic Virginia*, 250; Stevens, *House Tour*, 296–97.

45. Woods, *Albemarle*, 183–85; Wheeler, *Historic Virginia*, 249; Stevens, *House Tour*, 70; Bill Archer, "Woodland," study for Nichols, 1975; Welch, "Road to Secretary's Mill," bldg. no. 5.

46. *Central Gazette*, 19 Feb. 1825; *Virginia Advocate*, 11 Oct. 1828; *DP*, 14 Jan., 18 Feb. 1899, 17 July 1901; Woods, *Albemarle*, 341; Dan Friedman, *DP*, 9 Oct. 1977; Thomas Roby and Paul Stephens, "Wertland," study for Kayhoe, 1983; *DP*: Jon Sensbach, 6 Feb. 1983, Lane Thomasson, 11 Jan. 1992; Wheeler, *Historic Virginia*, 170; Stevens, *House Tour*, 48; Brush and Siracuse, "Fredericksburg Road Survey," bldg. no. 16.

47. Rawlings, *Ante-bellum Albemarle*, 54; John C. Wyllie, "Information on President James Monroe House and Monroe Hill," n.d., in my possession; Paul Douglas Martins and Lisa Marie Tucker, "Monroe Hill," study for Kayhoe, 1989; George Sidney Ford, "Recollections of the Past," in *From Porch Swings to Patios* (Charlottesville, Va., 1990), 113.

48. Woods, *Albemarle*, 175–76, 279; Rawlings, *Ante-bellum Albemarle*, 50; Calder Loth, "The Farm," study for Nichols, 1965; Robert E. Nalls, "The Farm," study for Nichols, 1975; Jennifer Patsos and Wayne Nelson, "The Farm," no. 130, SVA ser., 1992; Robert Brickhouse, *Inside UVA* 26 (12 July 1995); Robert Brickhouse, *UVA Alumni News*, Winter 1995; Ian Zack, *DP*, 11 Sept. 1995; Ian Zack, *Fredericksburg Free Lance-Star*, 21 Sept. 1995; Ian Zack, *Washington Post*, 23 Sept. 1995; Nancy L. Ross, ibid., 16 Nov. 1995. Its restoration resulted in a preservation award by the Thomas Jefferson Branch of the Association for the Preservation of Virginia Antiquities in 1996.

49. Cornelia Jefferson Randolph to Ellen Wayles Randolph Coolidge, 18 May 1827, Ellen Wayles Randolph Coolidge Papers, SC-VIU; drawing, Museum of Early Southern Decorative Arts, Winston-Salem, N.C.; fossé noted by architect Henry J. Browne, 1994, from earlier excavations; Mead, *Historic Homes*, 65–74; *DP*, 1 July 1893, 10 Nov. 1902, 25 Sept. 1903; Woods, *Albemarle*, 301–3; *Richmond Times-Dispatch*, 6 Mar. 1916; Rawlings, *Ante-bellum Albemarle*, 70; Olivia Taylor, "Edgehill, 1735–1902," *MACH* 30 (1972): 61–67; Reinberger and Tiller, "Three Notched Road Survey," bldg. no. 113; Dan Friedman, *DP*, 1 Sept. 1977; Mary Hughes, "History of the Landscape at Edgehill Farm," landscape architecture study for Prof. Robert Grese, UVA, 1986; Lisa Gilley, *DP*, 1 Apr. 1989; NRHP Nomination Form, VDHR; Ballard, "Edgehill"; drawings for Edgehill and The Farm indicate a Blackburn connection.

50. Rawlings, *Ante-bellum Albemarle*, 25; Stevens, *House Tour*, 60; Davis et al., "Staunton and James River Turnpike Survey," bldg. no. 30.

51. Woods, *Albemarle*, 239–40; Nancy A. Recchie, "John R. Jones House," study for Nichols, 1974; Charles M. Bowen, "John R. Jones House," study for Nichols, 1980.

52. Rawlings, *Ante-bellum Albemarle*, 44; Stevens, *House Tour*, 240; Dan Friedman, *DP*, 13 Nov. 1977; Pierre Crosby, "Brown's Gap Turnpike Survey," bldg. no. 43, VRT ser., 1982; Coons, "Brown," 67–69.

53. *Virginia Advocate*, 24 Sept., 5 Nov., 17 Dec. 1830; Woods, *Albemarle*, 242–44.

54. *DP*, 12 Feb. 1895, 27 June 1903; Woods, *Albemarle*, 277–79; Rawlings, *Ante-bellum Albemarle*, 42; Stevens, *House Tour*, 100; *DP*: Dan Friedman, 24 Nov. 1977, Richard Prior, 22 July 1979.

55. Jennifer Elvgren, *DP*, 17 Nov. 1997. During the year 1997 through September, twenty-two properties sold for more than $1 million each in the adjacent counties of Albemarle, Buckingham, Fluvanna, Greene, Louisa, and Nelson and another six for more than $3 million each. Rawlings, *Ante-bellum Albemarle*, 7; Wheeler, *Historic Virginia*, 243–44; Liz Dalton, *Richmond Times-Dispatch*, 5 May 1960; Rick Kniesler, "Morven and Verulum," study for Nichols, 1976; Edwards, Wenger, and Yetter, "Secretary's Road Survey," bldg. no. 57; DP: Daniel W. Lehman, 16 June 1985, Jane Dunlap Norris, 29 Nov. 1988; *Observer*, 28 Nov.–4 Dec. 1991; Calder Loth to Curry Roberts, 15 Mar. 1993.

56. Elizabeth B. Zeigler, "Esmont House," study for Nichols, 1970; Wayne Nelson, "Esmont," no. 132, AIV ser., 1992; NRHP Nomination Form, VDHR.

57. WPA Inventory; Rawlings, *Ante-bellum Albemarle*, 41; Ron Sibold, "Bel Aire," study for Nichols, 1980.

58. AC Deed Books 10:326 (1791), 16:587 (1808), 18:445 (1813), 20:85 (1816); John Kelly Correspondence, 1812–23, SC-VIU; correspondence, Margaret Fowler Clark with VDHR, 1968, and with me 6 Nov. 1978.

59. Jeff Bushman and Tim Revere, "Norris-McCue House," no. 27, SVA ser., 1976; Woods, *Albemarle*, 140–41; WPA Inventory; Moon, "Sketches," 73–82; Davis et al., "Staunton and James River Turnpike Survey," bldg. no. 6; Lenny Granger, *DP*, 16 Apr. 1978; Brian Ambroziak, Salvatore J. Canciello, and Marc A. Roehrle, "Barclay House," no. 96, SVA ser., 1990, awarded third place in the Peterson Prize Competition of the Historic American Buildings Survey.

60. AC Deed Books 23:343 (1822), 33:499 (1831), 36:424 (1838); AC Tax List, 1827; *Virginia Advocate*, 17 Dec. 1830; *DP*, 22 Mar. 1915; Marsha Glenn, "Livers's House," study for Nichols, 1975; R. Rasmussen, "Livers's House," study for Nichols, 1979; Robert P. Brennan, "Livers's House," study for Kayhoe, 1980; E. Scott Blackwell, "Livers's House," study for Nichols, 1981; Cheryl Hamilton, "Vowles's and Livers's Houses," study for Nichols, 1982; H. Warren Jones, "Livers's House," no. 81, SVA ser., 1983; David Elyea, Tina Moon, and Ken Anderson, "Livers's House," study for Kayhoe, 1989. Most of these studies misidentify the property deeds; the correct text information was conveyed to me by Eugenia Bibb, 15 Mar. 1996.

61. Carl Saladino, "John Vowles's Property," study for Nichols, 1967; Olga Barmine and Stephen Herr, "Vowles's Kitchen," no. 22, SVA ser., 1975; Anne Brewster Gibson, "Vowles's Townhouses," study for Nichols, 1975; J. Steven Frear, "Vowles's Townhouses," study for Nichols, 1980; Hamilton, "Vowles's and Livers's Townhouses," study for Nichols, 1982; Rachel Buchanan, *DP*, 3 Apr. 1989; J. Brian Dillard and Nathaniel Seymour McCormick, "Vowles's Townhouses," no. 103, SVA ser., 1993; Rawlings, *Early Charlottesville*, 108; David Armistead Dashiell III, "Carter-Gilmer House," study for Nichols, 1980; John Orgren, "Carter-Gilmer Outbuilding," study for Nichols, 1981; Pierre Crosby, "Carter-Gilmer House," no. 69, SVA ser., 1982; Rachel Buchanan, *DP*, 29 Dec. 1988; Mutual Assurance Society Policies, 19 Jan. 1797, 3 July 1809, 9 May 1833, 2 Dec. 1840, 25 Nov. 1846,

6 Oct. 1860; Robert Sangine, "Massie-Wills Townhouses," study for Nichols, 1965; Samuel Klingensmith, "Massie-Wills Townhouses," study for Nichols, 1974; David Akinaka and Peter Eckman, "Massie-Wills Townhouses," no. 98, SVA ser., 1993.

62. Mutual Assurance Society Policies, 12 May 1799, 18 July 1803, 18 Oct. 1810; Woods, *Albemarle*, 169–71; *Richmond Times-Dispatch*, 13, 22 Apr. 1938; Rawlings, *Ante-bellum Albemarle*, 22; correspondence between Charles E. Peterson and Milton L. Grigg, 12, 28 July 1950; William C. Allen, "Edgemont Plantation," study for Nichols, 1973; Desmond Guinness and Julius T. Sadler Jr., *Mr. Jefferson, Architect* (New York, 1973), 87–92; Marian Page, *Historic Houses Restored and Preserved* (New York, 1976), 99–105; Dan Friedman, *DP*, 6 Nov. 1977; Davis et al., "Staunton and James River Turnpike Survey," bldg. no. 38; Lenny Granger, *DP*, 11 Mar. 1979; *DP*, 19 Oct. 1980; David A. Maurer, *DP*, 9 Apr. 1992; Jennifer Kramer, "Historic Architecture: Edgemont, a Jeffersonian Riddle in Virginia," *Architectural Digest* 53, 6 (June 1996): 70–78.

63. Woods, *Albemarle*, 235–38; Gene Waddell, "The First Monticello," *Journal of Society of Architectural Historians* 46, 1 (Mar. 1987): 5–29; Ann Lucas, "Conjectural Plan: Monticello, First House and Dependencies," Apr. 1989, Thomas Jefferson Memorial Foundation Archives; Mills Lane, *Architecture of the Old South: Virginia* (Savannah, Ga., 1987).

64. For a more detailed study of Monticello, see Frederick D. Nichols and James A. Bear Jr., *Monticello* (Charlottesville, Va., 1967); William Howard Adams, *Jefferson's Monticello* (New York, 1983); Jack McLaughlin, *Jefferson and Monticello: The Biography of a Builder* (New York, 1988); Susan R. Stein, *The Worlds of Thomas Jefferson and Monticello* (New York, 1993). For the porticoes of Monticello, see John Wayles Eppes to Thomas Jefferson, 16 March 1804, Massachusetts Historical Society; Virginia Randolph to Nicholas Trist, 5 June 1823, Nicholas P. Trist Papers, Library of Congress; Jefferson to Thomas Mann Randolph Jr., Feb. 1796, Jefferson Papers, SC-VIU.

65. *Virginia Advocate*, 22 Mar., 19 July, 13 Dec. 1828.

66. Carter-Smith Papers, SC-VIU; John Coles II Account Books, 1745–1808, SC-VIU; Woods, *Albemarle*, 163–65; William B. Coles, *The Coles Family of Virginia* (New York, 1931); Francis A. Christian, *Homes and Gardens of Old Virginia* (Richmond, 1930), 388–93; Rawlings, *Ante-bellum Albemarle*, 10; B. Noland Carter, "The Carters of Redlands" (1962), private collection; Thacker Papers; Edwards, Wenger, and Yetter, "Secretary's Road Survey," bldg. no. 75; Dru Gatewood Haley, "Redlands" (Master of Architectural History thesis, UVA, 1977); Dan Friedman, *DP*, 31 July 1977; John J. Bernard, "Redlands," no. 91, SVA ser., 1982; Langhorne, Lay, and Rieley, *Virginia Family*, 54–65.

67. "The Autobiography of Mrs. William Cabell Rives", *Autobiography* (1851), private collection; Lewis A. Coffin Jr. and Arthur C. Holden, *Brick Architecture of the Colonial Period in Maryland and Virginia* (New York, 1919), 24; Rawlings, *Ante-bellum Albemarle*, 86; Philip R. Goyert Jr., "Farmington," study for Nichols, 1968; Bernard P. Chamberlain, "Farmington," *MACH* 29 (1971): 7–28; Guinness and Sadler, *Mr. Jefferson*, 83–86; Lapsley and Thomsen, "Three Notch'd Road Survey," bldg. no. 60; "Comments on the Massachusetts Historical Society Book on Jefferson's Drawings," 31 Mar. 1995, shared with me by A. Robert Kuhlthau; A. Robert Kuhlthau, "Summary of the Leigh Property," 20 July 1995, research notes, private collection.

68. Marlene Elizabeth Heck, "Palladian Architecture and Social Change in Post-Revolutionary Virginia" (Ph.D. diss., University of Pennsylvania, 1988); Lane, *Virginia*, 132.

69. Mutual Assurance Society Policies, 30 May 1805, 13 Dec. 1816; Richard Channing Moore Page, *Genealogy of the Page Family in Virginia*, 2d ed. (New York, 1893), 225–27; Mead, *Historic Homes*, 159–66; Woods, *Albemarle*, 288–89; Brush and Siracuse, "Fredericksburg Road Survey," bldg. no. 24.

70. Mutual Assurance Society Policies, 19 Apr., 18 July 1805, 28 Oct., 4 Nov. 1816; Brush, "Fredericksburg Road Survey," bldg. no. 40; Woods, *Albemarle*, 223–24; Rawlings, *Ante-bellum Albemarle*, 24; Bernard Chamberlain, "Sunny Bank Notes," 1974, photocopy in my possession; Jeff Berger, Charles Koch, and Nancy Recchie, "Sunny Bank," no. 16, SVA ser., 1974; NRHP Nomination Form, VDHR; Dudley and Mackie, "Staunton and James River Turnpike Survey," bldg. no. 40A.

71. *Virginia Advocate*, 17 Dec. 1830; photograph, c. 1890, SC-VIU; Sanborn Insurance Maps, Charlottesville, 1896, 1907, 1920, ACHS; Wheeler, *Historic Virginia*, 289; state of Howardsville obtained from my personal observations while a cleanup volunteer at Howardsville after the Nelson County flood from Hurricane Camille, 1969; Orlando Ridout, "An Architectural Survey of Howardsville," architectural history study, UVA, 1976, copy at VDHR.

72. Mutual Assurance Society Policy, 7 July 1812; Woods, *Albemarle*, 159–63; Rawlings, *Ante-bellum Albemarle*, 36; Stevens, *House Tour*, 100–101; Elizabeth Dabney Coleman, "Peter Carr of Carr's-Brook," *MACH* 4 (1943–44): 5–23; Guinness and Sadler, *Mr. Jefferson*, 41–44; *Charlottesville Observer*, June–July 1991, 3, 16.

73. AC Will Book 35:10; Woods, *Albemarle*, 219–22; Boyce Loving, *DP*, 13 Oct. 1966; Anne Carter Lee, "Mountain Grove," study for Nichols, n.d.; *DP*: Richard Prior, 29 Mar. 1981, Mary Jo Murphy, 18 Oct. 1981; John J. Bernard Jr., "Mountain Grove," no. 64, SVA ser., 1982; NRHP Nomination Form, VDHR; Lane, *Virginia*, 134–35.

74. Mutual Assurance Society Policies, 25 Nov. 1846, 16 Dec. 1853, 1 Aug. 1860; Rawlings, *Early Charlottesville*, 38–39; *DP*, 9, 10 Nov. 1954; *Richmond Times-Dispatch*, 13 May 1955.

75. Woods, *Albemarle*, 143, 148–49; Rawlings, *Ante-bellum Albemarle*, 53; Anne Freudenberg, "Oak Lawn," research notes, n.d., shared with me by author; Frederick D. Nichols,

"Oak Lawn," research notes, n.d., shared with me by author; Mary Kfoury and Travis McDonald, "Oak Lawn," study for Kayhoe, 1979; Dan Garofalo, "Oak Lawn," study for Nichols, 1980. Its restoration by local architect Douglas Gilpin resulted in a preservation award by the local branch of the Association for the Preservation of Virginia Antiquities in 1998.

76. Mutual Assurance Society Policies, 27 Jan. 1803, 21 Aug. 1806 (one-story frame house, 16 by 34 feet); Woods, *Albemarle*, 159–63, 192–93, 346–47; Vera V. Via, *DP*, 5 Feb. 1959; William Christian, "Belmont," study for Nichols, 1980; Thomas Dolan to K. Edward Lay, 18 Jan. 1985; Sandy Fitzpatrick, Nancy Harrington, and Rosalyn Keesee, "Belmont," no. 88, SVA ser., 1986; *Charlottesville Observer*, Dec. 1991; *DP*: Sherri Nee, 8 Feb. 1993, David A. Maurer, 21, 26 Feb., 7 Mar. 1993.

77. *Charlottesville Central Gazette*, 25 Dec. 1824.

78. Woods, *Albemarle*, 276–77; WPA Inventory; Dan Friedman, *DP*, 20 Oct. 1977; Rhinelander, "Dick Woods's Road Survey," bldg. no. 24; Rebecca Price-Wilkin, "Malvern," no. 74, SVA ser., 1982.

79. Mutual Assurance Society Policies, 20 May 1799, 1810; Woods, *Albemarle*, 172–73; Langhorne, Lay, and Rieley, *Virginia Family*, 11–37.

80. Woods, *Albemarle*, 294–95; Rawlings, *Ante–bellum Albemarle*, 56; Williams, "Wheeler's Road Survey," bldg. no. 2; Catherine Coiner, "John M. Perry and Montebello," *ACHS Bulletin* 9, 3 (June–July 1989): 3; Lynne C. Ely, "Montebello," study for Virginia Engineering Foundation, 1994, UVA; Andrea S. Madison, "Montebello," no. 160, AIV ser., 1994.

81. Talbot Hamlin, *Greek Revival Architecture in America* (1944; rept. New York, 1964), 192.

82. *Virginia Advocate*, 29 Mar. 1828; *DP*, 11 Sept. 1901, 17 Mar. 1903; Rawlings, *Ante–bellum Albemarle*, 84; Lapsley and Thomsen, "Three Notch'd Road Survey," bldg. no. 61; Jack Abgott, "Birdwood," study for Nichols, n.d.; Bernard Chamberlain, "History of Birdwood," n.d., "Birdwood" vertical file, ACHS; Gary Ross Shook, "Birdwood," study for Nichols, 1980; Andrea Mullenix Nadel, "Birdwood Icehouse," no. 61, SVA ser., 1982; Jane Flaherty Wells, "Thomas Jefferson's Neighbors," *MACH* 47 (1989): 1–13; Andrew Kim and Lorenzo Mattii, "Birdwood Water Tower," no. 102, SVA ser., 1993, awarded first place in the Peterson Prize Competition by the Historic American Buildings Survey in 1994; NRHP Nomination Form, VDHR.

83. Woods, *Albemarle*, 252–53, 287; Stevens, *House Tour*, 227.

84. *DP*, 3 Nov. 1899; Robert A. Lancaster Jr., *Historic Virginia Homes and Churches* (Philadelphia and London, 1915), 416; Lewis A. Coffin Jr. and Arthur C. Holden, *Brick Architecture of the Colonial Period in Maryland and Virginia* (New York, 1919), pl. III; Roberts Coles II, "The Coles Homes on the Green Mountain and Their Mistresses," 1926, MS shared with me by a Coles family descendant; Rawlings, *Ante–bellum Albemarle*, 21; Stevens, *House Tour*, 93; *DP*: Dan Friedman, 20 Nov.

1977, Lenny Granger, 24 Aug. 1978, Richard Prior, 2 Dec. 1979; *DP*, 19 Apr. 1981; Charlottesville Realtors, *Real Estate Digest*, June 1981; Jim Ketcham–Colwill, *DP*, 15 Apr. 1984; Langhorne, Lay, and Rieley, *Virginia Family*, 65, 74–93; Linda Sherman, *Charlottesville Observer*, 23–29 May 1991; NRHP Nomination Form, VDHR.

85. Wheeler, *Historic Virginia*, 281; John W. White III, "The White Family of Albemarle County, Virginia," 1977, MS 44, ACHS; Dudley and Mackie, "Staunton and James River Turnpike Survey," bldg. nos. 47 and 48; Claudia Harrison, "Linden Farm," no. 174, AIV ser., 1996; Rawlings, *Ante–bellum Albemarle*, 33.

86. *Charlottesville Chronicle*, 26 Feb. 1865; *DP*, 15 July 1897, 5 July 1928, 19 Feb. 1942; Coffin and Holden, *Brick Architecture*, pl. 117; Rawlings, *Ante–bellum Albemarle*, 19; Wheeler, *Historic Virginia*, 264; Osborne Mackie, "Tallwood," study for Nichols, 1980; Dudley and Mackie, "Staunton and James River Turnpike Survey," bldg. no. 35E; Lisa Umstattd, "Tallwood," no. 91, SVA ser., 1981; Langhorne, Lay, and Rieley, *Virginia Family*, 68–74.

87. Mead, *Historic Homes*, 89–98; Wheeler, *Historic Virginia*, 179; Stevens, *House Tour*, 49; Brush and Siracuse, "Fredericksburg Road Survey," bldg. no. 8; Cade Beach, "East Belmont," study for Nichols, n.d.

88. Byrd Oliver, "Monroe Hill Law Office," no. 59, SVA ser., 1981; Hunt H. Harris and DeTeel P. Tiller, "Monroe Law Office, Limestone," no. 37, SVA ser., 1976.

89. Gayle M. Schulman, "Court Square 1863 Recalled by Richard Thomas Walker Duke Jr.," *MACH* 52 (1994): 114–24; conversation with Floyd Johnson, 18 Mar. 1996; removal of iron railing to Mount Moriah Methodist Church brought to my attention by Eugenia Bibb.

90. AC Record of the Overseers of the Poor, 1786, Albemarle County Courthouse.

91. *A Map of Albemarle County, Virginia*, Green Peyton, Civil Engineer, 1875, SC-ViU; *A New and Historical Map of Albemarle County, Virginia*, Frank A. Massie, 1907, SC-ViU. Woods, *Albemarle*, 137–38; AC Deed Book, 8 Apr. 1806; "Recollections of Judge Richard Thomas Walker Duke Jr. (1853–1926)," SC-ViU, brought to my attention by Gayle M. Schulman; AC Deed Book 65:91; Nell Lee, *DP*, 9 Sept. 1979; Linda Gail Boggan, "Olde Poorhouse Farm," no. 142, AIV ser., 1994.

92. Thomas Jefferson to Dr. Thomas Cooper, 2 Nov. 1822, Jefferson Papers, SC-ViU.

93. Moore, *Albemarle*, 155.

94. Benson J. Lossing, *Biographical Sketches of Signers of the Declaration of American Independence* (Boston, 1856); John E. Remsburg, *Jefferson an Unbeliever* (Atchison, Kan., 1882); Remsburg, *Six Historic Americans . . . , the Fathers and Saviors of Our Republic, Freethinkers* (New York, 1906); Jessica Lowe, *Cavalier Daily*, 26 Mar. 1997; conversations with Mrs. Stanislaw J. Makielski Sr. and Earl Leake, Charlottesville, 1987.

95. Rawlings, *Early Charlottesville*, 46; Meade, *Old Churches*,

52; Vestry Minutes, 1838–95, Christ Church, Charlottesville, SC-ViU; Richard Silverman, "Contributions to the Architectural History of Christ Church, Charlottesville, Virginia, 1824–1895," architectural history study for Prof. Charles Brownell, UVA, 1990; Anne E. Bruder, "Evangelical Episcopalian Architecture: Christ Church, Charlottesville," *MACH* 55 (1997): 16–37. The footprint of the 1826 church can be seen on the 1877 O. W. Gray map of Charlottesville, SC-ViU.

96. Cannan, "Some Presbyterian Churches"; Alison Stone and James Vernon, "South Plains Presbyterian Church," no. 84, SVA ser., 1984; AC Deed Books 21:302, 26:381 (1827); Charlottesville Deed Books 5:166 (1770), 39:363 (1842), 51:488 (1853), 52:374 (1854); Rawlings, *Early Charlottesville*, 46, 56, 59, 89, 91. According to church historian Robert E. Simpson, the church contract was made on 1 Dec. 1827; Robert E. Simpson, "Presbyterian Church Buildings, Charlottesville, Virginia"; conversations with Robert E. Simpson, 1 July 1987.

97. Hill and Murphy, "Coursey's Road Survey," bldg. no. 13; *Sesquicentennial History of Liberty Baptist Church, 1829–1979* (n.p., 1979); *DP*, 11 Aug. 1979.

98. WPA Inventory; AC Deed Book 65:188; Woods, *Albemarle*, 136; Pegram, "Victorian Churches."

99. *DP*: David A. Maurer, 7 May 1995, Vera V. Via, 8 Sept. 1955; McLeod and Wenger, "Buck Mountain Road Survey," bldg. no. 21; Lapsley and Thomsen, "Three Notch'd Road Survey," bldg. no. 45.

100. Harry Edward Poindexter, "A History of the Charlottesville Woolen Mills" (M.A. thesis, UVA, 1955); Peter Sandbeck, "A History of the Charlottesville Woolen Mills," study for Nichols, 1975; Moore, *Albemarle*, 261; *DP*: Lenny Granger, 19 Nov. 1978, John Sensbach, 23 Dec. 1979, Mary Jo Murphy, 10 Jan. 1982, Robert Brickhouse, 12 Dec. 1982; Andy Meyers, "The Charlottesville Woolen Mills: Working Life, Wartime, and the Walkout of 1918," *MACH* 53 (1995): 70–113; O. Allan Gianniny Jr., "What Is the Photograph on the Cover of Last Year's Magazine?" ibid. 54 (1996): 68–82; Carolyn Kazen, *Real Estate Weekly*, 23–29 Mar. 1994. The mill's twenty–ton cloth dryer was relocated at the Church of Jesus Christ of Latter–Day Saints in Salt Lake City.

101. Dan Friedman, *DP*, n.d.; Bruce Davis and Chip Logan, "Hatton Grange Mill," no. 34, SVA ser., 1976; Boroughs, Chapman, and King, "James River Road Survey," bldg. no. 5.

102. Pawlett, *Albemarle County Roads*, 104; AC Order Books, 2 Feb. 1801: 263, 5 June 1801: 387; Mutual Assurance Society Policies, 27 Jan. 1803, 7 June 1805, 1812, 1815, 1816; Edwin Morris Betts, ed., *Thomas Jefferson's Farm Book* (1953; rept. Charlottesville, Va., 1976), 411; AC Order Book, 5 June 1815: 10; N. B. Jones, "A List of Manufactures," *MACH* 10 (1950): 25; Bruce, *History* 1:171f; Moore, *Albemarle*, 262.

103. Mead, *Historic Homes*, 249–50.

104. *DP*, 25 Feb. 1994, 19; Moore, *Albemarle*, 95.

105. Mutual Assurance Society Policy, 21 Mar. 1814; Moore, *Albemarle*, 262.

106. AC Personal Property Tax Lists, 1800; Woods, *Albemarle*, 57–61; Moore, *Albemarle*, 93; MacLeod and Wenger, "Buck Mountain Road Survey," bldg. no. 18; Mutual Assurance Society Policy, 7 Oct. 1816; Massie map, 1907; WPA Inventory, 16 Dec. 1937; Davis et al., "Staunton and James River Turnpike Survey," bldg. no. 40.

107. AC Land Tax Lists, 1815, 1820, 1821, 1830.

108. Mutual Assurance Society Policies, 27 Nov., 10 Dec. 1816; Garvey Winegar, *DP*, 26 May 1976; Dashiell and McKinney, "Rockfish Gap Turnpike Survey," bldg. no. 18; Dudley and Mackie, "Staunton and James River Turnpike Survey," bldg. no. 42; WPA Inventory; *DP*: Vera V. Via, 31 Mar. 1955, Boyce Loving, 7 June 1956; James Green, *Richmond Times–Dispatch*, 11 Apr. 1965; Reinberger and Tiller, "Three Notched Road Survey," bldg. no. 115; Cecile Clover Walters, "A Trip Back in Time to the Forgotten Village of Milton," *Albemarle Monthly* 1, 3 (July 1978): 10–21; Roulhac Toledano, *Charlottesville Observer*, 3 Dec. 1992, 12; Karen McIntyre, "Locust Grove Tavern," no. 143, AIV ser., 1994; *Virginia Advocate*, 6 Sept. 1828.

109. *Virginia Herald*, 15 Nov. 1824; Ward, *General Lafayette's Visit*, 94; Brandon, *Lafayette*, 3:13; AC Deed Book 10:187; Woods, *Albemarle*, 289–91; Rawlings, *Early Charlottesville*, 4, 53, 66–67; Golladay, "Nicholas Family," *MACH* 35–36 (1977–78): 123–56; *DP*, 12, 13 July 1940; Mutual Assurance Society Policies, 21 Oct. 1816, 20 June 1823; *Jefferson's Albemarle*, 84; Boyce Loving, *DP*, 3 May 1964; John Paul Hyde, "Jefferson's High Way," research notes, June 1994; Boroughs, Chapman, and King, "James River Road Survey," bldg. no. 13.

110. Mutual Assurance Society Policy, 21 Mar. 1814; AC Land Tax Lists, 1815, 1821; *Virginia Advocate*, 15 Dec. 1827; Wheeler, *Historic Virginia*, 341; Woods, *Albemarle*, 150–51, 217, 225–26; Towler, "Three Taverns," 50; Justin Lawhorne Green and Dudley Cabell Vest, "Rockfish Gap Turnpike Survey," bldg. no. 46, VRT ser., 1996.

111. Wheeler, *Historic Virginia*, 365; Green and Vest, "Rockfish Gap Turnpike Survey," bldg. no. 47; Woods, *Albemarle*, 195–97; Christopher Klein, "The Fretwell–Tilman House," no. 136, AIV ser., 1992; Judy Bitting and Robert Dripps, "Crossroads Tavern," no. 17, SVA ser., 1974; Dudley and Mackie, "Staunton and James River Turnpike Survey," bldg. no. 43; *Charlottesville Observer*, 1–7 Aug. 1991.

112. Woods, *Albemarle*, 214–16; WPA Inventory; Sarah Cogle, *DP*, 10 Mar. 1995; Pennington and Scott, *Courthouse Burned*, 86; Mutual Assurance Society Policy, 21 May 1833; Davis et al., "Staunton and James River Turnpike Survey," bldg. no. 5.

113. Mutual Assurance Society Policies, 7 May 1833, 2 Dec. 1840, 25 Nov. 1846, 24 Dec. 1853, 24 Aug., 18 Sept. 1860; Sanborn Insurance Company Maps, 1886, 1896; *Virginia Advocate*, 26 Jan., 22 Mar., 6 Dec. 1828; Rawlings, *Early Charlottesville*, 32; *Charlottesville Observer*, 8–14 Feb. 1990; Moore, *Albemarle*, 372; *DP*: Neil Osborn, 21 Jan. 1974, Robert Brickhouse, 27 Mar. 1983, David A. Maurer, 1 Sept. 1991, 14 June 1992.

114. AC Order Books, 13 Oct. 1785, 13 Oct. 1791, 11 Oct. 1792; Mutual Assurance Society Policies, 28 Mar. 1803, 12 Oct. 1816, 13, 14, 19 June 1823, 21 June 1827, 8, 9, 10 May 1833, 2 Dec. 1840, 25 Nov. 1846, 15 Dec. 1853, 24 Aug. 1860; Rawlings, *Early Charlottesville*, 2–8; Schulman, "Court Square 1863 Recalled by Duke"; Laura Weyrauch, "Number Nothing," study for Nichols, 1980.

115. Woods, *Albemarle*, 70; illustration of an oil painting of the university from the tollgate to the west, *MACH* 35–36 (1977–78): 19.

IV. The Greek Revival (1830–1860)

1. Asher Benjamin, *The Practical House Carpenter, Being the Complete Development of the Grecian Order of Architecture* (Boston, 1830), pls. 46, 47, 48.

2. Mead, *Historic Homes*, 249; Marcus Whiffen, *American Architecture since 1780* (Cambridge, Mass., 1969), 38–47; Virginia and Lee McAlester, *A Field Guide to American Houses* (New York, 1984), 178–95.

3. *Virginia Advocate*, 10 Sept. 1830, 3.

4. Wealth is based on the combined real estate (land book) and personal property taxes paid: AC Tax Lists, 1830. Dr. Mann Page was followed by Robert Rives in total wealth with thirty slaves and William Cabell Rives who owned thirty-nine slaves. Both Page and W. C. Rives owned about 3,700 acres of land, while Robert Rives had 2,186 acres. The second-highest valued buildings were Alexander Garrett's holdings at $17,600, followed by John S. Cocke's Cedars valued at $11,200 and John Winn's Belmont at $11,000. Next came Tucker Coles's Tallwood at $9,457, followed by Dr. Charles Cocke's Esmont at $8,700. Then came Robert Rives's Boiling Springs and John Coles III's Estouteville, both at $8,000. In the $7,000 range was Jacob Moon's Mount Air, and in the $6,000 range were the dwelling of William Morris at North Garden and Jesse Joplin's River Lawn. Next came house values in the $5,000 range: Micajah Woods's two dwellings on Ivy Creek, Dabney Minor's Carrsbrook, William Cabell Rives's Castle Hill, Hugh Nelson's Belvoir, which employed forty slaves, Samuel Dyer's Plain Dealing, which employed thirty-two, John Kelly's Park Street residence, John Rogers Jr.'s East Belmont, and Gen. John Hartwell Cocke's hotel on West Main Street in Charlottesville. In the $4,000 range were John Rodes Sr.'s Midway, David Higginbotham's Morven, John D. Craven's Rose Hill, John Fretwell's dwelling in the northwest part of the county, William Ramsay's Millburne on the Mechum's River, Thomas Jefferson Randolph's Tufton, John Minor's Gale Hill, Reuben Lindsay's Springfield, Richard Duke's mill complex, Andrew Leitch Jr.'s Charlottesville dwelling, Jefferson's Monticello, Mary Eliza Coles Carter's Redlands, Martha A. Cocke's Edgemont, William Tulloch's buildings, and Thomas Wells's Eagle Tavern in Charlottesville. In fact, seventeen taverns were listed in the 1830 tax records. David A. Maurer, *DP*, 19 Jan. 1992. Micajah Woods, who died in 1837, first married

Lucy Walker, then Sarah Rodes. His son was commonwealth's attorney and a Civil War hero.

5. Joseph Martin, ed., *A New and Comprehensive Gazetteer of Virginia . . .* (Charlottesville, Va., 1835).

6. For a good general history of these and subsequent developments in the nineteenth and early twentieth centuries, see Moore, *Albemarle*, 171ff.

7. David A. Maurer, *DP*, 30 Aug. 1992.

8. *DP*, 24 Feb. 1994, 11; AC Tax Lists, 1840. Buildings in the $6,000 range include Gilly M. Lewis's Albemarle Mills (Peter Field Jefferson's mill) on the Hardware River, Rice W. Woods and Nathaniel Burnley's Hydraulic Mills on Ivy Creek (purchased from John M. Perry in 1829 and owned until 1860), Eliza Bragg's rented building on Charlottesville lot no. 3, and Alexander Garrett's Midway Hotel in Charlottesville, as well as the dwelling of Robert Rives (from Nelson County) called Boiling Springs and William Garth's Birdwood. In the $5,000 building range were Tucker Coles's mill on the Hardware River, Richard Duke's mill complex on the Rivanna River, William Cabell Rives's Castle Hill, John Fray's dwelling at Advance Mills, William Hunter Meriwether's Pireus, the John N. C. Stockton estate's Carrsbrook, Tucker Coles's Tallwood, John S. Cocke's The Cedars, and university bursar Alexander Garrett's Oak Hill in Charlottesville. In the $4,000 building value range were Charlottesville area ones such as Mary E. Kelly's dwelling, Cynthia T. Norris's rented lot no. 4, John Russell Jones's rented lots no. 63 and 64, Valentine W. Southall's rented lots no. 9 and 10, the West Main Street hotel of Gen. John Hartwell Cocke of Bremo in Fluvanna County, and the brick house designed by John Neilson for George C. Blaetterman, university professor of modern languages, just south of the intersection of the old Lynchburg Road (Jefferson Park Avenue) and the Three Notch'd Road (University Avenue). In this range in the county were Buck Island Mills, the John Winn estate's Belmont, James P. Tyler's Brooksville, George Rives's Sherwood, David Higginbotham's Morven, Dr. Charles Cocke's Esmont, John Rodes Sr.'s Midway, Thomas Jefferson Randolph's Edgehill, William B. Phillips's Sunnyfields, John M. Perry's Montebello, Charles Harper's buildings on Ivy Creek seven miles from of town, Mary Eliza Coles Carter's Redlands, John Rogers Jr.'s East Belmont, William Garth's Chestnut Ridge on Ivy Creek five miles northwest of town, and Jesse Garth's 1805 Cherry Valley eight miles northwest.

9. *DP*, 25 Feb. 1994, 9; Moore, *Albemarle*, 151; 1850 Tax Lists, SC-ViU. In the $6,000 range in the county were Judge Alexander Rives's Carlton, William Garth's Birdwood, and James M. Bowen's Mirador. In this range were the rented lots in Charlottesville of George Carr and William P. Farish on a portion of lot no. 2, Eliza Bragg on lot no. 3, and Alexander Garrett's Midway Hotel on lot no. 120. In the $5,000 range were Thomas Jefferson Randolph's Edgehill, William Cabell Rives's Castle Hill, the John N. C. Stockton estate's Carrsbrook, Tucker Coles's Tallwood, John S. Cocke's The Cedars,

John Fray's dwelling at Advance Mills, and Stapleton C. Snead's buildings on 252 acres on the Rivanna River five miles southeast of town that had undergone $100 in improvements within the past year. In this range in the city were Alexander Garrett's Oak Hill and portions of lots no. 17 and 18 rented by Obediah B. Brown of Washington, D.C. In the $4,000 range in the county were William Garth's Chestnut Ridge on Ivy Creek five miles northwest of town, Jesse Garth's Cherry Valley, the John Rogers estate's East Belmont, the Francina Rodes estate's Midway, Bedford Brown's Esmont, William D. Bowy's building twenty-six miles southwest of Charlottesville, Mary Coles Carter's Redlands, William P. Farish's Hillcrest Farm, John O. Harris's Ellerslie, David Higginbotham's Morven, the William Morris estate's Lewis Level, William B. Phillips's Sunnyfields, George Rives's Sherwood, Robert Rives's Bolling Springs (old Nicholas place), and the Jonathan W. Beers estate's Brooksville. In this range in Charlottesville were several rented buildings on portions of lots: lot no. 39 rented by Hugh and I. J. Fry of Richmond, Mary E. Kelly's lot no. 97, Cynthia T. Norris's lot no. 4, Valentine W. Southall's lots no. 9 and 10, John Russell Jones's lots no. 63 and 64, and Benjamin C. Flannagan's lot no. 25. In this range adjacent to the town were John Cochran's millhouse, John H. Timberlake's dwelling one-quarter of a mile northeast, Gen. John Hartwell Cocke's West Main Street hotel, the Elijah Dunkum estate's Ridge Street dwelling, Slaughter W. Ficklin's Belmont, the Blaetterman estate's dwelling near the university, and George Wilson Spooner Jr.'s Montebello. *Statistics of U.S.: 1850 Census.*

10. *DP*, 25 Feb. 1994, 19; Moore, *Albemarle*, 172; *Charlottesville Advocate*, 16 Mar. 1860, 4.

11. Moore, *Albemarle*, 151–52; AC Tax Lists, 1860. Belmont and Estouteville were followed by Thomas L. Farish's The Farm just east of Charlottesville at $7,600 and William H. Cosby's mill west of town at $7,500. John S. Crosby's dwelling fifteen miles west of town and George W. Turpin's Farish House hotel on lot no. 1 in town were both listed at $7,000. Dwellings in the $6,000 range were Mrs. Eliza Bragg's brick dwelling on Charlottesville lot no. 3, Judge Alexander Rives's Carlton, Mrs. Julia Peyton's Farmington, Thomas Jefferson Randolph's Edgehill, Col. John Bowie Strange's brick house on Ridge Street, and John A. Marchant's double brick house and store on lots no. 23 and 24. Buildings other than houses in the $6,000 range were Nathaniel Burnley and Rice W. Wood's Hydraulic Mills, Monticello Bank on Charlottesville lot no. 39, the Albemarle Insurance Company on lot no. 19, Robert S. Jones's three-story brick store on lot no. 38, James Fife's building on lot no. 36, and Benjamin C. Flannagan's building on lot no. 25.

12. Claudia Craig, "Springdale Farm," no. 58, SVA ser., 1981.

13. Lapsley and Thomsen, "Three Notch'd Road Survey," bldg. no. 1.

14. *Charlottesville Advocate*, 16 Mar. 1860; O'Neal, *Primitive*.

15. AC Deed Book 11:402; Polly A. Spaar, "Tarry Farm," study, UVA, 1973; Dame and Sabadell, "Brown's Gap Turnpike Survey," bldg. no. 26.

16. WPA Inventory.

17. *DP*, 28 Aug. 1930; Rawlings, *Ante-bellum Albemarle*, 12; Stevens, *House Tour*, 72; Edwards, Wenger, and Yetter, "Secretary's Road Survey," bldg. no. 74; Dan Friedman, *DP*, 8 Sept. 1977; Welch, "Road to Secretary's Mill," bldg. no. 13; Camille Wells, "Round Top Chain of Title," 23 Aug. 1991, private collection.

18. Mutual Assurance Society Policy, 21 Nov. 1846.

19. Charlotte Crystal and Bryan McKenzie, *DP*, 23 Aug. 1994.

20. Lapsley and Thomsen, "Three Notch'd Road Survey," bldg. no. 56; A. Robert Kuhlthau, "Summary of the Leigh Property," 1995, in possession of author.

21. Mead, *Historic Homes*, 111–27; *DP*, 21, 24 Dec. 1894, 31 Oct. 1904, 7 Nov. 1929; Rawlings, *Ante-bellum Albemarle*, 75; Stevens, *House Tour*, 47; Brush and Siracuse, "Fredericksburg Road Survey," bldg. no. 12; Cade Beach, "Cismont Manor," study for Nichols, n.d.; Richard Prior, *DP*, 30 Dec. 1979.

22. *DP*, 27 July 1897; Woods, *Albemarle*, 260–62, 330–31; Mead, *Historic Homes*, 271–75; John Bowie Ferneyhough, ed., *Year-Book of the American Clan Gregor Society* (Richmond, 1929), 33–40; Rawlings, *Ante-bellum Albemarle*, 71; Stevens, *House Tour*, 43; Reinberger and Tiller, "Three Notch'd Road Survey," bldg. no. 116; *DP*, 10 Oct. 1991; Victoria Alexander, *Charlottesville Observer*, 22–28 Aug. 1991; L. B. Taylor Jr., *The Ghosts of Charlottesville and Lynchburg* (Lynchburg, Va., 1992), 34–35; Scott Cyphers, "Glenmore," no. 170, AIV ser., 1996.

23. Conversation with Mary Brice Sloan, 7 May 1990; Woods, *Albemarle*, 331–32.

24. Rawlings, *Ante-bellum Albemarle*, 47, 89; Boyce Loving, *DP*, 28 Apr. 1966; Crosby, "Brown's Gap Turnpike Survey," bldg. no. 38; Coons, "Brown," 70–75; *DP*, 18, 22 May 1906; NRHP Nomination Form, VDHR; Cerrone and Wagstaff, "Rockfish Gap Turnpike Survey," bldg. no. 33; *Jeffersonian Republican*, 2 Aug. 1860; Vera V. Via, *DP*, 2 Feb. 1956; MacLeod and Wenger, "Buck Mountain Road Survey," bldg. no. 16; Roulhac Toledano, *Charlottesville Observer*, 23–29 Apr. 1987.

25. Wheeler, *Historic Virginia*, 169; Richard Prior, *DP*, 17 June 1979.

26. Amy Lane Whitlock, "Clover Fields," no. 133, AIV ser., 1992; Sarah Dreller, Fiona Robertson, and Martha Teall, "Clover Fields," no. 111, SVA ser., 1997.

27. Ann V. Swallow, "Norris-Preston Cottage," no. 65, SVA ser., 1982; Woods, *Albemarle*, 308–10; Wheeler, *Historic Virginia*, 174; Brush and Siracuse, "Fredericksburg Road Survey," bldg. no. 2.

28. Davis et al., "Staunton and James River Turnpike Survey," bldg. no. 21; Ashley Shelton, "Three Scottsville Houses," no. 105, AIV ser., 1991; Alice Bojanowski, Shayn Bjornholm, Courtney Newcomer, and Patricia Sherwood, "Jeffries-Bruce House," no. 97, SVA ser., 1990.

29. WPA Inventory; Davis et al., "Staunton and James River Turnpike Survey," bldg. no. 19; Dan Friedman, *DP*, 22 Jan. 1978; Kate Black, "Old Hall," no. 76, SVA ser., 1982.

30. Rawlings, *Ante-bellum Albemarle*, 55; B. F. D. Runk, "John Patten Emmet," *MACH* 13 (1953): 54–67; NRHP Nomination Form, 1976, VDHR; Elizabeth Kahn, "Morea," study for Nichols, 1980; *DP*, 15 July 1984; Candace Smith and Sara Amy Leach, "Morea," study for Kayhoe, 1985; Bibb, "Charlottesville Landmark Survey," 1987.

31. Mutual Assurance Society Policy, 25 Sept. 1845.

32. Mead, *Historic Homes*, 75–88; Woods, *Albemarle*, 189–90.

33. *DP*, 10 Feb. 1906; Rawlings, *Ante-bellum Albemarle*, 32; Wheeler, *Historic Virginia*, 272; Stevens, *House Tour*, 90–91; Boroughs, Chapman, and King, "James River Road Survey," bldg. nos. 4 and 6.

34. Rawlings, *Ante-bellum Albemarle*, 59; Ronald J. Hansen, *DP*, 25 Feb. 1994.

35. Woods, *Albemarle*, 219–22, 260; Rawlings, *Ante-bellum Albemarle*, 73; Edwards, Wenger, and Yetter, "Secretary's Road Survey," bldg. no. 60; WPA Inventory.

36. Lenny Granger, *DP*, 17 Dec. 1978.

37. *DP*, 24 Dec. 1928; Rawlings, *Ante-bellum Albemarle*, 28; Stevens, *House Tour*, 89; Dan Friedman, *DP*, 30 Oct. 1977; Davis et al., "Staunton and James River Turnpike," bldg. no. 26; Chip Jones, *DP*, 27 Dec 1981; NRHP Nomination Form, VDHR; Shelton, "Three Scottsville Houses"; Jamie Simpson, *DP*, 14 Nov. 1993; Wheeler, *Historic Virginia*, 337; MacLeod and Wenger, "Buck Mountain Road Survey," bldg. no. 50.

38. Mead, *Historic Homes*, 231–40; Armistead C. Gordon, *William Fitzhugh Gordon* (New York, 1909), 56–63; Brush, "Fredericksburg Road Survey," bldg. no. 32; Linda Robinson, "Edgeworth," no. 166, AIV ser., 1995.

39. WPA Inventory; Reinberger and Tiller, "Three Notch'd Road Survey," bldg. no. 110.

40. Davis et al., "Staunton and James River Turnpike Survey," bldg. no. 22; Shelton, "Three Scottsville Houses"; Marita D. Fritz and John M. Lupinos, "Tipton-Blair House," no. 104, AIV ser., 1993; Mutual Assurance Society Policy, 18 Sept. 1860; Woods, *Albemarle*, 143.

41. Woods, *Albemarle*, 198–201, 283–85; Rawlings, *Ante-bellum Albemarle*, 85; Lapsley and Thomsen, "Three Notch'd Road Survey," bldg. no. 55; Rhinelander, "Dick Woods's Road Survey," bldg. no. 5.

42. Homer Richey, ed., *Memorial History of the John Bowie Strange Camp, United Confederate Veterans* (Charlottesville, Va., 1920); Moore, *Albemarle*, 197.

43. Papamichael, Tucker, and Whitehead, "Staunton and James River Turnpike Survey," bldg. no. 27.

44. Feldman, Mickler, and Perdue, "Buck Mountain Road Survey," bldg. no. 87; Mutual Assurance Society Policies, 14 Jan. 1854, 6 Oct. 1860; *DP*, 5–11 Apr. 1990; Todd R. Mozingo, "Hughes House," study for Nichols, 1973; Marianne Corriero, "Hughes House," study for Nichols, n.d.; Brent A. Campbell and Matthew T. Barnes, "Dr. John C. Hughes House," no. 101, SVA ser., 1993; information about the Hodges-Gleason house brought to my attention by Eugenia Bibb, 16 May 1995.

45. AC Deed Book 55:100 (1856); Woods, *Albemarle*, 296; Wheeler, *Historic Virginia*, 240; Edwards, Wenger, and Yetter, "Secretary's Road Survey," bldg. no. 64; correspondence with Sam C. Towler, 18 May 1990; correspondence with Calder Loth, 11 May, 29 Sept., 2 Oct. 1991; Calder Loth, NRHP Nomination Form, 1993, VDHR.

46. *DP*, 23 May 1906, 14 May 1927; Rawlings, *Ante-bellum Albemarle*, 34; Stevens, *House Tour*, 65; correspondence with Margaret Fowler Clark, 6 Nov. 1978; Chris Snowbeck, *DP*, 23 May 1996.

47. Mead, *Historic Homes*, 63–64; Wheeler, *Historic Virginia*, 212–13; Stevens, *House Tour*, 31; Reinberger and Tiller, "Three Notch'd Road Survey," bldg. no. 112.

48. *DP*, 25 Feb. 1899, 4 Jan. 1902; Woods, *Albemarle*, 216–19; Rawlings, *Ante-bellum Albemarle*, 8; Edwards, Wenger, and Yetter, "Secretary's Road Survey," bldg. no. 69; Fillmore Norfleet, "Two Prentis Letters," *MACH* 35–36 (1977–78): 161.

49. Woods, *Albemarle*, 172–73; Lancaster, *Historic Virginia Homes*, 413–14; Rawlings, *Ante-bellum Albemarle*, 17; Wheeler, *Historic Virginia*, 265–66; Boyce Loving, *DP*, 1 Sept. 1955; Langhorne, Lay, and Rieley, *Virginia Family*, 142–49; Roulhac Toledano, *Charlottesville Observer*, 11 Nov. 1993; John O. Pickett Jr., *Observer*, 18 Nov. 1993; Hawes Spencer, *C-ville Review*, 1–14 Dec. 1993; correspondence with Calder Loth and W. James Eddins, 12 Nov., 8 Dec. 1993, 19 Jan., 25 Jan., 7 Feb. 1994.

50. Langhorne, Lay, and Rieley, *Virginia Family*, 149–52.

51. Monticola Preservation Fund, *Monticola* (Howardsville, Va., 1988); David A. Maurer, *DP*, 9 June 1988, 30 June 1991, 8, 15, 22 May 1994; Jennifer L. Patsos, "Unique Interpretations of the Greek Revival," no. 130, AIV ser., 1992.

52. *Virginia Advocate*, 7 Apr. 1849; Mutual Assurance Society Policy, 18 Sept. 1860; Kevin Hildebrand, "Seamen Mansion," study for Nichols, 1982; Dan Genest, *DP*, 15 Jan. 1985; Susan Henneke and James Vernon, "200 South Street," study for Kayhoe, n.d.; Rachel Garfield, *Charlottesville Observer*, 31 Oct.–6 Nov. 1985; Mary Hosmer Lupton, *Bulletin of the ACHS* 11 (1991): 4.

53. Mead, *Historic Homes*, 110; Brush and Siracuse, "Fredericksburg Road Survey," bldg. no. 11; Mary Starke, *DP*, 2 Mar. 1969; Tammy Le, "Bonahora," no. 168, AIV ser., 1995.

54. Alice Bowsher, "Abell-Gleason House," study for Nichols, 1974; Laura Weyrauch, "Abell-Gleason House," study for Nichols, 1980; conversation with William Stevens, 24 Mar. 1994.

55. Richard Thomas Walker Duke Jr. Papers, SC-ViU; "Genealogical Column: Gilmer Family of Virginia," *Richmond Times-Dispatch*, 18 June 1905.

56. Rawlings, *Ante-bellum Albemarle*, 52; Skip Glenn, "Locust Grove," study for Nichols, n.d.; Robert L. Hillier, "Locust Grove Kitchen," no. 54, AIV ser., 1981.

57. Woods, *Albemarle*, 147–48; *DP*, 16 Apr. 1902, 18 June 1906; Langhorne Family Papers, SC-ViU; E. Pendleton Hogan, "El Mirador," *American Motorist* 7 (Nov. 1932): 17, 45; Wheeler, *Historic Virginia*, 360; *DP*: Boyce Loving, 23 Feb. 1974, Dan Friedman, 21 Aug. 1977; Grosskopf, Thaler, and Trischman-Marks, "Rockfish Gap Turnpike Survey," bldg. no. 2; David A. Maurer, *DP*, 23 Oct. 1994; NRHP Nomination Form, VDHR.

58. Mutual Assurance Society Policies, 1799, 1803, 19 May 1809, 9 Dec. 1816; Woods, *Albemarle*, 251–56, 295–96; WPA Inventory; Boynton Merrill Jr., *Jefferson's Nephews: A Frontier Tragedy* (Princeton, N.J., 1976), 4–5, 32–35.

59. Brush, "Fredericksburg Road Survey," bldg. no. 34.

60. Mead, *Historic Homes*, 240–46; *DP*, 6 June 1907; NRHP Nomination Form, VDHR; Richard Guy Wilson, *Arise and Build!* (Charlottesville, Va., 1995), 17.

61. Rawlings, *Early Charlottesville*, 23; *Virginia Advocate*, 7 Apr. 1849; Peter Briggs, Karen Myers, and Peter Sandbeck, "Number One Cottage Lane," no. 9, SVA ser., 1974; William Frazier, "Rugby Hall," study for Nichols, 1974.

62. Mutual Assurance Society Policy, 2 Dec. 1840; correspondence with Margaret Fowler Clark, 6 Nov. 1978; Debra Curtis and Kate Mahood, "Redland Club," study for Kayhoe, 1983.

63. W. Donald Rhinesmith, "The Old Rectory of Christ Episcopal Church," study for Nichols, 1965–66.

64. *DP*, 21 Apr. 1893, 8 July 1897; Thacker Papers; Tammy Poole, *DP*, 2 Nov. 1991; *C-ville Review*, 12–25 Nov. 1991; *DP*, 24 Nov. 1991.

65. Woods, *Albemarle*, 254–55; Wheeler, *Historic Virginia*, 311; Stevens, *House Tour*, 203; Hank Long, "Faulkner House," study for Nichols, 1975; Betsy Kulamer and Becky Pickens, *Declaration*, 16 Oct. 1975; Scharer, "Three Notch'd Road Survey," bldg. no. 64; Jeff O'Dell, NRHP Nomination Form, 1984, VDHR; Edward O. McCue III, *DP*, 28 Feb 1992; Mary Koonts, "Faulkner House," no. 171, AIV ser., 1996.

66. Stevens, *House Tour*, 290–91; Geoffrey B. Henry, NRHP Nomination Form, 1991, VDHR.

67. Woods, *Albemarle*, 259–60; Lapsley and Thomsen, "Three Notch'd Road Survey," bldg. no. 33; information about Pleasant Retreat brought to my attention by Dabney Wiant, 28 Mar. 1989; Coons, "Brown," 40–42.

68. Rawlings, *Ante-bellum Albemarle*, 5; Lucy Walker Snead, "Some Recollections of Fancy Hill," n.d., Thomas Jefferson Memorial Foundation Archives; *DP*, 20 June 1995.

69. Woods, *Albemarle*, 171; Cerrone and Wagstaff, "Rockfish Gap Turnpike Survey," bldg. no. 30; Geoffrey B. Henry, NRHP Nomination Form, VDHR; Towler, "Three Taverns," 52.

70. *DP*, 8 Apr. 1973, 21 Jan., 10, 19 Feb. 1974, 25 Jan. 1975, 5, 27 Feb., 30 Sept. 1981, 8 May 1987.

71. Meade, *Old Churches* 2:48–56; Roberts Coles, lecture, 1932, "History of Christ Church, St. Anne's Parish, 1832–1932," photocopy in my possession; WPA Inventory, R. E. Hannum, 27 Nov. 1936; Elizabeth Coles Langhorne, *A History of Christ Church, Glendower* (Charlottesville, Va., 1957), photocopy in my possession; Douglas L. Forsyth, "Brief History of St. Anne's Parish, Albemarle," Spring 1968, photocopy in my possession; Scott and Wyper, "Christ Church Glendower," 4; Frierson, "Five Episcopal Churches"; Langhorne, Lay, and Rieley, *Virginia Family*, 114–20; correspondence with Andy Johnson, with plan and detail drawings showing the original pew and communion rail locations, 4 Aug. 1991.

72. Grosskopf, Thaler, and Trischman-Marks, "Rockfish Gap Turnpike Survey," bldg. no. 7.

73. William Frazier and Angela Kim, "Scottsville Presbyterian Church," no. 6, SVA ser., 1973; Cannan, "Some Presbyterian Churches"; E. E. Dinwiddie, "Lebanon Church, West Hanover Presbytery," *Presbyterian of the South and the Presbyterian Standard* 105 (1931): 35; Elizabeth Morton Dinwiddie, "History of Lebanon Church, West Hanover Presbytery," *West Hanover Presbyterian Church Histories*, SC-ViU; Grosskopf, Thaler, and Trischman-Marks, "Rockfish Gap Turnpike Survey," bldg. no. 11; Hugh Henry, "A History of Tabor Church in West Hanover Presbytery, 1882," *MACH* 2 (1941): 24–27; Dashiell and McKinney, "Rivanna and Rockfish Gap Turnpike," bldg. no. 10.

74. Rawlings, *Early Charlottesville*, 46, 56, 59, 89, 91; *DP*, 14 Jan. 1960; Covey, "First United Methodist Church."

75. The name of Mount Ed is believed to have been derived from Joshua 22:34: "And the children of Reuben and the children of Gad called the altar Ed: for it shall be a witness between us that the Lord is God"; John B. Turpin, *A Brief History of the Albemarle Baptist Association* (Richmond, [1892]), 19; Russell H. Davis, "A History of Mount Ed Baptist Church," *MACH* 32 (1974): 8–38; Michael Francis Conner, "Mount Ed Baptist Church," no. 38, SVA ser., 1976; *DP*, 24 Sept. 1988; Papamichael, Tucker, and Whitehead, "Staunton and James River Turnpike Survey," bldg. no. 65; Edwards, Wenger, and Yetter, "Secretary's Road Survey," bldg. no. 56; AC Deed Book 62:431; Vera V. Via, "Free Union Church Named Town Which Grew Up There," *DP*, 2 Dec. 1954; MacLeod and Wenger, "Buck Mountain Survey," bldg. no. 36; Davis et al., "Staunton and James River Turnpike Survey," bldg. no. 23.

76. Douglas C. McVarish, "Antebellum Methodist Churches of the Central Piedmont, Virginia," no. 70, AIV ser., 1988; Mrs. Eldridge Jones, *Mount Moriah Methodist Church: Its Origin and Growth, 1834–1972* (n.p., 1972); Boyce Loving, *DP*, 4 Oct. 1962; MacLeod and Wenger, "Buck Mountain Road Survey," bldg. no. 22; Jane Dunlap Norris, *DP*, 14 June 1988; Pegram, "Victorian Churches."

77. Orlando Ridout, "Howardsville Survey," architectural history study, UVA, 1976, copy at VDHR.

78. Rawlings, *Early Charlottesville*, 91; Don Covey, "One Hundred Fifty Years: A History of First United Methodist Church, Charlottesville, 1834–1984," 1984, ACHS vertical files.

79. Woods, *Albemarle*, 213; Rawlings, *Early Charlottesville*, 89; *DP*, 14 Jan. 1960; "150th. Anniversary, First Christian Church, Charlottesville, Virginia, 1835–1985," typescript at First Christian Church, Charlottesville, Va.; James R. Boyd and Julia Henley, "Scottsville Disciples of Christ Church," no. 18, SVA ser., 1974; Davis et al., "Staunton and James River Turnpike Survey," bldg. no. 7.

80. Vera V. Via, "Earlysville Church Remained Free during 122 Year Use," *DP*, 19 May 1953; Feldman, Mickler, and Perdue, "Buck Mountain Road Survey," bldg. no. 70; Gina Haney and Jennifer Wimmer, "Earlysville Union Church," no. 106, SVA ser., 1995; Amy Lemley, *Charlottesville Observer*, 23–29 Nov. 1995.

81. Rhinesmith, "Rectory."

82. *DP*, 17 Nov. 1977.

83. For a general discussion, see Wilbur A. Nelson, *Geology and Mineral Resources of Albemarle County* (Charlottesville, Va., 1962).

84. Mead, *Historic Homes*, 189; *Charlottesville Advocate*, 16 Mar. 1860, 4:

"Slating! Slating!! Slating!!!

The undersigned having secured the service of a good workman, is at all times ready to execute work in his line of business, in all its branches, with more satisfaction to himself and patrons than heretofore; viz: slating roof in any part of the State, likewise he is prepared to receive orders for hearths for houses, head and tombstones for monuments; slab prefaces and squares for flagging sidewalks, etc. He has leased the Everettsville Quarries, Albemarle, (originally opened and worked by W. E. Elliott), where he is now working extensively and getting out superior slates, and will always have a supply on hand to fulfill any order at home or abroad.

Address, Anthony R. Cary, Keswick, Albemarle, Va. May 21, 1857."

85. 1864 Gilmer map; 1866 Hotchkiss map; 1875 Peyton map; 1907 Massie map; Davis et al., "Staunton and James River Turnpike Survey," bldg. no. 15.

86. *DP*, 29 Aug 1898; Thacker Papers.

87. U.S. Census, Schedule of Inhabitants, AC, 1840.

88. Stauffenberg, "Economic Survey," 51; U.S. Census, Schedule of Inhabitants, AC, 1850.

89. Margaret A. Pennington and Lorna S. Scott, *The Courthouse Burned: Book II* (Waynesboro, Va., 1986), 87; Davis et al., "Staunton and James River Turnpike Survey," bldg. no. 1; Jamie M. Barnett and Beth Cates, "Canal Warehouse, Scottsville," no. 99, SVA ser., 1993; A. B. Mullett & Co. drawings, 1897, private collection; *DP*: Robert Brickhouse, 15 Oct. 1979, Anne Richardson, 8 Jan. 1980.

90. Kimberly Merkel, "Woolen Mills Tavern," no. 36, SVA ser., 1976; C. Gene Spurgeon, "The Monticello Hotel Annex," study for Nichols, n.d.; *Jeffersonian Republican*, 10 Jan. 1861; Woods, *Albemarle*, 357–58; Sam C. Towler, "Three Taverns in Albemarle County, Virginia," *Central Virginia Heritage* 8, 4 (Winter 1990): 50–51.

91. Wagstaff and Cerrone, "Rockfish Gap Turnpike Survey," bldg. no. 31; Woods, *Albemarle*, 203–5; Dashiell and McKinney, "Rockfish Gap Turnpike Survey," bldg. no. 11; Ziad Shehab, "Evolution of the Garland A. Garth House," no. 137, AIV ser., 1992; AC Tax Lists, 1860.

92. Lapsley and Thomsen, "Three Notch'd Road Survey," bldg. no. 26.

93. James Wade Dizdar, "Charlottesville Banks before 1935," no. 73, AIV ser., 1988.

94. Moore, *Albemarle*, 38–39, 68, 206–7; Martin, *Gazetteer*.

95. Whitlock, "Clover Fields" ; Wagstaff and Cerrone, "Rockfish Gap Turnpike Survey," bldg. no. 33.

96. *Central Gazette*, 8 Jan. 1825; Woods, *Albemarle*, 199; Rawlings, *Ante-bellum Albemarle*, 85; Rhinelander, "Dick Woods's Road Survey," bldg. no. 5.

97. Mead, *Historic Homes*, 65–74; Olivia Taylor, "Edgehill, 1735–1902," *MACH* 30 (1972): 61–67; Richard Prior, *DP*, 19 July 1979; A. Robert Kuhlthau and Beulah O. Carter, "Baptist Education for Young Ladies in Charlottesville," *MACH* 53 (1995): 32–57.

98. Kean, "The C and O in Central Virginia"; Farm Journal for Clover Fields, courtesy of Sara Lee Barnes, 1994; Mead, *Historic Homes*, 249; Woods, *Albemarle*, 115–16; Newton Bond Jones, "Charlottesville and Albemarle County, Virginia, 1819–1860" (Ph.D. diss., UVA, 1950), 172; Moore, *Albemarle*, 188–89, 242–43; *DP*: Garvey Winegar, 6 June 1976, Mary Alice Blackwell, 14 July 1991.

99. Mead, *Historic Homes*, 263–66; *DP*, 4 Sept. 1909; Brush and Siracuse, "Fredericksburg Road Survey," bldg. no. 6; Sara Lee Barnes, "A Brief History of the Keswick Depot," 1993, typescript in my possession; Reinberger and Tiller, "Three Notched Road Survey," bldg. no. 114; Michael Zimney, "Shadwell Depot," no. 47, SVA ser., 1979; information about the Warren Depot brought to my attention by Thomas W. Dixon Jr.; Walter E. Berg, *Buildings and Structures of American Railroads* (New York, 1900), 251; John B. Farmer Jr. and Mark A. Kearney, "Warren Depot," no. 4, SVA ser., 1973; Boroughs, Chapman, and King, "James River Road Survey," bldg. no. 17; Pennington and Scott, *Courthouse Burned*, 85; Peggy Bruns and Frederick Schneider, "Scottsville Depot," no. 42, SVA ser., 1977.

V. BEYOND THE CLASSICAL REVIVAL

1. Evarts B. Greene and V. D. Harrington, *American Population before the Federal Census of 1790* (New York, 1932), 150, 152: 1755: 1,344 whites + 1,747 blacks = 3,091; AC Tax Lists, 1786; U.S. Census, Schedule of Inhabitants, AC, Virginia, 1790

and 1800; *Compendium of the Enumeration of Inhabitants of U.S. from Censuses, 1790*, bk. 1 (Philadelphia, 1791), 48; *Compendium, 1800*, bk. 1 (Washington, D.C., 1801); *DP*, 25 Feb. 1994, 9–10; Greene and Harrington, *American Population*, 154: 1790: 7,000 whites + 5,800 blacks (171 of whom were free) = 12,500.

2. WPA, "Inventory of the Church Archives of Virginia, Negro Baptist Churches in Richmond," iv, LVA; *DP*, 25 Feb. 1994, 9–10; Moore, *Albemarle*, 54, 113, 119; *Daily Chronicle*, 11 Mar. 1864. For a detailed essay on free blacks residing on East Main Street in Charlottesville during the first half of the nineteenth century, see Lucia Stanton, "Monticello to Main Street: The Hemings Family and Charlottesville," *MACH* 55 (1997): 94–126. Col. Thomas Bell (d. 1800) built a one-story frame house on the corner of Second and Main Streets, which c. 1920 became the location of the National Bank and Trust company. Bell fathered a daughter, Sally Jefferson Bell, by Mary Hemings (b. 1753), a Monticello slave. Sally Bell married Jesse Scott (1781–1862), whose mother was an Indian. Scott and his sons, Robert (1803–1899) and James (c. 1810–1888), were talented musicians who married black women. Scott's sons, as well as their mother, were born in this house.

3. Brush and Siracuse, "Fredericksburg Road Survey," bldg. no. 13; Carr house location brought to my attention by Corinne Nettleton, Dee Dee Smith, and William Rough, 13 Jan. 1997.

4. Robert Weise, "Shadwell Mills," study for Prof. Charles Perdue, UVA, 1991; Mead, *Historic Homes*, 80–81; AC Will Books 2:107, 27:293.

5. *Central Gazette*, 25 Dec. 1824 (quote); Langhorne, Lay, and Rieley, *Virginia Family*, 132–41.

6. U.S. Census, Schedule of Inhabitants, AC, 1900; *Enumeration*, 1810–1880, passim, and 1900, pt. 1, 1:396, 561, 605, 644; *Statistics of U.S.*, 1850.

7. U.S. Census, Schedule of Inhabitants, AC, 1920.

8. *Virginia Gazette*, 5 Mar. 1752; *Central Gazette*, 25 Dec. 1824; *DP*, 5 June, 13, 15, 18 July 1993, 6, 10 Feb., 5 May, 20 June 1994; *Inside UVA* (2 July 1993); Ian Zack, *DP*, 3 Dec. 1995, 5 Jan. 1997; Betts, *Garden Book*, 245; television program, *Thomas Jefferson: A View from the Mountain*, 9 Dec. 1995; AC Inventory Book 15:461; AC Will Book 24:8 (when Oldham's widow died, she left a slave, Dolly, and $100 for her support to William B. Phillips); *Central Gazette*, 27 May 1820. For more information on African Americans, see Ervin L. Jordan Jr., *Black Confederates and Afro-Yankees in Civil War Virginia* (Charlottesville, Va., 1995), and Michael Plunkett, *Afro-American Sources in Virginia: A Guide to Manuscripts* (Charlottesville, Va., 1990).

9. For more information on the impact of the war on this area, see Jean V. Berlin, "A Civil War Nurse in Charlottesville," *MACH* 52 (1994): 125–46; Ervin L. Jordan Jr., *Charlottesville and the University of Virginia in the Civil War* (Lynchburg, Va., 1988); skirmish at Rio Hill: Ben Critzer, *DP*, 1 Aug. 1975; Kay Collins Chretien, *Charlottesville Observer*, 19–25 Sept. 1996.

10. Moore, *Albemarle*, 208; John F. Brown, "Sheridan's Occupation of Charlottesville," *MACH* 22 (1963–64): 38.

11. *MACH* 22 (1963–64): 25–26, 31, 37–38, 43–44, 50, 60; a more accurate account of the war was brought to my attention by Paul Burke, 26 May 1992: *The War of the Rebellion: A Compilation of the Official Records*, ser. 1, no. 33 (1891), 161–69, and no. 46 (1894), 474–523.

12. *Charlottesville Chronicle*, 15 Feb. and 1 Mar. 1865; Ford, "Recollections of the Past," 113.

13. *MACH* 17 (1958–59): 22, 30; Moore, *Albemarle*, 203–13; R. T. W. Duke Jr., "Recollections," SC-ViU, brought to my attention by Gayle M. Schulman, transcriber.

14. David A. Maurer, *DP*, 24 Sept., 1 Oct. 1995.

15. Whiffen, *American Architecture*; McAlester, *American Houses*; Andrew Jackson Downing, *The Architecture of Country Houses* (New York, 1969), 42.

16. Rawlings, *Ante-bellum Albemarle*, 9; William McGroarty, "Four Virginia Blenheims," *Tyler's Quarterly* 29 (Apr. 1948): 241–48; Stevens, *House Tour*, 71; Edwards, Wenger, and Yetter, "Secretary's Road Survey," bldg. no. 71; Drucilla G. Haley and Marlene Heck, "Blenheim Library," no. 30, SVA ser., 1976; Langhorne, Lay, and Rieley, *Virginia Family*, 123–27; Peggy Udell Flick, *Charlottesville Observer*, 19 Apr. 1989; Dell T. Upton, NRHP Nomination Form, VDHR.

17. Woods, *Albemarle*, 181–82; Duke Papers, SC-ViU; Rawlings, *Ante-bellum Albemarle*, 43; Stevens, *House Tour*, 236; Ben Carstoiu, "Sunnyside," no. 167, AIV ser., 1995; Mary Ann Elwood and Fred T. Heblich, *Charlottesville and the University of Virginia: A Pictorial History* (Norfolk, 1982), 41.

18. Susan Holbrook, "Fowler House," no. 63, SVA ser., 1982.

19. AC Tax Lists, 1865. In the $7,000 range in the county were Thomas L. Farish's The Farm, George W. Turpin's Farish House hotel, John S. Crosby's property, and Eolus Mill from Walker Timberlake's estate. The $6,000 range included Benjamin C. Flannagan's property on Sixth Street between Main and Market, Randolph Frank Harris's Iron Foundry and Agriculture Machine Manufactory in Charlottesville, the Albemarle Insurance Company, and the Monticello Bank, all in town, as well as county properties: Mrs. Mary A. Harper's Farmington, Thomas Jefferson Randolph Jr.'s Edgehill, Judge Alexander Rives's Carlton, and J. M. Brown's property on Stockton Creek; Rawlings, *Early Charlottesville*, 26–27, 29, 109; William P. Farish resided at Hillcrest Farm and owned the Farish House hotel. His Monticello House was known at different times as the Stone Tavern and Central Hotel. John Vowles had become the proprietor of the Eagle Hotel in 1833; Moore, *Albemarle*, 211, 237–38.

20. Whiffen, *American Architecture*; McAlester, *American Houses*. Examples include Gervase Wheeler's *Rural Homes* (1851) and *Homes for People in Suburb and Country* (1855), Calvert Vaux's *Villas and Cottages* (1857), Henry Hudson Holly's *Holly's Country Seats* (1863) and *Modern Dwellings in Town And Country* (1878), *The American Woman's Home* by the Beecher

sisters, George E. Woodward's *Woodward's Country Homes* (1865) and *Woodward's National Architect* (1868), and the many pattern books by A. J. Bicknell and the Pallisers.

21. Moore, *Albemarle*, 216; AC Tax Lists, 1870. In the $8,000 range were Dr. Charles D. Everett's Belmont, Peyton Skipwith Coles's Estouteville, and Randolph T. Harris's lot no. 172 in Charlottesville. In the $7,000 range were Thomas L. Farish's The Farm, Mary A. Harper's Farmington, N. H. Massie's Eagle Hotel, and John Thornley's buildings on lot nos. 15 and 16 in town. In the $6,000 range were the Charlottesville buildings of Benjamin C. Flannagan on lot no. 25, Edward Benner on lot no. 34, the Albemarle Insurance Company on lot no. 19, and Col. John Bowie Strange's brick Ridge Street house. County buildings in this value range were Judge Alexander Rives's Carlton, John Mosby's building ten miles west of town on Mechum's River, the Walker Timberlake estate's Eolus Mill on the Hardware River, and the Nathaniel Burnley estate's Hydraulic Mills.

22. AC Surveyor's Book 1, Edmund Anderson's additions, surveys of 17 Dec. 1818, 2 Apr. 1819, 28 Sept. 1825; Department of Community Development, *Historic Landmark Study*, 3; Mary Rawlings, *Historical Guide to Old Charlottesville, with Mention of Its Statues and of Albemarle's Shrines* (Charlottesville, Va., 1958), [9]; *Charlottesville Central Gazette*, 26 Feb. 1820; Martha Randolph Carr, *DP*, 27 Oct. 1989.

23. E. F. Turner, *Annual Directory for the City of Charlottesville, 1888–1889* (Yonkers, N.Y., 1888).

24. Inventory, AC Will Book 27:480; account, ibid., 481; Turner, *Directory, 1888–1889*; AC Marriage Record, 1853; Prout and Fyler, *Directory of Charlottesville* (Charlottesville, Va., 1895).

25. Ford, "Recollections of the Past," 101–14; conversation with Alice Norris, 5 July 1996; Turner, *Directory, 1888–1889*.

26. AC Deed Books 82:138, 85:286; Charlottesville Deed Book 5:473; Turner, *Directory, 1888–1889*; Prout and Fyler, *Directory*, 1895; U.S. Census, Schedule of Inhabitants, AC, 1900; AC Marriage Record, 18 Nov. 1852, 26 July 1880, 5 June 1888; conversation with Alice Norris, 5 July 1996; Moore, *Albemarle*, 429; Prout and Fyler, *Directory*, 1890–91, 1902; Harris and Sharpe, *Directory of Charlottesville, Va.* (Charlottesville, Va., 1898).

27. *DP*, 24 Jan. 1921; AC Deed Book 37:412; AC Will Book 2:312; AC Marriage Record, 12 Jan. 1859; U.S. Census, Schedule of Inhabitants, AC, 1830, 1900; Turner, *Directory, 1888–1889*; Prout and Fyler, *Directory*, 1890–91, 1895, 1902, 1905; Harris and Sharpe, *Directory*, 1898; Oakwood Cemetery inscriptions; *Central Gazette*, 23 June 1820.

28. Chris Edwards, *Charlottesville Observer*, 24 Dec. 1992; Chris Meyer, *Real Estate Weekly*, 12–18 July 1995; Boroughs, Chapman, and King, "James River Road Survey," bldg. no. 1; Dudley and Mackie, "Staunton and James River Turnpike Survey," bldg. no. 35A; correspondence with James T. Wollen Jr., 17 Dec. 1993, 18 Jan. 1994.

29. Rawlings, *Early Charlottesville*, 44; Jeffrey Jacobson, "Watson House," SVA ser. (not cataloged), 1982; Nell Lee, *DP*, 6 Jan. 1980; Woods, *Albemarle*, 245–46; Wheeler, *Historic Virginia*, 208; Hill and Murphy, "Coursey's Road Survey," bldg. no. 4; *Weekly Chronicle*, 22 Sept. 1898; *DP*, 10 Jan. 1928; Wheeler, *Historic Virginia*, 267; Dudley and Mackie, "Staunton and James River Turnpike Survey," bldg. no. 35C; correspondence with Keith Van Allen, 5 July 1997.

30. Edwards, Wenger, and Yetter, "Secretary's Road Survey," bldg. no. 67; Leslie J. Vollmert, "Tower House," study for Nichols, 1974.

31. Philip Ovuka, "Marshall Rucker House," study for Nichols, 1975.

32. Frederick William Neve, "Autobiography of Frederick William Neve," from a typescript prepared by the Reverend Dennis Whittle from a handwritten copy dictated by Neve to family members in 1940, *MACH* 26 (1967–68): 5–73; Dennis Whittle, "Archdeacon Neve's Later Years," *MACH* 26 (1967–68): 75–79; Elizabeth Coles Langhorne, *Nancy Astor and Her Friends* (New York, 1974), 13–15.

33. Lapsley and Thomsen, "Three Notch'd Road Survey," bldg. no. 62; William Tucci and Joseph Debreczeni, "J. I. Maupin Store, Alberene," no. 2, SVA ser., 1973; Tom Dubuisson, Richard Hekimian, and Kenneth C. Magalis, "Alberene Company House," no. 29, SVA ser., 1976.

34. Mutual Assurance Society Policy, 1 Aug. 1860; Camille Wells, "The Poore House," study for Nichols, 1974; William C. Mott Jr., "427 Park Street," study for Nichols, n.d.; Brian Hughes and Denis Robert McNamara, "Price-Poore House," no. 105, SVA ser., 1993; *DP*, 6 June 1899, 28 Apr. 1900, 2 Aug. 1905; Blanche Sellers Ortman, *The Old House, and Other Stories* (Chicago, 1910); Lenny Granger, *DP*, 15 June 1978; Amy T. Gilbert, "Blue Ridge Farm," study for Nichols, 1980; Geoffrey B. Henry, NRHP Nomination Form, VDHR.

35. Richard P. Thomsen Jr., "The Old Jail and Jailor's House," study for Prof. Roy Graham, School of Architecture, UVA, 1975; Don Horn and Susan Harrison, "The Albemarle County Jail Complex," study for Kayhoe, n.d.; AC Minute Book, 1875: 126 (4 June), 128 (26 June); Moore, *Albemarle*, 360–61; Dan Fay and Lisa Smith, "Albemarle County Jail Number Five," no. 109, SVA ser., 1995. For more information about Albemarle County jails, see Frank William Hoffer, Floyd Nelson House, and Delbert Martin Mann, *The Jails of Virginia* (New York, 1933), 44–49.

36. *DP*, 11, 14 Feb., 2 Mar., 27, 28 May, 16 July, 16, 18, 26, 27, 28, 30 Sept., 3, 8 Oct., 16, 23 Nov. 1895; Barclay Rives, *A History of Grace Church, Cismont: Walker's Parish* (Charlottesville, Va., , 1993); Frierson, "Five Episcopal Churches."

37. Ruth E. Balluff, "Ivy Parish, Virginia, 1893–1963," VDHR architectural survey files; Moore, *Albemarle*, 342–43; Whittle, "Archdeacon Neve's Later Life," 5–73, 75–79; David A. Maurer, "Mountaineer Apostle Left an Indelible Mark," *DP*, 11 Nov. 1990.

38. Joseph Lee Vaughn and Omer Allan Gianniny Jr., *Thomas Jefferson's Rotunda Restored* (Charlottesville, Va., 1981), 34–39; O. A. Gianniny, "The Rotunda That Was Not Built: Mr. Jefferson's Pet Cast in Iron," MACH 40 (1982): 63; personal interview with O. A. Gianniny, 9 May 1985; Withey and Withey, *Biographical Dictionary*, 404; Wilson, *Arise and Build!*.

39. Robert Moje, Rod Temmick, and Dwight Young, "St. John's Episcopal Church," no. 19, SVA ser., 1974; Pegram, "Victorian Churches"; Sallie Smith, "St. Luke's Chapel," no. 55, SVA ser., 1981; Frierson, "Five Episcopal Churches"; John V. Berberich III, "Cemetery Plans," 1991, photocopy in my possession; Rebecca Trumbull, "Garth Chapel," no. 57, SVA ser., 1981.

40. Pegram, "Victorian Churches"; *Fluvanna County Historical Society Bulletin* 34 (Oct. 1982): 16; DP, 23 Dec. 1973; Charlottesville Deed Books 100:321, 197:321, 357:422.

41. Pegram, "Victorian Churches."

42. Woods, *Albemarle*, 59–60; Moore, *Albemarle*, 216; West Main Street Lutheran church information brought to my attention by Eugenia Bibb, 15 Mar. 1996.

43. Marjorie F. Irwin, *The Negro in Charlottesville and Albemarle County* (M.A. thesis, UVA, 1919), Phelps-Stokes Fellowship Papers, no. 9 (Charlottesville, Va., 1929); Helen Camp de Corse, *A Study of Negro Life and Personality* (master's thesis, UVA, 1933), Phelps-Stokes Fellowship Papers, no. 11 (Charlottesville, Va., 1933)); WPA, "Inventory of the Church Archives of Virginia, Negro Baptist Churches in Richmond," LVA; James Simms, *The First Colored Baptist Church in North America* (New York, 1969); Carter G. Woodson, *The History of the Negro Church* (1921; rept. Washington, D.C., 1972); Albert J. Raboteau, *Slave Religion* (New York, 1978); Rosanna Liebman and Matilda McQuaid, "A Study of Ten Black Baptist Churches in Albemarle County," no. 19, AIV ser., 1983; Moore, *Albemarle*, 80–81; 1864 Gilmer map and 1866 Hotchkiss map of Albemarle County.

44. Pegram, "Victorian Churches"; Liebman and McQuaid, "Ten Black Baptist Churches."

45. Pegram, "Victorian Churches"; Liebman and McQuaid, "Ten Black Baptist Churches"; DP, 19 Jan. 1986.

46. Orson Squire Fowler, *A Home for All; or The Gravel Wall and Octagonal Mode of Building* (New York, 1854); Mark Reinberger and Julie Semmelman, "Zion Baptist Church," no. 23, SVA ser., 1975.

47. John B. Boles, *A Bicentennial History of Chestnut Grove Baptist Church, 1773–1973* (Richmond, 1973).

48. Burnley, *Court House*, 9; Eugenia Bibb, "Historic Landmark Survey," 1989, Department of Community Development, Charlottesville; Doug Chambers and Shaun Eyring, "Mount Zion Baptist Church," study for Kayhoe, n.d.; Roberta C. Kerr, Mount Zion Baptist Church NRHP Nomination Form, Apr. 1991, VDHR; Linda Blackford, *Charlottesville Observer*, 22–28 Oct. 1992, 30 May–5 Apr. 1995.

49. *Jeffersonian Republican*, 2 Aug. 1860; Richard I. McKinney, "Keeping the Faith: A History of the First Baptist Church," MACH 39 (1980): 12–29; Liebman and McQuaid, "Ten Black Baptist Churches"; William James Sr., "First Baptist Church," *Advocate*, 18–25 Sept. 1992, 3; Ray Bell lecture on "Memories of Vinegar Hill" for ACHS, 21 Feb. 1993; Kay Collins Chretien, DP, 30 May–5 June 1996.

50. Liebman and McQuaid, "Ten Black Baptist Churches."

51. Nancy E. Willner, "A Brief History of the Jewish Community in Charlottesville and Albemarle," MACH 40 (1982): 1–24; conversation with Jeffrey Hantman, Charlottesville, Jan. 1994.

52. Nancy O. Elliot and T. Ricardo Quesada, "Woolen Mills Chapel," no. 11, SVA ser., 1973.

53. Thomas Jefferson to Dr. Woods, Jefferson Papers; Thomas Jefferson, *Notes on the State of Virginia*, 159, 291.

54. David A. Dashiell III, "Between Earthly Wisdom and Heavenly Truth: The Effort to Build a Chapel at the University of Virginia, 1835–1890," MACH 52 (1994): 86–113, and Master of Architectural History thesis, UVA, 1992; *University Journal*, 8 Feb. 1993; *Cavalier Daily*, 17 Feb. 1994.

55. Davis et al., "Staunton and James River Turnpike Survey," bldg. no. 9.

56. David Ives Bushnell, "Ancient Soapstone Quarry in Albemarle County, Virginia," *Journal of the Washington Academy of Sciences* 16 (18 Nov. 1926); Tucci and Debreczeni, "J. I. Maupin Store"; Thomas Dubuisson, Richard Hekimian, and Kenneth Magalis, "Alberene Company House," no. 29, SVA ser., 1976; Lenny Granger, DP, 9 Apr. 1978; Susan Tyler Hitchcock, "Soapstone from Alberene," *Commonwealth* 50 (July 1983): 29–32; David A. Maurer, DP, 1 Apr. 1990, 1 Sept. 1996; *Charlottesville Observer*, 26 Mar.–1 Apr. 1992, 16–17; Garth G. Groff, *Soapstone Shortlines: Alberene Stone and Its Railroads* (Charlottesville, Va., 1991).

57. *Manufactures of U.S. in 1860: 8th Census* (Washington, D.C., 1865), 604.

58. David A. Maurer, DP, 1 Dec. 1991, 30 Aug. 1992; AC Tax Lists, 1870.

59. "Cocke's Mill House and Cocke's Mill Site," NRHP Nomination Form, VDHR. The four mills that have been adapted into other uses are Peter Field Jefferson's mill, Thomas Walker Jr.'s mill, Warren Mill, and Crossroads Mill. Other extant mills that have not been adapted into other uses are Hatton Grange Mill, Merrie Mill, Smith's mill, Garth's mill, Wilhoit's mill, Wood's mill, and Gleco Mills. The Meadow Run Mill at Michie Tavern was relocated to that complex from the Shenandoah Valley.

60. Edward W. Hase II and Robert M. Hubbard, "Adolph Russow and the Monticello Wine Company," MACH 46 (1988): 16–27.

61. Stephen Price Maury, "Tale of a Black Sheep," memoirs, July 1926, private collection; Randolph Jefferson Kean, "Early Street Railways and the Development of Charlottesville," MACH 33–34 (1975–76): 1–52; Moore, *Albemarle*, 276–

307; Eugenia Bibb, "Charlottesville Landmark Survey," 1982, Department of Community Development, Charlottesville; David A. Maurer, *DP*, 24 Mar. 1991.

62. Elizabeth Respess, *DP*, 15 June 1975.

63. Ray McGrath, *DP*, 28 Oct. 1979.

64. AC Tax Lists, 1860.

65. *DP*: Jamie Gibson, 3 Nov. 1993, Charlotte Crystal, 31 Dec. 1995; *DP*, 27 Mar. 1975; Kay Collins Chretien, *Charlottesville Observer*, 9 Dec. 1993; Tucci and Debreczeni, "J. I. Maupin Store"; Rex Bowman, *DP*, 23 Feb. 1995; Dame and Sabadell, "Brown's Gap Turnpike Survey," bldg. no. 34; Boroughs, Chapman, and King, "James River Road Survey," bldg. no. 18; Lapsley and Thomsen, "Three Notch'd Road Survey," bldg. no. 44.

66. F. T. Heblich Jr. and Cecile Clover Walters, *Holsinger's Charlottesville, 1890–1925* (Charlottesville, Va., 1978), 78.

67. Mary Ann Elwood and Fred T. Heblich, *Charlottesville and the University of Virginia: A Pictorial History* (Norfolk, Va., 1982), 33; Timothy Bishop, "Inge's Store," no. 49, SVA ser., 1979; Lawrence P. Keitz, "Inge's Grocery Store," study for Nichols, n.d.; Ray McGrath, *DP*, 11 Nov. 1979; Leslie Cauley, *Charlottesville Observer*, 8–14 May 1980; *DP*: Audrey Ross, 19 Jan. 1989, David A. Maurer, 21 Jan. 1990.

68. *DP*: Douglas Pardue, 13 Jan. 1975, David A. Maurer, 10 Dec. 1989.

69. Mead, *Historic Homes*, 41–48; *DP*, 29 Nov. 1912, 18, 19 July 1929; Ron Shibley, *Jefferson Journal*, 2 Mar. 1972; Tom Lankford, *Declaration*, 19 Oct. 1973; Gail Hammerquist, NRHP Nomination Form, VDHR; Rhinelander, "Dick Woods's Road Survey," bldg. no. 38; correspondence with James Thomas Wollen Jr., 17 Dec. 1993, 7, 18 Jan. 1994; Kay Collins Chretien, *Charlottesville Observer*, 7–13 Mar. 1996.

70. Moore, *Albemarle*, 232.

71. AC Deed Book 97:316 (16 Feb. 1892); Moore, *Albemarle*, 320–21.

72. Frederick Spitzmiller, NRHP Nomination Form, 1977, VDHR; Bob Boucheron, *Real Estate Weekly*, 15–21 Sept. 1993; Will Morton, *DP*, 14 Sept. 1994; Association of Collegiate Schools of Architecture's Design + Energy National Competition, first place awarded to Peter Kutscha under the direction of Prof. K. Edward Lay, UVA, 1987, for a study to convert the Union Depot into an urban transportation and commercial center; *DP*: editorial, 21 Mar. 1991, Nick Johnson, 8, 19, 27 Mar. 1991, Bryan Mackenzie, 29 Mar. 1991, Lawrence M. Herbert, 14 Apr. 1991; Thomas W. Dixon Jr., "The C&O's Colonial Revival Stations," *Chesapeake and Ohio Historical Magazine* 19 (Jan. 1987): 4–8.

VI. The Eclectic Era (1890–1939)

1. Tania Durilin, "Bremo Recess," no. 71, AIV ser., 1988.

2. William Bertholet Rhoads, *The Colonial Revival*, 2 vols. (New York, 1977), lists several significant publications during this period. In 1876 Charles Wylls Elliott published his *Book on American Interiors*. The year 1891 witnessed Irving W. Lyon's *Colonial Furniture of New England*. During this period Batty Langley's eighteenth-century sourcebook *Examples from Ancient Masonry* was reprinted. William Rotch Ware's *The Georgian Period* came out in a journal series in 1898, exhibiting American architectural drawings and photographs, and was reprinted in 1923. Henry Lawrence Wilson's *The Bungalow Book* was published in 1908 promoting the cottage style in America. During this period the ubiquitous I-house competed with the bungalow and the foursquare house. Weyerhaeuser published an architectural periodical of measured drawings, *Pencil Points*, in its White Pine Series of Architectural Monographs between 1915 and the 1940s. Even the five books by America's first pattern-book author, Asher Benjamin, were reprinted in 1918. Other early publications pertaining to Virginia architecture included Joseph Everett Chandler's *Colonial Architecture of Maryland, Pennsylvania, and Virginia* (1892), Edward A. Crane's *Examples of Colonial Architecture in the South* (1899), Bishop William Meade's *Old Churches* (1900), William H. Snowden's *Some Old Historic Landmarks of Virginia* (1901), Dr. William Alexander Lambeth's *Jefferson as an Architect* (1913), Robert A. Lancaster's *Historic Virginia Homes and Churches* (1915), Lewis A. Coffin Jr.'s *Brick Architecture of the Colonial Period in Maryland and Virginia* (1919), Fiske Kimball's *Domestic Architecture of the American Colonies and Early Republic* (1922), Swepson Earle's *The Chesapeake Bay Country* (1924), Dora C. Jett's *In Tidewater Virginia* (1924), Paul Wilstach's *Tidewater Virginia* (1929), Henry I. Brock's *Colonial Churches in Virginia* (1930), I. T. Frary's *Thomas Jefferson: Architect and Builder* (1931), Thomas Tileston Waterman's *Domestic Colonial Architecture of Tidewater Virginia* (1932), William E. Carson's *Historic Shrines of Virginia* (1933), Wallace Nutting's *Virginia Beautiful* (1935), Richard H. Halsey's *The Homes of Our Ancestors* (1935), James L. Kibler's *Colonial Virginia Shrines* (1936), John W. Wayland's *Historic Homes of Northern Virginia* (1937), Marylou Rhodes's *Landmarks of Richmond* (1938), and Thomas Tileston Waterman's *The Mansions of Virginia* (1940).

3. Heblich and Walters, *Holsinger*, 15; *Historic Landmark Study*, 4.

4. For vitae on these and subsequent architects, see: Henry F. and Elsie R. Withey, *Biographical Dictionary of American Architects (Deceased)* (Los Angeles, 1956); George S. Koyl, ed., *American Architects' Directory* (New York, 1956); *American Art Annual* (Washington, D.C., 1924); and Rhoads, *Colonial Revival*; *DP*, 22 Mar. 1915, contains a promotional article concerning the city's building boom that was brought to my attention by A. Robert Kuhlthau.

5. Brought to my attention by Edna Tapscott Anderson, 18 July 1996, and Keith Van Allen, 22 June, 5 July 1997; Susan Hume Frazer, *Scottsville Museum Newsletter*, no. 7 (Mar. 1997), and Fraser's lecture 6 Apr. 1997 at the Scottsville Victory Hall.

6. Edward C. Mead, *DP*, 4, 5, 6, 7 Feb. 1895, 8 July 1914;

DP, 21 Apr. 1893, 16, 29 Mar. 1906; Gray M. Bryan, "Waddy Wood's Residences, Washington, D.C." (Master of Architectural History thesis, UVA, 1980).

7. For more information on Stanhope S. Johnson, see S. Allen Chambers Jr., *Lynchburg: An Architectural History* (Charlottesville, Va., 1981).

8. William B. O'Neal and Christopher Weeks, *The Work of William Lawrence Bottomley in Richmond* (Charlottesville, Va., 1985); George C. Longest, *Genius in the Garden: Charles F. Gillette and Landscape Architecture in Virginia* (Richmond, 1992).

9. AC Deeds, 1860–63, 1892–97; *DP*, 21 Feb. 1921; U.S. Census, Schedule of Inhabitants, AC, 1860, 1900; Prout and Fyler, *Directory*, 1890–91, 1895; AC Marriage Record, 10 May 1859; Oakwood Cemetery gravestone inscriptions.

10. Eugene Bradbury Architectural Drawings, SC-ViU; conversations with Francis Fife and Anne E. H. Freudenburg, Charlottesville, 1984.

11. Conversation with E. E. Burruss Jr., Charlottesville, 1982.

12. Sheet music brought to my attention by Steven Nock.

13. Moore, *Albemarle*, 271–73; Papamichael, Tucker, and Whitehead, "Staunton and James River Turnpike Survey," bldg. no. 63.

14. *DP*, 1 Feb. 1906; Walker, *The Daily Progress, Historical and Industrial Magazine*, 43; *DP*, 13 Oct. 1917; Richard Prior, *DP*, 2 Sept. 1979; Margaret P. Mickler, NRHP Nomination Form, 1980, VDHR; Lynn Crytzer, *History of Ednam*, Stevens and Co. (n.p., n.d.); *DP*: 1 Feb. 1981, Cindy Conte, 25 Oct. 1981, Tina Eshleman, 30 Mar. 1992.

15. Wheeler, *Historic Virginia*, 269; *DP*: Dan Friedman, 29 Jan. 1978, David A. Maurer, 14 Mar. 1993; correspondence with James T. Wollen Jr., 17 Dec. 1993, 18 Jan. 1994; Calder Loth and Margaret P. Mickler, NRHP Nomination Form, VDHR.

16. John Wells, "Buckingham Palace," no. 28, SVA ser., 1976; Tracy S. Scharer, "Three Notched Road Survey," bldg. no. 69; Helen Jameson, "Carr's Hill," study for Nichols, 1982; Tatiana S. Durilin and Heidi Rosenwald, "Carr's Hill Carriage House," study for Kayhoe, n.d.; Andrea Dickens, *University Journal*, 8 Feb. 1993; Charles Rosenblum, Carr's Hill lecture, 20 Oct. 1995; Ford, "Recollections of the Past," 113.

17. *Washington Post*, 13 Apr. 1937; Stevens, *House Tour*, 212; Robert Husbands, *Cavalier Daily*, 19 Apr. 1974; Jack Mazzeo and Elizabeth Bailey, ibid., 8 Dec. 1994; Wheeler, *Historic Virginia*, 303.

18. Stevens, *House Tour*, 52–53; *DP*, 11 Sept. 1977; Anne Taylor, "Edgewood," AIV ser., 1995 (uncataloged).

19. *DP*, 22 Mar. 1915; Ace Atkins, *C-ville Review*, 10–16 Dec. 1991; *Inside UVA*, 21 July 1995; Mary Hughes and Jennifer Steen, "U.VA.'s Lost 'Pleasure Ground,'" *University of Virginia Alumni News* 86, 3 (Fall 1997): 26–29.

20. Lance Phillips, *Folks I Knowed and Horses They Rode* (Ashland, Va., 1975); Roulhac Toledano, *Charlottesville Observer*, 5–11 June 1986.

21. Stevens, *House Tour*, 213; *DP*, 25 Feb. 1916.

22. *DP*, 18 Dec. 1965.

23. Wheeler, *Historic Virginia*, 314–16; Stevens, *House Tour*, 102, 202.

24. Wheeler, *Historic Virginia*, 320; George and Mary Roberts, *Triumph on Fairmount* (Philadelphia, 1959); Stevens, *House Tour*, 104; Calder Loth, NRHP Nomination Form, VDHR; Brownell et al., *Virginia Architecture*, 122.

25. Stevens, *House Tour*, 300; Grosskopf, Thaler, and Trischman-Marks, "Rockfish Gap Turnpike Survey," bldg. no. 10.

26. Rick Kniesler, "Morven and Verulam," study for Nichols, 1976.

27. *DP*, 16 June 1903; Stevens, *House Tour*, 83; Jane McHugh, *DP*: 10 Sept. 1987, Amanda Kell, 28 Aug. 1990, Richard Miller, 28 Mar., 7 Apr. 1991, James Blair Lovell, 6 May 1991, Mary Alice Blackwell, 7 Sept. 1991, Rey Berry, 28 Feb. 1992, Bob Gibson, 5 Sept. 1993, Ronald J. Hansen, 8, 10, 11, 12, 15, 16, 17 June, 21 July, 3 Oct. 1994, Sean Scully, 20 June 1994, Bob Gibson, 6 Oct. 1994.

28. Kevin Hildebrand, "Manley House," study for Nichols, 1980.

29. Stevens, *House Tour*, 282–83; Grosskopf, Thaler, and Trischman-Marks, "Rockfish Gap Turnpike Survey," bldg. no. 8.

30. Stevens, *House Tour*, 288–89; Barclay Rives, "Portrait: Lucy LeGrand," *Albemarle Magazine* 6 (Sept.–Oct. 1988); Grosskopf, Thaler, and Trischman-Marks, "Rockfish Gap Turnpike Survey," bldg. no. 5.

31. *Charlottesville Observer*, Jan. 1992, 3–4, 8, 11.

32. Green and Vest, "Rockfish Gap Turnpike Survey," bldg. no. 58.

33. Stevens, *House Tour*, 190–97.

34. *DP*, 3, 4 Oct. 1930; *Richmond Times-Dispatch*, 25 Apr. 1952; J. Ward Kuser, "Gallison Hall and Rose Hill," study for Nichols, 1969; Grosskopf, Thaler, and Trischman-Marks, "Road to Rockfish Gap Survey," bldg. no. 4; Koyl, *American Architects' Directory*, 22.

35. Wheeler, *Historic Virginia*, 321; Stevens, *House Tour*, 198–201; Kuser, "Gallison Hall and Rose Hill"; *DP*: Carla Malcolm Pace, 13 Oct. 1983, Sherri Nee, 16 Oct. 1992; Brownell et al., *Virginia Architecture*, 378.

36. Wheeler, *Historic Virginia*, 331–32; Stevens, *House Tour*, 234–35; telephone conversation with Mr. and Mrs. Howard L. Hamilton, 26 Sept. 1995.

37. "Mr. Robert B. Crawford's Villa at Keswick, Virginia," *Spur* 14 (1 Oct. 1914): 26–27, 48; *DP*, 5 Apr., 28 Sept. 1928; *Richmond Times-Dispatch*, Dec. 1982; *DP*, 5 Aug. 1983; *Charlottesville Observer*, 16–22 July 1992, 14.

38. *DP*: 7 Oct., 13 Nov., 13 Dec. 1902, 24 Mar. 1906, Allen Hale, 3 Sept. 1968; Moore, *Albemarle*, 153–54; Ann Holiday, *Richmond News Leader*, 16 Apr. 1987; *APVA Newsletter*, Fall 1990; Green and Vest, "Rockfish Gap Turnpike Survey," bldg. no. 57.

39. *DP*, 25 Sept. 1930; Ella Smith, *Tears and Laughter in Virginia and Elsewhere* (Verona, Va., 1972), 2, 10, 27, 86–87; Geoffrey B. Henry, NRHP Nomination Form for Casa Maria, VDHR; Grosskopf, Thaler, and Trischman-Marks, "Rockfish Gap Turnpike Survey," bldg. no. 3; *Albemarle*, no. 30 (Oct–Nov. 1992): 40–43; Agnes Rothery, *A Fitting Habitation* (New York, 1944).

40. Clem Labine, *Old-House Journal* 10 (Mar. 1982): 55–57.

41. Renee Kahn, ibid., 10 (May 1982): 99–102.

42. Kahn, ibid., 5 (Sept. 1977): 99–102.

43. Lenny Granger, *DP*, 17 Nov. 1978; Brent Tarter, "Theodore Roosevelt's Virginia Retreat," *Virginia Cavalcade* 32 (Spring 1984): 184–91; David A. Maurer, *DP*, 31 Mar. 1991; information from William H. Harbaugh, 16 Dec. 1992, 8, 9 Jan. 1993; NRHP Nomination Form, VDHR; William H. Harbaugh, "The Theodore Roosevelts' Retreat in Southern Albemarle: Pine Knot, 1905–1908," *MACH* 51 (1993): 1–50; David A. Maurer, *DP*, 22 Aug. 1993, 29 Oct. 1995; Matthew Lee, *DP*, 7 Nov. 1993; Wheeler, *Historic Virginia*, 237; Stevens, *House Tour*, 62–63; *DP*, 22 Aug. 1940.

44. Kahn, *Old-House Journal* 10 (Feb. 1982): 29–32.

45. Telephone conversation with Collett M. Thach, 21 Sept. 1995.

46. *Charlottesville Observer*, 7–13 May 1992, 16–17.

47. "House of Mrs. James A. Cole, Charlottesville, Va.: Kenneth Day, Architect," *Architectural Forum* 61 (Dec. 1934): 436–38.

48. A. Robert Kuhlthau and Harry W. Webb, "Sculpture in and around Charlottesville: Confederate Memorials," *MACH* 50 (1990): 1–57; *Historic Landmark Study*, 212–13; Bob Boucheron, *Charlottesville Area Real Estate Weekly*, 1–7 Dec. 1993; David A. Maurer, *DP*, 28 Apr. 1996.

49. According to a letter from Mrs. Frederic William Scott, 3 Dec. 1993, it is more likely that the statue depicts someone other than Homer; S. Waite Rawls III of Chicago, *University of Virginia Alumni News* 82 (Jan.–Feb. 1994): 2.

50. Kathryn Horn, *University Journal*, 8 Mar. 1994.

51. David A. Maurer, *DP*, 23 Mar., 27 Apr. 1997.

52. Moore, *Albemarle*, 357, 369–70; Rawlings, *Early Charlottesville*, 23.

53. Frierson, "Five Episcopal Churches"; Lamonte H. Tupper, "The Rock Church of Rio: A History, 1895–1970," 1970, ACHS vertical files; Lamonte H. Tupper, "The Church of Our Savior," 1981, ACHS vertical files.

54. Pegram, "Victorian Churches."

55. Conversations and correspondence with Mrs. Marshall S. Wells, Charlottesville, 1982–88; *DP*, 13 Apr. 1962; Charlottesville Deed Book 55:95.

56. A. L. Bennett, "A Century of Methodism in Charlottesville, Virginia," 1934, ACHS vertical files; Covey, "First United Methodist Church"; AC Deed Books 25:280, 416, 27:221, 29:394; the African Methodist Episcopal Church was brought to my attention by Patricia Edwards from the recollections of 105-year-old Dr. Rebecca F. McGinnis, 20 Oct. 1997.

57. Howard Newlon Jr., "A Brief History of University Baptist Church," *Word* 27 (Oct. 1975).

58. Dashiell and McKinney, "Rockfish Gap Turnpike Survey," bldg. no. 19; AC Deed Books 49:87–88, 338:327; Pegram, "Victorian Churches"; *DP*, 24 Dec. 1973.

59. Williams, "Wheeler's Road Survey" bldg. no. 15.

60. Roulhac Toledano, *Observer*, 5 Aug. 1993.

61. *DP*: 29 Jan. 1995, David A. Maurer, 5 May 1996.

62. Robert Brennan, "Fry's Spring Filling Station," no. 56, SVA ser., 1981; Wendy Hillis, "Colle Service Station," no. 107, SVA ser., 1995.

63. Margaret Fowler Clark, *The Golden Age of the Performing Arts* (Richmond, 1976); brought to my attention by Howard Newlon. Its proscenium-arch construction was similar to that in Robert Stuart's *A Dictionary of Architecture* (London, 1830), pl. c.22.i; Moore, *Albemarle*, 350–51.

64. Debra Lynn Alderson, "The Jefferson and Paramount Theaters," no. 106, AIV ser., 1991, 3–10; Nick Johnson, *DP*, 8 Mar. 1992.

65. Moore, *Albemarle*, 361–63.

66. Ibid., 388; Alderson, "Jefferson and Paramount," 10–17; Nell Lee, *DP*, 4 Sept. 1980; Mark Essig, *Declaration*, 20 Sept. 1990, 6–7, 10; Rhonda Minor, *DP*, 27 May 1995.

67. Moore, *Albemarle*, 468–69; *DP*: 8 Jan. 1951 (obituary), 24 Apr. 1972, David A. Maurer, 9 Apr. 1995.

68. Moore, *Albemarle*, 300.

69. David A. Maurer, *DP*, 15 Oct. 1995; Moore, *Albemarle*, 311; Roger Gregory Magruder, *Martha Jefferson Hospital* (Charlottesville, Va., 1985).

70. William B. O'Neal, *Pictorial History of the University of Virginia* (Charlottesville, Va., 1968), 92; Moore, *Albemarle*, 309–11, 366, 384; *DP*, 18 Aug. 1991; Magruder, *Martha Jefferson Hospital*; Robyn L. Davis, *DP*, 25 Feb. 1994.

71. *DP*, 25 Feb. 1994, 12.

72. Moore, *Albemarle*, 373, 451; David A. Maurer, *DP*, 11, 18 Sept. 1994; Pam Jiranek, *Real Estate Weekly*, 15–21 Feb. 1995; Kay Collins Chretien, *Observer*, 4–10 Apr. 1996.

73. Rob Busler, "Howardsville Masonic Lodge," no. 33, SVA ser., 1976; correspondence with Robert E. Simpson, 27 May 1995.

74. Moore, *Albemarle*, 346–47.

75. Ibid., 345; Wheeler, *Historic Virginia*, 304; *Spur* 14 (1 Oct. 1914): 26–27, 48; *Observer*, 16–22 July 1992, 14.

76. Moore, *Albemarle*, 345, 387.

VII. THE UNIVERSITY OF VIRGINIA AND THE JEFFERSONIAN LEGACY

1. Jefferson to Peter Carr, 7 Sept. 1814, quoted in Malone, *Jefferson* 6:243–44; Bruce, *History of the University of Virginia* 1:223, 5:152; Jefferson to James Dinsmore, 13 Apr. 1817, Jefferson Papers, quoted in *Thomas Jefferson's Academical Village: The Creation of an Architectural Masterpiece*, ed. Richard Guy Wilson (Charlottesville, Va., 1993), 15; Boyd Coons, K.

Edward Lay, and Douglas McVarish, "The Early Years of Architectural Education at the University—Part I," *Colonnade* 3 (Summer 1988); Boyd Coons, "History of the School of Architecture, University of Virginia," 1988, Fiske Kimball Fine Arts Library, UVA; Peterson, *Thomas Jefferson*, 968; "School of Architecture," in *University of Virginia Record* 63, 3 (1976–78): 323; *University of Virginia School of Architecture Graduate Programs* (Charlottesville, Va., 1989), 11.

2. Conversations with Mrs. S. J. Makielski Sr. and Earl C. Leake, Charlottesville, 1987; for more information about Makielski, see *University of Virginia Record*, 1919–65, in which he is mentioned frequently.

3. Jacqueline Melander, "The Architectural Contributions of A. Lawrence Kocher," *Center County Heritage* 22 (1944): 29–31; conversation and correspondence with Nick Pappas, architect of Colonial Williamsburg, 1987.

4. Successors to Campbell at the university's School of Architecture have been Frederick C. Disque, acting chair, 1950–53; Thomas K. Fitzpatrick, dean, 1953–66; J. Norwood Bosserman, acting dean, 1966–67, dean, 1967–75, 1976–80; K. Edward Lay, acting dean, Spring 1976; Jaquelin Taylor Robertson, dean, 1980–88; Harry W. Porter, acting dean, 1988–89, dean, 1989–93; Daphne Spain, acting dean, Spring 1994; William McDonough, dean, 1994–99; Karen Van Lengen, dean, 1999–.

5. Conversations and correspondence with Mrs. Marshall S. Wells, Charlottesville, 1982–88.

6. Conversations and correspondence with Mrs. Arthur C. Barlow, Charlottesville, 1982; conversations and correspondence with Mrs. Clarence W. Wenger, Charlottesville, 1982; Clarence W. Wenger Papers, SC-ViU; obituary, *DP*, 8 Feb. 1982.

7. Joseph Lasala, "Milton Grigg," no. 102, AIV ser., 1990; conversations and correspondence with Mrs. William Newton Hale and Mr. and Mrs. Milton L. Grigg, 1980–87; Milton L. Grigg Papers, SC-ViU.

8. Conversations with Floyd E. Johnson and Thomas W. S. Craven, Charlottesville, 1982–87; Sydney Burtner, *Charlottesville Observer*, 23–29 May 1996.

9. Conversations with Mr. and Mrs. Louis L. Scribner, Charlottesville, 1982–88.

10. Conversations with B. Henderson Heyward, Charlottesville, 1982–88, H. H. Taylor, Trumansburg, N.Y., 1987, R. B. Baker, New York, 1987.

11. Moore, *Albemarle*, 318; conversations and correspondence with Allaville and Evelina Magruder, Charlottesville, 1983–88.

12. Moore, *Albemarle*, 432.

13. The following is adapted from a tour I conducted for the Fourth Annual Architectural History Symposium at UVA during the autumn of 1991 and K. Edward Lay, "The American Renaissance at U.VA.," *University of Virginia Alumni News* 82, 7 (Nov.–Dec. 1993): 16–21 (includes those buildings erected during Jefferson's time through World War II but does not include the buildings in the Lawn gardens).

14. White's alteration of Jefferson's design brought to my attention by C. Allan Brown, 18 May 1998. Evidence exists that the steps and plinth for columns, and possibly the columns themselves, may already have been erected on the north portico by builder John Gorman (22 and 28 Mar. 1827, Proctor's Daybook, SC-ViU); Vaughn and Gianniny, *Thomas Jefferson's Rotunda Restored*, 38–39; Gianniny, "The Rotunda That Was Not Built," *MACH* 40 (1982): 63; interview with O. A. Gianniny, 9 May 1985; Wilson, *Arise and Build!*

15. See John Richard Andrews's letter to the editor, *University of Virginia Alumni News* 82 (Mar.–Apr. 1994): 72.

16. *DP*, 13 July, 9 Sept. 1905; see John Richard Andrews's letter to the editor, *University of Virginia Alumni News* 82 (Mar.–Apr. 1994): 72; Jessica Lowe, *Cavalier Daily*, 24 Sept. 1997.

17. S. Waite Rawls III of Chicago, *University of Virginia Alumni News* 82 (Jan.–Feb. 1994): 2.

18. Wilson, *Arise and Build!* 26; Virginius Dabney, *Mr. Jefferson's University* (Charlottesville, Va., 1981), 41.

19. See John Richard Andrews's letter to the editor, *University of Virginia Alumni News* 82 (Mar.–Apr. 1994): 72.

20. Craig Vandecastle, "A Resting Place of History: The Story of the University Cemetery," *University of Virginia Alumni News* 88, 2 (Summer 1998): 20–27.

21. Jessica Lowe, *Cavalier Daily*, 24 Sept. 1997.

Glossary

ARCHITRAVE TRIM: a door or window surround
asymmetrical
symmetrical

ATTENUATED MANTEL SHELF: the shelf over a fireplace opening that has been reduced in apparent thickness through a series of wooden layers, reducing in size, supporting it

BALLOON FRAMING: wooden framing where the studs extend from the top of the soleplate to the roof plate as opposed to being separate members for each floor as in platform framing

BANK BUILDING: a building built into the slope of the land so that the entrance is on the upper level where the building is one story in height with the land dropping off to the rear to make it two stories

BAYS: the number of openings across a building facade

BEADED JOISTS: wood structural members in the ceiling, supporting the floor above, that have rounded edges formed with a beading plane and meant to be left exposed

BEAM:
dragon beam: a short but large wooden beam that bisects the wall plate and the summer beam at an angle
summer beam: a large wooden beam supporting the ends of floor joists

BOARD AND BATTEN: exterior sheathing of wide vertical boards with narrower vertical boards covering their joints

BRACKET: projecting wooden member supporting roof eaves

BRICK BOND: the arrangement of the headers or ends of bricks that bind together brick masonry walls (see fig. 8)
American bond: rows of headers occurring every fourth or more courses with stretcher courses between
American with Flemish variant: rows of alternating headers and stretchers occurring every sixth or more courses with stretcher courses between
English bond: alternating courses of headers and stretchers
Flemish bond: each course consisting of alternating headers and stretchers arranged to form a plus-sign pattern in three courses
running bond: all courses laid as stretchers with vertical joints of one course falling midway between those of adjacent courses

BRICK CLOSERS: specially formed bricks used near building corners and openings to make brick patterns come out regularly such as in Flemish-bond brickwork
king's closer: about two-thirds the length of a brick stretcher
queen's closer: about two-thirds the length of a brick header

BRICK DIAPERING: diamond-or lozenge-shaped brick patterns made by glazed headers or the removal of those headers for ventilation

BRICK NOGGING: bricks laid between studs for fireproofing, ratproofing, soundproofing, or insulation

BRICK WASH: sloping surfaces of brick chimneys
tiled wash: bricks laid with flat sides to form slope
stepped wash: bricks corbeled or stepped to form slope

BRICK, PIE-SHAPED: triangular brick with a curving face used to form column shafts

CASTELLATIONS (CRENELLATIONS): battlements of repeated indentations on the tops of towers or walls

CARYATIDS: columns in the form of erect women

CAST-IRON CRESTING: a metal roof screen or railing

CHAMFERED: posts with corners beveled at a 45° angle

CHIMNEY:
buttress-type: in the form of two buttresses placed together with two washes on each side (double-ramped)
cat and clay (catted): wood poles laid in a horizontal manner to form a rectangular chimney shaft and covered with mud
chimney curtain: a brick parapet wall connecting two gable-end chimneys and masking the gable roof
chimney pent: a shed-roofed one-story structure between two chimneys used for various purposes such as a china press, book shelves, storage, or powdering room
diagonally set: fireplace set at a 45° angle in a chimney stack in order to service two separate rooms
pyramidal: angled in the form of a pyramid to its necking
T-plan: chimney stack in the form of a T in plan usually expressing separate flues

CHINA PRESS: a closet with shelving for dishes

CHINESE RAILING: graceful railings in the manner of Thomas Chippendale patterned after Chinese motifs

CHINKING: material used for filling the horizontal spaces between logs

CONSTRUCTION:

de l'Orme truss: a structural system for piecing together wooden ribs to form a dome in the 1561 book *Nouvelles inventions* by French architect Philibert de l'Orme

king-post truss: a triangular frame formed by two inclined members joined at the apex with a vertical member extending from there to the horizontal tie beam

post-and-beam (post-and-lintel): construction using vertical posts and a horizontal lintel to span an opening

CORNICE: on the exterior the trim at the meeting of the roof and the wall, or the top molding at the ceiling on an interior wall

modillion (dentil): bricks under a roof eave that project to form dentils

molded brick: specially molded bricks that when grouped together vertically form a cyma molding just under the roof eave and usually whitewashed

mousetooth (houndstooth): one or two rows of diagonally set brick under the roof eave

CROSSETTES: projections of architrave moldings around doors, windows, and fireplaces, usually at the extremities of the lintel, to form "ears"

CROW'S-STEP GABLE: a brick parapet with a stepped edge masking a pitched roof

DOOR:

aedicule doorway: a door framed by columns or pilasters and crowned with a pediment

batten: a door constructed of vertical boards held together by horizontal battens on the back side

double-leaf: two single doors hung in the same doorframe

false (blind): giving the appearance of a door leading to another space but over a solid wall and nonoperating

four-panel: appearing in the Greek Revival period often with separate applied moldings around the panels

rails: the horizontal pieces in a door

regency: early twentieth-century door with five horizontal panels

six-panel: popular in the Federal period and forming a cross above an open Bible below, often referred to as a Christian door

stiles: the vertical pieces in a door

DOOR HARDWARE:

butt: cast iron with two rectangular leaves

H: wrought iron in form of the letter H

HL: wrought iron in form of the letters H and L

self-closing: cast iron with an angled pin holder to enable the door to ride down to seal off the door at the floor and to rise over a carpet when opening

strap: elongated wrought iron often terminating in a circle

ENTABLATURE: classical feature consisting of three parts: cornice (top), frieze (middle), architrave (bottom)

FIGURAL SPACE: space that is nonorthogonal (nonrectangular) but shaped, for instance, as octagonal, oval, cyma, circular, or segmental

FOSSÉ: a foundation excavation of the earth from ground

level to cellar floor with retaining wall, keeping earth away from cellar wall for waterproofing

IMBRICATED SHINGLES: patterned slate shingles made up of different shapes and sometimes different colors

JACK ARCH: a flat lintel with gauged bricks

KEYSTONE: the central voussoir or wedge-shaped center unit of an arch

KITCHEN:

summer: detached kitchen from main house served for fire protection and to keep heat from the main house

winter: in the main house, usually located in the cellar and used mostly in the cold months

L-SHAPED CORNER POST: the wooden corner post of a building which has an L shape in section

LABEL MOLD: raised drip molding that extends across the top of an exterior opening, turning vertically downward for a short distance on the opening sides

LAMB'S TONGUE: the cyma transition between the chamfer and the square wooden post

LANDSCAPE:

ha-ha: a barrier in the form of a trench to prevent cattle from entering but devoid of a fence, thus allowing an unobstructed view from the building

parterres: terraced ground levels

serpentine wall: a twisting or winding garden wall one brick in thickness

LATH: thin narrow strips of split or sawn wood nailed to wall studs and ceiling joists and spaced apart to serve as a base for plaster

rivens: split pieces of wood to serve as lath

LINENFOLD PANELING: wood paneling appearing to form a linen scroll

LINTEL:

trabeated: flat lintels over openings

triangulated: flattened pediments over openings

LOG HOUSE: intended to be a permanent dwelling made of hewn logs

dogtrot (possum trot): two log pens with a center passage between, enclosed by vertical studs clad with horizontal weatherboards

saddlebag: two log pens on either side of a chimney

MARBLEIZING: the use of painting techniques on wood to achieve the appearance of marble

MOLDING:

acorn: ornament representing an acorn—symbol of plenty

baseboard: a horizontal wall molding at floor level

bead: a molding consisting of a series of beads

bead and reel: a semiround convex molding decorated with a pattern of alternating round and elongated beads

bolection: a molding that covers a joint between surfaces

bucrania: a sculptured composition ornament representing the skull of an ox—symbol of eternal life or fertility

candlestick (punch and dentil): small circular holes over the negative spaces between dentils to form the image of a lit candle

cavetto: a circular concave molding

MOLDING (continued)

chair rail: a horizontal wood molding affixed to a plaster wall at a height which prevents the backs of chairs from damaging the wall surface

cyma recta (ogee): a molding having a double curvature profile with concave at the outer edge and convex at the inner edge

cyma reversa (back bend, reverse ogee, Lesbian cyma): a molding having a double curvature profile with convex at the outer edge and concave at the inner edge

dentil: one of toothlike blocks

egg and dart: egg-shape ornaments alternating with dartlike ones

extrados: the surface of an arch

fluting: parallel grooves; the reverse of reeding

garlands: wreaths or festoons of leaves, fruits, or flowers

Greek fret (Greek key, meander, labyrinth fret): continuous lines arranged in rectangular forms

guilloche: bands twisted over each other, leaving circular openings

interlaces: intertwined bands of decoration

lidded urn: a vase with a top

ovolo: a convex molding, usually a quarter of a circle

patera (roundel): a rounded or oval figure often with radiating lines like a sunburst

picture mold: a molding near the ceiling used to support picture hooks

pineapple: ornament representing a pineapple — symbol of hospitality

reeding: adjacent, parallel, protruding, half-round moldings; the reverse of fluting

rope: a torus molding carved in imitation of a rope

scotia: a noncircular concave molding

swags (festoons): pendant semiloops with loose ends

torus: a convex molding, usually half a circle

wainscot (dado): a wood-paneled lower portion of a wall between the baseboard and chair rail

wall of Troy: a undulating line in a rectangular fashion to resemble the fortified walls of Troy

wave motif: a series of stylized representations of breaking waves

MORTISE-AND-TENON: wooden joinery formed by fitting a tongue at the end of one member into the rabbet in another; often fastened together with hardwood pegs and incised with Roman numerals to designate the members cut for a particular joint

MUNTIN: wooden framing member to hold panes (lights) of glass in window sash

Gothic lunette: containing muntins that cross forming pointed arches in a semicircular opening

NAIL:

cut: machine-sheared nails from sheet metal

roseheaded: wrought-iron nails with hammered heads resulting in a rosette

NOTCHING: methods of joining log construction

diamond: forms a diamond-shaped connection

full dovetail: forms a splayed-tenon connection like a dove's tail

half dovetail: forms half of the full dovetail

saddle: forms a crossing of the logs into concave connections

square: forms a square-shaped connection

V-notch: the most common but complex connection that sheds water away from the joint

ORDERS: a particular style of column with its entablature

arcade: a passageway enclosed with a series of arches supported by piers

colonnade: a passageway enclosed with a series of spaced columns

Composite: an elaboration of the Corinthian order, having acanthus leaves of its capital combined with the large volutes of the Ionic order

Corinthian: characterized by a capital with volutes and two rows of acanthus leaves and an elaborate cornice

Doric: the pure Greek Doric column differs from the Roman one in that it is fluted, has no base and is squatter

Ionic: the pure Greek Ionic capital has its volutes parallel to the building wall surface whereas the Roman one has its volutes projecting on the radius of the shaft

Tower of the Winds: a special composite column from the Tower of the Winds temple in Athens, Greece

Tuscan: a simplified version of the Doric order, having a plain frieze and no mutules in the cornice

OVERMANTEL: woodwork above the mantel shelf often where a "landskip" painting or mirror was displayed

PALLADIAN MOTIF (VENETIAN MOTIF, SERLIANO): a door or window opening in three parts, divided by posts, with a flat, lintel over each side by arched over the center

PARAPET: the part of a wall that extends above the roof and into which the roofing is flashed

PEDIMENT: the triangular gable end of a roof above its cornice

PENCILING: the painting of the mortar joints in brickwork with white lime lines

PENDANT: a hanging ornament, sometimes as a pineapple or acorn

PEN-LINED PANEL FIELD: lines painted around a wood panel to appear as if inlaid wood

PERISTYLE: a colonnade around an open space

PIANO NOBILE: the principal story of a house that is completely one story above the ground, often with an exterior stair to it, with the servant spaces below — derived from Renaissance architecture

PILASTER: a flat rectangular pillar on a wall with a capital and base

PILE: the number of rooms front to back of a building plan

single: one room front to back in a building

double: two rooms front to back in a building

PLAN:

H-plan: two parts of a house built parallel to each other with a connection space (hyphen) between, thus forming an H-shape in plan

hall-parlor: a two-room plan

I-house: a two-story, single-pile house with center

passage, essentially half front to back of the proto-typical Georgian plan

L-plan: a plan whose footprint forms an L

single-cell: a one-room plan

stack house: a single-pile house form that has but one room over a first-floor room

T-plan: a plan whose footprint forms a T

PLANK CONSTRUCTION: rectangular-shaped logs with tongues on the ends to slide into a groove in a vertical post, thus eliminating chinking

PLASTER MEDALLION: a composition ceiling plaque, often circular and with ornate decoration

PORTE COCHERE: a porch for a carriage

PORTICO: a covered entry area supported by columns

distyle-in-muris: two columns on the same plane as the facade with a recessed entry behind

paired-column: a tetrastyle portico with narrower spaces between the end columns and a much wider space in the center

piazza: a large porch, usually with more than four columns and two stories in height

tetrastyle: a four-column portico, usually two stories high

two-tier: a two-story portico with balcony engaged with the columns

PUNKAH: a large dining room fan from India kept in motion by a servant to cool the air over the table and chase away flies

PUTLOG HOLE: a brick left out in a wall to provide support for the horizontal member of scaffolding

QUOINS: a pattern of raised bricks or stones on the corners of buildings

RONDEL BLOCK: a circular piece within the square end blocks around architrave trim

ROOF:

bellcast: when the roof curves upward at the eaves

clipped (jerkinhead): having the gable ends truncated or cut out at an angle

dome: a curved roof structure spanning an area; often spherical

gable: a double-sloping roof from the ridge to the eaves

gambrel: a roof having a double slope on two sides, the lower slope being much steeper

hipped: a roof which slopes upward from all four sides

mansard: a roof having a double slope on all four sides, the lower slope being much steeper

pyramidal: a hipped roof on a square plan culminating in a peak, often with a finial

ROOF PEAK: the apex of the roof where the rafters meet

with ridgeboard: a longitudinal member at the apex of a roof into which the rafters are nailed

bellcote: a louvered tower with bells

belvedere (observatory): a glazed or open roof tower that is occupiable

cupola: a roof tower with louvered sides to admit air into the building

glazed monitor (lantern, skylight): a glazed superstructure crowning a roof to allow sunlight to the building interior

widow's walk (captain's walk): an occupiable open roof-peak deck with railing

without ridgeboard: rafters fastened by nailing or mortise-and-tenon or shiplapped and pegged

SAW MARKS:

circular: timbers sawn with a water- or steam-powered circular blade resulting in curving marks

pit-sawed (pitsawn): hand-sawn timber with the log supported over a pit for easy access by two persons using a double-ended saw resulting in slightly tilted uneven marks

reciprocating: water-powered vertically sawn timbers resulting in vertical, evenly spaced marks

STAIR:

banisters: the vertical members that support the stair rail

box: stair enclosed by partitions

closed string: fascia board supporting ends of steps cut at an angle to mask step profile

dogleg: a half-turn stair which has a landing between flights

elliptical (flying spiral, circular): a flight of stairs, curving in plan, whose treads wind around, seemingly unsupported

flying spiral stair: a flight of stairs with a curving plan, seemingly unsupported

open string: fascia board supporting ends of steps cut out to reveal each riser and tread

pyramidal: exterior steps that ascend on three sides, narrowing to a platform at the doorway

scroll brackets: ornament on sides of the stair steps; often the signature of the builder

welcoming arms: splayed exterior stairs that are wider at the ground level than at the doorway

winder: steps that spin around a corner with wedge-shaped treads

STRING (BELT) COURSE: a horizontal raised course of brick or brick recessed to receive stucco on the exterior between the first- and second-floor levels

SUMMER LIVING ROOM: usually a single-pile entry space without fireplaces to be used during the summer months

SUSPENDED BALCONY: a balcony that is hung on one side with wrought-iron rods from the underside of a portico and attached to the facade on the other side

TRANSOM: a window over a door

with sidelights with glass corner panels

with sidelights with solid corner panels

TYMPANUM: the triangular space within a pediment

VERGEBOARD (BARGEBOARD): a board which hangs from the projecting end of a gable roof, sometimes pierced or scalloped

WATER TABLE: the horizontal ledge of a brick wall often formed with specially molded bricks to take up the difference in the wall thickness between the first floor and the cellar

WEATHERBOARD: horizontal wall cladding usually of sawn wood

beaded: horizontal wood siding with a rounded edge formed with a beading plane

WEATHERBOARD (continued)

clapboard: a split board used for roofing or cladding

German siding: interlocking horizontal wood siding with a concave upper edge

plain: horizontal wood siding with a straight or plain edge

WINDOW:

barred: cellar windows usually with diagonally set horizontal or vertical wood or wrought-iron bars to prevent larger animals from entry

bull's-eye: a circular window

casement: sash hinged on one side

Diocletian therm: a large lunette with two vertical mullions

double-hung (guillotine): two vertically sliding sash

dual: two windows grouped side by side with a mullion between

false (blind): giving the appearance of a window but with a solid brick wall, usually covered with closed blinds

fanlight: windows with radiating muntins, often semicircular

Gothic: lintel curved to a point

jalousie: overlapping horizontal louvers which serve as sun shades over a window

jib: a two-leaf door at floor level below a double-hung window to allow access outdoors when the lower sash is raised and the doors open

lunette (thermal): a semicircular window

quatrefoil: a four-lobed pattern

segmental: lintel arched in the segment of a circle

trefoil: a three-lobed, cloverleaf pattern

tripartite: three windows grouped side by side usually with the middle one wider

triple-hung: three vertically sliding sash

Selected Bibliography

MANUSCRIPT SOURCES

Albemarle County and Charlottesville records (deed books; will books; inventory books; account books; surveyors' books; birth, marriage and death records; chancery records; minute and order books; miscellaneous records): Clerk of the Circuit Court, Court Square, Charlottesville The Library of Virginia, Richmond (in addition to above: land books, personal property tax lists, WPA records) Special Collections, University of Virginia Library, Charlottesville (all of the above records on microfilm)

Bishop, Timothy L. "Fraternity Houses at the University of Virginia, Their History, Their Architecture: An Independent Study." Charlottesville, Va., 1981. Fiske Kimball Fine Arts Library, University of Virginia.

Garrow & Associates, Inc. "From the Monacans to Monticello and Beyond: Prehistoric and Historic Contexts for Albemarle County, Virginia." Raleigh, N.C., 1995.

Lay, K. Edward, director. Architectural Pattern Associated with Virginia Road Traces series (surveys of over 500 buildings). 34 vols., 1976–96. VRT series, Fiske Kimball Fine Arts Library, University of Virginia.

———, director. Architecture in Virginia series (in-depth studies of buildings). 196 vols., 1979–98. AIV series, Fiske Kimball Fine Arts Library, University of Virginia.

———, director. Studies in Vernacular Architecture series (over 900 measured drawings to the Historic American Buildings Survey standards). 111 vols., 1973–97. SVA series, Fiske Kimball Fine Arts Library, University of Virginia.

List of Members of the University of Virginia Board of Visitors, 1819–1968. Special Collections, University of Virginia Library.

Sanborn Map Company. Sanborn Fire Insurance Maps: Virginia [microform]. Teaneck, N.J.: Chadwyck-Healey, 1983.

Specification Book for the University of Virginia, 18 July 1819. 28 slides. Fiske Kimball Fine Arts Library, University of Virginia.

University of Virginia. Minutes of Faculty, 1825–56. 7 vols. Special Collections, University of Virginia Library.

———. Minutes of Rector and Board of Visitors, 1817–1928. 9 vols. with index. Special Collections, University of Virginia Library.

———. Papers of the Office of the Proctor. Bound Ledgers, 1819–25, 1826–32 (index in front); Bound Journals, 1817–22, 1819–28; Loose Papers (many boxes by year of correspondence). Special Collections, University of Virginia Library.

BOOKS

Adams, William Howard. *Jefferson's Monticello*. New York, 1983.

———, ed. *The Eye of Thomas Jefferson*. Washington, D.C., 1976.

———, ed. *Jefferson and the Arts: An Extended View*. Washington, D.C., 1976.

Ballast, David Kent. *Architecture, Design, and Construction Word Finder*. Englewood Cliffs, N.J., 1991.

Bear, James A., Jr. *Jefferson at Monticello*. Charlottesville, Va., 1967.

Bear, James A., Jr., and Lucia C. Stanton, eds. *Jefferson's Memorandum Books: Accounts, with Legal Records and Miscellany, 1767–1826*. Princeton, N.J., 1997.

Bergh, Albert Ellery, ed. *The Writings of Thomas Jefferson*. 20 vols. Washington, D.C., 1907.

Betts, Edwin Morris, ed. *Thomas Jefferson's Farm Book*. 1953; rept. Charlottesville, Va., 1976.

———. *Thomas Jefferson's Garden Book, 1766–1824*. 1944; rept. Philadelphia, 1981.

Betts, Edwin Morris, and Hazlehurst Bolton Perkins. *Thomas Jefferson's Flower Garden at Monticello*. 3d ed., rev. and enlarged by Peter J. Hatch. Charlottesville, Va., 1986.

Blandford, Percy W. *Country Craft Tools*. New York, 1976.

Boyd, Julian P., et al., eds. *The Papers of Thomas Jefferson*. 27 vols. to date. Princeton, N.J., 1950– .

Bruce, Philip Alexander. *History of the University of Virginia*. 5 vols. New York, 1920.

Bucher, Ward, ed. *Dictionary of Building Preservation*. New York, 1996.

Burnley, William Samuel. *The Court House of Albemarle County in Old Virginia*. N.p., 1939.

Burr, Horace. *Albemarle County in the 1760's, from Viewmont to Castle Hill and from Locust Hill to Boswell's Tavern*. Charlottesville? Va: 196–? Map.

Cabell, Joseph. *Early History of the University of Virginia*. Richmond, 1856.

Clark, Margaret W. Fowler. *The Golden Age of the Performing Arts*. Richmond, 1976.

Dabney, Virginius. *Mr. Jefferson's University: A History*. Charlottesville, Va., 1981.

DeAlba, Susan. *Country Roads: Albemarle County, Virginia*. Natural Bridge Station, Va., 1993.

Deetz, James. *In Small Things Forgotten: The Archaeology of Early American Life*. Garden City, N.Y., 1977.

Dumbauld, Edward. *Thomas Jefferson, American Tourist*. Norman, Okla., 1946.

Embury, Aymar, II. *Asher Benjamin*. (Reprint of *Country Builders Assistant, American Builders Companion, Rudiments of Architecture, Practical House Carpenter*, and *Practice of Architecture*). New York, 1917.

Fisher, Leonard Everett. *Monticello*. New York, 1988.

Frary, Ihna Thayer. *Thomas Jefferson, Architect and Builder*. Richmond, 1931.

Garrett, Elisabeth Donaghy. *At Home: The American Family, 1750–1870*. New York, 1990.

Glassie, Henry. *Pattern in the Material Folk Culture of the Eastern United States*. Philadelphia, 1971.

Guinness, Desmond, and Julius Trousdale Sadler Jr. *Mr. Jefferson, Architect*. New York, 1973.

Harris, Cyril M. *Dictionary of Architecture and Construction*. New York, 1993.

Heblich, Fred T., and Mary Ann Elwood. *Charlottesville and the University of Virginia: A Pictorial History*. Norfolk, 1982.

Heblich, Fred T., and Cecile Clover Walters. *Holsinger's Charlottesville, 1890–1925*. Charlottesville, Va., 1976.

Historic Landmark Study: Charlottesville, Virginia. Charlottesville, Va., 1976.

Hogan, Pendleton. *The Lawn: A Guide to Jefferson's University*. Charlottesville, Va., 1987.

Jefferson, Thomas. *Notes on the State of Virginia*. Ed. William Peden. 1954; rept. New York, 1974.

Kimball, Fiske. *Thomas Jefferson, Architect: Original Designs in the Coolidge Collection*. Boston, 1916.

Lambeth, William Alexander, and Warren H. Manning. *Thomas Jefferson as an Architect and a Designer of Landscapes*. New York, 1913.

Lane, Mills. *Architecture of the Old South: Virginia*. Savannah, Ga., 1987.

Langhorne, Elizabeth. *The Golden Age of Albemarle: A Portrait Show, 1800–1860*. Charlottesville, Va., 1984.

———. *Monticello*. Chapel Hill, N.C., 1987.

Langhorne, Elizabeth, K. Edward Lay, and William D. Rieley. *A Virginia Family and Its Plantation Houses*. Charlottesville, Va., 1987.

Loth, Calder, ed., *The Virginia Landmarks Register*. 3d ed. Charlottesville, Va., 1986.

Malone, Dumas. *Jefferson and His Time*. 6 vols. Boston, 1948–81.

McLaughlin, Jack. *Jefferson and Monticello: The Biography of a Builder*. New York, 1988.

———, ed. *To His Excellency Thomas Jefferson: Letters to a President*. New York, 1991.

Mead, Edward C. *Historic Homes of the South-west Mountains Virginia*. 1898; rept. Harrisonburg, Va., 1978.

Moore, John Hammond. *Albemarle: Jefferson's County, 1727–1976*. Charlottesville, Va., 1976.

Moore, Virginia. *Scottsville on the James*. Charlottesville, Va., 1969.

Morris, James McGrath, and Persephone Weene, eds. *Thomas Jefferson's European Travel Diaries*. Ithaca, N.Y., 1987.

Nichols, Frederick D. *Thomas Jefferson's Architectural Drawings*. Charlottesville, Va., 1961.

Nichols, Frederick D., and James A. Bear Jr. *Monticello*. Charlottesville, Va., 1967.

Nichols, Frederick Doveton, and Ralph E. Griswold. *Thomas Jefferson, Landscape Architect*. Charlottesville, Va., 1978.

Noble, Allen George. *Wood, Brick, and Stone: The North American Settlement Landscape*. Amherst, Mass., 1984.

O'Neal, William B. *Architectural Drawing in Virginia, 1819–1969*. Charlottesville, Va., 1969.

———. *Jefferson's Buildings at the University of Virginia: The Rotunda*. Charlottesville, Va., 1960.

O'Neal, William Bainter. *Jefferson's Fine Arts Library: His Selections for the University of Virginia, Together with His Own Architectural Books*. Charlottesville, Va., 1976.

O'Neal, William B. *Pictorial History of the University of Virginia*. Charlottesville, Va., 1968.

Onuf, Peter, ed. *Jeffersonian Legacies*. Charlottesville, Va., 1994.

Pain, William. *The Builder's Pocket-Treasure, or Palladio Delineated and Explained*. Westmead, Farnborough, Hants., Eng., 1972.

Pain, William, and James Pain. *British Palladio*. Farnborough, Hants., Eng., 1969.

———. *Decorative Details of the Eighteenth Century*. London, 1946.

Palladio, Andrea. *The Four Books on Architecture*. Trans. Robert Tavernor and Richard Schofield. Cambridge, Mass., 1997.

Pawlett, Nathaniel Mason. *Historic Roads of Virginia: Albemarle County Road Orders, 1744–1748*. Charlottesville, Va., 1975.

———. *Historic Roads of Virginia: Albemarle County Road Orders, 1783–1816*. Charlottesville, Va., 1975.

———. *Historic Roads of Virginia: Albemarle County Road Orders, 1725–1816*. Charlottesville, Va., 1981.

———. *Historic Roads of Virginia: An Index to Roads in the Albemarle County Surveyors Books, 1744–1853*. Charlottesville, Va., 1976.

Pawlett, Nathaniel Mason, and K. Edward Lay. *Historic Roads of Virginia: Early Road Location, Key to Discovering Historic Resources?* Charlottesville, Va., May 1980.

Peterson, Merrill D. *Thomas Jefferson and the New Nation*. New York, 1970.

———, ed. *Writings/Thomas Jefferson*. New York, 1984.

Poesch, Jessie. *The Art of the Old South, 1560–1860*. New York, 1989.

Randolph, Sarah N. *The Domestic Life of Thomas Jefferson*. Rept. Charlottesville, Va., 1978.

Rawlings, Mary. *The Albemarle of Other Days*. Charlottesville, Va., 1925.

———. *Ante-Bellum Albemarle*. Charlottesville, Va., 1974.

———. *Early Charlottesville: Recollections of James Alexander, 1828–1874*. Charlottesville, Va., 1942.

———. *Historical Guide to Old Charlottesville*. Charlottesville, Va., 1958.

Rives, Barclay. *A History of Grace Church, Cismont: Walker's Parish*. Charlottesville, Va., 1993.

Shuffelton, Frank. *Thomas Jefferson: A Comprehensive Bibliography of Writings about Him (1826–1980)*. New York, 1983.

Shurtleff, Harold Robert. *The Log Cabin Myth*. Cambridge, Mass., 1939.

Sloane, Eric. *A Museum of Early American Tools*. New York, 1974.

———. *A Reverence for Wood*. New York, 1965.

Stein, Susan R. *The Worlds of Thomas Jefferson at Monticello*. New York, 1993.

Stevens, William T. *Virginia House Tour*. Charlottesville, Va., 1962.

Stilgoe, John R. *Common Landscape of America, 1580 to 1845*. New Haven, 1982.

Thurlow, Constance E., et al., comps. *The Jefferson Papers of the University of Virginia*. Charlottesville, Va., 1973.

Tocqueville, Alexis de. *Journey to America*. Garden City, N.Y., 1971.

United States War Department. *The Official Atlas of the Civil War*. New York, 1958.

Upton, Dell, ed. *America's Architectural Roots: Ethnic Groups That Built America*. New York, 1986.

Upton, Dell, and John Michael Vlach, eds. *Common Places: Readings in American Vernacular Architecture*. Athens, Ga., 1986.

Vaughan, Joseph Lee, and Omer Allan Gianniny Jr. *Thomas Jefferson's Rotunda Restored, 1973–1976: A Pictorial Review with Commentary*. Charlottesville, Va., 1981.

Wheeler, Roy. *Historic Virginia*. Richmond, 1946.

Wilbur, C. Keith. *Home Building and Woodworking in Colonial America*. Old Saybrook, Conn., 1992.

Williams, Dorothy Hunt. *Historic Virginia Gardens: Preservations by the Garden Club of Virginia*. Charlottesville, Va., 1975.

Wilson, Richard Guy, ed. *Thomas Jefferson's Academical Village: The Creation of an American Masterpiece*. Charlottesville, Va., 1993.

Wilson, Richard Guy, and Sara A. Butler. *The Campus Guide: University of Virginia*. New York, 1999.

Woods, Edgar. *Albemarle County in Virginia*. 1900; rept. Harrisonburg, Va., 1972.

Works Progress Administration. *Jefferson's Albemarle: A Guide to Albemarle County and to the City of Charlottesville, Virginia*. Charlottesville, Va., 1941.

ARTICLES

Lay, K. Edward. "The American Renaissance at U.Va.: A Walking Tour of Buildings Jefferson Did Not Design." *University of Virginia Alumni News* 82, 7 (Nov.–Dec. 1993): 16–21.

———. "Dinsmore and Neilson: Jefferson's Master Builders." *Colonnade, the Newsjournal of the University of Virginia School of Architecture* 6, 1 (Spring 1991): 9–13.

———. "European Antecedents of Seventeenth and Eighteenth Century Germanic and Scots-Irish Architecture in America." *Pennsylvania Folklife* 32, 1 (Autumn 1982): 2–43.

———. "Jefferson's Master Builders: They Gave Shape to the University and the Community around It." *University of Virginia Alumni News* 80, 1 (Oct. 1991): 16–19.

———. "Mills in the Central Piedmont Region of Virginia." *Pioneer America Society Echoes of History* 4, 4 (July 1974): 57–64.

Lay, K. Edward, and Martha Tuzson Stockton. "Castle Hill: The Walker Family Estate." *Magazine of Albemarle County History* 52 (1994): 38–64.

Lay, K. Edward, and Nathaniel Mason Pawlett. "Architectural Surveys Associated with Early Road Systems." *Bulletin of the Association for Preservation Technology* 12, 2 (1980): 3–36.

McVarish, Douglas, ed., with contributions by Ferol O. Briggs, Boyd Coons, K. Edward Lay, and George H. Yetter. "The History of Architectural Education at the University of Virginia." *Colonnade, the Newsjournal of the University of Virginia School of Architecture*, Summer 1988, Winter 1989, and 4, 2 (Summer–Autumn 1989): 27–37.

Nichols, Frederick Doveton. "The Early Architecture of Virginia: Original Sources and Books." *American Association of Architectural Bibliographers Papers* 1 (1965): 80–128, 2 (1966): 83–113.

Wenger, Mark R. "The Central Passage in Virginia: Evolution of an Eighteenth-Century Living Space." In *Perspectives in Vernacular Architecture*, ed. Camille Wells, 2 (1986): 137–49.

Dissertations and Theses

Corse, Helen Camp de. *Charlottesville: A Study of Negro Life and Personality*. M.S. Thesis, University of Virginia. Phelps-Stokes Fellowship Papers no. 11. Charlottesville, Va., 1933.

Cote, Richard C. "The Architectural Workmen of Thomas Jefferson in Virginia." Ph.D. diss., Boston University, 1986.

Grizzard, Frank E., Jr. "Documentary History of the Construction of the Buildings at the University of Virginia, 1817–1828." Electronic Ph.D. diss., University of Virginia, 1996. http://jefferson.village.Virginia.EDU/grizzard/construction.

Irwin, Marjorie Felice. *The Negro in Charlottesville and Albemarle County*. M.A. thesis, University of Virginia. Phelps-Stokes Fellowship Papers no. 9. Charlottesville, Va., 1929.

List of Sponsors

Anonymous
Jackie and Terry Batcheller
Mary and Carter Becker
Mrs. Robert Carter
Charlotte and Ralph Dammann
Margareta C. H. Douglas
Ann and Jim Eddins
George H. Fleming Jr.
Melinda and Henry Frierson
Mr. and Mrs. W. Douglas Gilpin Jr., FAIA
Vesta Lee Gordon
Hunter C. Gray
Mary and Jack Harrison
Andrew D. Hart Jr.
Mr. and Mrs. William Johnson
Joseph F. Johnston Jr.
Margaret F. Lay

Mr. and Mrs. Leigh B. Middleditch Jr.
George R. Minor, M.D.
Jenny and Martin Quarles
Mrs. Frederic W. Scott
Lloyd T. Smith Jr.
Virginia Stokes
Linda E. A. Wachtmeister
Gertrude Weber
Barbara and William Wright
Albemarle County Historical Society
Charlottesville-Albemarle Community Foundation
C. Venable Minor Expendable Gift Fund
Perry Foundation
Thomas Jefferson Branch of the Association for the
    Preservation of Virginia Antiquities
University of Virginia School of Architecture

Acknowledgments

My wife: Margaret F. Lay, artist and landscape architect, for her support of this project during the many years of its research and development.

All those countless persons who invited me into their homes.

Developmental editors: John S. Salmon, Staff Historian, Virginia Department of Historic Resources, and Emily J. Salmon, Associate Editor, Publications and Educational Services Division, The Library of Virginia, who enriched the manuscript with their scholarship and editorial expertise.

Computer and scanning assistance: Michael L. Tuite Jr., Administrator, New Media Center, University of Virginia; his staff Christine Madrid and William Rourk; and architect–computer expert Duncan Kincaid, without whose guidance, expertise, and dogged determination the CD-ROM containing the survey database would not have been realized.

Albemarle County Historical Society: Grateful appreciation is extended to the society for enthusiastic support and for handling contributions and disbursements for this project. In particular, thanks go to Executive Director Lynne C. Ely and former Executive Director Melinda B. Frierson; Administrative Assistant Sandra L. DeKay and Librarian Margaret M. O'Bryant; Board members Sara Lee Barnes, Vesta Gordon, Robert Kuhlthau, Howard Newlon, and Lloyd T. Smith Jr.; and volunteers Eugenia Bibb, Gayle Schulman, and George Worthington IV.

Research Assistants: Jonathan Balas, Chris Crowder, Dorothy Geyer, Leslie Giles, Charles Herrmann, Ann Lucas, Lauren Mitchell, Whitney Morrill, Woodrow Parrish, Paulette Roberts, Lisa Smith, Martha Tuzson Stockton, Alan Wong.

Readers: Eugenia Bibb, Melinda Frierson, Christine Madrid, Jeffrey Plank, Lloyd T. Smith Jr.

Early formative readers: S. Allen Chambers Jr., Calder Loth, Camille Wells.

Persons who joined me on field trips: Sara Lee Barnes, Eugenia Bibb, Ferol O. Briggs, Thomas Craven, Melinda Frierson, Frank Grizzard, Geoffrey Henry, Floyd Johnson, Robert Kuhlthau, Steven G. Meeks, Jeffrey O'Dell, Menger Ramsay, Pattie Sternheimer.

Map Assistance: Michael L. Tuite Jr.; Deborah Reade

UVA School of Architecture: Dean J. Norwood Bosserman, Dean Jaquelin T. Robertson, Dean Harry Porter, Acting Dean Daphne Spain, Dean William McDonough, Associate Dean Kenneth Schwartz, Associate Dean Elizabeth Fortune, Department Chair Peter Waldman.

UVA Special Collections: Francis L. Berkeley Jr., Michael F. Plunkett.

Virginia Department of Historic Resources: Jeffrey O'Dell, Calder Loth, Julie Vosmik, Marc Wagner, John Wells.

Realtors: Charlotte Dammann, Ted Dunstan, Frank Hardy, Geoffrey Henry, Michael May, Steve McLean, Percy Montague, Deborah Murdock, Frank J. Quayle, Charlotte Ramsey, John H. Royer Jr., Ross Stevens.

Masters of Architecture Students for whom I served as major thesis advisor: Edward Chappell, Barbara Hume Church, Genny Keller, Camille Wells.

Studies in Vernacular Architecture (SVA — Measured Drawings) Students: David Akinaka, Brian Ambroziak, Heather Archer, Janet Averill, Olga Barmine, Matt Barnes, Jamie Barnett, David Basham, Jeff Berger, John Bernard, Tim Bishop, Judy Bitting, Shayn Bjornholm, Kate Black, Brian Boehmke, Jonathan Bohm, Alice Bojanowski, Jim Boyd, Harry Bradley, Rob Brennan, Peter Briggs, Ruth Broderick, Peggy Bruns, Gray Bryan, John Burrows, Jeff Bushman, Rob Busler, Brent Campbell, Sal Canciello, Berry Candler, Jerry Carrier, Mary Cary, Alex Casserley, Beth Cates, Edward Chappell, Al Cheatham, Barbara Hume Church, Leslie Claytor, Hank Cochran, Michael Francis Conner, Martha Crabill, Pierre Crosby, Chris Crowder, Bruce Davis, Hornor Davis, Joe Debreczeni, Leslie Dill, Brian Dillard, Thomas Dolan, Susan Dornbusch, Bill Drake, Sarah Dreller, Robert Dripps, Tom Dubuisson, Pete Eckman, Nancy Elliot, David Elyea, Diane Engel, Amy Facca, John Farmer, Sally Favrao, Dan Fay, Sandy Fitzpatrick, Maureen Fox, William Frazier, Marita Fritz, Cathy Ganzel, Kathryn Gettings, John Graham, Cathy Haley, Drucilla Gatewood Haley, Gina Haney, Doug Harnsberger, Nancy Harrington, Harry Harris, Hunt Harris, Marlene Heck, Richard Hekimian, Julia Henley, Stephen Herr, Ted Hicks, Robert Hiller, Margaret Hilliard, Wendy Hillis, Susan Holbrook, Ellen Honigstock, Mary

Redenbaugh Howard, Brian Hughes, Jeff Jacobson, Tony James, Angela Jim, Diana Johnson, Warren Jones, Johanna Josephs, Mark Kearney, Rosalyn Keesee, Jeff Kidder, Wayne Kille, Andy Kim, Jane Kimball, Chris Kness, Chuck Koch, Leslie Kuhl, Kathryn M. Kuranda, Joe Ligon, Randy Liverman, Chip Logan, Debbie Lord, Matt Lowry, John Lupinos, M. Tabb Lynn, Glenn MacCullough, Ken Magalis, Kate Mahood, Mary Matter, Lorenzo Mattii, Peter Maxson, Foree McCauley, Nat McCormick, Duncan McCrea, Kathryn McCutchen, Denis McNamara, Louise McPhillips, Steve Meixner, Kim Merkel, Ann Brush Miller, Robert Moje, Tina Moon, Ayres Morison, Karen Myers, Andrea Mullenix Nadel, Wayne Nelson, Courtney Newcomer, Bill Newman, Byrd Oliver, Lloyd Ostby, Andrew Oyen, Vanessa Patrick, Jennifer Patsos, Bill Pohill, Becky Price-Wilkins, Sumpter Priddy, Rick Quesada, Nancy Recchie, Chris Redmann, Mark E. Reinberger, Karen Renick, Tim Revere, Orlando Ridout V, Fiona Robertson, John Robbins, Sharman Roberts, Marc Roehrle, Jim Rose, Peter Sandbeck, Meiko Sato, Eugene Scheel, Fred Schneider, Cathy Schultz, Russell Scott, Julie Semmelman, Ernest Shealy, Patricia Sherwood, Stuart Siegel, Lisa Smith, Sallie Smith, Theresa Stanley, Mike Stewart, Alison Stone, Kristie Struble, Mike Sullivan, Ann Swallow, Scott Taylor, Thomas Taylor, Martha Teall, Rod Temmick, Mark Thompson, Richard P. Thomsen Jr., DeTeel Pat Tiller, Robert Troxell, Rebecca Trumbull , Bill Tucci, Betsy Updike, Jim Vernon, Charley Watts, Claire Welch, Louise Weller, Camille Wells, John Wells, Kathy Williams, Steve Williams, Jennifer Wimmer, Jay Wyper, Dwight Young, Michael Zimny.

Virginia Road Traces (VRT — Architectural Surveys) Students: Jason Boroughs, Mary Cerrone, Dawn Chapman, Barbara Hume Church, Michael Francis Conner, Pierre Crosby, Buffy Dame, David A. Dashiell III, Margaret G. Davis, Margie Dudley, David Allan Edwards, Ann R. Fair, Lori Feldman, Justin Green, Belinda Grosskopf, Drucilla Gatewood Haley, M. Ward Hill, Lennie King, Karen Lang Kummer, Kathryn M. Kuranda, Guy M. Lapsley, Osborne Mackie, Cynthia Ann MacLeod, David D.McKinney, Margaret Pearson Mickler, Ann Brush Miller , Patricia A. Murphy, Tina Papamichael, Martin Perdue, Mark E. Reinberger, Charles Rhinelander, Silvia Sabadell-Johnson, Tracy S. Scharer, Stuart N. Siegel, A. James Siracuse, Jennifer Thaler, Richard P. Thomsen Jr., DeTeel P. Tiller, Jill Trischman-Marks, Hampton Tucker, Cabell Vest, Kevin Wagstaff, E. Claire Welch, Mark James Wenger, Mark Randolph Wenger, Jill Whitehead, Carolyn Leone Williams, George Humphrey Yetter.

Architecture in Virginia (AIV — Regional Architecture and Recording Historic Buildings) Students: Debbie Alderson, David Amundson, Heather Archer, Regina Arlotto, Melanie Arndt, Terry Averill, Sandy Babbidge, Victoria Ballard, Sara Lee Barnes, Susan Barto, Lee Batchelder, Gina Baylon, Emily Billheimer, Sally Bishop, Claire Blanchard, Linda Boggan, Leslie Booth, Virginia Booth, Andrew Boyd, Harry Bradley, Lynn Hickey Brennan, Terry Brooks, Anne Burkarth, Dave Bush, Debbie Cannan, Estaban Carazo, Ben Carstoiu, Beth Cates, Robert Champagne, Vivian Chi, Andy Conlon, Boyd Coons, Robert R. Costantino, Debra Curtis, Scott Cyphers, Hugh Darville, Marjie Daly, Ed Davis, Mary Claire Davis, Jeffrey P. Diglio, Wade Dizdar, Eric Dobson, Shirley Dorrier, William Drake, Sarah Driggs, Tania

Durilin, Albert Eck, Mehmet Elbirlik, Kathryn Ellenburg, Vera Embick, Susan Escherich, Kay Fanning, Craig Farnsworth, Arlene Fenlon, Joe Fordham, John Franklin, Melinda Frierson, Sara Gann, Cathy Ganzel, Joe Gelletich, Cindy Georgallis, Jere Gibber, Leslie Giles, Gwyn Gilliam, Luis Gonzalez, Gillian Goodwin, John Grier, Christoph Grier, Claudia Harrison, Rick Haughey, Dana Heiburg, Joe Heisler, Susan Hellman, Bob Henry, Lee Herbert, Jeanine Herbst, Becky Hill, Brooke Hodge, Elizabeth Hoge, Christine Holt, Mary Redenbaugh Howard, Elizabeth Hughes, Ann Huppert, David Johnson, Leigh Ann Johnson, Tracy Johnson, Amy Jordan, Marcia Joseph, Kristen Kaiser, Alena Kaplan, Suzanne Kelley, Maggie Kelly, Lynda Kemp, Pam Kirkland-Gottschalk, Howard Kittell, Chris Klein, Pam Klinger, Stefan Klosowski, Linda Komes, Mary Koonts, Lara Kozak, Debbie Kraybill, Caroline Kurrus, Jean Lakemper, Joe Lasala, Richard Laub, Tammy Le, Judith Leckrone, Brian LeCouteur, Rosanna Liebman, Tim Linblad, John Lockard, Andrea Madison, James N. Maiocco, Don Matheson, Kay McCarron, Pat McClane, Nancy McCollum, Dennis McFarland, Lisa McIntosh, Karen McIntyre, Matilda McQuaid, Doug McVarish, Mary Jo Mertz, Ann Brush Miller, Victor Montes, Tina Moon, Whitney Morrill, Sharon Morris, Roger Muckenfuss, Leslie Naranjo-Lupold, Francis Nathans, Debbie Nauta-Rodriguez, Traci Neenan, Pat Neill, Wayne Nelson, Courtney Newcomer, Traci Nottingham, Clare Novak, Robin O'Hara, Jay Oles, Alex Oporto, Libbie Pangburn, Jennifer Patsos, Nathaniel Mason Pawlett, LeAnn Pegram, Douglas Peterson, Donna Pivik, Michelle Plourde, Jane Posey, Chris Redmann, Cathy Ribble, Ray Pickens, Antoinette Roades, Linda Robinson, Amy Ross, Gwyn W. Rowland, Gregory Russell, Silvia Sabadell-Johnson, Joann Satullo, Susan Schager, Mark Schara, Claire Seifert, Werner Sensbach, Ziad Shehab, Ashley Shelton, Patricia Sherwood, Cindy Slater, Rick Smith, Mike Sobczak, Mike Stauffer, Jennifer Steingasser, Paul Stephens, Heather Sterling, Martha Tuzson Stockton, Alison Stone, Larry Streeter, Colleen Sullivan, Jean Sullivan, Paul Symes, Jennifer Tait, Anne Taylor, Martha Teall, Wendy Thomas, Joy Thompson, Babette Thorpe, Julia T. Thorson, Holly Tompkins, Lisa Tucker, Michael Tuite, Edward Tyner, Cabell Vest, Donald Viola, Shelley Wagner, Bill Walker, Tish Weichmann, Amanda Welch, Dan Welsh, Kimberlee Welsh, Lewis Wendell, Katie Whelahan, Amy Whitlock, Chris Wigren, Steve Williams, Margareta Williamson, Ridley Wills, Melanie Wilson, Jennifer Wimmer, Angela Wingard-Brusch, Susannah Wood, James E. Wootton, Charles Yudd, James Zinck.

Fieldwork in Preservation Students: Jack Abgott, Melanie Betz, Brad Bosher, Rob Brennan, Margaret G. Davis, Kit Garrett, Doug Harnsberger, Rebecca Harrison, Wayne Kille, Karen Kummer, Kathryn M. Kuranda, Bill Martin, Brian McDaniel, Phil Neuberg, Byrd Oliver, David Reese, Dick Ryan, Sylvia Sabadell-Johnson, Deborah Sheetenhelm, Stuart N. Siegel, Nora Pat Small, Sallie Smith, Rebecca Trumbull, E. Claire Welch, Carolyn Leone Williams, Mike Zimny.

Virginia Architecture of the 18th and 19th Century Seminar Participants: J. R. Andrews, Virginia Andrews, Suzanne Annand, Jane Axelrod, Betty Bailey, Charlotte Baker, Lisa Barker, Sara Lee Barnes, Graham Basto, Terry Batcheller, Jackie Batcheller, David Bearr, Robert Beck, Jim Beckwith, Diane Berkeley,

Arthur Bernstein, Sewell Biggs, Warren Bingham, Frances Boas, Jared Bockoff, Harvey Bomberger, Greg Bridgeford, Gina Bridgeford, C. Stanworth Brinkley, John Brittain, Charlotte Brittain, Bonita Busta, John Campbell, Cliff Cantrell, Jan Cantrell, Sondra Carver, Lawrence Case, Kenneth Cassada, Anne Cassada, John Chappell, Nancy Cichowicz, Terry Clark, Marcia Clark, Pat Clopper, Pat Coman, William Coman, Arthur Cree, Romelda Cree, Linda Cripps, Roger Critchlow, Nancy Critchlow, Lucy Crockin, Bill Cross, Lesley Cross, Brenda Curnin, Charlotte Dammann, Elizabeth Greenleaf Dana, Elizabeth David, Robert Dawson, Anna Dees, I. B. Dent, Page Dickson, Robert Dinsmore, Margareta C. H. Douglas, Ruth Edwards, Robert Eichberger, Bill Eley, William Ellis, Patricia Elton, Liz Ferrell, Josie Fox, Judy Franklin, Lena French, Kay Frye, Joan Galanis, Tom George, Malvina Glick, Barbara Goldberg, Marianne Graham, Gary Gray, Diane Hallisey, Abbie Harlin, Laurie Harper, Al Harris, David Hartman, Dorothy Hartman, Bob Henderson, Mary Henderson, Tom Higginson, Janice Hill, Mary Holbeck, Karl Hossli, Ava Humphrey, John Hyer, Leslie Infinger, Dorothy Infinger, Jean James, Kristin Johnson, Michael Johnson, Murray Johnson, William Johnston, Nancy Jones, Roy Jones, Virginia Jones, Sharon Keith, Kieran Kilday, Theodora Kinder, Margaret King, Pam Kirkland, Raymond Koplinka, Rosmarie Koplinka, William Kramer, Kathy Kucharski, Robert Kucharski, Carter Lively, Pam Luce, Steve Mano, Debbie Mano, Richard Marks Jr., Richard Marks III, Louise Mashburn, De-De Mayer, Mary McConnell, James McCormick, Nancy McCrea, Karen Medina, Dottie Mercer, Renee Miller, Bernard Mills, Lyle Minter, Mary Frances Morris, Rosanna Morris, Ruth Morris, Donna Morrison, Mary Muir, Paul Nelson, Clay Nightingale, Rose Nimmo, Bella Nusbaum, Margaret O'Bryant, Daniel O'Neill, Richard Oxsen, Dan Owens, Susan Owens, Suzanne Owens, Jennifer Parr, Lee Payne, Eunice Payne, Emarie Payne, Elizabeth Pearsall, George Pearson, Robert Pellegrini, Joyce Pierson, Charles Rappold, Robin Rawles, Jamie Rawles, Edmund Rennolds Jr., Douglas Roller, Helena Roller, Thomas Salley, Andrea Salley, Terry Sanderson, Donald Santarelli, Kara Schonberger, Nancy Snow, Marilyn Sommers, Patricia Stees, Patricia Stone, Margaret Story, Wilton Strickland, Alice Strickland, Wynne Stuart, Martha Stuart, Rebecca Stumpf, Elizabeth Sully, Thomas Sweeney, Norma Tarrow, William Taylor, Natalie Thatcher, Susan Thomas, Patricia Thompson, Paula Thomson, Dorothy Thorssell, Sarah Townsend-Harrison, Philip Trainer, Regina Trainer, William Tucker, Suzanne Tuite, Hank Tumpa, Renee Vance, Bill Walker, Tom Williams, Holland Wilmer, Lucy Wilmer, Mary Wilmeth, Judith Wilson, Margaret Winter, Matt Wirth, Elaine Wiser, David Wolford, Posey Wright, Jane Zamorski, Ron Zamorski.

Architecture of the Federal Period in Virginia Seminar Participants: Walter B. Armstrong, Diane Berkeley, Kirk Berkeley, Deborah S. Biddle, Robert Bower, Andrew Boyd, Robert Boyd, Albert Broughton, Haskell Brown, Todd W. Bullard, Kenneth D. Camp, Michael Carmagnola, Kamal Chaudbury, W. G. Clark, Ron W. Djuren, Timothy Galvin, Glenn German, Michael Goldfinger, Bruce Hobby, Lori Hoden, Henry C. Holle, Karl S. Hossli, Howard Johnson, Thomas H. King, Bruce M. Kriviskey, Alison F. Kriviskey, Joseph Lavigne, Dwight Matthews, Nancy McCarren, Tony Miller, Jonathan S. Monroe, James R. Nelson, James Noel, Thomas J. O'Neil, John Reid, Neal Riddle, Arnold C. Rodriguez, Carl Rogers, Candace M. P. Smith, Gene S. Stepp, Suzanne Stewart, Jeff L. Trussler, Gail H. Viner, James Walker, Jim O. White, Richard A. Whiteley, Terrance R. Williams, Robert P. Winthrop.

Thomas Jefferson Chapter of Association for the Preservation of Virginia Antiquities: W. Douglas Gilpin Jr., Michael May, James Wootton.

Preservation Piedmont: James Eddins, Deborah Murdock.

Virginia Highway and Transportation Research Commission: Howard Newlon, Ann Brush Miller, Nathaniel Mason Pawlett.

Monticello: Sara Lee Barnes, James Bear, William Beiswanger, Andrew Johnson, William Kelso, Ann Lucas, Robert Self, Lucia Stanton, Susan Stein, Douglas Wilson.

University of Virginia: Raymond Bice, James Murray Howard.

Ash Lawn/Highland: James Wootton.

Michie Tavern: Cindy Conte.

Iron furnaces: Thomas T. Brady, William W. Reynolds.

Civil War: J. Paul Burke, Richard Nicholas.

Land grants: Robert Vernon.

Colonial Williamsburg: Edward Chappell, Carl Lounsbury, Nick Pappas, Mark R. Wenger.

University photography: Pauline Page.

Others who shared information: William C. Allen, Anne Barnes, John V. Berberich III, Raymond Bice, Henry Browne, Charles E. Brownell, Margaret Fowler Clark, Linda Franklin, Milton L. Grigg, Elizabeth C. Langhorne, Allaville and Evelina Magruder, Frederick D. Nichols, William B. O'Neal, William D. Rieley, Barclay Rives, William Seale, Robert E. Simpson, Ashlin Smith, Bill Sublette, Don Swofford, Richard P. Thomsen, Sam Towler, Camille Wells, John Williamson.

Illustration Credits

Photographs or drawings are by the author unless otherwise noted.

Albemarle County Courthouse Records: figs. 4 (drawn by R. E. Moon), 6 (redrawn by Alan Wong)

Albemarle County Historical Society, Charlottesville: figs. 48 (drawn by Martha Tuzson Stockton), 178 (Rawlings Thomson), 186 (neg. PC 96j), 250, 252, 254 (church archives), 278, 314, 315, 350, 354 (1904)

Cordelia Ruffin Austin, Charlottesville: fig. 58

Author's field notes, redrawn by: figs. 5 (Jonathan Balas, Paulette Roberts); 8, 14, 15, 22, 76, 136, 144 (Paulette Roberts); 10 (Lauren Mitchell); 24 (Ed Ayres, Martha Tuzson Stockton); 46 (Paulette Roberts from Mutual Assurance Society policy, 1805); 51, 169, 205 (Martha Tuzson Stockton); 122 (Woody Parrish, Gillian Goodwin, Architecture in Virginia ser., no. 145); 163 (Robert Brennan); 208 (Woody Parrish, Martha Tuzson Stockton from Sanborn Insurance Society policies)

Author's coursework Studies in Vernacular Architecture series, School of Architecture, University of Virginia: figs. 26 (no. 10, Hornor Davis, Duncan McCrea, Peter Maxon), 33 (no. 91, Thomas Dolan), 72 (1st Place HABS Peterson Prize 1994, no. 102, Lorenzo Mattii, Andrew Kim), 116 (3d Place HABS Peterson Prize 1983, no. 70, Diana Johnson), 118 (1st Place HABS Peterson Prize 1984, no. 83, Harry Bradley, Mary Redenbaugh Howard), 127 (no. 46, Louise McPhillips), 141 (no. 100, Jennifer Patsos, Wayne Nelson), 150 (no. 103, Brian Dillard, Nathaniel McCormick), 151 (no. 103, Brian Dillard, Nathaniel McCormick), 153 (no. 91, John Bernard), 154 (no. 91, John Bernard), 161 (no. 64, John Bernard), 167 (no. 74, Becky Price-Wilkins), 174 (no. 91, Lisa Umstattd), 177 (no. 37, Hunt Harris, Pat Tiller), 185 (no. 84, Alison Stone, James Vernon), 196 (no. 34, Bruce Davis, Chip Logan), 202 (no. 17, Judy Bitting, Robert Dripps), 203 (no. 17, Judy Bitting, Robert Dripps), 211 (no. 91, Cathy Ganzel), 213 (no. 104, Marita Fritz, John Lupinos), 218 (no. 58, Claudia Craig), 227 (no. 97, Shayn Bjornholm, Alice Bojanowski, Courtney Newcomer, Pat Sherwood), 228 (no. 76, Kate Black), 229 (no. 76, Kate Black), 258 (no. 38, Barbara Church, Michael Conner), 270 (no. 99, Jamie Barnett, Beth Cates), 291 (no. 105, Brian Hughes, Denis McNamara), 347 (no. 56, Robert Brennan)

Bayly Art Museum, University of Virginia, Charlottesville: fig. 104 (artist John Toole)

Eugenia Bibb, Charlottesville: fig. 188 (from calendar)

Ferol Briggs, Albemarle County: fig. 83

Holmes M. and Mary Ellen Brown, Albemarle County: fig. 233

Barbara N. Chakmakian, Shepardstown, W.Va.: fig. 121

Christ Church archives, Charlottesville: figs. 182, 183

Brendan Clancy, South Street Inn, Charlottesville: fig. 237

Roberts Coles, Albemarle County: fig. 75 (1951)

Cynthia Conte, Albemarle County: fig. 34, 90 (Vestal Thomas Milton)

Dr. Lewis F. Cosby, Johnson City, Tenn. : fig. 102

Daily Progress, Charlottesville: figs. 49 (photograph by Rip Payne), 132 (photograph by Dan Friedman)

Margareta C. H. Douglas, Albemarle County: fig. 329

Hazel Dudley, Albemarle County: fig. 130

First Christian Church, Charlottesville, archives: fig. 264 (Gitchell Studios))

Sally G. Gieck, Albemarle County: fig. 29 (c. 1935)

Peter Hallock, Albemarle County: fig. 280

Frank Hardy, Inc., Realtors, Charlottesville: figs. 73 (with Roy Wheeler Realty Co., Charlottesville), 328

Elizabeth Oglesby Haugh, Albemarle County: fig. 143 (1930s)

Atcheson L. Hench, Charlottesville: fig. 105

Historic American Buildings Survey, National Park Service: fig. 32 (drawings 1934)

Ironworker, Lynchburg, Va.: fig. 103 (L. M. Sims)

Mrs. Harold L. Javins (Catherine B.), Charlottesville: fig. 212

Floyd E. Johnson, Albemarle County: figs. 84, fig. 160 (Bucky Forsythe)

Matthais E. Kayhoe student study, School of Architecture, University of Virginia: 164 (Mary Kfoury, Travis McDonald, redrawn by Martha Tuzson Stockton), 293 (Don Horn, Susan Harrison)

Chiles T. A. and Suzanne Larson, Albemarle County: fig. 41

Mrs. Fred G. Liady, Jr., Albemarle County: fig. 191

Jorg Lippuner, General Manager, Boar's Head Inn—A Country Resort at the University of Virginia: fig. 269

Allaville Magruder, Charlottesville (now deposited with the Albemarle County Historical Society): figs. 112 (c. 1908), 142, 162, 206 (Allen Perkins), 207, 241 (Barbara Rosser, L19C), 249, 267, 271, 272, 277, 345

Evelyn G. Marshall, Charlottesville: fig. 234

Massachusetts Historical Society, Boston, Thomas Jefferson drawings: figs. 123 (N-6, K-170, MHS-193), 155 (N-14, K-183, MHS-200), 156 (N-13, K-182, MHS-199)

Page Tapscott Massie and Edna Tapscott Anderson, Albemarle County: fig. 45

William D. Maupin III, Albemarle County: fig. 189

Polly P. McGavock Realtor, Charlottesville: figs. 159, 221

Paula I. Mell and Akwenasa, Albemarle County: fig. 236

Montague, Miller & Company Realtors and Polly P. McGavock Realtor, Charlottesville: fig. 187

Virginia Moore, *Scottsville on the James* (Charlottesville, Va.: 1969): fig. 25 (drawn by Floyd Johnson)

Dr. David L. Morris, Albemarle County: fig. 85 (c. 1900)

John Morris, Albemarle County: fig. 21

Mary Catharine Murphy, Albemarle County: fig. 204 (c. 1937)

Frederick D. Nichols's student studies, School of Architecture, University of Virginia: figs. 171, 172 (John Fornaro); 244 (Donald Rhinesmith)

Charlotte Ramsay, Inc. Realtors: map of Charlottesville

1740 Antiques, Albemarle County: fig. 101 (artist John Toole, c. 1850)

Mary Brice Sloan, Charlottesville: fig. 223 (Holsinger Studio)

Ashlin and Lloyd T. Smith, Jr., Charlottesville: fig. 288 (Holsinger Studio)

Stevens & Company, Albemarle County: fig. 240

A. Raymon Thacker, Scottsville: fig. 349 (W. E. Burgess)

William C. Thacker, Jr., North, Va.: fig. 78 (Thomas Martin Thacker sketch and notes)

UVA Alumni News: fig. 359 (Nov./Dec. 93)

Special Collections, University of Virginia Library, Charlottesville: figs. 1 (acc. no. 9408, neg. 4x5-203), 7 (Thomas Jefferson Papers, N-526, item a), 16 (c. 1890, pnts., neg. 4x5-390), 17 (A. L. Hench 1931, pnts. 12, neg. 4x5-385-B), 18 (1909, acc. no. 8116-a, neg. 4x5-515), 19 (c. 1890–1910, acc. no. RG 21/42.701, neg. 4x5-1798-B), 20 (1939, acc. no. 619, neg. 4x5-1798-L), 23 (F. B. Johnston, 1930s, pnts. 158-9.1), 30 (C. F. Gillette, 1933, acc. no. 11083, neg. 4x5-1858-B), 31 (acc. no. 4437, neg. 4x5-670-B), 35 (F. B. Johnston, 1930s, pnts. 158-33.1), 38 (C. F. Gillette, acc. no. 11083, neg. 4x5-1858-AQ), 43 (F. B. Johnston, 1930s, pnts. 158-15.8), 44 (F. B. Johnston, 1930s, pnts., neg. 158-47.2), 47 (pnts., neg. 4x5-211), 50 (F. B. Johnston, 1930s, pnts. 158-45.2), 64 (F. B. Johnston, 1930s, pnts. 158-28.2), 65 (1939, pnts., neg. 4x5-213), 70 (F. B. Johnston, 1930s, pnts. 158-14.1), 71 (F. B. Johnston, 1930s, pnts. 158-9.3), 77 (pnts., neg. 4x5-1788-I), 81 (acc. no. 10340-6, neg. 4x5-1178-H), 86 (F. B. Johnston, 1930s, pnts. 158-24.1), 92 (*Century Magazine*, 1887, neg. 35-86-A), 94 (engraving by Pierson, 19c, acc. no. 2535.40, neg. 4x5-187), 95 (Edward Sachse lithograph, 1856 Bohn print, acc. no. RG 5/7/2.762, neg. 1946), 97 (acc. no. 4527, neg. 4x5-1217), 98 (acc. no. 4527, neg. 35-7g), 100 (Thomas Jefferson Papers, acc. no. 6552, N-385), 126 (F. B. Johnston, 1930s, pnts. 158-19.1), 133 (acc. no. 6745-b, neg. 4x5-70), 139 (A. L. Hench, pnts. 130, neg. 1803-P.2), 140 (A. L. Hench, 1926, pnts. 130, neg. 4x5-1801-D.11), 145 (Holsinger Studio, 1913, acc. no. 9862, neg. X-1631-c-B), 149 (Holsinger Studio, 1914, acc. no. 9862, neg. X-2135-L-B1), 152 (F. B. Johnston, 1930s, pnts. 158-46.1), 158 (c. 1890, pnts., 13, neg. 4x5-902-B), 168 (Holsinger Studio, 1913, acc. no. 9862, neg. X-1327-B2), 170 (Holsinger Studio, 1917, acc. no. 9862, neg. X-5449-B1), 173 (F. B. Johnston, 1930s, pnts. 158-17.5), 180 (R. T. W. Duke, Jr., Papers, 1:133, acc. no. 9521-I, neg. 35-44-C), 192 (A. L. Hench, 1932, neg. 4x5-184), 197 (c. 1900, acc. no. 54, neg. 54.82), 199 (C. F. Gillette, 1933, acc. no. 11083, neg. 4x5-1858-V), 215 (acc. no. 4702-e, neg. 4x5-1799-O), 224 (A. L. Hench, pnts. 130, neg. 4x5-1803-B.1), 235 (Holsinger Studio, 1915, acc. no. 9862, neg. X-3012-B1), 239 (acc. no. 6589-a, neg. 4x5-219-A), 243 (McLemore Papers, acc. no. 10659-a, neg. 4x5-658-C), 245 (Holsinger Studio, 1917, acc. no. 9862, neg. X-4751-13), 255 (Holsinger Studio, 1917, acc. no. 9862, neg. X-4776-B), 256 (Holsinger Studio, 1917, acc. no. 9862, neg. X-4776-B2), 259 (pnts., neg. 4x5-1798-H), 262 (pnts., neg. 4x5-1455), 263 (Holsinger Studio, 1913, acc. no. 9862, neg. X-1795-B), 266 (pnts., neg. 4x5-1798-E), 274 (c. 1900, pnts., neg. 4x5-225), 275 (pnts., neg. 4x5-1799-G), 276 (Holsinger Studio, 1916, acc. no. 9862, neg. X-4900-B), 282 (Holsinger Studio, 1913, acc. no. 9862, neg. X-1920-B10), 284 (c. 1938, pnts., neg. 4x5-1798-D), 286 (acc. no. 3070-e, neg. 4x5-1099-E), 294 (pnts., neg. 4x5-608), 297 (pnts., neg. 4x5-1799-L), 301 (Holsinger Studio, 1917, acc. no. 9862, neg. X-4749-B), 302 (Holsinger Studio, 1917, acc. no. 9862, neg. X-4753-B), 305 (Holsinger Studio, 1913, acc. no. 9862, neg. X-1800-B), 307 (F. B. Johnston, 1930s, pnts. 158-18.1), 308 (F. B. Johnston, 1930s, pnts. 158-1.1), 311 (A. L. Hench, 1931, pnts. 130, neg. 4x5-1802-N), 312 (1903, pnts. 54, neg. 54.192), 316 (Holsinger Studio, 1917, acc. no. 9862, neg. X-5690-B17), 317 (pnts. 59, neg. 4x5-602), 318 (c. 1910, pnts., neg. 4x5-1799-E), 319 (pnts., neg. 4x5-1442), 322 (Holsinger Studio, 1914, acc. no. 9862, neg. X-2153-B4), 323 (Holsinger Studio, 1912, acc. no. 9862, neg. 4x5-907-N-13), 324 (Holsinger Studio, 1916, acc. no. 9862, neg. X-4524-B), 326 (Holsinger Studio, 1912, acc. no. 9862, neg. X-242-B9), 335 (Holsinger Studio, 1917, acc. no. 9862, neg. X-5620-B2), 336 (Holsinger Studio, acc. no. 9862, neg. X-1940-B2), 346 (William Lester Leap, M.A. thesis no. 416, 1930, neg. 4x5-1151-J), 348 (pnts., neg. 4x5-250), 351 (Holsinger Studio, 1919, acc. no. 9862, neg. X-7826-B), 353 (Holsinger Studio, 1917, acc. no. 9862, neg. X-5218-B2), 355 (Holsinger Studio, 1916, acc. no. 9862, neg. X-8x10-3982A-B), 357 (post card, 1909, pnts., neg. 4x5-1799-D), 358 (UVA File, neg. 4x5-1901), 366 (UVA File post card, neg. 4x5-514-C), 367 (Architects' Drawing, acc. no. 6846-p, neg. A7.6)

Virginia Transportation Research Council, Charlottesville: fig. 2 (Nathanial Mason Pawlett)

Roy Wheeler Realty Co., Charlottesville: fig. 147

James Dabney Wiant II, Albemarle County: fig. 246

George Worthington IV, Albemarle County, 1957: figs. 13, 200, 209, 217

Index

Jarman-Cree house, 15, 183–84
Jarman-Harris mill, 82
Jarman house, *109*
Jarman-Walker house, 180, *181*
Jefferson, Jane Randolph, 301 n.12
Jefferson, Lucy, 45
Jefferson, Maria (later Eppes). *See* Eppes, Maria Jefferson
Jefferson, Martha (later Carr). *See* Carr, Martha Jefferson
Jefferson, Martha (later Randolph). *See* Randolph, Martha Jefferson
Jefferson, Peter: gristmill, 10, 77–79; landholdings, 193; as magistrate, 27; mill, 77, 77–79, *78*, 99; at Shadwell, 37, 301 n.12, 301 n.19; as surveyor, 47, 73, 304 n.83
Jefferson, Peter Field, 43, 165, 214; mill, *166*, 325 n.59; warehouse, 17, 214, *214*
Jefferson, Thomas, 1–2, *3*, 89; acquaintances, 11, 155, 168, 215, 284–85; Agricultural Society membership, 26; and Albemarle County, 16, 21, 26; architecture, 37, 44, 107, 114, 115, 121, 138, 142, 154, 160, 267, 281; death, 170; debts, 132, 218; education, 29, 87; family, 10, 45, 51, 60, 72, 90, 99, 119, 145, 181, 197, 301 n.19; foundry, 54; as governor, 11–12; influence of, 89–96, 151, 226, 255; master builders, 13–14, 48, 93, 95–96, 99, 102, 103, 124, 154; Monticello, 56, 113, 114, 115, 139–40; Palladio's influence on, 92; Poplar Forest, 90–91, 115, 254, 260; as president, 101, 115; properties, 38, 318 n.4; and public education, 17, 303 n.72; on public education, 281; religion, 104, 158, 240; Revolution, 87; sawmill, 165; Shadwell, 27, 30, 76, 77–79, 165, 301 n.19; slaves, 224, 311 n.7, 311 n.8, 312 n.9; statue, 270, 289; University of Virginia, 281, 284; writings, 7, 11, 37, 158, 240, 281; youth, 8
Jefferson Bank building, 274
Jefferson High School, 278
Jefferson Hotel, 148, 170, *172*, 179, 180
Jefferson-Madison Regional Library, 20
Jefferson Memorial, Washington, D.C., 254
Jefferson National Bank, 275
Jefferson Opera House, 274, *274*
Jefferson Park Hotel, 245
Jefferson School, 249
Jefferson School for Boys, 216, *218*
Jefferson's mill. *See under* Jefferson, Peter
Jefferson Theater, 254, 274, 275
Jeffries, William, house, 193
Jeffries-Bruce house, 185, *186*

Jerdone, Francis, I, 141–42
Jessup house, 215, 243
Jett, Dora C., 326 n.2
Johns, Jay Winston, 38–40
Johnson, Albert, 223
Johnson, Catherine Elizabeth (later Vandegrift). *See* Vandegrift, Catherine Elizabeth Johnson
Johnson, Craven and Gibson firm, 273
Johnson, Floyd Elmer, 142, 157, 283
Johnson, Michael, 136
Johnson, Philip, 268
Johnson, Stanhope S., 20, 170, 254, 260, 262, 276
Johnson, William, 123
Johnson family, 82
Johnston, Frances Benjamin, 138, 200
Jones, Major Horace W., 148, 216; School for Boys, 148, 216
Jones, Brigadier General John Marshall, 226
Jones, John Russell, 318 n.8–9; house, 132
Jones, Robert S., 319 n.11
Jones-Willams house, *114*
Joplin, Jesse, 312 n.11, 318 n.4
Joplin, Joseph, 46, 154
Jordan, John, 12, *104*, 104–5, 115, 148, 157
Jordan, Lucy Winn, 104
Jouett, Jack, 11, 87
Jouett, John, Sr., 11, 29, 87, 149
Jourden family, 45
Julian, Raymond Hiroux, 161, 272, 283
Jumping Branch, 263
Justement, Louis, 293

Kappa Sigma house, 260, 285. *See also* Kenridge
Kearney, Brigadier General John Watts, 255, 258; house, 255
Kearney, Major General Philip, 258
Kearney, General Stephen Watts, 258
Keblinger, William M., 194
Keck, Charles, 259, 270
Keenan, William W., 229
Keene store, 245, *245*
Keller, John L., 47
Keller and George Jewelers building, 247
Kelley, John, 102
Kelly, Alexander, house, 223
Kelly, John, 92, 135; house, 132, *133*, 318 n.4
Kelly, Mary E., 318 n.8, 319 n.9
Kelso, William, 301 n.19
Kendall, William, 257
Kendrick, Drury W., 209
Kendrick, Washington C., 209
Kennedy, Edward M., 92
Kennedy, Fred, 257
Kennedy, Joan, 284

Kennedy, John F., 89
Kennedy, Robert F., 92
Kenridge, 20, 259–60. *See also* Kappa Sigma house
Kent, William, 91
Kenwood, 254
Keppel, William Anne, 9
Keswick, 57–59, *58*, 72, 179
Keswick Country Club, 280. *See also* Keswick Hall; Villa Crawford
Keswick Depot, 18, 220, *220*, *221*, 225
Keswick Hall, 19, 264, 280. *See also* Keswick Country Club; Villa Crawford
Keswick Hunt Club, 280
Key, J. Ben, 229
Key, James, 301 n.15
Key, John, 114, 230, 301 n.15; mill, 77
Key, Martin, 114
Key, Thomas Hewitt, 281
Key family, 40, 59
Key's meetinghouse, 209
Kibler, James L., 326 n.2
Kidd, L. Ashley, 255
Kilpatrick, Brigadier General H. Judson, 17–18
Kimball, Sidney Fiske, 19–20, 253, 260, 281–83, 287, 290, 293, 326 n.2
King, Charles, warehouses, 214
King, Martin, 73
King Solomon Masonic Lodge No. 194, 280
Kinloch, 43
Kinloch, Elizabeth (later Nelson). *See* Nelson, Eliza Kinloch
Kinloch, Francis, 312 n.9
Kinney, Jacob, 29, 82
Kinney (landowner), 238
Kinsolving, James, 44
Kirby, William, 124
Kirklea, 18, 232
Kluge, John Werner, 135
Kluge, Patricia, 240
Kluge Rehabilitation Center, 264
Kniffen, Fred B., 46
Kocher, Alfred Lawrence, 282
Koltukian, K. G., 255

Lafayette, marquis de, 86, 93, 168
Lafayette Theater, 274
Lafever, Minard, 15, 175
La Fourche Tavern (Travellers' Grove), 16, 86
Lambeth, Dr. William Alexander, 259, 284, 326 n.2
Lancaster, Clay, 149
Lancaster, Nancy Tree, 197
Lancaster, Robert A., 326 n.2
Land's End, 43